JAMES HOGG

Songs by
The Ettrick Shepherd

THE STIRLING / SOUTH CAROLINA RESEARCH EDITION OF
THE COLLECTED WORKS OF JAMES HOGG
FOUNDING GENERAL EDITOR – DOUGLAS S. MACK
GENERAL EDITORS – IAN DUNCAN AND SUZANNE GILBERT

THE STIRLING / SOUTH CAROLINA RESEARCH EDITION OF

THE COLLECTED WORKS OF JAMES HOGG

FOUNDING GENERAL EDITOR – DOUGLAS S. MACK

GENERAL EDITORS – IAN DUNCAN AND SUZANNE GILBERT

Volumes are numbered in the order of their publication in
the Stirling / South Carolina Research Edition

JAMES HOGG

Songs by
The Ettrick Shepherd

Edited by

Kirsteen McCue

with Janette Currie

EDINBURGH UNIVERSITY PRESS

2014

© Edinburgh University Press, 2014

Edinburgh University Press
22 George Square
Edinburgh
EH8 9LF

Typeset at the University of Stirling
Printed by CPI Antony Rowe, Chippenham, Wiltshire

ISBN 978 0 7486 3936 6

A CIP record for this book is available
from the British Library

The Stirling / South Carolina Research Edition of

The Collected Works of James Hogg

The Aims of the Edition

James Hogg lived from 1770 till 1835. He was regarded by his con-
temporaries as one of the leading writers of the day, but the nature of
his fame was influenced by the fact that, as a young man, he had been
a self-educated shepherd. The second edition (1813) of his poem *The
Queen's Wake* contains an 'Advertisement' which begins as follows:

> THE *Publisher having been favoured with letters from gentlemen in vari-
> ous parts of the United Kingdom respecting the Author of the* QUEEN'S
> WAKE, *and most of them expressing doubts of his being a Scotch Shep-
> herd; he takes this opportunity of assuring the Public, that* THE QUEEN'S
> WAKE *is really and truly the production of* JAMES HOGG, *a* common
> shepherd, *bred among the mountains of Ettrick Forest, who went to
> service when only seven years of age; and since that period has never
> received any education whatever.*

His contemporaries tended to regard the Scotch Shepherd as a man of
powerful and original talent, but it was felt that his lack of education

caused his work to be marred by frequent failures in discretion, in expression, and in knowledge of the world. Worst of all was Hogg's lack of what was called 'delicacy', a failing which caused him to deal in his writings with subjects (such as prostitution) which were felt to be unsuitable for mention in polite literature.

A posthumous collected edition of Hogg was published in the late 1830s. As was perhaps natural in the circumstances, the publishers (Blackie & Son of Glasgow) took pains to smooth away what they took to be the rough edges of Hogg's writing, and to remove his numerous 'indelicacies'. This process was taken even further in the 1860s, when the Rev. Thomas Thomson prepared a revised edition of Hogg's *Works* for publication by Blackie. These Blackie editions present a comparatively bland and lifeless version of Hogg's writings. It was in this version that Hogg was read by the Victorians, and he gradually came to be regarded as a minor figure, of no great importance or interest.

Hogg is thus a major writer whose true stature was not recognised in his own lifetime because his social origins led to his being smothered in genteel condescension; and whose true stature was obscured after his death because of a lack of adequate editions. The poet Douglas Dunn wrote of Hogg in the *Glasgow Herald* in September 1988: 'I can't help but think that in almost any other country of Europe a complete, modern edition of a comparable author would have been available long ago'. The Stirling / South Carolina Edition of James Hogg seeks to fill the gap identified by Douglas Dunn. When completed the edition will run to thirty-nine volumes, and it will cover Hogg's prose, his poetry, his letters, and his plays.

The late Douglas S. Mack founded the edition and served as General Editor, and driving force, from its inception until his death in December 2009. Peter Garside, Suzanne Gilbert, and Gillian Hughes joined the editorial team as Associate General Editors in 1998; and in 2000 Gillian Hughes was appointed joint General Editor (with Douglas Mack), a position she held for ten years. In 2009 Peter Garside retired from the editorial team, and Ian Duncan and Suzanne Gilbert were named General Editors.

General Editors' Acknowledgements

We record with gratitude the support given to the Stirling / South Carolina Research Edition of the Collected Works of James Hogg by the University of Stirling and by the University of South Carolina. Valuable grants or donations have also been received from the Arts and Humanities Research Council, from the Carnegie Trust for the Universities of Scotland, from the Modern Humanities Research Association, from the Association for Scottish Literary Studies, and from the James Hogg Society. The work of the Edition could not have been carried on without the support of these bodies. Douglas Mack initially served as the General Editor for the present volume; Suzanne Gilbert took over that role after Professor Mack's death.

Volume Editor's Acknowledgements

Firstly I am indebted to Douglas Mack for the invitation to become involved in this project at the very start, and for his enthusiasm and willingness to guide me so skilfully and with such humility through the waters of first-time textual editing. I have been most privileged to have learnt from him, and it is with great personal sadness that I was unable to discuss the final complex editorial decisions of this particular volume with him and that his untimely death has meant that he was unable to see the completion of the volume. I am most grateful to Wilma Mack for continuing this support and am especially indebted to the input of my new General Editor, Suzanne Gilbert, for her wisdom, humanity and sound advice, not to mention the hours of typesetting and checking. I would also like to thank Ian Duncan for his guidance and support, and for helping focus the volume at a crucial stage in the process. Thanks are also owed to Ian Davidson at EUP.

The volume would not have been possible without the major work undertaken as part of the Arts and Humanities Research Council-funded 'James Hogg Songs Project' between 2005 and 2008. Janette Currie was the full-time research assistant on this project, and her professionalism and skill in finding materials, and in researching so thoroughly the context to the songs in this volume, deserves particular acknowledgement. Her work is apparent in the Editorial Notes here, and she was responsible for producing the essay 'The Genesis of the Text' that follows the Introduction, the Explanatory Notes section of the note for each song, and the Glossary in this volume. Her research also heavily underpins the songs presented in the partner volume to this, namely Hogg's *Contributions to Musical Collections and Miscellaneous Songs*. Jennifer Orr undertook some fascinating research in Belfast on Hogg's reception in contemporary magazines and periodicals. I am also indebted to the assistance offered in more recent months by Megan Coyer and Linden Bicket. In advance of the 'James Hogg Songs Project' award, and on completion of a previous Arts and Humanities Research Board grant for the Collected Works of James Hogg, Douglas Mack was awarded a supplementary dissemination grant from the AHRC. This helped underpin some of the initial research on the Hogg Songs project and enabled me to present some of those findings to the Scottish

Romanticism and World Literatures Conference at the University of California, Berkeley in 2006. It also enabled the production of a CD of Hogg's songs ('I'll sing ye a wee bit sang') and the foundation of the James Hogg Research website, which is referred to several times in this volume. I would also like to acknowledge the help of the Stirling University Hogg fund, which supported the preparation of the text for this volume.

Special thanks are owed to a number of friends and colleagues who have been generous with advice. In particular I thank other editors of Hogg's songs, who have been so encouraging since the outset, namely Murray Pittock, Suzanne Gilbert, and Peter Garside and Richard Jackson, as well as Tom Richardson for his work on those songs also published in Blackwood's. I am also indebted to Gillian Hughes for her detailed knowledge of Hogg territory and her continued support of the project. Other scholars and friends who deserve acknowledgement here for listening, advising and commenting at various stages in this lengthy process are: Paul and Chris Banks, Christina Bashford, Rhona Brown, Carol Baranuik, Kenneth Elliott, Robin MacLachlan, Micah Gilbert, Meiko O'Halloran, Valentina Bold, Sharon Alker, Holly Faith Nelson, Hans de Groot, Douglas Gifford, Katherine Campbell, John Milne, Fiona Stafford, Alison Lumsden, David Hewitt, Susan Manning, Caroline McCraken-Flesher, Pauline Mackay, Maureen McLane, Jane Millgate, Pam Perkins, Penny Fielding, Patrick Scott, G. Ross Roy, Sheena Wellington, Jeffrey Robinson, Ian and Ingrid Ross, Leith Davis, Bill Zachs, Gordon Munro, Steve Newman, Anne Lorne Gillies, Vivien Williams, William Donaldson, and Sheona Low. Marjorie Rycroft has advised on things musical for many years and I am most grateful to her. Joanne Burns and Una Hunt gave valuable advice on connections with the songs of Thomas Moore. I would also like to thank Chris Wright at Tobar an Dualchais / Kist o Riches at the School of Scottish Studies for help with sourcing Gaelic melodies.

My close colleagues in Scottish literature at the University of Glasgow have all given support at various times, but I am indebted to Gerry Carruthers, who has been my sounding-post since the earliest stages of the process, who has wisely advised and given support when I most needed it. Nigel Leask, Head of the School of Critical Studies at the time of major work on this volume, has likewise supported the project with characteristic enthusiasm. I owe thanks to the University for helping facilitate conference presentations and additional expenses for images and library trips during the later stages of the project. I am also grateful for the support of Jeremy Smith, current Head of Critical Studies.

A large number of libraries and archives have aided the preparation of this volume. Specific acknowledgements are to: Almut Boehme and Tim Lawrence at the National Library of Scotland; the music staff at the British Library; Michelle Gait at Aberdeen University Special Collections; the staff of the music room at Cambridge University Library; Peter Ward Jones at the Bodleian Library, Oxford; the staff of the Glasgow University Special Collections; the staff at Stirling University Library; Peter Baxter and the staff of the Music Library of Edinburgh Central Library; Alasdair Pettinger at the Scottish Music Centre; Enda Ryan at the Mitchell Library, Glasgow; Sue Payne at the library of Perth Museum and Art Gallery; and the staff of the Newberry Library in Philadelphia. Patrick Scott, Elizabeth Sudduth, and their team at the Thomas Cooper Library at the University of South Carolina deserve special thanks for their hospitality and support when I visited there as W. Ormiston Roy Memorial Visiting Research Fellow in the summer of 2006.

Finally I would like to thank my parents, Pat and Bill, for beginning my love of song all those years ago. My father's singing and my mother's accompanying of 'When the kye comes hame' was my introduction to Hogg's songs when I was a child. During this project my mother has given me much-needed space (christened 'the Hoggery') and culinary support, and I am indebted to her. My children, Dora and Gregor, have been 'understanding' over much of their early childhoods about the importance of James Hogg in our lives and have even camped at St Mary's Loch with the midges to prove it. But my husband David has lived most closely with these songs, always willing to listen, discuss and accompany performances formal and informal. Words of thanks seem insufficient, but they are nonetheless offered most warmly.

Contents

Songs by The Ettrick Shepherd

Introduction

Songs by the Ettrick Shepherd (1831) and
Contributions to Musical Collections and Miscellaneous Songs

This volume of James Hogg's *Songs by the Ettrick Shepherd* (1831) is a scholarly edition of a small volume of some 113 songs by Hogg that was produced quickly in 1830 and published early in January 1831. The brief headnotes which introduce most of the songs in the volume are unusual in Hogg's published work and provide both entertaining anecdotal material and key information about the creative and/or publishing context of the songs in question. Many notes advertise the presence of the song in a contemporary musical collection or in song-sheet format. The editorial decision was made to present *Songs by the Ettrick Shepherd* as a single text-only volume, thus respecting the form of its initial publication. It was also decided to provide a companion volume of Hogg's *Contributions to Musical Collections and Miscellaneous Songs* that would present, where possible, facsimile copies of the collections and song-sheets to which Hogg refers in his headnotes, along with any other contemporary musical appearances of his songs. As such, the present edition is intended to be used in consultation with the volume entitled *Contributions to Musical Collections and Miscellaneous Songs*, and the editorial notes, provided on each song at the back of the present volume, will cross-refer to additional editorial annotation included in the *Contributions* volume.

1. James Hogg's Songs

Whether justly or unjustly it is hard to say, but it is the songs of the Shepherd which have done most to keep his name alive. Some were made to old tunes, some had tunes composed for them by himself, some were written and left to take their chance of finding a tune, but there are few which do not demand to be sung. He published them in his own volumes of poetry, in magazines, and in various "Garlands" with music by himself and others, and in 1831 he collected them nearly all into one volume with notes on the tunes and any stories of the publication or composition of the verses which he thought likely to interest the public.[1]

The above quotation is taken from Edith Batho's pivotal 1927 study *The Ettrick Shepherd*, where it introduces a discussion of James Hogg's *Songs by the Ettrick Shepherd* published by William Blackwood in Edinburgh in January 1831. While Batho rightly notes that it was Hogg's songs that had kept his name alive (at least prior to the subsequent rediscovery of *The Private Memoirs and Confessions of a Justified Sinner*), it is nonetheless notable that most Hogg criticism in the twentieth century spends little, if any, time discussing Hogg's song opus. It is only with the production of the new Stirling/South Carolina research edition of *The Collected Works of James Hogg* that this situation has changed. Pivotal scholarly and editorial work by Douglas Mack, Gillian Hughes, and Elaine Petrie, and more recently by Murray Pittock, Peter Garside, Richard Jackson, and Suzanne Gilbert, has opened up the topic of Hogg as songwriter. This activity has finally established a body of criticism around Hogg's songs and song-writing which rivals the interest shown by reviewers and journalists in the middle of the nineteenth century.[2] Batho's statement that Hogg's songs were published not just across his own work, but in 'magazines and in various "Garlands"' is testament to the importance of songs in Hogg's creative work and to their relative popularity with publishers during his lifetime. As Batho suggests, this is a story that Hogg is able to demonstrate most clearly in this final song collection. His decision to present what he (and the public) had deemed to be his best or most popular songs with his own notes was not simply to aid his reader's enjoyment, nor to reflect a new form of presentation found in other publications at that time. It was a clever and considered decision on Hogg's behalf to illustrate his importance as a national songwriter, to show how widely his songs had spread during his lifetime, and to indicate the considerable diversity of publications in which his songs might be found.

Hogg's early development as a songwriter is described by Peter Garside and Richard Jackson in the introduction to their new edition of Hogg's earlier song collection, *The Forest Minstrel*, which had appeared in 1810.[3] Suffice it to say songs were vitally important to Hogg from his earliest years, being a staple part of the domestic diet supplied by friends, family, and the Ettrick community where he grew up, most notably through his mother's performance of songs and ballads. As Garside and Jackson note, Hogg draws attention to this milieu from the first of his memoirs in 1807, by recounting how amazed he was to see songs and ballads in print, in Scott's *Minstrelsy of the Scottish Border* (1802), when he had only heard them sung before, and by people who could not read themselves. This memoir also includes the unforgettable account of Hogg buying his first fiddle, and of how, if he was not too tired after a day's shepherding, he would spend 'an hour or two every night in rubbing over my favourite old Scottish tunes'.[4] Moreover, Hogg notes that his earliest compositions, including 'The Way that the World goes on', were songs. Several comments in his *Highland Journeys*, undertaken between 1802 and 1804, also illustrate Hogg's musicality and interest in songs and singing, as well as providing evidence of his musical literacy. His first letter of 1802, initially printed in *The Scots Magazine*, presents his fellow Borderers as people with a 'generally musical ear' and discusses the shared provenance of many tunes or melodies from the Borders, the South West and up to Perthshire.[5] His 1803 *Journey* refers to a 'Dutch concert' (akin to a *ceilidh*) performed by the birds around him at Loch Katrine, 'from the small whistle of the wren, to the solemn notes of the cuckoo, sounded on E. and C. a double octave lower'.[6] Another detailed description of his friend John Grieve's 'musical ear' is found in his account of a visit to Lochgilphead in his 1804 *Journey*, where he refers to keys ('sharp key'), cadences, musical intervals ('a fifth') and note lengths ('a minim').[7] Such references show that Hogg had more than just an innate oral musicality.[8] He must also have developed a knowledge and understanding of musical terminology, perhaps through discussions with musicians or his own reading. This understanding is something he would use later in his career, notably in the second part of his long narrative poem *Pilgrims of the Sun* in 1815.[9]

Including songs in one's regular poetic publications was standard literary practice at this time; Robert Burns printed his first songs at the end of his *Poems, Chiefly in the Scottish Dialect* of 1786, for example. Having established a certain flare for writing songs at the start, Hogg included some in his first publication, *Scottish Pastorals* of 1801, and then alongside his longer ballads in *The Mountain Bard* in 1807 (and 1821). He was also contributing songs to *The Scots Magazine* at this time. But it was with *The Forest Minstrel* of 1810 that he took a notable step forward in his role as songster. While Hogg himself was unsure about the quality of many of these early songs – stating in his 1821 'Memoir' that 'in general they are not good'[10] – *The Forest Minstrel* does clearly illustrate his ability to adapt oral material for wider literary consumption. Garside's and Jackson's recent edition shows just how Hogg does this, and they give a detailed account of Hogg's awareness of the process of encapsulating songs from a rural environment and introducing them to the more literate folk of the town.[11] Hogg had boldly declared himself the font of knowledge of Scottish Border ballad tradition in *The Mountain Bard*.[12] And, though unsuccessful with the public, *The Forest Minstrel* project revealed his talents as a songwriter in addition to those of collector and editor. He produced the lyrics for more than half of the volume (some 56 of the

83 songs included), but this project involved Hogg collaborating with a number of new friends and colleagues in Edinburgh and publishing some of their songs beside his own. Hogg was moving in a new social environment, and his friendship with the Izett family in particular shaped his understanding of a new audience for his songs, both as readers and amateur performers.[13]

Setting aside this project as something of a learning curve, and appreciating where it had failed, Hogg then built his profile further with his representation of the 'Master Singers' in *The Queen's Wake* (1813).[14] The narrative structure of a bardic competition was not just an ingenious solution to incorporating a diverse range of ready-made songs and ballads; it was a major statement about Hogg's position as a national songwriter.[15] Across the three nights described in the poem, songsters and balladeers from all corners of the Scottish nation make their unique regional contributions. Hogg clearly shows himself to be adept at writing songs and ballads in all styles, with different regional and linguistic inflections, as well as projecting his own position as the Bard of the moment in the guise of the Bard of Ettrick. It is undoubtedly *The Queen's Wake* that first truly celebrated Hogg's role as Scotland's national songwriter.[16] By the time its popular fifth edition appeared in 1819, and arguably on the back of this success, Hogg had provided songs for two major London musical collections and made important connections with a number of key Scottish song editors, including Alexander Campbell, George Thomson, and the influential music publisher Nathaniel Gow & Sons. Songs also played their part from the 1810s onwards in Hogg's other published works: within dramas and longer narrative poems and in the fiction as well.

In 1821, when Hogg produced an updated 'Memoir', as preface to the second edition of *The Mountain Bard*, he was able to account for this activity and comment on his abilities as a 'natural songster' for the first time.[17] The end of the 'Memoir' refers to specific musical collaborations, and Hogg gives the impression that he is now sought after as a writer of songs, even by 'a celebrated composer of music'.[18] In this case the composer is William Heather, and the publication referred to is 'Sacred Melodies', which is in fact a series of *German Hebrew Melodies* for which Hogg contributed the lyrical component in 1816–17 (see *Contributions to Musical Collections and Miscellaneous Songs*). The penultimate paragraph of the 'Memoir' includes Hogg's plans to develop further the Edinburgh song collection (with music) entitled *A Border Garland* (published in [1819]), that he produced with the musician Niel Gow Junior and the publishing firm Nathaniel Gow & Sons. Moreover, the list of publications includes his 'Jacobite Relics of Scotland', in two parts featuring approximately 340 songs which Hogg had collected (some were his own), amended and edited for the Highland Society in 1819 and 1821.[19]

The ambitions Hogg shared here were realized in the 1820s. Firstly he chose to include many songs (texts only) in his four-volume *Poetical Works* of 1822, a publication to which he went back regularly for texts to include in *Songs by the Ettrick Shepherd*. Between 1821 and 1824 Hogg worked closely with Scottish composer Robert Archibald Smith on his collections of Scottish and Irish airs; and, with composer James Dewar, he expanded *A Border Garland*, creating a collection with twelve songs called *The Border Garland* around 1829. By this time Hogg's songs were appearing in Literary Gift Books and Annuals (*The Forget me Not* and *The Musical Bijou*).[20] He produced all the song texts for the major London collection *Select & Rare Scotish Melodies* with music by Sir Henry Bishop, published around 1828, and his songs were picked up and included in musical magazines such as *The Harmonicon*. From 1817 onwards Hogg was also contributing songs on a regular basis as the Shepherd of 'Noctes Ambrosianae' in *Blackwood's Edinburgh Magazine*. This role helped secure his reputation as a songwriter with a wide readership, and he was very keen to emphasise this in this final song collection in 1831.

Reclaiming songs that have appeared in so many different places and packaging them anew was the plan behind *Songs by the Ettrick Shepherd*. Pooling materials that had been scattered through periodicals and magazines was not a new venture for Hogg. The relationship between Hogg and Blackwood had seen happier times. Fewer of Hogg's pieces – with the notable exception of his songs – were appearing in *Blackwood's Edinburgh Magazine* by the late 1820s. Moreover, Hogg had become increasingly frustrated throughout 1828 with Blackwood's reluctance to publish *The Shepherd's Calendar*, a volume of his stories as they had appeared across the intervening years in 'the Magazine'. When the volume appeared in the spring of 1829, it was only with the at times heavy editorial involvement of Hogg's nephew Robert. This project signaled Hogg's intentions to reclaim his own work and, indeed, his 'self' as writer. But one might argue that this is a project he began in advance of his 1821 'Memoir' with *Winter Evening Tales*, published by Oliver and Boyd in 1820. This collection pulls together many, often reworked, pieces that had appeared over the preceding decade in Hogg's magazine *The Spy* and in a number of other magazines (including the early issues of *Blackwood's*) and chapbooks ('The Long Pack'), or which had failed to find outlets ('Connel of Dee'). Ian Duncan's recent edition of *Winter Evening Tales* draws attention to Hogg's creative process as being a self-confessed mixture of 'collecting' and 'writing over' or 'new-modelling', which is most certainly the case with his songs.[21] With *The Shepherd's*

Calendar Hogg was actively compiling his stories as they had appeared across the issues of one magazine. But, as with *Winter Evening Tales*, any compilation of his songs was clearly going to be rather more complex.

Both Gillian Hughes and Peter Garside have noted the proximity of Hogg's idea to the new 'magnum opus' edition of the works of Walter Scott (1829–33), in which Scott presented his work with his own notes and comments.[22] Hogg suggests in his letter to William Blackwood of 26 May 1830 that Blackwood might like to 'publish all my tales in numbers like Sir W Scott's', and Hogg says that that he would be prepared to improve them.[23] Hughes talks about the vogue for 'drawing-room sets of volumes'– especially those by Byron and Scott – and states that Hogg was 'remarkably quick in noting this new publishing opportunity'.[24] She also recounts that the period 1829 to 1830 was a time of gathering storm clouds for Hogg. There were difficulties with the lease on Mount Benger, and the new, young Duke of Buccleuch was not proving as generous a landlord as his father to Hogg. Hogg's debts were considerable and his creditors were also beginning to pressure him. Understandably then, Hogg was looking for publications of works that would sell. From April 1830 he piled on the pressure to have Blackwood consider what he later referred to as a 'cabinet edition' of his work. And it is worthy of note that this process, while it was never completed, was initiated by the appearance of *Songs by the Ettrick Shepherd* in 1831 and *A Queer Book* in 1832, containing a number of Hogg's shorter poems and ballads likewise pulled together from a variety of earlier sources. In his 1995 edition of *A Queer Book*, Peter Garside comments that it was clearly 'envisaged as a companion piece' to *Songs* and that when it was published it was 'virtually identical in appearance to its predecessor, the embossed cloth binding resembling several of the literary annuals'.[25] Hogg was also keen to push reissues of his most popular poetic work, *The Queen's Wake*, and his most popular prose writings, *Winter Evening Tales*, but neither of these appeared before his death in 1835.

2. Production of *Songs by the Ettrick Shepherd*

'Bye the Byes I am rejoiced to see his songs announced. They will make a capital volume.'

This quotation is taken from a letter written by D. M. or 'Delta' Moir to William Blackwood on 26 November 1830,[26] referring to the imminent arrival of *Songs by the Ettrick Shepherd*, which duly appeared at the beginning of January 1831. Hogg felt the same as Moir: he saw the potential of a popular volume of his songs some months before this, having first raised the idea with Blackwood in his letter of 11 April 1830 when he announced that he was in the process of selecting 'a pocket volume of my best songs out of all the periodicals in the kingdom &c.'.[27]

Blackwood took some persuading. On 21 June 1830 Hogg tried again, adding at the bottom of his letter that he 'forgot to mention that it has often been suggested to me that a neat volume of my songs would sell well'.[28] Again in his letter of 30 September he concluded: 'the only thing that I can see we can do on the instant is to publish a vol of select songs wholly my own in the manner Moore has done'.[29] This final comment referred to Thomas Moore's *Irish Melodies*, which had just appeared in a popular single-volume edition in 1827. Hogg continued that the volume of songs 'should be ready about New year', and that if this was really not an option then a new 12mo edition of *The Queen's Wake* would be the next best thing. Hogg was therefore seeing his songs on the same popular platform as *The Queen's Wake*, and this says much for the esteem in which he regarded his song opus. 'My songs', he asserted, 'have been scattered over the country and sung for the last twenty years and many of them highly popular and no author known.' Here Hogg drew attention not just to the wide circulation, but also to the fact that he felt peeved that some readers might not recognize some of these songs as being by him. His famous note to 'Donald MacDonald' – which appears as the first song in *Songs by the Ettrick Shepherd* – tells of his astonishment at witnessing two very different performances of the song where those performing and listening have no idea that Hogg is the song's creator. Hogg's decision to incorporate many of his 'Noctes' songs from *Blackwood's Edinburgh Magazine* in his 1831 collection suggests that he feels a similar anxiety about attribution here.

By the time of Hogg's letter of 20 October 1830, Blackwood had finally consented to the plan. In this letter Hogg sent the first twenty songs of the volume he was now calling 'Select songs of the Ettrick Shepherd', encouraging Blackwood to start the printing process and urging, once again, for a New Year's day publication.[30] His insistence on this date clearly indicates that Hogg was seeing his volume in the same category as the Christmas or New Year annuals – something of a keep-sake edition. He suggests that Blackwood call on his nephew Robert Hogg to facilitate the production of the volume and then gives details of how he wishes the volume to look. The process of Hogg's personal involvement with the final preparation and production of the volume is discussed in more detail in the present edition in Janette Currie's 'Note on the Genesis of the Text'. But it is worth noting here that Hogg wanted his volume to look like one of the popular annuals in circulation at this time; he wished the type not to be too large, but to enable the printing of the songs 'in long measure without breaking the lines'; and he intended adding 'simple notices to each song'. With a view to continuing his search for the best of his songs he also requested that Blackwood send him a copy of *The Forest Minstrel*. Garside and Jackson have commented that copies of this volume were hard to find, it having been something of a failure on its appearance and subsequently not reprinted. They suggest that even by 1830 copies had 'evidently become something of a rarity' and cite Hogg's requests to Blackwood for a copy as evidence of this – he had already asked for a copy in his letter of 11 April.[31] Hogg's letter of 20 October notes that he has a large number of songs 'scattered through all the periodicals almost of Britain' and that while he thus has plenty of songs from which to choose, he nonetheless plans to write more in future. With some frustration under the surface here, Hogg also makes reference to the possibility of a 'cabinet edition' of his work for the boudoir, suggesting that perhaps Robert Ackermann, the editor of London annuals including *Forget-me-Not*, might be better placed than Blackwood to undertake this.

Hogg's continual pressure seems to have paid off. The next month proved to be a busy one in terms of Hogg and Blackwood sending proofs back and forth. In his letter of 10 November 1830, Hogg encloses proofs and 'a few more songs' and reiterates his wish that the volume be published on New Year's day. Furthermore, he requests that Blackwood go ahead with an advertisement and even gives him the chosen wording for this: 'MR HOGG'S SONGS. A selection from the songs of the Ettrick Shepherd is in the press and will appear on New-year's-day Elegantly printed &c &c.'.[32] Hogg also refers in this letter to the incorporation of his songs in *Noctes* and suggests ways in which he will include some of them (and possibly also some of the dialogue from the magazine beside the presentation of these songs) in *Songs by the Ettrick Shepherd*. Proofs are again mentioned in his letter to Blackwood of 17 November and once more on 24 November.[33] On 30 November Hogg informs Blackwood that he has been 'confined to bed' with 'a disease in my gums and a dreadfully swelled face'. He asks Blackwood not to send more proofs for now as he is due to come to Edinburgh soon. In this letter he thanks Blackwood for his revised headnote to Hogg's song 'Donald M'Gillavry' in the volume. He also states: 'I have plenty of songs here such as they are but there are many many good ones that I want and will want though it is no great matter', suggesting that he was still undecided about some of the songs he wished to include.[34]

Such indecisiveness is revealed when one examines the almost complete fair-copy manuscript (principally found in the Blackwood Papers at NLS MS 4805) that the printer used for the production of *Songs by the Ettrick Shepherd*. Hogg had arrived in Edinburgh by 9 December (stated in his letter to his wife Margaret), and, as further exploration of the manuscript and the published volume indicate, he was making final changes almost at the printing press.[35] The fact that there is so little variation between manuscript and first printed edition is notable, and one is left concluding that this was a fast and intense process. There are only slight alterations, and gaps are sometimes filled by Hogg referring the printer to a published copy of a song in another volume, so that he refrains from writing it out in full. In general this manuscript acts as a very 'fair' copy of the published edition. Again this would suggest that neither Blackwood nor another editor is interfering with Hogg's plans. This had not been the case with *The Shepherd's Calendar*, nor was it to be the case with the companion volume to *Songs*, namely *A Queer Book*, which was quickly established as the next project within weeks of the publication of *Songs*. Here, as Peter Garside has shown, Robert Hogg's involvement was very noticeable and James had little control over final editorial decisions. Robert was also involved in *Songs*, but, as Janette Currie's work on the manuscript has shown, it is often impossible to know whether final 'tweaking' is Robert's doing or James's. There is no 'hacking' of existing texts, while there is sometimes rewriting and often a little delicate polishing, and some variants suggest that on occasions Hogg reverts to his memory rather than copying from a printed text. But aside from offering part of the note on 'Donald MacDonald' or potentially rewriting the note for 'The Minstrel Boy', it is indeed difficult to trace Robert's hand at all.

Hogg's 1830 Christmas break in Edinburgh to oversee the final production of *Songs* was helped significantly, as Gillian Hughes recounts, by bouts of shopping and social events with his curling friends.[36] Sadly for Hogg, his *Songs* failed to appear on New Year's day, as he explains to Margaret on the day itself when discussing his plans to return to Altrive: 'I am still uncertain the volume not being yet published'.[37] But, as the reviews below suggest, it must have appeared almost simultaneously – a pretty 'pocket volume' measuring some 4½ x 7 inches, with clean typeface and sensitive page-breaks (with notices in the same but smaller font size) and with an attractive embossed green cloth binding with gold lettering.

3. The headnotes and Hogg's editorial policy

As discussed above, Hogg's inspiration for his 'cabinet' edition was most probably Walter Scott's contemporaneous 'magnum opus' edition. Critics have already noted how Hogg's 'simple notices' to each of the songs in his new select collection mirror Scott's project.[38] With so many songs spread widely across his own work, and in such a diverse range of other publications, it would be impossible to see the whole picture of Hogg's songs so easily without his 'notices' or headnotes in *Songs by the Ettrick Shepherd*. And, arguably, this is exactly why Hogg wished to include them in the first place. These notes are of different lengths and are variously funny, entertaining, and informative of Hogg's creative process or biography; but, above all else, they allow Hogg himself to create a map of his work as a songwriter across his career.

The first song presented is 'Donald MacDonald', apparently written, as his note tells us, when Hogg was a shepherd boy. By 1830 it had already become a highly popular song, appearing in many different places across Hogg's work (already in *The Forest Minstrel* and in *The Mountain Bard*) and in independent song-sheet copies. This is one of very few songs in the collection to have both a headnote and a footnote, but both explain how the song has become part of popular tradition, without Hogg's name as creator. This is surely the key reason for Hogg including it here as the opening song: he had made a song so popular that it had become at once part of a printed culture and a living oral tradition. While this is an accolade, it was also a worry for Hogg, as the public awareness of his prowess in the area of songwriting was vitally important to his legacy. It was this which drove him to reclaim his songs, however positive and flattering such anonymous circulation may have been. And this is one of the reasons why his editorial role with *Songs by the Ettrick Shepherd* is worthy of further detailed consideration by its reader. Hogg's ability to sport a powerful and often artificial sense of modesty in these headnotes is a notable characteristic and mostly endears him to his audience. While on several occasions he is keen to draw attention to the popularity of his songs – indeed he almost protests this at times – the collection also includes songs which were relatively new. 'I hae Naebody Now', which appears later in the volume, had only just been printed in May 1830 in *Fraser's Magazine for Town and Country* (this was also the case with 'The Lass of Carlisle'). And after the publication of *Songs by the Ettrick Shepherd*, *Fraser's* periodically featured songs from the volume, suggesting the importance of Hogg's 1831 collection as a stimulus for further printings of his songs (e.g., 'The Frazer's in the Correi' which appeared in *Fraser's* in March 1834).

Only one of the 113 songs included was appearing for the first and only time in *Songs by the Ettrick Shepherd*: all others had appeared somewhere else first. There is no sense of chronology through the volume, nor does Hogg choose to categorise the songs here. While he includes songs which would fall under the headings 'Humorous', 'Love', 'Patriotic', or 'National', as employed in *The Forest Minstrel*, there appears to be a more relaxed mixing and matching of songs in his 1831 collection. Again this was nodding much more towards the trend for popular mixed collections of songs, rather than looking backwards to eighteenth-century collections such as those of David Herd, which had clearly been on Hogg's mind in those early years. This selection is no formal representation of Hogg's prowess in writing songs in specific genres, nor is it an antiquarian selection of lost but important pieces for future generations; it is created to be an enjoyable and diverse journey through the best of his work and to celebrate Hogg's considerable abilities across the range.

While the overall appearance is of a loose structure, closer inspection does show that Hogg often thought in terms of 'groups' of songs. For example the first dozen songs here were undoubtedly the bestselling ones or those which had been most widely published: 'Donald MacDonald', 'Scotia's Glens', 'The Broom Sae Green', 'Flora MacDonald's Farewell', 'Bonny Prince Charlie' 'The Skylark', 'Gang to the Brakens wi' Me', 'The Minstrel Boy', 'Farewell to Glen-Shalloch' and 'Caledonia'. This group is then quickly followed by a number of Blackwoodian songs: 'The Noctes Sang', 'I Lookit East, I Lookit West' and 'The Village of Balmaquhapple' from *Noctes,* amongst several Ettrick songs, including 'The Souters of Selkirk', a couple of Jacobite songs ('Callum-a-Glen' and 'The Three Men of Moriston') and Hogg's love song 'When the kye comes hame'. His decision to give songs from *Noctes* and *Blackwood's Edinburgh Magazine* such prominence here illustrates Hogg's awareness of their general popularity and his wide fame as 'the Shepherd'. But they also indicate his anxiety that he is not being given due respect as song creator in the *Noctes* itself, where he is often at the receiving end of disparaging remarks from Christopher North and Timothy Tickler. Although Hogg is not entirely consistent in his presentation of the *Noctes* songs in this 1831 collection, he does often choose to present the songs with the dialogue from the magazine to introduce and conclude the song. Not surprisingly, he does so when some flattering or positive remark is made about the Shepherd's song writing skills (e.g. 'I lookit East, I lookit West', 'Meg o'Marley' or 'Bonny Mary'). As Thomas Richardson has noted in his editions of Hogg's *Contributions to Blackwood's Edinburgh Magazine*, it is the *Noctes* songs which 'highlight the breadth of Hogg's song subjects', as Hogg had freedom in producing songs on any subject he chose regardless of the issues under discussion.[39] Many of the songs included in *Noctes* encompassed his popularity as 'occasional' songwriter and performer. These are exactly the qualities Hogg wishes to underline in his new collection. He purposefully includes a number of songs which he has been commissioned to write for specific purposes, such as 'I lookit East, I lookit West' (pp. 18–20), which was first performed at the institutionary dinner of the Caledonian Asylum in London in 1815 for the widows and families of Scottish soldiers who had died. Likewise 'A National Song of Triumph' (pp. 114–15) had been specially written for the return of the Allies from Paris in 1814, and 'The Ancient Banner' (p. 116–17) for the football match at Carterhaugh in 1815. Hogg's headnotes also frequently draw attention to his writing songs for particular friends or family members. 'Love Letter' and 'Mischievous Woman' are grouped together in the volume, and he notes that they were written for his wife Margaret. 'Athole Cummers', which immediately precedes these songs, was written at his mother's request. 'When Maggy Gangs Away' (pp. 36–37) was written for his daughter Maggy, and 'A Father's Lament', which appears beside it in the volume, was for a young friend, Robert Anderson, who had died in 1823 and to whose father Hogg had sent his song. In the case of 'O, weel Befa' the Maiden Gay' (pp. 53–55), Hogg explains that he wrote this competitively when staying amongst other writers in the Lake District.

There is a focus throughout the volume on what Hogg terms 'compositions of my early youth' (pp. 79–86), and the largest single number of songs to come from a previous publication is the group taken from *The Forest Minstrel*. Even accounting for Hogg's difficulties throughout 1830 in sourcing a copy of the volume, there are significant reasons for selecting these early songs and Hogg includes 18 of them in total. While some are scattered across the volume, there is a group of five of them in beginning with 'Auld Ettrick John' (p. 79) and including 'Doctor Munro', 'Sing On, Sing On, my Bonny Bird', 'Jock an' his Mother' and 'On Ettrick Clear'. These are all introduced by one over-arching headnote to 'Auld Ettrick John' in which Hogg notes that they are early and 'even in my own estimation they are below par in poetical merit'. But he states that they have nonetheless become popular 'among the class for which they were framed', so that he feels it unwise to leave them out of this later volume. He further comments that these songs are happily incorporated because they also connect directly to the 'shepherds, cottagers, and rosy servant maids'. Hogg is keen to emphasise his roots here, his direct and intimate knowledge of what he terms 'the sphere around the cottage hearth and the farmer's kitchen-ingle'. For Hogg, and thus his songs, these humble beginnings in which there was no thought of 'any higher distinction' is of great importance in indicating both the value of their oral roots and authenticity, and also in revealing just how far he has come.

Only a handful of songs in *Songs by the Ettrick Shepherd* appear without an introductory headnote, but, as is the case with this group from *The Forest Minstrel*, the reason is normally because they are linked to a grouping of songs within the volume. For example, towards the end of the collection, Hogg chooses to include three songs from *The Queen's Wake*, beginning with 'O Lady Dear' (p. 126). The second and third songs, 'The Spectre's Cradle Song' and 'Hymn to the God of the Sea', thus also appear without headnotes. And a small group of songs, at the very end of the volume, also appear without explanation. But, as Janette Currie's work on the fair-copy manuscript has shown, Hogg appears to have added songs at the very end of the process; the songs after 'O Lady Dear' either have no page numbers or are numbered out of sequence in the manuscript.

Hogg also includes a significant number of Jacobite songs in this final collection. His role in the publication of the two series of *The Jacobite Relics of Scotland* in 1819 and 1821 was principally as editor, or, as Murray Pittock terms it, involved Hogg in 'a process of interaction with as well as preservation of the texts he assembled'.[40] Hogg was collecting, amending, and presenting this material with his own informative notes at the back of the volume. As Pittock's edition illustrates, tracing songs which are principally Hogg's own creations can be complex and is sometimes impossible. While one might think that Hogg would only choose to include his own songs in this 1831 volume, attribution can still be tricky (e.g., 'Farewell to Glen-Shalloch' (pp. 12–13) and 'M'Lean's Welcome' (pp. 32–33). Hogg includes 11 songs from the *Relics* in *Songs* 1831, and notably they do not sit together as a group but are scattered throughout the volume: from his popular 'Flora MacDonald's Farewell' and 'Farewell to Glen-Shalloch', which appear in the very first group of songs, to 'Bauldy Frazer', one of the last songs in the collection. 'Flora MacDonald's Farewell' notwithstanding, they are most often high-spirited, war-like songs, celebrating the prowess of individuals or clans and portraying a certain sense of defiance, and they are most often combined with spirited and memorable tunes. While 'Bonny Prince Charlie', also known by its first line 'Cam' ye by Athole', was not included in *Relics* it proved to be one of Hogg's most popular songs, with a contemporary theatre life all its own, and so Hogg understandably wished to include it in the opening group in 1831. The other little group of Jacobite songs here, also missing from *Relics*, is the entertaining sequence of three Cumberland songs beginning with 'The Two Men of Colston' (p. 67), the first of which is written phonetically in Cumberland dialect. Although it can still be difficult to prove Hogg's authorship at times (even with songs like 'Charlie is my Darling'), his final choices of Jacobite songs for *Songs* 1831 are clearly those with which he wished his name to be closely associated.

True to his initial plan, Hogg's *Songs by the Ettrick Shepherd* does pull together songs from across his repertoire as a writer. In addition to those from *The Forest Minstrel, Blackwood's Edinburgh Magazine* and *Jacobite Relics*, another large group came from Hogg's early magazine *The Spy*. His protestation to Blackwood that his songs were scattered across 'the periodicals almost of Britain', was proven to be the case, for those already mentioned were joined by texts from *The Scots Magazine*, the *Edinburgh Magazine and Literary Miscellany*, the *Edinburgh Literary Journal (or Weekly Register of Criticism and Belles Lettres)*, and also from *Fraser's Magazine for Town and Country*. In addition to the small selection of songs from *The Queen's Wake* of 1813, Hogg also chose some from *Dramatic Tales* of 1817, namely one from *All-Hallow-Eve* and another two from *The Haunted Glen*. And a further two songs appear from Hogg's play *The Bush Aboon Traquair* (written in the early 1810s). He often includes songs which have appeared in numerous places across the years: for example his popular love song 'When the kye comes hame', which had already appeared in both *Blackwood's Edinburgh Magazine* and his novel *The Three Perils of Man* in 1823.

Hogg's 1831 headnote for 'The Moon Was A-Waning' (p. 112), one of the early songs taken from *The Forest Minstrel*, emphasises his role as a shepherd, where he had 'often heard my strains chanted from the ewe-bught and the milking-green with delight'. But in this note Hogg tells his reader of his 'exultation' at moving 'a step higher': this, he states, is the first of his songs that he heard 'sung at the piano'. One of the major editorial decisions that Hogg made in this final song collection was to include nearly every one of his songs which had appeared by 1830 in musical form, either in a major song collection or in single song-sheet format.[41] His headnotes actively advertise these publications, thus encouraging his reader to seek them out. Hogg often makes comments about the melodies, and he states clearly if he likes a musical setting or prefers the song in another musical form. But, regardless of his tastes, the reader of *Songs* 1831 is left in no doubt about the popularity of his songs with musicians, music publishers, and performers the length and breadth of the British Isles. These headnotes act as a useful promotional tool, advertising Hogg's success in this sphere, from the first volume of Alexander Campbell's collection *Albyn's Anthology* in 1816 to both *The Border Garland* (of Purdie in Edinburgh) and *Select & Rare Scotish Melodies* (of Goulding & D'Almaine in London) published within only a year of the appearance of *Songs by the Ettrick Shepherd*. Songs from some 10 major musical collections are included – notably also from R. A. Smith's *Irish Minstrel* (c.1825). The first edition of this volume had run into major copyright issues with Thomas Moore's publishers, The Power Brothers. Indeed the eight Irish songs by Hogg included here have most entertaining headnotes which refer to his annoyance about this and his direct competition with Moore's texts as found in *Irish Melodies*.[42] Other songs referred to had by this time appeared in several separate 'miscellaneous' song-sheets – see 'Flora MacDonald's Farewell' and 'Bonnie Prince Charlie' in particular. Hogg's headnotes to these songs thus celebrate his own musical celebrity and indicate just how widely sought-after and distributed his songs were musically. While his comments occasionally suggest disappointment with some of the musical settings, most of the time the headnotes reveal his pride at involvement in these collections.[43]

One final issue which Hogg raises in his headnotes regards his own prowess as musician and performer and indeed emphasizes the performance culture around him. His readership is made aware of his practical musicianship from the famous anecdote in his first 1807 'Memoir' about fiddle playing at Mr Scott of Singlee's house. His description tells us much about the way Hogg learned tunes and learned how tunes worked: a process he calls 'essaying'.[44] Several headnotes alert us to songs for which Hogg has composed the tunes himself: for example 'The Broom sae Green' (pp. 6–7), which Hogg says 'Is my greatest favourite at present', continuing, 'probably because the air is my own', and 'The Poor Man' and 'The Women Fo'k', which he places side by side in *Songs* 1831 (pp. 30–32) and which were both included in *A Border Garland* [1819] with Hogg's airs. He also sometimes draws attention to his fame as a singer. Accounts of Hogg performing songs are sprinkled throughout contemporary reports of Burns dinners and other social events, but Hogg himself is keen to highlight this in his headnotes. His introduction to 'The Women Fo'k' does not simply draw attention to his authorship of the tune, but notes that he was famed for performing the song himself: 'It is my own favourite humorous song, when forced to sing by ladies against my will, which too frequently happens; and notwithstanding my wood-notes wild, it will never be sung by any so well again' (p. 31). Hogg is also very keen to indicate when his songs were written for the 'singing' of others (e.g.,'The Souters of Selkirk' (p. 16), 'The Ladies Evening Song' (pp. 49–50), and 'The Flowers of Scotland' (pp. 5-6)). His headnotes or 'notices' are always emphasing that his songs are made for singing; they are not simply created for reading.

4. Reception of *Songs by the Ettrick Shepherd*

Though *Songs by the Ettrick Shepherd* did not arrive when Hogg had wished – on New Year's Day 1831 – its appearance had been anticipated in *The Edinburgh Literary Journal; or Weekly Register of criticism and belles lettres* in its section entitled 'Literary Chit-Chat and Varieties' for 11

December 1830.[45] The Journal briefly announced that 'A selection of Mr Hogg's best Songs is in the press, and to be published on Christmas day, in an elegant cabinet volume'. And it quotes 'a contemporary' who notes that Hogg is 'Educated in the great school which nature keeps on Tweedside and Yarrow' and that his 'verses are superior to the mushroom productions which that great middenstead, the College, produces'. The journal followed up this announcement on Christmas Day 1830, when it published a short article entitled 'The Ettrick Shepherd – Himself – His Portrait – and his Songs'.[46] It promoted the new song collection whilst also introducing the public to arguably the most famous of Hogg's portraits, by John Watson Gordon. The article drew attention to the importance of work of national and patriotic verve (nodding to Hogg's songs in this capacity) and discussed the difficulties (for Hogg) of his close proximity to Burns as writer of songs. In so doing it clearly suggested both to Hogg and his readership that if Hogg 'be not the successor of Burns, he has no successor living'. The article highlights that the range of songs covers the 'grave, gay, pathetic, comic, patriotic and amatory' and that they are 'unequal'. Many of them are 'admirable, full of genius, and moist with the natural dews of poetry'. Indeed, the anonymous reviewer also endorses the notion of Hogg as 'natural songster', stating that his songs 'sparkled up from his own soul, and came spontaneously to the surface, like foam bells in a fountain'. These songs, the article tells us, are sung 'on our streets and in our cottages,– at the jovial board, and by the peasant girl as she winds down the glen in the joyousness of her own innocent heart'. *The Edinburgh Literary Journal; or Weekly Register* had also included a piece entitled 'The Ettrick Shepherd's First Song' (about 'Donald MacDonald') back in May 1830,[47] thus establishing interest in the longevity of Hogg's songwriting several months in advance of this new collection.

Songs by the Ettrick Shepherd was, unsurprisingly, also anticipated in *Blackwood's Edinburgh Magazine* for December 1830 (No. CLXXIV, Vol. 28) in an issue entitled 'Winter Rhapsody' where North converses around the topic of Scottish song, starting with 'The Moon was a-waning'. North notes that a collection of the Shepherd's songs is 'published this very day' and quotes from Hogg's headnote to the song. This is where North also comments that James has been given 'the power of immortal song' – a quotation which Hogg later uses in his 'Reminiscences of Former Days' published as part of *Altrive Tales* in 1832.[48] The issue then proceeds to talk of song as 'the most undefinable of all undefinable kinds of poetic inspiration' and accuses Burns, Hogg, and Allan Cunningham of theft of these traditional 'Flowers of the Forest', as he terms it. For North, this is a 'Silver Age of Song'. The issue of *Noctes* of January 1831 (No. LLXXV, Vol. 29) once more announces the appearance of *Songs* with North stating: 'I am delighted to hear that Mr Blackwood is about to publish a volume of your inimitable Songs. 'Twill be universally popular, my dear James –'. North continues by speaking of Hogg and Burns holding hands as the two best songwriters of Scotland.[49]

On 1 January a proper review of *Songs by the Ettrick Shepherd* appeared in *The Literary Gazette: A Weekly Journal of Literature, Science, and the fine Arts* with the opening sentence: 'Of such a man his country may be proud'.[50] Written with no small sense of respect and admiration, this review welcomes Hogg's collection, noting that 'a strong feeling has gone straight from his heart to his song' and adding 'He is the poet of actual emotions'. Even this first review draws attention to the success of Hogg's headnotes: 'The running commentary on his own songs is one of the most amusing and original things we remember to have read'. And, as with most other reviews of the volume, numerous examples are presented. This first review talks about 'Donald MacDonald', 'The Skylark', 'The Broom sae Green', 'The Women Fo'k' and then refers to one of Hogg's Irish songs 'The Maid of the Sea' (it later refers also to 'O'er the Ocean Bounding'). It comments on Hogg's rivalry with Thomas Moore's *Irish Melodies*, highlighted by Hogg's headnotes, and concludes that the legal battle between writers had nothing to do with them as artists, but with the laws of 'musical copyright'. There is a brief discussion of 'Donald M'Gillavry', referring to the context of Blackwood's redrafted headnote, and the article also comments on 'Mary, canst thou leave me?', discussing the musical setting by Henry Bishop. 'O, weel befa' the Maiden Gay', which Hogg wrote in the Lake District, is also covered in the context of Hogg's long 1831 headnote. Full texts for 'The Broken Heart', 'When Maggy gangs Away' and 'Love Letter' are given before the conclusion which lists another group of songs the reviewer would like to have included. It ends with the comment:

> This volume will greatly raise the poet in the estimation of England, which is too apt to mistake him for a *Noctesian* roisterer, and, though an imaginative, a sometimes coarse prose writer.

So Hogg is proved right from the outset: namely in his decision to include his 'notices' or headnotes, and also in the necessity of reclaiming songs, especially from *Blackwood's*, to bolster his reputation as a songwriter of quality across the British Isles.

Following up its major pre-publication discussion, *The Edinburgh Literary Journal; or Weekly Register* also printed an article about the collection's appearance on 8 January 1831, stating:

> Having been favoured with a copy of this work in sheets, we should have noticed it sooner, had our Christmas or New-Year's-Day number contained reviews. We now hasten to introduce it to the acquaintance of our readers, fully satisfied that it will speedily acquire an extensive and well-merited popularity.[51]

Rather than give a full review of the work, primarily because its 25 December piece had already 'taken occasion to speak of the Shepherd's peculiar talents', this review simply presents extracts from the volume proper. It recommends *Songs* to its readership by quoting in full 'Donald MacDonald', 'The Broom sae Green', 'The Women Fo'k', 'O, weel, befa' the Maiden Gay', and 'A Father's Lament'. The journal includes Hogg's headnotes alongside these. It appeared on the same day as the formal announcement ('This day published') in *The Scotsman*, which also advertised *The Shepherd's Calendar* as having been 'lately published'.[52] On 12 January the same advertisement appeared in the London *Morning Chronicle* and the *Edinburgh Literary Journal*.[53] *The Scotsman*, while not publishing a full-blown review of the volume, continued to drip-feed information about it by printing on 2 February both 'The Skylark' and 'Flora Macdonald's Farewell' from 'A volume just published, entitled 'Songs by the Ettrick Shepherd''; and, on 5 February, 'The Ladies Evening Song'.

On 15 January the next major review of the collection appeared in *The Athenaeum* under the title 'The Songs of James Hogg, the Ettrick Shepherd'.[54] Again, this review, like that published in *The Edinburgh Literary Journal* on 8 January, is more of a promotional feature, quoting texts and information from Hogg's headnotes rather than offering much comment or opinion on the collection as a whole. Almost exactly the same group of songs appeared in this review as in those already in circulation. This article also appeared a week later, on 21 January, in the *Belfast News-Letter*.

On 22 January a short review appeared in the *Lancaster Gazette*, opening with reference to Hogg's role as 'only one of the old-established bards that perseveres in song'. Hogg, the article tells us, 'sings with a full heart', and the reviewer makes mention immediately of the success of Hogg's headnotes:

> Mr Hogg saves his life-writer all these pains: in the prefixes (they are hardly prefaces) he tells us the when and whereabouts of each individual copy of verse, and, furthermore, favours us with his own criticism upon it; thus forestalling the critic as well as the biographer. Many of these little pieces of prose are pleasant, and contain anecdotes of himself and friends, of a piquant description.[55]

The headnote for 'O weel befa' the Maiden Gay' is then discussed before attention moves once more to Hogg's role as 'a not unworthy successor of Burns'. The reviewer concludes that 'there are some dozens of songs in this book which no living bard could match'.

The New Monthly Magazine and Literary Journal for 1 February 1831 included a brief discussion of 'Songs, by the Ettrick Shepherd' in its substantial 'Critical Notices' section.[56] Like the *Literary Gazette* article from 1 January, this piece draws attention to the coverage of Hogg's songs to date, commenting that this collection will endear him to a newfound English audience. In contrast to the reviews which have appeared before it, this article does not quote song texts or headnotes, but offers opinion on Hogg's status as a songwriter, emphasising his rural roots and the necessity for his songs (as 'daises on the green hill side' of the Border) to be gathered and sent to 'market in city and in town'. The reviewer also notes how natural Hogg's songs are in their emotions and expression, and that they offer something new to challenge the 'affectation' of many city lyrics. Again Hogg's headnotes prompt comment:

> Many of these songs are tender and affectionate – some are of a festive, others of a national kind – and there are notes which tell us something of the author – a little about his vanity, perhaps, and much more to the honour of his head and heart.

The fact that the volume was announced in the *Belfast News-letter* on 21 January may well have inspired a more detailed review of the volume which appeared in May in the *The Ulster Magazine and monthly review of science and literature.*[57] This was also a highly complimentary review. Unsurprisingly, there is mention of Hogg's connection with Thomas Moore and the furore over the Irish songs included in *Songs by the Ettrick Shepherd*, but the connections and comparisons with Burns are also to the fore here. Hogg's 'Hymn to the Evening Star' is given as a 'beautiful specimen of his effusions' and 'Lock the Door Lariston' as a 'bold battle-song' being 'illustrative of the author's manly energetic style'. Once more there are comments on Hogg's natural ability as a songwriter (his 'untaught genius'), and the reviewer admires Hogg's success in rising to 'rank among the intellects of the mighty of the land'.

One major characteristic of the first batch of reviews was the positioning of Hogg as the 'worthy successor' to Robert Burns in Scotland's national song tradition. This was something which Hogg himself may already have been considering: John Wilson's essay entitled 'Some Observations on the Poetry of the Agricultural and that of the Pastoral Districts of Scotland, illustrated by a Comparative View of the

Genius of Burns and the Ettrick Shepherd', had appeared in *Blackwood's Magazine* in 1819, for example.[58] But it is nonetheless notable that Hogg's final 'Memoir of the Author's Life', published as part of *Altrive Tales* in 1832, made a great deal of his connection with the ploughman poet. While Burns had not been mentioned in previous versions of the 'Memoir', in 1832 he plays a prominent role. Hogg recounts how he first came to know of Burns and how he felt on hearing 'Tam o'Shanter', and he makes a case for Burns as the key inspiration for him to become a poet. He situates himself as the person best placed to inherit Burns's poetic prowess, stating: 'I have much more time to read and compose than any ploughman could have, and can sing more old songs than ever ploughman could in the world'.[59] The comparison between the poets and the competition for the crown of Scottish song continues in the periodical press for several decades beyond this.[60]

The appearance of Hogg's songs in musical collections is also part of the reception story of *Songs by the Ettrick Shepherd*, and such reviews are given, where available, in the introductions to those collections in *Contributions to Musical Collections and Miscellaneous Songs*. What is clear is that this early engagement with the collection is overwhelmingly positive, and Hogg's plan to produce a popular volume would appear to have been fulfilled. William Blackwood, who had taken so many months to come round to Hogg's thinking in 1830, was delighted with its commercial success, writing to Hogg on 26 February: 'Your Songs are liked by every body, and the sales are going well'.[61] The correspondence with Hogg at this time includes offers of copyright payment from Blackwood. Hughes explains that Blackwood offered Hogg £120 for the copyright of the volume. When Hogg declined, Blackwood then offered a lesser figure of £70 as a first instalment, with a further £50 when 1000 of the 1500 copies of the first print run had sold. Hogg immediately started pressing Blackwood to publish *A Queer Book* as the next volume in the new series, and work moved ahead with some speed. An American edition of *Songs by the Ettrick Shepherd* appeared quickly in 1832, published by William Stodart of New York. While clearly reset, this edition includes exactly the same song texts as the Edinburgh first edition. Stodart includes a brief preface, in which he speaks of its British popularity: 'The publisher hopes that this collection of Songs, which exhibits most strikingly the author's peculiar merits, and which has been so popular in Great Britain, will not prove unacceptable to the American public.'[62]

As various of the notes to individual songs in the present edition will show, some songs were selected for other collections and anthologies of Scots song throughout the nineteenth century, from well-known text-only collections such as those by Allan Cunningham and Robert

Chambers, to less well-known and anonymously edited collections such as the undated *Illustrated Book of Scottish Songs, from the Sixteenth to the Nineteenth Century*. Work to date across many of these collections would suggest that Burns came first in terms of popularity, with Robert Tannahill and Hogg often vying for second place. Key Hogg songs to appear included several from the first group he had chosen to present in *Songs by the Ettrick Shepherd*: 'Donald MacDonald', 'Flora Macdonald's Farewell', 'Bonnie Prince Charlie', 'The Skylark', 'When the Kye comes Hame'. Whether this was because these are indeed his finest songs, or whether this selection was aided by Hogg's own ordering of songs in his final 1831 collection, is difficult to ascertain.

Posthumous printings of *Songs by the Ettrick Shepherd* tended to be within larger collected works of Hogg. The fifth volume of the first multi-volume edition of *The Poetical Works of the Ettrick Shepherd*, produced by the Glasgow printer Blackie & Son in 1840, included a large number of the songs, and a separate section with Hogg's 'Sacred Melodies'. While most of the texts from *Songs by the Ettrick Shepherd* appeared here, they did so only roughly in order, as many were missing if they appeared elsewhere in the volumes as part of other collections such as *The Mountain Bard* or *The Queen's Wake*. This first edition of works then seems to have set the pattern for those published across the next few decades. Blackie issued a single volume entitled *Songs and Ballads by The Ettrick Shepherd* in 1842 which was exactly the same as this fifth volume of *Poetical Works*. Moreover, when the Revd. Thomas Thomson finalised his two-volume edition of *The Works of the Ettrick Shepherd* (published by Blackie 1865) it followed the same pattern of including collections like *The Mountain Bard* and *The Forest Minstrel* as separate sections. This also had a set of Hogg's 'Sacred Melodies' and a catch-all heading of 'Miscellaneous Songs', which included the bulk of the songs from *Songs by the Ettrick Shepherd*.

A representative grouping of the songs from *Songs* 1831 appeared in T.N. Foulis's attractive *Songs and Poems of the Ettrick Shepherd* in 1911 with memorable illustrations (especially of 'Kilmeny') by Jessie M. King. But only one much later edition of the complete *Songs by the Ettrick Shepherd* appeared, namely Jonathan Wordsworth's facsimile edition of 1989, published by Woodstock Books as part of its series entitled 'Revolution and Romanticism 1789–1834'.

5. The Present Edition

The present edition is based on *Songs by the Ettrick Shepherd* as it appeared in its first printed edition in January 1831. All 113 songs therein are included here and are presented in their original order. The decision to use the first printed edition as copy text is explained more fully above and with reference to Janette Currie's essay on 'The Genesis of the Text'. As explained, the emendations between the almost complete fair-copy manuscript and the printed text are relatively few. Excepting the editorial apparatus before and after the main body of the text, and with only a small number of emendations to correct printer errors or obvious mistakes, the present edition thus adheres closely to Hogg's original 1831 publication.

The new editors of Hogg's earlier song collection *The Forest Minstrel* of 1810, Peter Garside and Richard Jackson, decided to recreate the musical and performative contexts for each of the songs (where Hogg had included a tune title in the original publication) within the body of the text of their new edition. While, like *Songs by the Ettrick Shepherd,* this earlier collection was printed originally as a text-only volume, the new edition of 2006 thus presents musical sources alongside the texts of each of the songs, where appropriate sources have been located. Although Hogg frequently refers to musical settings and publications of songs in his headnotes to the songs included in his 1831 collection, it was decided to retain *Songs by The Ettrick Shepherd* as a text-only volume for the present edition. The reader is referred (in the editorial notes to each song) to the companion volume *Contributions to Musical Collections and Miscellaneous Songs* to see copies of the musical settings to which Hogg refers. Thus the reader of the present edition will share a very similar experience to the readers of Hogg's original publication who were encouraged to go and seek out the musical settings if they so wished, but were not compelled to do so if they preferred to 'read' the songs.

As the notes to the individual songs included will show, most of the contents in *Songs by the Ettrick Shepherd* had appeared (sometimes several times) elsewhere in Hogg's works or in other printed sources. As such, the collation process for each song included was often complex. The editorial notes at the back of the present edition aim to guide the reader through these difficulties, and where possible cross-refer the reader to the other appearances of these songs in their original editions and across the new *Collected Works of James Hogg.*

Notes

1   Edith Batho, *The Ettrick Shepherd* (Cambridge: Cambridge University Press, 1927), p. 149.

2   See for example, Elaine Petrie, 'Hogg as Songwriter', in *Studies in Hogg and His World,* 11 (1990), 19–29; and Murray G. H. Pittock, 'James Hogg: Scottish Romanticism, Song and the Public Sphere', in *James Hogg and the Literary Marketplace: Scottish Romanticism and the Working-Class Author,* ed. by Sharon Alker and Holly Faith Nelson (Farnham/Burlington: Ashgate, 2009), pp. 111–122.

3   James Hogg, *The Forest Minstrel*, ed. by Peter Garside & Richard Jackson (S/SC, 2006).

4   James Hogg, *The Mountain Bard*, ed. by Suzanne Gilbert, (S/SC, 2007), p. 9.

5   See James Hogg *Highland Journeys*, ed. by H. B. de Groot (S/SC, 2010), pp. 7–8. See also H. B. de Groot, 'Musical Notation in the *Highland Journeys*: Did Hogg have perfect pitch?', in *Studies in Hogg and his World*, 16 (2005), 127–30.

6   Hogg, *Highland Journeys*, ed. de Groot, p. 60.

7   Hogg, *Highland Journeys*, ed. de Groot, p. 167.

8   See Kirsteen McCue, 'Hogg and Music' in *The Edinburgh Companion to James Hogg*, ed. by Ian Duncan & Douglas S. Mack (Edinburgh: Edinburgh University Press, 2012), pp. 90–95.

9   See Kirsteen McCue, 'From the Songs of *Albyn's Anthology* to *German Hebrew Melodies*: the Musical Adventures of James Hogg', in *Studies in Hogg and his World*, 20 (2009), 67–83.

10 Hogg, *The Mountain Bard*, ed. Gilbert, p. 207.

11 Hogg, *The Forest Minstrel*, ed. Garside and Jackson, p. xxxvii.

12 Here Hogg was contesting Scott's place as Border ballad collector and imitator in the *Minstrelsy of the Scottish Border*. See *The Mountain Bard*, ed. Gilbert, pp. xxvi–xxviii.

13 See Janette Currie, 'James Hogg's Literary Friendships with John Grieve and Eliza Izett', in James Hogg, *Mador of the Moor*, ed. by James E. Barcus, (S/SC, 2005), pp. xliii–lvii.

14 See James Hogg, *The Queen's Wake*, ed. by Douglas S. Mack (S/SC, 2005), pp. xlviii–liii.

15 Hogg apparently had reservations about the quality of some of the songs and ballads and states in his 1821 'Memoir' that he thought *The Queen's Wake* was 'a very imperfect and unequal work' – see *The Mountain Bard*, ed. Gilbert, p. 215.

16 See Hogg's 1832 'Memoir of the Author's Life' in *Altrive Tales*, ed. by Gillian Hughes (S/SC, 2005), p. 24.

17 The quotation is: 'I was a natural songster, without another advantage on earth' – see *The Mountain Bard*, ed. Gilbert, p. 207.

18 This information is given in *The Mountain Bard*, ed. Gilbert, pp. 230–31.

19 See James Hogg, *The Jacobite Relics of Scotland*, 2 vols, ed. by Murray Pittock (S/SC, 2001, 2003).

20 See James Hogg, *Contributions to Annuals and Gift-Books*, ed. by Janette Currie and Gillian Hughes (S/SC, 2006).

21 See James Hogg, *Winter Evening Tales*, ed. by Ian Duncan (S/SC, 2004), p. xiii. The quotations are from a letter from Hogg to Archibald Constable 20 May 1813: see *The Collected Letters of James Hogg*, 3 vols, ed. by Gillian Hughes and others, (S/SC, 2004, 2006, 2008), II, pp. 145–46.

22 See Gillian Hughes, *James Hogg: A Life*, (Edinburgh: Edinburgh University Press, 2007), pp. 222–23; James Hogg, *A Queer Book*, ed. by Peter Garside (S/SC, 1995).

23 See *Letters*, II, pp. 384–86.

24 Hughes, *A Life*, p. 223.

25 See *A Queer Book*, ed. Garside, p. xiii.

26 D. M. Moir to William Blackwood, 26 November 1830 (NLS MS 4028 ff. 78–79 (78)). Thanks to Megan Coyer for alerting me to this.

27 *Letters*, II, p. 380.

28 *Letters*, II, p. 390.

29   *Letters*, II, pp. 400–03.

30   *Letters*, II, pp. 404–07.

31   See *The Forest Minstrel*, ed. Garside, p. xlix.

32   *Letters*, II, 407–09.

33   *Letters*, II, pp. 409–10 and pp. 412–13.

34   *Letters*, II, pp. 413–44.

35   *Letters*, II, pp. 414–16.

36   Hughes, *A Life*, pp. 225–26.

37   *Letters*, II, p. 421.

38   Hughes, *A Life*, p. 223.

39   James Hogg, *Contributions to Blackwood's Edinburgh Magazine*, 2 vols, ed. by Thomas Richardson (S/SC, 2008), I, pp. liv–lv.

40   Hogg, *The Jacobite Relics of Scotland*, ed. Pittock, I, p. xi. Pittock has as many as ten categories for his notes, revealing the complexity of the sources for these songs and the further complexity of Hogg's interaction with them.

41   The exception here is his *German Hebrew Melodies* [1817], which he included in his 1822 *Poetical Works* but left out of selection for *Songs* 1831. For further details, see *Contributions to Musical Collections and Miscellaneous Songs*.

42   See *Contributions to Musical Collections and Miscellaneous Songs*; see also Gillian Hughes, 'Irish Melodies and a Scottish Minstrel', *Studies in Hogg and his World*, 13 (2002), 36–45.

43   More detailed accounts of Hogg's involvement with each of these musical collections (and copies of the songs with music) can be found in James Hogg, *Contributions to Musical Collections and Miscellaneous Songs*.

44   See Hogg, *The Mountain Bard*, ed. Gilbert, p. 10.

45   *The Edinburgh literary journal, or, Weekly register of criticism and belles lettres*, (11 December 1830), 109.

46   *The Edinburgh Literary Journal; or Weekly Register of criticism and belles lettres*, (25 December 1830), 405–06.

47   *The Edinburgh Literary Journal; or Weekly Register of criticism and belles lettres*, (8 May 1830), 275–76.

48   See 'Reminiscences of Former Days', in Hogg, *Altrive Tales*, ed. Hughes, p. 55.

49   *Blackwood's Edinburgh Magazine*, Vol. 29, No. LLXXV, (January 1831), 18.

50   *The Literary Gazette : A weekly journal of literature, science, and the fine arts* (1 January 1831), 728; 5–6.

51   *The Edinburgh Literary Journal, or, Weekly register of criticism and belles lettres*, (8 January 1831), 23–25.

52   *The Scotsman* reprinted this advertisement on 15 January 1831.

53   *The Edinburgh Weekly Journal*, 34 (12 January 1831), Issue 1726. This advertisement was reprinted on 19 January.

54   Buckingham, James Silk (ed.), *The Athenaeum*, 168 (15 January, 1831), 36–38.

55   *The Lancaster Gazette and General Advertiser, for Lancashire, Westmorland, &c.* (Lancaster, England), (Saturday, January 22, 1831), Issue 1545.

56   S.C. Hall (ed.), *The New monthly magazine and literary journal* (January 1821–December 1836), 33.122 (February 1831), 56–67.

57   *The Ulster Magazine and monthly review of science and literature* 2, No. 17, (1831), 315–320 (Belfast: C.H Macloskie, at no. 35, Ann-Street). This volume is dated 1 May. Reference: Queen's University, Belfast Special Collections / h AP4.U4.

58   *Blackwood's Edinburgh Magazine* (4 Feburary 1819), 521–29.

59   See Hogg, *Altrive Tales*, ed. Hughes, p. 18. See also Kirsteen McCue, "Singing

'more old songs than ever ploughman could': The Songs of James Hogg and Robert Burns in the Musical Marketplace", in *James Hogg and the Literary Marketplace: Scottish Romanticism and the Working-Class Author*, ed. Alker and Nelson, pp. 123–138.

60   For example, see the article entitled 'The Songs of James Hogg' in *Chambers's Edinburgh Journal*, Feb. 1832–Dec. 1853; Oct 17, 1840; 455.

61   See Hughes, *A Life*, p. 226, and references to Blackwood's letters in fn. 63 on p. 326.

62   In the preface to *Songs by the Ettrick Shepherd*, (New York: William Stodart, 1832), p. vii.

The Genesis of the Text

Janette Currie

When Hogg first floated the idea of a collected edition of his songs to his publisher, William Blackwood, on 11 April 1830 he had recently received 'an absolute refusal' of the option to renew the lease on his Mount-Benger farm, and also been advised that a warrant ordering the roup of his 'stock and all effects' had been issued on behalf of the Duke of Buccleuch.[1] The idea was a sound one as the work could be put together quickly by selecting the 'best songs out of all the periodicals in the kingdom', that is, from the various periodicals and musical collections to which Hogg had contributed since the early 1800s, as well as from his previous early collections, such as *The Forest Minstrel* (1810). Working on the collection that would quickly evolve into *Songs by the Ettrick Shepherd* [hereafter *Songs* 1831] gave Hogg the opportunity of renewing his acquaintance with songs composed some thirty years previously, so that many of the songs within the collection are entirely redrafted while others remain in the same form in which they were originally created.

A major part of Hogg's holograph manuscript used in the preparation of *Songs* 1831 survives among the Blackwood Papers at the National Library of Scotland (NLS) at MS 4805. ff. 95–102.[2] Moreover, another five of Hogg's manuscript versions of songs in the finished volume are extant at NLS MS 3112, folios 280–81 and at NLS MS 10256, folios 64–66. Hogg's manuscript is heavily marked with printer's marks and other indications that it has been through the printing process. For example, above the song 'O Jeanie There's naething to fear ye' is the note '33–C' which corresponds to the printing in *Songs* 1831 on page 33 at gathering 'C', and written at the side of the text of 'The Broken Heart' is another printer's mark '273/S' which corresponds exactly with the position of this part of the song in *Songs* 1831, on p. 273, gathering 'S'. Taken together with Hogg's surviving correspondence with William Blackwood, the manuscript provides an almost unparalleled opportunity for tracing Hogg's text from manuscript to print.[3]

After two further requests, Blackwood finally agreed to 'publish a volume of select songs [...] in the manner Moore has done' (or, without musical notation), and also to a short publication deadline.[4] Hogg's letter to Blackwood of 20 October sets out the plan of the work in detail. He writes,

> I send you besides the first twenty songs of "Select Songs of the Ettrick Shepherd" that you may begin printing for they should be ready on New-Year's-day but I would particularly reccommend [*sic*] the utmost neatness and elegance in printing and fitting up the work and that you would send for Robert Hogg and consult with him for I think he has good taste in these things. It should be much like one of the Annuals. It will not contain one third of my songs and it is impossible that I can know the best but I think [I/we] cannot go wrong in taking all which have been popular in the first place. Therefore in the course of printing you may *defer* any song you like till we see if we cannot get a handsome volume made up of better ones. The type should not be large but calculated to get in the songs in long measure without breaking the lines. I have added simple notices to each song which I think will interest all such as are attached to them which notices should be printed in the same type with the songs. You must by all means endeavour to get me a copy of "The Forest Minstrel" published long ago by Constable I cannot go on without that although out of the whole vol. I do not think I could take above half a dozen But indeed they are scattered through all the periodicals almost of Britain and can never be recovered by me [...]. [...] in the meantime there can be nothing to prevent the going on of the songs as quickly as you please as I can send you twenty songs every week if you require them.

Hogg concludes by thanking Blackwood 'with the most lively gratitude for your ready assistance in an extremity'.[5] In order to keep to the eleven-week publication deadline Hogg outlines every detail of the finished volume, from his request that his nephew is involved, to the selection of typeface, and also thinking ahead to the outward appearance of the volume so that it conforms to the seasonal literary Annuals. Significantly, at this point Hogg also relinquishes much of the editorial control over the contents of the volume to Blackwood, giving him authority to '*defer* any song' as the work proceeds. Further, he indicates (in his letter above) that Blackwood should simply reprint 'one of the songs which can be printed from the book' rather than wait for a fresh version.[6]

Robert Hogg, as Douglas Mack revealed in his S/SC edition of *The Shepherd's Calendar*, removed many of his uncle's 'indelicate' passages prior to publication in 1829. For example, Robert cut 'almost two thousand words' from 'Mary Burnet'.[7] Robert Hogg adds his stamp to the finished version of *Songs* 1831. For example, it was he who communicated the second anecdote appended to the published version of 'Donald M,Donald'. In an undated letter to William Blackwood he writes,

> my uncle has omitted an anecdote which I have heard him tell in relation to Donald Macdonald, which appeared to me very interesting, not only as a proof of the extensive popularity of the song, but of its popularity among a class to inspire whom with devotion to the cause of their country was at the time a matter of no little consequence

He goes on to relate an anecdote about Hogg hearing 'a soldier who seemed to be either travelling home upon furlough or returning to his regiment' sing 'Donald M,Donald' and concludes by noting that this anecdote 'is worth twenty of that he has given about hearing the song sung in the Lancaster Theatre'.[8] Robert Hogg's extra anecdote appears in the published version of *Songs* 1831 below another by Hogg in which he relates an account of being present during a performance of the song 'in the theatre at Lancaster' (see pp. 4–5 of the present text).

Robert Hogg seems to have worked differently on the text of *Songs* 1831 than on *The Shepherd's Calendar*. While there is evidence of some literary polishing it is not extreme, nor is it clear whether the 'polishing' is by Hogg or his nephew. For example, there are substantive additions in the published version of 'The Minstrel Boy' that are not within Hogg's holograph manuscript (NLS MS ff. 31v–32r). Following Hogg's statement that cancellation of the earlier version of the song was 'the most ridiculous of all things', the phrase 'in my opinion' has been added to the printed headnote, which separates Hogg from his publishers, presumably in case of any future litigation proceedings. Furthermore, Hogg ends with the exclamatory 'take that!', but someone has added the proverbial phrase 'as Gideon Laidlaw said when the man died who had cheated him' in the published version. It is not clear whether Hogg made these alterations during the printing process or whether it is the work of Robert Hogg, softening Hogg's indignation. Whatever the case, Hogg was in Edinburgh during the final few weeks prior to publication so that he would have regained overall editorial control of the finished volume and had time to correct, replace or reject any part of the text.

As printing commenced on the volume, the proofs were dispatched from Ballantyne and Company, the Edinburgh printers, to Hogg at Altrive in Yarrow. Hogg's concern that the work continue speedily provokes a query, as he asks Blackwood on 10 November,

Before I go farther inform me of this Do proof sheets go free? for our carrier now passes between us only once a fortnight and if they come by post I get them every Monday and every Friday after the post arrives [...] I also return proofs and a few more songs that the press may be going on for I want the volume published on New-year's day and you may announce it in some way as follows "MR HOGG'S SONGS. A Selection from the songs of the Ettrick Shepherd is in the press and will appear on New-year's day Elegantly printed &c &c" [.][9]

On 24 November Hogg's anxiety resurfaces in a complaint to Blackwood: 'I have been wondering the proofs have come so slow none have yet arrived by post'.[10] By 30 November, Hogg is in bed with a severe toothache but still the work continues: 'I have nevertheless dashed you off a few songs as they came to hand to keep the press going' he writes to Blackwood.[11]

NLS MS 4805, ff. 26–94 (ending with 'The Wee Housie', f. 94v) comprises what seems to be a combination of a working copy and also Hogg's fair-copy holograph of the manuscript he prepared for *Songs* 1831. For example, there are two holograph manuscript versions of 'The Minstrel Boy', at NLS MS ff. 31–32 and at f. 57. The page number '12' is written at the top left hand corner of f. 31v, and this number follows a sequence of pagination that begins with 'p 1' of 'Donald M, Donald' (f. 26r) and ends at '26' and the conclusion of 'The Village of Balmaquhapple' (f. 38v). MS 4805, f. 57r is not paginated. However, immediately below the title is a note (not in Hogg's hand) stating 'Already Printed at page 20' and another note at the top right-hand of the manuscript, which is in Hogg's hand, stating 'p 113 from the proofs but Love's like a dizziness wanting'. What appears to have happened is that as Hogg worked through the proofs he simply forgot that 'The Minstrel Boy' was already included within his collection. Indeed, the text of NLS MS 4805, ff. 31v–32r is printed in *Songs* 1831 at p. 20. The text of both songs is identical in both manuscripts. However, Hogg wrote out a new headnote for the second version of the song which is not included in the printed version:

The Minstrel Boy
Is one likewise on the proscription list an inter-communed rebel against the sovereign authority of Thomas Little the Great and really I believe it is treading too hard on the heels of his dignity though I am sure it was through no ill intention. It was harmonized by Smith to an Irish air called <u>The Moreen</u> and engraved but like the rest the edition was burnt and the plate destroyed.[12]

In the same letter of 30 November (above), Hogg informs Blackwood 'I am much pleased with your introduction to Donald M,Gillavry'.[13] There is a very full introductory headnote in the published volume (pp. 41–42 of the present text). However, Hogg's holograph manuscript states simply,

(There are two droll quotations which Mr Blackwood will please to cause be inserted here neither of which I have by me. The one is from the Edin. Review of the Jacobite Relics relating to this song the other the answer to it in Maga) (f. 47v)

NLS MS 4805, ff. 26–94 comprises a number of sheets cut to different sizes, the majority being 12cm x 19cm, but also including sheets of 15cm x 18.5cm and 13cm x 21cm. For some songs, Hogg squeezed the text around the edges of the page to prevent the text slipping onto the next (for example, at the end of 'Red Clan-Ranald's Men, f. 64r). On other occasions he left the verso of the sheet blank and started a new song on a fresh sheet ('The Frazer's in the Correi', f. 59r). Mostly, Hogg writes the text in a continuous stream and separates the headnotes from the songs by drawing a short line between them; he also separates each new song with a longer line drawn across the page below the last line of the song. It would appear, therefore, that when compiling the text Hogg was also paying very close attention to how it would fit into the finished 'pocket-sized' volume.

Hogg's manuscript has its own sequence or sequences of pagination that, at times, do not correspond with the printed text. 'Donald M,Donald' is on pp. 1–3 of *Songs* 1831 (spelled 'Donald MacDonald' in the printed text), and this is the song Hogg writes in the headnote that he 'places [...] the first' in his collection. This song does indeed begin with 'p 1' written at the top right-hand of the page in Hogg's hand (NLS MS 4805, folio 26r). Hogg's pagination proceeds until a break occurs at 'page 26' at the conclusion of 'I lookit East, I lookit West' (folio 38r) and begins again at 'page 29' with 'The Women Fo'k' (folios 39–40). The missing songs are found in NLS MS 10256, folios 64r–66v, which contain the songs 'Lenachan's Farewell', the title and headnote of 'The Stuarts of Appin', and 'The Poor Man'. Hogg has paginated these songs 'pp. 25–28' which almost corresponds to the missing sequence. Moreover, the ordering of the songs corresponds to their placing within *Songs* 1831 (pp. 56–64). There are further breaks in NLS MS 4805, for example at the end of the song 'The Frazer's in the Correi', numbered '69' in the manuscript's pagination. The page numbering begins again on a double-page numbered '114–115', indicating that there are 69 'pages' missing. However, the above songs take up only 10 pages of the printed text of *Songs* 1831 at pages 129–138. Such gaps in the page-numbering might indicate that Hogg deliberately left space for songs that were ultimately left out of the printed version, or perhaps some songs were deleted at the final printing stage, or, more possibly, Hogg did not keep track of the numbering of the pages he sent off in batches from Altrive to Edinburgh.

In his letter to Blackwood of 30 November (above) Hogg continues to press on with the work of compiling the volume:

> I hardly think you need send out any more proofs as I must see you asson [*sic*] as able to ride. I have plenty of songs here such as they are but there are many many good ones that I want and will want though it is no great matter. Good and ill they are all manifestly pears of the same tree [.]

And he concludes with a footnote requesting, 'For God's sake send me some of your fine large paper again to Selkirk before Friday as I cannot do without it and I am sure you cannot say but I have been thrifty of it [...].'[14]

By 9 December Hogg was in Edinburgh (he informs Margaret 'I am here in safety and hope to return in a forthnight [*sic*]'.[15] In the end, though, the work must have been more complicated and time-consuming than Hogg had imagined as he was still in Edinburgh on 1 January 1831.[16]

At the top left-hand corner of 'O Lady Dear' (NLS, MS 4805, folio 88v) Hogg has written the page-number '202' and this song is followed by an unpaginated section of songs from *The Queen's Wake* that (Hogg writes in the headnote to 'Hymn to the God of the Sea') 'might be successfully set to music' (p. 127 of the present text). This section of the manuscript has no page numbers. However, 'Mary Gray' (NLS, MS 3112, folio 281) is page-numbered '203' and '204' and follows the sequential page numbering after 'O Lady Dear'. Initially, therefore, 'Mary Gray' followed 'O Lady Dear' within the collection, but at some point prior to printing Hogg added further songs from *The Queen's Wake*. In his letter to Blackwood of 20 October (mentioned above) Hogg had also suggested publication of a new edition of *The Queen's Wake*, and this idea is clearly behind his decision to include additional songs from his most successfully published work. The songs entitled 'Ode on hearing of the death of Mr Pitt', 'Busaco', and 'Ode to the Genius of Shakespeare' are numbered differently: the number '1' is written in the top right hand corner of the first song, followed by '2' and '3' for each song. These songs are printed at the end of *Songs* 1831 where the running order of the printed version corresponds to their ordering in the manuscript. The final song in the printed version, 'Good Night and Joy', corresponds with a note by Hogg written in the top right-hand of the manuscript: 'This to be on the last leaf of the vol'. There is no page number on the leaf, which exists separately from the bulk of the manuscript, at NLS MS 3112, folio 280. It may be, therefore, that this version of the song, along with the songs that do not directly follow the page numbering of the majority of the manuscript, were written while Hogg was in Edinburgh during December 1830 to oversee the printing of *Songs* 1831.

The printer's marks and alterations clearly indicate that the surviving manuscripts mentioned above were a significant part of the process of bringing Hogg's songs to publication; that he was actively involved in every aspect of the preparation of *Songs* 1831. Given Hogg's close involvement with the publication process and the fact that he gives no indication that he was unhappy with the final copy, that he would have chosen different songs, rearranged the collection, or edited the finished volume differently, we have no reason to assume that he was less than satisfied with the published text. For these reasons the copy text for the present text is the first published edition of *Songs by the Ettrick Shepherd*.

Douglas S. Mack's essay, 'The Stirling/South Carolina Edition of James Hogg: Thoughts on Editorial Policy', helpfully provided a guiding framework to establish a clear editorial policy on establishing the copy text for the present volume. Mack points to the significance of Jerome McGann's view that we should see 'the conversion of the author's manuscript into print, not so much as a corruption of the purity of the original utterance, but rather as a collaborative process of preparation of the text for its public appearance'.[18] In deciding the copy text, Mack writes, an editor should take account of all of the 'social processes' involved in bringing a text to print, that 'in editing Hogg, the choice of copy text will depend on the circumstances of the particular case'.[19] In Mack's view, if Hogg's involvement in the detailed preparation of a text for publication was active and consensual, then it is likely that the first edition rather than the manuscript will be the appropriate choice as copy text. Given Hogg's close involvement and obvious controlling influence during the preparation and publication process, the editorial team decided that the first published version of *Songs* 1831 would be the copy text for the present S/SC edition. However, we have also given a full account in the textual notes of the various interesting textual differences between the manuscript and the first edition.

Overall, the finished volume of *Songs by the Ettrick Shepherd* represents a sustained collaborative effort between songwriter, editor, and publisher working together to produce 'a handsome volume' of Hogg's 'best' songs with 'simple' authorial annotation. What they finally end up with is a volume of 113 songs comprising pastoral songs, love songs, pathetic songs, political songs, national songs, Jacobite songs, ballads and non-classifiable lyrics.[17] *Songs* 1831 is a truly 'select' collection representing thirty years of Hogg's songs.

Notes

1. The present essay revises and clarifies many of the observations I raised in 'Editing the Text and Music of James Hogg's *Songs by the Ettrick Shepherd* (1831)', written with Kirsteen McCue, *Scottish Studies Review*, 8.2 (Autumn 2007), 54–68. See Hogg's letters to Walter Scott of 7 January and 7 March 1830, in *The Collected Letters of James Hogg, 1820–1831*, ed. by Gillian Hughes (S/SC, 2006), pp. 369–79 and 377 respectively (hereafter *Letters*, II).

2. Folios 26–94 comprise songs included in the finished volume, while folios 95–102 are earlier drafts and fair-copy versions of songs contained in the volume.

3. Peter Garside provides another example of Hogg's close involvement in the publication of his work in the introduction to *The Private Memoirs and Confessions of a Justified Sinner* (S/SC, 2001), pp. lv–lxvi. However, in that case, Hogg's manuscript is not extant.

4. See Hogg's letters to Blackwood of 21 June and 30 September 1830, in *Letters*, II, 390 and 400–01.

5. *Letters*, II, 404–06.

6. *Letters*, II, 404–06 (p. 406).

7. *The Shepherd's Calendar*, ed. by Douglas S. Mack (S/SC , 2002), p. xvii.

8. See NLS MS 4079, folios 202–203.

9. *Letters*, II, 407–08.

10. *Letters*, II, 412.

11. *Letters*, II, 413–414.

12. NLS MS 4805, f. 57r.

13. *Letters*, II, 414.

14. *Letters*, II, 413–414 (p. 414).

15. *Letters*, II, 414–15 (p. 414).

16. See his letter to Margaret of this date in *Letters*, II, 421. No doubt he returned to Altrive in between this date (see his letter addressed from Altrive of 16 December in *Letters*, II, 417–18). Hughes records an advertisement of *Songs by the Ettrick Shepherd* 'Just published' in the *Edinburgh Weekly Journal* of 12 January 1831 (*Letters*, II, 422n.).

17. 'Ode to the Genius of Shakespeare' (*Songs* 1831, pp. 304–06), for example, is a non-classifiable lyric.

18. *Studies in Hogg and his World*, No. 4 (1993), 83–90 (p. 86).

19. Ibid., p. 87.

S O N G S,

BY

THE ETTRICK SHEPHERD.

NOW FIRST COLLECTED.

WILLIAM BLACKWOOD, EDINBURGH:
AND T. CADELL, LONDON.
MDCCCXXXI.

Donald MacDonald.

I PLACE this song the first, not on account of any intrinsic merit that it possesses,—for there it ranks rather low,—but merely because it was my first song, and exceedingly popular when it first appeared. I wrote it when a barefooted lad herding lambs on the Blackhouse Heights, in utter indignation at the threatened invasion from France. But after it had run through the Three Kingdoms, like fire set to heather, for ten or twelve years, no one ever knew or enquired who was the author.—It is set to the old air, "Woo'd an' married an' a'."

MY name it is Donald M'Donald,
   I leeve in the Heelands sae grand;
I hae follow'd our banner, and will do,
   Wherever my Maker has land.
When rankit amang the blue bonnets,   5
   Nae danger can fear me ava;
I ken that my brethren around me
   Are either to conquer or fa'.
      Brogues an' brochin an' a',
      Brochin an' brogues an' a';   10
      An' is nae her very weel aff
      Wi' her brogues an' brochin an' a'?

What though we befriendit young Charlie?—
   To tell it I dinna think shame;
Poor lad, he cam to us but barely,   15
   An' reckon'd our mountains his hame.
'Twas true that our reason forbade us;
   But tenderness carried the day;—
Had Geordie come friendless amang us,
   Wi' him we had a' gane away.   20
      Sword an' buckler an' a',
      Buckler an' sword an' a';
      Now for George we'll encounter the devil,
      Wi' sword an' buckler an' a'!

An' O, I wad eagerly press him   25
   The keys o' the East to retain;
For should he gie up the possession,
   We'll soon hae to force them again.
Than yield up an inch wi' dishonour,
   Though it were my finishing blow,   30

He ay may depend on M'Donald,
  Wi' his Heelanders a' in a row:
    Knees an' elbows an' a',
    Elbows an' knees an' a';
    Depend upon Donald M'Donald,   35
    His knees an' elbows an' a'!

Wad Bonaparte land at Fort-William,
  Auld Europe nae langer should grane;
I laugh when I think how we'd gall him,
  Wi' bullet, wi' steel, an' wi' stane;   40
Wi' rocks o' the Nevis and Garny
  We'd rattle him off frae our shore,
Or lull him asleep in a cairny,
  An' sing him—Lochaber no more!
    Stanes an' bullets an' a',   45
    Bullets an' stanes an' a';
    We'll finish the Corsican callan
    Wi' stanes an' bullets an' a'!

For the Gordon is good in a hurry,
  An' Campbell is steel to the bane,   50
An' Grant, an' M'Kenzie, an' Murray,
  An' Cameron will hurkle to nane;
The Stuart is sturdy an' loyal,
  An' sae is M'Leod an' M'Kay;
An' I, their gudebrither, M'Donald,   55
  Shall ne'er be the last in the fray!
    Brogues an' brochin an' a',
    Brochin an' brogues an' a';
    An' up wi' the bonny blue bonnet,
    The kilt an' the feather an' a'! *   60

---

* I once heard the above song sung in the theatre at Lancaster, when the singer substituted the following lines of his own for the last verse:

  'For Jock Bull he is good in a hurry,
    An' Sawney is steel to the bane,
  An' wee Davie Welsh is a widdy,
    An' Paddy will hurkle to nane;
  They'll a' prove baith sturdy and loyal,
    Come dangers around them what may,
  An' I, their gudebrither, M'Donald,
    Shall ne'er be the last in the fray!" &c.

It took exceedingly well, and was three times encored, and there was I sitting in the gallery, applauding as much as any body. My vanity prompted me to tell a jolly Yorkshire manufacturer that night, that I was the author of the song. He laughed excessively at my assumption, and told the landlady that he took me for a half-crazed Scots pedlar.

Another anecdote concerning this song I may mention; and I do it with no little pride, as it is a proof of the popularity of Donald M'Donald among a class, to inspire whom with devotion to the cause of their country was at the time a matter of no little consequence. Happening upon one occasion to be in a wood in Dumfries-shire, through which wood the highroad passed, I heard a voice singing; and a turn of the road soon brought in sight a soldier, who seemed to be either travelling home upon furlough, or returning to his regiment. When the singer approached nearer, I distinguished the notes of my own song of Donald M'Donald. As the lad proceeded with his song, he got more and more into the spirit of the thing, and on coming to the end,

> "An' up wi' the bonny blue bonnet,
> The kilt an' the feather an' a'!"

in the height of his enthusiasm, he hoisted his cap on the end of his staff, and danced it about triumphantly. I stood ensconced behind a tree, and heard and saw all without being observed.

Scotia's Glens

WAS written the same year with the foregoing, and published in several papers the following year; a feeble attempt to contribute my mite for the defence of my country, the only way that it was in my power. It became popular in India. The original name of the air is "Lord Ballenden's delight"—a fine one, but hard to sing—to be found in some of the old collections.

> 'MANG Scotia's glens and mountains blue,
> Where Gallia's lillies never grew,
> Where Roman eagles never flew,
>   Nor Danish lions rallied,
> Where skulks the roe in anxious fear,   5
> Where roves the swift an' stately deer,
> There live the lads to freedom dear,
>   By foreign yoke ne'er galled!
>
> There woods grow wild on every hill,
> There freemen wander at their will,   10
> And Scotland will be Scotland still,
>   While hearts so brave defend her!

Fear not, our sovereign Liege, they cry,
We've flourish'd fair beneath thine eye;
For thee we'll fight, for thee we'll die,   15
    Nor aught but life surrender!

Since thou hast watch'd our every need,
And taught our navies wide to spread,
The smallest hair from thy grey head
    No foreign foe shall sever;   20
Thy honour'd age in peace to save,
The sternest enemy we'll brave,
Or stem the fiercest ocean wave,
    Nor heart nor hand shall waver!

Though nations join yon tyrant's arm,   25
While Scotia's noble blood runs warm,
Our good old man we'll guard from harm,
    Or fall in heaps around him!
Although the Irish Harp were won,
And England's Roses all o'errun,   30
'Mong Scotia's glens, with sword and gun,
    We'll form a bulwark round him!

The Broom Sae Green

Is my greatest favourite at present,—probably because the air is my own,
as well as the verses; for I find I have a particular facility in approving of
such things. It is beautifully set by Bishop, in Goulding and D'Almaine's
Select Scottish Melodies.

LANG I sat by the broom sae green,
    An' O, my heart was eerie!
For aye this strain was breathed within,
    Your laddie will no come near ye!
Lie still, thou wee bit fluttering thing,   5
What means this weary wavering?
Nae heart returns thy raptured spring,
    Your laddie will no come near ye!

His leifu' sang the robin sung
    On the bough that hung sae near me,   10
Wi' tender grief my heart was wrung,
    For O, the strain was dreary!

The robin's sang it coudnae be
That gart the tear-drap blind my ee;
How ken'd the wee bird on the tree 15
    That my laddie wad no come near me?

The new-wean'd lamb on yonder lea
    It bleats out through the braken,
The herried bird upon the tree
    Mourns o'er its nest forsaken;– 20
If they are wae, how weel may I?
Nae grief like mine aneath the sky,
The lad I lo'e he cares nae by
    Though my fond heart is breaking!

Flora MacDonald's Farewell

WAS composed to an air handed me by the late lamented Niel Gow, junior. He said it was an ancient Skye air, but afterwards told me it was his own. When I first heard the song sung by Mr Morison, I never was so agreeably astonished,–I could hardly believe my senses that I had made so good a song without knowing it.

FAR over yon hills of the heather sae green,
    An' down by the correi that sings to the sea,
The bonny young Flora sat sighing her lane,
    The dew on her plaid, and the tear in her ee.
She look'd at a boat wi' the breezes that swung 5
    Away on the wave, like a bird of the main,
An' aye as it lessen'd, she sigh'd and she sung,
    Fareweel to the lad I shall ne'er see again!
Fareweel to my hero, the gallant an' young,
    Fareweel to the lad I shall ne'er see again! 10

The moorcock that craws on the brows of Ben-Connal,
    He kens of his bed in a sweet mossy hame;
The eagle that soars o'er the cliffs of Clan-Ronald,
    Unawed and unhunted, his eyry can claim;
The solan can sleep on the shelve of the shore, 15
    The cormorant roost on his rock of the sea,
But, ah! there is one whose hard fate I deplore,
    Nor house, ha', nor hame, in his country has he–
The conflict is past, and our name is no more–
    There's nought left but sorrow for Scotland and me! 20

The target is torn from the arm of the just,
    The helmet is cleft on the brow of the brave,
The claymore for ever in darkness must rust,
    But red is the sword of the stranger and slave;
The hoof of the horse, and the foot of the proud,   25
    Have trod o'er the plumes on the bonnet of blue!
Why slept the red bolt in the breast of the cloud
    When tyranny revell'd in blood of the true?
Fareweel, my young hero, the gallant and good!
    The crown of thy fathers is torn from thy brow!   30

Bonny Prince Charlie.

Is it not singular how this song should have been so popular? There can
be no dispute that it is one of my worst. The air was likewise given me
by my friend the late Mr Niel Gow, and to it I dashed down the words
at random. Afterwards, when there was like to be a dust among the
music-sellers about the tune, Mr Robertson wrote to me about it, and
to justify his appropriation, assured me that the air was that of "Gala
Water!" I answered that I would not dispute his authority, but after
that, no man was entitled to disbelieve that a horse-hair would turn an
eel.—For the music of this and the foregoing song, the best sets are to
be found in Mr Purdie's Border Garland, by Dewar.

CAM ye by Athol, lad wi' the philabeg,
Down by the Tummel, or banks o' the Garry,
Saw ye our lads, wi' their bonnets and white cockades,
Leaving their mountains to follow Prince Charlie?
    Follow thee! follow thee! wha wadna follow thee?   5
    Lang hast thou loved and trusted us fairly!
    Charlie, Charlie, wha wadna follow thee,
    King o' the Highland hearts, bonny Prince Charlie?

I hae but ae son, my gallant young Donald;
But if I had ten, they should follow Glengarry!   10
Health to M'Donnell and gallant Clan-Ronald,
For these are the men that will die for their Charlie!
    Follow thee! follow thee! &c.

I'll to Lochiel and Appin, and kneel to them,
Down by Lord Murray, and Roy of Kildarlie;   15
Brave M'Intosh he shall fly to the field with them;
These are the lads I can trust wi' my Charlie!
    Follow thee! follow thee! &c.

Down through the Lowlands, down wi' the Whigamore!
Loyal true Highlanders, down wi' them rarely! 20
Ronald an' Donald, drive on, wi' the broad claymore,
Over the necks of the foes o' Prince Charlie!
   Follow thee! follow thee! wha wadna follow thee?
   Lang hast thou loved and trusted us fairly!
Charlie, Charlie, wha wadna follow thee, 25
King o' the Highland hearts, bonny Prince Charlie?

The Skylark.

A LITTLE pastoral song, worth half-a-dozen of the foregoing.–For the fine original air, see Mr Purdie's Border Garland.

    BIRD of the wilderness,
    Blithesome and cumberless,
Sweet be thy matin o'er moorland and lea!
    Emblem of happiness,
    Blest is thy dwelling-place— 5
O to abide in the desert with thee!
    Wild is thy lay and loud,
    Far in the downy cloud,
Love gives it energy, love gave it birth.
    Where, on thy dewy wing, 10
    Where art thou journeying?
Thy lay is in heaven, thy love is on earth.

    O'er fell and fountain sheen,
    O'er moor and mountain green,
O'er the red streamer that heralds the day, 15
    Over the cloudlet dim,
    Over the rainbow's rim,
Musical cherub, soar, singing, away!
    Then, when the gloaming comes,
    Low in the heather blooms 20
Sweet will thy welcome and bed of love be!
    Emblem of happiness,
    Blest is thy dwelling-place—
O to abide in the desert with thee!

Gang to the Brakens wi' Me.

THIS pastoral ballad is likewise set to music by Bishop, in Goulding and D'Almaine's Select Melodies, but I confess not much to my taste, as he has ruined the simplicity of my favourite air, which I deemed a masterpiece.

I'LL sing of yon glen of red heather,
    An' a dear thing that ca's it her hame,
Wha's a' made o' love-life thegither,
    Frae the tie o' the shoe to the kaime.
Love beckons in every sweet motion,   5
    Commanding due homage to gie;
But the shrine o' my dearest devotion
    Is the bend o' her bonny eebree.

I fleech'd an' I pray'd the dear lassie
    To gang to the brakens wi' me;   10
But, though neither lordly nor saucy,
    Her answer was–"Laith wad I be!
I neither hae father nor mither,
    Sage counsel or caution to gie;
An' prudence has whisper'd me never   15
    To gang to the brakens wi' thee."

Dear lassie, how can ye upbraid me,
    An' try your ain love to beguile?
For ye are the richest young lady
    That ever gaed o'er the kirk-stile.   20
Your smile, that is blither than ony,
    The bend o' your cheerfu' eebree,
An' the sweet blinks o' love there sae bonny,
    Are five hunder thousand to me!

She turn'd her around, an' said, smiling,   25
    While the tear in her blue eye shone clear,
"You're welcome, kind sir, to your mailing,
    For, O, you hae valued it dear:
Gae make out the lease, do not linger,
    Let the parson indorse the decree;   30
An' then, for a wave o' your finger,
    I'll gang to the brakens wi' thee!"
There's joy in the bright blooming feature,

When love lurks in every young line;
There's joy in the beauties of nature,   35
    There's joy in the dance and the wine:
But there's a delight will ne'er perish,
    'Mang pleasures all fleeting an' vain,
And that is to love and to cherish
    The fond little heart that's our ain!   40

The Minstrel Boy

WAS written as a *per contra* to Mr Moore's song to the same air. But either he or his publishers, or both, set up their birses, and caused it and a great many more to be cancelled,—the most ridiculous of all things, in my opinion, I ever knew. It was manifestly because they saw mine were the best. Let them take that! as Gideon Laidlaw said when the man died who had cheated him.

THE Minstrel Boy to the glen is gone,
    In its deepest dells you'll find him,
Where echoes sing to his music's tone,
    And fairies listen behind him.
He sings of nature all in her prime,   5
    Of sweets that around him hover,
Of mountain heath and of moorland thyme,
    And trifles that tell the lover.

How wildly sweet is the minstrel's lay,
    Through cliffs and wild woods ringing,   10
For, ah! there is love to beacon his way,
    And hope in the song he's singing!
The bard may indite, and the minstrel sing,
    And maidens may chorus it rarely;
But unless there be love in the heart within,   15
    The ditty will charm but sparely.

Farewell to Glen-Shalloch.

THIS Jacobite song is set to an old Highland melody, by the late Mr R. A. Smith, to whom the vocal melodies of Scotland are more indebted than to any man that ever existed. The song itself was composed from a scrap of a translation in prose of what Mrs Fraser said was a Gaelic song.

FAREWELL to Glen-Shalloch,
  A farewell for ever!
Farewell to my wee cot
  That stands by the river!
The fall is loud sounding   5
  In voices that vary,
And the echoes surrounding
  Lament with my Mary.

I saw her last night,
  'Mid the rocks that enclose them,   10
With a child at her knee,
  And a child at her bosom:
I heard her sweet voice
  'Mid the depth of my slumber,
And the sang that she sung   15
  Was of sorrow and cumber.

"Sleep sound, my sweet babe,
  There is nought to alarm thee;
The sons of the valley
  No power have to harm thee!   20
I'll sing thee to rest
  In the balloch untrodden,
With a coronach sad
  For the slain of Culloden!

"The brave were betray'd,   25
  And the tyrant is daring
To trample and waste us,
  Unpitying, unsparing!
Thy mother no voice has,
  No feeling that changes,   30
No word, sign, or song,
  But the lesson of vengeance!
"I'll tell thee, my son,
  How our laurels are withering;

I'll bind on thy sword 35
   When the clansmen are gathering;
I'll bid thee go forth
   In the cause of true honour,
And never return
   Till thy country hath won her! 40

"Our tower of devotion
   Is the home of the reaver;
The pride of the ocean
   Is fallen for ever!
The pride of the forest, 45
   That time could not weaken,
Is trod in the dust,
   And its honours are shaken!

"Rise, spirits of yore,
   Ever dauntless in danger! 50
For the land that was yours
   Is the land of the stranger.
O come from your caverns,
   All bloodless and hoary,
And these fiends of the valley 55
   Shall tremble before ye!"

Caledonia.

IT is rather curious that the only time I ever heard this song sung, except by one young lady (Miss Forrest), was in the theatre at Lancaster, by the same man who sung Donald M'Donald, a Scotsman, I think, of the name of M'Rae. He sung it to a monotonous tune, and it did not take well. They were both announced for a future night; but I came off and left them. It happened to be the time of the assizes, and in two days, out of near forty offenders, they cast twenty-four for execution, the whole trials taking up little more time than in Scotland would have been taken for the trial of one. I had gone to make the tour of Wales; but it appeared to me that all these fellows were just men that they had brought in to be hanged. So I thought I was long enough there, and the next morning set off for Scotland by the Lakes of Westmoreland and Cumberland; and so ended my tour to Wales. Niel Gow, jun. composed the air to which it is set in the Border Garland, but it is oftener sung to another composed by a young lady.

CALEDONIA! thou land of the mountain and rock,
   Of the ocean, the mist, and the wind–
Thou land of the torrent, the pine, and the oak,
   Of the roebuck, the hart, and the hind:
Though bare are thy cliffs, and though barren thy glens,   5
   Though bleak thy dun islands appear,
Yet kind are the hearts, and undaunted the clans,
   That roam on these mountains so drear!

A foe from abroad, or a tyrant at home,
   Could never thy ardour restrain;   10
The marshall'd array of imperial Rome
   Essay'd thy proud spirit in vain!
Firm seat of religion, of valour, of truth,
   Of genius unshackled and free,
The muses have left all the vales of the south,   15
   My loved Caledonia, for thee!

Sweet land of the bay and the wild-winding deeps,
   Where loveliness slumbers at even,
While far in the depth of the blue water sleeps
   A calm little motionless heaven!   20
Thou land of the valley, the moor, and the hill,
   Of the storm and the proud rolling wave–
Yes, thou art the land of fair liberty still,
   And the land of my forefathers' grave!

The Noctes Sang

WAS made one day in Edinburgh, for singing in Ambrose's at night, on a particular occasion, when a number of foreign literary gentlemen were to be of the party. I did not sing it till late at night, when we were all beginning to get merry; and the effect on the party was like electricity. It was encored I know not how oft, and Mr Gillies ruffed and screamed out so loud in approbation, that he fell from his chair, and brought an American gentleman down with him. I have lost a verse of it, but it is likely to have been preserved in the Noctes Ambrosianæ. It has been always the first song at our jovial meetings ever since. The air is my own, and a very capital one. I believe it is preserved in the Noctes, and nowhere else.

IF e'er you wad be a brave fellow, young man,
Beware o' the Blue an' the Yellow, young man;

For if ye wad be strang,
An' wad wish to live lang,
Come join wi' the lads that get mellow, young man!   5
Like the crack of a squib that is thrawn on, young man,
Compared wi' the roar of a cannon, young man,
          Sae is a Whig's blow
          To the pith that's below
The brand of auld Geordie Buchanan, young man.   10

I heard a bit burd in the braken, young man,
It sung till the Whigs were a' quakin', young man;
          An' aye the sad lay
          Was, Alack for the day!
For the Blue an' the Yellow's forsaken, young man!   15
If ye wad hear tell o' their pingle, young man,
Gae list that wee burd in the dingle, young man;
          Its notes o' despair
          Are sae loud in the air,
That the windows of heaven play jingle, young man!   20

I'll gie you a toast of the auldest, young man,
The loyal heart ne'er was the cauldest, young man;
          Our King an' his Throne,
          Be his glory our own,
An' the last o' his days aye the bauldest, young man!   25
But as for the rogue that wad hector, young man,
And set us at odds wi' a lecture,* young man,
          May he dance Cutty-mun,**
          Wi' his neb to the sun,
An' his doup to the General Director,*** young man!   30

---

* A celebrated London professor was lecturing here then.

** *Cutty-mun;* an old Scottish tune of exceedingly quick and cramp time.

*** This is a mysterious allusion to the common place of execution in Edinburgh. C. N. *Blackwood's Magazine.*

The Souters o' Selkirk

Was written at the request, and for the singing, of Dr Clarkson of Selkirk, who liked the old air, and sung it well. Of course, the song is meant to express his own sentiments. He said he did not wish for a long song—a short song, by all manner of means. But when he got it he was in a mighty passion, because there was no more of it. "It was no song at all," he said; "it was not well begun till it was done."

Up wi' the Souters o' Selkirk,
  The sons of an auld pedigree!
An' up wi' the lads o' the Forest,
  Renown'd for their leal loyaltye!
I may be mista'en, but I carena,   5
  My error I never shall rue;
Of all manly virtues I value
  The heart that is loyal and true.

    Sing umptidy-tumptidy tearhim,
      Sing umptidy-tumptidy tee;   10
    Then up wi' the Souters o' Selkirk!
    The sons o' auld heroes for me!

Let them brag o' their factious republics,
  Of brawling an' plebeian birth;
The land that has got a good sovereign,   15
  Has got the best blessing on earth.
Then up wi' our auld-fashion'd structure,
  An' Willie the tap o' the tree!
An' up wi' the Souters o' Selkirk!
  The sons o' auld heroes for me!   20

    Sing umptidy-tumptidy tearhim,
      Sing umptidy-tumptidy tee;
    Then up wi' the Souters o' Selkirk!
    The sons o' auld heroes for me!

O, Jeanie, There's Naething to Fear Ye!

HAPPENING to spend an evening, as I had done many, with Patrick Maxwell, Esq., he played the old air, "Over the Border," so well, that I could get no rest or sleep till I had composed the following verses for it that I could croon to myself. The late Mrs Gray went over and corrected them next day. It has been by far the most popular love-song I ever wrote.–For the air, see The Border Garland.

O, MY lassie, our joy to complete again,
    Meet me again i' the gloaming, my dearie;
Low down in the dell let us meet again–
    O, Jeanie, there's naething to fear ye!
Come, when the wee bat flits silent and eiry,   5
Come, when the pale face o' Nature looks weary;
        Love be thy sure defence,
        Beauty and innocence–
O, Jeanie, there's naething to fear ye!

Sweetly blows the haw an' the rowan-tree,   10
    Wild roses speck our thicket sae breery;
Still, still will our walk in the greenwood be–
    O, Jeanie, there's naething to fear ye!
List when the blackbird o' singing grows weary,
List when the beetle-bee's bugle comes near ye,   15
        Then come with fairy haste,
        Light foot, an' beating breast–
O, Jeanie, there's naething to fear ye!

Far, far will the bogle an' brownie be,
    Beauty an' truth, they darena come near it;   20
Kind love is the tie of our unity,
    A' maun love it, an' a' maun revere it.
'Tis love makes the sang o' the woodland sae cheery,
Love gars a' nature look bonny that's near ye;
        That makes the rose sae sweet,   25
        Cowslip an' violet–
O, Jeanie, there's naething to fear ye!

Arabian Song.

THESE verses were written to an Arabian air, sent me by R. A. Smith, which I lost. They were subsequently set to music by Bishop, to an air which I liked much better.—See Select Scottish Melodies, by Goulding and D'Almaine.

MEET me at even, my own true love,
Meet me at even, my honey, my dove,
    Where the moonbeam revealing
    The cool fountain stealing
    Away and away   5
    Through flow'rets so gay,
Singing its silver roundelay.

Love is the fountain of life and bliss,
Love is the valley of joyfulness;
    A garden of roses,   10
    Where rapture reposes
    A temple of light,
    All heavenly bright—
O, virtuous love is the soul's delight!

I Lookit East, I Lookit West.

TICKLER.
Cease your funning, James, and give us a song.

SHEPHERD *sings.*
I LOOKIT east, I lookit west,
    I saw the darksome coming even;
The wild bird sought its cozy nest,
    The kid was to the hamlet driven;
    But house nor hame aneath the heaven,   5
Except the skeugh o' greenwood tree,
    To seek a shelter in, was given
To my three little bairns an' me.

I had a prayer I couldna pray,
    I had a vow I couldna breathe,   10
For aye they led my words astray,
    And aye they war connected baith
    Wi' ane wha now was cauld in death:

I lookit round wi' watery ee,
 Hope wasna there—but I was laith   15
To see my little bairnies dee.

Just as the breeze the aspen stirr'd,
 And bore aslant the falling dew,
I thought I heard a bonny bird
 Singing amid the air sae blue.   20
 It was a lay that did renew
The hope deep sunk in misery;
 It was of ane my waes that knew,
And some kind hearts that cared for me.

O sweet as breaks the rising day,   25
 Or sunbeam through the wavy rain,
Fell on my soul the cheering lay—
 Was it an angel pour'd the strain?
 Whoe'er has kend a mother's pain,
Bent o'er the babe upon her knee,   30
 O they will bless, and bless again
The generous hearts that cared for me!

A cot was rear'd by Mercy's hand,
 Amid the dreary wilderness;
It rose as if by magic wand,   35
 A shelter to forlorn distress.
 And weel I ken that Heaven will bless
The heart that issued the decree;
 The widow and the fatherless
Can never pray, and slighted be.   40

TICKLER.

Very touching, James, indeed. You are a tragic poet after Aristotle's own heart; for well you know how to purge the soul by pity and terror.

SHEPHERD.

Ay, that I do, sir; an' by a' sorts of odd humour too. Snap your thumbs.—NOCTES AMBROSIANÆ, No. XXVIII.

Some explanation is necessary still towards the understanding of the above song. It was written many years ago, at the joint request of Mr Galt and some other literary friends, for singing at the first meeting of some benevolent society in London, the denomination of which I have forgot; but it was for the purpose of relieving the wives and families of Scottish soldiers who had fallen in our sanguine wars abroad. The song was well received, having been sung by professional singers to the Scottish air of "The Birks of Invermay."

The Village of Balmaquhapple.

NORTH.

Stop, stop, Beelzebub, and read aloud that bit of paper you have in your fist.

BEELZEBUB.

Yes, sir.

SHEPHERD.

Lord sauf us, what a voice! They're my ain verses, too. Whisht, whisht!

BEELZEBUB *sings* "*The Great Muckle Village of Balmaquhapple*," *to the tune of* "*The Sodger Laddie*."

D'YE ken the big village of Balmaquhapple,
The great muckle village of Balmaquhapple?
'Tis steep'd in iniquity up to the thrapple,
An' what's to become o' poor Balmaquhapple?
Fling a' aff your bannets, an' kneel for your life, fo'ks,   5
And pray to St Andrew, the god o' the Fife fo'ks;
Gar a' the hills yout wi' sheer vociferation,
And thus you may cry on sic needfu' occasion:

"O, blessed St Andrew, if e'er ye could pity fo'k,
Men fo'k or women fo'k, country or city fo'k,   10
Come for this aince wi' the auld thief to grapple,
An' save the great village of Balmaquhapple
Frae drinking an' leeing, an' flyting an' swearing,
An' sins that ye wad be affrontit at hearing,
An' cheating an' stealing; O, grant them redemption,   15
All save an' except the few after to mention:

"There's Johnny the elder, wha hopes ne'er to need ye,
Sae pawkie, sae holy, sae gruff, an' sae greedy;
Wha prays every hour as the wayfarer passes,
But aye at a hole where he watches the lasses;   20
He's cheated a thousand, an' e'en to this day yet,
Can cheat a young lass, or they're leears that say it.
Then gie him his gate; he's sae slee an' sae civil,

Perhaps in the end he may wheedle the devil.

"There's Cappie the cobbler, an' Tammie the tinman,   25
An' Dickie the brewer, an' Peter the skinman,
An' Geordie our deacon, for want of a better,
An' Bess, wha delights in the sins that beset her.
O, worthy St Andrew, we canna compel ye,
But ye ken as weel as a body can tell ye,   30
If these gang to heaven, we'll a' be sae shockit,
Your garret o' blue will but thinly be stockit.

"But for a' the rest, for the women's sake, save them,
Their bodies at least, an' their sauls, if they have them;
But it puzzles Jock Lesly, an' sma' it avails,   35
If they dwell in their stamocks, their heads, or their tails.
An' save, without word of confession auricular,
The clerk's bonny daughters, an' Bell in particular;
For ye ken that their beauty's the pride an' the staple
Of the great wicked village of Balmaquhapple!"   40

NORTH (aside to TICKLER.)

Hogg's, bad.

SHEPHERD.

What's that you twa are speaking about? Speak up!

NORTH.

These fine lines must be preserved, James. Pray, are they allegorical?

SHEPHERD.

Preserve's, what a dracht's in that lum! &c.–NOCTES AMBROSIANÆ,
No. XXVI.

Christopher might well ask such a question, for I cannot conceive what
could induce me to write a song like this. It must undoubtedly have
some allusion to circumstances which I have quite forgot.

Callum-a-Glen.

THE air of this Jacobite song is to be found in Smith's Scottish Minstrel.
It was first published by Captain Fraser.

WAS ever old warrior of suffering so weary?
    Was ever the wild beast so bay'd in his den?
The southron bloodhounds lie in kennel so near me,
    That death would be freedom to Callum-a-Glen.
My sons are all slain, and my daughters have left me,   5
    No child to protect me, where once there were ten;
My chief they have slain, and of stay have bereft me,
    And wo to the grey hairs of Callum-a-Glen!

The homes of my kinsmen are blazing to heaven,
    The bright sun of morning has blush'd at the view;   10
The moon has stood still on the verge of the even,
    To wipe from her pale cheek the tint of the dew:
For the dew it lies red on the vales of Lochaber,
    It sprinkles the cot, and it flows in the pen;
The pride of my country is fallen for ever—   15
    Death, hast thou no shaft for old Callum-a-Glen?

The sun in his glory has look'd on our sorrow,
    The stars have wept blood over hamlet and lea;
O! is there no day-spring for Scotland—no morrow
    Of bright renovation for souls of the free?   20
Yes, One above all hath beheld our devotion,
    Our valour and faith are not hid from his ken;
The day is abiding of stern retribution
    On all the proud foes of old Callum-a-Glen.

The Three Men of Moriston.

THIS ballad is beautifully set to music by Thomson;—the accompani-
ments by the immortal Haydn. The editor adds, that he has given this
excellent ballad as it came to him; but though it commemorates three
worthies only, it has been said that there were six of them, namely, the
three trusty Macdonalds, Peter Grant, Hugh Chisholm, and Colin
Fraser, by whom the Prince was concealed and supported in a cave in
Glen-Moriston, for above five weeks. One of the Macdonalds went often
in disguise into the English camp, to procure some wheaten bread for

their guest, and pick up what intelligence he could. There he regularly heard, at the drum-head, a proclamation in English and Gaelic, of a reward of fifty thousand pounds, to any one who would produce the Pretender. But though the guardians of the cave had not a shilling among them all, they despised enriching themselves by an act of treachery. How painful it is to add, what the editor has been assured is true, that one of these magnanimous poor fellows was afterwards hanged for stealing a cow! On the ladder he declared that he had never taken either sheep or cow from any of his own clan or their friends, nor from any man who had not risen against the house of Stuart. Consequently, all attempts to persuade him to acknowledge the justice of his sentence were fruitless."

The ballad was once much longer and more particular; but Mr Thomson shortened it to suit a page, and, as usual, I have no original copy.

Now cease of auld ferlies to tell us,
    That happen'd nane living kens when;
I'll sing you of three noble fellows
    Wha lived in the wild Highland glen.
The times were grown hard to brave Donald,   5
    For lost was Culloden's sad day;
The hearts o' the chiefs were a' broken,
    And O, but poor Donald was wae!

They keekit out o'er the wild correi,–
    The towers of Clan-Ranald were gone;   10
The reek it hung red o'er Glengarry;
    Lochaber was herried and lone!
They turn'd them about on the mountain,
    The last o' their shealings to see;
"O, hon a Righ!" cried poor Donald;   15
    "There's naething but sorrow for me!"

Now our three noble lads are in hiding,
    Afar in Glen-Moriston's height;
In the rock a' the day they are biding,
    And the moon is their candle by night.   20
And oft their rash rising they rued it,
    As looking o'er ravage and death,
And blamed their ain prince, Charlie Stuart,
    For causing the Highlands sic skaith.

Ae night they sat fearfu' o' danger,   25
    And snappit their kebbuck fu' keen,

When in came a stately young stranger,
    As ragged as man e'er was seen.
They hadna weel lookit around them
    Till tears cam happing like rain—   30
"You're welcome, young Dugald M'Cluny;
    For a' you see here is your ain!"

Each kend the brave wreck of Culloden,
    But dared not to mention his name,
Lest one of the three had betray'd him,   35
    And cover'd their country wi' shame.
They served him with eager devotion,
    They clad him from shoulder to tae,
Spread his board from the moor and the ocean,
    And watch'd o'er him a' the lang day.   40

They had not a plack in their coffer,
    They had not a ewe on the brae,
Yet kend o' mair goud in their offer
    Than they could have carried away.
Now crack o' your Grecian and Roman!   45
    We've cast them a' back in the shade;
Gie me a leal-hearted M'Donald,
    Wi' nought but his dirk and his plaid!

The sun shines sweet on the heather,
    When tempests are over and gane;   50
But honour shines bright in all weather,
    Through poverty, hardship, and pain.
Though we had ne'er heard o' Clan-Ronald's
    Nor gallant Glengarry's wild sway,
The names of the loyal M'Donalds   55
    Had flourish'd for ever and aye!

When the Kye Comes Hame.

In the title and chorus of this favourite pastoral song, I choose rather to violate a rule in grammar, than a Scottish phrase so common, that when it is altered into the proper way, every shepherd and shepherd's sweetheart account it nonsense. I was once singing it at a wedding with great glee the latter way, ("when the kye come hame,") when a tailor, scratching his head, said, "It was a terrible affectit way that!" I stood corrected, and have never sung it so again. It is to the old air of "Shame fa' the gear and the blathrie o't," with an additional chorus. It is set to music in the Noctes, at which it was first sung, and in no other place that I am aware of.

> Come all ye jolly shepherds
>   That whistle through the glen,
> I'll tell ye of a secret
>   That courtiers dinna ken:
> What is the greatest bliss   5
>   That the tongue o' man can name?
> 'Tis to woo a bonny lassie
>   When the kye comes hame.
>   When the kye comes hame,
>   When the kye comes hame,   10
>   'Tween the gloaming and the mirk,
>   When the kye comes hame.
>
> 'Tis not beneath the coronet,
>   Nor canopy of state,
> 'Tis not on couch of velvet,   15
>   Nor arbour of the great—
> 'Tis beneath the spreading birk,
>   In the glen without the name,
> Wi' a bonny, bonny lassie,
>   When the kye comes hame.   20
>   When the kye comes hame, &c.
>
> There the blackbird bigs his nest
>   For the mate he loes to see,
> And on the topmost bough,
>   O, a happy bird is he;   25
> Where he pours his melting ditty,
>   And love is a' the theme,
> And he'll woo his bonny lassie
>   When the kye comes hame.
>   When the kye comes hame, &c.   30

When the blewart bears a pearl,
  And the daisy turns a pea,
And the bonny lucken gowan
  Has fauldit up her ee,
Then the laverock frae the blue lift   35
  Doops down, an' thinks nae shame
To woo his bonny lassie
  When the kye comes hame.
      When the kye comes hame, &c.

See yonder pawkie shepherd,   40
  That lingers on the hill,
His ewes are in the fauld,
  An' his lambs are lying still;
Yet he downa gang to bed,
  For his heart is in a flame,   45
To meet his bonny lassie
  When the kye comes hame.
      When the kye comes hame, &c.

When the little wee bit heart
  Rises high in the breast,   50
An' the little wee bit starn
  Rises red in the east,
O there's a joy sae dear,
  That the heart can hardly frame,
Wi' a bonny, bonny lassie,   55
  When the kye comes hame!
      When the kye comes hame, &c.

Then since all nature joins
  In this love without alloy,
O, wha wad prove a traitor   60
  To Nature's dearest joy?
Or wha wad choose a crown,
  Wi' its perils and its fame,
And *miss* his bonny lassie
  When the kye comes hame?   65
      When the kye comes hame,
      When the kye comes hame,
    'Tween the gloaming and the mirk,
      When the kye comes hame!

I composed the foregoing song I neither know how nor when; for when the "Three Perils of Man" came first to my hand, and I saw this song put into the mouth of a drunken poet, and mangled in the singing, I had no recollection of it whatever. I had written it off hand along with the prose, and quite forgot it. But I liked it, altered it, and it has been my favourite pastoral for singing ever since. It is too long to be sung from beginning to end; but only the second and antepenult verses can possibly be dispensed with, and these not very well neither.

Lenachan's Farewell.

ALEXANDER STUART of Lenachan was a man of gigantic strength, and an officer of the regiment of Appin. He was obliged to make his escape to America, several years subsequent to the *Forty-Five*, to elude the vengeance of the Campbells. The song is set to music by Smith, in The Scottish Minstrel.

> FARE thee weel, my native cot,
>   Bothy o' the birken-tree!
> Sair the heart an' hard the lot
>   O' the man that parts wi' thee!
> My good grandsire's hand thee rear'd—   5
>   Then thy wicker-work was full;
> Many a Campbell's glen he clear'd,
>   Hit the buck, an' hough'd the bull.
>
> In thy green and grassy crook
>   Mair lies hid than crusted stanes;   10
> In thy bein and weirdly nook
>   Lie some stout Clan-Gillian banes.
> Thou wert aye the kinsman's hame—
>   Routh and welcome was his fare;
> But if serf or Saxon came,   15
>   He cross'd Murich's hirst nae mair!
>
> Never hand in thee yet bred
>   Kendnae how the sword to wield;
> Never heart of thine had dread
>   Of the foray or the field!   20
> Ne'er on straw, mat, bulk, or bed,
>   Son of thine lay down to dee;
> Every lad within thee bred
>   Died beneath heaven's open ee!

Charlie Stuart he came here   25
  For our king, as right became;
Wha could shun the Bruce's heir,
  Or desert his royal name?
Firm to stand and free to fa',
  Forth we march'd right valiantlie—   30
Gane is Scotland's king and law,
And wo to Appin and to me!

Freeman yet, I'll scorn to fret;
  Here nae langer I maun stay,
But when I my hame forget,   35
  May my heart forget to play!
Fare thee weel, my father's cot,
  Bothy o' the birken-tree!
Sair the heart and hard the lot
  O' the warrior leaving thee!   40

The Stuarts of Appin.

No national calamity has ever given me so much pain as the total be-
reavement of the brave Clans who stood to the last for the cause of the
House of Stuart. It is a stain on the annals of our Legislature which can
never be blotted out. Of course, the following effusion, among many
others, was sincerely from the heart. The song is set to a fine warlike
air, by Peter M'Leod, Esq.

I SING of a land that was famous of yore,
  The land of Green Appin, the ward of the flood,
Where every grey cairn that broods o'er the shore,
  Marks grave of the royal, the valiant, or good.
The land where the strains of grey Ossian were framed,—   5
  The land of fair Selma, and reign of Fingal,—
And late of a race, that with tears must be named,
  The noble Clan Stuart, the bravest of all.
    Oh-hon, an Righ! and the Stuarts of Appin!
    The gallant, devoted, old Stuarts of Appin!   10
      Their glory is o'er,
      For the clan is no more,
And the Sassenach sings on the hills of green Appin.

In spite of the Campbells, their might and renown,
   And all the proud files of Glenorchy and Lorn,   15
While one of the Stuarts held claim on the crown,
   His banner full boldly by Appin was borne.
And ne'er fell the Campbells in check or trepan,
   In all their Whig efforts their power to renew,
But still on the Stuarts of Appin they ran,   20
   To wreak their proud wrath on the brave and the few.

     Oh-hon, an Righ! and the Stuarts of Appin, &c.

In the year of the Graham, while in oceans of blood
   The fields of the Campbells were gallantly flowing–
It was then that the Stuarts the foremost still stood,   25
   And paid back a share of the debt they were owing.
O, proud Inverlochy! O, day of renown!
   Since first the sun rose o'er the peaks of Cruachin,
Was ne'er such an host by such valour o'erthrown,
   Was ne'er such a day for the Stuarts of Appin!   30

     Oh-hon, an Righ, and the Stuarts of Appin, &c.

And ne'er for the crown of the Stuarts was fought
   One battle on vale, or on mountain deer-trodden,
But dearly to Appin the glory was bought,
   And dearest of all on the field of Culloden!   35
Lament, O, Glen-Creran, Glen-Duror, Ardshiel,
   High offspring of heroes, who conquer'd were never,
For the deeds of your fathers no bard shall reveal,
   And the bold clan of Stuart must perish for ever!

     Oh-hon, an Righ! and the Stuarts of Appin, &c.   40

Clan-Chattan is broken, the Seaforth bends low,
   The sun of Clan-Ranald is sinking in labour;
Glencoe, and Clan-Donnachie, where are they now?
   And where is bold Keppoch, the lord of Lochaber?
All gone with the house they supported!–laid low,   45
   While dogs of the south their bold life-blood were
       lapping,
Trod down by a proud and a merciless foe–
   The brave are all gone with the Stuarts of Appin!

     Oh-hon, an Righ! and the Stuarts of Appin, &c.

They are gone! they are gone! the redoubted, the brave!   50
    The sea-breezes lone o'er their relics are sighing,
Dark weeds of oblivion shroud many a grave,
    Where the unconquer'd foes of the Campbell are lying.
But, long as the grey hairs wave over this brow,
    And earthly emotions my spirit are wrapping,   55
My old heart with tides of regret shall o'erflow,
    And bleed for the fall of the Stuarts of Appin!

     Oh-hon, an Righ! and the Stuarts of Appin!
     The gallant, devoted, old Stuarts of Appin!
       Their glory is o'er,   60
       For their star is no more,
And the green grass waves over the heroes of Appin!

The Poor Man.

THE air of this song is my own, and is to be found in The Border Garland, with accompaniments by Dewar–Mr Purdie's edition.

LOOSE the yett, an' let me in,
    Lady wi' the glistening ee,
Dinna let your menial train
    Drive an auld man out to dee.
Cauldrife is the winter even,   5
    See, the rime hangs at my chin
Lady, for the sake of Heaven,
    Loose the yett, an' let me in!

Ye shall gain a virgin hue,
    Lady, for your courtesye,   10
Ever beaming, ever new,
    Aye to bloom an' ne'er to dee.
Lady, there's a lovely plain
    Lies beyond yon setting sun,
There we soon may meet again–   15
    Short the race we hae to run.

'Tis a land of love an' light;
    Rank or title is not there,
High an' low maun there unite,
    Poor man, prince, an' lady fair;   20

There, what thou on earth hast given,
    Doubly shall be paid again!
Lady, for the sake of Heaven,
    Loose the yett, an' let me in!

Blessings rest upon thy head,   25
    Lady of this lordly ha'!
That bright tear that thou didst shed
    Fell nae down amang the snaw.
It is gane to heaven aboon,
    To the fount of charitye;   30
When thy days on earth are done,
    That blest drop shall plead for thee.

The Women Fo'k.

THE air of this song is my own. It was first set to music by Heather, and
most beautifully set too. It was afterwards set by Dewar, whether with
the same accompaniments or not, I have forgot. It is my own favourite
humorous song, when forced to sing by ladies against my will, which too
frequently happens; and, notwithstanding my wood-notes wild, it will
never be sung by any so well again.—For the air, see the Border Garland.

O SAIRLY may I rue the day
    I fancied first the womenkind;
For aye sinsyne I ne'er can hae
    Ae quiet thought or peace o' mind!
They hae plagued my heart an' pleased my ee,   5
    An' teased an' flatter'd me at will,
But aye, for a' their witcherye,
    The pawky things I lo'e them still.
        O the women fo'k! O the women fo'k!
            But they hae been the wreck o' me;   10
        O weary fa' the women fo'k,
            For they winna let a body be!

I hae thought an' thought, but darena tell,
    I've studied them wi' a' my skill,
I've lo'ed them better than mysell,   15
    I've tried again to like them ill.
Wha sairest strives, will sairest rue,

To comprehend what nae man can;
When he has done what man can do,
  He'll end at last where he began.   20
    O the women fo'k, &c.

That they hae gentle forms an' meet,
  A man wi' half a look may see;
An' gracefu' airs, an' faces sweet,
  An' waving curls aboon the bree;   25
An' smiles as soft as the young rose-bud,
  An' een sae pawky, bright, an' rare,
Wad lure the laverock frae the cludd–
  But, laddie, seek to ken nae mair!
    O the women fo'k, &c.   30

Even but this night nae farther gane,
  The date is neither lost nor lang,
I tak ye witness ilka ane,
  How fell they fought, and fairly dang.
Their point they've carried right or wrang,   35
  Without a reason, rhyme, or law,
An' forced a man to sing a sang,
  That ne'er could sing a verse ava.
    O the women fo'k! O the women fo'k!
      But they hae been the wreck o' me;   40
    O weary fa' the women fo'k,
      For they winna let a body be!

M'Lean's Welcome.

I VERSIFIED this song at Meggernie Castle, in Glen-Lyon, from a scrap of prose said to be the translation, *verbatim*, of a Gaelic song, and to a Gaelic air, sung by one of the sweetest singers and most accomplished and angelic beings of the human race. But, alas! earthly happiness is not always the lot of those who, in our erring estimation, most deserve it. She is now no more, and many a strain have I poured to her memory. The air is arranged by Smith.–See the Scottish Minstrel.

COME o'er the stream, Charlie,
Dear Charlie, brave Charlie;
Come o'er the stream, Charlie,
   And dine with M'Lean;
And though you be weary,   5
We'll make your heart cheery,
And welcome our Charlie,
   And his loyal train.
We'll bring down the track deer,
We'll bring down the black steer,   10
The lamb from the braken,
   And doe from the glen,
The salt sea we'll harry,
And bring to our Charlie
The cream from the bothy   15
   And curd from the pen.

Come o'er the stream, Charlie,
Dear Charlie, brave Charlie;
Come o'er the stream, Charlie,
   And dine with M'Lean;   20
And you shall drink freely
The dews of Glen-sheerly,
That stream in the starlight
   When kings do not ken,
And deep be your meed   25
Of the wine that is red,
To drink to your sire,
   And his friend the M'Lean.

Come o'er the stream, Charlie,
Dear Charlie, brave Charlie;   30
Come o'er the stream, Charlie,
   And dine with M'Lean;
If aught will invite you,
Or more will delight you,
'Tis ready, a troop of   35
   Our bold Highlandmen,
All ranged on the heather,
With bonnet and feather,
Strong arms and broad claymores,
   Three hundred and ten!   40

The Maid of the Sea

Is one of the many songs which Moore caused me to cancel, for nothing
that I know of, but because they ran counter to his. It is quite natural
and reasonable that an author should claim a copyright of a sentiment;
but it never struck me that it could be so exclusively his, as that another
had not a right to contradict it. This, however, seems to be the case in
the London law; for true it is that my songs were cancelled, and the
public may now judge on what grounds, by comparing them with Mr
Moore's. I have neither forgot nor forgiven it; and I have a great mind to
force him to cancel Lalla Rookh for stealing it wholly from the Queen's
Wake, which is so apparent in the plan, that every London judge will
give it in my favour, although he ventured only on the character of one
accomplished bard, and I on seventeen. He had better have let my few
trivial songs alone.—It was once set to music by Smith.

COME from the sea,
Maiden, to me,
Maiden of mystery, love, and pain!
Wake from thy sleep,
Low in the deep,   5
Over thy green waves sport again!
Come to this sequester'd spot, love,
Death's where thou art, as where thou art not, love;
Then come unto me,
Maid of the Sea,   10
Rise from the wild and stormy main;
Wake from thy sleep,
Calm in the deep,
Over thy green waves sport again!

Is not the wave   15
Made for the slave,
Tyrant's chains, and stern control;
Land for the free
Spirit like thee?
Thing of delight to a minstrel's soul,   20
Come, with thy song of love and of sadness,
Beauty of face and rapture of madness;
O, come unto me,
Maid of the Sea,
Rise from the wild and surging main;   25
Wake from thy sleep,

Calm in the deep,
Over thy green waves sport again!

Go Home to your Rest.

ANOTHER of the proscribed M'Gregors; but here he is again, and sung
to the well-known old air of "The Dandy O."

Go home, go home to your rest, young man,
The sky looks cold in the west, young man;
    For should we rove
    Through Morna's grove,
A noontide walk is the best, young man;   5
Go sleep, the heavens look pale, young man,
And sighs are heard in the gale, young man:
    A walk in the night,
    By the dim moonlight,
A maiden might chance to bewail, young man!   10

When all the world's awake, young man,
A proffer of love I may take, young man;
    But the star of truth,
    The guide of my youth,
Never pointed to midnight wake, young man.   15
Go sleep till rise of the sun, young man,
The sage's eye to shun, young man;
    For he's watching the flight
    Of demons to-night,
And may happen to take thee for one, young man!   20

The Harp of Ossian.

I HAVE been sorely blamed by some friends for a sentiment expressed
in this song; but I have always felt it painfully that the name of SCOT-
LAND, the superior nation in every thing but wealth, should be lost, not
in Britain, for that is proper, but in England. In all dispatches we are
denominated *the English*, forsooth! We know ourselves, however, that
we are not English, nor ever intend to be.–This song is finely set by H.
R. Bishop, in one of the Musical Bijous.

OLD harp of the Highlands, how long hast thou slumber'd
    In cave of the correi, ungarnish'd, unstrung!
Thy minstrels no more with thy heroes are number'd,
    Or deeds of thy heroes no more dare be sung.
A seer late heard, from thy cavern ascending,   5
    A low sounding chime, as of sorrow and dole,
Some spirit unseen on the relic attending,
    Thus sung the last strain of the warrior's soul:

"My country, farewell! for the days are expired
    On which I could hallow the deeds of the free;   10
Thy heroes have all to new honours aspired,
    They fight, but they fight not for Scotia nor me.
All lost is our sway, and the name of our nation
    Is sunk in the name of our old mortal foe;
Then why should the lay of our last degradation   15
    Be forced from the harp of old Ossian to flow?

"My country, farewell! for the murmurs of sorrow
    Alone the dark mountains of Scotia become;
Her sons condescend from new models to borrow,
    And voices of strangers prevail in the hum.   20
Before the smooth face of our Saxon invaders
    Is quench'd the last ray in the eye of the free;
Then, oh! let me rest in the caves of my fathers,
    Forgetful of them as forgetful of thee!"

When Maggy Gangs Away.

A VERY different strain from the foregoing. I heard a girl lilting over the
first line to my little daughter Maggy, and forthwith went in and made
a song of it.—It is set to a lively old strain by Bishop, and is beginning
to be a favourite.

O WHAT will a' the lads do
    When Maggy gangs away?
O what will a' the lads do
    When Maggy gangs away?
There's no a heart in a' the glen   5
    That disna dread the day.
O what will a' the lads do
    When Maggy gangs away?

Young Jock has ta'en the hill for't—
   A waefu' wight is he;   10
Poor Harry's ta'en the bed for't,
   An' laid him down to dee;
An' Sandy's gane unto the kirk,
   And learnin' fast to pray.
And, O, what will the lads do   15
   When Maggy gangs away?

The young laird o' the Lang-Shaw
   Has drunk her health in wine;
The priest has said—in confidence—
   The lassie was divine—   20
And that is mair in maiden's praise
   Than ony priest should say:
But, O, what will the lads do
   When Maggy gangs away?

The wailing in our green glen   25
   That day will quaver high,
'Twill draw the redbreast frae the wood,
   The laverock frae the sky;
The fairies frae their beds o' dew
   Will rise an' join the lay: 30
An' hey! what a day will be
   When Maggy gangs away!

A Father's Lament.

A YOUNG friend of mine, whom I greatly admired for every manly and amiable virtue, was cut off suddenly in the flower of his age, (Mr R—— A——n.) The next time that I visited the family, his parent's distress and expressions of fond remembrance affected me so deeply, that I composed the following verses in his character. I likewise composed an air for it, which I thought adapted to the words. It is finely set by Bishop, in his Select Melodies.

How can you bid this heart be blithe,
   When blithe this heart can never be?
I've lost the jewel from my crown—
   Look round our circle, and you'll see

That there is ane out o' the ring   5
　　Who never can forgotten be—
Ay, there's a blank at my right hand,
　　That ne'er can be made up to me!

'Tis said as water wears the rock,
　　That time wears out the deepest line;   10
It may be true wi' hearts enow,
　　But never can apply to mine.
For I have learn'd to know and feel—
　　Though losses should forgotten be—
That still the blank at my right hand   15
　　Can never be made up to me!

I blame not Providence's sway,
　　For I have many joys beside,
And fain would I in grateful way
　　Enjoy the same, whate'er betide.   20
A mortal thing should ne'er repine,
　　But stoop to the Supreme decree;
Yet, oh! the blank at my right hand
　　Can never be made up to me!

There's Gowd in the Breast.

I HAVE forgot whether this is one of the proscribed ones or not; I think
it is: but I have not Mr Moore's songs by me. It is set by Smith to a fine
old Irish air, ycleped "The Red Fox;" but I know not if it is in existence,
as these cancelled things are hard to come at.

THERE'S gowd in the breast of the primrose pale,
　　An' siller in every blossom;
There's riches galore in the breeze of the vale,
　　And health in the wild wood's bosom.
Then come, my love, at the hour of joy,   5
　　When warbling birds sing o'er us:
Sweet nature for us has no alloy,
　　And the world is all before us.

The courtier joys in bustle and power,
  The soldier in war-steeds bounding,   10
The miser in hoards of treasured ore,
  The proud in their pomp surrounding:
But we hae yon heaven, sae bonny and blue,
  And laverocks skimming out o'er us;
The breezes of health and the valleys of dew—   15
  O the world is all before us!

Why Weeps Yon Highland Maid?

THIS song was written to a cramp air sent me by Smith. It is, however, very beautiful and pathetic.

WHY weeps yon Highland maid
Over the tartan plaid—
Is it a pledge of care,
Or are the blood drops there?
Tell me, thou hind of humble seeming,   5
Why the tears on her cheek are gleaming,
  Why should the young and fair
  Thus weep unpitied there?

Stranger, that Highland plaid
Low in the dust was laid;   10
He who the relic wore,
He is, alas! no more:
He and his loyal clan were trodden
Down by slaves on dark Culloden.
  Well o'er a lover's pall,   15
  Well may the teardrops fall!

Where now her clansman true,
Where is the bonnet blue,
Where the claymore that broke
Fearless through fire and smoke?   20
Not one gleam by glen or river,
It lies dropp'd from the hand for ever.
  Stranger, our fate deplore,
  Our ancient name's no more!

My Emma, my Darling.

I HAVE nothing to tell about this one at all; for I do not remember aught about it, save that I think it is in one of the Musical Bijous.

MY Emma, my darling, from winter's domain
Let us fly to the glee of the city again,
Where a day never wakes but some joy it renews,
And a night never falls but that joy it pursues;
Where the dance is so light, and the ball is so bright,   5
And life whirls onward one round of delight.
Would we feel that we love and have spirits refined,
We must mix with the world, and enjoy humankind.

Mute nature is lovely in earth and in sky,
It cheers the lone heart and enlivens the eye;   10
But nowhere can beauty and dignity shine,
So as in the human face fair and divine.
'Mongst these could I love thee, and that love enjoy,
But, ah! in the wilderness fond love would cloy;
To the homes of our kindred our spirits must cling,   15
And away from their bosoms at last take their wing!

The Mermaid's Song

CONSISTS here only of the singing verses of a long ballad which I wrote many years ago, in the house of Mr Aitken, then living at Dunbar. The original ballad is to be found printed in some work, but where I know not. The air is my own, but I cannot boast much of it: it is rather humdrum. It was first arranged by young Gow, and latterly by Dewar, in Mr Purdie's edition of the Border Garland.

LIE still, my love, lie still and sleep,
   Long is thy night of sorrow;
Thy maiden of the mountain deep
   Shall meet thee on the morrow.
But O, when shall that morrow be,   5
   When my true love shall waken,
When shall we meet, refined and free,
   Amid the moorland braken?
Full low and lonely is thy bed,

The worm even flies thy pillow;   10
Where now the lips, so comely red,
   That kiss'd me 'neath the willow?
O, I must smile, and weep the while,
   Amid my song of mourning,
At freaks of man in life's short span,   15
   To which there's no returning.

Lie still, my love, lie still and sleep,
   Hope lingers o'er thy slumber;
What though thy years beneath the steep
   Should all its flowers outnumber;   20
Though moons steal o'er, and seasons fly
   On time-swift wing unstaying,
Yet there's a spirit in the sky,
   That lives o'er thy decaying.

In domes beneath the water-springs   25
   No end hath my sojourning;
And to this land of fading things
   Far hence be my returning.
For all the spirits of the deep
   Their long last leave are taking.–   30
Lie still, my love, lie still and sleep
   Till the last morn is breaking.

Donald M'Gillavry

WAS originally published in the Jacobite Relics, without any notice of its being an original composition; an omission which entrapped the Edinburgh Review into a high but unintentional compliment to the author. After reviewing the Relics in a style of most determined animosity, and protesting over and over again that I was devoid of all taste and discrimination, the tirade concluded in these terms: "That we may not close this article without a specimen of the good songs which the book contains, we shall select the one which, for sly, characteristic Scotch humour, seems to us the best, though we doubt if any of our English readers will relish it." The opportunity of retaliating upon the reviewer's want of sagacity was too tempting to be lost; and the authorship of the song was immediately avowed in a letter to the Editor of Blackwood's Magazine. "After all," said this avowal, "between ourselves, Donald M'Gillavry, which he has selected as the best specimen of the true old Jacobite song, and as remarkably above its fellows for 'sly, characteristic

Scotch humour,' is no other than a trifle of my own, which I put in to fill up a page!"

I cannot help remarking here, that the Edinburgh Review seems to be at fault in a melancholy manner whenever it comes to speak of Scottish songs. My friend Mr William Laidlaw's song of Lucy's Flitting appeared first in the Forest Minstrel, and immediately became popular throughout Scotland. It was inserted in every future selection of Scottish songs, and of course found a place in Allan Cunningham's collection. Here it is to be supposed the Edinburgh reviewer saw and heard of it for the first time; and, with some words of praise, he most condescendingly introduced it to public notice, after it had been sung and appreciated from the cottage to the palace for a space of nearly twenty years. This reminds me of an old gentleman, who, as he said, "always liked to have people known to each other;" so one day he made a party for the purpose of introducing two cousins who had been brought up under the same roof. The company took the matter with gravity, and the joke passed off very well at the old gentleman's expense.–For the air, see Jacobite Relics, vol. i.

> DONALD'S gane up the hill hard an' hungry,
> Donald's come down the hill wild an' angry;
> Donald will clear the gouk's nest cleverly;
> Here's to the king an' Donald M'Gillavry!
> Come like a weigh-bauk, Donald M'Gillavry,   5
> Come like a weigh-bauk, Donald M'Gillavry;
> Balance them fair, an' balance them cleverly,
> Off wi' the counterfeit, Donald M'Gillavry!
>
> Donald's come o'er the hill trailin' his tether, man,
> As he war wud, or stang'd wi' an ether, man;   10
> When he gaes back, there's some will look merrily;
> Here's to King James an' Donald M'Gillavry!
> Come like a weaver, Donald M'Gillavry,
> Come like a weaver, Donald M'Gillavry;
> Pack on your back an elwand o' steelary,   15
> Gie them full measure, my Donald M'Gillavry!
>
> Donald has foughten wi' reif and roguery,
> Donald has dinner'd wi' banes an' beggary;
> Better it war for whigs an' whiggery
> Meeting the deevil than Donald M'Gillavry.   20
> Come like a tailor, Donald M'Gillavry,
> Come like a tailor, Donald M'Gillavry;
> Push about, in an' out, thimble them cleverly–
> Here's to King James an' Donald M'Gillavry!

Donald's the callant that bruiks nae tangleness, 25
Whigging an' prigging an' a' newfangleness;
They maun be gane, he winna be baukit, man;
He maun hae justice, or rarely he'll tak it, man.
Come like a cobler, Donald M'Gillavry,
Come like a cobler, Donald M'Gillavry; 30
Bore them, an' yerk them, an' lingel them cleverly–
Up wi' King James an' Donald M'Gillavry!

Donald was mumpit wi' mirds and mockery,
Donald was blindit wi' bladds o' property;
Arles ran high, but makings war naething, man; 35
Gudeness, how Donald is flyting an' fretting, man!
Come like the deevil, Donald M'Gillavry,
Come like the deevil, Donald M'Gillavry;
Skelp them an' scadd them pruved sae unbritherly–
Up wi' King James an' Donald M'Gillavry! 40

O'er the Ocean Bounding

Is another of the proscription list; but here, let them turn the blue bon-
net wha can. Our forefathers had *cried down* songs, which all men and
women were strictly prohibited from singing, such as "O'er Boggie,"
and "The wee Cock Chicken," &c., because Auld Nick was a proficient
at playing them on the pipes. The London people have done the same
with a number of mine; but I hereby cry them up again, and request
every good singer in Britain and Ireland, and the East Indies, to sing
the following song with full birr to the sweet air, "Maid of the valley."–It
was set by Smith, but the edition was burnt.

O'ER the ocean bounding,
Other lands surrounding,
Love, I will think of thee!
Though new skies me cover,
And other stars shine over, 5
Yet thou art still with me.
When, at morn or even,
Low I kneel to Heaven,
Be my sins forgiven
As my love shall be! 10
When my hopes are dearest,
And my soul sincerest,
Then I remember thee!

Thee, my soul's sole pleasure,
　Thee, its dearest treasure,　　　　　　　　15
Life, health, all to me.
　All of land or ocean,
　All a world's commotion,
Knits me the more to thee.
　When new passions move me,　　　　　　20
　When I cease to love thee,
　May the heavens above me,
Chasten my perfidy!
　Even in woe and cumber,
　Even in death's last slumber,　　　　　　25
I will remember thee!

Charlie is my Darling.

ALTERED from the original, at the request of a lady who sung it sweetly—
and published in the Jacobite Relics.

'TWAS on a Monday morning,
　Right early in the year,
That Charlie came to our town,
　The Young Chevalier.
　　An' Charlie is my darling,　　　　　　5
　　　My darling, my darling,
　　Charlie is my darling,
　　　The Young Chevalier.

As Charlie he came up the gate,
　His face shone like the day;　　　　　　10
I grat to see the lad come back
　That had been lang away.
　　An' Charlie is my darling, &c.

Then ilka bonny lassie sang,
　As to the door she ran,　　　　　　　　15
Our king shall hae his ain again,
　An' Charlie is the man:
　　For Charlie he's my darling, &c.

Outower yon moory mountain,
 An' down the craigy glen,   20
Of naething else our lasses sing
 But Charlie an' his men.
   An' Charlie he's my darling, &c.

Our Highland hearts are true an' leal,
 An' glow without a stain;   25
Our Highland swords are metal keen,
 An' Charlie he's our ain.
   An' Charlie he's my darling,
    My darling, my darling;
   Charlie he's my darling,   30
    The young Chevalier.

If E'er I Am Thine

WAS written to an Irish air, called "The Winding Sheet," and harmonized by Smith; but was, I believe, one of the suppressed ones.

IF e'er I am thine, the birds of the air,
 The beasts of the field, and fish of the sea,
Shall in our love and happiness share,
 Within their elements fair and free,
And rejoice because I am thine, love.   5

We'll have no flowers, nor words of love,
 Nor dreams of bliss that never can be;
Our trust shall be in Heaven above,
 Our hope in a far futurity
Must arise, when I am made thine, love.   10

And this shall raise our thoughts more high
 Than visions of vanity here below;
For chequer'd through life our path must lie,–
 Mid gleams of joy and shades of woe
We must journey, when I am thine, love.   15

Meg o' Marley.

NORTH.

You were once so good as to flatter me, by saying that I ought to go into Parliament. Now, James, if you wish it, I'll bring you in.

SHEPHERD.

I haena the least ambition. Sae far frae envying the glory o' the orators i' that house, I wadna swap ane o' my ain wee bits o' sangs wi' the langest-windit speech that has been "Hear! hear'd!" this session.

TICKLER.

James, let us have Meg o' Marley.

SHEPHERD (*sings.*)
O KEN ye Meg o' Marley glen,
    The bonny blue-eed dearie?
She's play'd the deil amang the men,
    An' a' the land's grown eery;
She's stown the "Bangor" frae the clerk,   5
    An' snool'd him wi' the shame o't;
The minister's fa'n through the text,
    An' Meg gets a' the blame o't.

The ploughman ploughs without the sock;
    The gadman whistles sparely;   10
The shepherd pines amang his flock,
    An' turns his een to Marley;
The tailor lad's fa'n ower the bed;
    The cobler ca's a parley;
The weaver's neb's out through the web,   15
    An' a' for Meg o' Marley.

What's to be done, for our gudeman
    Is flyting late an' early?
He rises but to curse an' ban,
    An' sits down but to ferly.   20
But ne'er had love a brighter lowe
    Than light his torches sparely
At the bright een an' blithesome brow
    O' bonny Meg o' Marley.

NORTH.

A simple matter, but well worth Joseph Hume's four hours' speech, and forty-seven resolutions.—NOCTES AMBROSIANÆ, NO. XXV.

Bonny Mary

Is one of the songs of my youth, and there are some good verses in it. It is much too long for singing. Should it turn a favourite with any one, three verses are easily selected. It is preserved in the Noctes, and was published long before, Gudeness kens where.

WHERE Yarrow rows amang the rocks,
　An' wheels an' boils in mony a linn,
A brisk young shepherd fed his flocks,
　Unused to wranglement or din;
But love its silken net had thrown　　　　　　5
　Around his breast, so brisk an' airy,
An' his blue eyes wi' moisture shone,
　As thus he sang of bonny Mary.

O Mary, thou'rt sae mild and sweet,
　My very being clings about thee;　　　　　　10
This heart would rather cease to beat,
　Than beat a lonely thing without thee.
I see thee in the evening beam—
　A radiant, glorious apparition;
I see thee in the midnight dream,　　　　　　15
　By the dim light of heavenly vision!

When over Benger's haughty head
　The morning breaks in streaks sae bonny,
I climb the mountain's velvet side,
　For quiet rest I get nae ony.　　　　　　20
How dear the lair on yon hill cheek,
　Where many a weary hour I tarry,
For there I see the twisting reek
　Rise frae the cot where dwells my Mary!

When Phœbus keeks outower the muir,　　　　　　25
　His gowden locks a' streaming gaily;
When Morn has breathed her fragrance pure,
　An' life an' joy ring through the valley,
I drive my flocks to yonder brook—
　The feeble in my arms I carry,　　　　　　30
Then every lammie's harmless look
　Brings to my mind my bonny Mary!

Oft has the lark sung ower my head,
   And shook the dewdrops frae his wing,—
Oft hae my flocks forgot to feed,   35
   An' round their shepherd form'd a ring.
Their looks condole the lee-lang day,
   While mine are fix'd and never vary,
Aye turning down the westlin brae,
   Where dwells my loved, my bonny Mary!   40

When gloaming, creeping west the lift,
   Wraps in deep shadow dell and dingle,
An' lads an' lasses mak a shift
   To raise some fun around the ingle,
Regardless o' the wind or rain,   45
   Wi' cautious step and prospect wary,
I often trace the lonely glen
   To steal a sight o' bonny Mary!

When midnight draws her curtain deep,
   An' lays the breeze amang the bushes,   50
An' Yarrow in her sounding sweep,
   By rock and ruin raves and rushes,
Though sunk in deep and quiet sleep,
   My fancy wings her flight so airy,
To where sweet guardian spirits keep   55
   Their watch around the couch of Mary!

The exile may forget his home
   Where blooming youth to manhood grew;
The bee forget the honey-comb,
   Nor with the spring his toil renew;   60
The sun may lose his light and heat,
   The planets in their rounds miscarry,
But my fond heart shall cease to beat
   When I forget my bonny Mary!

TICKLER.

Equal to any thing in Burns!

NORTH.

Not a better in all George Thomson's collection. Thank you, James—God bless you, James. Give me your hand. You're a most admirable fellow, and there's no end to your genius.

SHEPHERD.

A man may be sair mista'en about many things, sic as yepics, an' trag-
edies, an' tales, an' even lang set elegies about the death o' great public
characters, an' hymns, an' odes, an' the like, but he canna be mista'en
about a sang. As sune as it's down on the sclate, I ken whether it's gude,
bad, or middlin'. If ony o' the twa last, I dight it out wi' my elbow,—if
the first, I copy it ower into writ, and then get it aff by heart, when it's
as sure o' no being lost as it war engraven on a brass plate. For though
I hae a treacherous memory about things in ordinar, a' my happy sangs
will cleave to my heart till my dying day; an' I shouldna wonder gin I
war to croon a verse or twa frae some o' them on my deathbed.–Noctes
Ambrosianæ, No. XXVII.

The Ladies' Evening Song

Was written long ago, for the singing of a young lady in a house where
we drank very deep, rather too deep for me, though "it's no little that
gars auld Donald pech." It is beautifully set by Bishop in Goulding
and D'Almaine's Select Scottish Melodies, to an air something like
Dumbarton Drums, if not indeed the very same.

O THE glass is no for you,
  Bonny laddie O!
The glass is no for you,
  Bonny laddie O!
The glass is no for you,   5
For it dyes your manly brow,
An' it fills you roarin' fu',
  Bonny laddie O!

Then drive us not away
  Wi' your drinkin' O!   10
We like your presence mair
  Than you're thinkin' o'.
How happy wad you be
In our blithesome companye,
Taking innocence and glee   15
  For your drinking O!

Now your een are glancing bright,
  Bonny laddie O!
Wi' a pure an' joyfu' light,
  Bonny laddie O!   20

But at ten o'clock at night,
Take a lady's word in plight,
We will see another sight,
   Bonny laddie O!

There's a right path an' a wrang,   25
   Bonny laddie O!
An' you needna argue lang,
   Bonny laddie O!
For the mair you taste an' see
O' our harmless companye,   30
Aye the happier you will be,
   Bonny laddie O!

Mary, Canst Thou Leave Me?

Is finely set by Bishop to a melody of my own. I cannot aver that it is
thoroughly my own; but if it is not, I know not where I heard it. But it is
of no avail: since I think it is mine, it is equally the same as if it were so.

MARY, canst thou leave me?
   Is there nought will move thee?
Dearest maid, believe me,
   I but live to love thee.
When we two are parted,   5
   When the seas us sever,
Still this heart, deserted,
   Clings to thee for ever.
Days so dull and dreary,
Nights so mirk and eerie,   10
Is there nought can cheer me?
   Never! my love, never!

Connal, cease to borrow
   Rueful words to chide me!
From this land of sorrow   15
   Haste, O, haste to hide thee!
Spirits round us hover,
   Breathing death and plunder;
But when this is over,
   Which we tremble under,   20
Then, dear youth, believe me,

Though this time I grieve thee,
Kindly I'll receive thee,
    Never more to sunder!

Black Mary

WAS set by young Gow to a fine Gaelic air, called "Is fallain gun dith
thainig thu;" but I have forgot where it is to be found. My songs, bad
as many of them are, have been for these last thirty years published in
newspapers and other periodicals over all Britain, and there is only one
person alive who ever can collect them, Mr John Aitken, of the house
of Constable and Co.

MARY is my only joy,
Mary is blithe, and Mary is coy,
Mary's the goud where there's nae alloy—
    Though black, yet O she's bonny!
Her breath is the birken bower o' spring,   5
Her lips the young rose opening,
An' her hair is the hue o' the raven's wing,
    She's black, but O she's bonny!

The star that gilds the e'ening sky,
Though bright its ray, may never vie   10
Wi' Mary's dark and liquid eye—
    Though black, yet O she's bonny!
In yon green wood there is a bower,
Where lies a bed of witching power;
Under that bed there blooms a flower,   15
    That steals the heart unwary.

O, there is a charm, and there is a spell,
That, O an' alack! I know too well;
A pang that the tongue may hardly tell,
    Though felt baith late an' early.   20
The beauteous flower beneath the tree,
The spell o' the wildest witcherye,
The goud an' the gear an' a' to me
    Is my black but bonny Mary!

Love Is Like a Dizziness.

THE following ridiculous song, which was written twenty-six years ago, has been so long a favourite with the country lads and lasses, that for their sakes I insert it, knowing very well they would be much disappointed at missing it out of this volume.—It is to the Irish air called "Paddy's Wedding."

I LATELY lived in quiet case,
   An' never wish'd to marry, O!
But when I saw my Peggy's face,
   I felt a sad quandary, O!
Though wild as ony Athol deer,   5
   She has trepann'd me fairly, O!
Her cherry cheeks an' een sae clear
   Torment me late an' early, O!
     O, love, love, love!
       Love is like a dizziness;   10
     It winna let a poor body
       Gang about his biziness!

To tell my feats this single week
   Wad mak a daft-like diary, O!
I drave my cart outow'r a dike,   15
   My horses in a miry, O!
I wear my stockings white an' blue,
   My love's sae fierce an' fiery, O!
I drill the land that I should plough,
   An' plough the drills entirely, O!   20
     O, love, love, love! &c.

Ae morning, by the dawn o' day,
   I rase to theek the stable, O!
I keust my coat, an' plied away
   As fast as I was able, O!   25
I wrought that morning out an' out,
   As I'd been redding fire, O!
When I had done an' look'd about,
   Gudefaith, it was the byre, O!
     O, love, love, love! &c.   30

Her wily glance I'll ne'er forget,
   The dear, the lovely blinkin o't
Has pierced me through an' through the heart,
   An' plagues me wi' the prinkling o't.
I tried to sing, I tried to pray,   35
   I tried to drown't wi' drinkin' o't,
I tried wi' sport to drive't away,
   But ne'er can sleep for thinkin' o't.
      O, love, love, love! &c.

Nae man can tell what pains I prove,   40
   Or how severe my pliskie, O!
I swear I'm sairer drunk wi' love
   Than ever I was wi' whisky, O!
For love has raked me fore an' aft,
   I scarce can lift a leggie, O!   45
I first grew dizzy, then gaed daft,
   An' soon I'll dee for Peggy, O!
      O, love, love, love!
       Love is like a dizziness
      It winna let a poor body   50
      Gang about his biziness!

O, Weel Befa' the Maiden Gay.

THIS song was written at Ellery, Mr Wilson's seat in Westmoreland, where a number of my very best things were written. There was a system of competition went on there, the most delightful that I ever engaged in. Mr Wilson and I had a Queen's Wake every wet day—a fair set-to who should write the best poem between breakfast and dinner, and, if I am any judge, these friendly competitions produced several of our best poems, if not the best ever written on the same subjects before. Mr Wilson, as well as Southey and Wordsworth, had all of them a way of singing out their poetry in a loud sonorous key, which was very impressive, but perfectly ludicrous. Wilson, at that period, composed all his poetry, by going over it in that sounding strain; and in our daily competitions, although our rooms were not immediately adjoining, I always overheard what progress he was making. When he came upon any grand idea, he opened upon it full swell, with all the energy of a fine foxhound on a hot trail. If I heard many of these vehement aspirations, they weakened my hands and discouraged my heart, and I often said to myself, "Gudefaith, it's a' ower wi' me for this day!" When we went over the poems together in the evening, I was always anxious to learn what parts of the poem had excited the sublime breathings which

I had heard at a distance, but he never could tell me.

There was another symptom. When we met at dinner-time, if Mr Wilson had not been successful in pleasing himself, he was desperate sulky for a while, though he never once missed brightening up, and making the most of the subject. I never saw better sport than we had in comparing these poems. How manfully each stood out for the merits of his own! But Mrs Wilson generally leaned to my side, nominally at least. I wrote the "Ode to Superstition" there, which, to give Mr Wilson justice, he approved of most unequivocally. He wrote "The Ship of the Desert" against it–a thing of far greater splendour, but exceedingly extravagant. I likewise wrote "The Stranger" and "Isabelle" there, both to be found in the Poetic Mirror; and I know some of the poems that Mr Wilson wrote against these too, if I were at liberty to tell. The one he wrote that day on which I composed the following song, was not a song, but a little poem in his best style. What with sailing, climbing the mountains, driving with Bob to all the fine scenery, dining with poets and great men, jymnastics (as Wilson spells it in the Noctes), and going to tell our friends that we were *not* coming to dine with them–these were halcyon days, which we shall never see again!

> O, WEEL befa' the maiden gay,
>   In cottage, bught, or penn,
> An' weel befa' the bonny May
>   That wons in yonder glen;
> Wha loes the modest truth sae weel,   5
> Wha's aye kind, an' aye sae leal,
> An' pure as blooming asphodel
>   Amang sae mony men.
> O, weel befa' the bonny thing
>   That wons in yonder glen!   10
>
> 'Tis sweet to hear the music float
>   Along the gloaming lea;
> 'Tis sweet to hear the blackbird's note
>   Come pealing frae the tree;
> To see the lambkin's lightsome race–   15
> The speckled kid in wanton chase–
> The young deer cower in lonely place,
>   Deep in her flowery den;
> But sweeter far the bonny face
>   That smiles in yonder glen!   20
>
> O, had it no' been for the blush
>   O' maiden's virgin flame,

Dear beauty never had been known,
   An' never had a name;
But aye sin' that dear thing o' blame   25
Was modell'd by an angel's frame,
The power o' beauty reigns supreme
   O'er a' the sons o' men;
But deadliest far the sacred flame
   Burns in a lonely glen!   30

There's beauty in the violet's vest—
   There's hinney in the haw—
There's dew within the rose's breast,
   The sweetest o' them a'.
The sun will rise an' set again,   35
An' lace wi' burning goud the main—
The rainbow bend outow'r the plain,
   Sae lovely to the ken;
But lovelier far my bonny thing
   That wons in yonder glen!   40

Cameron's Welcome Hame.

THIS song was written to the Highland air bearing that name, and is harmonized by Smith in the sixth volume of the Scottish Minstrel.

O STRIKE your harp, my Mary,
   Its loudest, liveliest key,
An' join the sounding correi
   In its wild melody;
For burn, an' breeze, an' billow,   5
   Their sangs are a' the same,
And every waving willow
   Soughs "Cameron's welcome hame."

O list yon thrush, my Mary,
   That warbles on the pine,   10
His strain, sae light an' airy,
   Accords in joy wi' thine;
The lark that soars to heaven,
   The sea-bird on the faem,

Are singing, frae morn till even,   15
    Brave "Cameron's welcome hame."

D'ye mind, my ain dear Mary,
    When we hid in the tree,
An' saw our Auchnacarry
    All flaming fearfully?   20
The fire was red, red glaring,
    An' ruefu' was the scene,
An' aye you cried, despairing,
    My father's ha's are gane!

I said, my ain dear Mary,   25
    D'ye see yon cloud sae dun,
That sails aboon the carry,
    An' hides the weary sun?
Behind yon curtain dreary,
    Beyond, and far within,   30
There's Ane, my dear wee Mary,
    Wha views this deadly sin.

He sees this waefu' reaving,
    The rage o' dastard knave,
He saw our deeds of bravery,   35
    And He'll reward the brave.
Though all we had was given
    For loyalty an' faith,
I still had hopes that Heaven
    Would right the hero's skaith.   40

The day is dawn'd in heaven
    For which we a' thought lang;
The good, the just, is given
    To right our nation's wrang.
My ain dear Auchnacarry,   45
    I hae thought lang for thee;
O sing to your harp, my Mary,
    An' sound its bonniest key!

Oh-hon, Oh Righ!

Is a trivial song, written to a simple Gaelic air of a cross measure. It is
harmonized by Smith.

OH-HON, oh righ! there's something wanting,
  Oh-hon, oh righ! I'm weary;
For nae young, blithe, or bonny lad
  Comes o'er the knowe to cheer me.
      When the day   5
      Wears away,
Sad I look adown the valley;
      Ilka sound
      Wi' a stound
Sets my heart a-thrilling.   10

When I see the plover rising,
  Or the curlew wheeling,
Then I trow some bonny lad
  Is coming to my shieling.
      Why should I   15
      Sit and sigh,
While the greenwood blooms sae bonny?
      Laverocks sing,
      Flowerets spring–
A' but me are cheery.   20

My wee cot is blest and happy–
  O 'tis neat and cleanly!
Sweet the brier that blooms beside
  Kind the heart that's lanely!
      Come away,   25
      Dinna stay,
Herd, or hind, or boatman laddie
      I hae cow
      Kid an' ewe,
Goud an' gear to gain ye.   30

The Frazer's in the Correi

Is one of those Jacobite things, relating to the persecuted state of the
Highlanders after the slaughter at Culloden, of which I have written so
many. The air is originally to be found in Captain Frazer's collection,
but is well harmonized by Mr Dewar in the Border Garland, last edition.

"WHERE has your daddy gone, my little May?
Where has our lady been a' the lang day?
Saw you the red-coats rank on the ha' green?
Or heard you the horn on the mountain yestreen?"
"Auld carle greybeard, ye speer na at me,   5
Gae speer at the maiden that sits by the sea;
The red-coats were here, and it wasna for good,
For the raven's grown hoarse wi' the waughtin' o' blood.

"O listen, auld carle, how roopit his note,
The blood o' the Frazer's too hot for his throat;   10
I trow the black traitor's of Sassenach breed,
They prey on the living, and he on the dead.
When I was a baby, we call'd him in joke
The harper of Errick, the priest of the rock;
But now he's our mountain companion no more,   15
The slave of the Saxon, the quaffer of gore."

"Sweet little maiden, why talk you of death?
The raven's our friend, and he's croaking in wrath;
He will not pick eye from a bonneted head,
Nor mar the loved form by the tartans that's clad.   20
But point me the cliff where the Frazer abides,
Where Foyers, Culduthel, and Gorthaly hides;
There's danger at hand, I must speak with them soon,
And seek them alone by the light of the moon."

"Auld carle greybeard, a friend you should be,   25
For the truth's on your lip and the tear in your ee;
Then seek in yon correi, that sounds from the brae,
An' sings to the rock when the breeze is away.
I sought them last night with the haunch of the deer,
And deep in their cave they were hiding in fear: 30
There, at the last crow of the brown heather-cock,
They pray'd for their prince, kneel'd, and slept on the rock.
"O tell me, auld carle, what will be the fate

Of those who are killing the gallant and great;
Who force our brave chiefs to the correi to go, 35
And hunt their own prince like the deer or the roe?
I know it, auld carle, as sure as yon sun
Shines over our heads, that the deeds they have done
To those who are braver and better than they,
There's one in this world or the next will repay!" 40

Ye Breezes that Spring

HAS nothing to recommend it, save that it is set to an original air by
Bishop, with very fine accompaniments.

YE breezes that spring in some land unknown,
Or sleep on your clouds of the eider down,
Come over the mountain and over the dale,
More sweet than Arabia's spicy gale!
Come over the heath-flower's purple bloom, 5
And gather the birk's and the thyme's perfume!
For these are the sweets that bring no alloy
To dark Caledonia's mountain joy.

But O, thou breeze of the valley and hill!
Thou canst bring a richer offering still: 10
The kindly wish from the hall and the cot,
And the poor man's blessing, that's never forgot,
The shepherd's proud boast over every degree,
And the song of the maiden the dearest to me.
Come laden with these, thou breeze of the hill! 15
And the lay of the Minstrel shall hail thee still.

Come Rowe the Boat

WAS written long ago to a boat-song that I heard in the Highlands, sung
by the rowers. It is a short cross measure,—one of those to which it is
impossible to compose good or flowing verses, but, when sung, is very
sweet. It has since been set in modern style by Bishop. See Goulding
and D'Almaine's Select Scottish Melodies.

COME rowe the boat, rowe the boat,
Ply to the pibroch's note,
Steer for yon lonely cot
    O'er the wild main;
For there waits my dearie,   5
Both lonesome and eery,
And sorely she'll weary
    To hear our bold strain.

Then rowe for her lover,
And play, boys, to move her,   10
The tide-stream is over,
    And mild blows the gale.
I see her a-roaming
Like swan in the gloaming,
Or angel a-coming   15
    Her Ronald to hail!

The deer of Ben-Aitley
Is comely and stately,
As tall and sedately
    She looks o'er the dale.   20
The sea-bird rides sprightly
O'er billows so lightly,
Or boldly and brightly
    Floats high on the gale.

But O, my dear Mary,   25
What heart can compare thee
With aught in the valley,
    The mountain, or tide?
All nature looks dreary
When thou art not near me,   30
But lovely and dearly
    When thou'rt by my side.

The Highlander's Farewell

Is one of those desperate Jacobite effusions, which, in the delirium
of chivalry, I have so often poured out when contemplating the dis-
interested valour of the clans, and the beastly cruelty of their victors.
It is a mercy that I live in a day when the genuine heir of the Stuarts
fills their throne, else my head would only be a tenant at will of my

shoulders. I have composed more national songs than all the bards of Britain put together. Many of them have never been published; more of them have been, under various names and pretences: but few of them shall ever be by me again.—The song is set by Smith, in the Scottish Minstrel.

O WHERE shall I gae seek my bread,
　Or where shall I gae wander,
O where shall I gae hide my head,
　For here I'll bide nae langer?
The seas may rowe, the winds may blow, 　　　　5
　And swathe me round in danger,
But Scotland I maun now forego,
　And roam a lonely stranger!

The glen that was my father's own,
　Maun be by his forsaken; 　　　　　　　　10
The house that was my father's home
　Is levell'd with the braken.
Oh hon! oh hon! our glory's gone,
　Stole by a ruthless reaver—
Our hands are on the broad claymore, 　　　　15
　But the might is broke for ever!

And thou, my Prince, my injured Prince,
　Thy people have disown'd thee—
Have hunted and have driven thee hence,
　With ruined Chiefs around thee. 　　　　　20
Though hard beset, when I forget
　Thy fate, young, hapless rover,
This broken heart shall cease to beat,
　And all its griefs be over.

Farewell, farewell, dear Caledon, 　　　　　25
　Land of the Gael no longer!
Strangers have trod thy glory on,
　In guile and treachery stronger.
The brave and just sink in the dust,
　On ruin's brink they quiver— 　　　　　　30
Heaven's pitying eye is closed on thee;
　Adieu, adieu for ever!

A Witch's Chant.

THIS is a most unearthly song, copied from an unearthly tragedy of my own, published anonymously with others, in two volumes, in 1817, by Messrs Longman and Co., and John Ballantyne. The title of the play is All-Hallow Eve. It was suggested to me by old Henry Mackenzie. After a short but intimate acquaintance, I threw it aside, and my eyes never fell upon it till this night, the last of November, 1830. The poetry of the play has astounded me. The following is but a flea-bite to some of it.

THOU art weary, weary, weary,
    Thou art weary and far away,
Hear me, gentle spirit, hear me,
    Come before the dawn of day.

I hear a small voice from the hill,   5
The vapour is deadly, pale, and still—
A murmuring sough is on the wood,
And the witching star is red as blood.

And in the cleft of heaven I scan
The giant form of a naked man,   10
His eye is like the burning brand,
And he holds a sword in his right hand.

All is not well. By dint of spell,
Somewhere between the heaven and hell
There is this night a wild deray,   15
The spirits have wander'd from their way.

The purple drops shall tinge the moon
As she wanders through the midnight noon;
And the dawning heaven shall all be red
With blood by guilty angels shed.   20

Be as it will, I have the skill
To work by good or work by ill;
Then here's for pain, and here's for thrall,
And here's for conscience, worst of all.

Another chant, and then, and then,   25
Spirits shall come or Christian men—

Come from the earth, the air, or the sea,
Great Gil-Moules, I cry to thee!

Sleep'st thou, wakest thou, lord of the wind,
Mount thy steeds and gallop them blind;   30
And the long-tailed fiery dragon outfly,
The rocket of heaven, the bomb of the sky.

Over the dog-star, over the wain,
Over the cloud, and the rainbow's mane,
Over the mountain, and over the sea,   35
   Haste—haste—haste to me!

Then here's for trouble, and here's for smart,
And here's for the pang that seeks the heart;
Here's for madness, and here's for thrall,
And here's for conscience, the worst of all!   40

How Dear to Me the Hour.

THIS is likewise on the proscription list—a proscribed rebel against the sovereign authority of Mr Little the Great; but if I have trod too near the heels of his dignity, I am sure it was through no ill intention. The verses were once harmonized by Smith to an Irish air called "The Twisting of the Rope."

How dear to me the hour when daylight springs,
   And sheds new glories on the opening view,
When westward far the towering mountain flings
   His shadow, fringed with rainbows on the dew,
And the love-waken'd lark enraptured springs   5
   To heaven's own gate, his carols to renew!

In every flowering shrub then life is new,
   As opening on the sun its gladsome eye;
So is life's morning—blithely we pursue
   Hope's gilded rainbow of the heavenly dye,   10
Till worn and weary we our travel rue,
   And in life's cheerless gloaming yearn and die!

The Hill of Lochiel.

A JACOBITE song, suggested by the name of the air. To be found in the
Scottish Minstrel.

LONG have I pined for thee,
Land of my infancy,
Now will I kneel on thee,
    Hill of Lochiel!
Hill of the sturdy steer,   5
Hill of the roe and deer,
Hill of the streamlet clear,
    I love thee well!

When in my youthful prime,
Correi or crag to climb,   10
Or tow'ring cliff sublime,
    Was my delight;
Scaling the eagle's nest,
Wounding the raven's breast,
Skimming the mountain's crest,   15
    Gladsome and light.

Then rose a bolder game,—
Young Charlie Stuart came,
Cameron, that loyal name,
    Foremost must be!   20
Hard then our warrior meed,
Glorious our warrior deed,
Till we were doom'd to bleed
    By treachery!

Then did the red blood stream,   25
Then was the broadsword's gleam
Quench'd; in fair freedom's beam
    No more to shine!
Then was the morning's brow
Red with the fiery glow;   30
Fell hall and hamlet low,
    All that were mine.

Far in a hostile land,
Stretch'd on a foreign strand,
Oft has the tear-drop bland   35
    Scorch'd as it fell.
Once was I spurn'd from thee,
Long have I mourn'd for thee,
Now I'm return'd to thee,
    Hill of Lochiel!   40

The Flowers of Scotland

WAS written to the popular air of "The Blue Bells of Scotland," at the request of a most beautiful young lady, who sung it particularly well. But several years afterwards I heard her still singing the old ridiculous words, which really, like the song of the whilly-whawp, "is ane shame till heirre." I never thought her so bonny afterwards; but neither she was.

WHAT are the flowers of Scotland,
    All others that excel?
The lovely flowers of Scotland,
    All others that excel!
The thistle's purple bonnet,   5
    And bonny heather bell,
O they're the flowers of Scotland
    All others that excel!

Though England eyes her roses,
    With pride she'll ne'er forego,   10
The rose has oft been trodden
    By foot of haughty foe;
But the thistle in her bonnet blue,
    Still nods outow'r the fell,
And dares the proudest foeman   15
    To tread the heather bell.

For the wee bit leaf o' Ireland,
    Alack and well-a-day!
For ilka hand is free to pu'
    An' steal the gem away: 20
But the thistle in her bonnet blue
    Still bobs aboon them a';
At her the bravest darena blink,
    Or gie his mou a thraw.

Up wi' the flowers o' Scotland,   25
    The emblems o' the free,
Their guardians for a thousand years,
    Their guardians still we'll be.
A foe had better brave the deil
    Within his reeky cell,   30
Than our thistle's purple bonnet,
    Or bonny heather bell.

The Bonny Lass of Deloraine

WAS written on one of the flowers of the Forest nearly thirty years ago. There were two very lovely sisters of the family, and I never said to any one which was meant, hoping that each would take the compliment to herself in good part. But now, when both of them have children ready either to make songs, or have songs made of them, I must confess it was Elizabeth—Mrs W. B. Shaw.—It has never been set to music.

STILL must my pipe lie idle by,
    And worldly cares my mind annoy?
Again its softest notes I'll try,
    So dear a theme can never cloy.
Last time my mountain harp I strung,   5
    'Twas she inspired the simple strain,
That lovely flower so sweet and young,
    The bonny lass of Deloraine.

How blest the breeze's balmy sighs
    Around her ruddy lips that blow,   10
The flower that in her bosom dies,
    Or grass that bends beneath her toe!
Her cheek's endued with powers at will
    The rose's richest shade to drain,
Her eyes what soft enchantments fill,   15
    The bonny lass of Deloraine.

Let Athole boast her birchen bowers,
    And Windermere her woodlands green,
And Lomond of her lofty shores—
    Wild Ettrick boasts a blither scene;   20
For there the evening twilight swells
    With many a wild and melting strain,

And there the pride of beauty dwells,
    The bonny lass of Deloraine.

May health still cheer her beauteous face,   25
    And round her brows may honour twine,
And Heaven preserve that bosom's peace,
    Where meekness, love, and duty join.
But all her joys shall cheer my heart,
    And all her griefs shall give me pain,   30
For never from my soul shall part
    The bonny lass of Deloraine.

The Two Men of Colston;
or,
The True English Character.

RETURNING to my old friends the Jacobites again, I venture to present my readers with three pretended Cumberland ones, which I introduced in an old Magazine as follows:–"Two Scotsmen come to a poor widow's house in Cumberland, in search of old songs, having heard that she was in possession of some. She tells them that she has plenty, but that they were all written by her *brwother Twommy*, and proceeds to say, 'Whoy, didst thou neaver heaur of Twommy? I thowt all Cooamberland had knwoan brwother Twommy. Him wos a swart oof, a keynd of a dwomony, whoy had mwore lear nwor wot to guyde it; and they ca'd him the leympyng dwomony, for heym wos a creypple all the days of heym's layfe. A swort of a treyfling nicky-nacky bwody he wos, and neiver had the pooar to dey a gude turn eyther to the sel o' heym, or wony yan belaunged till heym. Aweel, thou'lt no hender Twommy, but he'll patch up a' the feyne ould sangs i' the weyde warld, and get them prentit in a beuk. And sae, efter he had spent the meast pairt o' him's leyfe gathering and penning, he gyangs his ways to Caril, whoy but he, to maik a greyt fortune. Whew! the prenter woad neaver look at nowther heym nor his lawlyess syangs. Twommy was very crwoss than, and off he sets wey them crippling all the way till Edinborough, and he woffers them till a measter prenter for a greyte swom of mwoney. Ney, he would nae byite! Then he woffers them till anwother measter prenter. He wos reather better, for he woffered Twommy a beuk o' prented syangs for his wretten yans. 'Wow, Twommy, man!' quoth I, 'but thou wast a great feul no till chap him, for then thou wadst hae had a beuk that every body could heave read, wheyras thou hast now neything but a batch o' scrawls, that nay body can read but the sell o' thee.' Twommy brought

heame his beuk o' grand syangs yance myair; but at last there cwoms
a Scots chap to Caril, speering after ooar Twommy's syangs, and then,
peur man, he was up as heyly as the wund, expecting to pouch the hale
mony o' the keuntrey. But afore the Scots gentleman came back, there
cwomes anwother visitor, by the bye, and that was Mr Palsy, and he
teuk off peur Twommy leyke the shot of a gun, and then all his grand
schemes war gyane leyke a blast o' wunn. The syangs are all to the
fore, and for ney euse, that I can sey, but meaking sloughs to the wheeal
spindle.'"–Of course, the three following Jacobite ballads are extracted
from "Twommy's beuk."

"WHOY, Josey mon, where be'st thou gwoing
    Woth all thyne own horses and keye,
With thy pocks on thy back, leyke a pether,
    And bearnies and baggage forby?"
"Whoy, dom it, mun, wost thou nwot hearing   5
    Of all the bwad news that are out,
How that the Scwots rascals be cwoming
    To reave all our yauds and our nout?

"So I's e'en gwoing up to the muirlands,
    Amang the weyld floshes to heyde,   10
With all my heall haudding and gyetting,
    For fear that the worst should betyde.
Lword, mon! hast thou neaver been hearing,
    There's noughts bwot the deavil to pay,
There's a Pwope cwoming down fro' the Heylands,   15
    To herry, to bworn, and to slay?

"He has mwore nor ten thwosand meale weyming,
    The fearswomest creatures of all,
They call them Rebellioners–dom them!
    And cannie-bulls swome do them call.   20
Whoy, mon, they eat Chreastians lyke robbits,
    And bworn all the chworches for fwon;
And we're all to be mwordered togyther,
    Fro' the bearn to the keyng on the thrwone.

"Whoy, our keyng he sends out a greyt general,   25
    With all his whole army, nwo less;
And what dwoes this Pwope and his menzie?
    Whoy, Twommy mon, feath thou'lt nwot guess?
Whoy, they fwalls all a-rwaring and yelling,
    Leyke a pack of mad hounds were their gowls;   30

And they cwomes wopen-mouth on our swodgers,
   And eats them wop, bwodies and sowls!

"Whoy, Heaster, what deavel's thou dwoing?
   Come, caw up the yaud woth the cart;
Let us heaste out to Bwarton's weyld shieling,   35
   For my bloud it runs could at my heart.
So fare thee weal, Twommy—I's crying—
   Commend me to Mwoll and thyne wyfe;
If thou see'st oughts of Jwhony's wee Meary,
   Lword, tell her to rwon for her lyfe!"   40

"Whoy, Josey mon, surely thou'st raving,
   Thou'st heard the wrong seyd of the treuth;
For this is THE TRUE KEYNG that's cwoming,
   A brave and mwoch-wrong'd rwoyal yeuth.
Thou's ignorant as the yaud that thou reyd'st on,   45
   Or cauve that thou dreyv'st out to the lwone;
For this Pwope is the Prince Charles Stuart,
   And he's cwome bwot to clayme what's his own.

"His feythers have held this ould keyngdom
   For a meatter of ten thowsand years,   50
Till there cwomes a bit dwom'd scrwogy bwody,
   A theyvish ould rascal, I hears;
And he's stown the brave honest lad's crown fro'm,
   And kick'd him out of house and hould,
And rewin'd us all with taxations,   55
   And hang'd up the brave and the bwold.

"Now, Josey mon, how wod'st thou lyke it,
   If swome crabbit, half-wotted lown
Should cwome and seize on they bit haudding,
   And droyve thee fro' all that's theyne own?   60
And, Josey mon, how wod'st thou lyke it,
   If thou in theyne freands had swome hwope,
If they should all tworn their backs on thee,
   And call thee a thief and a Pwope?"

"Whoy, Heaster, where deavil's thou gwoing,   65
   Thou'lt droyve the ould creature to dead;
Hould still the cart till I conseyder,—

Gyang, take the ould yaud bee the head.
Whoy, Twommy mon, what wast thou saying?
    Cwome, say't all again without feal;   70
If thou'lt swear unto all thou has tould me,
    I've had the wrong sow bee the teal."

"I'll swear unto all I has tould thee,
    That this is our TRUE SOVEREIGN KEYNG;
There never was house so ill gueydit,   75
    And bee swuch a dwort of a theyng."
"Bwot what of the cannie-bulls, Twommy?
    That's reyther a doubtful concern;
The thoughts of these hworrid meale weeyming
    Make me tremble for Heaster and bearn?"   80

"They're the clans of the Nworth, honest Josey,
    As brave men as ever had breath;
They've ta'en the hard seyde of the quorrel,
    To stand by the reyght until death.
They have left all their feythers and mwothers,   85
    Their weyves and their sweethearts and all,
And their heames, and their dear little bearnies,
    With their true prince to stand or to fall."

"Oh, Gwod bless their sowls, honest fellows!
    Lword, Twommy! I's crying like mad!   90
I dwont know at all what's the matter,
    But 'tis summat of that rwoyal lad.
Hoy, Heaster! thou fusionless hussey,
    Tworn back the yaud's head towards heame;
Get wop on the twop of the panniels,   95
    And dreyve back the rwod that thou keame.

"Now, Twommy, I's dwone leyke mee betters,
    I's changed seydes, and sey let that stand,
And, mwore than mwost gentles can say for,
    I've changed both with heart and with hand;   100
And, since this lad is OUR TRUE SOVERING,
    I'll geave him all that I possess,
And I'll feyght for him too, should he need it,—
    Can any true swobject do less?"

"Now geave me theyne hand, honest Josey,   105
    That's spoke lyke a true Englishman;
He needs but a pleyne honest stworey,
    And he'll dwo what's reyght if he can.
Cwome thou down to ould Nanny Cworbats,
    I'll give thee a quart of good brown,   110
And we'll dreynk to the health of Prince Charles,
    And every true man to his own."

Red Clan-Ranald's Men

Is likewise a pretended transcript from the "Dwomony's beuk," and relates to the skirmish on Clifton Moor, on the 18th of December, 1745, where a party of M'Donalds, left to guard the baggage, so gallantly repulsed two regiments of cavalry, killing one hundred and fifty of them, and wounding more, while the Highlanders lost only twenty-four in all.

THERE'S news—news—gallant news,
    That Caril disna ken, joe;
There's gallant news of tartan trews,
    And red Clan-Ranald's men, joe.
There has been blinking on the bent,   5
    And flashing on the fell, joe;
The red-coat sparks hae got their yerks,
    But Caril darena tell, joe.

The prig dragoons they swore by 'zoons
    The rebels' hides to tan, joe;   10
But when they fand the Highland brand,
    They funkit and they ran, joe.
And had the frumpy froward Duke,
    Wi' a' his brags o' weir, joe,
But met our Charlie hand to hand,   15
    In a' his Highland gear, joe;

Had English might stood by the right,
    As they did vaunt fu' vain, joe,
Or played the parts of Highland hearts,
    The day was a' our ain, joe.   20
We darena say the right's the right,
    Though weel the right we ken, joe;

But we dare think, and take a drink
    To red Clan-Ranald's men, joe.

Afore I saw our rightfu' prince   25
    Frae foreign foggies flee, joe,
I'd lend a hand at Cumberland
    To rowe it in the sea, joe.
Come fill a cup, and fill it up,
    We'll drink the toast ye ken, joe,   30
And add, beside, the Highland plaid,
    And red Clan-Ranald's men, joe.

We'll drink to Athole's gallant band,
    To Cluny of the Glen, joe,
To Donald Blue, and Appin true   35
    And red Clan-Ranald's men, joe;
And cry our news—our gallant news,
    That Caril disna ken, joe,
Our gallant news of tartan trews,
    And red Clan-Ranald's men, joe.   40

Up An' Rin Awa', Geordie.

It is a pity that we cannot father this on the ideal "Dwomony" altogether.
However, it is not just so bad when considered that it is an answer to a
Whig song of 1746, beginning, "Up an' rin awa', Charlie," &c.

Up an' rin awa', Geordie,
Up an' rin awa', Geordie,
For feint a stand in Cumberland
    Your troops can mak ava, Geordie.
Your bauld militia are in qualms,   5
    In ague fits an' a', Geordie,
And auntie Wade, wi' pick an' spade,
    Is delving through the snaw, Geordie.
        Up an' rin awa', Geordie, &c.

The lads o' Westmoreland came up,   10
    An' wow but they were braw, Geordie,
But took the spavie in their houghs,

An' limpit fast awa', Geordie.
O had ye seen them at their posts,
   Wi' backs against the wa', Geordie,   15
Ye wad hae thought—It matters not—
   Flee over seas awa', Geordie.
        Up an' rin awa', Geordie, &c.

These Highland dogs, wi' hose an' brogs,
   They dree nae cauld at a', Geordie;   20
Their hides are tann'd like Kendal bend,
   An' proof to frost an' snaw, Geordie.
They dive like moudies in the yird,
   Like squirrels mount a wa', Geordie;
An' auld Carlisle, baith tower an' pile,   25
   Has got a waesome fa', Geordie.
        Up an' rin awa', Geordie, &c.

Brave Sir John Pennington is fled,
   An' Doctor Waugh an' a', Geordie;
And Humphrey Stenhouse he is lost,   30
   And Aeron-bank's but raw, Geordie.
And Andrew Pattison's laid bye,
   The prince of provosts a', Geordie;
'Tis hard to thole, for gallant soul
   His frostit thumbs to blaw, Geordie.   35
        Up an' rin awa', Geordie, &c.

Prince Charlie Stuart's ta'en the road,
   As fast as he can ca', Geordie,
The drones to drive frae out the hive,
   An' banish foreign law, Geordie.   40
He's o'er the Mersey, horse an' foot,
   An' braid claymores an' a', Geordie;
An' awsome forks, an' Highland durks,
   An' thae's the warst of a', Geordie.
        Up an' rin awa', Geordie, &c.   45

I canna tell, ye ken yoursell,
   Your faith, an' trust, an' a', Geordie;
But 'tis o'er true your cause looks blue,
   'Tis best to pack awa', Geordie.
An' ye maun tak your foreign bike,   50

Your Turks, an' queans, an' a', Geordie,
To pluff an' trig your braw new wig,
 An' your daft pow to claw, Geordie.
   Up an' rin awa', Geordie, &c.

There's ae thing I had maist forgot,   55
 Perhaps there may be twa, Geordie:
Indite us back, when ye gang hame,
 How they received you a', Geordie.
An' tell us how the langkail thrive,
 An' how the turnips raw, Geordie;   60
An' how the seybos an' the leeks
 Are brairding through the snaw, Geordie.
   Up an' rin awa', Geordie, &c.

That Hanover's a dainty place,
 It suits you to a straw, Geordie;   65
Where ane may tame a buxom dame,
 An' chain her to a wa', Geordie.
An' there a man may burn his cap,
 His hat, an' wig, an' a', Geordie;
They're a' sae daft, your scanty wits   70
 Will ne'er be miss'd ava, Geordie.
   Up an' rin awa', Geordie, &c.

You've lost the land o' cakes an' weir,
 Auld Caledonia, Geordie;
Where fient a stand in a' the land,   75
 Your Whigs can mak ava, Geordie.
Then tak leg-bail, an' fare-ye-weel,
 Your motley group an' a', Geordie;
There's mony a ane has rued the day
 That ye cam here ava, Geordie.   80
  Up an' rin awa', Geordie,
  Up an' rin awa', Geordie,
 For fient a stand in all England
  Your Whigs dare mak ava, Geordie!

My Love's Bonny

Is sung by the country people to a fine ballad air, but has never been set to music. It is introduced in character in one of my printed dramas, but I have forgot which, and cannot find it.

My love's bonny as bonny can be,
My love's blithe as the bird on the tree;
But I like my bonny lass, an' she loes me,
   An' we'll meet by our bower in the morning.
O, how I will cling unto my love's side,   5
And I will kiss my bonny, bonny bride;
And I'll whisper a vow, whatever betide,
   To my little flower in the morning.

Her breath is as sweet as the fragrant shower
Of dew that is blawn frae the rowan-tree flower;   10
Oh! never were the sweets of vernal bower,
   Like my love's cheek in the morning.
Her eye is the blue-bell of the spring,
Her hair is the blackbird's bonny wing;
To her dear side, oh! how I'll cling,   15
   On our greenwood walk in the morning.

The Gloamin'

Is one of my very earliest songs. The futile efforts of an untutored muse to reach the true pathetic are quite palpable, and bordering on the ridiculous.—It has never been set to music.

The gloamin' frae the welkin high
   Had chased the bonny gouden gleam;
The curtain'd east, in crimson die,
   Lay mirror'd on the tinted stream;
The wild-rose, blushing on the brier,   5
   Was set wi' draps o' pearly dew,
As full and clear the bursting tear
   That row'd in Ellen's een o' blue.

She saw the dear, the little cot,
    Where fifteen years flew sweetly by,   10
An' sair she wail'd the hapless lot
    That forced her frae that hame to fly.
Though blithe an' mild the e'ening smiled,
    Her heart was rent wi' anguish keen;
The mavis ceased his music wild,   15
    And wonder'd what her plaint could mean.

A fringe was round the orient drawn,
    A mourning veil it seem'd to be;
The star o' love look'd pale and wan,
    As if the tear were in her ee.   20
The dowy dell, the greenwood tree,
    With all their inmates, seem'd to mourn;
Sweet Ellen's tears they doughtna see,
    Departing never to return.

Alas! her grief could not be spoke,   25
    There were no words to give it name;
Her aged parents' hearts were broke,
    Her brow imbued with burning shame.
That hame could she ne'er enter mair,
    Ilk honour'd face in tears to see,   30
Where she so oft had join'd the prayer
    Pour'd frae the heart so fervently.

Ah, no! the die was foully cast,
    Her fondest earthly hope was gone;
Her soul had brooded o'er the past,   35
    Till pale despair remain'd alone.
Her heart abused, her love misused,
    Her parents drooping to the tomb,
Weeping, she fled to desert bed,
    To perish in its ample dome.   40

Liddel Bower,
A Ballad,

WAS written for Albyn's Anthology, where it appeared to an old Border
air of one part, which Mr Campbell had picked up. I have an impression
that the ballad was founded on some published legend, but where it is
to be found I have quite forgot.

"O WILL you walk the wood, ladye,
    Or will you walk the lea,
Or will ye gae to the Liddel bower,
    An' rest a while wi' me?"
"The dew lies in the wood, Douglas,   5
    The wind blaws on the lea,
An' when I gae to the Liddel bower,
    It shall not be wi' thee."

"The stag bells on my hills, ladye,
    The hart but an the hind,   10
My flocks spread o'er the Border dales,
    My steeds outstrip the wind.
At ae blast o' my bugle-horn
    A thousand tend my ca';
With Douglas at the Liddel bower,   15
    No ill can thee befa'.

"D'ye mind when in that lonely bower
    Meeting at eventide,
I kiss'd your young and rosy lips,
    An' woo'd you for my bride?   20
I saw the blush break on your cheek,
    The tear stand in your ee;
O could I ween, fair Lady Jane!
    That then ye loed nae me?"

"But sair, sair hae I rued that day,   25
    An' sairer yet may rue!
Ye thought nae on my maiden love,
    Nor yet my rosy hue.
Ye thought nae on my bridal bed,
    Nae vow nor tear o' mine—   30
Ye thought upon the lands o' Nith,
    And how they might be thine.

"Away, ye cruel fause leman!
   Nae mair my bosom wring;
There is a bird into yon bower,   35
   O gin ye heard it sing!"
"Lady, beware! Some words there are
   That secrets may betray—
No utterance gives them to the air—
   What dares your wee bird say?"   40

"It hirples on the bough, and sings,
   'O wae's me, dame, for thee!
An' wae's me for the comely knight
   That sleeps beneath the tree!
His cheek is on the cauld, cauld clay,   45
   Nae belt or brand has he;
His blood is on a kinsman's spear—
   O wae's me, dame, for thee!'"

"My yeomen line the wood, ladye,
   My steed stands at the tree,   50
An' you maun dree a dulefu' weird,
   Or mount an' ride wi' me."
What gars Caerlaverock yeomen ride
   Sae fast in belt and steel?
What gars the Jardine mount his steed,   55
   An' scour o'er moor and dale?

The Johnstones, with an hundred strong,
   Have pass'd the sands o' Dryfe,
As if some treasure they had lost
   That dearer was than life.   60
Why seek they up by Liddel bower,
   And down by Tarras linn?
The heiress of the lands of Nith
   Is lost to all her kin.

O lang, lang may her mother greet,   65
   Down by the salt sea-faem;
An' lang, lang may the Maxwells look,
   Afore their bride come hame.
And lang may every Douglas rue,
   An' ban the deed for aye—   70
That deed was done at Liddel bower,
   About the break of day.

Auld Ettrick John.

THIS, and the four songs that follow, are all compositions of my early youth, made for the sphere around the cottage hearth and the farmer's kitchen-ingle, without the most distant prospect of any higher distinction. Therefore, with all the hankerings of early youth, even in my own estimation they are below par in poetical merit, and ought not to have been here. But they have been such general favourites among the class for which they were framed, for the last thirty years, that to them the leaving out of these songs would make a petrifying blank; it would be like a parent denying the first of his offspring. For the sakes, therefore, of the shepherds, cottagers, and rosy servant maids, these homely songs are preserved, while scores of more polished ones are left out; for nothing can be more satiating than a whole volume of songs all of the same grade.

THERE dwalt a man on Ettrick side,
   An honest man I wat was he,
His name was John, an' he was born
   A year afore the thretty-three.
He wed a wife when he was young,   5
   But she had dee'd, and John was wae;
He wantit lang, at length did gang
   To court Nell Brunton o' the Brae.

Auld John cam daddin' down the hill,
   His arm was waggin' manfullye,   10
He thought his shadow look'd nae ill,
   As aft he keek'd aside to see;
His shoon war four punds weight a-piece,
   On ilka leg a ho had he,
His doublet strang was large an' lang,   15
   His breeks they hardly reach'd his knee;

His coat was thread about wi' green,
   The moths had wrought it muckle harm,
The pouches war an ell atween,
   The cuff was fauldit up the arm;   20
He wore a bonnet on his head,
   The bung upon his shoulders lay,
An' by its neb ye wad hae read
   That Johnnie view'd the milky way:

For Johnnie to himsell he said,   25
    As he came duntin' down the brae,
"A wooer ne'er should hing his head,
    But blink the breeze an' brow the day;"
An' Johnnie said unto himsell,
    "A wooer risks nae broken banes;   30
I'll tell the lassie sic a tale
    Will gar her look twa gates at anes."

But yet, for a' his antic dress,
    His cheeks wi' healthy red did glow;
His joints war knit and firm like brass,   35
    Though siller-grey his head did grow.
An' John, although he had nae lands,
    Had twa gude kie amang the knowes;
A hunder punds in honest hands,
    An' sax-an-thretty doddit yowes.   40

An' Nelly was a sonsy lass,
    Fu' ripe an' ruddy was her mou',
Her een war like twa beads o' glass,
    Her brow was white like Cheviot woo;
Her cheeks were bright as heather-bells,   45
    Her bosom like December snaw,
Her teeth war whiter nor egg-shells,
    Her hair was like the hoody craw.

John crackit o' his bob-tail'd yowes;
    He crackit o' his good milk-kie,   50
His kebbucks, hams, an' cogs o' brose,
    An' siller out at trust forby;
An' aye he show'd his boordly limb,
    As bragging o' his feats sae rare,
An' a' the honours paid to him   55
    At kirk, at market, or at fair.

Wi' sicklike say he wan the day,
    Nell soon became his dashin' bride;
But ilka joy soon fled away
    Frae Johnnie's canty ingle side;   60
For there was fretting late an' ear',
    An' something aye a-wanting still,
The saucy taunt an' bitter jeer—
    Now, sic a life does unco ill.

An' John will be a gaishen soon;   65
   His teeth are frae their sockets flown;
The hair's peel'd aff his head aboon;
   His face is milk-an'-water grown;
His legs, that firm like pillars stood,
   Are now grown toom an' unco sma';   70
She's reaved him sair o' flesh an' blood,
   An' peace o' mind, the warst of a'.

May ilka lassie understand
   In time the duties of a wife;
But youth wi' youth gae hand in hand,   75
   Or tine the sweetest joys o' life.
Ye men whase heads are turning grey,
   Wha to the grave are hastin' on,
Let reason a' your passions sway,
   An' mind the fate o' Ettrick John.   80

Ye lasses, lightsome, lythe, an' fair,
   Let pure affection win the hand;
Ne'er stoop to lead a life o' care
   Wi' doited age, for gear or land.
When ilka lad your beauty slights,   85
   An' ilka blush is broke wi' wae,
Ye'll mind the lang an' lanesome nights
   O' Nell, the lassie o' the Brae.

Doctor Monroe.

"DEAR Doctor, be clever, an' fling aff your beaver,
   Come, bleed me an' blister me, dinna be slow;
I'm sick, I'm exhausted, my prospects are blasted,
   An' a' driven heels o'er head, Doctor Monroe!"
"Be patient, dear fellow, you foster your fever;   5
   Pray, what's the misfortune that troubles you so?"
"O, Doctor! I'm ruin'd, I'm ruin'd for ever—
   My lass has forsaken me, Doctor Monroe!

"I meant to have married, an' tasted the pleasures,
   The sweets, the enjoyments from wedlock that flow; 10
But she's ta'en another, an' broken my measures,
   An' fairly dumfounder'd me, Doctor Monroe!

I am fool'd, I am dover'd as dead as a herring—
   Good sir, you're a man of compassion, I know;
Come, bleed me to death, then, unflinching, unerring,   15
   Or grant me some poison, dear Doctor Monroe!"

The Doctor he flang aff his big-coat an' beaver,
   He took out his lance, an' he sharpen'd it so;
No judge ever look'd more decided or graver—
   "I've oft done the same, sir," says Doctor Monroe,   20
"For gamblers, rogues, jockeys, and desperate lovers,
   But I always make charge of a hundred, or so."
The patient look'd pale, and cried out in shrill quavers,
   "The devil! do you say so, sir, Doctor Monroe?"

"O yes, sir, I'm sorry there's nothing more common;   25
   I like it—it pays—but, ere that length I go,
A man that goes mad for the love of a woman
   I sometimes can cure with a lecture, or so."
"Why, thank you, sir; there spoke the man and the friend
      too;
   Death is the last reckoner with friend or with foe,   30
The lecture then, first, if you please, I'll attend to;
   The other, of course, you know, Doctor Monroe."

The lecture is said—How severe, keen, an' cutting,
   Of love an' of wedlock, each loss an' each woe,
The patient got up—o'er the floor he went strutting,   35
   Smiled, caper'd, an' shook hands with Doctor Monroe.
He dresses, an' flaunts it with Bell, Sue, an' Chirsty,
   But freedom an' fun chooses not to forego;
He still lives a bachelor, drinks when he's thirsty,
   An' sings like a lark, an' loves Doctor Monroe!   40

Sing On, Sing On, my Bonny Bird.

SING on, sing on, my bonny bird,
   The sang ye sung yestreen, O,
When here, aneath the hawthorn wild,
   I met my bonny Jean, O!
My blude ran prinklin' through my veins,   5
   My hair begoud to steer, O;
My heart play'd deep against my breast,
   When I beheld my dear, O!

O weel's me on my happy lot,
   O weel's me o' my dearie,   10
O weel's me o' the charming spot
   Where a' combined to cheer me!
The mavis liltit on the bush,
   The laverock o'er the green, O,
The lily bloom'd, the daisy blush'd,   15
   But a' war nought to Jean, O!

Sing on, sing on, my bonny thrush,
   Be nouther fley'd nor eerie;
I'll wad your love sits in the bush,
   That gars ye sing sae cheerie.   20
She may be kind, she may be sweet,
   She may be neat an' clean, O,
But O, she's but a drysome mate
   Compared wi' bonny Jean, O!

If love wad open a' her stores,   25
   An' a' her blooming treasures,
An' bid me rise, an' turn an' choose,
   An' taste her chiefest pleasures,
My choice wad be the rosy cheek,
   The modest beaming eye, O;   30
The auburn hair, the bosom fair,
   The lips o' coral dye, O!

A bramble shade around our head,
   A burnie popplin by, O;
Our bed the sward, our sheet the plaid,   35
   Our canopy the sky, O!
An' here's the burn, an' there's the bush,
   Around the flowery green, O;
An' this the plaid—an' sure the lass
   Wad be my bonny Jean, O!   40

Hear me, thou bonny modest moon,
   Ye sternies, twinklin' high, O,
An' a' ye gentle powers aboon,
   That roam athwart the sky, O!
Ye see me gratefu' for the past,   45
   Ye saw me blest yestreen, O,
An' ever till I breathe my last,
   Ye'll see me true to Jean, O!

Jock an' his Mother.

Air–"*Jackson's cog i' the morning.*"

"Now, mother, since a' our fine lasses ye saw
Yestreen at the wedding, sae trig an' sae braw,
Say, isna my Peggy the flower o' them a',
    Our dance an' our party adorning?
Her form is sae fair, an' her features sae fine,   5
Her cheek like the lily anointit wi' wine,
The beam o' her bonny blue ee does outshine
    The starn that appears i' the morning."

"Away, ye poor booby! your skeel is but sma',
Gin ye marry Peggy ye'll ruin us a';   10
She lives like a lady, an' dresses as braw,
    But how will she rise i' the morning?
She'll lie in her bed till eleven, while ye
Maun rise an' prepare her her toast an' her tea;
Her frien's will be angry an' send ye to sea,   15
    Dear Jock, tak a thought an' some warning."

"O, mother, sic beauty I canna forego,
I've sworn I will have her, come weel or come woe,
An' that wad be perjury black as a crow
    To leave her an' think of another."   20
"An' if you should wed her, your prospects are fine,
In meal-pocks and rags you will instantly shine;
Gae break your mad vow, an' the sin shall be mine–
    O pity yoursell an' your mother!"

"I'm sure my dear Peggy is lovely as May,   25
An' I saw her father this very same day,
An' tauld him I was for his daughter away."
    "Sure, Jock, he wad tak it for scorning?"
"He said he wad gie me a horse an' a cow,
A hunder good yowes, an' a pack o' his woo,   30
To stock the bit farm at the back o' the brow,
    An' gie Maggy wark i' the morning."

"Your Peggy is bonny, I weel maun allow,
An' really 'tis dangerous breakin' a vow;
Then tak her–my blessing on Peggy an' you   35
    Shall tarry baith e'ening an' morning."

So Jock an' his Peggy in wedlock were bound,
The bridal was merry, the music did sound,
They went to their bed, while the glass it gaed round,
   An' a' wished them joy i' the morning.   40

On Ettrick Clear.

ON Ettrick clear there blooms a brier,
   An' mony a bonny budding shaw,
But Peggy's grown the fairest flower
   The braes o' Ettrick ever saw.
Her cheek is like the woodland rose,   5
   Her ee the violet set wi' dew;
The lily's fair without compare,
   Yet in her bosom tines its hue.

Had I as muckle gowd an' gear
   As I could lift unto my knee,   10
Nae ither lass but Peggy dear
   Should ever be a bride to me.
O she's blithe, an' O she's cheerie,
   O she's bonny, frank, an' free:
The sternies bright nae dewy night   15
   Could ever beam like Peggy's ee.

Had I her hame at my wee house,
   That stands aneath yon mountain green,
To help me wi' the kie an' yowes,
   An' meet me on the brae at e'en,   20
O sae blithe, an' O sae cheerie,
   O sae happy we wad be;
The lammie to the yowe is dear,
   But Peggy's dearer far to me.

But I may sigh an' stand abigh,   25
   An' greet till I tine baith my een;
For Peggy's dorty, dink, an' shy,
   An' disna mind my love a preen.
O I'm sad, an' O I'm sorry,
   Sad an' sorry may I be;   30
I will be sick, an' very sick,
   —But I'll be unco sweer to dee.

Athol Cummers.

I MUST add one other of the same quality, for two, with me, potent reasons.

1st, The song was composed at the request of a beloved parent. I remember it well. One evening in the winter of 1800, I was sawing away on the fiddle with great energy and elevation, and having executed the strathspey called Athol Cummers, much to my own satisfaction, my mother said to me, "Dear Jimmie, are there ony words to that tune?"— "No that I ever heard, mother."—"O man, it's a shame to hear sic a good tune an' nae words till't. Gae away ben the house, like a good lad, and mak' me a verse till't." The request was instantly complied with.

2d, It was a great favourite with my kind friend, Mr R. P. Gillies, who sung it every night with great glee; and after he had done, and taken a laugh at it, he uniformly put his hand across his mouth, and made the following remark—"Well, I certainly do think it is a most illustrious song, Athol Cummers."

DUNCAN, lad, blaw the bummers,
Play me round the Athol cummers;
A' the din o' a' the drummers,
Canna rouse like Athol cummers.
When I'm dowie, wet or weary,   5
Soon my heart grows light an' cheery,
When I hear the sprightly nummers
O' my dear, my Athol cummers!

When the fickle lasses vex me,
When the cares o' life perplex me,   10
When I'm fley'd wi' frightfu' rumours,
Then I lilt o' Athol cummers.
'Tis my cure for a' disasters,
Kebbit ewes an' crabbit masters,
Drifty nights an' dripping summers—   15
A' my joys is Athol cummers!

Ettrick banks an' braes are bonny,
Yarrow hills as green as ony;
But in my heart nae beauty nummers
Wi' my dear, my Athol cummers.   20
Lomond's beauty nought surpasses,
Save Breadalbane's bonny lasses;
But deep within my spirit slummers
Something sweet of Athol cummers.*

* Maidens.

Love Letter.

THIS and the following song were both written in 1811, forming parts
of humorous letters to the young lady who afterwards became my wife.

AH, Maggy, thou art gane away,
   And left me here to languish,
To daunder on frae day to day,
   Swathed in a sort o' anguish.
My mind's the aspen o' the vale,   5
   In ceaseless waving motion;
'Tis like a ship without a sail,
   On life's unstable ocean!

I downa bide to see the moon
   Blink o'er the hill sae dearly,   10
Late on a bonny face she shone,
   A face that I loe dearly.
An' when down by the water clear
   At e'en I'm lonely roaming,
I sigh, an' think if ane war here,   15
   How sweet wad fa' the gloaming.

Ah, Maggy, thou art gane away,
   An' I nae mair shall see thee;
Now a' the lee-lang simmer day,
   An' a' the night I weary;   20
For thou wert aye sae sweet, sae gay,
   Sae teazing an' sae canty,
I dinna blush to swear an' say,
   In faith I canna want thee!

O, in the slippery paths o' love   25
   Let prudence aye direct thee,
Let virtue every step approve,
   And virtue will respect thee.
To ilka pleasure, ilka pang,
   Alack! I am nae stranger,   30
An' he wha aince has wander'd wrang,
   Is best aware of danger.

May still thy heart be kind an' true,
   A' ither maids excelling,
An' heaven shall shed its purest dew   35

Around thy rural dwelling.
May flow'rets spring, an' wild birds sing
    Around thee late an' early,
An' oft to thy remembrance bring
    The lad that loes thee dearly!   40

Mischievous Woman.

COULD this ill warld hae been contrived
    To stand without mischievous woman,
How peacefu' bodies might hae lived,
    Released frae a' the ills sae common;
But since it is the waefu' case   5
    That man maun hae this teazing crony,
Why sic a sweet bewitching face?
    O had she no been made sae bonny!

I might hae roam'd wi' cheerfu' mind,
    Nae sin or sorrow to betide me,   10
As careless as the wandering wind,
    As happy as the lamb beside me;
I might hae screw'd my tunefu' pegs,
    And caroll'd mountain airs fu' gaily,
Had we but wantit a' the Megs,   15
    Wi' glossy een sae dark an' wily.

I saw the danger, fear'd the dart,
    The smile, the air, an' a' sae taking,
Yet open laid my wareless heart,
    An' gat the wound that keeps me waking.   20
My harp waves on the willow green,
    Of wild witch-notes it has nae ony
Sin' e'er I saw that pawky quean,
    Sae sweet, sae wicked, an' sae bonny!

Lock the Door, Lariston.

THIS Border song was published in my own weekly paper, THE SPY, March 30, 1811, and found its way into the London papers, and partially through Britain, as the composition of my friend Mr Gray, now in India. I never contradicted it, thinking that any body might have known that no one could have written the song but myself. However, it has appeared in every collection of songs with Mr Gray's name. Although I look upon it as having no merit whatever, excepting a jingle of names, which Sir Walter's good taste rendered popular, and which in every other person's hand has been ludicrous, yet I hereby claim the song as one of my own early productions,—mine only, mine solely, and mine for ever.

LOCK the door, Lariston, lion of Liddisdale,
Lock the door, Lariston, Lowther comes on,*
    The Armstrongs are flying,
    Their widows are crying,
The Castletown's burning, and Oliver's gone;   5
Lock the door, Lariston—high on the weather gleam
See how the Saxon plumes bob on the sky,
    Yeomen and carbineer,
    Billman and halberdier;
Fierce is the foray, and far is the cry.   10

Bewcastle brandishes high his broad scimitar,
Ridley is riding his fleet-footed grey,
    Hedley and Howard there,
    Wandale and Windermere,—
Lock the door, Lariston, hold them at bay.   15
Why dost thou smile, noble Elliot of Lariston?
Why do the joy-candles gleam in thine eye?
    Thou bold Border ranger,
    Beware of thy danger—
Thy foes are relentless, determined, and nigh.   20

Jock Elliot raised up his steel bonnet and lookit,
His hand grasp'd the sword with a nervous embrace;
    "Ah, welcome, brave foemen,
    On earth there are no men
More gallant to meet in the foray or chase!   25

* For I defy the British nation
  To match me at alliteration. *Lit. Jour.*

Little know you of the hearts I have hidden here,
Little know you of our moss-trooper's might,
    Lindhope and Sorby true,
    Sundhope and Milburn too,
Gentle in manner, but lions in fight!   30

I've Margerton, Gornberry, Raeburn, and Netherby,
Old Sim of Whitram, and all his array;
    Come all Northumberland,
    Teesdale and Cumberland,
Here at the Breaken Tower end shall the fray."   35
Scowl'd the broad sun o'er the links of green Liddisdale,
Red as the beacon-light tipp'd he the wold;
    Many a bold martial eye
    Mirror'd that morning sky,
Never more oped on his orbit of gold!   40

Shrill was the bugle's note, dreadful the warrior shout,
Lances and halberds in splinters were borne;
    Halberd and hauberk then
    Braved the claymore in vain,
Buckler and armlet in shivers were shorn.   45
See how they wane, the proud files of the Windermere,
Howard—Ah! woe to thy hopes of the day!
    Hear the wide welkin rend,
    While Scots' shouts ascend,
"Elliot of Lariston, Elliot for aye!"   50

Fair Was thy Blossom;

AN elegiac song on the death of a natural child, of the most consum-
mate beauty and elegance. It was first published in THE SPY, but some
of the original stanzas are omitted, as too particular.

FAIR was thy blossom, bonny flower,
    That open'd like the rose in May,
Though nursed beneath the chilly shower
    Of fell regret for love's decay.
How oft above thy lowly bed,   5
    When all in silence slumber'd low,
The fond and filial tear was shed,
    Thou child of love, of shame, and woe!

Fair was thy blossom, bonny flower,
 Fair as the softest wreath of spring,   10
When late I saw thee seek the bower,
 In peace thy morning hymn to sing.
Thy little foot across the lawn
 Scarce from the primrose press'd the dew;
I thought the spirit of the dawn   15
 Before me to the greenwood flew.

The fatal shaft was on the wing,
 Thy spotless soul from guilt to sever;
A tear of pity wet the string,
 That twang'd, and seal'd thine eye for ever.   20
I saw thee late the emblem true
 Of beauty, innocence, and truth,
Stand on the upmost verge in view,
 'Twixt childhood and unstable youth.

But now I see thee stretch'd at rest—   25
 To break that rest shall wake no morrow—
Pale as the grave-flower on thy breast,
 Poor child of love, of shame, and sorrow!
May thy long sleep be sound and sweet,
 Thy visions fraught with bliss to be!   30
And long the daisy, emblem meet,
 Shall shed its earliest tear o'er thee!

Courting Song;

Or the singing verses of a love ditty written in 1810, and since set to music.

The day-beam's unco laith to part,
 It lingers o'er yon summit low'ring,
While I stand here with beating heart,
 Behind the brier and willow cow'ring.
The gloamin' stern keeks o'er the yoke,   5
 An' strews wi' goud the stream sae glassy;
The raven sleeps aboon the rock,
 An' I wait for my bonny lassie.

Weel may I tent the siller,
    That comes at eve sae saftly stealing;   10
The silken hue, the bonny blue,
    O' nature's rich an' radiant ceiling.
The lily lea, the vernal tree,
    The night-breeze o'er the broomwood creeping;
The fading day, the milky way,   15
    The star-beam on the water sleeping.

For gin my lassie were but here,
    The jewel of my earthly treasure,
I'll hear nought but her accents dear,
    Whisper'd in love's delicious measure.   20
Although the bat, wi' velvet wing,
    Wheels round our bower so dark an' grassy,
O I'll be happier than a king,
    Placed by thy side, my bonny lassie!

Nae art hast thou, nae pawky wile,   25
    The rapid flow of love impelling;
But O the love that lights thy smile,
    Wad lure an angel frae his dwelling!
There is a language in thy ee,
    A music in thy voice of feeling,   30
The mildest virgin modestye,
    An' soul that dwells within revealing.

She comes with maiden's cautious art,
    Her stealing steps to tears impel me,
For, ah! the beatings of her heart   35
    Come flichterin' on the breeze to tell me.
Flee, a' ye sorrows, on the wind,
    Ye warldly cares, I'll lightly pass ye;
Nae thought shall waver through my mind,
    But raptures wi' my bonny lassie.   40

There's Nae Laddie Coming,

Is set to a sweet original air by Bishop, and published in Goulding and D'Almaine's Select Scottish Melodies.

THERE's nae laddie coming for thee, my dear Jean,
There's nae laddie coming for thee, my dear Jean;
I hae watch'd thee at mid-day, at morn, an' at e'en,
An' there's nae laddie coming for thee, my dear Jean.
But be nae down-hearted though lovers gang by,   5
Thou'rt my only sister, thy brother am I;
An' aye in my wee house thou welcome shalt be,
An' while I hae saxpence, I'll share it wi' thee.

O Jeanie, dear Jeanie, when we twa were young,
I sat on your knee, to your bosom I clung;   10
You kiss'd me, an' clasp'd me, an' croon'd your bit sang,
An' bore me about when you hardly dought gang.
An' when I fell sick, wi' a red watery ee,
You watch'd your wee brother, an' fear'd he wad dee;
I felt the cool hand, and the kindly embrace,   15
An' the warm trickling tears drappin aft on my face.

Sae wae was my kind heart to see my Jean weep,
I closed my sick ee, though I wasna asleep;
An' I'll never forget till the day that I dee,
The gratitude due, my dear Jeanie, to thee!   20
Then be nae down-hearted, for nae lad can feel
Sic true love as I do, or ken ye sae weel;
My heart it yearns o'er thee, and grieved wad I be
If aught were to part my dear Jeanie an' me.

Appie M'Gie.

THIS favourite lively song is likewise set to original music by Bishop; but his air is quite different from that to which it is sung in Scotland, and to which the words were at first adapted, taken from Captain Fraser's collection.

O LOVE has done muckle in city an' glen,
In tears of the women, an' vows of the men;
But the sweet little rogue, wi' his visions o' bliss,
Has never done aught sae unhallow'd as this.

For what do ye think?—at a dance on the green,   5
Afore the dew fell through the gloaming yestreen,
He has woundit the bosom, an' blindit the ee,
Of the flower o' our valley, young Appie M'Gie.

Young Appie was sweet as the zephyr of even,
And blithe as the laverock that carols in heaven;   10
As bonny as ever was bud o' the thorn,
Or rose that unfolds to the breath o' the morn.
Her form was the fairest o' Nature's design,
And her soul was as pure as her face was divine.
Ah, Love! 'tis a shame that a model so true,   15
By thee should be melted and moulded anew.

The little pale flow'rets blush deep for thy blame;
The fringe o' the daisy is purple wi' shame;
The heath-breeze, that kisses the cheeks o' the free,
Has a tint of the mellow soft-breathings of thee.   20
Of all the wild wasters of glee and of hue,
And eyes that have depths o' the ocean of blue,
Love, thou art the chief! And a shame upon thee,
For this deed thou hast done to young Appie M'Gie.

The Gathering of the Clans.

THIS Jacobite ballad is likewise harmonized by Bishop, in the Select
Melodies, but was originally composed to the popular Irish air, "St
Patrick's Day in the Morning."

THERE'S news come ower the Highlands yestreen
Will soon gar bonnets an' broadswords keen,
An' philabegs short an' tartans green,
    Shine over the shore in the morning.
He comes, he comes, our spirits to cheer,   5
To cherish the land he holds so dear,
       To banish the reaver,
       The base deceiver,
And raise the fame of the clans for ever:
       Our Prince's array   10
       Is in Moidart bay,
    ·   Come, raise the clamour
       Of bagpipes' yamour,
And join our loved Prince in the morning.

Come, brave Lochiel, the honour be thine,   15
The first in loyal array to shine;
If bold Clan-Ranald and thee combine,
   Then who dares remain in the morning?
Glengarry will stand with arm of steel,
And Keppoch is blood from head to heel;   20
The Whiggers o' Sky may gang to the deil,
      When Connal and Donald,
      And gallant Clan-Ranald,
      Are all in array,
      And hasting away   25
   To welcome their Prince in the morning.

The Appin will come while coming is good,
The stern M'Intosh is of trusty blood,
      M'Kenzie and Fraser
      Will come at their leisure,   30
   The Whiggers of Sutherland scorning;
The Atholmen keen as fire from steel,
M'Pherson for Charlie will battle the deil,
      The hardy Clan-Donnoch
      Is up in the Rannoch,   35
Unawed by the pride of haughty Argyle,
      And lordly Drummond
      Is belted, and coming
   To join his loved Prince in the morning.

Come all that are true men, steel to the bane,   40
Come all that reflect on the days that are gane,
Come all that hae breeks and all that hae nane,
   And all that are bred unto sorning—
Come Moidart and Moy, M'Gun and M'Craw,
M'Dugalds, M'Donalds, M'Devils, an' a',   45
      M'Duffs an' M'Dumpies,
      M'Leods an' M'Lumpies,
      With claymores gleaming,
      And standards streaming,
      Come, swift as the roe,   50
      For weel or for woe,
      That Whigs in their error
      May quake for terror,
   To see our array in the morning.

I Hae Naebody Now

Was published lately in Fraser's Magazine, and received with higher encomiums than it deserved. It was written in the character of a disconsolate parent, whose desolate condition I witnessed; but, Heaven be thanked, as yet having no relation to any breach in my own family. Many of my warm and sincere friends were alarmed at seeing it, and condoled with me; but to such I answer, as I have done already, that if such poetical licenses were not allowable, what a limited hold the bard would occupy!–This song has been set to music both in Scotland and England. It is said that a Mr Ebsworth, an accomplished musician in Edinburgh, has set it beautifully.

I hae naebody now, I hae naebody now
　To meet me upon the green,
Wi' light locks waving o'er her brow,
　An' joy in her deep blue een;
Wi' the raptured kiss an' the happy smile,　　　　　5
　An' the dance o' the lightsome fay,
An' the wee bit tale o' news the while
　That had happen'd when I was away.

I hae naebody now, I hae naebody now
　To clasp to my bosom at even,　　　　　10
O'er her calm sleep to breathe the vow,
　An' pray for a blessing from heaven
An' the wild embrace, an' the gleesome face
　In the morning that met my eye,
Where are they now, where are they now?　　　　　15
　In the cauld, cauld grave they lie.

There's naebody kens, there's naebody kens,
　An' O may they never prove,
That sharpest degree o' agony
　For the child o' their earthly love–　　　　　20
To see a flower in its vernal hour
　By slow degrees decay,
Then calmly aneath the hand o' death
　Breathe its sweet soul away.

O dinna break, my poor auld heart,　　　　　25
　Nor at thy loss repine,
For the unseen hand that threw the dart
　Was sent frae her Father and thine;

Yet I maun mourn, an' I *will* mourn,
    Even till my latest day,   30
For though my darling can never return,
    I can follow the sooner away.

The Forty-Second's Welcome to Scotland

WAS written, at the suggestion of Mr George Thomson, on the return
of that gallant regiment from Waterloo, and harmonized beautifully by
him to the old air bearing the name of the regiment. It is to be found,
I think, in Mr Thomson's first volume, small edition.

OLD Scotia! wake thy mountain strain,
    In all its wildest splendours,
And welcome back the lads again,
    Your honour's dear defenders.
Be every harp and viol strung,   5
    Till all the woodlands quaver;
Of many a band your bards have sung,
    But never hail'd a braver.
      Raise high the pibroch, Donald Bane,
        We're all in key to cheer it;   10
      And let it be a martial strain,
        That warriors bold may hear it.

Ye lovely maids, pitch high your notes
    As virgin voice can sound them,
Sing of your brave, your noble Scots,   15
    For glory blazes round them.
Small is the remnant you will see,
    Lamented be the others,
But such a stem of such a tree
    Take to your arms like brothers.   20
      Then raise the pibroch, Donald Bane,
        Strike all the glen with wonder;
      Let the chanter yell, and the drone-notes swell,
        Till music speaks in thunder.

What storm can rend your mountain-rock,   25
    What wave your headlands shiver?
Long have they stood the tempest's shock,
    Thou know'st they will for ever.

Sooner your eye those cliffs shall view
    Split by the wind and weather,   30
Than foeman's eye the bonnet blue
    Behind the nodding feather.
        O raise the pibroch, Donald Bane!
            Our caps to the sky we'll send them.
        Scotland, thy honours who can stain,   35
            Thy laurels who dare rend them!

Highland Tay

WAS written on leaving one of the loveliest scenes in Athol, if not in the world, and one of the sweetest maidens; therefore the song is truly no fiction. It was so true, that a beloved female friend of mine could never endure to hear it sung. It was never published, that I remember of.—It is to the air of "The Maid of Isla."

WEAR away, ye hues of spring,
    Ye dyes of simmer, fade away;
Round the welcome season bring
    That leads me back to Highland Tay.
Dear to me the day, the hour,   5
    When last her winding wave I saw,
But dearer still the bonny bower
    That lies aneath yon birken shaw.

Aye we sat, and aye we sigh'd,
    For there was ane my arm within;   10
Aye the restless stream we eyed,
    And heard its soft and soothing din.
The sun had sought Glen-Lyon's glade,
    Forth peer'd the e'ening's modest gem,
An' every little cloud that stray'd,   15
    Look'd gaudy in its gouden hem.

The playful breeze across the plain
    Brought far the woodlark's wooer tale,
An' play'd along the mellow grain
    In mimic waves adown the dale.   20
I saw the drops of dew so clear
    Upon the green leaf trembling lie,
But sweeter far the crystal tear

That trembled in a lovely eye.
When lovers meet, 'tis to the mind   25
    The spring-flush o' the blooming year;
But O their parting leaves behind
    Something to memory ever dear!
On Ettrick's fairy banks at eve,
    Though music melts the breeze away,   30
The gloamin' fall could never leave
    A glow like that by Highland Tay.

I'll No Wake wi' Annie.

I COMPOSED this pastoral ballad, as well as the air to which it is sung, whilst sailing one lovely day on St Mary's Loch; a pastime in which, above all others, I delighted, and of which I am now most shamefully deprived. Lord Napier never did so cruel a thing, not even on the high seas, as the interdicting of me from sailing on that beloved lake, which if I have not rendered classical, has not been my blame. But the credit will be his own,—that is some comfort.—The song was first harmonized by Mr Heather, London, and subsequently by Mr Dewar of Edinburgh; and is to be found in the Border Garland, last edition, published by Mr Purdie.

O, MOTHER, tell the laird o't,
    Or sairly it will grieve me, O,
That I'm to wake the ewes the night,
    And Annie's to gang wi' me, O.
I'll wake the ewes my night about,   5
    But ne'er wi' ane sae saucy, O,
Nor sit my lane the lee-lang night
    Wi' sic a scornfu' lassie, O:
        I'll no wake, I'll no wake,
            I'll no wake wi' Annie, O;   10
        Nor sit my lane o'er night wi' ane
            Sae thraward an' uncanny, O!

Dear son, be wise an' warie,
    But never be unmanly, O;
I've heard ye tell another tale   15
    Of young an' charming Annie, O.

The ewes ye wake are fair enough,
  Upon the brae sae bonny, O;
But the laird himsell wad gie them a'
  To wake the night wi' Annie, O.   20
    He'll no wake, he'll' no wake,
      He'll no wake wi' Annie, O;
      Nor sit his lane o'er night wi' ane
      Sae thraward an' uncanny, O!

I tauld ye ear', I tauld ye late,   25
  That lassie wad trapan ye, O;
An' ilka word ye boud to say
  When left alane wi' Annie, O!
Take my advice this night for aince,
  Or beauty's tongue will ban ye, O,   30
An' sey your leal auld mother's skill
  Ayont the muir wi' Annie, O.
    He'll no wake, he'll no wake,
      He'll no wake wi' Annie, O,
      Nor sit his lane o'er night wi' ane   35
      Sae thraward an' uncanny, O!

The night it was a simmer night,
  An' oh the glen was lanely, O!
For just ae sternie's gowden ee
  Peep'd o'er the hill serenely, O.   40
The twa are in the flow'ry heath,
  Ayont the muir sae flowy, O,
An' but ae plaid atween them baith,
  An' wasna that right dowie, O?
    He maun wake, he maun wake,   45
      He maun wake wi' Annie, O;
      An' sit his lane o'er night wi' ane
      Sae thraward an' uncanny, O!

Neist morning at his mother's knee
  He blest her love unfeign'dly, O;   50
An' aye the tear fell frae his ee,
  An' aye he clasp'd her kindly, O.
"Of a' my griefs I've got amends,
  In yon wild glen sae grassy, O;
A woman only woman kens,—   55

Your skill has won my lassie, O.
　　I'll aye wake, I'll aye wake,
　　I'll aye wake wi' Annie, O,
An' sit my lane ilk night wi' ane
　　Sae sweet, sae kind, an' canny, O!"　　60

The Lass o' Carlisle.

I WROTE this daftlike song off-hand one day to fill up a page of a letter
which was to go to Fraser by post, being averse to his paying for any
blank paper. I did not deem it worthy of publication anywhere else; but
after its having appeared in print, why, let it have a place here.

I'LL sing ye a wee bit sang,
　A sang i' the aulden style,
It is of a bonny young lass
　Wha lived in merry Carlisle.
An' O but this lass was bonny,　　5
　An' O but this lass was braw,
An' she had gowd in her coffers,
　An' that was best of a'.
　　Sing hey, hickerty dickerty,
　　　Hickerty dickerty dear;　　10
　　The lass that has gowd an' beauty
　　　Has naething on earth to fear!

This lassie had plenty o' wooers,
　As beauty an' wealth should hae;
This lassie she took her a man,　　15
　An' then she could get nae mae.
This lassie had plenty o' weans,
　That keepit her hands astir;
And then she dee'd and was buried,
　An' there was an end of her.　　20
　　Sing hey, hickerty dickerty,
　　　Hickerty dickerty dan,
　　The best thing in life is to make
　　　The maist o't that we can!

My Love She's But a Lassie Yet

WAS written at the request of Mr Thomson, to the old air bearing that name. But after the verses were written, he would not have them, because they were not good enough. "He did not like any verses," he said, "that had the lines ending with O's, and joes, and yets, &c. as they were very poor expedients for making up the measure and rhyme." He was quite right; but what was a poor fellow to do, tied to a triple rhyme like this?–The song was afterwards published in the *Literary Journal.*

My love she's but a lassie yet,
A lightsome lovely lassie yet;
    It scarce wad do
    To sit an' woo
Down by the stream sae glassy yet.   5
But there's a braw time coming yet,
When we may gang a-roaming yet;
    An' hint wi' glee
    O' joys to be,
When fa's the modest gloaming yet.   10

She's neither proud nor saucy yet,
She's neither plump nor gaucy yet;
    But just a jinking,
    Bonny blinking,
Hilty-skilty lassie yet.   15
But O her artless smile's mair sweet
Than hinny or than marmalete;
    An' right or wrang,
    Ere it be lang,
I'll bring her to a parley yet.   20

I'm jealous o' what blesses her,
The very breeze that kisses her,
    The flowery beds
    On which she treads,
Though wae for ane that misses her.   25
Then O to meet my lassie yet,
Up in yon glen sae grassy yet;
    For all I see
    Are nought to me,
Save her that's but a lassie yet!   30

The Moon.

SHEPHERD.

Here, sir, tak the prospeck, an' gie's a screed o' philosophy, for I'm
gaun to gie ye anither sang.

NOW fare-ye-weel, bonny Lady Moon,
    Wi' thy still look o' majestye;
For though ye hae a queenly face,
    'Tis e'en a fearsome sight to see.
Your lip is like Ben-Lomond's base,   5
    Your mouth a dark unmeasured dell;
Your eebrow like the Grampian range,
    Fringed with the brier an' heather-bell.

Yet still thou bear'st a human face,
    Of calm an' ghostly dignity;   10
Some emblem there I fain wad trace
    Of Him that made baith you an' me.
But fare-ye-weel, bonny Lady Moon,
    There's neither stop nor stay for me;
But when this joyfu' life is done,   15
    I'll take a jaunt an' visit thee.

The Witch o' Fife;

ANOTHER balloon song, notable for nothing save its utter madness.

HURRAY, hurray, the jade's away,
    Like a rocket of air with her bandalet!
I'm up in the air on my bonny grey mare,
    But I see her yet, I see her yet.
I'll ring the skirts o' the gowden wain   5
    Wi' curb an' bit, wi' curb an' bit;
An' catch the Bear by the frozen mane,—
    An' I see her yet, I see her yet.

Away, away, o'er mountain an' main,
    To sing at the morning's rosy yett;   10
An' water my mare at its fountain clear,—
    But I see her yet, I see her yet.

Away, thou bonny witch o' Fife,
    On foam of the air to heave an' flit,
An' little reck thou of a poet's life,   15
    For he sees thee yet, he sees thee yet.

Row on, Row on,

WAS written to an old Border air, ycleped "Tushilaw's Lines," which
has never been published. The words were meant to suit the plaintive
notes of the tune.

Row on, row on, thou cauldrife wave,
    Weel may you fume, and growl, and grumble—
Weel may you to the tempest rave
    And down your briny mountains tumble;
For mony a heart thou hast made cauld,   5
    Of firmest friend and fondest lover,
Who lie in thy dark bosom pall'd,
    The garish green wave rolling over.

Upon thy waste of waters wide,
    Though ray'd in a' the dyes o' heaven!   10
I never turn my looks aside,
    But my poor heart wi' grief is riven;
For then on ane that loe'd me weel
    My heart will evermair be turning;
An' oh! 'tis grievous aye to feel   15
    That nought remains for me but mourning.

For whether he's alive or dead,
    In distant land for maiden sighing,
A captive into slavery led,
    Or in thy beds of amber lying,   20
I cannot tell;—I only know
    I loved him dearly, and forewarn'd him;
I gave him thee in pain and woe,
    And thou hast never more return'd him.

Still thou rowest on with sullen roar—   25
    A broken heart to thee is nothing;
Thou only lovest to lash the shore,
    And jabber out thy thunder, frothing.

Thy still small voice send to this creek,
   The wavy field of waters over;   30
Oh! Spirit of the Ocean, speak!
   And tell me where thou hold'st my lover!

Marion Graham;

A PASTORAL ballad, written expressly for the first Number of the *Literary Journal*, and published there.

AWAKE, my bonny Marion Graham,
   And see this scene before it closes,
The eastern lift is a' on flame,
   And a' besprinkled o'er wi' roses;
It is a sight will glad your ee,   5
A sight my Marion loes to see.

Here are the streaks of gowden light,
   Fair as my Marion's locks o' yellow;
And tints of blue as heavenly bright
   As smile within her ee sae mellow;   10
Her cheeks, young roses, even seem
To dimple in yon heavenly beam.

Awake, my bonny Marion Graham,
   Ye never saw sae bright adorning;
I canna bear that my sweet dame   15
   Should lose the pleasures o' this morning;
For what wad a' its beauties be
Without some likeness unto thee?

I see thee in the silver stream,
   The budding rose, and gracefu' willow;   20
I see thee in yon morning beam,
   And beauty of the glowing billow;
I see thy innocence and glee
In every lamb that skims the lea.

And could you trow it, lovely May,   25
   I see thee in the hues of even,

Thy virgin bed the milky way,
　Thy coverlet the veil of heaven!
There have I seen a vision dim
Hush'd by an angel's holy hymn.　　　　　　　　30

And, Marion, when this morn, above
　The gates of heaven, I saw advancing
The morning's gem—the star of love,
　My heart with rapture fell a-dancing;
Yet I in all its rays could see,　　　　　　　　35
And all its glories, only thee.

Ah! Marion Graham! 'tis e'en ower true,
　And Gude forgie my fond devotion!
In earth's sweet green, and heaven's blue,
　And all the dyes that deck the ocean,　　　　40
The scene that brings nae mind o' thee
Has little beauty to my ee.

Get up, ye little wily knave!
　I ken your pawky jinks an' jeering,
You like to hear your lover rave,　　　　　　　45
　An' gar him trow ye dinna hear him;
Yet weel this homage you'll repay,—
Get up, my love, an' come away!

The Flower

WAS published in the Forest Minstrel, upwards of twenty years ago, and
has been partially popular ever since.—It was beautifully harmonized to
a Gaelic air, by Miss C. Forest, in a single sheet.

O SOFTLY blaw, thou biting blast,
　O'er Yarrow's lonely dale,
And spare yon sweet and tender bud
　Exposed to every gale!
Long has she hung her drooping head,　　　　　5
　Despairing to survive;
But partial sunbeams through the cloud
　Still kept my flower alive.

One evening, when the sun was low,
 Through yon lone dell I stray'd,   10
While little birds from every bough
 Their music wild convey'd.
The sunbeam lean'd across the shower,
 The rainbow girt the glen,
There first I saw my lovely flower   15
 Far from the walks of men.

Her cheek was then the ruddy dawn,
 Stole from the rising sun;
The whitest feather from the swan
 On her fair breast was dun.   20
Her mould of modest dignity
 Was form'd the heart to win;
The dewdrop glist'ning in her eye,
 Show'd all was pure within.

But frost on cold misfortune borne,   25
 Hath crush'd her in the clay;
And ruthless fate hath rudely torn
 Each kindred branch away.
That wounded stem will never close,
 But bleeding still remain;   30
Relentless winds, how can you blow,
 And nip my flower again!

Birniebouzle.

IT is said "the multitude never are wrong;" so be it. Well, then, this has been a popular street song for nearly thirty years. How does the instance justify the adage? Not well. However, bowing with humility to the public voice, in preference to my own judgment, I give it a place.

AIR—*Braes of Tullimett.*

WILL ye gang wi' me, lassie,
 To the braes o' Birniebouzle?
Baith the yird an' sea, lassie,
 Will I rob to fend ye.
I'll hunt the otter an' the brock,   5
The hart, the hare, an' heather cock,

An' pu' the limpet aff the rock,
   To batten an' to mend ye.

If ye'll gang wi' me, lassie,
   To the braes o' Birniebouzle,   10
Till the day you dee, lassie,
   Want shall ne'er come near ye.
The peats I'll carry in a skull,
The cod an' ling wi' hooks I'll pull,
An' reave the eggs o' mony a gull,   15
   To please my denty dearie.

Sae canty will we be, lassie,
   At the braes o' Birniebouzle,
Donald Gun and me, lassie,
   Ever sall attend ye.   20
Though we hae nowther milk nor meal,
Nor lamb nor mutton, beef nor veal,
We'll fank the porpy and the seal,
   And that's the way to fend ye.

An' ye sall gang sae braw, lassie,   25
   At the kirk o' Birniebouzle,
Wi' littit brogues an' a', lassie,
   Wow but ye'll be vaunty!
An' you sall wear, when you are wed,
The kirtle an' the Heeland plaid,   30
An' sleep upon a heather bed,
   Sae cozy an' sae canty.

If ye'll but marry me, lassie,
   At the kirk o' Birniebouzle,
A' my joy shall be, lassie,   35
   Ever to content ye.
I'll bait the line and bear the pail,
An' row the boat and spread the sail,
An' drag the larry at my tail,
   When mussel hives are plenty.   40

Then come awa wi' me, lassie,
   To the braes o' Birniebouzle;
Bonny lassie, dear lassie,

You shall ne'er repent ye.
For you shall own a bught o' ewes,   45
A brace o' gaits, and byre o' cows,
An' be the lady o' my house,
    An' lads an' lasses plenty.

I Hae Lost my Love.

A BITTER song against the women.

I HAE lost my love, an' I dinna ken how,
    I hae lost my love, an' I carena;
For laith will I be just to lie down an' dee,
    And to sit down an' greet wad be bairnly;
But a screed o' ill-nature I canna weel help,   5
    At having been guidit unfairly;
An' weel wad I like to gie women a skelp,
    An' yerk their sweet haffits fu' yarely.

O! plague on the limmers, sae sly and demure,
    As pawkie as deils wi' their smiling;   10
As fickle as winter, in sunshine and shower,
    The hearts o' a' mankind beguiling;
As sour as December, as soothing as May,
    To suit their ain ends, never doubt them;
Their ill faults I couldna tell ower in a day,   15
    But their beauty's the warst thing about them!

Ay, that's what sets up the haill warld in a lowe;
    Makes kingdoms to rise and expire;
Man's micht is nae mair than a flaughten o' tow,
    Opposed to a bleeze o' reid fire!   20
'Twas woman at first made creation to bend,
    And of nature's prime lord made the fellow!
An' 'tis her that will bring this ill warld to an end,
    An' that will be seen an' heard tell o'!

Allan Dhu.

I LIKE to see you, Allan Dhu,
   I like wi' you to meet,
But dinna say to me you loe,
   For that wad gar me greet.
I like to see you smile on me   5
   Amang our maidens a',
But, oh! ae vow o' love frae you
   I cou'dna stand ava.

Ay, ye may smile, but dinna speak;
   I ken what ye've to say;   10
Sae, either haud your tongue sae sleek,
   Or look another way;
For, should it be of love to me,
   In manner soft and bland,
I wadna ye my face should see   15
   For a' Breadalbin's land.

Oh! Allan Dhu, 'tis nought to you
   Of love to gibe and jeer;
But little ken ye of the pang
   A maiden's heart maun bear,   20
When a' on earth that she hauds dear,
   The hope that makes her fain,
Comes plump at aince–Oh, me! the thought
   'Maist turns my heart to stane!

No, Allan, no–I winna let   25
   You speak a word the night:
Gang hame, an' write a lang letter,
   For weel ye can indite.
And be it love, or be it slight,
   I then can hae my will,   30
I'll steal away, far out o' sight,
   An' greet, an' greet my fill.

Love's Visit.

LOVE came to the door o' my heart ae night,
   And he call'd wi' a whining din—
"Oh, open the door! for it is but thy part
   To let an old crony come in."
"Thou sly little elf! I hae open'd to thee 5
   Far aftener than I dare say;
An' dear hae the openings been to me,
   Before I could wile you away."

"Fear not," quo' Love, "for my bow's in the rest,
   And my arrows are ilk ane gane; 10
For you sent me to wound a lovely breast,
   Which has proved o' the marble stane.
I am sair forspent, then let me come in
   To the nook where I wont to lie,
For sae aft hae I been this door within 15
   That I downa think to gang by."

I open'd the door, though I ween'd it a sin,
   To the sweet little whimpering fay;
But he raised sic a buzz the cove within,
   That he fill'd me with wild dismay; 20
For first I felt sic a thrilling smart,
   And then sic an ardent glow,
That I fear'd the chords o' my sanguine heart
   War a' gaun to flee in a lowe.

"Gae away, gae away, thou wicked wean!" 25
   I cried, wi' the tear in my ee;
"Ay! sae ye may say!" quo' he, "but I ken
   Ye'll be laith now to part wi' me."
And what do you think?—by day and by night,
   For these ten lang years and twain, 30
I have cherish'd the urchin with fondest delight,
   And we'll never mair part again.

The Moon Was A-Waning

Is one of the songs of my youth, written long ere I threw aside the shepherd's plaid, and took farewell of my trusty colley, for the bard's perilous and thankless occupation. I was a poor shepherd half a century ago, and I have never got farther to this day; but my friends would be far from regretting this, if they knew the joy of spirit that has been mine. This was the first song of mine I ever heard sung at the piano, and my feelings of exultation are not to be conceived by men of sordid dispositions. I had often heard my strains chanted from the ewe-bught and the milking green, with delight; but I now found that I had got a step higher, and thenceforward resolved to cling to my harp, with a fondness which no obloquy should diminish,—and I have kept the resolution.—The song was first set to music and sung by Miss C. Forest, and has long been a favourite, and generally sung through a great portion of Scotland.

THE moon was a-waning,
    The tempest was over;
Fair was the maiden,
    And fond was the lover;
But the snow was so deep,   5
    That his heart it grew weary,
And he sunk down to sleep,
    In the moorland so dreary.

Soft was the bed
    She had made for her lover,   10
White were the sheets
    And embroider'd the cover;
But his sheets are more white,
    And his canopy grander,
And sounder he sleeps   15
    Where the hill foxes wander.

Alas, pretty maiden,
    What sorrows attend you!
I see you sit shivering,
    With lights at your window;   20
But long may you wait
    Ere your arms shall enclose him,
For still, still he lies,
    With a wreath on his bosom!

How painful the task 25
    The sad tidings to tell you!–
An orphan you were
    Ere this misery befell you;
And far in yon wild,
    Where the dead-tapers hover, 30
So cold, cold and wan
    Lies the corpse of your lover!

O, What Gart Me Greet?

WAS written in 1810, on an affecting incident related to me by a lady. It was published in THE SPY that year, and has never been set to music, but I have heard it chanted to "Bonny Dundee," an air of more general utility than any in Scotland.

O WHAT gart me greet when I partit wi' Willie,
    While at his gude fortune ilk ane was sae fain?
My neighbours they shamed me, an' said it was silly,
    When I was sae soon to see Willie again.
He gae me his hand as we gae'd to the river, 5
    For O he was aye a kind brother to me:
Right sair was my heart frae my Willie to sever,
    And saut was the tear-drop that smartit my ee.

It wasna the kiss that he gae me at parting,
    Nor yet the kind pressure I felt o' my hand– 10
It wasna the tear frae his blue ee was starting,
    As slow they were shoving the boat frae the land.
The tear that I saw ower his bonny cheek straying,
    It pleased me indeed, but it doubled my pain;
For something within me was constantly saying, 15
    "Ah, Jessie! ye'll never see Willie again!"

The bairn's unco wae to be taen frae its mother,
    The wee bird is wae when bereaved o' its young,
But oh, to be reft of a dear only brother,
    It canna be spoken–it canna be sung! 20
I dream'd a' the night that my Willie was wi' me,
    Sae kind to his Jessie–at meeting sae fain,
An' just at the dawning a friend came to see me,
    An' tauld me I never wad see him again!

I hae naebody now to look kind an' caress me,   25
   I look for a friend, but nae friend can I see;
I dinna ken what's to become o' poor Jessie—
   Life has nae mair comfort or pleasure for me!
Hard want may oppress me, an' sorrow harass me,
   But dearest affection shall ever remain,   30
An' wandering weary this wilderness dreary,
   I'll lang for the day that shall meet us again!

A National Song of Triumph

THE following song was written for, and sung at, a large social meeting
of friends, who met by appointment at Young's tavern, to celebrate the
entry of the Allies into Paris in 1814.

Now, Britain, let thy cliffs o' snaw
   Look prouder o'er the marled main;
The bastard eagle bears awa',
   An' ne'er shall ee thy shores again.
Come, bang thy banners to the wain,   5
   The struggle's past, the prize is won;
Well may thy lion shake his mane,
   And turn his grey beard to the sun.

Lang hae I bragg'd o' thine an' thee,
   Even when thy back was at the wa',   10
Now thou my proudest sang shalt be
   As lang as I hae breath to draw.
Where now the coofs wha boded wae,
   An' cauldness o'er thy efforts threw;
An' where the proudest, fellest fae   15
   Frae hell's black porch that ever flew?

O he might conquer feckless kings—
   Those bars in Nature's onward plan—
But fool is he the yoke that flings
   O'er the unshackled soul of man.   20
'Tis like a cobweb o'er the breast,
   That binds the giant while asleep;
Or curtain hung upon the east
   The daylight from the world to keep.

Here's to the hands sae lang upbore   25
    The Rose and Shamrock, blooming still;
An' here's the burly plant of yore,
    The Thistle o' the norlan' hill!
Lang may auld Britain's banners pale
    Stream o'er the seas her might has won;   30
Lang may her Lions paw the gale,
    An' turn their dewlaps to the sun!

The Fall of the Leaf.

THE following are the singing verses of a pastoral effusion, published
long ago.

THE flush of the landscape is o'er,
    The brown leaves are shed on the way,
The dye of the lone mountain flower
    Grows wan, and betokens decay;
The spring in our valleys is born,   5
    Like the bud that it fosters, to die,
Like the transient dews of the morn,
    Or the vapour that melts in the sky.

So youth, with its visions so gay,
    Departs like a dream of the mind,   10
To pleasure and passion a prey,
    That lead to the sorrows behind;
Its virtues too buoyant to grow,
    Its follies too latent to die—
We shall reap of the seeds we then sow,   15
    When the stars have dissolved in the sky.

All silent the song of the thrush,
    Bewilder'd she cowers in the dale;
The blackbird sits lone on the bush—
    The fall of the leaf they bewail.   20
All nature thus tends to decay,
    And to drop as the leaves from the tree
And man, just the flower of a day,
    How long, long his winter will be!

The Ancient Banner.

THIS song was written for, and sung at, the great football match at Cart-
erhaugh, on the 5th of December, 1815, when the old tattered banner
of Buccleuch was displayed at the head of the combatants. It was the
first rallying standard of the clan, and is very ancient.

AND hast thou here, like hermit grey,
　　Thy mystic characters unroll'd,
O'er peaceful revellers to play,
　　Thou emblem of the days of old!
Or com'st thou with the veteran's smile,　　　　　　5
　　Who deems his day of conquest fled,
Yet loves to view the bloodless toil
　　Of sons whose sires he often led?

Not such thy peaceable intent,
　　When over Border waste and wood,　　　　　　10
On foray and achievement bent,
　　Like eagle on his path of blood.
Symbol to ancient valour dear,
　　Much has been dared and done for thee;
I almost weep to see thee here,　　　　　　15
　　And deem thee raised in mockery.

But no—familiar to the brave,
　　'Twas thine thy gleaming moon and star
Above their manly sports to wave,
　　As free as in the field of war;　　　　　　20
To thee the faithful clansman's shout,
　　In revel as in rage, was dear—
The more beloved in festal rout,
　　The better fenced when foes were near.

I love thee for the olden day,　　　　　　25
　　The iron age of hardihood,
The rather that thou led'st the way
　　To peace and joy through paths of blood;
For were it not the deeds of weir,
　　When thou wert foremost in the fray,　　　　　　30
We had not been assembled here,
　　Rejoicing in a father's sway.

And even the days ourselves have known
    Alike the moral truth impress,
Valour and constancy alone   35
    Can purchase peace and happiness.
Then hail! memoiral of the brave,
    The liegeman's pride, the Border's awe;
May thy grey pennon never wave
    O'er sterner field than Carterhaugh!   40

A Widow's Wail.

ONE of my early songs, made so long ago that my mind retains no re-
membrance of the time, but I see it was published in the Forest Minstrel
in 1810, and several times since, with some slight alterations.–It is sung
to the air of "Gilderoy," but never was set to music.

O THOU art lovely yet, my boy,
    Even in thy winding-sheet;
I canna leave thy comely clay,
    An' features calm an' sweet!
I have no hope but for the day   5
    That we shall meet again,
Since thou art gone, my bonny boy,
    An' left me here alane!

I hoped thy sire's loved form to see,
    To trace his looks in thine;   10
An' saw with joy thy sparkling ee
    With kindling vigour shine!
I thought, when auld an' frail, I might
    Wi' you an' yours remain;
But thou art fled, my bonny boy,   15
    An' left me here alane!

Now closed an' set thy sparkling eye,
    Thy kind wee heart is still,
An' thy dear spirit far away
    Beyond the reach of ill!   20
Ah! fain wad I that comely clay
    Reanimate again;
But thou art fled, my bonny boy,
    An' left me here alane!

The flower now fading on the lea   25
    Shall fresher rise to view,–
The leaf just falling from the tree
    The year will soon renew;
But lang may I weep o'er thy grave
    Ere thou reviv'st again;   30
For thou art fled, my bonny boy,
    An' left me here alane!

Auld Joe Nicholson's Nanny

Was written the year before last, for Friendship's Offering, but has since become a favourite, and has been very often copied. I have refused all applications to have it set to music, having composed an air for it myself, which I am conscious I will prefer to any other, however much better it may be.

THE daisy is fair, the day-lily rare,
    The bud o' the rose as sweet as it's bonny;
But there ne'er was a flower, in garden or bower,
    Like auld Joe Nicholson's bonny Nanny!
       O, my Nanny!   5
       My dear little Nanny!
My sweet little niddlety-noddlety Nanny!
       There ne'er was a flower,
       In garden or bower,
Like auld Joe Nicholson's bonny Nanny!   10

Ae day she came out, wi' a rosy blush,
    To milk her twa kie, sae couthy and canny;
I cower'd me down at the back o' the bush,
    To watch the air o' my bonny Nanny.
       O, my Nanny, &c.   15

Her looks that stray'd o'er nature away,
    Frae bonny blue een sae mild an' mellow,
Saw naething sae sweet in nature's array,
    Though clad in the morning's gowden yellow.
       O, my Nanny, &c.   20

My heart lay beating the flowery green
  In quaking, quivering agitation,
An' the tears cam' tricklin' down frae my een,
  Wi' perfect love an' wi' admiration.
            O, my Nanny, &c.   25

There's mony a joy in this warld below,
  An' sweet the hopes that to sing were uncanny
But of all the pleasures I ever can know,
  There's nane like the love o' my bonny Nanny.
            O, my Nanny!   30
            My dear little Nanny!
My sweet little niddlety-noddlety Nanny!
            There ne'er was a flower,
            In garden or bower,
Like auld Joe Nicholson's bonny Nanny!   35

The Broken Heart

WAS written in detestation of the behaviour of a gentleman (can I call
him so?) to a dearly-beloved young relative of my own, and whom, at
the time I wrote this, I never expected to recover from the shock her
kind and affectionate heart had received. It has, however, turned out a
lucky disappointment for her.

        NOW lock my chamber door, father,
            And say you left me sleeping;
        But never tell my step-mother
            Of all this bitter weeping.
        No earthly sleep can ease my smart,   5
            Or even a while reprieve it;
        For there's a pang at my young heart
            That never more can leave it!

        O, let me lie, and weep my fill
            O'er wounds that heal can never;   10
        And O, kind Heaven! were it thy will,
            To close these eyes for ever;
        For how can maid's affections dear
            Recall her love mistaken?
        Or how can heart of maiden bear   15
            To know that heart forsaken?

O, why should vows so fondly made,
  Be broken ere the morrow,
To one who loved as never maid
  Loved in this world of sorrow?   20
The look of scorn I cannot brave,
  Nor pity's eye more dreary;
A quiet sleep within the grave
  Is all for which I weary!

Farewell, dear Yarrow's mountains green,   25
  And banks of broom so yellow!
Too happy has this bosom been
  Within your arbours mellow.
That happiness is fled for aye,
  And all is dark desponding,   30
Save in the opening gates of day,
  And the dear home beyond them!

As a note to the above song, I may quote a stanza from another poem written at the same time:—

Woe to the guileful tongue that bred
  This disappointment and this pain!
Cold-hearted villain! on his head
  A minstrel's malison remain!
Guilt from his brow let ne'er depart,
  Nor shame until his dying day;
For he has broke the kindest heart
  That ever bow'd to nature's sway!

John o' Brackadale.

WRITTEN for, and published in, Albyn's Anthology.

HEY, John, ho, John,
  Hey, John o' Brackadale;
Auld John, bauld John,
  Brave John o' Brackadale!
Came ye o'er by Moravich,   5
  Saw ye John o' Brackadale,
At his nose a siller queich,
  At his knee a water-pail?

Copper nose an' haffets grey,
 Bald head an' bosom hale,   10
John has drunken usquebae
 Mair than a' Loch Brackadale!
  Hey, John, ho, John, &c.

Sic a carle! to wear away,
 An' lye down quiet i' the yird,   15
Just when the glorious usquebae
 Is growing cheaper by a third;—
It winna do—I'll no believe it,
 For ne'er was carle sae blithe an' hale;
Then hey for routh o' barley bree,   20
 An' brave John o' Brackadale!
  Hey, John, ho, John,
   Hey, John o' Brackadale;
  Auld John, bauld John,
   Brave John o' Brackadale!   25

Bauldy Frazer

Is a rant which I composed for my own singing, in the broken Highland
dialect, when I was a shepherd.

AIR—*Whigs o' Fife.*

HER name pe Bauldy Frazer, man,
She's puir and oult, and pale and wan;
She proke her shin, and tint a han',
 Upon Cullotin's lea, man.
Our Heelant clans pe creat forworn,   5
Els tem hat geen te loons ter corn;
But sic a tey was nefer porn
 For Heelant mans to tee, man.

Och, sic a hurly-purly rase,
Te fery lift was in a plase,   10
As all te teils had won ter ways,
 On Heelant mans to flee, man.
Te cannon an' te pluff trakoon,
Sore proke her rank an' pore her toon,
Her nain sell ne'er cot sic a stoon,   15
 As Cot shall answer me, man.

Pig Satan sent te plan frae hell,
Or put our chiefs peside hersell,
To plant tem on te open fell,
   In pase artillery's ee, man.   20
For had she met te gruesome Tuke
At ford of Spey or Prae-Calrook,
Te ploot of every foreign pouk
   Had dyed te Cherman sea, man.

She fought for all she loved or had,   25
And for te right; put Heavin forpade,
And mony a bonny Heelant lad
   Lay pleeding on te prae, man.
Fat could she too, fat could she say?
Te crand M'Tonald was away,   30
And her nown chief tat luckless tay
   Pe far peyond Dunvey, man.

M'Pherson and M'Gregor poth,
Te men of Moidart and Glen-quoich,
And cood M'Kenzies of te Doich,   35
   All absent from te field, man.
Te sorde was sharp, te arm was true,
Pe honour still her nainsell's tue,
Impossibles she cou'd not do,
   Though laith she pe to yield, man.   40

When Sharles first wi' the flighters met,
Praif lad, he thought us pack to ket,
"Turn, turn," he cry't, "and face tem yet,
   We'll conquer, or we'll tee, man!"
Put her nainsell shumpit owre te purn,   45
And sweart pe Cot she wudna turn,
For ter was nought put shoot and purn,
   And hanging on te tree, man.

Fie, ploody Tuke, fat ail't her ten,
To rafage every Heelant glen?   50
Her crime was truth, and lofe to ane,
   She had no hate at tee, man.
And you, and yours, will yet pe klad
To trust te honest Heelant lad;
Te ponnit plue and pelted plaid   55
   Will stand te last of tree, man.

Hymn to the Evening Star.

WRITTEN in 1811. All the pieces which I wrote at that age have a melody in them, which, since that period, I have never been able to reach; but they are often deficient in real stamina.

ARISE, arise, thou queen of Love,
　　Thy bed is chill'd with evening dew
Thy robe the virgin fays have wove,
　　And rear'd thy canopy of blue.
O, let me see thy golden breast,　　　　　　　　　5
　　Thy amber halo o'er the hill,
And all the chambers of the west
　　Thy coronal with glory fill.

O, come–the evening colours fade,
　　Soft silence broods o'er lawn and lee;　　　　10
And beauty in the greenwood shade,
　　Uplifts a longing eye for thee.
Thy temple be this silvan bower,
　　Where wounded lovers kneel confest;
Thine altar-cloth the daisy flower,　　　　　　　15
　　Thy tabernacle, beauty's breast.

Be this thy dearest, holiest shrine,
　　Thy breviary two beaming eyes;
And aye I'll pant to see thee shine–
　　Beloved star, arise, arise!　　　　　　　　　20
As slowly steals an angel's wing,
　　Thy light pavilion down the sky;
Before thee let young seraphs sing
　　The softest love-sick melody.

And here, on thy beloved shrine,　　　　　　　25
　　Where fragrant flowers of incense glow,
Pure as that heavenly breast of thine,
　　And fairer than the virgin snow;–
Here will I worship with delight,
　　And pay the vows I made to thee,　　　　　　30
Until thy mild and modest light
　　Is cradled on the heaving sea.

Ohon-a-Righ!

A HUMBLE petition from the Ettrick Shepherd to his late loved sovereign,
King George IV., to restore the titles of the last remnants of the brave
defenders of the rights of their ancient dynasty.

OHON-a-righ!
Ohon-a-righ!
There's nought but alteration;
  The men that strove
  Our throne to move,   5
And overturn the nation,
  Are a' come round,
  Wi' wit profound,
To those they branded sairly
  An' show more might   10
  For George's right
Than e'er they did for Charlie.

  The day is past,
  It was the last
Of suffering and of sorrow   15
  And o'er the men
  Of northern glen
Arose a brighter morrow.
  The pibroch rang
  With bolder clang   20
Along the hills of heather;
  An' fresh an' strong
  The thistle sprung
That had begun to wither!

  Our sovereign gone,   25
  Whom we think on
As sons on sire regarded,
  Of the plaided north
  Beheld the worth
And loyalty rewarded.   30
  Return'd their own,
  And to the throne
Bound all their spirits lordly,
  Now who will stand,
  With dirk or brand,   35
As Donald does for Geordie?

Beannaich-an-righ!
Beannaich-an-righ!
Her nainsell now be praying.
Though standard praw, 40
And broadsword law,
She all aside be laying,
With Heelant might,
For Shorge's right,
Cot! put she'll braolich rarely, 45
Gin lords her nain
Pe lords ackain,
That fell for sake of Charlie!

The Laddie that I Ken O'.

THERE'S a bonny, bonny laddie that I ken o',
There's a bonny, bonny laddie that I ken o',
An' although he be but young,
He has a sweet wooing tongue,
The bonny, bonny laddie that I ken o'. 5

He has woo'd me for his own, an' I trow him, O,
For it's needless to deny that I loe him, O;
When I see his face come ben,
Then a' the lads I ken,
I think them sae far, far below him, O. 10

There is Annie, the demure little fairy, O,
Our Nancy, an' Burns' bonny Mary, O;
They may set their caps at him,
An' greet till they gae blin',
But his love for his Jean will never vary, O. 15

He'll come to me at e'en though he's weary, O,
An' the way be baith langsome an' eery, O,
An' he'll tirl at the pin,
An' cry, "Jeanie, let me in,
For my bosom it burns to be near ye, O!" 20

He's a queer bonny laddie that I ken o',
He's a dear bonny laddie that I ken o';
For he'll tak me on his knee,
An' he'll reave a kiss frae me,
The bonny, bonny laddie that I ken o'. 25

O Lady Dear.

COPIED from the Queen's Wake. Queen Mary hears an ancient bard singing it to her at a distance, and is deeply affected. It was set to music on a single sheet by Mr Monzanni. I also composed an air for it, since known by the name of "The Cameronian's Midnight Hymn." See the Brownie of Bodsbeck.

O LADY dear, fair is thy noon,
But man is like the inconstant moon;
Last night she smiled o'er lawn and lea,
That moon will change and so will he.
Thy time, dear lady, 's a passing shower,   5
Thy beauty is but a fading flower;
Watch thy young bosom and virgin eye,
For the shower must fall, and the flow'ret die.

The Spectre's Cradle Song.

HUSH, my bonny babe!–hush, and be still!
Thy mother's arms shall guard thee from ill;
Far have I borne thee in sorrow and pain,
To drink the breeze of the world again.
The dew shall moisten thy brow so meek,   5
And the breeze of midnight fan thy cheek;
And soon shall we rest in the how of the hill–
Hush, my bonny babe!–hush, and be still!

For thee have I travail'd in weakness and woe,
The world above and the world below;   10
My heart was kind, and I fell in the snare,
Thy father was cruel, but thou wert fair.
I sinn'd, I sorrow'd–I died for thee,
Then O, my bonny babe, smile on me!
And weep thou not for thy mother's ill–   15
Hush, my bonny babe!–hush, and be still!

See yon thick clouds of the murky hue,
Yon star that peeps from its window blue
Above yon clouds that are wandering far,
Away and beyond yon little star,–   20

There's a home of peace that soon shall be thine,
And there shalt thou see thy father and mine,
Away from sorrow, away from ill—
Hush, my bonny babe!—hush, and be still!

The flowers of this world will bud and decay,   25
The trees of the forest be weeded away,
And all yon stars from the milky way,
But thou shalt bloom for ever and aye.
The time will come I shall follow thee,
But long, long hence that time shall be.   30
O weep not so for thy mother's ill!—
Hush, my bonny babe!—hush, and be still!

Hymn to the God of the Sea.

THIS and the foregoing songs are copied, with a slight variation, from the Queen's Wake, as pieces that might be successfully set to music.

O THOU, who makest the ocean to flow,
Thou, who walkest the channels below,
To thee the incense of song we heap,—
Thou, who knowest not slumber nor sleep,
Journeying with everlasting motion,   5
Great spirit that movest on the face of the ocean,
To thee!—to thee!—we sing to thee,
God of the western wind! God of the sea!

To thee, who breathest in the bosom'd sail,
Who rulest the shark and the rolling whale,   10
Who bid'st the billows thy reign deform,
Laugh'st in the whirlwind, sing'st in the storm,
Who flingest the sinner to downward grave,
Who light'st thy lamp on the mane of the wave—
To thee!—to thee!—we sing to thee,   15
God of the western wind! God of the sea!

To thee, who leadest forth in the air,
The things that be not, are not there,
That rise like mountain amid the sea,
Where mountain was never, and never will be,   20
Who mov'st thy proud and thy pale chaperoon,

Mid walks of the angels and ways of the moon—
To thee!—to thee!—we sing to thee,
God of the western wind! God of the sea!

To thee, who bid'st those mountains of brine   25
Softly to sink in the fair moonshine,
And spreadest thy couch of mellow light,
To lure to thy bosom the Queen of the night,
Who weavest the cloud of the ocean dew,
And the mist that sleeps on her breast of blue—   30
To thee!—to thee!—we sing to thee,
God of the western wind! God of the sea!

To thee, whose holy calm is spread
For nymphs of the ocean's wooing bed,
When the murmurs die at the base of the hill,   35
And the shadows lie rock'd and murmuring still,
And the solan's young and the lines of foam
Are scarcely heaved on thy peaceful home—
To thee!—to thee!—we sing to thee,
God of the western wind! God of the sea!   40

Angel's Morning Song to the Shepherd.

WAKEN, drowsy slumberer, waken!
Over gorse, green broom, and braken,
From her sieve of silken blue,
Dawning sifts her silver dew,
Hangs the emerald on the willow,   5
Lights her lamp below the billow,
Bends the brier and branchy braken—
Waken, drowsy slumberer, waken!

Round and round, from glen and grove,
Pour a thousand hymns to love;   10
Harps the rail amid the clover,
O'er the moon-fern whews the plover,
Bat has hid and heath-cock crow'd,
Courser neigh'd and cattle low'd,
Kid and lamb the lair forsaken—   15
Waken, drowsy slumberer, waken!

Mary Gray.

SOME say that my Mary Gray is dead,
  And that I in this world shall see her never;
Some say she is laid on her cold death-bed,
  The prey of the grave and of death for ever!
Ah, they know little of my dear maid, 5
  Or kindness of her spirit's giver;
For every night she is by my side—
  By the morning bower, or the moonlight river.

My Mary was bonny when she was here,
  When flesh and blood was her mortal dwelling; 10
Her smile was sweet, and her mind was clear,
  And her form all virgin forms excelling.
But oh, if they saw my Mary now,
  With her looks of pathos and of feeling,
They would see a cherub's radiant brow, 15
  To ravish'd mortal eyes unveiling.

The rose is the fairest of earthly flowers,
  It is all of beauty and of sweetness,—
So my dear maid in the heavenly bowers,
  Excels in beauty and in meekness! 20
She has kiss'd my cheek, she has kaim'd my hair,
  And made a breast of heaven my pillow,
And promised her God to take me there
  Before the leaf falls from the willow!

Farewell, ye homes of living men, 25
  I have no relish for your pleasures;
In the human face I naething ken
  That with my spirit's yearning measures.
I long for onward bliss to be,
  A day of joy—a brighter morrow, 30
And from this bondage to be free—
  Farewell this world of sin and sorrow!

Ode on Hearing of the Death of Mr Pitt.

THIS and the two following are inserted as pieces that might be set to music, though as yet they never have been, and probably never will be.

AND art thou departed, ere yet from the field
 The tidings of glory are borne?
And art thou departed, our bulwark, our shield,
 And live I thy exit to mourn?
My country's horizon for ever is shorn   5
 Of the splendour that over it shone;
The darkness is shed, and the storm is gone forth,
Our sun and our moon have both dropp'd to the earth,
The child of the mighty hath come to the birth,
 But the strength of the parent is gone.   10

O, Pitt, I may wail thee, and wail without blame,
 For here cannot party deride!
'Twas in the lone wild I first heard of thy name,
 With Nature alone for my guide,
Who taught me to love thee—my boast and my pride 15
 From thence thou hast been and shalt be;
I read and I wonder'd, but still I read on,
My bosom heaved high with an ardour unknown,
But I found it congenial in all with thine own,
 And I set up my rest under thee.   20

I wonder'd when senators sternly express'd
 Disgust at each measure of thine;
For I was as simple as babe at the breast,
 And their motives I could not divine.
I knew not, and still small the knowledge is mine, 25
 Of the passions that mankind dissever,
That minds there are framed like the turbulent ocean,
That fumes on its barriers with ceaseless commotion,
On the rock that stands highest commanding devotion,
 There dash its rude billows for ever. 30

They said thou wert proud;—I have ponder'd it long,
 I have tried thee by plummet and line,
Have weigh'd in the balance the right and the wrong,
 And am forced in the charge to combine:
They call'd thee ambitious;—a censure condign— 35

I know it—I own it was true;
But it was of thy country alone thou wert proud,
Thy ambition was all for her glory and good,
For there thy wrung heart a wild torrent withstood,
    Which broke what it could not subdue.   40

Be hallow'd thy memory, illustrious shade!
    A shepherd can ill understand,
But he weens that as clear and unbiass'd a head,
    As clean and less sordid a hand,
Or a heart more untainted did never command   45
    The wealth of a nation on earth;
And he knows that long hence, when his head's low as
        thine,
That the good and the great, and the brave and benign,
And the lovers of country and king, will combine
    To hallow the hour of thy birth.   50

Busaco.

BEYOND Busaco's mountains dun,
When far had roll'd the sultry sun,
And night her pall of gloom had thrown
    O'er nature's still convexity,
High on the heath our tents were spread,   5
The green turf was our cheerless bed,
And o'er the hero's dew-chill'd head
    The banners flapp'd incessantly.

The loud war-trumpet woke the morn,
The quivering drum, the pealing horn,   10
From rank to rank the cry is borne,
    "Arouse! for death or victory!"
The orb of day in crimson dye
Began to mount the morning sky,
Then what a scene for warrior's eye   15
    Hung on the bold declivity!

The serried bay'nets glittering stood,
Like icicles on hills of blood,

An aerial stream, a silver wood,
    Reel'd in the flickering canopy.   20
Like waves of ocean rolling fast,
Or thunder-cloud before the blast,
Massena's legions, stern and vast,
    Rush'd to the dreadful revelry.

The pause is o'er, the fateful shock,   25
A thousand thousand thunders woke,
The air grows sick, the mountains rock,
    Red ruin rides triumphantly!
Light boil'd the war-cloud to the sky,
In phantom towers and columns high;   30
But dark and dense their bases lie,
    Prone on the battle's boundary.

The thistle waved her bonnet blue,
The harp her wildest war-notes threw,
The red rose gain'd a fresher hue,   35
    Busaco, in thy heraldry!
Hail, gallant brothers! woe befall
The foe that braves thy triple wall!
For even the slumbering Portugal
    Arouses at thy chivalry!   40

Ode to the Genius of Shakespeare.

SPIRIT all limitless,
    Where is thy dwelling place,
Spirit of him whose high name we revere?
    Come on thy seraph wings—
    Come from thy wanderings,   5
And smile on thy votaries who sigh for thee here!

    Whether thou journey'st far
    On by the morning star,
Dream'st in the shadowy brows of the moon;
    Or linger'st in fairyland   10
    Mid lovely elves to stand,

Singing thy carols all lightsome and boon;–
    Whether thou tremblest o'er
    Green grave of Elsinore,
Stay'st o'er the hill of Dunsinnan to hover,   15
    Bosworth or Shrewsbury,
    Egypt or Philippi,
Come from thy roamings the universe over!

    Come, O thou spark divine,
    Rise from thy hallow'd shrine!   20
Here in the vales of the north thou shalt see,
    Hearts true to Nature's call,
    Spirits congenial,
Proud of their country, yet bowing to thee.

    Here thou art call'd upon,   25
    Come thou to Caledon,
Come to the land of the ardent and free–
    The land of the lone recess,
    Mountain and wilderness,
This is the land, thou wild meteor, for thee!   30

    And here, by the sounding sea,
    Torrent and green-wood tree,
Here to solicit thee cease shall we never!
    Meteor, effulgence bright,
    Here must thy flame relight,   35
Or vanish from nature for ever and ever!

The Wee Housie.

I LIKE thee weel, my wee auld house,
    Though laigh thy wa's an' flat the riggin',
Though round thy lum the sourock grows,
    An' rain-draps gaw my cozy biggin'.
Lang hast thou happit mine and me,   5
    My head's grown grey aneath thy kipple,
And aye thy ingle cheek was free
    Baith to the blind man an' the cripple.

What gart my ewes thrive on the hill,
    An' kept my little store increasin'?   10
The rich man never wish'd me ill,
    The poor man left me aye his blessin'.
Troth I maun greet wi' thee to part,
    Though to a better house I'm flittin';
Sic joys will never glad my heart   15
    As I've had by thy hallan sittin'.

My bonny bairns around me smiled,
    My sonsy wife sat by me spinning,
Aye lilting o'er her ditties wild,
    In notes sae artless an' sae winning.   20
Our frugal meal was aye a feast,
    Our e'ening psalm a hymn of joy;
Sae calm an' peacefu' was our rest,
    Our bliss, our love, without alloy.

I canna help but haud thee dear,   25
    My auld, storm-batter'd, hamely shieling;
Thy sooty lum, an' kipples clear,
    I better love than gaudy ceiling.
Thy roof will fa', thy rafters start,
    How damp an' cauld thy hearth will be!   30
Ah! sae will soon ilk honest heart,
    That erst was blithe an' bauld in thee!

I thought to cower aneath thy wa',
    Till death should close my weary een,
Then leave thee for the narrow ha',   35
    Wi' lowly roof o' sward sae green.
Fareweel, my house an' burnie clear,
    My bourtree bush an' bowzy tree!
The wee while I maun sojourn here,
    I'll never find a hame like thee.   40

Good Night, and Joy.

THIS song was written for, and published as the concluding song of, Smith's Scottish Minstrel; a work, the music of which is singular for its sweetness and true Scottish simplicity. The song, with a little variation, forms an appropriate conclusion to these simple lyrical effusions.

THE year is wearing to the wane,
    An' day is fading west awa',
Loud raves the torrent an' the rain,
    And dark the cloud comes down the shaw;
But let the tempest tout an' blaw   5
    Upon his loudest winter horn,
Good night, an' joy be wi' you a',
    We'll maybe meet again the morn!

O, we hae wander'd far and wide
    O'er Scotia's hills, o'er firth an' fell,   10
An' mony a simple flower we've cull'd,
    An' trimm'd them wi' the heather-bell!
We've ranged the dingle an' the dell,
    The hamlet an' the baron's ha',
Now let us take a kind farewell,—   15
    Good night, an' joy be wi' you a'!

Though I was wayward, you were kind,
    And sorrow'd when I went astray;
For O, my strains were often wild
    As winds upon a winter day.   20
If e'er I led you from the way,
    Forgie your Minstrel aince for a';
A tear fa's wi' his parting lay,—
    Good night, an' joy be wi' you a'!

THE END.

Note on the Text

The Introduction to the present edition gives a full account of the publishing history of *Songs by the Ettrick Shepherd* 1831 along with a detailed account of the relationship between the first printed edition and Hogg's fair-copy manuscript for the volume, now chiefly located amongst the Blackwood Papers at NLS MS 4805 ff. 95–102. This note thus focusses on the copy text for the present edition, namely the first printed edition of *Songs by the Ettrick Shepherd*, published by William Blackwood of Edinburgh and Thomas Cadell of London in January 1831.

As explained by Janette Currie in 'The Genesis of the Text' (pp. xli-xlviii), the relationship between Hogg's fair-copy manuscript for this volume, which is largely complete, and the first edition published in 1831 is very close. There is clear evidence, as Currie maps out, of Hogg's residency in Edinburgh during December 1830 and his physical involvement in the preparation of the printed volume. This is clear from markings on the fair-copy manuscript. The emendations between manuscript and first edition are slight: frequently there are no changes between the manuscript of a song and the printed text. As such, it was decided that the first printed edition of January 1831 would be a suitable copy text for this new edition.

Any changes which did take place between manuscript and printed version are clearly explained in editorial notes to the song in question. There is one notable inconsistency in the titles of songs throughout 1831. In the first edition these are most often followed by a full-stop, but, on occasion there is no punctuation and sometimes there is a semi-colon or a comma. The present edition has adhered to the punctuation given in 1831 and has not standardised the presentation of song titles. We have also adopted Hogg's presentation in his printed 1831 text of names beginning with 'Mc'. There are inconsistencies between manuscript and print, but in the printed text they are consistently presented as a reverse apostrophe, and we have adhered to this practice. On a few occasions it is clear that Hogg's hand-writing was misread by the printer. On occasions when the song had appeared several times elsewhere, and in cases where there is a clear record of stability between earlier versions, then the text here has been emended. The present edition also makes a small number of emendations in order to correct what appear to be printer's errors (e.g. 'Shakespeare' for 'Shakspeare' on p. 132). These emendations are given below with the emended version first, followed by the original 1831 version. References for page and line number are listed using the system adopted in the Editorial Notes.

11, l. 7 of moorland] moorland ['of' is included in both NLS MS 4805 and in the first printed text of 1825 in R. A. Smith's *The Irish Minstrel*: see Editorial Notes.]

16, ll. 9–12
Sing umptidy-tumptidy tearhim,
  Sing umptidy-tumptidy tee;
Then up wi' the Souters o' Selkirk!
  The sons o' auld heroes for me!] Sing umpity-tumptidy tearhim, &c
[The first line of the chorus alone is given with the first verse in 1831
and in the manuscript no chorus is given at all for verse 1 and only the
first line with verse 2: see Editorial Notes.]

19, l. 20 blue.] blue

20 [opening dialogue of Shepherd] Whisht, whisht!] Whisht, whisht 1
[printer's error]

20, l. 22 say it.] say it

22, l. 10 sun] steep ['sun' appears in two earlier printings of the text: see
Editorial Notes].

31, l. 28 snaw.] snaw

31, l. 32 thee.] thee

33, l. 19 stream] sea ['stream' appears in NLS MS 4805 and in earlier
printings: see Editorial Notes.]

33, ll. 35–36
'Tis ready, a troop of
Our bold Highlandmen,] 'Tis ready, a troop of our bold Highlandmen,

40, l. 5 ball] hall [While 'hall' also makes sense, 'ball' appears both in NLS
MS 4805 and also in the version which appears in *The Musical Bijou*:
see Editorial Notes.]

46, l. 4 eery;] eery [There is no punctuation in 1831 but the earlier ap-
pearance in *Blackwood's Edinburgh Magazine* uses a semi-colon.]

54, l. 18 flowery] flowing ['flowery' appears in NLS MS 4805 and in earlier
printings of the text: see Editorial Notes.]

57, l. 28 cow] now ['cow' appears in NLS MS 4805 and in all earlier print-
ings of the text: see Editorial Notes.]

57, l. 30 ye.] ye

58, l. 22 Gorthaly] Gorthaleg ['Gorthaly' appears in NLS MS 4805 and
also in earlier printings of the text – though understandably has been
misread from ms by the printer: see Editorial Notes.]

58, l. 30 fear:] fear [There is no punctuation in 1831 but in *JR II* the text
appears with a colon.]

60, l. 20 dale.] dale [There is no punctuation in 1831 but a full-stop appears in the text printed in *Select & Rare Scottish Melodies.*]

71, l. 6 flashing] slashing [While both make sense, 'flashing' appears in NLS MS 4805 and in early printing of the text: see Editorial Notes].

71, l. 13 froward Duke] frowardDuke

80, l. 61 ear'] air ['ear' clearly means 'early' and appears in NLS MS 4805: see Editorial Notes].

81, l. 81 lythe] blithe ['lythe' appears in NLS MS 4805 and appears to have been misread by the printer: see Editorial Notes].

86, l. 1 bummers] cummers ['cummers' makes no sense here and 'bum-mers' appears clearly in NLS MS 4805 and in earlier printing of the text: see Editorial Notes.]

90, l. 35 fray."] fray.

109, l. 18 Makes] Make's [printer's error]

114, l. 4 again.] again

124, l. 12 Charlie.] Charlie

130, l. 20 rest] nest ['rest' appears in NLS MS 4805 and in earlier print-ing of the text – this is most probably a misreading by the printer: see Editorial Notes.]

130, l. 28 fumes] foams ['fumes' appears in the earlier printing of the text, and while difficult to read, also in NLS MS 4805 – this is most probably a misreading by the printer: see Editorial Notes.]

132 [Title] Shakespeare] Shakspeare [clearly 'Shakespeare' in NLS MS 4805 – printer's error: see Editorial Notes.]

Hyphenation List

Below is the single case in which a word hyphenated at the end of the line in the present edition should be retained in making quotations. References are given using the system adopted in the Editorial Notes.

40 The Mermaid's Song [headnote] hum-drum

Editorial Notes

Editorial notes are provided here for the 113 songs which appear in *Songs by the Ettrick Shepherd* of 1831. Notes are given under the title of each song with reference to page numbers in this Stirling/South Carolina (hereafter S/SC) edition: individual songs were not numbered in the 1831 first edition which was used as copy text for this new edition. Because many of the songs in this volume had already appeared elsewhere (sometimes in several different publications) prior to 1831, these individual song histories are often complex. The notes are thus arranged in clearly defined sections.

The first section of each note – Creative Context – provides information about the Creative Context of the song and includes details about related manuscript sources. The relationship between the fair-copy manuscript for *Songs by the Ettrick Shepherd* (1831), chiefly located at NLS MS 4805, ff. 26–102 (Blackwood Papers), and the 1831 edition is discussed in more detail by Janette Currie in her essay on 'The Genesis of the Text', pp. xli–xlviii. Any substantive variants are mentioned in the notes when the manuscript is discussed. If the song has been amended across Hogg's lifetime this will be traced and, where evidence is available, explained.

The second section of the editorial note – Publication History – then provides a short chronological listing of the song's appearance in Hogg works, before and after 1831 providing brief references to the relevant sources. Citations from first editions are given and, where possible, readers are also referred to the new S/SC editions of Hogg's work. Unauthorised versions of the song in question, if applicable, will also be listed here. Such unauthorised and later versions are an important part of the overall picture of Hogg's songs and their wider dissemination and reception. However, this list is by no means exhaustive, and only notable appearances which we have identified to date are given here. The dating of the musical collections and miscellaneous song sheets is complex: if the date is given in square brackets (i.e. [1828]) it denotes a publication with no clear date of publication on the copy, but where a dated preface or additional concrete evidence has allowed a clear year or date of publication to be surmised. If a date appears with circa (i.e., *c.*1828) this denotes a publication where no exact date is published on the copy and no exact date has been able to be surmised through other sources, but where an approximate date range has been able to be established. Full details of the dating of collections and individual song-sheets will be given in either the Introductory notes to the collection in which the song appears or in the editorial notes to that particular song-sheet in the accompanying volume of Hogg's songs, *Contributions to Musical Collections and Miscellaneous Songs* (S/SC, 2014).

The third section of the editorial notes – Musical Context – then discusses the musical context of the song, giving details of the melodies or airs associated with the song and often referring the reader to a musical setting discussed by Hogg in his headnote for the relevant song. Copies of these settings and further information about these musical collections and Hogg's involvement with them are given in the aforementioned *Contributions to Musical Collections and Miscellaneous Songs*.

The final section of the editorial notes – Explanatory Notes – gives further necessary information to elucidate the lyrics themselves, where this is deemed helpful to the reader. The definitions of single words are given in the Glossary at the back of the present edition. In the Explanatory Notes references to songs include page and line numbers in the present edition.

Quotations from the Bible are from the King James version, the translation most familiar to Hogg and his contemporaries. The notes make reference to standard works such as *The Oxford Dictionary of National Biography*, abbreviated to *ODNB*, *The Oxford English Dictionary*, abbreviated to *OED*, and *The Dictionary of the Scottish Language,* http://www.dsl.ac.uk [accessed September 2005–June 2008], abbreviated to *DSL*. This online resource incorporates the twelve-volume *Dictionary of the Older Tongue*, edited by William Craigie, et. al. (Oxford: Oxford University Press, 1931–2002) and the ten-volume *Scottish National Dictionary*, edited by William Grant and David Murison (Edinburgh: Scottish National Dictionary Association, 1931–1976).

The first editions of Hogg's work are cited in 'Publication History' and, where possible, references are given alongside these to the new S/SC edition of the same work. Unless otherwise specified, the references given are to the first editions with a short title and page references only. The short titles used are as follows, in order of publication:

The Mountain Bard: *The Mountain Bard* (Edinburgh: Archibald Constable; London: John Murray, 1807)

The Forest Minstrel: *The Forest Minstrel* (Edinburgh: Archibald Constable; London: Hunter, Park and Hunter, 1810)

The Queen's Wake: *The Queen's Wake: A Legendary Poem* (Edinburgh: George Goldie; London: Longman, Hurst, Rees, Orme, and Brown, 1813)

Jacobite Relics I: *The Jacobite Relics of Scotland. First Series* (Edinburgh: William Blackwood; London: T. Cadell and W. Davies, 1819)

Jacobite Relics II: *The Jacobite Relics of Scotland. Second Series* (Edinburgh: William Blackwood; London: W. Davies: London, 1821)

Poetical Works: *The Poetical Works of James Hogg*, 4 vols (Edinburgh: Archibald Constable; London: Hurst, Robinson & Co., 1822)

Songs 1831: *Songs by the Ettrick Shepherd* (Edinburgh: William Blackwood; London: T. Cadell, 1831)

A Queer Book: *A Queer Book* (Edinburgh: William Blackwood; London: T. Cadell, 1832)

Likewise there are a number of key musical collections to which Hogg contributes. Full information about each of these, and copies of all Hogg's songs therein, are given in *Contributions to Musical Collections and Miscellaneous Songs*. Short titles of key collections listed in 'Publication History' are as follows in order of publication, excepting Thomson's volumes which are grouped together.

Albyn's Anthology: *Albyn's Anthology, or, A Select Collection of the Melodies & Vocal Poetry peculiar to Scotland & the Isles, hitherto unpublished,* 2 vols (Edinburgh: Oliver & Boyd, 1816, 1818)

Twelve Vocal Pieces: *Twelve Vocal Pieces Most of them with Original Poetry […] by John Clarke Mus. Doc.Cam.* […] (London: Birchall, [1817])

George Thomson, **A Select Collection of Original Scottish Airs:** *A Select Collection of Original Scottish Airs* , folio vol 5 (London: Preston; Edinburgh: Thomson, 1818, 1826, 1831)

George Thomson, **The Select Melodies of Scotland:** *The Select Melodies of Scotland Interspersed with those of Ireland and Wales united to the Songs of Robt. Burns […],* octavo 1822–23 (vols 1–5) (London: Preston; Edinburgh: Thomson)

George Thomson, **Thomson's Collection of the Songs of Burns:** *Thomson's Collection of the Songs of Burns, Sir Walter Scott Bart. And Other Eminent Lyric Poets Ancient and Modern […],* octavo [1825] [1830] (vols 1–6) (London: Preston; Edinburgh: Thomson)

George Thomson, **Melodies of Scotland:** *The Melodies of Scotland with Symphonies and Accompaniments […] The Poetry Chiefly by Burns […]* (London: Coventry & Hollier; Edinburgh: Thomson, folio 1831/1838 (vols 1–5) and 1841 (vol 6))

A Border Garland: *A Border Garland containing Nine New Songs by James Hogg. The Music Partly Old Partly Composed by Himself and Friends And Arranged with Symphonies and Accompaniments for the Pianoforte* (Edinburgh: Engraved Walker & Anderson; sold by Nathaniel Gow & Son, [1819])

The Scotish Minstrel: *The Scotish Minstrel A Selection from the Vocal Melodies of Scotland, Ancient and Modern, Arranged for the Voice and Piano Forte by R.A. Smith,* 6 vols (Edinburgh: Robt Purdie, [1821–24] and (c.1828–37))

The Irish Minstrel: *The Irish Minstrel A Selection from the Vocal Melodies of Ireland, Ancient and Modern, Arranged for the Piano Forte by R.A. Smith* (Edinburgh: Robt Purdie, [1825]; second edition c.1828)

Select & Rare Scotish Melodies: *Select & Rare Scotish Melodies The Poetry by the Celebrated Ettrick Shepherd The Symphonies & Accompaniments composed & the Whole Adapted & Arranged by Henry R. Bishop* (London: Goulding, D'Almaine & Co., [1828])

The Border Garland: *The Border Garland Containing Twelve New Songs the Poetry by James Hogg the Celebrated Ettrick Shepherd, Several of the Airs composed by Himself and Friends Arranged with Symphonies and Accompaniments by James Dewar* (Edinburgh: Robt Purdie, c.1829)

Original Scottish Melodies: *Original Scottish Melodies Composed by Peter McLeod* (Edinburgh: Wood & Co., [1834])

References to volumes from *The Collected Works of James Hogg* in the Stirling/South Carolina Edition, published by Edinburgh University Press, are noted with the abbreviation 'S/SC' and the date of first publication given in parentheses. Several of the references to Hogg's songs are quoted from or cross-reference notes to the following S/SC editions with the kind permission of the editors: *The Three Perils of Woman* (1823), edited by Antony Hasler and Douglas S. Mack (S/SC, 2002, paperback edition); *The Spy*, edited by Gillian Hughes (S/SC, 2000); *The Jacobite Relics of Scotland*. First Series, edited by Murray G. H. Pittock (S/SC, 2002); *The Jacobite Relics of Scotland*, Second Series, edited by Murray G. H. Pittock (S/SC, 2003); *Contributions to Annuals and Gift Books*, edited by Janette Currie and Gillian Hughes (S/SC, 2006); *The Forest Minstrel*, edited by Peter Garside and Richard Jackson (S/SC, 2006); *The Mountain Bard* (1807 and 1821), edited by Suzanne Gilbert (S/SC, 2007); *The Bush Aboon Traquair and the Royal Jubilee*, edited by Douglas S. Mack, (S/SC, 2008); *Contributions to Blackwood's Edinburgh Magazine*, I, 1817–1828, edited by Thomas B. Richardson (S/SC, 2008); *Contributions to Blackwood's Edinburgh Magazine*, II, 1828–1835, edited by Thomas B. Richardson (S/SC, 2012); and *The Collected Letters of James Hogg*, I, 1800–1819, edited by Gillian Hughes (S/SC, 2004; *The Collected Letters of James Hogg*, II, 1820–1831, edited by Gillian Hughes (S/SC, 2006); and *The Collected Letters of James Hogg*, III, 1832–1385, edited by Gillian Hughes (S/SC, 2008).

Books frequently used in the Notes are referred to by the following abbreviations:

Child: *The English and Scottish Popular Ballads*, ed. by Francis James Child, 5 vols (New York: The Folklore Press, 1957)

Dick: *The Songs of Robert Burns and Notes on Scottish Songs by Robert Burns*, by James C. Dick. Together with *Annotation of Scottish Songs by Burns*, by Davidson Cook (Hatboro, Pennsylvania: Folklore Associates, 1962)

Glen: John Glen, *Early Scottish Melodies* (Edinburgh: R. & J. Glen, 1900)

Gooch and Thatcher: *Musical Settings of British Romantic Literature: A Catalogue*, 2 vols (New York and London: Garland Publishing, 1982)

Graham: *The Songs of Scotland Adapted to their Appropriate Melodies, arranged with Pianoforte Accompaniments* by G. F. Graham, T. M. Mudie, J. T. Surenne, H. R. Dibdin, Finlay Dun, &c.: Illustrated with Historical, Biographical, and Critical Notices by George Farquhar Graham, 3 vols in 1 (Edinburgh: Wood and Co, 1848–49)

Groome: *Ordnance gazetteer of Scotland: a survey of Scottish topography, statistical, biographical, and historical*, edited by Francis H. Groome, 6 vols (Edinburgh : Thomas C. Jack, 1882–1885)

Humphries & Smith: Charles Humphries and William C. Smith, *Music Publishing in the British Isles from the Beginning until the middle of the nineteenth century* (Oxford: Blackwell, 1970)

SMM: *The Scots Musical Museum 1787–1803*, edited by James Johnson and Robert Burns, 6 vols. A two volume facsimile reprint, introduced by Donald A. Low (Aldershot: Scolar Press, 1991)

Stenhouse: *Illustrations of the Lyric Poetry and Music of Scotland*, William Stenhouse [with additional notes and illustrations by David Laing and C. K. Sharpe], (Edinburgh: William Blackwood and Sons, 1853)

Donald MacDonald. (pp. 3–5)

Creative Context:
A full account of the textual and publishing history of 'Donald Macdonald' (and a detailed history of the tune 'Woo'd an married an a' which is closely associated with the text) is given in *The Forest Minstrel* (S/SC, 2006). Further context and Explanatory Notes to the text are found in *The Mountain Bard* (S/SC, 2007).

In summary, Hogg states in his 1831 headnote that this was his 'first song', and his 1832 'Memoir' specifically dates the song to 1800 (*Altrive Tales* (S/SC, 2003), p. 20). But research for the editions above concur that it is more probable that Hogg wrote the song in 1803. Not only was he undertaking his second, more extensive Highland journey at this time, but this was also during a second wave of anxiety about Napoleonic invasion. This is supported by Hogg's decision to partner 'Donald MacDonald' with 'Scotia's Glens', the next song in *Songs* 1831, which Hogg notes was written in the same year and with reference to the same political context (see 'Scotia's Glens' below). For further discussion of the dating of 'Donald MacDonald' see R. G., 'The Ettrick Shepherd's First Song', in the *Edinburgh Literary Journal* of 8 May 1830 (275–76), and, most recently, Peter Garside, 'The Origins and History of James Hogg's "Donald MacDonald"', *Scottish Studies Review*, 7.2 (Autumn 2006), 24–39.

'Donald MacDonald' is central to Hogg's song opus, as it was indeed the first of his songs to appear with musical accompaniment in a broadsheet for voice, piano and German flute, published, in two slightly different versions, by John Hamilton of Edinburgh in *c*.1803. Moreover Hogg's references to the song in his 1832 'Memoir' and his 'Anecdotes of Scott' would suggest that he frequently performed the song himself and that it was thus well circulated and well known during his lifetime. It appeared as text alone in the 1807 edition of *The Mountain Bard* and in *The Forest Minstrel* of 1810. Hogg did not include it in the revised and extended edition of *The Mountain Bard* in 1821. Its appearance as the first song in *Songs* 1831 was its next, and its last, authorised printing.

While an early holograph version of the song is extant at NLS MS 10279, f. 83 (see *The Forest Minstrel* (S/SC, 2006), p. 349), the fair-copy manuscript for 1831 is found at NLS MS 4805, ff. 26r–27r. There are notable variants between 1831 and earlier printings, particularly regarding Hogg's decision to omit the second stanza in 1831. Reasons for this emendation are given by Garside and Jackson in in *The Forest Minstrel* (S/SC, 2006), p. 351. But it is the information in Hogg's headnote for the song and the footnote supplied by his nephew Robert Hogg, which make the 1831 edition particularly important. Robert Hogg, supplied the second paragraph of the textual note in an undated letter to William Blackwood, which was sent after the songs for *Songs* 1831 had been set in proof. However this note does appear in Hogg's fair-copy manuscript. Robert Hogg told Blackwood that the extra anecdote ought to be included with the song because it 'is worth twenty of that he has given about hearing the song sung in the Lancaster Theatre': see NLS MS 4719, f. 202–03. In the present edition, Robert Hogg's additional note is included because there is no indication that Hogg declined this contribution of additional anecdotal material to illuminate his first song.

The first anecdote recalls hearing a very successful performance of the song at the Lancaster Theatre, most likely in the 1810s after publication of *The Forest Minstrel* (see 'Caledonia', pp. 13–14). The second anecdote recalls Hogg overhearing a soldier singing the song in Dumfriesshire. Both stories substantiate the claim that Hogg's songs were widely performed at the time, with specific reference to theatrical performance, and this anecdotal evidence has often been used by scholars to highlight Hogg's role as a tradition bearer. While not printed again by Hogg in his lifetime, 'Donald MacDonald' is one of several Hogg songs which continued to be included in popular chapbook format and in anthologies of Scots song right through the nineteenth century. There is further evidence of international popularity. Steve Newman has found a report of the Highland Society Dinner in Bombay on 21 March 1823 in *The Calcutta Journal* (April 16, 1823) which states: 'Our northern brethren being more famous for the willing hand and heart than the ready tongue, had previously arranged that no healths of those present should be drunk; but the song was not forgotten. – Scots wha he' wi' Wallace bled; The death of Abercromby. – Donald McDonald – The Kail brose of auld Scotland – and many others, were sung in excellent style and added not a little to the hilarity of the evening'. Mention of the song is also made in 'Letters from India' or the correspondence of a 'young Artillery Officer in the East India Company's service' published in the Albany *Zodiac, A Monthly Periodical devoted to Science, Literature and the Arts* (New York) between the months of July and September 1835. The unknown Officer's 'Letter III, To a Distinguished Scotch Poet' is addressed to Hogg who is informed that his 'fame has even travelled into the wild of India, where your Donald McDonald is almost as great a favorite as "Scots wha hae wi' Wallace bled", or "Auld Lang Syne" '(I, No. 2 (August 1835), 18–19). For further information on Hogg and the *Zodiac*, see Janette Currie, 'From Altrive to Albany: James Hogg's Transatlantic Publication', Revised, March 2007 for the *James Hogg Research* website http://www.jameshogg.stir.ac.uk. See also the note for 'Scotia's Glens' below.

Hogg writes more expansively about the creation and contemporary performances of 'Donald MacDonald' in his 1832 'Memoir' (in *Altrive Tales* (S/ SC, 2003), p. 20. His suggestion, in the 1831 headnote, that he was a 'lad' (or 'boy' as it is in MS 4805) is a wild exaggeration, as Hogg would have been in his thirties at the time of its creation. But this reference highlights Hogg's intention to present his songs with personal details in *Songs* 1831, thus enabling him to create a public persona of himself as songwriter and creator.

Publication history:

*c.*1803 – 'Donald M'Donald, A Favorite New Scots Song set for the Voice, Piano-Forte, and Ger. Flute, written by James Hog.' [*sic*] dated *c.* 1801 – see *Contributions to Musical Collections and Miscellaneous Songs* (S/SC, 2014)

*c.*1803 – 'Donald McDonald' – Edinburgh, Printed & Sold by J. Hamilton at his Music Library No. 24 North Bridge Street. – see *Contributions to Musical Collections and Miscellaneous Songs* (S/SC, 2014)

1807 – in *The Mountain Bard*, pp. 179–82 – see (S/SC, 2007), pp. 108–09, 178–79, and 454–55

1810 – in *The Forest Minstrel*, pp. 190–93 – see (S/SC, 2006), pp. 176–78 and 348–352

1831 – in *Songs by the Ettrick Shepherd*, pp. 1–5 – see (S/SC, 2014), pp. 3–5

Unauthorised versions:
Often found in contemporary chapbooks: see for example, *Donald M'Donald; to which are added, Merry Maggy Cameron, Sandy o'er the Lee, Fairfa' the Lasses, O* (Stirling, Printed by W. Macnie, 1824), an eight-page chapbook where 'Donald M 'Donald' appears on pp. 2–5 (NLS, L.C. 2874 (9). Also notably in *The Caledonian Musical Repository* (Edinburgh: Oliver & Co., *c*.1806) pp. 72–75). Other unauthorised printings include a version, without musical notation, in *The Harp of Caledonia*, 2 vols (Glasgow: Khull, Blackie &Co.; Edinburgh: A. Fullarton, n.d. [*c*.1818]), Vol. II, 197–99. This song is also usually found amongst Hogg's contributions to major Scots song collections right through the 1900s (see *Contributions to Musical Collections and Miscellaneous Songs*).

Musical Context:
The traditional Scottish tune 'Woo'd and Married an' a'' was nominated as the chosen melody for this song from the first early song sheets up to and including its appearance in *Songs* 1831. This was a tune with a long history of publication, regarded as one of the most popular Scottish tunes of the period which was regularly in print from the 1750s onwards. An account of its history can be found in *The Forest Minstrel* (2006), pp. 350–52. For further information on the song sheets published by John Hamilton see: *Contributions to Musical Collections and Miscellaneous Songs*.

Explanatory Notes:
See *The Mountain Bard* (S/SC, 2007), pp. 454–56.

Scotia's Glens (pp. 5–6)

Creative Context:
A full account of the textual and publishing history of 'Scotia's Glens' (and a detailed history of the tune 'Lord Ballenden's Delight' to which Hogg refers in his 1831 headnote), is given in *The Forest Minstrel* (S/SC, 2006). Further details and Explanatory Notes to the text are found in *The Mountain Bard* (S/SC, 2007).

As noted above in the context of 'Donald MacDonald', Hogg's headnote in *Songs* 1831 tells us that this song was created in the same year as his 'first song' ('Donald MacDonald') and in the context of the anxieties over Napoleonic Invasion. In summary, 'Scotia's Glens' had appeared initially in *The Scots Magazine* in October 1803. It was subsequently printed (with variants) in *The Mountain Bard* in 1807 (but not in its 1821 edition) and again in *The Forest Minstrel* in 1810, before appearing finally in *Songs* 1831. Hogg had difficulties laying his hands on a copy of *The Forest Minstrel* at the time of preparing *Songs* 1831 for print, so it is thought that Hogg redrafted some of these songs from memory, rather than copying from a previous edition. There are some variants in 1831 but nothing substantive.

No earlier manuscript has been located. The fair-copy manuscript for 1831 is found at NLS MS 4805, ff. 27–28. The pages are numbered '4' and '5' in the top right had corners. The spelling of the air is changed from 'Lord Ballendine's delight' in the manuscript to 'Lord Ballenden's delight' for the printed text.

As is the case with 'Donald MacDonald' the 1831 headnote supplies the reader with evidence of Hogg's apparent patriotism, but with tantalising information about the song's international reputation. Evidence of the popularity of Hogg's songs in India is found in a series of 'Letters from India' reprinted in the Albany

Zodiac, A Monthly Periodical devoted to Science, Literature and the Arts (New York) between the months of July and September 1835, one of which includes mention of the Indian reception of Hogg's songs. For further information see the above note to 'Donald MacDonald'.

Publication history:
1803 – in *The Scots Magazine*, 65 (October 1803), 725
1807 – in *The Mountain Bard*, pp. 177–78 – see (S/SC, 2007), pp. 107 and 453–54
1810 – in *The Forest Minstrel*, pp. 170–71 – see (S/SC, 2006), pp. 158 and 332–34
1831 – in *Songs by the Ettrick Shepherd* on pp. 6–8 – see pp. 5–6 in the present edition
Unauthorised versions:
*c.*1818 – The song clearly remained in circulation after 1810 as revealed by an unauthorised printing in *The Harp of Caledonia*, 2 vols (Glasgow: Khull, Blackie &Co.; Edinburgh: A. Fullarton, n.d. [*c.*1818]), vol 2, pp. 242–43.

Musical Context:
Hogg's 1831 headnote refers to 'the original name of the air' (or melody) as 'Lord Ballenden's delight'. This is, in Hogg's opinion, a 'fine' tune but one which is 'hard to sing'. This would suggest that the tune he had in mind was a variant of an older instrumental tune, not initially designed with the voice in mind. Further evidence of his intention that existing instrumental tunes be adapted for song lyrics as necessary can be located in his 'Preface' to the *Forest Minstrel* (S/SC, 2006, p. 7). In the case of this song, he notes: 'the tune of *Scotia's Glens* is not *Lord Ballendine's delight* as it appears in general; but is one of our finest Scottish airs, and seems to be taken from it' (p. 7). Richard Jackson's research into the tune for *The Forest Minstrel* has, however, unearthed no tune with the name Hogg cites, nor any variant which adapts to the lyrics Hogg created. Many variant titles are extant and appeared in contemporary sources. For further information see *The Forest Minstrel* (2006), pp. 333–34.

Explanatory Notes:
See *The Mountain Bard* (S/SC, 2007), p. 454.

The Broom Sae Green (pp. 6–7)

Creative Context:
'The Broom Sae Green' was created most probably in early January 1828 by Hogg for inclusion in the musical collection *Select & Rare Scotish Melodies* which had musical settings by Sir Henry Bishop and was published in London around October 1828 by the music publisher Goulding D'Almaine & Co. A full history of Hogg's involvement in this collection and copies of the 13 Hogg songs printed there can be found in *Contributions to Musical Collections and Miscellaneous Songs*. It is most likely that Hogg's letter to the Edinburgh music publisher Robert Purdie dated 18 January 1828 (see *Letters*, II, p. 284) included this song as one of the 'eight more songs' Hogg sent him for Goulding & D'Almaine, but he only mentions 'The brakens wi' me' by name. Purdie aided the publication of several of Hogg's songs, as part of his own production of Robert Archibald Smith's *The Scotish Minstrel* and also *The Irish Minstrel* in the mid-1820s (see *Contributions to Musical Collections and Miscellaneous Songs*). He also negotiated on behalf of Hogg with Goulding and

with other London firms (see *Letters*, II, pp. 512–14).

Its recent publication in London most probably accounts for Hogg's inclusion of the song in *Songs* 1831. Hogg further draws attention to it by confessing, in his headnote, that it is 'my greatest favourite at present'. Modesty not permitting, Hogg explains that this is because both the words and the melody are his own.

The fair-copy manuscript is the only extant manuscript and is found at NLS MS 4805, f. 28. There are no substantive variants between the manuscript and its printed version in *Songs* 1831. However the text for the musical setting does vary slightly from that printed in 1831, notably the final line of the first verse in *Select & Rare Scotish Melodies* reads 'My Laddie he'll no come near me', clearly indicating that the song is for the female voice. Hogg's emendation to 'Your laddie will no come near ye' in 1831 suggests the song might be sung by either man or woman. Other notable variants to the text for 1831 include replacing the vividly depicted 'gowden broom' with the unremarkable 'bough that hung' (l. 10), and a revision of the 'robin' in the second stanza with the metaphoric 'wee bird' (l. 13) and 'Redbreast' (l. 15).

Publication history:
[1828] – in *Select & Rare Scotish Melodies*, pp. 41–44 – see *Contributions to Musical Collections and Miscellaneous Songs* (S/SC, 2014)
1831 – in *Songs by the Ettrick Shepherd*, pp. 9–10 – see pp. 6–7 in the present edition

Musical Context:
Hogg's headnote leads the reader directly to the authorised musical publication of the song in *Select & Rare Scotish Melodies*. While Hogg is not always complimentary about musical settings of his songs, he clearly likes this one and congratulates Henry Bishop here on a fine setting of Hogg's own melody. Hogg composed his own melodies for several of his finest songs (see also *A Border Garland* in *Contributions to Musical Collections and Miscellaneous Songs*). The melody Hogg created for this lyric is clearly inspired by his fiddle playing. There is a wide range of well over an octave and many leaps (notably in the first phrase of the tune) which are easier to play than to sing. It also has a modal quality which links it strongly to the folk tradition. This melody illustrates Hogg intimate love and knowledge of the Scottish fiddle tradition on which he comments so notably in his 1807 'Memoir' (see *The Mountain Bard* (S/SC, 2007), pp. 9–10.

Explanatory Notes:
6 [Title] broom is a shrub, *Sarothamnus* or *Cytisus Scoparius*, part of the *Leguminosæ* family. It bears large yellow flowers and is found on sandy banks, pastures, and heaths in Britain, and diffused over Western Europe (OED).
7, l. 17 new-wean'd lamb, sets the song in Spring-time.

Flora Macdonald's Farewell (pp. 7–8)

Creative Context:
This song already had a significant history before *Songs* 1831. It appeared firstly in a song sheet published by Nathaniel Gow & Son with the title 'The Lament of Flora Macdonald' which was advertised in 1819 (see *Contributions to Musical Collections and Miscellaneous Songs*). But it is likely that Hogg created it for his major collection of *Jacobite Relics* where it appeared as 'SONG XCII' in the Second Series of 1821. Hogg provided a note of explanation as to its creation:

I got the original of these verses from my friend Mr Niel Gow, who told me they were a translation from the Gaelic, but so rude that he could not publish them, which he wished to do on a single sheet, for the sake of the old air. On which I versified them anew, and made them a great deal better without altering one sentiment. (*Jacobite Relics*, II, 369)

Hogg's letter to George Thomson of 14 December 1821 (*Letters*, II, pp. 131–35) replicates this story about the song, noting that Niel Gow (1795–1823) also picked up the tune. The original Gaelic source has not been identified. Hogg was collecting a great deal of material for *Jacobite Relics* at this time, and consequently his interest in the contexts and personalities of Jacobite song was at its height.

There is scant information about the collaboration between Gow and Hogg. Only two of Hogg's letters to Gow are extant from around the time Hogg was working on *Jacobite Relics* (from 21 May 1819 (*Letters*, I, 407–08) and 27 July 1822 (*Letters*, II, 169–71)). In the second of these Hogg makes the interesting remark that while Gow appears 'quite disinterested' in transactions with Hogg, he is a nonetheless a shrewd businessman. Apparently Hogg speaks from the experience of working with Gow and his father Nathaniel on the recent production of the musical collection *A Border Garland* in [1819].The letter of 27 July 1822 refers to Hogg's new version of 'Carle and the King come' which he has written for the forthcoming visit of George IV to Edinburgh. He is referring Gow to the earlier appearance of this song in the First Series of *Jacobite Relics*, (SONG XXIII, pp. 39–40), but the 1822 letter also refers to the proposed publication of a new separate song sheet. This illustrates the Gows' practice of producing independent song sheets for songs which they believe will have certain popularity with their public. 'The Lament of Flora Macdonald' clearly falls into this catetory. For more information on Hogg's involvement with the Gows see *Contributions to Musical Collections and Miscellaneous Songs*.

Hogg's decision to include the song in *Songs* 1831 appears to have been for two reasons: firstly this song was popular, having already appeared in numerous musical publications; and secondly Hogg was particularly pleased with it. His modesty is endearingly presented in the headnote which declares how 'agreeably astonished' he was to hear the song performed, and he continues: 'I could hardly believe my senses that I had made so good a song without knowing it'. This is the first of several Jacobite songs to appear in *Songs* 1831 and, appropriately, it precedes 'Bonny Prince Charlie' (see below), which also has a melody by Niel Gow junior. As such these two Jacobite songs might be regarded as a pair.

Mr Morison, to whose singing Hogg refers in his 1831 headnote, is most likely John Morison (1782–1853), surveyor and artist of Kirkcudbrightshire in Galloway. Hogg met Morison during his time in Dumfriesshire in 1806 (see Gillian Hughes, *James Hogg. A Life* (Edinburgh: Edinburgh University Press, 2007), p. 70). In 1819, around the time that Hogg composed the song, Morison was surveying Abbotsford for Hogg's friend Walter Scott. Douglas Mack notes that the 'fifth' bard mentioned in 'Night the First' of *The Queen's Wake* (1813) contains an unflattering portrait of Morison (ll. 546–47), and that after his complaints Hogg 'made the description still harsher in the fifth edition' published in 1819 (*The Queen's Wake*, 2005), p. 411 and 448–49. See also Paul Barnaby, 'John Morison's Relations with Scott and James Hogg' on Edinburgh University's Walter Scott Digital Archive at http://www.walterscott.lib.ed.a.uk [accessed September 2007].

The manuscript source for the text in *Songs* 1831 is NLS MS 4805, ff. 28–30.

No earlier manuscript of the song has been found. It is significant that Hogg chooses to give the song the title 'Flora Macdonald's Farewell' in MS 4805 which is followed in *Songs* 1831. This is a substantive variant from all other earlier appearances of the song which are titled 'The Lament of Flora Macdonald'. Hogg gives no reasons for this change.

A comparison of the four authorised musical publications of the song – the undated Gow song sheet; the version in *Jacobite Relics*, II, 1821; the appearance in George Thomson's *Select Melodies of Scotland* in 1822; and finally the version found in *The Border Garland c.*1829 – with the text in *Songs* 1831 shows a number of other non-substantive variants, demonstrating that the song before 1831 was uniform. Non-substantive variants include, for example: 'sae' of 1.1 in 1831 is 'so' in all earlier versions; 'wi" of 1.5. in 1831 is 'with' in all earlier versions; 'eyry' of 1.14 in 1831 is 'eiry' in all earlier versions. The only line which does appear to have varied is 1.5–6, which has a variety of different punctuation in the earlier appearances of the song.

Like 'Donald Macdonald' (see above) and 'Bonnie Prince Charlie' (see below) this song was one of Hogg's most popular and appeared throughout the nineteenth century in general collections of Scots song.

Publication History:

[*c.*1819/1822] – 'The Lament of Flora MacDonald, An Original and Favorite Jacobite Air.' The Poetry Imitated from the Gaelic by James Hogg. Arranged with Symphonies & Accompaniments for the Piano forte or harp by Niel Gow, Junr. (Edinburgh: Nathaniel Gow and Son, 60 Princes Street). No first edition of the song has been found and so information given here is from the second edition a copy of which can be found in *Contributions to Musical Collections and Miscellaneous Songs*. Gillian Hughes records notices from the *Edinburgh Evening Courant* of 20 December 1819 and 5 January 1822 advertising the first and second editions of the song sheet of 'The Lament of Flora MacDonald', and noting that it is described as 'one of Gow's most popular compositions'. Hughes comments that the second edition of the song dates from early 1822 (*Letters*, II, 134).

1821 – in *Jacobite Relics*, II, 179–80 and 369 – see also (S/SC, 2003), p. 520

1822–23 – in George Thomson, *The Select Melodies of Scotland*, IV, 13–14 (octavo edition), with a note stating 'A new song by J. Hogg pubd singly by N. Gow & son, & given here by their authority' – see *Contributions to Musical Collections and Miscellaneous Songs*.

*c.*1829 – 'The Lament of Flora Macdonald, A Jacobite Song', The Air composed by a friend of the Poet, Arranged with Symphonies & Accompaniments by James Dewar in *The Border Garland*. Hogg arranged in November 1828 that Purdie, the publisher of *The Border Garland* would be allowed copyright of eight of the nine songs in the original *A Border Garland* of [1819]. He also negotiated three further songs to make his new publication one which included twelve songs. 'The Lament of Flora Macdonald' was one of the three additional songs Hogg provided. For more information on this collection and a copy of the song See *Contributions to Musical Collections and Miscellaneous Songs* (S/SC, 2014).

1826/1831 – Thomson reprinted 'The Lament of Flora Macdonald' in further editions of his collections of national songs: in 'New Edition, with many additions and improvements' of *A Select Collection of Original Scottish Airs*, folio edition of 1826, III, 150. And then in *Melodies of Scotland*, folio edition of 1831, III, 149.

Both of these versions included the same note below the title 'the Sym & Acc by N.Gow Junr And here pubd by permission of N.Gow & Son 1822'. Collation of the two editions would suggest that Thomson used the same musical plates. See *Contributions to Musical Collections and Miscellaneous Songs* (S/SC, 2014)

1831 – in *Songs by the Ettrick Shepherd*, pp. 11–12 – see pp. 7–8 in the present edition
Unauthorised versions:
This song was frequently reprinted in chapbooks. See, for example, 'Flora's Lament' in *Five Favourite Songs* (Falkirk, n.d.), pp. 3–4. A Gaelic version of the song was also published under the title 'Cumha Flori Nicdhomhnuill', alongside a parallel English translation of 'Flora Macdonald's Lament' in *The Celtic Garland*, by 'Fionn' (Glasgow: Archibald Sinclair, 1881), pp. 90–93.

Musical Context:
The success of the song undoubtedly has something to do with Niel Gow's very fine, lilting melody which provides an expansive musical foundation on which Hogg paints a detailed picture of highland landscape and Flora's emotions. The structure of the melody – with its little 4-bar coda at the end – allows an additional couplet in which Hogg is able to provide a sentimentally powerful conclusion to each verse. Hogg's notes to the song in *Jacobite Relics* make it clear that he and Gow were wishing to rework the song 'for the sake of the old air'. It is thus difficult to know how much of this 'old air' Gow incorporated in his new melody. A tune with the title 'Tha mi fodh ghruaim' or 'Flora McDonald's Adieu to the Prince' does appear, as noted by Pittock, in Simon Fraser's influential *The Airs and Melodies Peculiar to the Highlands of Scotland* of 1816. However the melody in Fraser's collection is wild and chromatic and bears little resemblance to the rather refined tune attributed to Gow. Gow also included a basic setting of his new melody in his *Sixth collection of Strathspeys, reels and slow tunes for the piano forte, harp, violin & violoncello*. Dedicated to the most noble the Marchioness of Huntly by Niel Gow & Songs (Edinburgh: Published by Nathaniel Gow & Son, [1822?], p. 20, where the note below the music reinforces the Hogg connection to Gow's tune: 'This beautiful Jacobite Air is published separately as a Song, words by the Ettrick Shepherd'. More information about Gow's musical setting of the song is found in See *Contributions to Musical Collections and Miscellaneous Songs*, (S/SC, 2014).

Explanatory Notes:
7 **[Title]** Flora Macdonald (1722–1790) became famous for aiding the escape Prince Charles Edward Stuart's escape from the mainland by boat to Skye following the defeat of the Jacobites at Culloden in 1746.
7, l. 3 **bonny young Flora** James Boswell, who met Flora while touring the Highlands with Samuel Johnson in 1773, describes Flora as 'a little woman of genteel appearance, and uncommonly mild and well bred' (*ODNB*, 'Flora Macdonald').
7, l. 5–6 **She look'd at a boat […]** | **like a bird of the main** accounts of the escape suggest that Flora did not watch the Prince set sail from Skye, but clearly an imagined farewell provided Hogg with great potential for a lyric mourning the loss of the Prince and also the failure of the Jacobite cause. Notably, Sir Harold Boulton might well have had Hogg's song in mind when he wrote 'The Skye Boat Song' in 1884, as this line is echoed in the chorus: 'Speed bonny boat, like a bird on the main'.
7, l. 8 **the lad I shall ne'er see again** Charles Edward was picked up by French

ships off the Scottish mainland on 19 September 1746 and did not return to Scotland.

7, l. 10 Ben-Connal 'Ben-na-Cailleach, a mountain in the S of the Isle of Skye, Inverness-shire, 3 miles W by S of Broadford. It is shaped somewhat like Vesuvius, and has a peaked summit' (Groome).

7, l. 12 Clan-Ronald Ranald (the younger) of Clan Ranald (*d.* 1766). The Clan Ranald lands of the Western Highlands included Moidart where the Prince first landed in Scotland. See also note 8, l. 12 and 'Red Clan-Ranald's Men', pp. 71–72 and Notes.

7, l. 18 The conflict is past a general amnesty was declared in July 1747, signalling the end of the Jacobite uprising.

7, l. 19 nought left but sorrow for Scotland and me Flora, and her husband Allan MacDonald of Kingsburgh (1722–1792) emigrated to North Carolina in 1774. She returned to Skye in 1779 where she lived until her death.

8, l. 25 plumes on the bonnet of blue see note 3, l. 5. Regimental bonnets were topped with six black ostrich plumes.

8, l. 26 Why slept the red bolt [...] | When tyranny revell'd in blood of the true? Echoes the narrator's concluding questioning of God's plan in *The Three Perils of Woman* (1823): (S/SC, 2002 [rev. paperback]), p. 407).

Bonny Prince Charlie (pp. 8–9)

Creative Context:
Hogg appears to have created this song for the musical collection *A Border Garland*, published by Nathaniel Gow & Sons in Edinburgh in [1819]. His 1831 headnote states that he 'dashed down the words at random' after receiving the melody from his friend Niel Gow junior. But there is no further information about the song's creation. Presumably the immediacy of Hogg's work on *Jacobite Relics* (1819–21) was his inspiration, though 'Bonny Prince Charlie' does not appear in either series of *Jacobite Relics*. While 'Bonny Charlie', 'Charlie is my Darling', 'Charlie Stuart' and 'O'er the Water to Charlie', all of which appear in the Second Series of *Jacobite Relics*, call for support of the rightful King, Hogg's 'Bonny Prince Charlie' rather praises the loyalty of specific highland men whom he names, and celebrates their prowess. As such its content is reminiscent of the first song in *Songs* 1831, namely 'Donald Macdonald' (see above pp. 3–5). 'Bonny Prince Charlie' is one of a number of Jacobite lyrics in *Songs* 1831. There is a close connection with this song and 'Flora Macdonald's Farewell', as both have melodies by Niel Gow junior and were widely performed at the time, and it is notable that Hogg places these two songs next to one another in *Songs* 1831.

Hogg's apparent dissatisfaction with the song, as stated so forcefully in the 1831 headnote, is perplexing. Why he should think of it as 'one of my worst' when it is clearly so popular is not easily explained, though it does follow a pattern of pseudo-complaint about the quality of other so-called 'popular' songs he also chooses to include in *Songs* 1831. In the case of this song, however, his apparent displeasure is also suggested in a letter to George Thomson of 15 August 1829 (*Letters*, II, 350), where he informs Thomson that Robert Purdie now owns the copyright to 'Cam' ye by Athol' and, as such, Thomson is not permitted to publish it. Instead Hogg suggests that he might create a better version to a better tune for Thomson when he has time. However, Hogg appears not to have re-written the song at a later date and Thomson accepts the legality of the agreement with Purdie and does not include it in his collections. It is Purdie's publication of James

Dewar's setting for *The Border Garland* (*c*.1829) which Hogg singles out in his 1831 headnote.

The fair-copy manuscript of the version of the song as it appears in *Songs* 1831is found in NLS MS 4805, f. 30. No other manuscript is extant. Most emendations between MS 4805 and *Songs* 1831 are non-substantive. Hogg did not repeat the refrain after the first verse when writing out a fresh version of his song in MS 4805, however these lines have been added at some point in the printing process for *Songs* 1831. A comparison of the 1831 text alongside its two major musical settings of *c*.1819 (Gow) and *c*.1829 (Dewar) reveal some non-substantive variants such as changes of spelling (Bonny/Bonnie or Cam/Came) and the spelling of names (M'Intosh/Mackintosh), or 'brave' for 'gallant'. The only substantive variant is the change from 'Charlie, Charlie' at the beginning of all three refrains to 'Follow thee! Follow thee!' in 1831 Hogg changes the first stanza to refer to a group of 'lads' rather than the singular 'lad' in *c*.1819 and *c*.1829. However the earlier Dewar setting of 1825 published by Alexander Robertson is the only musical copy to use the spelling of the title 'Bonny Prince Charlie' presented in 1831.

Publication History:

[1819] – in *A Border Garland* (Walker & Anderson; Nathaniel Gow & Son, Edinburgh) with musical setting by Niel Gow Junior, pp. 4–5 – see *Contributions to Musical Collections and Miscellaneous Songs* (S/SC, 2014)

c.1819–23 – 'Bonny Prince Charlie'. An Admired Scotish Melody. As Sung by Miss Stephens & Miss Noel. The Words Written by James Hogg the Ettrick Shepherd. The Music composed and Arranged for the Piano-Forte by Niel Gow Junr. (Edinburgh: Nathaniel Gow & Son, 60 Princes Street and London: John Gow & Son, 162 Regent Street) Ent. Stat. Hall Price 1/6. Footnote: 'This Song was first Published in the Border Garland the property of Nathaniel Gow & Son' – see *Contributions to Musical Collections and Miscellaneous Songs* (S/SC, 2014).

c.1825 – 'Bonny Prince Charlie', As Sung With the most distinguished applause by Miss Noel, In the National Play of REDGAUNTLET; Arranged with Symphonies & An Accompaniment for the Piano Forte by James Dewar. Ent Sta Hall Price 1/6. Edinburgh Published by Alexr. Robertson at the Music Saloon 47 Princes St. This was formerly thought to date from *c*.1845, but the dates at which Robertson was located at 47 Princes Street (*c*.1820–1833) points more clearly to an earlier date of publication and this has been narrowed due to the appearance of a dated 'Second Edition' (see below) to be *c*.1825. A copy of this song sheet is included in *Contributions to Musical Collections and Miscellaneous Songs* (S/SC, 2014).

c.1825 – 'Second Edition. Bonny Prince Charlie. As sung with the most distinguished applause by Miss Noel. The Poetry by James Hogg Esq. The Ettrick Shepherd. Arranged with Symphonies and An Accompaniment for the Piano Forte by James Dewar. Ent Sta. Hall Price 1/6. Published by Alexr. Robertson 47 Princes Street Edinburgh. Copies examined at BL H 1652 (15) and Cambridge University Library MRS 290.80.263. Watermark of 1825. With the exception of the amended title, this song sheet uses the same musical plates as that listed directly above and is thus not included in *Contributions to Musical Collections and Miscellaneous Songs* (S/SC, 2014).

c.1829 – in *The Border Garland*, pp. 1–3. The song appears with the elaborate heading: 'Bonnie Prince Charlie, The Favourite Jacobite Song', as Sung by Madame Stockhausen, from The Border Garland, Written by James Hogg the Celebrated Ettrick Shepherd, the air composed by a friend of the Author, and arranged with Symphonies & Accompaniments by James Dewar (Ent. Stat. Hall; Edinburgh: Printed & Sold by Robt Purdie at his Music & Musical Instrument Warehouse 83 Princes St). This is the setting to which Hogg refers in his 1831 headnote. See *Contributions to Musical Collections and Miscellaneous Songs* (S/SC, 2014).

1831 – in *Songs by the Ettrick Shepherd*, pp. 13–14 – see pp. 8–9 in the present edition

*c.*1828–37 – in *The Scotish Minstrel*, II, 104–05 – see *Contributions to Musical Collections and Miscellaneous Songs* (S/SC, 2014)

*c.*1835–47 – Bonnie Prince Charlie. A Favourite Scotch Ballad sun by Miss Clara Novello, and Madame Stockhausen Written by the Ettrick Shepherd. Newly Arranged with Symphonies and Accompts. By I. L. Hatton. Ent. Sta. Hall Price 1/6. Liverpool. Published by Hime and Son, Church Street […]. See *Contributions to Musical Collections and Miscellaneous Songs* (S/SC, 2014).

Unauthorised versions:

The song appears in several chapbooks of the 1810s, for example, in *Six Fashionable Songs* (Kilmarnock: Printed for the Booksellers, 1815). Later versions with new arrangements include, 'Bonnie Prince Charlie', Words by James Hogg. Music by Neil Gow, arranged by T. S. Gleadhill, p. 236–37, *The Casquet of Lyric Gems* (Glasgow: Bell & Bain, n.d.); 'Cam' ye by Athol? Jacobite War Song, Part Song for S.C.T.B, Arranged by H. S. Roberton (London: Bayley& Ferguson, 1914). The song also appears in text only anthologies of Scots song throughout the nineteenth century.

Musical Context:

As Hogg states in his 1831 headnote there is some confusion over the title of the melody. In *A Border Garland* [1819] it appears with the note: 'Air, by a friend of the Editor', but the friend is not named. Hogg clears up this mystery in the 1831 headnote, when he states categorically that the air (or melody) was 'given me by my friend the late Mr Niel Gow'. The headnote then tells the story of Hogg's disagreement with Mr Robertson (presumably the Alexander Robertson who prints the song in 1825) over the title of the tune which Robertson believed to be 'Gala Water'. Hogg clearly and forcefully disagrees and indeed contemporary appearances of 'Gala Water' show a different melody, with a different structure and time signature, but with similarities in melodic shape (see SMM, II, no. 125). Notably all musical settings of Hogg's lyric feature this melody by Niel Gow, with only slight variations in key and rhythm. This was one of Hogg's most popular songs both in his lifetime and throughout the 19th century and appeared often with music. For further, later musical settings see: Gooch and Thatcher, I, 8608–8615 (p. 788).

Explanatory Notes:

8 [headnote] **a horse-hair would turn an eel:** refers to the folkloric notion that if a horsehairs put into water it will turn into a 'rampar eel' or 'lamprey'.

8, l. 1 **Athol** 'a mountainous district in the north of Perthshire' (Groome).

8, l. 2 **Tummel** […] **Garry** the rivers Tummel and Garry run through the centre of Athol.

8, l. 3 **white cockades** The White Cockade was the distinctive badge of the House of Stuart.

8, l. 11 **Glengarry** the glen traversed by the river Garry.

8, l. 12 Health to M'Donell [...] **Clan-Ronald** The Macdonnells are a branch of the MacDonald Clan. The Clan Ronald lands of the Western Highlands included Moidart where the Prince first landed in Scotland. See also 'Flora Macdonald's Farewell' above 7, l.12.

8, l. 14 Lochiel and Appin Lochiel is both sea loch on the border of Argyllshire and Invernesshire and the title for Donald, Chief of the Clan Cameron (*c.*1700 –1748) whose lands extended around the Loch. The lands of the Stewarts of Appin extended from western Argyllshire to the Athol region: see also 'The Stuarts of Appin', pp. 28–30 and Notes.

8, l. 15 Lord Murray [...] **Roy of Kildarlie** 'Lord George Murray (*c.*1700–60), of Blair Atholl, shared overall command of the Prince's army with the Duke of Perth and the Prince himself' (AH/DSM). John Roy Stuart (1700–*c.*1747), Jacobite spy and soldier-poet. Kildary is a 'hamlet in Kilmuir-Easter parish, Rosshire..

8, l. 16 M'Intosh Aeneas Mackintosh, chieftain of clan Mackintosh remained a loyalist during the Jacobite campaign.

9, l. 19 Down through the Lowlands, down wi' the Whigamore! Hogg's association of Lowland Scots with whiggism over-simplifies the political map of Scotland, turning the Jacobite campaigns into a civil war of Highlander versus Lowlander. In 'The Gathering of the Clans', Hogg more accurately mentions loyalist clans who refused to 'come out' for the Prince, including 'the Whiggers of Sky' (l. 21) and 'the Whiggers of Sutherland' (l. 31), see pp. 94–95.

The Sky Lark (p. 9)

Creative Context:
This is one of Hogg's most successful songs and was frequently set by composers after his death and well into the 20th century. It was created initially for John Clarke-Whitfeld's musical collection *Twelve Vocal Pieces* published in London in [1817]. For further information about Hogg's involvement in this collection and a copy of the song see *Contributions to Musical Collections and Miscellaneous Songs*.

'The Sky Lark' was created in 1816 in response to a letter from Clarke-Whitfeld, most probably relating to Walter Scott's involvement with Clarke's project. Hogg's letter to Clarke-Whitfeld dated 8 April [1816] (see *Letters*, I, 275), is clearly in response to an appeal for a contribution and Hogg sends his text for 'The Lark' noting that he has 'this morning composed the song on the next page, so that if it is not the best on my list it is at all events the newest I wrote it for you and dedicate it to your work alone but if it does not suit you may have another and another'. Hogg gives the impression that his lyric is an exclusive gift to Clarke-Whitfeld, and so the composer decided to publish both of Hogg's songs (the other lyric is 'Naething to fear ye' see 'O, Jeanie, There's Naething to Fear Ye' also included in *Songs* 1831, p. 17) with the proviso that these lyrics, 'being Copyright; whoever reprints it shall be prosecuted' (on the Index beside Hogg's titles). Hogg seems to have ignored this copyright agreement and included both songs with few variants shortly thereafter in his first Edinburgh musical collection *A Border Garland* published by Nathaniel Gow and Son in [1819] (for further information about Hogg's involvement and copies of the nine songs in this collection see *Contributions to Musical Collections and Miscellaneous Songs*). It is possible that Hogg was inspired by Psalm 55 vv. 1–7, though he makes no specific reference to this as a source for the song. Hogg may also have been inspired by Wordsworth's earlier 'To a Sky-Lark' first published in 1807 which bears some similarities to Hogg's text.

The first use of the title 'The Skylark' was in the enlarged edition of *The Border Garland: Containing Twelve New Songs by James Hogg*, with arrangements by James Dewar, published by Robert Purdie in Edinburgh in *c*.1829 . Apart from the altered title, the wording of this version is exactly that of the earlier *A Border Garland* (further information about Hogg's involvement in *The Border Garland* and copies of the 12 songs can be found in *Contributions to Musical Collections and Miscellaneous Songs*.

At around the same time Hogg also contributed 'The Sky Lark: A Song' to Rudolph Ackermann, for publication in the London-based annual *Forget Me Not* around November 1828. In transmitting the song to the Christmas literary market, Frederic Shoberl, the annual's editor, made several important changes. For example, the words 'A Song' written below the title of Hogg's manuscript do not appear in *The Forget Me Not*. Moreover Shoberl changes l.18 which is revised from 'Musical cherubim hie thee away!' to 'Musical cherub, hie, hie thee away!'. For a full discussion of the textual transmission see *Contributions to Annuals and Gift Books* (S/SC, 2006), pp. 295–7.

With so much attention drawn to the lyric around this time, Clarke-Whifeld's publisher, Lonsdale Mills & Co., became aware of a breach in Clarke's earlier copyright agreement with Hogg. A full account of their subsequent argument is given in *Contributions to Musical Collections and Miscellaneous Songs*. Ultimately Hogg decided that 'to avoid all litigation and bad blood I shall write a new song in its place and convey the copyright to you provided you allow *The Lark* to stand in the collection where it is'. While Lonsdale and Mills appear not to have reprinted the song, Hogg thus made some changes to the lyric for subsequent use: notably the earlier l. 18 'Musical cherubin, hie thee away!' became 'Musical cherub, soar, singing away!' and in l. 22 he chose to repeat the 'Bird of the wilderness' refrain of the first line. Hogg then ensured that this new version (in its 12-line stanza form, as opposed to the earlier appearances which gave the text in four 6-line stanzas) appeared as one of the first songs in *Songs* 1831.

This background thus accounts for Hogg's preference, in his headnote, of the musical setting in *The Border Garland* of *c*.1829 rather than referring to Clarke-Whitfeld's collection as a source for his reader. Hogg places 'The Skylark' sixth in his 1831 collection, but notes that this 'little pastoral song' is 'worth half-a-dozen of the foregoing'. Interestingly 'the foregoing' includes 'Donald MacDonald', 'Flora Macdonald's Farewell', and 'Bonny Prince Charlie', all of which had gained assured popularity during Hogg's lifetime, and which are to this day regarded as the best of his songs. But his 1831 headnote reveals that Hogg regarded this song most highly. While critics such as Louis Simpson are less enthusiastic (see Louis Simpson, *James Hogg: A Critical Study* (New York: St Martin's Press, 1962), p. 77), the Victorian British domestic music market loved this song – see Kirsteen McCue, '"The Skylark": the popularity of Hogg's 'Bird of the Wilderness', November 2009, on the *James Hogg Research* website at: http://www.jameshogg. stir.ac.uk.

Hogg's awareness of the potential for wider popularity may well account for a number of extant manuscripts and signed holographs of this lyric. The manuscript of the earliest version of the song survives in Hogg's letter to Clarke [Whitfeld] dated 8 April [1816] at NLS MS 9634: the full text of 'The Lark', contributed by Hogg to *Twelve Vocal Pieces* is reprinted in *Letters*, I, (p. 275). The manuscript of 'The Skylark' that Hogg contributed to Rudolph Ackermann for publication in *The Forget Me Not* for 1828 survives in the Huntington Library, San Marino, California, MS HM 12409 (see also Hogg's letter to Ackermann dated 1 April

1827 in *Letters*, II, 260). The text of Hogg's unedited manuscript is reprinted in full on p. 39 of *Contributions to Annuals and Gift Books* (S/SC, 2006). There are also two signed holographs in existence: one is clearly a presentation holograph and is addressed to 'W. Forbes Mackenzie Esq Stobo Castle', dated 'Altrive-Lake Septr 7th 1832' (NLS ACC. 8879) while the other at NLS MS 10279, f. 83 is undated with no watermark to indicate the likely date of composition. Interestingly, this manuscript follows the entirely new beginning of line 3 which reads, 'Light be thy matin' that Hogg had written in the revised version of the song he contributed to Rudolph Ackermann's *Forget Me Not* in April 1827. NLS MS 8879 has 'gives' for 'gave' in the second stanza, and chooses 'Musical Cherubim, hie thee away!' at the end of verse 3.

Hogg's fair-copy holograph version prepared for *Songs* 1831 survives at NLS MS 4805, ff. 30, where there is only one slight revision in the title to 'The Sky Lark', which follows the wording of the title in the earlier version of the song Hogg contributed to Ackermann in 1827, and also the wording of the two surviving holographs.

Publication History:
[1817] – in *Twelve Vocal Pieces* (Volume I, No. V (text, p. 8; music, pp. 41–44)) – see *Contributions to Musical Collections and Miscellaneous Songs* (S/SC, 2014)
[1819] – in *A Border Garland* pp. 14–15 – see *Contributions to Musical Collections and Miscellaneous Songs* (S/SC, 2014)
1828 – in *The Forget Me Not*, p. 27– see *Contributions to Annuals and Gift Books* (S/SC, 2006), p. 39, notes, pp. 295–97
c.1829 – in *The Border Garland* pp. 13–15 – see *Contributions to Musical Collections and Miscellaneous Songs* (S/SC, 2014)
1831 – in *Songs by the Ettrick Shepherd*, pp. 15–16 – see p. 9 in the present edition
Unauthorised versions:
This song's subsequent popularity is unrivalled in terms of musical interest in Hogg's songs. A wide variety of different musical settings, most post-dating Hogg's death, are available to view (and some to hear) on the *James Hogg Research* website at: http://www.jameshogg.stir.ac.uk. Moreover further musical settings of the text are listed in Gooch and Thatcher's *Musical Settings of British Romantic Literature* Vol 2. (New York & London: Garland, 1982), pp. 787–809, where they cite little short of 60 settings from the 1810s to the 1950s. The editors of *Contributions to Annuals and Gift Books* argue that the musical setting by J. Clifton – *Bird of the Wilderness: A Favourite Scotch Song*' with music by J. Clifton, (London: Collard & Collard, *c*.1835) – was possibly related to the appearance of the lyric in *The Forget Me Not* and thus may have been authorised by Hogg (see *Contributions to Musical Collections and Miscellaneous Songs* (S/SC, 2014).

Hogg's work was frequently reprinted in American periodicals during the nineteenth century. 'The Skylark' appeared in *The Baltimore Literary Monument. A Weekly Journal Devoted to Literature, Science and the Fine Arts* (Baltimore: T. S. Arthur), within a longer article entitled, 'Parnassian Pastimes' that contrasted Blake's 'Tiger, Tiger' with Hogg's 'Skylark' from the version published in *The Forget Me Not* for 1828 (p. 27), II, No. 1 (May 1839), 17–18. A further two American musical settings of 'The Skylark' have been located. Further details can be found in the *Listing of Hogg Items in the American Periodical Press*, by Janette Currie, at the online *James Hogg Research* website hosted by the Division of Literature and Languages, School of Arts and Humanities, Stirling University, http://www.jameshogg.stir. ac.uk.

The text appeared in *The Casquet of Literary Gems*, 2 vols, ed. Alex. Whitelaw (Glasgow: Blackie, Fullerton, 1829) using the text from the *Forget me Not* for 1828 and in *The Book of Gems: The Modern Poets and Artists of Great Britain* ed. S C. Hall, 3 Vols (London: Saunders & Otley, 1836–38), Vol. III, 129–33 and in other similar publications after 1835 (See *Contributions to Annuals and Gift Books* (S/SC, 2006), pp. 280–81). The song was also often reprinted in text-only anthologies of Scots song throughout the nineteenth century.

Musical Context:
There are several different melodies associated with this song. Its first musical setting, by John Clarke-Whitfeld for *Twelve Vocal Pieces*, is a standard vocal aria of the period. Hogg's letter to the publisher Lonsdale & Mills of 16 December 1830 (see *Letters*, II, pp. 417–18) suggests that Hogg wrote the melody for this setting himself, but there is no evidence of Hogg having sent a tune alongside his lyric in 1816. The melody in *Twelve Vocal Pieces* may well be by Hogg, but it is unlike any other which Hogg created for his songs. In *A Border Garland* the melodies employed are more traditional in nature, and this is the case with the 'Air, Old' which is used for the song's appearance in this collection in [1819]. This tune is very much like a fiddle tune and follows the common structure of fiddle tunes and thus many Scottish vocal airs or melodies of the period. It is likely that the musical setting for *A Border Garland* was created by the London composer William Heather, with whom Hogg was also working at this time on *German Hebrew Melodies* (see *Contributions to Musical Collections and Miscellaneous Songs*). Heather certainly created the setting for 'Naething to fear ye' also included in this little collection, but 'The Lark' is not named specifically in correspondence with Heather (see Musical Context of 'O! Jeanie, there's Naething to Fear Ye!'). If Heather is not the composer of the setting, then it is likely that Niel Gow junior is. The next setting in *The Border Garland* of *c.*1829 is by James Dewar and, while more elaborate than the setting for *A Border Garland* of [1819] it does use the same 'traditional' melody. This is the musical source to which Hogg refers in his 1831 headnote, noting that it has a 'fine original air'. Other posthumous settings listed above vary dramatically in style and are set for a variety of performers from solo singer with piano, to settings for voice, piano and violin obligato, to vocal duets, part songs and even a setting for children's choir. For further discussion see *Contributions to Musical Collections and Miscellaneous Songs*.

Explanatory Notes:
See *Contributions to Annuals and Giftbooks*, p. 371.

Gang to the Brakens wi' Me (pp. 10–11)

Creative Context:
A full account of the textual and publishing history of 'Gang to the Brakens wi' Me' and information about the song's melody 'Driving the steers' (also with melodic notation) is given in *Contributions to Blackwood's Edinburgh Magazine* I. In summary, this song was first published in *Blackwood's* on 18 December 1825 where it appears, as do a number of Hogg's songs also included in *Songs* 1831, in the *Noctes Ambrosianae* (in this particular case in No. XXIII). There is no further evidence about the date or context of its creation and the original manuscript for Blackwood has not survived.

The popularity of the Shepherd's songs in *Noctes* must surely have been the reason for Hogg deciding to include a number of them in *Songs* (see the Introduction). In the case of 'The Noctes Sang', 'I Lookit East, I Lookit West' or 'The Village of Balmaqhapple' (see below) the Blackwoodian context is clear. But Hogg does not give 'Gang to the Brakens wi Me' its dialogical context in *Songs* 1831. Rather than discuss this initial source, Hogg chooses to make reference in his 1831 headnote to the inclusion of the song in the recent collection *Select & Rare Scotish Melodies* published in London by Goulding & D'Almaine, with new musical settings by the London theatre composer Henry Bishop: see *Contributions to Musical Collections and Miscellaneous Songs*.

A revised version of the Blackwood song, with the same title, was sent to Robert Purdie on 18 January 1828 (*Letters*, II, pp. 284–85). Hogg refers to 'The brakens wi' me' in this letter, telling Purdie that it had 'found its way into a Magazine several years ago' and that 'the notice which it then attracted makes me desirous that it should appear in such a respectable collection as this now getting up'. There are substantive variants between the earlier *Blackwood's* version of the song and that published in *Select & Rare Scotish Melodies*. The variants are discussed by Thomas Richardson in his notes to the song in *Contributions to Blackwood's* I (p. 513). Suffice it to say that Hogg revised the lyric to remove any earlier sexual connotations. The 1825 song presents the heroine as only too ready and willing to engage in the narrator's proposed love affair. The version for *Select & Rare Scotish Melodies* (with an altogether new fourth verse) presents a young lady who is prudent and only too aware of the trap into which the narrator wishes to lure her, noting that she will only enter such an arrangement with the parson's approval. Such revisions suggest Hogg was well aware of the female clientele for such musical collections. There are few variants between the text as published by Goulding in 1829 and that in *Songs* 1831, suggesting that Hogg was happy to go with the later and newer version. NLS MS 4805, ff. 30v–31v is Hogg's fair-copy holograph manuscript of the song used in *Songs* 1831, and is the only manuscript version of the song to survive. Variants between MS 4805 and *Songs* 1831 are non-substantive.

Publication History:
1825 – in *Blackwood's Edinburgh Magazine*, 18 (December 1825), 753–54 – see (S/SC, 2008), pp. 181–82, 370, and 513–14
[1828] – in *Select & Rare Scotish Melodies* pp. 45–50 – see *Contributions to Musical Collections and Miscellaneous Songs* (S/SC, 2014)
1831 – in *Songs by the Ettrick Shepherd*, pp. 17–19 – see pp. 10–11 in the present edition

Musical Context:
Hogg makes detailed reference both to the melody or air for this song and its new setting by Henry Bishop for *Select & Rare Scotish Melodies* in his 1831 headnote. In *Blackwood's* the song appeared with the melody 'Driving the Steers', which Hogg clearly regarded most highly. More information about the Gaelic roots of this air – found in Simon Fraser's *The Airs and Melodies Peculiar to the Highlands of Scotland* (1816) – is given by Thomas Richardson in *Contributions to Blackwood's* I, p. 514. The tune was also apparently intended by Hogg for his unpublished 'Ode on the Death of Lord Byron'. The melody printed in *Blackwood's* is the type of tune which Hogg's predecessor in Scots song, Robert Burns, would have referred to as having 'a degree of wild irregularity' so common to many such tunes (see *Robert Burns's Commonplace Book 1783–1785*, ed. David Daiches (Sussex: Centaur Press, 1965), p. 38). It is a modal tune with both rhythmic irregularity and strange

dissonances. A composer such as Henry Bishop, formally taught and working in the London theatre, would arguably have little idea of what to make of such a melody. He therefore adheres generally to the shape and line of 'Driving the Steers', but refines it and removes these melodic and rhythmic irregularities. The melody in *Select & Rare Scotish Melodies* therefore loses the strange sadness of the tune as it appears in *Blackwood's* and which Hogg obviously liked very much. It is noteable that Tickler's comment after he hears the song in *Blackwood's* is: 'I'm never merry, when I hear sweet music' and he says this as he passes '*his hand across his eye*'. In the case of other songs in *Select & Rare Scotish Melodies* Hogg is highly complimentary of Bishop's arrangements, but in this case the amendments to the melody were unacceptable to him. For more information on the musical setting see *Contributions to Musical Collections and Miscellaneous Songs*.

Explanatory Notes:
10, l.9 'I fleech'd an' I pray'd possible allusion to Robert Burns's song lyric 'Duncan Gray'. In the version Burns gave to George Thomson, the song included the line: 'Duncan fleech'd and Duncan pray'd; | Meg was deaf as Ailsa craig' (see Robert Burns, *The Poems and Songs*, ed. James Kinsley (Oxford: Clarendon Press, 1969), II, No. 394, pp. 666–68, and III, pp. 1415–16.

The Minstrel Boy (p. 11)

Creative Context:
There is no information about the creation of Hogg's song 'The Minstrel Boy'. It was first published in Robert Archibald Smith's collection *The Irish Minstrel* in Edinburgh in its first edition of [1825] with the melody 'The Moreen'. This melody was already associated with a song with the same title by Thomas Moore. Moore's powerful lyric beginning 'The Minstrel-Boy to the war is gone/ In the ranks of death you'll find him' was first published in 1813 in the fifth number *Irish Melodies* (vi) and thereafter frequently reprinted both as text and with music. Hogg's song is clearly his own attempt at lyrics for the same beautiful tune, but his text is different in poetic theme and content.

Information about Hogg's involvement in R.A. Smith's *The Irish Minstrel* (first and second editions) and copies of Hogg's songs included in this collection are found in *Contributions to Musical Collections and Miscellaneous Songs*. In summary, Hogg's 1831 headnote refers to a copyright wrangle which appears to have ensued between Smith's publisher Robert Purdie in Edinburgh and Moore's publishers the Power brothers of London and Dublin, who were themselves at the heart of a major music publishing copyright battle in the courts after the brothers went their separate ways in 1817.

There are two different versions of Hogg's 'The Minstrel Boy' in the fair-copy manuscript for *Songs* 1831 at NLS MS 4805, at ff. 31v–32r and at f. 57r. The page-number '12' is written at the top left hand corner of f. 31v, and this number follows a sequence of pagination discussed in Janette Currie's 'The Genesis of the Text' (pp. xli–xlviii). MS 4805, f. 57r is not paginated in the same way as that above, but immediately below the title is a note (not in Hogg's hand) stating 'Already Printed at page 20'. There is another note at the top right-hand of the manuscript, which is in Hogg's hand, stating 'p 113 from the proofs but Love's like a dizziness wanting'. During the latter part of 1830, batches of the proofs of *Songs* 1831 were exchanged between Hogg in Altrive and Blackwood's Edinburgh premises. What appears to have happened is that as Hogg worked through the proofs he simply forgot that

'The Minstrel Boy' was already included within his collection. Indeed, the text of NLS MS 4805, ff. 31v–32r is the one printed in *Songs* 1831. The text of both songs is identical in both manuscripts. However, Hogg wrote out a new headnote for the second version of the song:

> The Minstrel Boy
> Is one likewise on the proscription list an inter-communed rebel against the sovereign authority of Thomas Little the Great and really I believe it is treading too hard on the heels of his dignity though I am sure it was through no ill intention. It was harmonized by Smith to an Irish air called *The Moreen* and engraved but like the rest the edition was burnt and the plate destroyed. (NLS MS 4805, f. 57r)

Clearly Hogg blames Moore ('Thomas Little the Great') for being too precious about his 'melodies' (namely the lyrics). The texts of both Hogg manuscript versions of the song share the same non-substantive differences with the printed version. Notably, next to Hogg's statement that cancellation of the earlier version of the song was 'the most ridiculous of all things' the phrase 'in my opinion' has been added for *Songs*, which was clearly to separate Hogg from his publishers in case of any future litigation proceedings. The manuscript ends with the exclamatory 'take that!' but someone has added the proverbial phrase 'as Gideon Laidlaw said when the man died who had cheated him.' It is not clear whether Hogg made these alterations later in the printing process or whether it is the work of Robert Hogg, softening Hogg's indignation.

The *Songs* 1831 version follows closely that of [1825] and it is likely that Hogg consulted *The Irish Minstrel* when preparing the song for inclusion in his collection. One alteration to the printed text occurs in both manuscript versions and also in *The Irish Minstrel*: 'Of mountain heath and of moorland thyme' (v. 1, l. 7) is altered to 'Of mountain heath and moorland thyme' in the printed text. The second 'of' is necessary to fit the melody properly, and it is probable that its omission in *Songs* 1831 was an error in transmission.

Publication History:
[1825] – in *The Irish Minstrel*, pp. 14–15 – see *Contributions to Musical Collections and Miscellaneous Songs*, (S/SC, 2014)
1831 – in *Songs by the Ettrick Shepherd*, pp. 20–1 – see p. 11 in the present edition

Musical Context:
Hogg refers to 'the same air' as that used by Thomas Moore in his headnote for 1831 but does not name the air. It is, however, named clearly as 'Air – The Moreen' in R.A. Smith's *The Irish Minstrel* alongside the setting of Hogg's lyric on pp. 14–5. It is a wide-ranging and melancholic tune, still best known in association with Moore's lyric from *Irish Melodies*, yet often set by composers, such as Beethoven, with a more aggressive war-like tempo. A published source for the air before its appearance with Moore's text in 1813 has not been found and it is reasonable to conclude that Moore may have received it in manuscript form. The melody did appear in 1816 in the second volume of George Thomson's *A Select Collection of Irish Airs*. It would appear that Smith uses Moore's *Irish Melodies* as his source for the tune which is even in the same key.

Explanatory Notes:

11 (a) per contra adv. 'On the opposite side; on the other hand' (*OED* online at
http://dictionary.oed.com, accessed 6/11/09).

11 (b) Gideon Laidlaw a Gideon Laidlaw appears in the marriage and christening
records of Ettrick parish: Gideon Laidlaw married Agnes Biggar on 9 January
1767 and their son Alexander was subsequently christened on 12 November
1769. The Laidlaws are described as 'indwellers of Midgehope': see OPR of
Selkirk Parish, m/film no. 1067924. It is not known whether Hogg was closely
connected to the Laidlaws of Midgehope. We have not found further details
which would explain this comment.

Farewell to Glen-Shalloch (pp. 12–13)

Creative Context:
This is another of the batch of Jacobite songs included by Hogg in *Songs* 1831. It
is not clear when Hogg created this song. It first appeared in the Second Series of
The Jacobite Relics of Scotland in 1821. The note 'From the Gaelic' is printed beneath
the title of the song, which would suggest that Hogg had collected it. Murray
Pittock's note for the S/SC edition concludes that it is 'probably by Hogg'.

The headnote for *Songs* 1831 gives more detail about its creation. Hogg notes
categorically that the song 'was composed of a scrap of translation in prose of
what Mrs Fraser said was a Gaelic song'. It may then be one of the 'few Gaelic
translations of Jacobite songs' on which Hogg was working on 4 March 1820
when he informed David Laing how he 'translated' the Gaelic songs he received.
Hogg stated to Laing that some of his correspondents would send him 'disjointed
sentences of overstrained English which they aver to be literal translations of
Gaelic' and that Hogg would then turn these 'into regular Scotch songs though
although I stick close by the sense they may rather be called imitations from the
Gaelic than translations' (see *Letters*, II, pp. 13–14). Mrs Fraser is not known but
may have been one such correspondent.

Hogg's headnote also refers to the song's appearance in *The Scotish Minstrel*
edited by Robert Archibald Smith published in Edinburgh by Robert Purdie
between 1821 and 1824: see *Contributions to Musical Collections and Miscellaneous
Songs*. This song appeared in the fifth volume of *The Scotish Minstrel* (p. 9) and was
clearly lifted from *Jacobite Relics*. Smith produced several editions of his collection
through to the mid-1830s but the lyric for 'Farewell to Glen-Shalloch' remained
unaltered. In 1828, when Purdie decided to produce *The Border Garland*, with
new musical settings by James Dewar, Hogg assigned the copyright of this song,
amongst others, to Purdie (see *Letters*, II, pp. 315–16), but it did not appear in the
12 songs included in this collection.

Hogg's 1831 text is slightly altered from the *Relics* version. For example, Hogg
gives 'child' in place of 'babe' (v. 2, ll. 3 and 4) and 'gird' for 'bind' (v. 5, l. 5). But
there is only one substantive change which occurs in the penultimate verse where
Hogg replaces 'pine', which had appeared in every previous version of the song,
to 'pride' (v. 6, l. 5). Originally, mention of the loss of the 'pine' from the glen lent
a metaphorical association with the Clearances. Hogg's alteration removes such
political overtones and instead, reinforces the clansman's dignity.

The only extant manuscript of the song is found at NLS MS 4805, ff. 32r–33r,
Hogg's fair-copy manuscript of *Songs* 1831. Aside from the usual addition of
punctuation and one non-substantive change ('inclose' is printed as 'enclose', v. 2,
l. 2), it is transmitted cleanly to the printed text.

Publication History:

1821 – in *Jacobite Relics*, II, 160–62 and 355 – see also (S/SC, 2003), p. 518

[1823] – in *The Scotish Minstrel*, V, 9 – see *Contributions to Musical Collections and Miscellaneous Songs* (S/SC, 2014)

1831 – in *Songs by the Ettrick Shepherd*, pp. 22–25 – see pp. 12–13 in the present edition

Musical Context:

A complicated story relates to the melody or air associated with 'Farewell to Glen-Shalloch'. Hogg's initial note in *Jacobite Relics* refers to a beautiful 'original air', but he notes that this is not the air published in *Relics*. He states that William Stenhouse has chosen a traditional Gaelic tune entitled "*M 'Gregor-a-Ruara*" which Hogg argues might be easier to sing. But beside Hogg's note to the song he gives another melody which he refers to as the 'true air' from Simon Fraser's *The Airs and Melodies Peculiar to the Highlands of Scotland* of 1816 where it apparently titled 'Bodhan an Eassain'. It is this 'true air' which Smith then uses for the song in *The Scotish Minstrel*, though he slightly amends it by setting it in a much lower key (so that it is easier for the voice) and he irons out some of the more intricate rhythms. The Stenhouse choice of Gaelic tune is quite unlike this 'true air'. It is much more regular with a more militaristic feel than the Fraser tune, which may well have piping origins, and which hints at loss and lament. Murray Pittock notes the similarities with another tune in Patrick MacDonald's *Highland Airs* of 1784 (see *Jacobite Relics*, II, 518). For further information on Smith's setting see *Contributions to Musical Collections and Miscellaneous Songs*.

Explanatory Notes:

12 (a) Title Glen-Shalloch or Glen salach, 'a glen in Ardchattan parish, Argyllshire, extending 51/2 miles north-north-westward from Loch Etive, near Ardchattan House, to Loch Creran, near Barcaldine' (Groome). 'Glen-Shalloch' is uncle to Alaster Mackenzie, Sally Niven's Highland lover in *The Three Perils of Woman* of 1823 (S/SC, 2002 [rev. paperback]), p. 377)

12, l. 24 slain of Culloden reference to the battle of Culloden (also known as Drumossie Moor).

12, l. 26 tyrant Prince William Augustus, Duke of Cumberland (1721–1765).

13, l. 42 **Is the home of the reaver** Pittock notes 'despite the ferocity of official action, the continuing presence of armed Jacobite units in the field ensured "the growth of banditry, not only in such traditional haunts of Lochaber and Rannoch Moor, but in most mountainous districts of the southern and central Highlands"' (*Jacobitism*, p. 130).

13, ll. 43 The pride of the ocean possible reference to the Motto of the Clan MacDonald, 'Per mare per terras: By sea and by land'.

13, l. 52 the land of the stranger 'Ten years after Culloden, there were no fewer than 60 British Army patrols and outposts in Scotland' (Pittock, *Jacobitism*, p. 130).

Caledonia (pp. 13–14)

Creative Context:

A full account of the textual and publishing history of 'Caledonia' (and a detailed history of the tune 'Lord Aboyne' which is associated with the text) is given in *The Forest Minstrel* (S/SC, 2006).

In summary, there is no printing or manuscript of this song prior to its appearance in *The Forest Minstrel* in 1810, though Hogg refers here in his 1831 headnote to having heard it performed alongside his own 'Donald MacDonald' in the Lancaster Theatre (see notes to 'Donald MacDonald' above). It is thought that 'Caledonia' is thus one of Hogg's early songs dating from the same period as 'Donald MacDonald' and 'Scotia's Glens' (with which it shares its national fervour and imagery). These two songs have appeared just before it in *Songs* 1831.

The editors of *The Forest Minstrel* suggest that the likely date for this Lancaster performance is the summer of 1804, when Hogg visited England briefly after completing his Highland Journey, and this is reiterated in Gillian Hughes's *James Hogg: A Life* (pp. 57–58). Hogg's 1831 headnote provides further information as he places the trip to Lancaster as the first stage of a planned tour to Wales. For whatever reason, he decided not to travel further south after Lancaster, returning North via the Lakes. Hogg's only noted trip to the Lakes is not until September 1814 (see Hughes, *James Hogg: A Life*, pp. 125–27). But this later date would not coincide with the Lancaster 'assizes', or trials, also mentioned in detail in his 1831 headnote. These took place in April and August every year at Lancaster Castle, and appear to have been busy social times for the city, with many visitors and much entertainment. For further information see 'Lancaster and the Assizes 1800–1910', by Christine Goodier, from Lancaster Castle website, http://www.lancastercastle. com [accessed November 2007]. Hogg presumably then experienced these trials in the late summer of 1804. His 1832 'Memoir' refers to his having spent 'the remainder of the summer' in England (see *Altrive Tales*, (S/SC, 2005), p. 22). His reference to the differences between the legal systems here and in his native Scotland enhances the nationalism of his song. Moreover, the mention of both Wales and the Lakes provides a comparative pictorial context for the dramatic description of the Scottish mountains which he then gives in 'Caledonia'.

The editors of *The Forest Minstrel* give a detailed account of any printed variants between the publications of the song. Hogg notes here that it appeared with a melody and setting by Niel Gow junior in *A Border Garland* in [1819]. It was also included in *The Border Garland* of *c*.1829: see *Contributions to Musical Collections and Miscellaneous Songs*.

The 'young lady' mentioned at the end of the headnote is clearly the 'Miss Forrest' from the beginning of the note, namely, Miss Chalmers Forrest (*b*. 3 March 1790), a niece of Hogg's early literary confidant, Eliza Izett. Hogg describes her as 'the amiable lady C. Forest' in his letter to Izett of 11 December 1808 (*Letters*, I, 97–99). She was, by all accounts, a competent musician, and set many of Hogg's early songs to music. He was clearly fond of her and recalls with affection hearing her perform them: see also 'The Flower', pp. 106–07 and 'The Moon was a-waning', pp. 112–13. For further information 'Notes on Correspondents, *Letters*, I, 457–460).

Hogg's fair-copy holograph version of the song as it appears in *Songs* 1831 is the only extant manuscript and is found at MS4805, ff. 33v–34r where the pages are numbered '16' and '17' in the top left and right hand corners respectively. Hogg's unpunctuated text is transferred cleanly to the printed version with one slight variant occurring in the headnote: 'would have been done' of MS 4805, f. 33v becomes 'would have taken' in the printed version. At some stage prior to printing, the word 'trials' has been added to the headnote and it is included in the printed version.

Publication history:
1810 – in *The Forest Minstrel*, pp. 221–22 – see (S/SC, 2006), pp. 202–03 and 374–76
[1819] – in *A Border Garland*, pp. 16–17 – see *Contributions to Musical Collections and Miscellaneous Songs* (S/SC, 2014)

*c.*1829 – in *The Border Garland,* pp. 19–20 – see *Contributions to Musical Collections and Miscellaneous Songs* (S/SC, 2014)

1831 – in *Songs by the Ettrick Shepherd,* pp. 26–27 – see pp. 13–14 in the present edition

Musical Context:

The song is initially published in *the Forest Minstrel* to the tune entitled 'Lord Aboyne' and further information about the history of this melody is found in *The Forest Minstrel* (S/SC, 2006) pp. 375–76. The editors note that although this tune exists in many variants it 'is unsuited metrically to the words of Hogg's song'. Hogg's 1831 headnote would suggest that neither this tune, nor the unidentified Mr M'Rae's singing of it impressed him. Instead Hogg refers to two other possible melodies: the first by Niel Gow junior for *A Border Garland* of [1819], which is also set in the *c.*1829 *The Border Garland* by James Dewar, and finally 'another composed by a young lady' (namely, Chalmers Forrest mentioned above). The Gow tune is a hymn-like anthem, a dignified tune (notably with an impressive octave leap in the first bar) to match Hogg's lofty and proud lyric. For further information on the musical settings see *Contributions to Musical Collections and Miscellaneous Songs.*

There is no extant copy of the melody 'oftener sung' with Hogg's words, namely the melody created by Chalmers Forrest. Charles Rogers, in his *The Modern Scottish Minstrel* (6 vols (Edinburgh: Adam and Charles Black, 1855), mentions another newly composed air by 'Mr Walter Burns of Cupar-Fife which has been arranged with symphonies and accompaniments for the pianoforte by Mr Edward Salter, of St Andrews' (see Vol. II, p. 100). No copy has yet been found.

Explanatory Notes:

13 [Title] 'Roman name for part of what is now Scotland; literary name for Scotland' (*DSL*).

14, l. 5 barren thy glens an aside to the contemporary political issue of Highland Clearance and a topical sore that runs throughout Hogg's songs depicting Scottish landscape.

14, ll. 11–12 The marshall'd array of imperial Rome | Essay'd thy proud spirit in vain reiterating a commonly held misconception that the Romans never conquered Scotland combined with reference to the more recent failure (1800–1815) of the Imperial French army under Napoleon to invade Britain.

The Noctes Sang (pp. 14–15)

Creative Context:

A full account of the textual and publishing history of the first version of this song, with the title 'If E'er You Would Be a Brave Fellow', and information about the song's melody 'O Whistle, and I'll come to ye, my Lad', is given in *Contributions to Blackwood's Edinburgh Magazine* I, (S/SC, 2008).

In summary, this song, given the new title of 'The Noctes Sang' by Hogg in his 1831 *Songs,* first appeared in *Blackwood's* in March 1825, as part of the series *Noctes Ambrosianae* No. XIX, where it is sung by the Shepherd. The complex history of Hogg's involvement in the magazine and in the *Noctes* series is discussed by Thomas Richardson in his Introduction to *Contributions to Blackwood's Edinburgh Magazine* I (pp. xliv–lvii) and also in the Introduction to the current volume. Richardson traces the textual differences between the two printed versions of the lyric in 1825 and 1831, noting that the later song has only three verses rather than four: he omits the verse beginning 'O wha wadna laugh at their capers, young man?'. Hogg himself draws attention to this difference in his 1831 headnote for the song, when he states: 'I have lost a verse of it'.

The Blackwoodian appearance of this song has its own very specific context of the topical and conversational *Noctes Ambrosianae*, which appeared as part of *Blackwood's* from 1822 until 1835 (though not regularly). Hogg clearly feels the need to contextualise the song for his 1831 reader. His headnote does two important things: firstly, it emphasises the connection between drinking and singing, as do several of Hogg's *Noctes* songs; and secondly, he gives the song the best possible introduction, by referring to its electrical effect when performed at Ambrose's. This lyric symbolises precisely what the *Noctes* creators represented – a jovial and spirited group of, apparently, fine Tory gentlemen working against the rival Whigs and their *Edinburgh Magazine* – so it makes sense for Hogg to change the name to the generic 'Noctes Sang'. Furthermore, his headnote includes a description of Ambrose's – the Edinburgh tavern where the *Noctes* took place, either in reality or imaginatively – and references to individuals involved in the creation of these printed conversations.

Robert Pierce Gillies (1789–1858), for example, was, like Hogg, an early contributor to the magazine and appeared in *Noctes* as the character of 'Kemperhausen', signifying his interest in German and Danish literature. Hogg and Gillies were good friends and worked often together between 1813 and the late 1820s, when Gillies moved to London. In his article, 'Concerning the *Noctes Ambrosianae*', Alan L. Strout notes that the details of this particularly riotous meeting at Ambrose's tavern, recorded by Hogg in his 1831 headnote, are confirmed by recollections of R.P. Gillies, published in *Fraser's Magazine* in October 1839: see *Modern Language Notes*, 51, No 8 (December 1936), 493–504, p. 501. It is not inconceivable however, that Gillies's anecdote was derived from Hogg's headnote. The 'American gentleman' is also referred to in Gillies's 'Some Recollections of James Hogg':'"twa grand Americans"' were 'young men of respectable demeanour (who personally knew several of the Transatlantic authors, and who wore frills and hand-ruffles, in the style of 1794)', *Fraser's Magazine*, 20 (October 1839), 428–29, quoted in, *Modern Language Notes*, 51, No 8 (December 1936), 493.

Thomas Richardson gives an account of the specific changes to the text between its appearance in *Blackwood's* and in 1831.

No early copy of this song has survived in manuscript. NLS MS 4805, ff. 34v–35r is Hogg's fair-copy manuscript version. The song is transmitted cleanly to the printed page with the usual changes in capitalisation and in lengthening and shortening of words. There are two significant additions to Hogg's headnote in the printed volume. Originally, Hogg writes 'screamed out till he fell' which is extended to 'screamed out so loud in approbation, that he fell' in the printed text. Further, Hogg originally writes, 'preserved in the Noctes' which is extended to 'preserved in the Noctes, and nowhere else'.

Publication history:

1825 – in *Blackwood's Edinburgh Magazine*, 17 (March 1825), 382–83 – see (S/SC, 2008), pp. 162–63, 367, and 504–05

1831 – in *Songs by the Ettrick Shepherd*, pp. 28–30 – see pp. 14–15 in the present edition

Musical Context:
Hogg states in the headnote that 'the air is my own, and a very capital one. I believe it is preserved in the Noctes, and nowhere else'. However he does not name the air in 1831. The title given alongside the earlier *Blackwood's* version of the song is 'AIR, – Whistle, and I'll come to ye, my Lad' but musical notation is not included there in 1825. This melody has, however, a much older history than Hogg's headnote would imply – and it is thus most unlikely to be his own creation. Robert Burns wrote words to this already popular tune which were published in the *SMM* (1788), II, No. 106: see Dick, 'Historical Notes', p. 417. The history of the tune is discussed by John Glen in his *Early Scottish Melodies* (p.92) where he accounts for its apparent Irish origins through its appearance in the comic opera by John O'Keefe entitled *The Poor Soldier* of (1783). Glen also quotes William Stenhouse, who believed the tune to have been composed by the late John Bruce, a fiddler in Dumfries in the mid 1750s (see Stenhouse *Illustrations*, pp. 109–10). Notably the Irish connection is maintained by Hogg's collaborator R. A. Smith, as the tune appears in his *The Irish Minstrel* in the mid 1820s with Burns's lyric and the title 'Noble Sir Arthur'.

Explanatory Notes:
See *Contributions to Blackwood's Edinburgh Magazine* I (S/SC, 2008), pp. 504–05.
Note that Hogg does give his own brief Explanatory Notes after the lyric in *Songs* (see p. 15).

The Souters of Selkirk (p. 16)

Creative Context:
There is scant information about the creation of this song. Hogg's 1831 headnote states that it was written for one Dr Clarkson, for his own singing. This is clearly Ebeneezer Clarkson (1799–1844) who was both a surgeon, and Bailie (*sic.*) and Provost of Selkirk' (*Letters*, I, 8). At the beginning of Hogg's writing career Clarkson was as one of his literary confidants, advising on *Scottish Pastorals* (1801) and other early works (see *Letters*, I, 7 and 9). Hogg's letters to his wife Margaret in [August 1828] refer to Hogg attending 'Yair': a dinner given to 'mark the disbanding of the Selkirkshire Yeomanry by their Captain, Alexander Pringle of Whytbank and Yair'(see *Letters*, II, 302–05). Hogg notes that Clarkson was present and so it is probable that the song was composed for and sung at this event. Certainly the demonstrative defiance of the lyric would fit this Creative Context.

The song first appeared in print in [1828] in *Select & Rare Scotish Melodies* with a musical setting by Sir Henry Bishop, published in London by Goulding, D'Almaine & Co.: see *Contributions to Musical Collections and Miscellaneous Songs*. Hogg had sent eight songs (all but 'The brakens wi' me' are unnamed) in a letter to Robert Purdie in January 1828 to forward to Goulding for inclusion in *Select & Rare Scotish Melodies* (see *Letters*, II, p. 284). However, it is possible that others were sent later in 1828 – at this point Hogg was involved in sending songs (mostly through Purdie) to Goulding for inclusion in *Select & Rare* but also in its annual *The Musical Bijou*.

It would appear that Hogg used the text from [1828] for his *Songs* 1831. But there are some notable differences. The first and most significant reveals that Hogg prepared the manuscript after June 1830 when King William IV (1765–1837) acceded to the throne following the death of his elder brother George IV. Hogg has removed the name 'Geordie' in the second verse (l. 6) and it is replaced with 'Willie'. The second alteration clears up a misprint that occurred within the text of *Select & Rare Scotish Melodies* where the printer presumably misread Hogg's handwriting: 'heroes' replaces 'hevas' (v. 2, l. 8) in the final line of the song for *Songs* 1831. This is also noted within a presentation copy of *Select & Rare Scotish Melodies*, inscribed to 'Miss Foster', where Hogg corrected the obvious misprint, scoring out the 'va' of 'hevas' and writing 'ro' above to indicate to the singer that 'heroes' should be sung instead (Beinecke Rare Book Room and Manuscript Library, Call No. 1974+69). Interestingly, the version of the song within *Select & Rare Scotish Melodies* does not include a chorus. It is not known whether the chorus was omitted in this collection or was added later by Hogg. But it is interesting that the earlier appearance of a song with this name, and the same melody, in *SMM*, also has no chorus.

The only extant manuscript version of the song is located within the fair-copy manuscript of *Songs* 1831, at NLS MS 4805 f. 35v. The headnote is amended to soften Hogg's comment that Clarkson was 'in a devil of a passion': the printed version describes him in 'a mighty passion'. The song itself is transferred cleanly to the printed page with the usual addition of punctuation. Interestingly Hogg does not write out the chorus in the manuscript either. Clearly Hogg or his printer decided to add one for the printed text. It may well be that the song was often performed with a chorus and thus it was decided to include one for the final publication of *Songs*.

Publication History
Authorised versions:
[1828] – in *Select & Rare Scotish Melodies* (London: Goulding & D'Almaine), pp. 23–25 – see *Contributions to Musical Collections and Miscellaneous Songs* (S/SC, 2014)

1831 – in *Songs by the Ettrick Shepherd*, pp. 31–32 – see p. 16 in the present edition

Musical Context:
Hogg refers to 'the old air' in his headnote. Clearly the tune was already well-known. Burns informed Thomson, in the marginalia of the manuscript version of 'The Sutors of Selkirk' for *SMM*, that "This tune can be found anywhere" (James C. Dick (p. 490)). Burns' version is in the sixth volume of *SMM* (1796, No. 438). Dick notes that the earliest appearance of 'the tune with the title' was in *A Collection of the Choicest Scots Tunes* by Adam Craig (Edinburgh, 1730). The tune was reprinted in most of the major eighteenth-century fiddle collections, including those by Aird and McGibbon. However, Thomas Crawford cautions against accepting traditional interpretations of the song at face value and classifies the song amongst 'trade-songs' of 'fairly recent oral transmission' (*Society and the Lyric: a Study of the Song Culture of Eighteenth-Century Scotland* (Edinburgh: Scottish Academic Press, 1979), p. 125). Bishop sets the tune as it appears in *SMM* (in the same key and with only slight variants).

Explanatory Notes:
16 [Title] from a traditional song. Hogg had earlier titled a short story with this same title which appeared within his 'Shepherd's Calendar' series in *Blackwood's Edinburgh Magazine* of May 1827. 'George Dobson's Expedition to Hell and The Souters of Selkirk' were published together under the heading of 'Dreams and Apparitions' and in the latter story a 'souter' or shoemaker named George Dobson sings the words traditionally associated with the song:

see Douglas S. Mack (ed.) James Hogg, *The Shepherd's Calendar* (S/SC, 1995, pp. 118–141 (126–141).

16, l. 2 auld pedigree Selkirk is 'a post and market town, a royal and parliamentary burgh and a parish in Selkirkshire' (Groome).

16 l. 3 lads o' the Forest Ettrick Forest, an ancient Royal hunting ground in Selkirkshire. Jean Elliott composed lyrics in the eighteenth century to accompany the tune 'The Flowers of the Forest', a traditional lament for seventy Selkirk men who died fighting for James IV at the Battle of Flodden in 1513.

16, l. 14, our auld fashion'd structure in the atmosphere of 1830–31 during the lead up to the 1832 Reform Bill the 'structure' of the British political establishment was a 'hot' topic.

16, l. 15, Willie King William IV (1765–1837). He acceded to the throne on 26 June 1830 following the death of his elder brother, King George IV (1762–1830).

O, Jeanie, There's Naething to Fear Ye! (p. 17)

Creative Context:
The only information about this song's creation is found in this 1831 headnote. Hogg's mention of the involvement of 'Mrs Gray' provides evidence that he most probably wrote the song in the early 1810s, during his first prolonged stay in Edinburgh. There he frequented the home of his friend and early literary mentor James Gray (1770–1830). Mary Gray, neé Peacocks, (1767–1829) was James's second wife, having married him in 1808. She was a keen writer, who had already corresponded with Burns during the 1790s and she contributed several articles to Hogg's magazine *The Spy* in 1810–1811. Hogg's headnote provides further evidence of her literary skill, as she 'corrected' his text the day after its composition. Further information about her can be found in 'Notes on Contributors' in *The Spy*, (S/SC, 2000), pp. 562–64. She had died in India in March 1829 and so Hogg potentially had commemoration of her in mind when he included the song.

'Patrick Maxwell Esq.' appears also to have been part of the Edinburgh literary circles within which Hogg moved at this time. Maxwell provided both the *Memoir* and *Notes* of *The Poetical Works of Miss Susanna Blamire* (Edinburgh: John Menzies, 1842) where he shows his knowledge of both the Scottish song tradition and also Hogg's songs (e.g. he quotes from ll. 13–20 of 'Donald Macdonald' (p. 176)). Hogg's headnote clearly suggests that he was a competent musician.

Hogg notes that 'O, Jeanie, There's Naething to Fear Ye 'has been by far the most popular love-song I ever wrote', and it was included in a number of contemporary song collections. Its first appearance in print was alongside Hogg's lyric 'The Lark' in John Clarke-Whitfeld's *Twelve Vocal Pieces* published in London in [1817] with the abbreviated title 'Naething to Fear Ye'. After receiving Hogg's 'The Lark'(see notes for 'The Skylark' p. 9), Clarke-Whitfeld requested further songs by Hogg and he sent another four in his letter to Clarke-Whiffeld of 11 November 1816 (*Letters*, I, 280–81). While unnamed, Gillian Hughes believes that one of these was 'Naething to Fear Ye' and another, referred to by Hogg as 'The border song', was most probably 'Lock the Door Lariston', a song which also has associations with James Gray (see Hughes's notes in *Letters*, I, 281 and also notes below for 'Lock the Door Lariston'). While Hogg confesses to having written 'The Lark' especially for Clarke-Whifeld, the four songs he subsequently sent are from existing manuscripts, again helping to date the song to earlier in the 1810s.

Hogg's letter of 16 December 1830 to the publisher Lonsdale & Mills refers to the two songs in *Twelve Vocal Pieces* as having 'been both published in ten different ways since, in periodicals in single sheets and collections of engraved music': see *Letters*, II, 417–8.

As was the case with 'The Lark' Hogg included 'Naething to Fear ye' in his first Scottish musical collection *A Border Garland* in [1819] and it was then included later in *The Border Garland* of *c*.1829 where the longer title as found in 1831 appears. The initial musical setting in *A Border Garland* appears to have been by William Heather. Gow & Galbraith then also issued the song as a separate song sheet with a different (though with similiarites) arrangement by Niel Gow Junr. between *c*.1823 and 1826. For more information of Hogg's involvement in all three musical collections and copies of all these musical settings, see *Contributions to Musical Collections and Miscellaneous Songs*.

There are surprisingly few textual variants between the appearances of the song from 1817 until 1831. The wording of the first and last verses remains stable in each version (with slight differences in spellings only). Verse 2 is subtly more sexual in its reference to 'our bed in the greenwood' in all early versions of the song, as opposed to 'our walk in the greenwood' of the 1831 text (17, l.12). Also in 1831 Hogg emends 'Note' (l.14) to 'List', whereas it is stable in the musical printings of the song; and 'blithesome' (l.16) is changed to 'fairy' in 1831, while it is stable in all other versions. One final change is the addition of the opening ''Tis' in l.23 in 1831. In performance, the refrain – 'O, Jeanie, There's Naething to Fear Ye' – is repeated after the conclusion of each verse. Whatever the reason for the changes, they show Hogg re-engaging with the song, rather than simply copying it out from a printed text.

There are two extant manuscripts. Hogg sent the first verse and chorus in his letter of 1 April 1818 to the composer William Heather [Boston Public Library/ Rare Books Department/ Mss. Acc. 70]. This text relates to Heather's setting of the song for *A Border Garland* (see Musical Context below). NLS MS 4805, f. 36 is Hogg's fair-copy holograph manuscript of the complete text. A printer's mark '33–C' written at the top right-hand side of f. 36r shows signs that the manuscript has been through the printing process. Moreover, the song is page-numbered '21' and '22' and follows consecutively within the printed order. Hogg's unpunctuated text is transferred relatively cleanly to the printed page. One alteration occurs in the headnote: 'went over and corrected it' is changed to 'went over and corrected them'.

Publication history:

[1817] – in *Twelve Vocal Pieces* (Vol. II, No. III (text, p. 5; music, pp. 28–33)) – see *Contributions to Musical Collections and Miscellaneous Songs* (S/SC, 2014)

[1819] – in *A Border Garland* pp. 6–7 – see *Contributions to Musical Collections and Miscellaneous Songs* (S/SC, 2014)

c.1822–23 – as the song sheet: 'Jeanie, There's naething to Fear ye', music arranged for Piano Forte by Niel Gow, Jr. (Edinburgh: Gow & Galbraith, 60 Princes Street, and Gow and Son, 162 Regent Street) – see *Contributions to Musical Collections and Miscellaneous Songs* (S/SC, 2014)

c.1829 – in *The Border Garland* pp. 7–9 – see *Contributions to Musical Collections and Miscellaneous Songs* (S/SC, 2014)

1831 – in *Songs by the Ettrick Shepherd*, pp. 33–34 – see p. 17 in the present edition

Musical Context:
Hogg refers in his headnote to a tune with the title 'Over the Border'. The melody included in John Clarke-Whitfeld's *Twelve Vocal Pieces* of [1817] is a spirited tune, more like a traditional Scottish tune than that employed for the setting of 'The Lark'. However, it is not the traditional tune to which Hogg refers in his headnote, which would appear to be the melody found with the song in *A Border Garland* in [1819]. It is this melody which also appears in *The Border Garland* of *c*.1829 and in the independent song sheet published by Gow & Galbraith around *c*.1822–23. The melody as printed in musical versions after Clarke-Whitfeld, is better known as 'Blue Bonnets over the Border', which is named in full, presumably as a marketing tool, in the separate Gow & Galbraith song sheet. In *A Border Garland* [1819] where it appears first, the tune is simply called 'Air, old', and it is unnamed in the setting by James Dewar in *The Border Garland* in *c*.1829, but it is almost exactly the same melody, even in the same key. The tune is a rousing march which might seem a rather strange choice for the tenor of the lyric. But, like the melody for Hogg's 'Bonny Prince Charlie' (see note above) the tune was to gain huge popularity in the early 19th century.

This may have to do with the appearance of new words for 'the ancient air of 'Blue Bonnets Over the Border' which Walter Scott presented in his novel *The Monastery* in 1820 (Vol. II, pp. 322–23, Chapter XI). R. A. Smith set them to music in *The Scotish Minstrel* in the mid 1820s to an air which he titled 'Blue Bonnets'. This appears to bear remarkable similarity to the tune published with Hogg's song 'O, Jeanie, There's Naething to Fear Ye' from 1819 onwards. And perhaps this context helps explain Gow & Galbraith's decision to sell their song sheet with the title 'Blue Bonnets over the Border' in full.

Both Scott's and Hogg's knowledge of a pre-existing 'ancient' tune was clear. In his letter of 13 December 1829 to Thomas Proudfoot Hogg refers to 'the fine old air of "Over the Border" which I am sure a true Borderer and his lady must know': see *Letters*, II, 366. But there are numerous variant melodies associated with the title 'Blue Bonnets'. Hogg's song 'Turn the Blue Bonnets wha can' which is also a rousing marching song is found in *The Border Garland* of *c*.1829 with a musical setting by James Dewar, but is altogether different from the tune for 'Jeanie'. In his *Songs of Scotland* (III, 55), George Farquhar Graham notes that Scott's song was based on an old Cavlaier song which Hogg had included in 1819 in *Jacobite Relics*, I (pp. 5–7) entitled 'Lesley's March' and he gives that melody for his reader to compare with the new popular tune associated with Scott's text.

Arabian Song (p. 18)

Creative Context:
There is scant information about the creation of this song. Hogg refers, in his 1831 headnote, to an earlier 'Arabian Song' which he had composed to a tune sent to him by Robert Archibald Smith. Hogg's correspondence with Smith dates from February 1818 until January 1824. His songs were included in two of Smith's collections: *The Scotish Minstrel* (1821–24) and *The Irish Minstrel* [1825] – for further information and copies of the relevant songs see *Contributions to Musical Collections and Miscellaneous Songs*.

Smith was, however, also working on a collection of 'national songs' entitled *Select Melodies, with appropriate words, chiefly original, collected and arranged with symphonies and accompaniments for the pianoforte* (Edinburgh: Robert Purdie (n.d.), *c.*1827). Although not containing any of Hogg's songs, he does include some by Hogg's nephew, Robert Hogg, including 'A German Maid am I', 'from the German of Klopstock' (pp. 26–27). Smith's plans for the collection can be traced in his correspondence with William Motherwell: see GUL MS Robertson 3, ff. 88–89, ff. 111–13 and ff. 115–16.

No further information about the 'earlier' song has been found. So Hogg must have rewritten the lyric which appears in *Songs* 1831. By this time the song had appeared in the London music collection *Select & Rare Scotish Melodies*, with a musical setting, referred to in Hogg's headnote, by Sir Henry Bishop and published by Goulding & D'Almaine in [1828]. For further information and copies of the relevant songs see *Contributions to Musical Collections and Miscellaneous Songs*. This probably means that 'Arabian Song' was included within Hogg's letter to Robert Purdie of 18 January 1828 when he writes he 'encloses eight more songs for your correspondents with such airs as I knew they could not command in London': see *Letters*, II, 284. Purdie was acting as Goulding & D'Almaine's London agent at this time and several of Hogg's songs also appeared in Goulding's annuals and gift books (see *Contributions to Annuals and Gift Books* (S/SC, 2006)).

Hogg clearly used the version of 'Arabian Song' from *Select & Rare Scotish Melodies* as his copy text when preparing the version found in *Songs* 1831, as it is transferred from the earlier collection without change. There is only one extant manuscript found at NLS MS 4805, ff. 36–37v, within the fair-copy manuscript used in the preparation of *Songs* 1831. The pages are numbered '22' and '23' Hogg's unpunctuated text has been transmitted cleanly to the printed version.
'Arabian Song' is singled out in a review of *Select & Rare Scotish Melodies* published in the *Edinburgh Literary Journal*, no. 8 (3 January 1829), 101–03. The unnamed critic states: 'but we like our author when he keeps on the north side of the Tweed; the air, composed by Bishop, is simple and beautiful, but strikes me as a little out of place' (p. 103).

Publication History:
[1828] – in *Select & Rare Scotish Melodies*, pp. 30–32 – see *Contributions to Musical Collections and Miscellaneous Songs* (S/SC, 2014)
1831 – in *Songs by the Ettrick Shepherd*, pp. 35–36 – see p. 18 in the present edition
Unauthorised versions:
Arabian Song' appears in a number of posthumous collections and anthologies, suggesting that the lyric was popular amongst the Victorians. Usually later versions are taken from the text as printed in 1831 and sometimes the song appears with music. It was published, for example, in *A Parting Gift* (Edinburgh, (n.d.), *c.*1845), p. 247, a gift book designed for the Christmas market of 1845: see *Contributions to Annuals and Gift Books* (S/SC, 2006), pp. 358–59, it was also reprinted in *Englische Dichter – English Poets. A Selection from the Works of the British Poet from Chaucer to Tennyson*, with a German Translation, edited by O.L.C. H.....r. (Leipzig: George Wigand, 1856), which contains two items by Hogg: 'An Arabian Song' on p. 552 with a German translation ('Ein Arabische Lied') on p. 553 and also 'The Wee Hausie' (see pp. 133–34 of the present volume). Gooch and Thatcher list two further musical settings of the lyric (see; Gooch & Thatcher, 8606–8607). 'The Garden of Roses', is a setting arranged for pianoforte and voices and is included as 'No. 1' of the 'Vocal Quartetts Series', which was published around 1863 by the London music publisher Robert Cocks & Co., publishers to 'the Queen, H. R. H. the Prince of Wales & the Emperor

Napoleon III'. The composer is Sigr. F. Paer' and the textual editor is named as William Hills. It was sold for 2/6. While the text of *Songs* 1831 is unchanged, the words are ordered differently, so that, for example, the song begins with the second verse. The setting ends with the repeated refrain 'A garden of roses', of l. 10, from where the sheet derives its title. A further music score is listed within the holdings of the Royal College of Music (MI529.5): *Three Vocal Duetts, with English and German words,* comprising 'Time Flies Away' by Cliem, 'An Arabian Song' by Hogg, and 'The Evening Star' by Campbell, the music is composed by H. S. Oakley (1830–1903).

Musical Context:
Hogg notes his preference for Bishop's musical setting of his lyric rather than the 'Arabian air' sent to him by R.A. Smith. As the latter is now lost, it is not possible to discuss the reasons for this preference. Bishop's melody does not seem particularly 'eastern' in tenor, but is a simple aria common of domestic song books of the period and in keeping with his other settings for *Select & Rare Scotish Melodies.*

Explanatory Notes:
18, l. 7 roundelay 'a short simple song with a refrain' (*OED*).
18, l. 14 O, virtuous love is the soul's delight! the song contains echoes of Hogg's series of 'Eastern Apologues', published in the *Forget Me Not* for 1829, pp. 309–323. In particular, in 'The Beauty of Women', Ismael convinces Sadac, the Prince, to uphold the 'beauties of virtue, mercy, and benevolence' above mere surface beauty of 'the skin' when seeking 'happiness with women': reprinted in *Contributions to Annuals and Gift Books* (S/SC, 2006), pp. 48–56, p. 54.

I Lookit East, I Lookit West (pp. 18–20)

Creative Context:
A full account of the textual and publishing history of 'I Lookit East, I Lookit West' is given in *Contributions to Blackwood's Edinburgh Magazine*, I (S/SC, 2008).

In summary, this song appeared in *Blackwood's* on 20 October 1826 as the first of three songs sung by the Shepherd in the *Noctes Ambrosianae* No. XXVIII (the other two being 'Tam Nelson' and 'There's some Souls 'ill Yammer and Cheep', neither of which Hogg included in *Songs* 1831). Its context is clear – even without an explanatory headnote in 1831 – because Hogg includes the relevant 'Tickler' and 'Shepherd' dialogue of the original *Noctes.* But Hogg does decide, in 1831, that an 'afterword' is required to place the song in terms of his overall work as a songwriter and, undoubtedly, to better contextualise the content of the lyric itself. Thus he notes that the song was 'written many years ago' and that it was created at the request of John Galt and other literary friends for a new organisation which was 'for the purpose of relieving the wives and families of Scottish solidiers who had fallen in our sanguine wars abroad'. It was first performed at the institutionary dinner of the Caledonian Asylum held at the Freemason's Tavern in London on Saturday 11 March 1815. Thomas Richardson's notes for the song in *Contributions to Blackwood's* give further details as to the first printing of the song and refer to Gillian Hughes's discovery of its appearance in the *Edinburgh Evening Courant* of 13 March 1815, as part of the paper's account of the dinner. See also Gillian Hughes 'James Hogg, and Edinburgh's Triumph Over Napoleon', *Scottish Studies Review* (Spring 2003), 98–111. The song as it appeared separately in print is found in *Contributions to Musical Collections and Miscellaneous Songs.* Richardson's notes also account for the textual history of the song from then until 1831 – the *Blackwood's* text is the one Hogg uses for *Songs*. Richardson also gives details of the manuscript of the song Hogg sent to the publisher George Thomson which is held at the British Library among Thomson's letterbooks MS 35, 265, fol. 340, but which was apparently not published.

The fair-copy manuscript for *Songs* 1831 is found within NLS MS 4805, ff. 37r–38r. A correction was made to the text of the 'afterword' prior to publication. Hogg's phrase 'sanguine wars against the French' is scored through and the word 'abroad' is inserted above so that the printed version ends more generally with 'sanguine wars abroad'. Notably Hogg might be remembering that the song's appearance in *Blackwood's* immediately follows a discussion of 'The Shepherd's' beheading (while he remains conscious) in France as part of the proceedings of the Revolution. Apart from this alteration the manuscript text is transferred cleanly to the printed page with the usual minor orthographic alterations of lengthening words such as 'stirr'd' with the insertion of an 'e' (l. 17).

Publication History:
1815 – 'SONG,/ BY THE ETTRICK SHEPHERD, / *Sung at the Institutory Dinner of the CALEDONIAN ASSYLUM, at the Freemason's Tavern, Saturday, March 4th, 1815* – see *Contributions to Musical Collections and Miscellaneous Songs* (S/SC, 2014)
1815 – in *Edinburgh Evening Courant*, 13 March 1815
1826 – in *Blackwood's Edinburgh Magazine*, 20 (October 1826), 622–23 – see (S/SC, 2008), pp. 253–54 and 529–31
1831 – in *Songs by the Ettrick Shepherd*, pp. 37–40 – see pp. 18–20 in the present edition

Musical Context:
Hogg's 'afterword' to the song's appearance in *Songs* 1831 refers to its London premiere by 'professional singers' – the account in the *Edinburgh Evening Courant* mentions a Master Millar as the singer, and notes that he was a pupil of 'Mr Addison', who was presumably the composer and singer John Addison (*c.*1766–1844). Hogg also explains that the tune to which his lyrics were sung was 'The Birks of Invermay'. Glen states that the tune (p. 80), also often called 'The Birks of Endermay', did not appear in print until 1733 where it was included in William Thomson's *Orpheus Caledonius* (Vol. II, p. 98). The opening two stanzas most often printed with the song in the 18th century begin 'The smiling morn, the breathing spring' and are by David Mallet (or Malloch). Additional stanzas often appear and are thought to have been created by the Rev. Doctor Bryce of Kirknewton. The tune is frequently printed in standard collections of Scots tunes from 1733 onwards, including those by William McGibbon, Francesco Barsanti and James Oswald. Hogg may well have known it from its appearance in *SMM* (1787), No. 72 (p. 73). It is a wistful and slightly haunting tune, well chosen for the tenor of Hogg's lyric, which speaks so expressively of a destitute widow and her three children finding Divine comfort. According to John Galt, who had 'commissioned' Hogg, the songs performed at the institutionary dinner were published by Chappell (*The Autobiography of John Galt*, I, 273). But neither such a collection, nor any later musical settings of Hogg's song have been found. The river May has its source among the Ochil-hills and is about 8 miles from The Earn. At the turn of the century Invermay is also the residence of Colonel Bleches, and was regarded, the *The Satistical Account of Scotland* (1791–99) as one of the most romantic and pleasant spots in this part of Perthshire'.

Explanatory Notes:

18 [Title] possibly from a traditional ballad known to Hogg. In *The Mountain Bard* (1807) Hogg included an extract from a traditional song (with the line: 'The dow flew east, the dow flew west'), which he attaches to his ballad 'Sir David Graeme', claiming that the words are adapted from 'a beautiful old rhyme which I have often heard my mother repeat, but of which she knows no tradition' (see *The Mountain Bard*, (S/SC, 2007), p. 25 (text), pp. 403–05 (notes). Similar lines are included in 'The Herone. A very Ancient Song' included in Hogg's story 'The Bride of Polmood' (*Winter Evening Tales* (S/SC, 2004), pp. 309–11 and notes on p. 576).

18 [headnote] Tickler a character based on Robert Sym, WS (1752–1845), uncle of John Wilson, who from February 1818 contributed regularly to *Blackwood's* under the name 'Timothy Tickler'. See Hogg's 'Reminiscences of Former Days', a section appended to 'Memoir of the Author's Life' in *Altrive Tales* (1832). Sym contributed anonymously to Hogg's magazine *The Spy*: see 'Notes on Contributors' in *The Spy* (S/SC, 2000), pp. 570–71. However, according to Hogg, it was not until 'long afterwards', when Hogg became acquainted with the Wilsons around 1814, that he discovered who Sym was and the nature of his relationship to John Wilson (*Altrive Tales* (S/SC, 2003), p. 77).

18, l. 5 house nor hame a typical pathetic balladic phrase, see for example, 'Richie Storie' (Child 232A). Also found in 'Flora Macdonald's Farewell', l. 18.

19, l. 39 the widow and the fatherless | Can never pray and slighted be it was a rule of Judaic and Mosaic Law that the helpless were under God's protection. See, Malachi 3:5, Zechariah 7:10, Exodus 22:22 and Psalm 68:5: 'A father of the fatherless, and a judge of the widows, is God in his holy habitation.'

19 [afterword] Mr Galt and some other literary friends no record of Galt's request has apparently survived. In 1833, Galt recorded in his autobiography how he 'undertook to assist in raising the funds which were afterwards employed in building and endowing the National Caledonian Asylum, which stands a little to the north of Pentonville, in the Fields' (*The Autobiography of John Galt*, 2 vols (London: Cochrane & McCrone, 1833), I, 272).

The Village of Balmaquhapple (pp. 20–21)

Creative Context:
An account of the textual and publishing history of 'The Village of Balmaquhapple' otherwise entitled 'The Great Muckle Village of Balmaquhapple', and information about the tune 'The Sodger Laddie, is given in *Contributions to Blackwood's Edinburgh Magazine* I (S/SC, 2008).

In summary, as is the case with 'I Lookit East, I Lookit West' and 'The Noctes Sang', which were already included in *Songs* 1831, 'The Village of Balmaquhapple' is also associated with Hogg's role as the Shepherd Songster of the series *Noctes Ambrosianae*, where it appeared on 19 June 1826 (739–40) in *No. XXVI*. It was therefore printed just a few months before 'I Lookit East, I Lookit West' discussed above. The song is part of a discussion between the *Noctes* personae of Christopher North, The Shepherd and the Devil, or Beelzebub, who sings the song which has been created by the Shepherd. Hogg decided, in 1831, to include the Noctean dialogue before and after the song – he sets up 'I Lookit East, I Lookit West' in this way too – and gives no 'headnote'. But, as with 'I Lookit East' he chooses to give an afterword, noting his lack of memory about the creation of this nonsense song.

Gillian Hughes believes that Hogg sent the song in response to Blackwood's urgent appeal for material for the magazine. In his letter of 9 March 1826 Blackwood wrote: 'If you happen to have any Songs ready, and could send them by return of post they could still be in time for this Nᵒ·' (*Letters*, II, 243–444, p. 244). Hughes believes the two songs Hogg sent were 'The Great Muckle Village of Balmaquhapple' and 'Meg o' Marley' (see below)). It is not known when precisely Hogg composed the song, but these were the two songs which appeared in the June issue of *Noctes*. Hogg appears to have been characteristically downhearted with his efforts, referring to the enclosed songs as 'very useless' in his letter to Blackwood of 19 March 1826. But this might also be connected to Hogg's annoyance with Blackwood, as he writes: 'I would send you plenty of things to Maga provided they were either inserted or returned which they never are Worse encouragement cannot be than that', and he goes on to list a number of rejected contributions (*Letters*, II, 243–444, p. 243). Hogg's complaint is even included within the *Noctean* dialogue in this No.: 'The Shepherd' is propelled across the room by the force of the opened lid of the 'Balaam box' causing 'Tickler' to remark, 'My dear Shepherd, why, you are a rejected contributor!' It's notable that Hogg retains this context in 1831, by choosing to include the dialogue following the song, in which North comments (aside to Tickler) that 'Hogg's bad'[this emends the original Blackwoodian text which reads: 'Bad, Hogg's']. Hogg includes only a little of the dialogue after the song and breaks off after one sentence of a rather more lengthy response by the Shepherd, again alluding to his depression at the burning or rejection of his creative work.

In *Songs* 1831 Hogg chooses to revise the original title, to the less comic 'The Village of Balmaquhapple', though he keeps the original title in the dialogue which precedes the lyric. He also amends several other elements of the text for 1831: for example, the 'poor village' becomes a 'great village' (l. 12), and 'way' is altered to the Scots 'gate' in l. 23 which does not alter the sentient but in the next line the Scots word 'wheedle' ('to persuade (a person) into a way of thinking or course of action': *DSL*) is changed to the Anglified 'cheat', which adds a more menacing tone. Further alterations include the naming of 'Jock Linton' who becomes 'Jock Lesley' (l. 35), and the alteration of 'frown' to 'word' (l. 37).

The fair-copy manuscript of the song for 1831 is found in NLS MS 4805, ff. 25–26. But this manuscript is incomplete, and the first section stops abruptly at the end of the text for this song on f. 26r of the manuscript just after the words 'Hogg's bad' (see Janette Currie: 'Genesis of the Text', pp. xli–xlviii). Hogg's unpunctuated text is transferred cleanly to the printed page – the title is missing in the manuscript.

Publication History:

1826 – in *Blackwood's Edinburgh Magazine*, 19 (June 1826), 739–40 – see (S/SC, 2008), pp. 188–89, 363–64, 373, and 517

1831 – in *Songs by the Ettrick Shepherd*, pp. 41–44 – see pp. 20–21 in the present edition

Musical Context:

The tune Hogg mentions in the context of this song is 'The Sodger Laddie' and musical notation is provided by Thomas Richardson in *Contributions to Blackwoods* noted above, though no music was printed in *Blackwood's*. This is a popular melody, which appeared in various musical publications during the 18ᵗʰ century, notably in William Thomson's *Orpheus Caledonius* in 1725, and it was also included in Johnson's *SMM*, Vol IV, no. 323. It was known by the time of Hogg's song as the tune associated with Burns's lyric 'I once was a Maid, tho' I cannot tell when', which was the second song of his cantata 'Love and Liberty' also known as 'The Jolly Beggars' (see Robert Burns *The Poems and Songs*, ed. J Kinsley (Oxford: Clarendon, 1968), II, no. 84, (text) III). Hogg would presumably have seen 'The Jolly Beggars', as it had been published by George Thomson as the second part of Volume 5 of *A Select Collection of Original Scottish Airs* in 1818 (the first part of which included three of Hogg's songs). Burns's cantata was set to music by Sir Henry Bishop, who would later set 13 of Hogg's songs for *Select & Rare Scottish Melodies*.

Explanatory Notes:
Also see *Contributions to Blackwood's Edinburgh Magazine*, I (S/SC, 2008), p. 517.
21 [afterword] what a dracth's in that lum this particular *Noctean* conversation had included an episode where the contents of the 'Balaam box' were burnt in the fire by 'The Incrementers' or 'firemen belonging to the Sun Fire Office', and the Devil. The Scots use of 'Balaam' was intended: 'where second-rate material kept in reserve in manuscript or type by a printer or publisher to be used only when needed to fill a gap in a newspaper or magazine or in case-room work' (*DSL*). The Scots usage apparently originated in *Blackwood's*, 'no doubt in allusion to the Biblical story of Balaam (Numbers xxii) and the speech of an ass' (*DSL*).
21 [afterword] It must undoubtedly have some allusion to circumstances as was normal practice, the entire *Noctean* conversation had included references to topical events. In this Number, topics included the 'Catholic Question' and Scottish preaching, and had concluded with a remark on 'Joseph Hume's four hours' speech, and forty-seven resolutions'. Hume (1777–1855) was a radical and a politician, well known for his lengthy, digressive speeches (see V. E. Chancellor's essay in *ODNB*). He was born at Montrose in Fife, on the east coast of Scotland near St. Andrews, which might indicate that he rather than a particular village in Fife was the object of Hogg's satire.

Callum-A-Glen (p. 22)

Creative Context:
It is not known when Hogg composed this song, but it is one of the group of Jacobite songs taken from the Second Series of *Jacobite Relics* of 1821 to appear here in *Songs* 1831. In the *Relics* it was given the title 'Callum-a-Glen. From the Gaelic'. For further information see *Jacobite Relics* II (S/SC, 2003). As with 'Farewell to Glen-Shalloch' (pp. 12–13) it may well have been one of the 'few Gaelic translations of Jacobite songs' that Hogg mentions in his letter of 4 March 1820 to David Laing (see *Letters*, II, 13–14). In his note to *Jacobite Relics*, Hogg suggests that it is difficult for him to talk about the songs objectively, because 'I have too much a hand in these songs from the Gaelic'. Murray Pittock states that there is too little textual evidence to be able to ascertain Hogg's creative input in this song. Both in *Jacobite Relics* and in *Songs* 1831 Hogg is more concerned with the melody than with information about his handling of the text.

The song, collected and amended by Hogg for *Relics*, appeared twice more in authorised musical publications before he picked it up for *Songs* 1831. Robert Archibald Smith included it in the sixth and final volume of *The Scotish Minstrel* [1824], where the copy text is the version found in *Jacobite Relics*. Across the several editions of his collection ranging through the 1830s the song is found without any major textual variation. For further information about Hogg's involvement in Smith's collection and copies of his songs therein see *Contributions to Musical Collections and Miscellaneous Songs*.

Hogg assigned 'sole Copyright' of a group of his songs to Smith's publisher, Robert Purdie in November 1827 including 'Callum-A-Glen (see *Letters*, II, 315–16). However Hogg noted that he was still 'reserving to myself the right of publishing any one or all of these songs in a literary work or new edition of the Jacobite Relics'. While no such edition was to be forthcoming Hogg could thus legally include the song in his 1831 collection.

There is no extant manuscript of the song: this is one of the songs missing in Hogg's fair-copy manuscript (NLS MS 4805) for this 1831 collection. Hogg most probably used the *Relics* version of this song for 1831. There is only one strange alteration in l. 10, where 'bright sun of the morning' is printed as 'bright steep of the morning'.

Publication History:
1821 – in *Jacobite Relics*, II, 155–56 and 353–54 – see also (S/SC, 2003), p. 517
[1824] – in *The Scotish Minstrel*, VI, 56–57 – see *Contributions to Musical Collections and Miscellaneous Songs* (S/SC, 2014)
1831 – in *Songs by the Ettrick Shepherd*, pp. 45–46 – see p. 22 in the present edition
Unauthorised versions:
'Callum-a-Glen' was reprinted in several collections after its original appearance in *Jacobite Relics*. In addition to appearing in important 19th century Scottish song collections such as those edited by Allan Cunningham and Robert Chambers, this song also appeared, as noted by Murray Pittock in a mid-nineteenth-century penny broadside ballad-sheet titled 'Callum O'Glen' and sold at 'Overgate, Dundee' (NLS L.c. Folio 70 fol 87): *Jacobite Relics*, II, 517. In musical terms Gooch and Thatcher list a further three unauthorised and later versions: 8644–8646.

Musical Context:
As noted above, Hogg is more concerned, in both *Jacobite Relics* and in *Songs*, to present information about the melody for the song, as he disagrees with William Stenhouse's choice of tune in *Relics*. Thus, as he does for 'Farewell to Glenshalloch', Hogg chooses to give an 'older' Gaelic tune in full in his note for *Relics*. The tune is 'Callum a ghlinne' [Malcolm of the Glen] from Simon Fraser's influential collection *The Airs and Melodies Peculiar to the Highlands and Islands* (Edinburgh, 1816) p. 103, no. 229. This is also the tune used by Smith for *The Scotish Minstrel* in [1824]. Stenhouse's choice of tune for *Jacobite Relics* is understandable, as the tessitura of the melody is much lower than Fraser's tune and in general it is easier to sing. But it does lack the character and the wildness of Fraser's tune, which Hogg clearly much preferred. The Fraser tune has a wide range, reminiscent of pipe tunes and a wonderful flattened seventh of the scale (common to the myxolydian mode) which makes the tune particularly expressive and thus ideal for the tenor of the lyric of old Callum. Information about a melody with the title 'Callum a Ghlinne' is also given by Donald Campbell in his essay on 'The Music, Poetry, and Traditions of the Highlands' in *Tait's Edinburgh Magazine* for May 1849 (271–81). Donald Campbell reprints the song in simultaneous English ('Malcolm of the Glen') and Gaelic ('Callum a Ghlinne') phonetic texts in his book-length study, *A Treatise on the Language, Poetry, and Music of the Highland Clans: Illustrative Traditions and Anecdotes and Numerous Ancient Highland Airs* (Edinburgh: D. R. Collie, 1862), pp. 251–52. See also Anne Lorne Gillies's *Songs of Gaelic Scotland*

(Edinburgh: Birlinn, 2005), pp. 506–08, which gives information about the creation of a song of this name which she believes was composed by 'Malcolm Maclean (Calumn of the glen) of Kinlochewe, Rosshire, who flourished in the first half of the eighteenth century' (p. 508).

Explanatory Notes:

22, l. 1 Was ever old warrior of suffering so weary? 'Callum-A-Glen'contains echoes of a song titled 'Lament for Abercrombie', written by Thomas Mouncey Cunningham and published in *The Forest Minstrel* in 1810 (pp. 163–65). Although the setting is in Dumfries-shire, and the time-period and battle-campaign of the late-eighteenth-century rather than the Jacobite campaigns, the protagonist, also named 'Malcolm' [or Callum], shares the battle-weariness of Hogg's hero. 'Lament for Abercrombie' is reprinted in *The Forest Minstrel* (2006), pp. 327–29.

22, l. 3 The southron bloodhounds lie in kennel so near me as becomes clear, the song is set in the Lochaber district of the north-western Highlands of Scotland. During the 1720s, after the initial attempted Jacobite uprisings, the British Government embarked on a military expedition to 'quell' the future Highland rebellions and to police the area. Under the direction of Major-General Wade, a series of roads and bridges were built linking a number of newly created garrisons at Fort Augustus, Fort George, Inverness, Ruthven and Fort William.

22, l. 5 My sons are all slain 'Possibly as many as 2000 men were hacked to death as they fled from Culloden. Drummossie Moor was turned into a killing field that day': see Explanatory Note, 12, l. 26.

22, l. 7 My chief they have slain in *The History of the Rebellion in the Year 1745* (1802), John Home records that 'the Highlanders who attacked sword in hand, were the Maclachlans and Macleans (making one regiment); the Macintoshes, the Frasers, the Stuarts, and the Camerons. Most of the Chiefs who commanded these five regiments were killed' (p. 238). 'Macdonald of Keppoch' from Lochaber also died sword in hand. See also the Explanatory Note to 122, ll. 45–46.

22, l. 23 The day is abiding of stern retribution echoes the conclusion of Hogg's novel of 1823, *The Three Perils of Woman*: see Explanatory Note, 8, l. 26.

The Three Men of Moriston (pp. 22–24)

Creative Context:

This song was suggested by and created for the Edinburgh song editor George Thomson in 1821–22. Hogg corresponded with Thomson between 1814 and 1829 and contributed several songs to his collection of Scottish airs. For further information about their relationship and copies of the songs in Thomson's collections see: *Contributions to Musical Collections and Miscellaneous Songs*.

In his letter of 30 November 1821 – in addition to requesting permission to reprint Niel Gow's setting of Hogg's 'The Lament of Flora Macdonald' – Thomson asked that Hogg consider producing more songs for his collection, and he sent three airs or melodies and suggested a Jacobite theme. In fact Thomson had initially been reluctant to think of including such politically charged material in his Scottish collection, but he did ultimately publish several Jacobite songs. By 1821, Hogg was already known as editor of Jacobite songs and he was in the process of completing the second series of his *Jacobite Relics* (see *Jacobite Relics*, I, xix–xx). Thomson wrote to Hogg:

> You have brought the <u>Tartan</u> so much into fashion, and such is the
> admiration of the prowess enthusiasm & fidelity of the Highlanders in
> the cause of Prince Charlie, that you could give nothing which would be
> more relished than a ballad on that theme to the canty tune of <u>Woo'd and</u>
> <u>married and a'.</u> What say you to the three honest thieves, the magnanimous
> Outlaws, who concealed the Prince in their cave, nor ask'd what owner
> rear'ed the beeves they killed for his supper? One of these brothers we are
> told went every day into the english camp to procure wheaten bread, &c and
> there he regularly heard proclaim'd on the drum head in english & gaelic
> the reward of thrice ten thousand pound to be given for the head of their
> royal guest!!! Are not such outlaws worthy of a deathless song? By Jupiter I
> envy you the pleasure of immortalizing these Macdonalds. (British Library,
> Add. MS 35, 268, fols. 72–74)

This historical context behind the song is explained by both Thomson and Hogg
in their respective notes to the song's appearance firstly in Thomson's *The Select*
Melodies of Scotland Interspersed with those of Ireland and Wales united to the Songs of
Robt. Burns in 1822–25 and thereafter in Hogg's *Songs* 1831. There are one or two
emendations, but the accompanying note printed by Thomson is almost identical
to that included by Hogg in his headnote, except that Hogg frames the 'story'
surrounding the subject of the song, with comments about Thomson's edition.

Hogg had problems creating the new song, not least because this initial
choice of melody – Woo'd and married an' a' – was the tune already famously
associated with his own 'Donald MacDonald' and he felt he was unable to
better this creation.   On 14 December 1821, Hogg wrote to Thomson to
explain his problem (*Letters*, II, 131–33, p. 1331), but Thomson's note from a
letter of 5 March 1822 clarifies that Hogg did eventually produce the songs.
British Library: Add MS 35, 265, ff. 104–05 is a copy of the 10 stanzas with
chorus which Hogg sent to Thomson to match the tune 'Woo'd and married
an' a''. Against the heading 'Mr Hogg, Altrive Lake, by Selkirk' Thomson
wrote:

> Letter sent, acknowledging receipt of three Songs of his writing, viz. a
> Jacobite ballad called The three men of Moriston [...] approving much of
> the first, but proposing to shorten it to 7 stanzas, and some slight alterations.
> (British Library, Add. MS 35, 268, fol. 88)

It was common for Thomson to tinker with the contributions of his poets and this
is a fine example. Possibly to aid Hogg's dilemma, Thomson revised the song to
match another melody of similar structure and spirit and sent it back to Hogg
for approval on 16 March 1822, when he noted: 'Wrote to Hogg, with his song
of the three men of Moriston, altered by me, in order to suit the air of 'Fy let us a'
to the wedding', begging him to consider the alterations, and to return the song,
revised by him in its new shape' (BL. Add. MS 35, 268, f. 90). Hogg seems to
have taken this well and indeed further revised the song for Thomson, informing
him in his letter of 21 March 1822: 'At first sight I was going to give up the ballad
in utter despair but have once more run slightly over leaving you the choice of
the new or the old lines as you think meet' (*Letters*, II, 156–58, pp. 156–59). Gillian
Hughes provides both Thomson's revised lyric (British Library Add. MS 35, 265,
ff. 115–116) alongside Hogg's comments here, allowing the reader to see just how

many revisions Thomson suggested and how the editor and poet worked together to finalise the text for publication.

Hogg's revised version was subsequently published, with further slight alterations by Thomson, in the third volume of his new 'octavo' edition of Thomson's *The Select Melodies of Scotland Interspersed with those of Ireland and Wales united to the Songs of Robt. Burns* in 1822–25. It is this musical appearance of the song which is used by Hogg for *Songs* 1831. Notably when Thomson presents it he does so without referring to Hogg's creative input: Hogg's name is found only in the index to the volume. This was common in Thomson, if he felt the lyric could be promoted as belonging to an active oral tradition.

This is one of the songs missing from the fair-copy manuscript for *Songs*, namely NLS MS 4805 (see Janette Currie, 'Genesis of the Text', pp. xli–xlviii). As such it is thought that Hogg simply supplied the printer with a copy of Thomson's song. Hogg had altered several things in the text between his final version and Thomson's first printing of the song, some of which Thomson retained and some of which he ignored. For example Hogg had altered the word 'Chiefs' to 'brave' (l. 7) but Thomson had printed 'Chiefs' in the *Select Melodies of Scotland*: see *Letters*, II, 156–57. Interestingly Hogg sticks with 'Chiefs' (l. 7) in *Songs* 1831. There are several slight orthographic alterations, such as 'keekit' in place of 'keeket' (l. 9), and also some alterations to the accidentals which are most likely the work of the printer. Overall, the text is that of the 1822–25 Thomson version.

As mentioned above, two of Hogg's holograph manuscripts of the earliest versions of 'The Three Men of Moriston', composed between November 1821 and March 1822, are extant within the Thomson papers at the British Library: Add MS 35, 265, ff. 104–05 and Add. MS 35, 265, ff. 115–16, the latter of which is reprinted in *Letters*, II, 156–57. Collation of the various versions of the lyrics shows just how much editing Thomson undertook with his commissioned verses. Hogg refers to this in his 1831 headnote by commenting that his initial commission was 'once much longer and more particular; but Mr Thomson shortened it to suit a page, and as usual, I have no original copy'.

Publication History:
1822–23 – in George Thomson, *The Select Melodies of Scotland*, III, 30. See *Contributions to Musical Collections and Miscellaneous Songs*, (S/SC, 2014)
1831 – in *Songs by the Ettrick Shepherd*, pp. 47–50 – see pp. 22–24 in the present edition

Musical Context:
Hogg draws attention to the musical setting of this song at the beginning of his 1831 headnote, by noting that it has been 'beautifully set to music by George Thomson' with 'the accompaniments by the immortal Haydn'. This refers to Thomson's editorial process: most often Thomson used an existing, often traditional, melody or air, and then commissioned new musical arrangements or settings of these airs by living composers. At the same time he sent off a commission for a new set of words to match the air from a living writer. When he'd received the two elements, he then matched them together, often amending them as he saw fit. In the case of this song Hogg was the poet and Joseph Haydn (1732–1809) the composer. More details about Thomson's project can be found in *Contributions to Musical Collections and Miscellaneous Songs*. Haydn, by then a mature and famous Austrian composer, had been introduced to 'Scots songs' during

his extended visit to London in the 1790s and had supplied the Scottish music publisher William Napier with arrangements before Thomson made contact with him. In the last years of his life Haydn set over 400 Scottish and Welsh songs, with just over 200 of these commissioned by George Thomson. Although Haydn died in 1809, Thomson republished many of his settings in the later editions and issues of his collections, in both folio and octavo format. Thus, Haydn's extant arrangement of the melody entitled 'The Blythsome Bridal' or 'Fy let's a' to the bridal' (it had already appeared in Thomson's collection first in 1805 in Vol, IV, 187) was married to Hogg's new lyric in 1822. For further information on the musical relationship between Thomson and Haydn, see Marjorie Rycroft, 'Eingriffe des Verlegers in Haydns Bearbeitungen Schottische Lieder', in *Haydn & Das Clavier,* ed. Georg Feder & Walter Reicher (Tutzing: Schneider, 2002), pp. 51–76 and also *Volksliedbearbeitungen. Schottische Lieder für George Thomson, Joseph Haydn Werke,* Band 3 (ed. Marjorie Rycroft, with Warwick Edwards and Kirsteen McCue).

The reasons behind Thomson changing his mind over the melody for this song – from 'Woo'd and married an' a'" to 'Fy let's a' to the wedding' or, as he prints, 'Fy let's a' to the bridal' – is given in 'Creative Context' above. Both melodies are uplifting in spirit and have the same metre. They are thus easily interchangeable, and Thomson often made such editorial choices. This tune also had notable Jacobite connotations by this time as discussed by William Donaldson in *The Jacobite Song* (pp. 31–35) who notes its use as a 'model' for others. The song (without music) had first appeared as 'The Blythesome Bridal' in James Watson's *Choice Collection* in 1706 where it had been united with a lyric entitled 'The Treaty of Union' – thereafter it became a model for popular Scottish political and Jacobite songs. The details of the history of the tune, which appeared frequently in collections across the 18th century – from William Thomson's 1725 *Orpheus Caledonius* (No. 36), to James Johnson's *SMM* under the heading 'An the Kirk wad let me be' 1787 (No. 58) – is given in detail in Glen's *Early Scottish Melodies* (pp. 75–76). Burns had more recently used the tune for the second of his Heron Ballads, a political satire beginning 'Fy let's a' to Kirkcudbright': see James Dick's *The Songs of Robert Burns,* (pp. 457–58).

Explanatory Notes:
22 [Title] As Hogg's (and Thomson's) accompanying notes to the song state, it is founded on historical details and legendary lore surrounding the events of July 1746, when Prince Charles Edward Stuart was in hiding in the Scottish Highlands. According to one historian of the early nineteenth century, the Prince went to Glen Moriston to wait until the passes through the mountains to Lochiel's country in Lochaber were safe: see *History of the Transactions in Scotland in the Years 1715–16, and 1745–46: [...], Together with an Authentic Detail of the Dangers Prince Charles Encountered after the Battle of Culloden,* by George Charles (Leith, 1817), 2 vols, II, 415–419 [hereafter *History of the Transactions in Scotland*]. Glen Moriston is located in the southern region of Loch Ness.
22 [headnote] Six of them the story of how the Prince and Glenaladale, his travelling companion, came to meet up with the six men is given in *History of the Transactions in Scotland* (1817), II, 419–20.
22 [headnote] Peter Grant George Charles describes Peter Grant as 'the most active of the Glenmoriston men', *History of the Transactions in Scotland* (1817), II, 423.

22 [headnote] Hugh Chisholm is one of the six men mentioned above, and Hogg's ill-fated protagonist, Sally Niven, is helped by Hugh Chisholm in the concluding section of *The Three Perils of Woman* (1823), (S/SC, 2002 [paperback]), p. 373.

22 [headnote] the Prince was concealed and supported in a cave in Glen-Moriston, for above five weeks according to George Charles, the six men initially took the Prince 'to a natural cave called Cairagoth, and in this grotto made up a bed for him of fearns and tops of heath (*History of the Transactions in Scotland* (1817), II, 421). After three days they moved to 'a place called Corieyeroch' and he remained there for five weeks and three days' (*History of the Transactions in Scotland*, II, p. 426 note).

22 [headnote] There he regularly heard [...] not a shilling among them all as above, this information is also found in *History of the Transactions in Scotland* (1817): see II, 421.

22, ll. 10–12 The towers of Clan-Ranald [...] | The reek it hung red o'er Glengarry; | Lochaber was herried and lone see also notes to 'Flora MacDonald's Farewell (pp. 7–8). George Charles provides a graphic account of the Hanoverian destruction of the areas Hogg mentions (*History of the Transactions in Scotland* (1817), II, 344–45).

23, l. 15 "O,hon a Righ!' Thomson originally suggested using the phrase 'O hon ha ma chrie!', to which Hogg responded, 'This surely is not the common Gaelic exclamation that means "Oh alas for the king" be sure to get it': BL. Add. MS 35, 265, ff. 115–16, l. 15, reprinted in *Letters*, II, 156. Hogg uses this phrase repeatedly in his Jacobite songs, as *Songs* 1831 reveals. See also, for example, 'Ohon-a-Righ!' (pp. 124–25), composed in 1822 around the same time as Hogg was completing 'The Three Men of Moriston'.

24, l. 31 Dugald M'Cluny on entering the hut of the six thieves one of them recognised the Prince but did not want to draw this to the attention of the other five. Charles tells the story of the Prince's 'nickname', used by his hosts to conceal his true identity: see (*History of the Transactions in Scotland* (1817), II, 420).

When the Kye Comes Hame (pp. 25–27)

Creative Context:
'When the Kye Comes Hame' is now regarded as one of Hogg's best known and best loved songs and was also a personal favourite of the poet. It has an established history in print before Hogg includes it in *Songs* 1831. Details about its earlier publications in Hogg's novel *The Three Perils of Man* and in *Blackwood's Edinburgh Magazine* in can be found in the new S/SC editions of both texts (see below).

In summary, before appearing in either of the above publications, Hogg had sent an early copy of this song to the Edinburgh song editor George Thomson with his letter of 14 December 1821 (see *Letters*, II, 131–133). Thomson did not publish the song at this point but did include it in his final sixth folio volume of *The Melodies of Scotland* in 1841 under the title, 'Come all ye jolly Shepherds' (p. 256) with a previously unpublished musical setting by Joseph Haydn (see 'Musical Context' below).

Thomas Richardson's notes to the song account for the first appearance of the lyric in Hogg's novel *The Three Perils of Man* in 1822 and the subsequent version which is sung by the Shepherd in *Noctes Ambrosianae No. VIII* published in *Blackwood's Edinburgh Magazine* in May 1823. It is noteworthy that the Blackwoodian dialogue revolves around a comparison of Hogg's song with a French song of the period by Pierre Jean de Béranger – suggesting that Hogg's, or the Shepherd's, songs have wider correspondence with contemporary European song culture. Moreover the figures of Tickler and Odoherty are highly complimentary of Hogg's song, noting, after its performance, that Hogg has 'done nothing so sweet these three years'. The Blackwoodian dialogue also acts as a fine promotion for *The Three Perils of Man*, for Hogg chastises Odoherty for not having read it. Hogg contributed the first verse and chorus of 'When the kye come hame' to Robert Archibald Smith in February 1823 (see: 'Preface to the 6th Volume. By the Editors', Glasgow University Library Robertson MS 3, fols 32–33), but Smith never published the song.

Richardson accounts for two manuscript versions of the song – the first in Hogg's letter to Thomson and the second to a Mr 'Blakie' which appears to have been written after the *Blackwood's* appearance (Edinburgh University Library, MS Dc. 4. 101–03). Gillian Hughes believes this correspondent may have been David Blaikie, subsequently editor of the *Edinburgh Evening Post* (the full text of the song is reproduced with Hogg's letter in *Letters*, II, 217–219). It may also be possible that Hogg was sending his song to Andrew Blaikie (d. 1841), an 'engraver and copperplate printer' with premises in Paisley at 175 Causey-side from 1820–1825, and at Abbey Street from 1829–1841 (*Scottish Book Trade Index*): see also the 'Bibliography' in *The Forest Minstrel* (p. 377), where Blaikie is described as 'a friend of James Hogg'.

The details of the manuscript relating to the song's appearance in *The Three Perils of Man* are given by Judy King and Graham Tulloch in *The Three Perils of Man* (S/SC, 2012) pp. xxxvi–vii. They also detail the changes to the text through its various appearances.

A holograph manuscript titled 'When the Kye Come Hame' is within the manuscript holdings of Dean Castle Museum, Ayrshire: digital collection no. EADO109n. Comprising the first verse and the chorus written out in full it is end-signed "Autograph of James Hogg, the Ettrick Shepherd, Written by him, for R.A. Smith, at Edinburgh. 27th Feb. 1823'. The holograph is presumably a contribution to the fifth volume of Smith's *Scotish Minstrel* which was published in May of that year, although no version of this song was included (for further information about Smith and Hogg's songs published in this collection see *Contributions to Musical Collections and Miscellaneous Songs*. The textual variants between the Thomson and Blakie manuscripts and all published versions are discussed by Richardson in *Contributions to Blackwood's Edinburgh Magazine* I, pp. 488–90 and by King and Tulloch.

The inclusion of this lyric in *Songs* 1831 is unsurprising as Hogg clearly feels this to be not simply one of his best but, moreover, one of his most popular songs. It is one of very few songs – Donald MacDonald being another obvious example – where Hogg presents it with both a headnote and 'afterword' or 'footnote'. His headnote states clearly that this is a 'favourite pastoral song' and refers to Hogg's own performance of it, thus endorsing his songs as contemporary living art. Moreover this anecdote of a performance allows Hogg to explain the reason for his having made a grammatical error in its title and in the refrain, 'When the kye comes hame'. All previous versions print the refrain: 'When the kye come hame'. Hogg takes this opportunity to explain that his use of the wrong elision of the verb is a deliberate mistake, noting that the correct 'come' sounded too 'affectit' in performance. It may also be that the phonetic effect of adding the 's' better served the continuity or fluidity of the melody or tune (see 'Musical Context' below).

His afterword modestly accounts for Hogg having forgotton the Creative Context of the song. Gillian Hughes surmises that Hogg 'probably began to prepare *The Three Perils of Man* in the summer of 1818' with 'the bulk of his manuscript' being offered to the Edinburgh publishing firm of Oliver and Boyd on 5 May 1821: see 'Recovering Hogg's Personal Manuscript for *The Three Perils of Man*', by Gillian Hughes, *SHW*, 13 (2002), 104–26, 110–11. It is interesting to find that Hogg's letter to George Thomson, dated 14 December 1821, which accompanied a revised version of the song with three verses and a chorus, was written barely a month after proofs of the novel had been recalled for revision, indicating that revision of the song was concurrent with revising his novel: see *Letters*, II, 131–33, which reprints Hogg's contribution to Thomson in full. Having forgotton this history Hogg explains in 1831 that he was delighted to hear the song again, and decided to revise it.

Having apparently 'forgotton' its earlier appearance, it is not clear which version of the song Hogg used for his 1831 revision. He changes one or two things from earlier printed versions. For example, in verse two the word 'coronet' replaces 'burgonet' as found in *The Three Perils of Man* and *Blackwood's*, and 'banner' of the version sent to Blakie *c.*1824. The ordering of the verses most closely resembles the version sent to Blakie, with Hogg retaining the new lines he created there for verse six, although in this version for *Songs*, verses six and seven are transposed.

The song was more widely circulated after 1831. The Northampton peasant poet John Clare wrote to Thomas Pringle on 5 July 1831 (and to John Taylor four days later) : 'I saw a song of Hoggs in a newspaper this spring 'When the Kye comes home' which delighted me it is the sweetest pastoral I have seen for many a day'. On 8 February 1832, while replying to Pringle's discussion of Hogg's London visit, Clare reminds Pringle of the pleasure he had derived from Hogg's song: 'give my hearty good wishes to James Hogg I am ill but I would travel ten miles to shake him by the hand & wish him success – I saw a ballad of his in a paper sometime back on the Herding at eve from the pasture which delighted me – tell him to go on with such old fashioned pastorals & time will pay him for all dissapointments [*sic*]. See *The Letters of John Clare*, ed. Mark Storey (Oxford: Clarendon Press, 1985), p. 543, p. 545 and pp. 571–573 respectively. Storey notes that the song was reprinted in the *Stamford Champion* on 1 February 1831 (*Letters of John Clare*, p. 543). This suggests that it had been picked up from the newly produced *Songs* 1831.

George Thomson published the song in 1841 but he did not use the manuscript version sent to him by Hogg in 1821, nor does he refer to *Songs* 1831. Thomson's lyric is much shorter (see *Contributions to Musical Collections and Miscellaneous Songs*. The now familiar opening two lines of the version printed in *Blackwood's* replace those which Hogg had informed Thomson he 'didnt like', while the second verse supplied by Hogg is omitted and replaced by a long verse of eight lines made up from a combination of an altered version of the third verse from Hogg's letter of 1821 and the verse beginning 'See, yonder pawky shepherd, that lingers on the hill' (at verse six but noted 'Verse the Fifteenth' in *Three Perils of Man*, verse six of *Blackwood's*, and verse five of *Songs*, 1831). Moreover Thomson changes the refrain to ensure that his printing is grammatically correct and so it appears as 'When the kye come hame'. Thomson also chooses to set the song to a melody quite unlike Hogg's initial choice, a variant of which was to become famous with the lyric (see 'Musical Context' below). Thomson's 'cobbling together' of existing materials, which were now published posthumously for both Hogg, who died in 1835, and Haydn, who had died in 1809, is explained in Thomson's preface to this final volume which he was issuing for the first and only time: 'being in possession of about half a volume of Melodies with Symphonies and Accompaniments which had been composed for them by those greatest of masters, Haydn and Beethoven', he found it 'inexcusable in allowing such charming things to remain dormant in his portfolio'.

This is one of the songs missing in Hogg's fair-copy manuscript for *Songs*, namely NLS MS 4805 (see Janette Currie, 'The Genesis of the Text').

Publication History:
1822 – in *The Three Perils of Man*, (Vol. III, pp. 19–22)) – see (S/SC, 2012), pp. 281–84
1823 – in *Blackwood's Edinburgh Magazine*, 13 (May 1823), 598 – see (S/SC, 2008) pp. 138, 361–62, 366, and 488–90
1831 – in *Songs by the Ettrick Shepherd*, pp. 51–55 – see pp. 25–27 in the present edition
1841 – in George Thomson, *The Melodies of Scotland*, VI (1841), 256 – see *Contributions to Musical Collections and Miscellaneous Songs* (S/SC, 2014)
Unauthorised versions:
This is one of a small group of Hogg's songs, including 'Donald MacDonald', 'Flora MacDonald's Farewell' and 'Bonnie Prince Charlie', which were frequently anthologised after Hogg's death and this one has remained one of his most popular songs to the present day, for it can be traced in general Scots song collections (both text only and with music) from the early Victorian period to the 21st century. In *The Works of the Ettrick Shepherd, Volume Two: Poems & Ballads*, Thomas Thomson reprints two versions, that of *Songs* 1831, and that of *Blackwood's* (II, 413–14). Later nineteenth-century reprintings include a music pamphlet containing two songs titled *O What will a' the Lads Do? and When the Kye Come Hame: Two Popular Songs, Written by Hogg, the Ettrick Shepherd*, with music by William Rogers, published in 1844 by the Boston music-publishing company, G. P. Reed, where in the ordering of verses illustrates that the text is derived from the version in *Blackwood's*. The text of this American version contains more Scotticisms than earlier versions, which was clearly, along with the reference to the 'Ettrick Shepherd', intended to highlight the Scottishness of the song which includes a helpful glossary to guide singers in such unfamiliar words as 'bigs', 'pawkie', and 'fauld' [Above information is derived from the 'Music for the Nation: American Sheet Music, ca. 1820–1860', part of the important *American Memory* project managed by the Library of Congress at http://memory.loc.gov/ammem, accessed August 2013]. An example of cheap reprinting is found on a version published *c.*1840, without authorial ascription, on a foolscap sheet without music, together with a song entitled 'The Brisk Young Lad', by W. McCall, Printer, 4 Cartwright Place, Byrom Street, Liverpool. Gooch and Thatcher list thirteen later versions of this popular song: 8770–8782.

Musical Context:
Hogg states in his 1831 headnote that the tune for this song is found in *Noctes* and 'in no other place that I am aware of'. Interestingly, as it is clearly one of Hogg's most famous songs, it has no other musical appearance during Hogg's lifetime. But it does appear in Thomson's final folio volume (see above) of *The Melodies of Scotland* in 1841 and shortly thereafter in George Farquhar Graham's *The Songs of*

Scotland. Of these appearances Graham's is by far the more important as it is in this collection that the revised version of the *Noctes* melody is given for the first time. The *Noctes* melody, published in *Contributions to Blackwood's* (see above) is entitled 'The Blathrie o't' and appears to be a variant of an already extant fiddle tune, found earlier in both Oswald's *Caledonian Pocket Companion* Book 5 and also in McGibbon's Third Collection of 1755. Further information about the history of the melody can be found in Stenhouse's *Illustrations* (No. XXXIII, pp. 32–33) and in Glen's *Early Scottish Melodies* (p. 68). The *Noctes* variant is wild and modal and, as with many instrumental tunes, demands a great deal of the singer. But its modality is particularly expressive in terms of the poignancy of the lyric and the tune fits that genre of melody which Hogg clearly appreciated. Graham's setting takes this basic fiddle tune, as printed in *Noctes*, and smoothes out some of the wider intervals and enharmonic twists. Indeed the version of the melody which appears with a lyric collected by Burns for Johnson's *SMM* in 1787 (Vol. 1, no.33) appears to be the melody used by Graham. Graham's notes state that 'the air to which Hogg adopted his words is not a true version of "The Blaithrie o't," but one considerably altered' (III, 82–83). In the 'Appendix', Graham goes further: 'The air given by Hogg resembles one in 6/8 time, to words beginning "O bonnie lassie, blink of the burn,"' said to have been written by the Rev. James Honeyman, minister of Kinneff, in Kincardineshire, and to have been set to music by an itinerant teacher of music, who visited that district'(III, 'Appendix', 170). A variant of Graham's tune is the one still popularly performed with Hogg's lyric today. Thomson's setting is of an altogether different tune, much easier to sing (though with a couple of chromatic corners). His index to the Sixth Volume gives the title of the tune as 'Come all ye jolly shepherds – Air from the Beggar's Opera. The musical arrangement is by Joseph Haydn (see 'Musical Context' for 'The Three Men of Moriston' above). The melody is very similar to that used for the second song (Act 1, Scene ii) in John Gay's *The Beggar's Opera* sung by Filch with the lyrics beginning ''Tis woman that seduces all mankind'. Gay sets this song to the traditional tune of English origin entitled 'The bonny grey-eyed morn'(see *The Beggar's Opera Written by John Gay. The Overture composed and the Songs arranged by John Chrisoph Pepusch*, ed. Edward J. Dent (Oxford: Oxford University Press, 1954), pp. 6–7.

Stenhouse's history of the song also accounts for the lyrics previously published with the melody from the early 1720s onwards. The song, traditionally, focussed on the marriage of a young girl to a wealthy old man. Thereafter, variants of the song, which are published by Herd, Ritson and collected to by Burns, concentrate on the virtue of true love over wealth and goods: i.e. 'the gear and the bagrie [blathrie] o't'. Hogg's reference to this line in his headnote to 1831 suggests he knew about some of these variants.

Explanatory Notes:
See Explanatory Notes in *Contributions to Blackwood's Edinburgh Magazine* I, (S/SC, 2008) p. 490. Also *The Three Perils of Man* (S/SC, 2012), pp. 526–27.

Lenachan's Farewell (pp. 27–28)

Creative Context:
This is another of Hogg's Jacobite songs to appear in *Songs* 1831 and to have come, initially, from the Second Series of *The Jacobite Relics of Scotland* of 1821. For further information see *Jacobite Relics*, II (S/SC, 2003).

While there is little evidence as to the date of its creation, it first appeared in *Jacobite Relics* in 1821 and thereafter, as his headnote attests, in Robert Archibald Smith's *The Scotish Minstrel* where it was included in the sixth and final volume in [1824]. In the first edition the song is printed on p. 45 but later moved to p. 49 in the second, third and subsequent editions. For further information about Hogg's involvement in this collection and a copy of the song see *Contributions to Musical Collections and Miscellaneous Songs*.

Hogg's note in *Jacobite Relics* refers to his having collected the song from Mr John Stewart, who had in turn translated it from a Gaelic emigrant by the name of Macmurich. This would suggest that Hogg is simply a vehicle for transmission, and Murray Pittock notes the lack of textual evidence for Hogg's creation of the song.

Hogg uses the song from *Jacobite Relics* for his reworking of it for 1831. Yet there are a number of changes for 1831: l. 4, 'lad' is changed to 'man' while l. 28 changes from 'Wha could tine our royal name?', which includes a repetition of the beginning of l. 27, to 'Or desert his royal name?' The last lines of verses four and five are freshly drafted. Previously, verse five concluded with 'Wo to the Highlands and to me'. The alteration here is presumably for continuity with Hogg's headnote mention of 'Appin.' In the original version, in l. 33 the comma was placed after the word 'yet', but in *The Scotish Minstrel* the comma is placed after the word 'Freeman', which moves the emphasis from 'yet'and, in doing so, slightly diminishes the boldness of the final verse. Hogg reverts to 'Freeman yet,' (l. 33) for *Songs*. The last line of the concluding verse is also new with Hogg replacing the youthful 'lad' of all previous versions with 'warrior' (l. 40). His headnote emphasises the strength and power of the named Jacobite Alexander Stuart (see Explanatory Notes below), and thus these changes are fitting.

The popularity of many of Hogg's Jacobite songs accounts for his decision to include this one in *Songs* 1831. In November 1828, Hogg had assigned 'sole Copyright' of his songs 'contained in the Scottish Minstrel and Irish Minstrel' to the Edinburgh publisher of these collections, Robert Purdie, with the proviso that he reserved 'to myself the right of publishing any one or all of these songs in a literary work or new edition of the Jacobite Relics'. Hogg then lists the first lines of 17 songs, 14 of which are in the *Scotish Minstrel*, including 'Fare thee weel my native cot': see *Letters*, II, 315–16. While no new edition of the *Relics* was forthcoming, Hogg therefore retained the copyright of the text of 'Lenachan's Farewell', and was able to include it in *Songs* 1831, pp. 56–58. See also notes to 'Farewell to Glen-Shalloch' (p. 12).

The manuscript of 'Lenachan's Farewell' for *Songs* 1831 is missing from the fair-copy manuscript for the collection at NLS MS 4805 (see Janette Currie, 'The Genesis of the Text', pp. xli–xlviii). However, 'Lenachan's Farewell' is found in NLS MS 10256, ff. 64–66 which comprises Hogg's fair-copy holograph manuscript versions of three songs: 'Lenachan's Farewell' (f. 64), the title of 'The Stuarts of Appin' (ff. 64v–65r), and 'The Poor Man' (f. 65). There are only two small emendations between the manuscript and *Songs*, both of which refer to Hogg's headnote: 'escape' is changed to 'elude', while 'The song' replaces 'It is', probably for the sake of clarity. The manuscript also shows signs that Hogg changed his mind as he redrafted the song. At line four he originally writes 'lad', a word found in all previous printed versions. However, he scores it through and writes 'man' above, which is retained in *Songs* 1831.

Publication History:
1821 – in *Jacobite Relics*, II, 189–90 and 370 – see also (S/SC, 2003), p. 522
[1824] – in *The Scotish Minstrel*, VI, 45 – see *Contributions to Musical Collections and Miscellaneous Songs* (S/SC, 2014)
1831 – in *Songs by the Ettrick Shepherd*, pp. 56–58 – see pp. 27–28 in the present edition

Musical Context:
Hogg's headnote refers only to the new musical setting by R. A. Smith for *The Scotish Minstrel* see above. The melody, however, is named in Hogg's notes for the song in the Second Series of *Jacobite Relics* (see above) where he states that the tune 'Ho cha neil mulad oirn' is included in Simon Fraser's *The Airs and Melodies Peculiar to the Highlands of Scotland* of 1816 (no. 226). Hogg clearly admired Fraser's collection, as noted in the case of a number of Jacobite melodies. This one, as printed in *Relics* is both bold but slightly melancholic, and sounds very much like a pipe tune. It is this tune (in a different key) which Smith sets for *The Scotish Minstrel*. In all editions of the *Scotish Minstrel*, Smith prints the Gaelic spelling of the tune with a translation alongside, 'Ho cha neil mulad oir', or 'The Emigrant's Adieu'.

Explanatory Notes:
27 **[headnote] ALEXANDER STUART of Lenachan was a man of gigantic strength, and an officer of the regiment of Appin** Leanachan Glen is situated on the lower slopes of Aonach Mor in Appin. See also 'The Stuarts of Appin'(pp. 28–30). No one named Alexander Stuart has been located, although an Appin man fitting Hogg's description is given in the account of the parish of Lismore and Appin in the first volume of *The Statistical Account of Scotland* (1791). This solider of the 42nd Regiment was named as Carmichael and was more than six feet and was 'the stoutest or thickest man in Britain, or even perhaps in Europe, at the time' (482–502, p. 502). He was obliged to make his escape to America at least three ships with Appin emigrants sailed for North Carolina in the later eighteenth century: see note 28, ll. 12–13.
27, l. 5 **My good grandsire's 'good/gude-brother'** denotes 'brother-in-law' (*DSL*), so that the familial relationship is through marriage.
27, l. 7 **mony a Campbell's glen he cleared** for over four centuries the Campbell lands surrounded the land of the Appin Stuarts, placing the song within the clan's history: see also note 29, l. 14.
27, l. 8 **Hit the buck, an' hough'd the bull** the crest of Clan Campbell is the head of a boar.
27, l. 10 **crusted stanes** a reference to the curious stones found on the island of Lismore as recorded in *The Statistical Account of Scotland* (1791) (I, 494).
27, l. 12 **Clan-Gillian banes** the name appears in Scott's 'War-Song of Lachlan, High Chief of Maclean. From the Gaelic' beginning 'Clan Gillian is to ocean gone'. In a footnote Scott writes: 'The clan of Maclean, literally the race of Gillian': see *The Works of Sir Walter Scott*, 8 vols (Edinburgh: Archibald Constable, 1813), 183–85 (p. 184).
27, l. 15 **Saxon** the English. See Murray Pittock, 'James Hogg: Scottish Romanticism, Song, and the Public Sphere', in *James Hogg and The Literary Marketplace: Scottish Romanticism and the Working Class Author*, eds. Sharon Alker & Holly Faith Nelson, (Surrey: Ashgate, 2009), p. 119. Pittock notes that for Scott

the Saxon was a lowlander, but for Hogg the Saxon was the English.

27, l. 16 Murich's hirst see Hogg's notes to the song in *Jacobite Relics* in 'Creative Context' above. The translation of the song which Hogg collected was apparently taken from a man named Macmurich. In Scots 'hirst' can mean a hillock or ridge and also refer to a gravel bank in the harbour (*DSL*).

28, l. 25 Charlie Stuart he came here Charles Edward Stuart raised the Royal Stuart standard at Glenfinnan in Appin in 1745 : see note 8, l. 2.

28, l. 27 the Bruce's heir Robert the Bruce (1274–1329). In his entry for Bruce in the *ODNB*, G. W. S. Barrow reveals the relationship between the Bruce through 'his mother's earldom of Carrick' and the Appin region.

The Stuarts of Appin (pp. 28–30)

Creative Context:
A full account of the textual and publishing history of 'The Stuarts of Appin' is given in *Contributions to Blackwood's Edinburgh Magazine* I (S/SC, 2008).

In summary, the song is first mentioned in Hogg's letter to William Blackwood of 1 August 1828 (see *Letters*, II, 299–300), but a fair-copy manuscript with a watermark of 1827 is held by Dunedin Public Libraries, New Zealand. The song first appeared in *Blackwood's Edinburgh Magazine* on 24 October 1828 in *Noctes Ambrosianae No. XXXVIII* . In the case of *Songs* 1831 Hogg removes the Noctean context, but the conversation between North and the Shepherd in the magazine makes mention of an honorary dinner for General David Stewart of Garth for which the Shepherd has written two songs. The Shepherd explains that, due to floods, he did not manage to attend the event, but that one of his songs was 'The Stuarts of Appin'. Information about Garth is given in Thomas Richardson's note to *Blackwood's*. Suffice it to say that Garth's Jacobite connections were impressive and he was a supporter of Highland culture. A friend of Walter Scott, Garth was also the man who had initiated the Jacobite Relics' project (see *Jacobite Relics* I, 'Introduction'). It is not known when Hogg met Stewart. In a letter from Alexander Campbell to Stewart dated 16 February 1816, Campbell informs him, 'Mr Hog's (*sic*) friends expect him to town in a few days [...] I know he values you a one of his best friends (quoted from *The First Highlander. Major-General David Stewart of Garth, C. B.*, by James Irvine Robertson (Phantassie, East Lothian: Tuckwell Press, 1998, p. 78). As stated in the 'Noctes', Stewart was appointed Governor and Military Commander of St. Lucia in the summer of 1828. The dinner referred to in the *Noctes* was a real event held by Highland Club of Scotland, in Edinburgh in September 1828. A detailed account of this 'public dinner' which reported the nationalist and patriotic songs, toasts and guests in attendance was printed in *The Edinburgh Evening Courant* of Monday 15 September. Professor Wilson was present, however, there is no mention of Hogg at the dinner.

Richardson's note for the *Blackwood's* appearance of the song also gives an account of its manuscript sources, including the existence of the fair-copy manuscript in the Dunedin Public Libraries, New Zealand mentioned above. A presentation holograph of verses 1, 5 and 6 of the song, titled 'The Appin Coronach' (Gaelic term for a lament), is located at NLS, Acc. 10001. Written neatly in Hogg's hand on paper with an '1815' watermark, the song was presented to Mrs Mary Anne Hughes on her visit to Abbotsford in August 1828: see Hughes's notes in *Letters*, II, , 299–300. The song is end-dated 'Mount-Benger July 27th 1828'. Collation between the holograph and the *Blackwood's* version reveals little re-writing on Hogg's part.

This song is missing from the fair-copy manuscript for *Songs* 1831 at NLS MS 4805, but, as with 'Lenachan's farewell' (above) and 'The Poor Man' (below), a fair copy is found in NLS MS 10256, ff. 64–66 (see 'The Genesis of the Text', pp. xli–xlvii). Hogg clearly uses the *Blackwood's* version for *Songs* 1831: Hogg notes '(Here copy this song from Maga, of which I have no copy)'. There are no major alterations to the text. A fragment of a further holograph manuscript of 'The Stuarts of Appin', written while Hogg was in London in the early months of 1832, is located at the Fales Library, New York. This version relates to the music sheet published by Chappell in *c.*1831–32 (see 'Musical Context' below).

Publication History:

1828 – in *Blackwood's Edinburgh Magazine*, 24 (October 1828), 535 – see (S/SC, 2008), pp. 348–50 and 557–661

1831 – in *Songs by the Ettrick Shepherd*, pp. 59–62 – see pp. 28–30 in the present edition

*c.*1831–32 – The Stuarts of Appin, music by Peter McLeod, arranged by John Thomson (London: S Chappell, 50 New Bond Street) – see *Contributions to Musical Collections and Miscellaneous Songs* (S/SC, 2014)

[1838] – in *Original National Melodies of Scotland*, Composed by Peter McLeod (London: George Virtue, 26 Ivy Lane, Paternoster Row; Edinburgh: A. Crichton, 27 West Register Street, n.d.)[1838]), pp. 192–98. Note: the same song as that published by Chappell in *c.*1831–32. For further information on Hogg's involvement with Peter M'Leod see *Contributions to Musical Collections and Miscellaneous Songs* (S/SC, 2014).

Musical Context:

Hogg writes in his headnote to 'The Stuarts of Appin': 'The song is set to a fine warlike air, by Peter M'Leod, Esq.' (1831, p. 59). The earliest musical setting to be found is that published by the famous London music publisher Samuel Chappell in *c.*1831–32. The song, comprising only the first and last verses, with a melody composed by M'Leod and arranged by the Edinburgh composer John Thomson, appeared almost exactly a year after publication of *Songs* 1831: for more information see *Contributions to Musical Collections and Miscellaneous Songs.* Writing to M'Leod from London on 27 February 1832, Hogg informs him of its recent publication and relates how he had been present in Chappell's shop when Thomson had performed several songs attempting to interest him in a collection of Scottish songs. Hogg writes how 'Thomson [...] did them ample justice': see NLS, MS 2208, fols. 39–40. While Hogg's headnote, written in 1830, reveals that M'Leod's music was composed for the song before Hogg's London visit, it is not known when M'Leod first composed the music, nor how Thomson came to arrange it.

A holograph manuscript of the song in the Fales Library, New York appears to be the copy text of the Chappell music sheet. This is confirmed by Hogg's directions at the beginning and end of the manuscript where he directs that 'singing stanzas' and 'the chorus of each song to be printed in full' and by his end note stating it was 'Written off-hand in the British Coffee-House on the 21st of Janr 1832 – for a queer callant they ca' John Mc Crone – By the Ettrick Shepherd': see Fales Manuscript Collection, Box 89, folder 21. Although the manuscript consists of three verses of the song (1, 3 and 6 of *Songs,* 1831), Chappell omitted the second verse so that only the first and last verse and chorus appear on the song sheet.

'Lament for the Stuarts of Appin' is a further printing of the song as a music score. It appeared in the third and final edition of *Original National Melodies of Scotland*, Composed by Peter M'Leod (London: George Virtue, 26 Ivy Lane, Paternoster Row; Edinburgh: A. Crichton, 27 West Register Street, n.d.)[1838]), pp. 192–98. Collation with Chappell's score of 1832 reveals only one substantive alteration: the omission of Hogg's gloss to the Gaelic refrain that was inserted as a footnote to p. 3.

Explanatory Notes:
See *Contributions to Blackwood's Edinburgh Magazine* I (S/SC, 2008), pp. 559–61.

The Poor Man (pp. 30–31)

Creative Context:
It is most likely that this song was composed in the mid-1810s for inclusion in *A Border Garland*, Hogg's collection of nine songs produced by the Edinburgh music publisher Nathaniel Gow & Sons in [1819]: for further information see *Contributions to Musical Collections and Miscellaneous Songs*. There is scant information about the context for its creation. It does fall into a popular category of the 'Fensterlied' or 'Window song' in which the (in most cases) female protagonist is encouraged to let her lover in either to her garden, in this case, or through her window in many other cases. This song changes little over its many appearances in Hogg's lifetime. Hogg's headnote here refers to the later musical setting of the song, by James Dewar, in *The Border Garland c.*1829: see *Contributions to Musical Collections and Miscellaneous Songs*.

There is only one extant fair-copy manuscript for the song, namely that found alongside 'Lenachan's Farewell' and 'The Stuarts of Appin' as NLS MS 10256, ff. 64–66: 'The Poor Man' (f. 65). Hogg's manuscript is page-numbered 27 and 28 and his unpunctuated text is transferred cleanly to the printed volume, with the exception of 'beaming' (line 11) becoming 'bonny', the latter of which appears in the previously published musical versions of the song. Hogg's text for 1831 clearly comes from the text as published in its two musical versions, though he makes a change to the final line from 'O how it shall plead for thee' to 'That blest drop shall plead for thee'.

Publication history:
[1819] – in *A Border Garland*, pp. 12–13 – see *Contributions to Musical Collections and Miscellaneous Songs* (S/SC, 2014)
*c.*1829 – in *The Border Garland*, pp. 22–24 – see *Contributions to Musical Collections and Miscellaneous Songs* (S/SC, 2014)
1831 – in *Songs by the Ettrick Shepherd*, pp. 63–64 – see pp. 30–31 in the present edition

Unauthorised versions:
The song was included in *The Spirit of British Song*, a miscellaneous collection of poems and songs edited by John Goldie which originally appeared in numbers in 1825–26. It was issued by the Glasgow publisher W. R. McPhun and was dedicated to the celebrated contemporary singer 'Miss Stephens' who also had associations with Hogg's song 'Bonnie Prince Charlie' (see *Contributions to Musical Collections and Miscellaneous Songs*). Further information about Goldie and his collection can be found in *The Contemporaries of Burns, and the More Recent Poets of*

Ayrshire (Edinburgh: Hugh Paton, Carver & Gilder, 1840), pp. 213–32.

Musical Context:
Hogg's headnote states that he has composed this melody or air himself. Its first musical appearance in *A Border Garland* [1819] states that the 'Air' is 'By a Friend of the Editor' and its later appearance in *The Border Garland c.*1829 states: 'Air, by a Friend of the Poet'. This is one of few songs where Hogg claims authorship of the music and the nature of the melody, both simple and fiddle-like, would certainly support Hogg's claim, but no further evidence has been sourced to prove his authorship. The setting in *A Border Garland* of [1819] is most likely by William Heather. James Dewar's later setting for *The Border Garland* is the setting which Hogg promotes in his 1831 headnote. Dewar sets the same melody with slight variants, though it is transposed to a lower key which is much easier to sing.

Explanatory Notes:
30 [Title] caring for the poor is a central Christian tenet of the New Testament Gospels, found, for example, in Matt. 19. 21, 'If thou wilt be perfect, go and sell that thou hast, and give to the poor, and thou shalt have treasure in heaven'.
30, ll. 9–10 Ye shall gain a virgin hue, | Lady, for your courtesye as a Presbyterian who worshipped in the Church of Scotland, Hogg would have been taught according to the tenets of the *Westminster Confession of Faith* that mankind is born into the 'Original Sin' of Adam and Eve and therefore sinful. Hogg's song implies that the 'lady' can enter a state of grace, or be redeemed from this sin by practicing Christian charity or 'Good Works'.
31, ll. 21–22 what thou on earth hast given, | Doubly shall be paid again! see Matt. 5.12 (part of Christ's Sermon on the Mount): 'great is your reward in heaven.'

The Women Fo'k (pp. 31–32)

Creative Context:
A full account of the textual and publishing history of 'The Women Fo'k' is given in *Contributions to Blackwood's Edinburgh Magazine* I (S/SC, 2008).

In summary, as with 'The Poor Man' which immediately precedes it in *Songs* 1831, 'The Women Fo'k' appears to have been created in collaboration with the composer William Heather for Hogg's musical collection *A Border Garland* [1819] and the first verse and chorus of the song is mentioned in Hogg's letter to Heather of 1 April 1818 (*Letters*, I, 343–45). Hogg reminds Heather that this song is 'of two parts and a chorus which I think is set on two sharps'. More information about Heather and Hogg's involvement with him is given in *Contributions to Musical Collections and Miscellaneous Songs.*

It was then included in *Blackwood's Edinburgh Magazine*, in December 1822 where it was 'performed' by 'Hogg' as part of *Noctes Ambrosianae* No. VI as an interlude to the conversation of the latest publications between 'Tickler', 'Blackwood', 'North', 'Kempherhausen', and 'Hogg'. As Richardson notes, it is the first appearance of Hogg as 'Hogg' and not as the 'Shepherd' in *Noctes Ambrosianae* No. VI. Interestingly Hogg makes no reference in his 1831 headnote to its Blackwoodian context, nor does he give the contextual discussion from *Noctes*. Instead he chooses to refer to its appearances in *A Border Garland* [1819] and *The Border Garland* of *c.*1829.

Richardson notes that there are only minor variants in spelling and punctuation between the different versions of the song. There is one later appearance of part of the song (its third stanza) as 'Song X' in the Blackie published version of Hogg's drama 'The Bush Aboon Traquair' Act III, Scene 1 in *Tales and Sketches* of 1836–37 (see: *The Bush Aboon Traquair*, ed. Douglas Mack, (S/SC, 2008).

The fair-copy manuscript for *Songs* 1831 is found at NLS, MS 4805, ff. 39r–40r. Hogg makes several emendations to the headnote in relation to the song's Musical Context (see below). Hogg has numbered the pages in the top corners beginning with '29' (f. 39r) and ending with '31' (f. 40r) which has been scored through. At the left-hand side of f. 39r, beside the title, is the printer's mark 'C/65'. This matches its place in the printed volume.

Publication History:

[1819] – in *A Border Garland*, pp. 6–7 – see *Contributions to Musical Collections and Miscellaneous Songs*, (S/SC, 2014)

1822 – in *Blackwood's Edinburgh Magazine*, 12 (December 1822), 705–06 – see (S/SC, 2008), pp. 95, 365, and 474–75

*c.*1829 – in *The Border Garland*, pp. 31–33 – see *Contributions to Musical Collections and Miscellaneous Songs* (S/SC, 2014)

1831 – in *Songs by the Ettrick Shepherd*, pp. 65–67 – see pp. 31–32 in the present edition

1836–37 – an extract only in *Tales & Sketches*, (Glasgow: Blackie & Son, 1836–37) – see (S/SC, 2008), pp. 102, 180. See also the fair-copy manuscript in the Alexander Turnbull Library, New Zealand (pp. 45, 175–76).

Musical Context:

Hogg's headnote emphatically states that the air or melody for this song is 'my own'. His emendations to the manuscript suggest that he thought twice about this descriptor. At the end of the headnote, Hogg originally wrote the words 'No air. It is my own composition' but this is then scored out. He initially began the headnote with the words 'This song' but scores this out and begins more emphatically, 'The air of this song is my own', which is retained in the published version. This information is given also in its first musical appearance in *A Border Garland* of [1819] where it states: 'Air, by James Hogg', and in the later *The Border Garland* of c.1829, the song is presented as 'Words and Melody' by Hogg. It is a characteristically bold and rhythmic tune. While the melody is the same in both musical collections, the two musical settings (firstly by William Heather and secondly by James Dewar) are in different keys, only the Heather setting adhering to the 'two sharps' referred to in Hogg's letter. Musical notation of Hogg's melody was also provided for the song's appearance in the *Noctes*, and it is probable that the source for this was *A Border Garland* [1819]. For further information and to view these settings see *Contributions to Musical Collections and Miscellaneous Songs*.

A further setting of the song was 'composed expressly for the musical magazine the *Harmonicon*' by Edwin J. Nielson (see *Contributions to Musical Collections and Miscellaneous Songs*). Hogg may have authorised the publication of this version of the song, which coincided with Hogg his visit to London at the beginning of 1832. The text is clearly derived from *Songs* 1831 as the second verse contains the newly created words 'I hae thought an' thought' (l. 1). It appeared in *The Harmonicon*, Vol. 10, Pt. 2 (London, 1832), 70–71. A separate song sheet version of this setting by Nielson appeared with the heading 'The Women Fo'k. A Ballad. The Poetry by the Ettrick Shepherd. Composed by Edwin J Nielson, Member of the Royal Academy of Music London', (Philadelphia: Fiot, Meignen & Co. Philadelphia, [1835]. Neither of these settings, however, uses Hogg's air or melody.

M'Lean's Welcome (pp. 32–33)

Creative Context:

This is one of the key group of Jacobite songs included by Hogg in *Songs* 1831 and he gives new information about the creation of this song in his 1831 headnote.

The song had previously appeared with another informative note by Hogg in *Jacobite Relics* II in 1821. Murray Pittock's editorial note (S/SC, 2003) concludes that this song is Hogg's own creation, even though Hogg himself suggests that he 'versified' it from a Gaelic source. In his 1831 headnote, however, Hogg gives even more specific Creative Context noting that his inspiration for the song was a visit to Meggernie Castle in Glen-Lyon and the performance of the song by 'one of the sweetest singers'. It is possible that this singer was the lady of the house, Mrs Menzies of Culdares, who died in 1829, and after whom a fiddle tune had been named which had appeared in fiddle collections by Joshua Campbell and the Gow family from the 1780s onwards. Indeed some Hogg's headnote echoes phrases contained within a letter of 1 June 1816 to Mrs Anne Bald: 'I write to you from a very romantic and beautiful spot indeed yet the greatest beauty about the castle is its lady who is one of those beings that grace out nature and form the combining link be[tween?] angels and the human race' (*Letters*, I, 277–78, p. 278). If this is the case, then composition of the song predates, by more than a year, the commission to collect and edit Jacobite Relics in 1817: see Murray Pittock's Introduction to *Jacobite Relics*, I, xix–xx. Further evidence that this is Hogg's own composition and not a true Jacobite song is found in the Turnbull MS in New Zealand, which, as Pittock notes, identifies this as 'a late song'.

Hogg refers to Robert Archibald Smith's setting of the song in [1823] in the first edition of the fifth volume of *The Scotish Minstrel*: see *Contibutions to Musical Collections and Miscellaneous Songs*. While there are one or two emendations it is clear that the *Relics* text had been used by Smith. For *Songs* 1831 Hogg sticks to this text with few emendations. In 1831, for the first time, the refrain is written in full at the beginning of each verse and the layout of each verse changes from four lines to eight shorter lines.

Hogg's fair-copy holograph version of the text found in *Songs* 1831 is in the fair-copy manuscript for the collection at NLS MS 4805, ff. 40r–41r. Overall, Hogg's unpunctuated manuscript is transferred cleanly to the printed text.

Publication History:

1821 – in *Jacobite Relics*, II, 90–92 and 300–01 – see (S/SC, 2003), also pp. 505–06

[1823] – in *The Scotish Minstrel*, V, 54–55 – see *Contributions to Musical Collections and Miscellaneous Songs* (S/SC, 2014)

1831 – in *Songs by the Ettrick Shepherd*, pp. 68–70 – see pp. 32–33 in the present edition

Unauthorised versions:

Two unauthorised printings appear to be taken from the version in *The Scotish Minstrel* with several textual variants. The first is printed under a different title, 'M'Lean's Invitation to Prince Charles', ascribed to 'Hogg' in Robert Chambers' *Scottish Songs*, 2 vols (Edinburgh: William Tait, 1829), II, 438–39. The second unauthorised version to appear in Hogg's lifetime is an American version reprinted in an anthology titled, *The Souvenir Minstrel: A Choice Collection of the Most Admired Songs, Duets, Glees, Choruses, etc* edited by Co. Soule Cartee (Philadelphia: Marshall, Clark & Co,, 1833), pp. 162–63. In this version, the title is taken from the first line 'Come O'er the Stream Charlie'. No author is ascribed, and, while a note states it has been 'adapted to Music', it does not say either where or by whom. Gooch and Thatcher list a further ten unauthorised and later versions of the song: 8732–8741.

Musical Context:
Hogg's note to the song in *Jacobite Relics* is very useful here for he refers to the variant of the melody included in Simon Fraser's *The Airs and Melodies Peculiar to the Highlands of Scotland* of 1816 and notes also that 'his [Fraser's] are always 'the best sets I have either seen or heard. Hogg is often critical of William Stenhouse's notation for the *Relics*. In this case Stenhouse's simple unnamed melody is that also used (in the same key) by Smith in *The Scotish Minstrel*.

Explanatory Notes:
33, l. 1 COME o'er the stream the MacLeans of Drimin held lands in Morvern, Argyllshire, 'on the Sound of Mull, opposite Tobermory, 121/2 miles NW of Morvern hamlet' (Groome).
33, ll. 9–16 We'll bring down the track deer, [...] and curd from the pen William Donaldson writes that these lines are 'far from the beggary and want traditionally associated with the *Gaidhealtachd*': see *The Jacobite Song: Political Myth and National Identity* (Aberdeen: Aberdeen University Press, 1988), pp. 103–04 (p. 103).
33, l. 10 black steer according to Marianne McLean's study, *The People of Glengarry: Highlanders in Transition, 1745–1820*, black cattle were an important livestock for the Highlanders (Montreal & Quebec: McGill–Queen's Press, 1993), p. 31.
33, ll. 21–24 And you shall drink freely [...] When kings do not ken William Donaldson comments, 'in Hogg's Highland Elysium, even ardent spirits lose their harsher connotations, and illicit poteen is transported into a lyrical and exalted substance' *The Jacobite Song: Political Myth and National Identity* (Aberdeen: Aberdeen University Press, 1988), pp. 103–04 (p. 103). Prior to the passing of the Excise Act in 1823 there were many illicit whisky stills over the Highlands and Islands of Scotland.
33, l. 22 Glen-sheerly a fictitious place-name, possibly a reference to the sheer or high mountainous sides of Glenlyon.
33, l. 40 Three hundred and ten figures giving the strength of the MacLeans in the campaign of 1745 vary in different historical accounts between 200 and 500. Hogg's precise number '310' is possibly taken from John Home's account of the number of casualties inflicted on the Government side at Culloden: see *The History of the Rebellion in the Year 1745* (1802), p. 237.

The Maid of the Sea (pp. 34–35)

Creative Context:
As with 'The Minstrel Boy' (p. 11) this is one of the group of eight Irish songs Hogg includes in *Songs* 1831 and which were created initially for Robert Archibald Smith's musical collection *The Irish Minstrel* of [1825], where this song appeared under the title of its first line 'Come from the Sea'. For further information on this set of songs and Hogg's involvement in Smith's collection and their wrangle with Thomas Moore's publishers, the Power brothers, alluded to in Hogg's headnote see: *Contributions to Musical Collections and Miscellaneous Songs*.

Comparison might be made with Thomas Moore's version of the song, titled 'Come o'er the sea', first published in the sixth number of *Irish Melodies* in 1815 (i). Hogg's headnote for 1831 notes that he intends to 'contradict' Moore.

Hogg clearly used the copy of his song in *The Irish Minstrel* as his copy text for *Songs* 1831 and there is only slight alteration in punctuation and one word change: line 11 'surging' becomes 'stormy'.

Hogg's fair-copy holograph version of the text found in *Songs* 1831 is extant at NLS MS 4805, ff. 41r–42r. Overall, Hogg's unpunctuated manuscript is transferred cleanly to the printed text without change.

Publication History:
[1825] – in *The Irish Minstrel*, pp. 100–01 – see *Contributions to Musical Collections and Miscellaneous Songs* (S/SC, 2014)
1831 – in *Songs by the Ettrick Shepherd*, pp. 71–72 – see pp. 34–35 in the present edition

Musical Context:
Hogg refers his reader to R. A. Smith's setting mentioned above. The Irish air 'Cuishlih ma chree' is used. The melody which Smith uses is in the same key and is very close to that found in Moore's *Irish Melodies*, which suggests that this was Smith's source. There is only one notable difference when Smith deletes the F sharp Moore inserts in bar 12, preferring instead G followed by A. There are few possible printed sources for Moore although a manuscript – Dr Kelly's music book – is named by Veronica Ní Chinnéide. In July 1814, Moore writes about Kelly's book 'which contains no less than four or five very pretty airs for our purpose' and promises to send a completed one in a few days. 'Cuishlah mo chree' is dispatched to his publisher James Power soon after; the poet later writes to Power to ask for the correct spelling of the air 'according to Dr Kelly' which accounts for the slight alteration in the title: see Veronica Ní Chinnéide, 'The Sources of Moore's Irish Melodies', *Journal of the Royal Society of Antiquaries of Ireland* (1959), 111–12.

Explanatory Notes:
34, ll. 1–2 COME from the sea, | Maiden, to me the opening two lines of Hogg's song echo the beginning of Moore's song: 'Come o'er the sea, | Maiden! with me' (ll. 1–2).
34, l. 8 Death's where thou art, as where thou art not, love contains strong echoes of the eighth line of Moore's song. However, Hogg's version reverses Moore's more positive romantic imagery. In Moore's song, there is 'life where thou art' and 'death where thou art not!' (l. 8).
34, ll. 15–16 Is not the wave | Made for the slave, | Tyrant's chains, and stern control once again Hogg reverses Moore's imagery. In Moore's song, the sea is 'Made for the free' while 'Lands' are 'for courts and chains alone?' (l. 15 and l. 17).

Go Home to your Rest (p. 35)

Creative Context:
As above, this is another of the eight Irish songs, here referred to as 'the proscribed M'Gregors', which Hogg includes in *Songs* 1831 and were written initially for Robert Archibald Smith's *The Irish Minstrel* in [1825]. For further information on

this set of songs and Hogg's involvement in Smith's collection and their wrangle with Thomas Moore's publishers, the Power brothers, alluded to in Hogg's headnote see: *Contributions to Musical Collections and Miscellaneous Songs.*

This song appeared initially under the title 'Go home, Go Home' and it is a contrasting lyric to Thomas Moore's 'The Young May-Moon' first published in the fifth number of his *Irish Melodies* in 1813 (v), to the tune 'The Dandy O' with which is may be closely compared. The copy text of the *Songs* 1831 version of Hogg's 'Go Home to Your Rest' is that of *The Irish Minstrel.* The text remains unaltered with only slight changes to punctuation.

Hogg's fair-copy holograph version of the text found in Songs 1831 is extant within NLS MS 4805, f. 42r directly below the conclusion of 'The Maid of the Sea'. Hogg directs the printer to rearrange the layout of line three with the words 'new line' written after the word 'rove' to indicate that the line should be split into two, as it is in the original version. Hogg's direction is carried out in the printed volume. Overall, Hogg's unpunctuated manuscript is transferred cleanly to the printed text. The song appears on pp. 73–74 in *Songs by the Ettrick Shepherd* (1831).

Publication History:
[1825]– in *The Irish Minstrel,* p. 88 – see *Contributions to Musical Collections and Miscellaneous Songs* (S/SC, 2014)
1831 – in *Songs by the Ettrick Shepherd,* pp. 73–74 – see p. 35 in the present edition

Musical Context:
As Hogg states in his headnote, the traditional Irish air of 'The Dandy, O' is used for this lyric. Although Smith's setting is in a different key (B flat) to Moore's (in C) and there are some rhythmical differences, there are enough similarities to suggest that Smith used Moore's *Irish Melodies* as his source. Moore probably got the tune from Shield's *Robin Hood* (1784) where it is noted as an Irish tune, but its name is a misnomer. The title belongs to another tune which Moore used in his song 'Eveleen's Bower' (*Irish Melodies*, II, vii) although in the latter Moore gives the title as 'unknown'. Veronica ní Chinnéide cites Moffat as the source of a theory that Moore's name for the air originated from part of the second verse of the song in Shield's work, which reads: 'And I'm her a-dandy O': see Veronica Ní Chinnéide: 'The Sources of Moore's Irish Melodies', *Journal of the Royal Society of Antiquaries of Ireland* (1959), 123.

Explanatory Notes:
35, l. 4 **Morna's grove** in Fingalian legend, Morna is 'fairest of women, daughter of Cormac-Carbre': see *Fragments of Ancient Poetry* XV, reprinted in *The Poems of Ossian and Related Works,* edited by Howard Gaskill, with an Introduction by Fiona Stafford (Edinburgh: Edinburgh University Press, 1996), pp. 29–30 (p. 29). The name 'Muirne or Morna' denotes 'a woman beloved by all' (*The Poems of Ossian and Related Works,* note, p. 567).

The Harp of Ossian (pp. 35–36)

Creative Context:
This song was created for the London music publisher Goulding & D'Almaine who published thirteen of Hogg's songs, with musical settings by Sir Henry Bishop, as *Select & Rare Scotish Melodies* in [1828]. For more information about Hogg's involvement with Goulding & D'Almaine and copies of the songs in

Select & Rare Scotish Melodies see: *Contributions to Musical Collections and Miscellaneous Songs.* Although it is not known exactly when or how the publisher approached him, Hogg sent a number of songs to them, through their Edinburgh agent Robert Purdie in 1828, and he was keen to alert them to songs and melodies from the North, which they might not otherwise know. This song is particularly nationalistic in its sentiment and this is clearly referred to in Hogg's headnote for its appearance in *Songs* 1831. However, this particular song was not included by Goulding & D'Almaine in *Select & Rare Scotish Melodies.* Instead they published it along with Hogg's 'My Emma, My Darling' (see p. 40 and notes), in one of their musical annuals, the *Musical Bijou for MDCCCXXIX [1829]*, edited by F. H. Burney with Henry R. Bishop's musical arrangement.

The copy text for the *Songs* 1831 version is the song as it appears in the *Musical Bijou*, although there are a number of variants, which enhance the nostalgic sentiment of the song. More substantive changes include the move of emphasis from the 'old harp of Ossian' to the 'harp of old Ossian' (l. 16)'. 'Thy fathers', becomes the more personal 'my fathers' (l. 23). And in the final line the emphasis moves from the Highlander completely as 'forgetful of me' changes to 'forgetful of thee' (l. 24).

The fair-copy version of the song Hogg revised for inclusion in *Songs* 1831 survives within NLS MS 4805, ff. 42v–43r. Hogg is clearly fine-tuning his work for the new collection in l.14, where he scores out the repetition of the word 'lost' and replaces it with 'sunk' written above, a change which is retained in the printed version. Aside from the usual addition of punctuation 'The Harp of Ossian' is transmitted cleanly to the printed version.

Publication History:

1829 – in *The Musical Bijou for MDCCCXXIX [1829]*, edited by F. H. Burney (London: Goulding and D'Almaine), p. 2 (text), pp. 3–7 (music): see *Contributions to Annuals and Gift Books*, (S/SC, 2006), pp. 143–48 (text); pp. 392–93 (notes)

1831 – in *Songs by the Ettrick Shepherd*, pp. 75–76 – see pp. 35–56 in the present edition

Musical Context:

The choice of melody and musical arrangement were those of Sir Henry Bishop and, as his headnote suggests, Hogg regarded them most highly.

Explanatory Notes:

See *Contributions to Annuals and Gift Books*, (S/SC, 200), pp. 392–93.

When Maggy Gangs Away (pp. 36–37)

Creative Context:

As with 'The Harp of Ossian' which immediately precedes it on *Songs* 1831, this song was created for inclusion in the London publisher Goulding & D'Almaine's *Select & Rare Scotish Melodies* in [1828], where it appeared with the title 'O What Will a' the Lads Do?'. For more information about Hogg's involvement with Goulding & D'Almaine and copies of the songs in *Select & Rare Scotish Melodies* see: *Contributions to Musical Collections and Miscellaneous Songs.*

There are two possible subjects for the song: Hogg's wife, Margaret, and his second daughter, Margaret Laidlaw Hogg. Hogg's 1831 headnote suggests that it was his daughter he had in mind. Hogg's wife, Margaret Phillips came from

Dumfriesshire and Hogg's reference to 'the laird of Langshaw' (l. 17) may refer to the historical estate and laird's house at Langshaw near Dumfries. But there is also a ruined 'Langshaw House' in the Borders (see Peter Garside's note to *The Private Memoirs and Confessions of a Justified Sinner* (S/SC, 2002, p. 207). Hogg's correspondence to his wife from the summer of 1827 onwards makes reference to the family's need to leave Ettrick and travel regularly to Edinburgh (see *Letters*, II, 301–08), hence the content of Hogg's song.

Hogg clearly uses the text as it appears in *Select & Rare Scotish Melodies* for *Songs* 1831 with one notable change: the third stanza, from 'The priest in confidence has said' to 'The priest has said – in confidence – ' in *Songs* 1831 (l. 3).

Hogg's fair-copy manuscript of the 1831 text is included in NLS MS 4805, ff. 43–44. Hogg scores out 'rue' and replaces it with 'dread' (l. 6). Otherwise the song is cleanly transferred to *Songs* 1831.

Publication History:
[1828] – in *Select & Rare Scotish Melodies*, pp. 5–9 – see *Contributions to Musical Collections and Miscellaneous Songs* (S/SC, 2014)
1831 – in *Songs by the Ettrick Shepherd*, pp. 77–78 – see pp. 36–37 in this edition
*c.*1834–1858 – O! What Will a' the Lads Do, A Popular Scotch Air. Arranged as a Duet. The Poetry Written by The Ettrick Shepherd. The Music Arranged by Sir Henry Bishop. London D'Almaine & Co, 20 Soho Square – in *Contributions to Musical Collections and Miscellaneous Songs* (S/SC, 2014)

Unauthorised versions:
This song was clearly popular. Later nineteenth-century versions include an American music pamphlet titled *O What will a' the Lads Do? and When the Kye Come Hame: Two Popular Songs, Written by Hogg, the Ettrick Shepherd*, with music by William Rogers, published in 1844 by the Boston music-publishing company, G. P. Reed. Although the spelling of 'Maggie' has been altered, the text is closest to the version in *Songs* 1831. And the tune is not that used by Bishop and referred to by Hogg in 1831. [Above information is derived from the 'Music for the Nation: American Sheet Music, *c.*1820–1860', part of the important *American Memory* project managed by the Library of Congress at http://memory.loc.gov/ammem, accessed August 2013]. A version derived from *Songs* was reprinted in the Philadelphian *Lady's Book*, 3 (October 1831), 227. Further details of the American publication of Hogg's songs can be found in the *Listing of Hogg Items in the American Periodical Press*, by Janette Currie, at the online *James Hogg Research* website hosted by the Division of Literature and Languages, School of Arts and Humanities, Stirling University, http://www.jameshogg.stir.ac.uk.

Musical Context:
The musical arrangement to which Hogg refers is that of Sir Henry Bishop in *Select & Rare Scotish Melodies* and clearly Hogg approved of his setting, as he states in his headnote to 1831. The tune bears a close similarity to the tune for which Burns wrote his lyrics beginning 'I'll ay ca' in by yon toun' which appeared in the *SMM* , Vol V (1796), No 458 (p. 470–71). The melody is known as 'I'll gae na [nae] mair to your [yon] town' and Glen notes that the tune had appeared in Oswald's *Caledonian Pocket Companion* (book x, p. 15). Gore's *Scottish Fiddle Index* notes its popularity across a wide range of musical collections and that it also had connections with the dance tune 'The Eight Men of Moidart'.

A Father's Lament (pp. 37–38)

Creative Context:

Hogg's headnote explains the Creative Context for this song, written in memory of his young friend Robert Anderson who had died on 20 November 1823. Hogg enclosed the song in a letter to Robert's father, Adam, of 28 April 1828 in which he remembered the 'acute feelings I had at that time by putting myself in your place' (*Letters*, II, 290–91).

After noting in his letter to Anderson that he intended this song to be a 'private memorial', Hogg then sent the lyric as one of a group of songs to the London music publisher Goulding & D'Almaine in 1828 and a revised version of the song appeared under the title 'I downa laugh, I downa sing' in *Select & Rare Scotish Melodies* in [1828] with a musical setting by Sir Henry Bishop. This was reprinted then in the musical magazine *The Harmonicon* in 1829. This version clearly advertised it as 'just published by GOULDING & D'ALMAINE' and it prints Bishop's setting but using new musical plates. It also advertises that this issue of the magazine included a review of *Select & Rare Scotish Melodies*. For further information see *Contributions to Musical Collections and Miscellaneous Songs*. As with other songs included in *Select & Rare*, Gouldling & D'Almaine did reissue the song as a separate song sheet and copies of this have been found with the same pagination and the note in the bottom of the musical plate 'Songs of the Ettrick Shepherd. B. 1'.

Gillian Hughes has noted that a version of the song with the title 'The Blank at My Right Hand' then appeared in the short-lived *Monthly Musical and Literary Magazine* in May 1830. There were few variants, though Hughes notes one significant change: 'the supreme decree' becomes 'the devine decree' in l. 22. See Hughes, 'Hogg and the Monthly Musical and Literary Magazine, in *Studies in Hogg and his World*, 15 (2004), 120–25.

The manuscript of the first version of the song entitled 'In Memory of Mr Robert Anderson' was included in Hogg's letter to Adam Anderson, dated 28 April 1828 (NLS, MS 3112, fols 278–79, with a typescript copy in NLS, MS 1758, fols 7–9: the full text is reproduced in *Letters*, II, 290–91). The manuscript of 'I Downa Laugh, I Downa Sing' for *Select & Rare Scotish Melodies* has not survived. But the copy of the song used for *Songs* 1831 is found in NLS MS 4805, f. 44. When composing his headnote Hogg scored out the word 'his' which is an unnecessary addition, and changes his mind over the word 'reccollection' changing it to 'remembrance'; both authorial changes are retained in the printed version.

Publication History:

[1828] – in *Select & Rare Scotish Melodies*, pp. 15–18 – see *Contributions to Musical Collections and Miscellaneous Songs* (S/SC, 2014)

1829 – in *The Harmonicon*, VII, Part 2 (January 1829), pp. 8–9 – see *Contributions to Muscial Collections and Miscellaneous Songs* (S/SC, 2014)

1830 – as 'The Blank in My Right Hand' in the *Monthly Musical and Literary Magazine* (May 1830), 94

1831 – in *Songs by the Ettrick Shepherd*, pp. 79–80 – see pp. 37–38 in the present edition

Unauthorised versions:

1835 – 'A Father's Lament. By James Hogg', in *The Zodiac, A Monthly Periodical devoted to Science, Literature and the Arts* 2 vols (Albany, New York: E. Perry, 1835–

36), I, No. 9, March 1835, p. 144. This version may have derived from the 1832 American edition of Hogg's songs published in New York by William Stodart. Further details of the American publication of Hogg's songs can be found in the *Listing of Hogg Items in the American Periodical Press,* by Janette Currie, at the online *James Hogg Research* website hosted by the Division of Literature and Languages, School of Arts and Humanities, Stirling University, http://www.jameshogg.stir. ac.uk.

Musical Context:
Hogg gives no indication as to a melodic starting point for the song's creation. It is thought that Bishop created both the melody and setting for this song and as with the two songs which precede it in *Songs* 1831, Hogg refers to the song as being 'finely set by Bishop'.

There's Gowd in the Breast (pp. 38–39)

Creative Context:
This is another of the eight 'proscribed' Irish songs which Hogg includes in *Songs* 1831 and which he wrote initially for Robert Archibald Smith's *The Irish Minstrel* in [1825]. For further information on this set of songs and Hogg's involvement in Smith's collection and their wrangle with Thomas Moore's publishers, the Power brothers, alluded to in Hogg's headnote see: *Contributions to Musical Collections and Miscellaneous Songs.*

It was first published in *The Irish Minstrel* of [1825] and like the other Irish songs Hogg includes in *Songs* 1831 it has a counterpart or companion lyric by Thomas Moore. In this case the partner is Moore's 'Let Erin Remember' which is set to the Irish tune 'The Red Fox' and appeared in the second number of *Irish Melodies* in 1808 (viii). Hogg's reference, in his 1831 headnote, that he does not have 'Mr Moore's songs by me' is notable in the case of his songs for the first edition of *The Irish Minstrel,* most of which bear a dangerously close resemblance to Moore's originals. Moore's *Irish Melodies* was published in ten numbers between 1808 and 1834 and also in a single volume that printed the text of the songs without the musical settings. In his letter to William Blackwood of 30 September 1830 Hogg suggests publishing 'a vol of select songs wholly my own in the manner Moore has done': see *Letters,* II, 407–08 (p. 408). Hughes notes (p. 409) 'the *Irish Melodies* [...] were published without the accompanying music in a single volume by J. Power of London in 1821 [...]. [...]. An eighth edition had been published in 1827, and this popular volume was clearly a model for *Songs by the Ettrick Shepherd.*'

Edith Batho has already commented (Batho, *The Ettrick Shepherd,* 1927, p. 152) that the tune 'The Red Fox' is, however, the only point of similarity between the lyrics of Hogg and Moore in the case of this song. Hogg's text is altogether different and, as a result, it is one of only three of the Irish songs to be granted a place in Smith's second edition of *The Irish Minstrel.*

The copy text of the *Songs* 1831 version of 'There's Gowd in the Breast' is the first edition of *The Irish Minstrel* [1825]. The text is altered, slightly, in both verses. Firstly, 'Sweet nature to us has no alloy' becomes 'Sweet nature for us has no alloy' (l. 7); secondly, 'The proud in the pomp around them' becomes 'The proud in their pomp surroundings' (l. 12). Such slight verbal variation of the wording suggests that Hogg rewrote the song from memory.

Hogg's fair-copy manuscript of the text found in *Songs* 1831 is extant at NLS MS 4805, f. 45r. The words 'it is' are additional to the printed volume and are clearly added to clarify the syntax of the phrase 'I know not if [it is] in existence'.

Publication History:
[1825] – in *The Irish Minstrel*, p. 76 – see *Contributions to Musical Collections and Miscellaneous Songs* (S/SC, 2014)
*c.*1828 – in *The Irish Minstrel*, p. 76 – see *Contributions to Musical Collections and Miscellaneous Songs* (S/SC, 2014)
1831 – in *Songs by the Ettrick Shepherd*, pp. 81–82 – see pp. 38–39 in the present edition

Musical Context:
The traditional Irish air of 'The Red Fox' is nominated as the melody for the song in both editions of *The Irish Minstrel* and there are enough similarities to suggest that Smith used Moore's *Irish Melodies* as his source. Smith's setting is in F Major rather than G Major and the Moore setting is more jaunty or militaristic in its rhythms and with a different ending, but otherwise the two songs are close. Moore most probably sourced the tune from Smollet Holden's *A Collection of Old Established Irish Slow and Quick Tunes,* book II (Dublin c1805) where it is called 'The red dog or fox'. There are actually two versions printed in Holden (called 'sets') which follow each other in Fleischmann's records, but the first of these is closer to Moore's version of the air: see Aloys Fleischmann, ed.: *Sources of Irish Traditional Music c.1600–1855,* 2 vols. (New York andLondon: Garland, 1998), p. 838.

Why Weeps Yon Highland Maid (p. 39)

Creative Context:
'Why Weeps Yon Highland Maid' is another of the eight 'proscribed' Irish songs which Hogg includes in *Songs* 1831 and which he wrote initially for Robert Archibald Smith's *The Irish Minstrel* in [1825]. For further information on this set of songs and Hogg's involvement in Smith's collection and their wrangle with Thomas Moore's publishers, the Power brothers, alluded to in Hogg's headnote see: *Contributions to Musical Collections and Miscellaneous Songs.*

In *The Irish Minstrel* [1825] this song appeared directly after 'There's Gowd in the Breast' as it does in *Songs* 1831. But interestingly Hogg makes no reference to *The Irish Minstrel* or to Thomas Moore in the 1831 headnote for this song. Like the other Irish songs Hogg includes in *Songs* 1831 this one has a counterpart or companion lyric by Moore: 'How Oft has the Banshee Cried – the dirge', first published in the second number *Irish Melodies* in 1808 (v). Both songs are set to the traditional Irish tune 'The Dear Black Maid'. While Hogg's song shares the theme of mourning over the loss of national heroic warriors, he refers to Culloden in 1746, whereas Moore's text refers to the heroism of the Irish and makes empathetic reference to the loss of English warriors, with specific mention of Nelson. Hogg's text is thus different enough to allow it to be reprinted in the second edition of Smith's *The Irish Minstrel* in *c.*1828.

The copy text for 1831 is that of *The Irish Minstrel* with several variants. For example, lines 7–8 are changed from 'Woe that the young and fair | Should weep unpitied there!' to 'Why should the young and fair | Thus weep unpitied there?'. He alters the description of 'the clansman' to 'her clansmen'(l. 17), while the final line originally ended 'Scotia's name's no more', which in this version becomes 'Our ancient name's no more!' (l. 24).

Hogg's fair-copy manuscript of the text found in *Songs* 1831 is in NLS MS 4805, ff. 26–102 (Blackwood Papers), on ff. 45v–46r. Hogg's unpunctuated text is transferred cleanly to the printed volume.

Publication History:
[1825] – in *The Irish Minstrel*, p. 77 – see *Contributions to Musical Collections and Miscellaneous Songs* (S/SC, 2014)
*c.*1828 – in *The Irish Minstrel*, p. 77 – see *Contributions to Musical Collections and Miscellaneous Songs* (S/SC, 2014)
1831 – in *Songs by the Ettrick Shepherd*, pp. 83–84 – see p. 39 in the present edition

Musical Context:
This tune used by Moore and Hogg is the Irish air 'The Dear Black Maid', but Hogg does not refer to it by name in *Songs* 1831, rather he notes that Smith has sent him 'a cramp air' which is 'however, very beautiful and pathetic'. This tune does not have the wide range of other plaintive tunes Hogg comments on favourable in other headnotes to *Songs* 1831, but is rather more focussed. The flat key (E flat) lends it a particularly mournful character. While this is in a different key to the tune in Moore's *Irish Melodies* (where it is in F) and while there are some rhythmic differences, the similarities are enough to suggest that Smith uses *Irish Melodies* as his source. Moore appears to have used Bunting's 1796 collection as his source, where the tune is named by both its English and Irish title: 'A bhean dubh rún dileas dubh' (see Edward Bunting, *A General Collection of the Ancient Irish Music* (London: Preston and son, 1796), I, 40. Fleischmann gives an erroneous source: 'The Bonny Black Irish Maid', which is no. 6b in B. Cooke's: *Cooke's Selection of twenty one favourite original Irish Airs* (Dublin, *c.*1795), a variant of the air. Donal O'Sullivan tells us that the tune was collected by Bunting at Ballinascreen, Co Sligo.' – see D. J. O'Sullivan, ed.: 'The Bunting Collection of Irish Folk Music and Song, edited from the Original Manuscripts'; *Journal of the Irish Folk Song Society*, II, 17 [NLI shelf number is: Ir 7844 I 3].

Explanatory Notes:
39, ll. 9–10 **Highland plaid | Low in the dust was laid** a reference to one of the measures implemented after the battle of Culloden. The wearing of the tartan plaid was unlawful under an act of Parliament that came was force from 1 August 1746 until the act was repealed in 1782.
39, l. 18 **bonnet blue** *OED* notes this garment was 'A broad round horizontally flattened bonnet or cap of blue woollen material, formerly in general use in Scotland'. While seventeeth century Presbyterians and Covenanters were termed 'blue bonnets', by the nineteenth century the term simply implied the wearer was a Scotsman.
39, l. 24 **Our ancient name's no more!** both previous versions of the song end slightly differently with, 'Scotia's name's no more'. 'Scotia' is the literary name for Scotland. See also notes to 'Scotia's Glens' (pp. 5–6), Hogg's song of nationalist pride relating to British victories over Napoleonic forces in the early 1800s.

My Emma, My Darling (p. 40)

Creative Context:
Hogg's almost flippant 1831 headnote gives little Creative Context for this song. But his reference to 'one of the Musical Bijous' connects it with 'The Harp of Ossian' which also appears in *Songs* 1831 (see pp. 35–36), for both songs first appeared together in the London *Musical Bijou for MDCCCXXIX [1829]*, with musical settings by Henry Bishop. Further information can be found in *Contributions to Annuals and Gift Books*, (S/SC, 2006). As Hughes and Currie note, this was one of a group of songs Hogg contributed to the London music publishers Goulding and D'Almaine, probably late in 1827 or early 1828. Thirteen of Hogg's songs – not including this one – were published with musical settings by Sir Henry Bishop in *Select & Rare Scotish Melodies* [1828] and four songs within the 1829 and 1830 editions of *The Musical Bijou, An album of Music, Poetry, and Prose*. Hughes and Currie note that the content of the song reflects the movement of members of fashionable society (who were the main clientele for such publications) from their summer country residences to their winter town houses.

The copy text for the *Songs* 1831 version is the *Musical Bijou*, although there are some non-substantive variants (in capitalisation and punctuation). One variant within the text of the *Songs* 1831 occurs in l. 5 where the word 'ball' becomes 'hall'. In his fair-copy manuscript Hogg has clearly written 'ball', so that the change is probably a printer's error and not authorial.

The fair-copy version of the song Hogg revised for inclusion in *Songs* 1831 is in NLS MS 4805, ff. 26–102 (Blackwood Papers), f. 46r. On the whole, Hogg's unpunctuated text is transferred cleanly to the printed text.

Publication History:
[1829] – in *The Musical Bijou MDCCCXXIX [1829]*, edited by F. H. Burney, p. 93 (text) with Bishop's musical arrangement , pp. 100–03 – see *Contributions to Annuals and Gift Books*, (S/SC, 2006), pp. 143–48 (text); pp. 392–93 (notes)
1831 – in *Songs by the Ettrick Shepherd*, pp. 85–86 – see p. 40 in this edition

Musical Context:
This is Henry Bishop's own musical creation, and does not use an already established melody.

The Mermaid's Song (pp. 40–41)

Creative Context:
Hogg's headnote helps to date this song with some accuracy, for he refers to 'the singing verses of a long ballad which I wrote many years ago, in the house of Mr Aitken, then living at Dunbar' (see p. 40). This was the literary patron John Aitken (1793–1833) and Hogg made a visit to his home in Dunbar in April 1819 (see *Letters*, I, 'Notes on Correspondents', 440–42, for details). Ten days later Hogg attended the annual celebrations of the Shakespeare Club of Alloa, which took place on the anniversary of Shakespeare's birthday (on 23 April). Hogg was 'Poet Laureate' of this Club and probably composed this song for the occasion. See also 'Ode to the Genius of Shakespeare' which Hogg also included later in *Songs* 1831 (pp. 132–33).

The song 'The Mermaid. A Scottish Ballad. By James Hogg' first appears in the *Edinburgh Magazine & Literary Miscellany* for May 1819, immediately after a report of the 'Alloa Speeches' from this Shakespeare Club dinner (398–99). The *Edinburgh Evening Courant* for 8 May 1819 announced that the 'singing verses' were also published as the fourth song in *A Border Garland* published in [1819] by Hogg's Edinburgh collaborators Gow & Galbraith (see *Letters*, I, 408n). While the ballad is clearly related to the song in *A Border Garland* there are some significant changes. Verses four and five are omitted from the song in *A Border Garland* prompting an alteration of ll. 29–30: 'I leave this grave, and glassy deep | A long last farewell taking' becomes a wider lament 'For all the spirits of the deep | Their long last leave are taking'. One further variant at l. 20 revises the original description of the 'flowers' ['beneath the steep' (l. 19)] to 'stones', more accurately depicting a seascape. For more information on *A Border Garland* see: James Hogg *Contributions to Musical Collections and Miscellaneous Songs*.

'The Mermaid's Song' was then published in the second volume of Hogg's four volume *Poetical Works* in 1822 as the final section of the longer ballad now titled 'The Mermaid'. In this publication the song is set in quatrains and is textually close to the version in *A Border Garland*, although there is further alteration to the wording of l. 29, which becomes, 'Spirits now have left the deep'. Verses four and five of the original are omitted, as in the *Border Garland* version. However, some of the wording from these omitted verses is included in two additional quatrains at the conclusion of the song.

As was the case with all nine songs in *A Border Garland*, 'The Mermaid's Song' was included in *The Border Garland* (*c*.1829) published in Edinburgh by Robert Purdie with new musical settings by James Dewar. For more information see James Hogg *Contributions to Musical Collections and Miscellaneous Songs*. The copy text is the earlier *A Border Garland* version with two verbal variants which may simply be printing errors: 'fuming freaks' (l. 15) becomes 'funning freaks' and 'stones' becomes 'stores' (l. 20).

When Hogg included it in *Songs* 1831 he made several changes to the text. For example, l. 13 changes from 'O I must laugh do as I can' of all previous versions to 'I must smile and weep the while'. l. 15 is redrafted: 'At all the funning freaks of man' becomes 'At freaks of man in life's short span'. The word 'flowers' is reinstated at l. 20 and the last line is slightly altered from 'The day is near the breaking' to 'Till the last morn is breaking' (l. 32), which gives the whole song an air of finality.

Hogg's fair-copy manuscript of the version of the song included in *Songs* 1831 survives at NLS MS 4805, ff. 46–47. Folio 46 is written over with printers' marks ('87–23' and 'PP'. This corresponds to its place in the printed volume. Hogg initially wrote the word 'brag' in his headnote but this is printed as 'boast' within the volume. Along with the usual addition of punctuation the remainder of Hogg's text is transmitted cleanly to the printed text.

Publication History:
1819 – in *Edinburgh Magazine & Literary Miscellany* (May 1819), 400–01
[1819] – in *A Border Garland*, pp. 8–9 – see *Contributions to Musical Collections and Miscellaneous Songs* (S/SC, 2014)
1822 – in *Poetical Works*, II, 230–37. The song text appears as part of the ballad now titled simply 'The Mermaid'; ('The Mermaid's Song', pp. 235–37).
c.1829 – in *The Border Garland*, pp. 28–30 – see *Contributions to Musical Collections and Miscellaneous Songs* (S/SC, 2014)
1829 – in *The Harmonicon* (November 1829, Vol. 7, Pt. 2) – see *Contributions to Musical Collections and Miscellaneous Songs* (S/SC, 2014)

1831 – in *Songs by the Ettrick Shepherd*, pp. 87–89 – see pp. 40–41 in the present edition

Musical Context:

In each version of the song the air is identified as Hogg's own. Unlike the spirited melody for 'The Women Fo'k', which Hogg also includes in *A Border Garland*, 'The Mermaid's song' is an atmospheric lament with several enharmonic twists which give it a sense of wildness. James Dewar's later setting for *The Border Garland* was reprinted in the musical magazine *The Harmonicon* in November 1829, flagged as 'from the Border Garland' (Vol. 7, Pt. 2). The newly extended edition of *The Border Garland* (*c*.1829) was reviewed in this same issue (Pt. I, 281–82), so that the reprinting within the *Harmonicon* offered a 'specimen' of both Hogg's text and Dewar's arrangement. The editors express the hope that the song 'will have as many charms for others as it has for us' (p. 281). For further information on both settings see: *Contributions to Musical Collections and Miscellaneous Songs*.

Donald M'Gillavry (pp. 41–43)

Creative Context:

As Hogg's headnote states, this song originates as part of his work on the Jacobite Relics project, where it appeared as 'Song LX' in the First Series of 1819. Pittock gives the manuscript source as: [S.L.] V. 15 p. 88, a notebook Hogg used in the preparation of the *Jacobite Relics* series. In the *Relics* Hogg presents the song as having been part of a living tradition, but his headnote in *Songs* 1831 states categorically that Hogg was rather teasing his reader with his initial factual annotation for *Relics* and that the song is in fact his own 'original composition'.

This song has one of the longest headnotes in *Songs* 1831 and presents in some detail the story behind Hogg's wish to mislead the critics of *The Edinburgh Review*. Both William Donaldson (*The Jacobite Song*, (Aberdeen, 1988), pp. 100–01) and Murray Pittock (editor of the S/SC edition) draw attention to this prank of Hogg's. Donaldson accounts for the triumphant tone of Hogg's note, as Francis Jeffrey's hostile review of the first series of the *Relics* (*Edinburgh Review*, 34 (August 1820)) had specifically mentioned 'Donald Macgillavry' as being one of the finest specimens of old Jacobite songs in the collection. Hogg's 1831 headnote does not just take some comfort in making this claim, but Hogg continues to criticise the *Review* for its treatment of Scottish songs in general, using his friend William Laidlaw's song 'Lucy's Flitting' as an example of the *Review* being seriously out of touch with the popular songs of the day. This song had appeared in Hogg's first text-only collection of songs *The Forest Minstrel* in 1810 (see *The Forest Minstrel*, (S/SC, 2006), pp. 21–23 and pp. 223–28. He also challenges the *Review* for its negative reception of his friend Allan Cunningham's *The Songs of Scotland, Ancient and Modern* (1825), which included Laidlaw's song and a number of songs by Hogg (see *Edinburgh Review* 1828). This negative review was also mentioned in the *Noctes Ambrosianae* of *Blackwood's* at the same time (*Blackwood's Edinburgh Magazine*, 23 (May 1828), 787–88.

For its appearance in *Songs* 1831 Hogg uses the *Relics* version as his copy text, though the manuscript for *Songs* 1831, NLS MS 4805, f. 47 shows evidence of some redrafting. For example, l. 9 is freshly drafted from, 'Donald's run o'er the hill but his tether, man' of the *Relics* version, to the more obvious, 'Donald's come o'er the hill trailin' his tether, man'. Similarly, the wording in l. 15 within the same verse is changed from 'Pack on your back, and elwand sae cleverly', to the more precise, 'Pack on your back an' elwand o' steelary'. Further redrafting is found within l. 31, where Hogg intensifies the shoemaking imagery by adding 'yerk' in place of 'bore' which moves to replace 'beat' at the beginning of the line.

One change within the *Songs* 1831 version is probably not authorial. Within l. 39 the demonstrative pronoun 'that' appears to be missing from the sentence: 'Skelp them an' scadd them pruved sae unbritherly–'. The *Jacobite Relics* version includes 'that' after 'scadd them'. Unfortunately, this portion of Hogg's holograph manuscript for *Songs* 1831 is missing, so that it is not known whether the error occurred at the printing stage or was an authorial slip. The headnote within the printed text is also missing from the manuscript which just includes a note from Hogg as follows:

> (There are two droll quotations which Mr Blackwood will please to cause be inserted here neither of which I have by me. The one is from the Edin. Review of the Jacobite Relics relating to this song the other the answer to it in Maga) (f. 47r)

Presumably Blackwood, or an assistant, subsequently wrote the text of the headnote using the material directed by Hogg. Writing from his sick bed, on 30 November 1830, Hogg wrote to Blackwood, 'I am much pleased with your introduction to Donald M,Gillavry': see *Letters*, II, 414–15. Overall, Hogg's unpunctuated text of the song is transferred cleanly to the printed volume.

Publication History:
1819 – in *Jacobite Relics*, I, 100–102 and 279–80 – see (S/SC, 2002), also pp. 455–56
1831 – in *Songs by the Ettrick Shepherd*, pp. 90–93 – see pp. 41–43 in the present edition
Unauthorised versions:
Unauthorised printings during Hogg's lifetime include a version published, along with a portion of Hogg's annotation from *Jacobite Relics*, in *The Songs of Scotland, Ancient and Modern*, edited by Allan Cunningham, 4 vols (London: John Taylor, 1825), III, 229–31. Here the copy text is clearly the *Jacobite Relics* version, with no mention of its being Hogg's own composition. A further unauthorised version was published in *The Jacobite Minstrelsy, with Notes* (Glasgow: R. Griffin, 1829), pp. 70–71. The copy text is *Jacobite Relics*, as is clear from the discussion in the footnote where attention is given to 'the Ettrick Shepherd's idea' that the song was 'used to signify the whole of the Scottish Clans' (p. 70).

Musical Context:
Stenhouse's musical notation is printed over pp. 100–01 in *Jacobite Relics*, but there is no tune title or additional information from Hogg about the melody. William Donaldson gives a detailed account of the tune and Hogg's marriage of words with it (in *The Jacobite Song: Political Myth and National Identity* (Aberdeen: Aberdeen University Press, 1988), pp. 102–03), where he notes the modal qualities of the air and where he concludes that Hogg shows himself to be a 'sensitive craftsman' in his textual response to the tune. It remains something of a mystery that this clearly popular Jacobite song did not capture the attention of musicians in the same way as other of Hogg's Jacobite songs included in *Songs* 1831 which appeared in musical collections and on independently published song sheets during Hogg's lifetime (e.g. 'Flora Macdonald's Farewell' or 'Cam' ye by Athole'). We have been unable to source any song sheets of this song before 1835 and it is notable in its absence from the musical collections of Scots songs to which Hogg contributed.

Explanatory Notes:

41 [headnote] the authorship of the song was immediately avowed in a letter to the Editor of Blackwood's Magazine Hogg is referring to his 'Letter from James Hogg to his Reviewer' in *Blackwood's Edinburgh Magazine*, 8 (October 1820), 67–75. In fact, the authorship was not within this 'Letter' (see below).

41–42 [headnote] "After all," said this avowal, "between ourselves [...] fill up a page!" Hogg's quotation is actually taken from the covering letter he sent to William Blackwood enclosing the 'Letter from James Hogg to his Reviewer'. In a footnote to Hogg's 'Letter', 'C.N.' notes, 'the above letter was enclosed in the following one to us', and Hogg's covering letter is then printed on pp. 75–76.

42, l. 3 gouk's nest 'gouk' is the Scots word for the cuckoo and also a fool. Hogg transfers the meaning from the cuckoo, and the known ornithological fact that the female cuckoo lays her eggs in the nests of other birds, into a satirical reference to George I (1714–27) as fool and, by association, the Hanoverian dynasty as unlawful possessors of the British throne. 'Song LXVII' titled 'The Cuckoo' is published in *Jacobite Relics* I, 111–12 (S/SC, 2003).

42, l. 4 the king as becomes clear on l. 12, the king in question is James Francis Edward Stuart (1688–1766), known to Jacobites as King James VIII and III– the Old Pretender or Old Chevalier. He was brought up in exile in Palais St. Germains-en-lye, near Paris and succeeded his father, James VII and II (1633–1701).

42, l. 15 elwand o' steelery 'elwand' is a form of measurement (weight), as in an ell-measure, so that, figuratively, the meaning is 'put on armour'.

42, l. 19 whigs and whiggery the term 'whig' was originally a derogatory term in use in Scotland during the seventeenth-century to denote a covenanter or 'whiggamore'. After 1688, the term was commonly used throughout Britain to denote opposition to Jacobitism.

O'er the Ocean Bounding (pp. 43–44)

Creative Context:

This is another of the eight 'proscribed' Irish songs which Hogg includes in *Songs 1831* and which he wrote initially for Robert Archibald Smith's *The Irish Minstrel* in [1825]. For further information on this set of songs and Hogg's involvement in Smith's collection and their wrangle with Thomas Moore's publishers, the Power brothers, alluded to in Hogg's headnote see: *Contributions to Musical Collections and Miscellaneous Songs.*

As with Hogg's other Irish songs, 'O'er the Ocean Bounding' shares a traditional Irish tune with one of Moore's *Irish Melodies*, in this case, 'Maid of the Valley' which accompanies Moore's song 'Go Where Glory Waits Thee', published in the first number of *Irish Melodies* in 1808(i). Both songs share the theme of love and have 'Remember me' as their refrain. But Hogg's song is both shorter and more secular than Moore's. While Hogg gives the impression in his headnote that this one was destroyed along with most of his other songs in the first edition of *The Irish Minstrel*, in fact it was deemed different enough to Moore's original to be one of only three of Hogg's songs to be reprinted in the second edition of *The Irish Minstrel* in *c.*1828.

In the headnote Hogg's anger with the Power brothers, who challenged Smith's publication, is palpable, but it also allows him to advertise the availability and increasingly popularity of his songs in London and Ireland and even the East Indies (see also the note to 'Donald MacDonald' pp. 3–5).

The copy text of the *Songs* 1831 version is that of *The Irish Minstrel* with slight textual alteration to the wording of l. 6. 'Yet I am still with thee' becomes 'Yet thou art still with me'. No manuscript version of the text has been located. This is one of the songs missing in the main surviving manuscript for *Songs* 1831: NLS MS 4805, ff. 26–102.

Publication History:
[1825] – in *The Irish Minstrel*, pp. 80–81 – see *Contributions to Musical Collections and Miscellaneous Songs* (S/SC, 2014)

*c.*1828 – in *The Irish Minstrel*, pp. 80–81 – see *Contributions to Musical Collections and Miscellaneous Songs* (S/SC, 2014)

1831 – in *Songs by the Ettrick Shepherd*, pp. 94–95 – see pp. 43–44 in the present edition

Musical Context:
The traditional Irish air 'Maid of the Valley' is nominated as the melody for the song in both editions of *The Irish Minstrel*. While the Smith song is in a different key (E flat) to Moore's (in F) the melodies are close enough to suggest that Smith used Moore's *Irish Melodies* as his source. Moore seems to have used Edward Bunting's 1796 collection as his source for the melody: see Edward Bunting, *A General Collection of the Ancient Irish Music* (London: Preston and son, 1796), 47.

Explanatory Notes:
43 [headnote] **turn the blue bonnet wha can** the title of a Jacobite song. Hogg prints a version as 'Song LI' in *Jacobite Relics*, II (see S/SC, 2003, pp. 95–96). Pittock notes 'it is doubtful if this is a song of the Jacobite period', and he suggests it is Hogg's own composition (pp. 506–07).

43 [headnote] **"O'er Boggie," and "The wee Cock Chicken,"** &c., the phrase 'o'er bogie' refers to a marriage unsanctioned by the Church. It is also the title of a traditional tune, found, for example, in Thomson's *Orpheus Caledonius* (1725). Burns contributed words to the melody which were published in the second volume of the S*MM* (1788), No. 168 (175–76). 'The Wee Cock Chicken' has not been identified.

43 [headnote] **Auld Nick** familiar Scots name for the Devil.

43 [headnote] **The London people have done the same with a number of mine** Hogg refers here to his wrangle with London publisher Lonsdale & Mills. See the introduction to to *Twelve Vocal Pieces* in *Contributions to Musical Collections and Miscellaneous Songs*.

Charlie is my Darling (pp. 44–45)

Creative Context:
This is another Jacobite song related to Hogg's work on the Jacobite Relics project between 1817and 1821. It first appeared as 'Song XLIX' in *Jacobite Relics* II in 1821, below what Hogg terms the 'Modern' verses. Interestingly, although the song was composed by Hogg, Pittock assigns it as category 'II' (of Jacobite provenance, but 'with significant variations': see p. 481). He notes that Hogg's song 'is a direct version of the lost lover song [...] tradition which refers to 'Charles's entry to

Glasgow in January 1746' (p. 506). Pittock also records several earlier versions of the 'original' song in eighteenth-century song collections, broadside ballads and in manuscript, the most familiar being Robert Burns's version which he adapted for the *SMM* (1796), No. 428. See also Pittock's *Poetry and Jacobite Politics in Eighteenth-century Britain and Ireland* (Cambridge: Cambridge University Press, 1994), Chapter Two, pp. 59–93.

Hogg gives two slightly different versions of how the song originates. In his notes to the song in *Relics* he claims that he wrote it 'some years ago, at the request of a friend, who complained that he did not like the old verses' (p. 301). Gillian Hughes suggests that George Thomson is the 'friend' in question: see *Letters*, I, 348, note to Hogg's letter to Thomson dated 9 May 1818. But in his very brief headnote in *Songs* 1831 Hogg claims that he altered the original verses at the 'request of a lady who sung it sweetly'. There is no evidence as to who this 'lady' was, but it is also notable that Thomson did not publish this song in any of his collections.

Its next appearance is not until *Songs* 1831. The copy text is the *Jacobite Relics* version and, with the exception of some insubstantive (e.g. l.20 'The craigy glen' becomes 'yon craigy glen') and orthographic variants, the text is the same. Gillian Hughes records an early version of the song in manuscript within the Beinecke Library Manuscript Collections: Osborn MSS, Folder 7423. Titled 'The Young Chevalier', but she notes that the mss is 'not in Hogg's hand'. The provenance is not known.

This is one of a group of songs missing from the main fair-copy manuscript for *Songs* 1831: at NLS MS 4805, ff. 26–102 (Blackwood Papers).

Publication History:
1821 – in *Jacobite Relics*, II, 92–94 and 301 – see also (S/SC, 2003), p. 506
1831 – in *Songs by the Ettrick Shepherd*, pp. 96–97 – see pp. 44–45 in the present edition

Unauthorised versions:
'Charlie is my Darling – Second Set', was published in *The Jacobite Minstrelsy, with Notes*, immediately below the 'original' version (Glasgow: R. Griffin, 1829), pp. 190–91. The copy text is *Jacobite Relics*, as is admitted in a footnote: 'This is the Ettrick Shepherd's version of the preceding song. [...] Hogg's usual felicity of thought and expression seem to be awanting here' (p. 190). See also *Letters*, II, 341 and 343.

Musical Context:
The song appears in the *Relics* with a melody which William Stenhouse states is 'a genuine copy of the old air' (*Illustrations*, p. 380). G. F. Graham's notes to the song discuss its popularity: 'it has been the fate of this air to undergo several odd transformations'. He mentions that the air printed by Hogg in *Jacobite Relics* is 'very different from the air No. 428 in Johnson's Museum, "modernized" by Mr. Stephen Clark' [...], and complains of Clark's alterations to the tune, putting 'semitones where tones were; and many other alterations' (Graham I, p. 91).

Explanatory Notes:
44, l. 4 Young Chevalier Prince Charles Edward Stuart (1720–1788), eldest son of the uncrowned James VIII and III: see note 3, l. 13.
44, ll. 11–12 I grat to see the lad come back | That had been lang away the Prince was born in exile.

44, l. 16 Our king shall hae his ain again words with particular resonance in the Jacobite tradition. The song titled 'The King shall enjoy his own again' is 'Song I' in *Jacobite Relics*, I, 1–3.

If E'er I am Thine (p. 45)

Creative Context:

This is another of the eight 'suppressed' Irish songs which Hogg includes in *Songs* 1831 and which he wrote initially for Robert Archibald Smith's *The Irish Minstrel* in [1825]. For further information on this set of songs and Hogg's involvement in Smith's collection and their wrangle with Thomas Moore's publishers, the Power brothers, alluded to in Hogg's headnote see: *Contributions to Musical Collections and Miscellaneous Songs*.

As with Hogg's other Irish songs, 'If E'er I Am Thine' shares a traditional Irish tune with one of Moore's *Irish Melodies*: in this case it is the air 'The Winnowing Sheet' which was matched with Moore's song 'If thou'lt be mine', in the seventh number of *Irish Melodies* (1815, viii). Hogg's song is similar to Moore's in theme and form (comprising quintains), and at times, such as in the title, it strays textually close to Moore's. For example, Moore begins with: 'If thou'lt be mine, the treasures of air'; and Hogg's song opens with: 'If e'er I am thine, the birds of air'. There are many reflections of lines and images in the Moore lyric (see Explanatory Notes), and as such it was not one of the songs which Smith was able to reprint in the second edition of *The Irish Minstrel* in *c*.1828.

The copy text of the *Songs* 1831 version of 'If E'er I am Thine' is that of *The Irish Minstrel* (above), with two variants: 'in' becomes 'to' in l. 9 while on the concluding line 'travel' is changed to 'journey' (l. 15).

This is another of the songs missing from the main body of the fair-copy manuscript for *Songs* 1831, namely NLS MS 4805, ff. 26–102 (Blackwood Papers).

Publication History:

[1825]– in *The Irish Minstrel*, p.98 – see *Contributions to Musical Collections and Miscellaneous Songs* (S/SC, 2014)

1831 – in *Songs by the Ettrick Shepherd*, pp. 98–99 – see p. 45 in the present edition

Musical Context:

The traditional Irish air 'The Winnowing Sheet' is nominated as the accompaniment to the song in the first edition of *The Irish Minstrel*. Smith appears to have used Moore's *Irish Melodies* (VII, viii) as his source: he keeps the melody in the same key although there are some rhythmical differences. This air belongs to a song entitled *An Cháitheach Róin (The Winnowing Sheet)* connected to the following process: a sheet was spread on the ground and the oats and chaff dropped from a height. This enabled the heavier seed to be collected as the lighter chaff is taken away by the wind. Moore's source is certainly Edward Bunting's collection (II, 1809), and is a tune collected from the County Leitrim harper, Charles Byrne. The version used by Moore is almost identical to Bunting in every respect (see: D.J. O'Sullivan, ed.: *The Bunting Collection of Irish Folk Music and Song*, parts 1–VI, 1927–1939: VI, 27 (NLI catalogue no. Ir 7844 I 3).

Explanatory Notes:

45, ll. 1–2 IF e'er I am thine, the birds of the air, | The beasts of the field, and fish of the sea echoes Moore's wording of the opening of 'If thou'lt be mine':

'If thou'lt be mine, the treasures of the air, | Of earth, and sea shall lie at they feet' (ll. 1–2).

45, l. 5 because I am thine, love echoes the wording of Moores' refrain at the end of each verse: 'if thou wilt be mine, love' (l. 5, etc.).

45, l. 6 We'll have no flowers contradicts Moore's image: 'Bright flowers shall bloom' (l. 6).

45, l. 11 And this shall raise our thoughts more high a further echo of Moore's song: 'And thoughts, whose source is hidden and high' (l. 11).

45, l. 13 our path must lie similar to Moore's song: 'like meads, that lie' (l. 13).

Meg o'Marley (p. 46)

Creative Context:

An account of the textual and publishing history of 'Meg O'Marley' is given in *Contributions to Blackwood's Edinburgh Magazine* I. In summary, Gillian Hughes notes that Hogg contributed this song, along with 'The Great Muckle Village of Balmaquhapple' (see *Songs* 1831, pp. 20–21), in response to Blackwood's urgent appeal for material. In short 'Meg o'Marley is another of Hogg's songs delivered in his role as the Shepherd Songster and it was first published in *Blackwood's Edinburgh Magazine* in June 1826 as part of the series *Noctes Ambrosianae* (No. XXVI of 19 (June 1826), 756). This number also includes 'The Village of Balmaqhapple'. As with other *Noctes* songs in *Songs* 1831, Hogg decided to include a little of the surrounding *Noctean* dialogue to contextualise the song for his reader. In this case he is nicely drawing attention to his wish to remain a songster rather than to take up the challenge of parliamentary speech-writing. Thus Joseph Hume (1777–1855), well known for his lengthy, digressive speeches, is mentioned after the song. An early holograph manuscript of the first verse of the song is end-dated 'Altrive Lake, March 25 1825' (Saint Andrews University Rare Books and Manuscript Library, msPR4791.05<ms14787>). But this is one of the songs missing from the fair-copy manuscript for *Songs* 1831.

Hogg clearly used the *Blackwood's* song as copy text for 1831. There are some variants to the later version of the song: e.g, 'tailor' becomes a 'tailor lad' (l. 13) and the 'weaver's neb's out through the web' rather than simply the 'weaver' (l. 15). The earlier *Blackwood's* version of the song had concluded with the 'goodman' valiantly preparing for love-making with the words, 'O light his torches warly', but in his latest version Hogg alters this to 'Than light his torches sparely' (l. 22).

Publication history:

1826 – in *Blackwood's Edinburgh Magazine*, 19 (June 1826), 756 – see *Contributions to Blackwood's Edinburgh Magazine* I, (S/SC, 2008), pp. 189–90 and 518

1831 – in *Songs by the Ettrick Shepherd*, pp. 100–102 – see p. 46 in the present edition

Musical Context:

Hogg does not indicate a particular tune for the song. It was printed without musical notation in *Blackwood's* and does not appear to have been set to music.

Explanatory Notes:

See *Contributions to Blackwood's Edinburgh Magazine* I, p. 518.

Bonny Mary (pp. 47–48)

Creative Context:

This is regarded as one of Hogg's favourite songs and it appears in print several times before *Songs* 1831. An account of the textual and publishing history of this song is found in *The Forest Minstrel* (S/SC, 2006), and also in *Contributions to Blackwood's Edinburgh Magazine* I, (S/SC, 2008). There were significant alterations to the text between its first appearance in *the Forest Minstrel* in 1810, its publication in Hogg's *Poetical Works* of 1822 and *Blackwood's* in 1826. Garside and Jackson include a detailed account of the major alterations to the text in the four different versions of the song listed below (including its appearance in 1831), and Thomas Richardson also discusses the variations between the 1822 and *Blackwood's* versions.

In summary, it is Hogg's 1831 headnote which suggests that 'Bonny Mary' was 'one of the songs of my youth' and Garside and Jackson believe that the song probably relates to Hogg's Nithsdale period between 1805–09. Indeed they also note that Hogg may have had Burns's 'My Bony Mary' in mind when he wrote this song. As with 'The Village of Balmaquapple' and 'Meg o'Marley'(which directly precedes it in *Songs* 1831), this song appears as part of the Shepherd's contributions to the *Noctes Ambrosianae* (No. XXVII, July 1826, 93–94). The Burns connection – Burns's song had first appeared in 1790 in the second volume of the *SMM*, No. 231 (p. 240) – is alluded to in the *Blackwood's* appearance of the song where 'Tickler' notes, after the Shepherd's performance, that it is 'equal to anything of Burns'. It is unclear whether Hogg, or his Blackwoodian collaborators, had made the change to the title of the song from 'Bonny Mary' to 'My Bony Mary' especially because of Burns: only the last three verses of Hogg's fair-copy manuscript of the version of the song that was published in *Blackwood's* is extant, at NLS, MS 4017, fol. 141 (see Manuscript Versions below). The Noctean dialogue also makes mention of George Thomson's opulent collections to which Hogg also contributed – see *Contributions to Musical Collections and Miscellaneous Songs*. This is significant as it reiterates the received quality of Hogg's songs.

It is notable that Hogg seems to have forgotton the song's initial appearance in *The Forest Minstrel* and also in his *Poetical Works* and that he refers only to the *Blackwood's* version in his headnote in 1831. But it is doubtless because he wishes to draw attention to the content of the Noctean dialogue which he includes with the song. This means that his supremacy to Burns and the following monologue about what songs mean to him as 'the Shepherd Songster' are both able to be presented to the readers of *Songs* 1831, thus aiding Hogg in his presentation of himself as the key Scottish songwriter after Burns.

Unsurprisingly it is the *Blackwood's* appearance of the song which Hogg uses for 1831, with some variants. The first four lines of sixth stanza beginning 'When gloaming, creeping west the lift' in 1831 is substantially different from this stanza in *Blackwood's* version, beginning 'When gloaming o'er the welkin steals'.

Two manuscript versions of 'Bonny Mary' are extant. NLS, MS 4017, fol. 141 is the manuscript closely related to the Blackwoodian version of the song and is discussed in detail by Garside and Jackson, and by Richardson. NLS, MS 4805, ff. 48r–49r is Hogg's fair-copy manuscript of the version of 'Bonny Mary' published in *Songs* 1831. The manuscript is incomplete and begins with the second verse so that it is not known whether Hogg himself returned to the earliest known title of the song or whether the decision was made by Robert Hogg or the printer. Hogg's unpunctuated text has been cleanly transferred to the printed version with one or two slight but insignificant alterations.

Publication History:

1810 – in *The Forest Minstrel*, pp. 47–50 – see (S/SC, 2006), pp. 51–53 and 253–54

1822 – in *Poetical Works*, IV, 341–44

1826 – in *Blackwood's Edinburgh Magazine*, 20 (July 1826), 93–94 – see (S/SC, 2008), pp. 190–92 and 518–19

1831 – in *Songs by the Ettrick Shepherd* , pp. 103–07 – see pp. 47–48 in the present edition

Musical Context:

Hogg notes, in his Preface to *The Forest Minstrel*, that this is one of the songs which has no designated tune, but for which the 'choice for suitable airs' is 'left to the discernment of the singer: *The Forest Minstrel* (2006), p. 7. As Richard Jackson notes: 'no tune is nominated in any of the versions described, though the title of the tune was also that of a well-known tune [...] one that Burns found attractive' (2006, p. 254). The tune Jackson selects to match Hogg's lyric in *The Forest Minstrel* is a variant of the tune 'Bonny Mary' from James Oswald's *Curious Scots Tunes* of *c*.1740, p. 15. For all of its popularity it is interesting that this was not a song contributed to any key musical collection nor has any published musical setting been located.

Explanatory Notes:

See *Contributions to Blackwood's Edinburgh Magazine*, I, (S/SC, 2008), p. 519.

The Ladies' Evening Song (pp. 49–50)

Creative Context:

This song appears to have been created in 1827–28 when Hogg was involved in sending songs to the London music publisher Goulding, D'Almaine & Co. for their collection *Select & Rare Scotish Melodies* [1828] with musical settings by Sir Henry Bishop. For more information about this collection and Hogg's involvement in it, and for copies of the songs, see *Contributions to Musical Collections and Miscellaneous Songs*.

'The Ladies Evening Song', however, is a recreation of an earlier song which Hogg alludes to in his headnote in *Songs* 1831. The song to which he refers as being 'written long ago' is 'The Drinkin' O. A Sang for the Edinburgh Ladies' which appeared in *The Scots Magazine* for November 1805 (vol. 67, p. 864). It was also included by Hogg in *The Forest Minstrel* in 1810 and discussion of it can be sourced in the new edition of that volume (S/SC, 2006). Garside and Jackson note that with its 'reference to a day-time rattling of guns and clinking of swords (stanzas 1 and 5)' the original song is most probably related to the topical discussions of 'threatened invasion from France in 1805' (see *The Forest Minstrel* (S/SC, 2006), p. 31 and also notes for 'Donald MacDonald' above). The 'young lady' to whom Hogg refers in his 1831 headnote has not been identified.

Garside and Jackson note details of a further reprinting of the song, 'The Drinkin' O. A Sang for the Greenock Ladies', in *The Greenock Advertiser* for Friday 13 December 1805. With a further modification to the title this version of the song was subsequently included in Hogg's 1810 song-collection, *The Forest Minstrel*. The complete text of 'The Drinkin' O. A Sang for the Ladies' is found in the recent

S/SC edition of this collection (2006), on pp. 128–29 with notes on pp. 310–12.

Hogg clearly refashioned this song into 'The Ladies Evening Song' which was probably one of the 'eight more songs for your correspondents' that Hogg sent with his letter to Robert Purdie of 18 January 1828: see *Letters*, II, 284. In redrafting this version of the song Hogg omits early contemporary references, retaining only the barest elements from the original. In this new version he reuses only the wording from ll. 17 and 18 and also a modified form of l. 8. He also changes the format from six quintets to four octets and shortens the lines.

The copy text of the *Songs* 1831 version is that of *Select & Rare Scotish Melodies* (above), without change.

The only surviving manuscript version of the song is that in Hogg's fair-copy manuscript for *Songs* 1831, where it is found at NLS MS 4805, f. 49. Hogg's unpunctuated text is transferred cleanly to the printed volume.

Publication History:

[1828] – in *Select & Rare Scotish Melodies*, pp. 26–29: see *Contributions to Musical Collections and Miscellaneous Songs* (S/SC, 2014)

1831 – in *Songs by the Ettrick Shepherd*, pp. 108–109 – see pp. 49–50 in the present edition

Unauthorised versions:

1831 – The song's popularity is revealed in an unauthorised American version of 'The Ladies Evening Song' reprinted in *The Liberator* of Boston for Saturday, 30 April 1831, where the text is flagged 'from Songs by the Ettrick Shepherd, just published' (p. 72). Although at first glance it would seem unusual that such a song would appear in this anti-slavery newspaper, the paper's editor, William Lloyd Garrison, frequently published Scottish-derived material. Further details of the American publication of Hogg's songs can be found in the *Listing of Hogg Items in the American Periodical Press*, by Janette Currie, at the online *James Hogg Research* website hosted by the Division of Literature and Languages, School of Arts and Humanities, Stirling University, http://www.jameshogg.stir.ac.uk.

Musical Context:

Since its first publication in 1805 'Dumbarton Drums' is the tune nominated as providing a suitable accompaniment to the song. The history of this the traditional Scottish tune is discussed at length in *The Forest Minstrel* (S/SC, 2006), pp. 310–12. It is a variant of this tune which Henry Bishop uses for his setting in *Select & Rare Scotish Melodies* in [1828], an arrangement of which Hogg appears to have approved as he states this clearly in his headnote for 1831. A version of this tune was included in *SMM* (1788), II, no. 161, (169). The tune 'Dumbarton Drums' is nominated below the title of the version of 'The Drinkin' O. A Sang for the Ladies' in *The Forest Minstrel* (1810), pp. 131–32.

Mary, Canst Thou Leave Me? (pp. 50–51)

Creative Context:

As with 'The Ladies' Evening Song' above this song appears to have been created in 1827–28 when Hogg was involved in sending songs to the London music publisher Goulding, D'Almaine & Co. for their collection *Select & Rare Scotish Melodies* [1828] with musical settings by Sir Henry Bishop. For more information about this collection and Hogg's involvement in it, and for copies of the songs, see

Contributions to Musical Collections and Miscellaneous Songs.

Its appearance in *Select & Rare Scotish Melodies* comprises 28 lines but Hogg omitted ll. 17–20 for the version he included in *Songs* 1831 and he also altered the name of the male protagonist from 'Colin' (l.13) to 'Connal'.

Hogg's fair-copy holograph manuscript of the version he prepared for *Select & Rare Scotish Melodies*, most probably sent in correspondence with the publisher's agent, Edinburgh-based Robert Purdie, is extant among the James Hogg papers at the Alexander Turnbull Library, New Zealand. (2 verses of 8 lines each) MS Papers 42, (), No. 66 (i). See Peter Garside, 'An Annotated Checklist of Hogg's literary manuscripts in the Alexander Turnbull library, Wellington, New Zealand' in *The Bibliotheck,* 5–23 (p. 5). Within a presentation copy of *Select & Rare Scotish Melodies,* inscribed to 'Miss Foster', Hogg's revision is evident on p. 3 where 'Haste, O haste to hide me' is crossed out and 'thee' written above (Beinecke Rare Book Room and Manuscript Library, Call No. 1974+69). This revision is carried into the *Songs* 1831 version (l. 16).

The version Hogg publishes in *Songs* 1831 is included in the fair-copy manuscript for this collection at: NLS MS 4805, f. 50r. The text covers a single folio page-numbered '57' (where Hogg has squeezed in the last line with the mark '+') and follows immediately after 'The Ladies Evening Song', thus concurring with the sequence of pagination and order of songs found also in *Songs* 1831. Hogg's unpunctuated text is transferred cleanly to the printed version.

Publication History:

[1828] – in *Select & Rare Scotish Melodies,* pp. 1–4 – see *Contributions to Musical Collections and Miscellaneous Songs* (S/SC, 2014)

1831 – in *Songs by the Ettrick Shepherd,* pp. 110–11 – see pp. 50–51 in the present edition

Musical Context:

Hogg's headnote to *Songs* 1831 notes that this is to 'a melody of my own', but he then continues by declaring that he's not so sure it is 'thoroughly my own'. His note draws attention clearly to the overlap between songs and tunes which are in the popular domain, and illustrates how quickly they become mixed up with others of original composition. His end note to the first song in the collection, 'Donald MacDonald' also emphasises this point, as the song is accepted as belonging to popular tradition and Hogg's involvement as creator goes unrecognised. Sometimes Bishop creates his own melodies for the songs in *Select & Rare Scotish Melodies* (as with 'Arabian Song'). But at times he refines a traditional tune (as with 'Gang to the Brakens wi' me') or sets a traditional tune (as with 'The Souters of Selkirk'). In this case the tune has the range and modality of a traditional fiddle tune, so it is likely that it may well have been Hogg's air or a variant of a known fiddle tune which Bishop has adapted.

Black Mary (p. 51)

Creative Context:

This is the first of six songs in *Songs* 1831 to have originally appeared in Alexander Campbell's collection entitled *Albyn's Anthology, or, A Select Collection of the Melodies & Vocal Poetry peculiar to Scotland & the Isles, hitherto unpublished,* published in Edinburgh by Oliver & Boyd in two volumes in 1816 and 1818. For further information on this collection, Hogg's involvement with it and copies of the songs see: *Contributions to Musical Collections and Miscellaneous Songs*.

As the Introduction to the collection in *Contributions to Musical Collections and Miscellaneous Songs* notes, Campbell had visited Hogg at Altrive in October 1816 seeking contributions for his collection and Hogg took him around Ettrick to visit several singers and provided songs himself. It is thus highly probable that the original version of 'Black Mary' was composed during this period. It was first published in February 1818 in the second volume of *Albyn's Anthology* and it then appeared in a further two versions before Hogg included it in *Songs* 1831. Notably the text remains remarkably stable through all its publications up to and including *Songs* 1831, and *Albyn's Anthology* appears to be the copy text for all the different printings.

It was published with the title 'Mary is My only Joy' in the third volume of Hogg's *Poetical Works* of 1822, with the usual orthographic alterations (such as changing 'y' to 'ie'). The first line of the song bears much resemblance to another popular Scots song beginning 'Robin is my only Jo[e]' which Stenhouse notes was included by David Herd in his *Ancient and Modern songs* in 1776, but Stenhouse believes it is much older than this (Stenhouse, p.421–22): a version of the text appears in *SMM* IV, no. 478 p. 492.

After 1822, Hogg's text then appeared with no title in the newly established *Edinburgh Literary Journal; or, Weekly Register of Criticism and Belles Lettres* for Saturday, 27 December 1828. Hogg had begun to contribute to this magazine in November 1828 partly due to the increasing difficulties of his relationship with William Blackwood. His song 'Marion Graham', which he also included in *Songs* 1831, appeared in the *Journal* for 15 November 1828 (see 'Marion Graham' pp. 105–06). The rivalry with *Blackwood's* is clear. 'Black Mary' was included within an ironically titled article, 'Noctes Bengerianæ By the Ettrick Shepherd', which was clearly pointing directly to *Blackwood's* long-running *Noctes Ambrosianæ* series. As in the *Noctes*, Hogg mixes songs and comic dialogue. This episode is held together loosely by the unexpected arrival of a vagrant known as 'The Man', or 'Lord Archbald' at Mount Benger, Hogg's farm in the Yarrow valley. Towards the end of the article, Hogg's servants entertain 'Lord Archbald' with songs, and a 'tall girl' named 'Nancy' sings 'Black Mary'. The text of this version of the song follows that in *Albyn's Anthology*, with two significant changes (from the word 'hue' to 'flue' l. 7) and fresh wording at line 12 ('The gem that cheers our valley'). Such slight changes probably indicate that Hogg was writing from memory.

Under the new title 'Black Mary', the copy text of the version in *Songs* 1831 is also that of *Albyn's Anthology*. Hogg reverts to the original wording at l. 12 but retains the word 'flue' in the second verse to describe the raven's wings (l. 7).

The only manuscript is in the fair-copy manuscript for *Songs* 1831 at: NLS MS 4805, ff. 50v–51r. The manuscript is page-numbered '58' and '59' and follows immediately after 'Mary Canst thou Leave Me', concurring with the printed volume. Hogg's unpunctuated text is transferred reasonably cleanly to the printed volume, with the exception of a misreading of 'flue' in Hogg's hand which is printed as 'hue' in line 7. This may simply have been an oversight in transmission, however the *OED* notes that 'flue' is 'a woolly or downy substance; soft downy feathers' so Hogg may have been using it specifically in this context.

Publication History:
1818 – in *Albyn's Anthology*, II, 46–47 – see *Contributions to Musical Collections and Miscellaneous Songs* (S/SC, 2014)
1822 – in *Poetical Works*, III, 371–72

1828 – in the *Edinburgh Literary Journal* for 27 December (No. 7, 87–90 (pp. 89–90))
1831 – in *Songs by the Ettrick Shepherd*, pp. 112–13 – see p. 51 in the present edition

Musical Context:
The musical setting by Alexander Campbell in *Albyn's Anthology* uses the same Gaelic melody as Hogg mentions in his headnote to *Songs* 1831. Hogg writes that the tune 'was set by young Gow', presumably referring to Niel Gow, junior (1795–1823), who set several of Hogg's songs including 'Flora MacDonald's Lament' and who was involved in *A Border Garland* of [1819] – see *Contributions to Musical Collections and Miscellaneous Songs*. A song sheet entitled 'Chai' banachag na bouille o bhouchaileachd earrich oirn. Black Mary. A favourite old Gaelic song, set for the voice, piano forte, flute or violin' was printed by J. Watlen and published in Edinburgh and London around 1795 has been found: see BL H.1653.g.(18.). However, a setting for 'Black Mary' with the melody 'Is fallain gun dith thainig thu' by Niel Gow Jr. has not come to light. Hogg may have simply forgotten the original version of the song with its Gaelic melody in *Albyn's Anthology*. Campbell's own editorial note with the song explains that he was sent the air ' by Colonel David Stewart of Garth, to whom it was communicated by the learned and ingenious author of "Elements of Gaelic Grammar," namely, the Rev. Alexander Stewart of Dingwall; but without the Gaelic words of the song' (*Albyn's Anthology*, II, 46). Campbell also notes that he supplied Hogg with the tune, 'to suit which Mr Hogg composed his stanzas' (II, 46).

Explanatory Notes:
51 [headnote] John Aitken of the house of Constable and Co. John Aitken (1793–1833), Hogg's close friend and confidant. Hogg claims to have composed 'The Mermaid's Song' at Aiken's house (see p. 40 and notes). He was editor of 'Constable's Miscellany' during the crash of 1826, and continued to work for the firm until 1831. (Information derived from *Letters*, I, 'Notes on Correspondents', pp. 440–42). Gillian Hughes also writes that Aitken 'had taken a prominent part in establishing the *Edinburgh Literary Journal*' (*Letters*, I, p. 441).

Love Is Like a Dizziness (pp. 52–53)

Creative Context:
This is another song with a long Publication History and established popularity before it reaches inclusion in *Songs* 1831. Hogg says, in his 1831 headnote, that he wrote the song 'twenty-six years ago' which dates the date of composition to *c.*1805. The first publication of the song, with the title 'Love's like a Dizziness' is not until *The Forest Minstrel* of 1810. However, Garside's and Jackson's notes to the song (S/SC, 2006) suggest that several references in the lyric, including mention of 'Corryvrichen', which Hogg saw on his second Highland Journey in 1803, and the explorer Mungo Park (1771–1806), who was just embarking on his last trip to Africa in 1805, may well support an earlier genesis of the song focusing on the years 1804–05. No earlier version of the song than that in the section of 'Humorous' songs in *The Forest Minstrel*, has been located.

If the song was created sometime between 1805 and its first publication in 1810 then the references to 'Peggy' may well relate to Hogg's early relationship with Margaret Phillips, his future wife. Hogg met Margaret in Edinburgh some time during the years 1807–1810 when he was moving in the City's refined social circles that included Chalmers Forrest and Eliza Izett (see 'Caledonia', pp. 13–14). Reference to the 'Athol deer' (l. 5) has associations with the area around Kinnaird House in the Athol valley, which was the Izetts' summer residence from 1805 to 1810 when they made it their permanent home. Furthermore, the description of 'Peggy' is borrowed from other images of Margaret that Hogg composed in the 1810s. For example, 'Her wily glance I'll ne'er forget | The dear, the lovely blinkin' o't' (ll. 31–32) is derived from 'Scotch Song', a song concerning his love-enthralment of Margaret that first appeared in *The Spy*, No. 15 (8 December 1810), p. 120. Hogg repeated this line in his correspondence with Margaret dated 27 July 1811, where he writes, 'and I would watch thy witching smile and glossy een sae dark and wiley': see *The Spy* (S/SC, 2000), p. 163, and *Letters*, I, 112–13. Moreover, the song's love-beguiled atmosphere is similar to that found in 'Love Letter' and 'Mischievous Woman' (or 'Scotch Song'), two songs that Hogg writes were originally 'parts of humorous letters to the young lady who afterwards became my wife': see 'Love Letter', pp. 87–88 (p. 87) and 'Mischievous Woman', p. 88.

The song next appeared, with slight variations, in the third volume of Hogg's *Poetical Works* of 1822. There are only two substantive changes as noted by Garside and Jackson. Prior to its appearance in *Songs* 1831 the 'Shepherd' character in *Blackwood's* interrupts a *Noctean* discussion about 'perspective and landscape' to sing the chorus of 'Love is Like a Dizziness' (*Noctes Ambrosianae*, No. XLVIII (April 1830)). The text is an amalgam of the two earlier versions in *The Forest Minstrel* and *Poetical Works*. For example, the first line, 'O! love! love! love!' follows that found in *Poetical Works* while the third line 'Love's like a dizziness' is from *The Forest Minstrel* version.

For *Songs* 1831 Hogg most probably referred back to *The Forest Minstrel* but, as Garside and Jackson suggest, he doubtless removed the fifth stanza referring to Park, as it was no longer topical. Minor alterations include changing 'harass' to 'torment' (l. 8) and drafting a new opening for the third stanza which was 'Soon as the dawn had brought the day' in previous versions.

The only extant manuscript is that in Hogg's fair-copy manuscript for *Songs* 1831 at NLS MS 4805, at f. 51r and v. The manuscript is page-numbered '59' and '60' and the text is transferred cleanly to the printed page. As usual practice, Hogg only writes the chorus in full after the first verse in the manuscript. He notes to the printer at the end of the song that the chorus should be printed 'in full' and this is how it appears in the printed text.

Publication History:
1810 – in *The Forest Minstrel*, pp. 114–16 – see (S/SC, 2006), pp. 115–17 and 299–301
1822 – in *Poetical Works*, III, 380–83
1830 – in *Blackwood's Edinburgh Magazine*, 27 (April 1830), 659–94 (p. 665)
1831 – in *Songs by the Ettrick Shepherd*, pp. 114–16 – see pp. 52–53 in the present edition

Unauthorised versions:
The song was popular in Hogg's lifetime and reprinted in many of the major song-collections, such as *The Harp of Caledonia*, 2 vols (Glasgow and Edinburgh, n.d. [*c*.1818]), I, 264–66 and 'Robert Chambers's *The Scottish Songs*, 2 vols (Edinburgh: William Tait, 1829), I, 152–53' (see *The Forest Minstrel*, 2006, p. 300). Interestingly, both these collections use the version of the song found in *The Forest Minstrel* as

copy text. Details of posthumous printings of the song are found in *The Forest Minstrel* (S/SC, 2006), p. 300.

Musical Context:
As Hogg states in his headnote for 1831, the song is set to a spirited Irish air called 'Paddy's Wedding' which was also noted at its air in *The Forest Minstrel* in 1810. Full details about the history of the tune can be found in *The Forest Minstrel* (S/SC, 2006), pp. 300–301. As Garside and Jackson note, the tune appears to have come to public attention through the English song composer Charles Dibdin who included it with the title 'The Irish Wedding' as one of several ballads in a show called 'The General Election' first performed in London in 1796 (see *The Forest Minstrel* (S/SC, 2006), pp. 300–01). The tune Hogg had in mind is, as Garside and Jackson indicate, a variant of this tune. They note that several variants were published in fiddle collections by Pringle, Gow and Cooper between *c.*1801 and *c.*1806.

O, Weel Befa' the Maiden Gay (pp. 53–55)

Creative Context:
As is the case with 'Love is like a Dizziness' (immediately preceding it in *Songs* 1831) this song has a long Publication History before 1831. An account of its textual and publishing history is given by Thomas Richardson in *Contributions to Blackwood's Edinburgh Magazine* I, (S/SC, 2008). There is also a detailed account of the song also in *Contributions to Annuals and Gift Books* (S/SC, 2006,), p. 154 (text), pp. 319–21 (notes) and 393 (Explanatory Notes).

In summary, the song beginning 'O weel befa' the guileless heart' first appears as one of several songs (also including 'My Love's Bonny', p. 75) in *The Haunted Glen*, published within Hogg's two volume collection of *Dramatic Tales* in 1817. It appears as the final song in this dramatic tale. But it is Hogg's headnote in *Songs* 1831 which accounts for its creation. He claims that this was one of several pieces (often songs) which he wrote in the competitive environment of Ellery (Elleray), 'Mr Wilson's seat in Westmorland'. Hogg references *The Queen's Wake*, his narrative poem about a bardic competition, which had appeared to acclaim in 1813. This context, if reliable, would date the song's creation to September–October 1814, when Hogg spent time in the Lakes, and stayed with Wilson at his house as well as visiting the Wordsworths in Rydal Mount and spending time with Robert Southey (see Hughes, *James Hogg A Life*, (2007), pp. 126–29). That Hogg chooses to refer in detail to this process of creating songs in *Songs* 1831 again emphasises the importance of his role as a songwriter within this notable grouping of 'poets and great men'.

The song appeared next within *The Haunted Glen* in the second volume of *Poetical Works* in 1822. When it was included in *Blackwood's Edinburgh Magazine* as part of the *Noctes Ambrosianae* series in 1826 (No. XXVII) it was substantially revised and its first line became 'O weel befa' the maiden gay'. Richardson accounts for the major revisions to the song and also accounts for a number of subsequent revisions in the version Hogg sent to the London music publisher Goulding, D'Almaine & Co.: see also notes by Hughes and Currie in *Contributions to Annuals and Gift Books*. It is notable that this is one of several songs from *Noctes* in 1826 to be included in *Songs* 1831 (see also: 'The Village of Balmaquapple', 'Meg o'Marley' and 'Bonny Mary').

It would appear that Hogg contributed the revised version of the song, along with 'My Bonny Mary', to *Blackwood's*, following a request for "one or two pastoral love songs" (see 'Bonny Mary', pp. 47–49). Although only a fragment of 'Bonny Mary' survives along with Hogg's note to Blackwood (NLS, MS 4017, fol. 141), Gillian Hughes conjectures that the other song was probably 'O Weel Befa' the Maiden Gay', as both songs were published together within the same *Noctean* dialogue (*Letters*, II, note, p. 248). Blackwood was apparently more than satisfied with Hogg's 'two capital Songs' which he received 'just in time for the Noctes'. He informed Hogg in his letter of 24 June 1826, 'They enliven the Noctes, and I hope you will send me some more very soon. I have credited your acc with two Guineas for them.' (*Letters*, II, note, p. 248).

It was this 1826 version of the song in *Blackwood's* that Hogg used as his copy text for *Songs* 1831 (with some small changes as noted by Richardson), but he removes all *Noctean* dialogue, which refers in part to the wider circulation of Hogg's songs. The character of 'North' notes that some of James's songs have been included in Allan Cunningham's recently published *Songs of Scotland* (1825), and he concludes that it is 'A very good collection indeed'. But Hogg leaves these comments out of his headnote, choosing to include instead his account of the song-writing competitions in the Lakes.

As Hughes and Currie note, before including it in *Songs* 1831 Hogg had also sent a copy of the song, in its earlier iteration ('O weel befa' the guileless heart') to his London music publisher Goulding, D'Almaine & Co. in his letter of 24 August 1829. This letter included a group of three 'fairy' songs which Hogg thought they could publish (see *Letters II*, 351–54). Hughes and Currie include the texts of all three songs in their edition of *Contributions to Annuals and Gift Books* (pp. 155–57). Hogg was hopeful that their house composer Sir Henry Bishop, who had just recently completed setting thirteen of Hogg's songs for *Select & Rare Scotish Melodies* [1828], would set this one for their annual *The Musical Bijou*, but this did not happen. Instead the text of this song (with some variants as discussed by Hughes and Currie) appeared in the *Monthly Musical and Literary Magazine* in February 1830 (p. 30). See Gillian Hughes: 'Hogg and the *Monthly Musical and Literary Magazine*, in *Studies in Hogg and his World*, 15 (2004), 120–25. For more information on Hogg's relationship with Goulding, D'Almaine & Co. and Sir Henry Bishop see *Contributions to Musical Collections and Miscellaneous Songs*.

Just following the publication of 'O weel befa' the maiden gay' in *Songs* 1831, the song appeared again in *Blackwood's* in March 1831, sung by the Shepherd as part of *Noctes Ambrosianae* No. LV. As Richardson notes, this second appearance in *Noctes* was by way of advertising the recent publication of Hogg's *Songs by the Ettrick Shepherd* (1831). The magazine did not print a review of Hogg's collection, but the dialogue alongside this second appearance of the song quotes the Shepherd as saying: 'Noo, I'll sing you a bit sang, out o' the colleckshun'.

While using the first 1826 *Blackwood's* version as the copy text for *Songs* 1831 (with some small revisions) the 1831 *Blackwood's* appearance uses the text from *Songs* 1831, sticking with its revised final line, but restoring 'sae' in l.6 from the earlier version, which Hogg had amended for *Songs* 1831. The fair-copy manuscript of the song for *Songs* 1831 is in NLS MS 4805, ff. 52r–53v. Within the headnote, Hogg has scored out the title of the poem' "The Gude Greye Katt"' and written "Isabelle" above, an alteration that is retained in the published text. These two poems were published in *The Poetic Mirror* in 1816 as supposed contributions from leading poets, such as Wordsworth ('The Stranger', mentioned in the headnote) and Coleridge ('Isabelle'), and Hogg himself ('The Gude Greye Katt').

Hogg's unpunctuated text is transferred reasonably cleanly to the printed version. As noted above, however, the printer appears to have misinterpreted Hogg's hand-writing when copying the second verse at l. 8. Hogg had closely followed previous versions and written 'flowery den' but this is printed as 'flowing den' in *Songs* 1831.

Publication History:
1817 – in *Dramatic Tales* (Edinburgh: John Ballantyne and London: Longman, Hurst, Rees, Orme, and Brown), II, pp. 269–70
1822 – in *Poetical Works*, II, 179–228 (song on pp. 227–28)
1826 – in *Blackwood's Edinburgh Magazine*, 20 (July 1826), 90–109 (p. 108) – see (S/ SC, 2008), pp. 192–93, 519–20
1830 – as 'Song. By the Ettrick Shepherd' in the *Monthly Musical and Literary Magazine* (February 1830), 30
1831 – in *Songs by the Ettrick Shepherd*, pp. 117–20 – see pp. 53–55 in the present edition
1831 – in *Blackwood's Edinburgh Magazine*, 29 (March 1831), 546–47 – see notes on the song in 1826 appearance

Musical Context:
Hogg makes no mention of a melody in his 1831 headnote. But when he sent the song to Goulding & D'Almaine on 24 August 1829, he stated: 'The above song was written to a very old air the original of The Wauking o' the Fauld. If Mr Bishop would therefore approximate the air to that it would please me best' (*Letters*, II, p. 353). Glen notes that this air is 'apparently very ancient' even though copies have not been traced, he says, before William Thomson's *Orpheus Caledonius* of 1733. However Glen believes that it is included by Robert Bremner in his 1760 edition of 'Music to the Songs in the Gentle Shepherd' and earlier in Oswald's *Caledonian Pocket Companion* in 1751: see Glen, p. 85. It is also included by Johnson in *SMM*, I, 88. We have traced a reference to a song sheet by John Daniel published in Edinburgh by Small, Bruce & Co.,which is reviewed in *The Harmonicon* in 1832, but no copy has been found. This publisher was at 54 Princes Street, Edinburgh between 1830–33.

Explanatory Notes:
See *Contributions to Blackwood's Edinburgh Magazine*, I, p. 520 and *Contributions to Annuals and Gift Books*, p. 393.

Cameron's Welcome Hame (pp. 55–56)

Creative Context:
This song (which shares its theme with 'The Hill of Lochiel' also included in *Songs* 1831 see pp. 64–65) was most probably created in the early 1820s when Hogg was working on songs for inclusion in George Thomson's forthcoming octavo edition of *Select Melodies of Scotland* (1822–25). For further information about Hogg's involvement with Thomson's collections see *Contributions to Musical Collections and Miscellaneous Songs*. Hogg had already collaborated with Thomson from 1815 on songs for the fifth folio volume of *A Select Collection of Original Scottish Airs* which appeared in 1818.

'Cameron's Welcome Hame' was first mentioned in Hogg's letter to Thomson of March 1822. Here Hogg sent his original text of the song titled 'Pull Away' (Notes to 'Pull away Jolly Boys' in *Contributions to Musical Collections and Miscellaneous*

Songs, and he states: 'I wrote one [a song] for Rattling roaring Willie last week but I have mislaid it and cannot get it to day if I should die' (*Letters*, II, 149). Hogg must have quickly discovered his 'lost' manuscript and he submits a copy of the song titled 'Cameron's Welcome Hame' to the 'Air Rattling Roaring Willie' to Thomson later in March, informing him: 'I know you will be proposing some alterations let the song be as good as it will I send you the original sketch of this song as I found it fallen by without altering a word': see NLS MS Acc. 9789, with Hogg's accompanying letter; it is reprinted in *Letters*, II, 153–55 (p. 153).

It was typical of Thomson's editorial practice to ask for changes to his writers' contributions. Thomson was not satisfied with the song and did not publish it in any of his collections (see Thomson's note of 16 March 1822 at BL. Add. MS 35, 268, f. 900. Hogg was undeterred and informed Thomson on 21 March that, although 'a little astonished' he was 'not dissapointed [sic] as I am very anxious to publish it myself to the same air and shall let you see it in a month'. He requested that, as he had 'no copy and do not reccollect [sic] a line of it [...]. Be sure to return my copy or another of the same': see *Letters* II, 157–58. There is evidence that Hogg also gave a copy of the song to the artist William Bewick (1795–1866) in 1823, when Bewick was sketching Hogg: see *The Life and Letters of William Bewick*, ed. by Thomas Landseer, 2 vols (London: Hurst and Blackett, 1871), (I, 259–60).

The song was subsequently published under the title 'O Strike Your Harp, My Mary' in the sixth and final volume of *The Scotish Minstrel*, edited by Robert Archibald Smith and published by Robert Purdie of Edinburgh in [1824]. In the first edition the song is printed over pp. 70–71, but appears on pp. 20–21 in the second and third editions. The sixth volume was completed in January 1824. For further information about Hogg's involvement with this collection and for a copy of the song see *Contributions to Musical Collections and Miscellaneous Songs*.

Collation between Hogg's original manuscript submitted to Thomson in March 1822 and the version published in the first edition of *The Scotish Minstrel* reveals significant redrafting of verses three and five. For example, 'When ye sat on my knee' (l. 18) becomes 'When we sat in the tree'. And the focus moves to 'Mary' as single protagonist of the song with the change from ' "Our hame's now gane for aye" to 'My father's ha's are gone' (l. 24). In verse five, there is evidence of two levels of redrafting as Hogg writes above ll. 37–40, removing potentially sensitive political material. At ll. 39–40 Hogg originally wrote 'He'll raise some kindred monarch | To right poor Scotia's skaith', which he then redrafts to 'I still had hopes that heaven | Would right poor Scotia's skaith', which is retained in *The Scotish Minstrel* version.

The copy text for *Songs* 1831 is the version in *The Scotish Minstrel* with slight verbal variations. For example, at l. 22 'pine' is changed to 'scene', a change that corrects an obvious misreading of Hogg's hand by the printer or engraver of *The Scotish Minstrel*. Further variants include 'Behind yon cloud sae dreary' to 'Behind yon curtain dreary' (l. 29).

Hogg's fair-copy holograph manuscript of the original version submitted to Thomson in March 1822 survives at NLS MS Acc. 9789, together with Hogg's accompanying letter and a typescript. The holograph is undated and there is no watermark so that the original date of composition is not known. The full text of the song and Hogg's letter to Thomson are reprinted in *Letters*, II, 153–55. The fair-copy manuscript of the song for *Songs* 1831 is at NLS MS 4805, ff. 55v–59r. The pages are numbered '64', '65', and '66' and follow sequentially from the previous song. Aside from one alteration, where the printer misreads Hogg's hand at l. 33, writing 'waefu'' in place of 'ruefu'', Hogg's text is transferred cleanly to the printed version.

Publication History:
[1824] – in *The Scotish Minstrel*, VI, 20–21 (thereafter pp. 70–71 in later editions) – see *Contributions to Musical Collections and Miscellaneous Songs* (S/SC, 2014)
1831 – in *Songs by the Ettrick Shepherd*, pp. 121–23 – see pp. 55–56 in the present edition

Musical Context:
Hogg's 1831 headnote states clearly that the 'song was written to the Highland air bearing that name' and he understandably refers his reader to Smith's *The Scotish Minstrel* for a musical setting. Originally composed to match the spirited tune 'Rattling, Roaring Willie' for Thomson's collections, Smith chooses to set the lyric to a melody with very different mood. 'Rattling Roaring Willie' was a spirited traditional border tune best know to Burns's lyric with this title: see Donald A. Low's, *The Songs of Robert Burns* (London: Routledge, 1993), pp. 276–77 (p. 276) and also in Stenhouse, p. 184. This tune had already appeared in Johnson's *SMM*, II, no. 192.

But the first edition of *The Scotish Minstrel* notes that the air is 'Cameron's welcome hame' and Smith notes on the musical plate that the melody has been 'written from the singing of Mrs Maxwell Senr. of Bredliand . This is also marked 'lively' but the tune bears no resemblance to "Rattling Roaring Willie'.

Explanatory Notes:
55 [Title] and **56, ll. 19–20 Auchnaccarry** the Clan Cameron lands were traditionally at Achnacarry in Inverness-shire. Hogg passed by Achnacarry on his journey through the Highlands in the summer of 1803, referring to it as 'the residence of the brave Lochiel, who was wounded at the battle of Culloden, and escaped with prince Charles to France.' Hogg goes on to describe the setting: 'The whole scene is romantic beyond conception: on the banks of Loch-Arkaig beyond it, there are large forests of wood, which in many places are perfect thickets' (*Highland Journeys*, ed. by Hans de Groot (S/SC, 2010), pp. 80–81. See also Hogg's note to Thomson in *Letters*, II, 153.
56, ll. 43–44 The good, the just, is given | To right our nation's wrang probably a reference to the forfeited Cameron estates which were restored to Donald Cameron (1769–1832), the grandson of 'the brave Lochiel', under the General Amnesty of 1784.

Oh-hon, Oh Righ! (p. 57)

Creative Context:
This song appeared in several publications before Hogg included it in *Songs* 1831. It was first presented to Alexander Campbell as one of the thirteen songs Hogg contributed to his two volume collection *Albyn's Anthology* of 1816 and 1818. It appeared with the title, 'Why Should I Sit and Sigh' in Vol. 1 of 1816. For further information on Cambpell's collection, Hogg's involvement with it and copies of the songs, see *Contributions to Musical Collections and Miscellaneous Songs*. This is a popular Gaelic tune and shows Hogg's specific interest in Highland material which he had developed since his first journeys to the Highlands in 1802. It should be noted that this song is very different to another in *Songs* 1831 with a

very similar title, namely 'Oh hon-a-Righ!' on pp. 124–25 of the present volume.

The song was next included as one of several songs in the fourth volume of Hogg's *Poetical Works* of 1822, where the copy text is the *Albyn's Anthology* version, without change. Both versions include the same nominated 'air' or melody entitled "*Cnochd a Bheanneihd*" below the title.

Hogg then redrafted the song for inclusion in the sixth and final volume of Robert Archibald Smith's musical collection *The Scotish Minstrel* published in [1824]. For further information on Smith's collection, Hogg's involvement with it and copies of the songs, see *Contributions to Musical Collections and Miscellaneous Songs*. Textually the song is the same, but Smith chooses to present a variant of the same tune 'Cnochd a Bheanneihd' (in a different key) and to present the verse first rather than the chorus. This means that the order of the lines has to be rearranged: rather than beginning the lyric with 'Why should I sit and sigh' as in the version for Campbell, Smith begins with 'Oh hon a ri! There's something wantin'' and gives the lines of text following this as the first part of the stanza (to match the lower-set part of the tune for the verse), following it with the four lines beginning 'Why should I sit and sigh' (to match the higher-set part of the tune for the chorus). This means that Smith omits Hogg's earlier refrain 'Ochon, o ri! there's something wanting' that had concluded each verse. In the second and third editions of the *Scotish Minstrel* the song moves to p. 60 of volume six. On the new plates used for the second and third editions, the orthography of some of the wording is slightly changed by the removal of the final 'g' in words such as 'rising' and 'wheeling' (ll. 9–10).

The copy text of the *Songs* 1831 version is that of the first edition of *The Scotish Minstrel* with a slight modification of the title to 'Oh-hon, oh Righ!'. The layout of the song is also slightly altered from the octet format to three ten-line verses formed by reducing the length of ll. 5–6 and ll. 8–9. Hogg's headnote mentions 'a simple Gaelic air of cross measure'and, if anything, this new layout of the text visibly accentuates this, for the short lines link to the most notable short phrases of the tune or air. The orthography and punctuation is also altered, no doubt for the sake of consistency within the volume, so that, for example, words ending 'ie' are changed to 'y'.

The only extant manuscript version of the song is Hogg's fair-copy manuscript for *Songs* 1831 at NLS MS 4805, ff. 26–102 at f. 55, immediately below the conclusion of 'Cameron's Welcome Hame' (which was also included in the sixth volume of Smith's *The Scotish Minstrel*). Hogg adds relatively rare punctuation to his mss version of the song in the form of an exclamation mark inserted after the opening word of the title. However, in the printed version the exclamation mark appears at the end of the title and the phrase within the song itself. An error occurs in translating Hogg's text to the printed page so that the word 'cow' (in all previous versions) is rendered 'now' (ll. 28–29). The rest of Hogg's unpunctuated text is transferred cleanly to the printed version.

Publication History:

1816 – in *Albyn's Anthology*, I, 14–15 – see *Contributions to Musical Collections and Miscellaneous Songs* (S/SC, 2014)

1822 – in *Poetical Works*, IV, 321–22

[1824] – in *The Scotish Minstrel*, VI, 61 – see *Contributions to Musical Collections and Miscellaneous Songs* (S/SC, 2014)

1831 – in *Songs by the Ettrick Shepherd*, pp. 124–25 – see p. 57 in the present edition

Musical Context:

Beside this song in *Albyn's Anthology* Campbell prints a fragment of six lines of a Gaelic song titled 'Cnochd a Bheannichd'. He notes: 'the remaining verses of this song have not come to the Editor's hand—in truth, Mr Hogg has caught the general spirit of the piece, and highly improved the subject' (I, p. 14). Smith's setting in *The Scotish Minstrel* is simpler and the tune is titled 'Gaelic Air'. It is in a different key and is not identical to the Campbell tune, but it is clearly a variant of the same tune.

Explanatory Notes:

57 **[Title]** a Gaelic refrain meaning 'Alas for the King' that Hogg used frequently
  in his writing. See also 'The Stuarts of Appin', pp. 28–29, and 'Oh hon-a-Righ!',
  pp. 124–25 of the present volume.

The Frazer's in the Correi (pp. 58–59)

Creative Context:

This is another of the batch of Jacobite songs included by Hogg in *Songs* 1831, indeed his headnote states clearly that this 'Jacobite thing' is one 'of which I have written so many'. It first appeared in *Jacobite Relics* II in 1821 as 'Song LXXXV'. 'Farewell to Glen-Shalloch' appears just three songs earlier in the same series and was included as one of the first songs in *Songs* 1831. It appeared with 'From the Gaelic' printed beneath the title of the song. While this might suggest that Hogg collected it, both this 1831 headnote and Murray Pittock's recent work on the song for *Jacobite Relics* suggests that Hogg probably created it himself. That the song was building on an older variant is noted by Hogg in *Jacobite Relics* where he states: 'I must beg pardon of the Highlanders for adding so much to the original idea in this song, by which it is nothing improved' (p. 356). The idea for the song may have originated with historical information included in Simon Fraser's 'Letter and Prospectus relative to the Airs and Melodies Peculiar to the Highlands of Scotland', end-dated '1 November 1815'. Fraser's *Airs and Melodies Peculiar to the Highlands of Scotland* first appeared in 1816, and was one of the first printed colletions of Highland melodies. Hogg often refers most favourably to Fraser's work in *Jacobite Relics*. In his letter Fraser explains that his 'paternal grandfather' along with 'Thomas Fraser of Gorthleck, the Editor's maternal grandfather (from the circumstance of the Pretender having passed the night after the Battle of Culloden in the house of the latter gentleman), were obliged to secret themselves in the recesses of the mountains, unable to approach their families or private concerns, and with little employment but ruminating on passing events' (reprinted in the second edition of *The Airs and Melodies Peculiar to the Highlands of Scotland*, edited by Angus Frawer (Inverness: Hugh Mackenzie, 1874). Fraser also gives additional information about the tune (see below in 'Musical Context'). The hero of the song's title is James Fraser, 9th of Foyers, who hid in a cave in Stratherrick, near to the Falls of Foyers in Inverness-shire for seven years after Culloden to avoid prosecution for his part in the rebellion. The Lovat Frasers owned the lands around Stratherrick from the sixteenth century which was forfeited to the crown in 1746 (excluding the lands of Foyers). The Frasers of Foyers are a branch of this Clan, and their Chieftain during the Jacobite campaign was Sir Simon Fraser, eleventh Lord Lovat.

The song had not appeared in the first *A Border Garland* of [1819], but it was one of four additional songs to appear with musical settings by Edinburgh composer James Dewar in the extended edition of *The Border Garland* in *c*.1829. For further information and to see this copy of the song see: *Contributions to Musical Collections and Miscellaneous Songs*. Robert Purdie, who edited the volume for the publisher Alexander Robertson & Co., simply reprinted the text from the *Jacobite Relics* version. Collation between these versions reveals small verbal and non-verbal variants, but too few to amount to whole scale redrafting on Hogg's part.

In 1834, Hogg published a story of the same title in which he fleshed out the details of the song more fully: see *Fraser's Magazine*, 9 (March 1834), (pp. 273–278). A further version of the song was included at the conclusion of the story (p. 278). Collation reveals this version to be a further redrafting of the song, with Hogg retaining elements from both the *Jacobite Relics* version and also the version found in *Songs* 1831 to create, in effect, a new version.

The copy text for the song as it appears in *Songs* 1831 is the version found in *Jacobite Relics* rather than the slightly altered text in *The Border Garland*. Hogg returns to the singular 'traitor's' of l.11, the reinsertion of the word 'now' (l. 15), and the return to 'the loved form' (l. 20) , although the correction of the word 'eye' is retained at l.19. 'And the raven's turn'd hoarse' (l.8) becomes 'For the raven's grown hoarse', and 'seek in the correi that sounds on the brae' becomes 'seek in yon correi that sounds from the brae' (l. 27). The most significant change is found in the closing four lines of the last verse which are new in the *Songs* 1831 version. These lines were originally spoken by the 'auld carle' in response to the young girl's questioning:

> "My sweet little maiden, beyond yon red sun
> "Dwells one who beholds all the deeds that are done:
> "Their crimes on the tyrants one day he'll repay,
> "And the names of the brave shall not perish for aye."

The rest of the dialogic exchange within the song is retained, so that Hogg's motive for the change of the last four lines is not clear.

The only extant manuscript version of the song is Hogg's fair-copy manuscript for *Songs* 1831 at NLS MS 4805, ff. 55v–56r. The pages are numbered '68' and '69', which follows 'Oh-hon, oh Righ' within the sequence of both MS4805 and *Songs* 1831. In transferring Hogg's text to the printed volume, the printer misreads Hogg's hand in the spelling of 'Gorthaly', which is printed as 'Gorthaleg' (l. 22). Aside from this one slip, Hogg's unpunctuated text is transferred cleanly to the printed version.

Publication History:

1821 – in *Jacobite Relics*, II, 166–67 and 356 – see also (S/SC, 2003), p. 519
c.1829 – in *The Border Garland*, pp. 34–36 – see *Contributions to Musical Collections and Miscellaneous Songs* (S/SC, 2014)
1831 – in *Songs by the Ettrick Shepherd*, pp. 126–28 – see pp. 58–59 in the present edition
1834 – in *Fraser's Magazine*, 9 (March 1834), 273–78
Unauthorised versions:
1829 –'The Fraser's in the Correi' was published in *The Jacobite Minstrelsy, with Notes* (Glasgow: R. Griffin, 1829), pp. 267–69, where the copy text is *Jacobite Relics*. Further information on this publication is given in the notes to *The Border Garland* in *Contributions to Musical Collections and Miscellaneous Songs* (S/SC, 2014). See also *Letters*, II, 341 and 343.

Musical Context:

Hogg's notes to the song in *Jacobite Relics* state that there is a fuller 'set of the air' 'to the same name' in Simon Fraser's *The Airs and Melodies Peculiar to the Highlands of Scotland*, edited by Simon Fraser (1816). Pittock notes that no air of this name is in that collection. However, Fraser's note about the story of the hiding Highlanders, quoted above, is clearly connected to the tune titled 'The Jacobites in their Hiding Places' or 'Nach bocdh a bhi'm falach'["the Rebels in their Hiding Places"] (See Fraser's *Airs and Melodies*, p. 58). It is a variant of this tune which is used for the song in *Jacobite Relics* and which James Dewar also chooses to set (with slight variants) in *The Border Garland*.

Explanatory Notes:

58, l. 3 the red-coats rank the Hanoverian forces were garrisoned at Fort Augustus on Loch Ness, close to the mansion house of Foyers on the banks of the river by the falls.

58, l. 11 Sassenach breed the English.

58, l. 14 The harper of Errick the River Errick is in Stratherrick, 'rising in the mountains of Strathdearn, and entering Loch Ness at Boleskine': see *The Statistical Account of Scotland* (1791–99), vol. 20; 'Parish of Boleskine and Abertarff', p. 20

58, l. 16 the Saxon a further reference to the English as the enemy of the Jacobites.

58, l. 19 pick eye from a bonneted head Jacobites traditionally wore blue bonnets. According to tradition, Fraser of Foyers was known locally as 'Bonaid Odhar (Dun bonnet), so that the country people could talk of him openly': see 'Tales of Old Days on the Aldourie Estate', by Lieut. Colonel Neil Fraser-Tytler, in *Transactions of the Gaelic Society of Inverness*, vol. 32 (1924–25), 144–57.

58, l. 20 by the tartans that's clad for a well-informed discussion of 'tartan's symbolic link with (militant) Jacobitism in the first half of the eighteenth century', see, Murray G. H. Pittock, *The Myth of the Jacobite Clans* (Edinburgh: Edinburgh University Press, 1995), pp. 112–14 (p. 113).

58, ll. 21 the cliff where the Frazer abides no contemporary published account of Fraser's concealment has been located. Hogg may have received details of Fraser's cave directly from Simon Fraser's note in his *Airs* as noted above.

58, l. 22 Where Foyers, Culduthel, and Gorthaleg hides Culduthel and Gorthaly were Frasers in Stratherrick. Simon Lovat, the Fraser Clan Chieftain sheltered with the Prince the night after Culloden at the farmhouse of Gorthaly before taking to the hills of the Western Highlands. Hogg was certainly familiar with Jacobite traditions surrounding the Falls of Foyer as he includes an incident involving the murder of four red-coats who are drowned in the Falls in the concluding section of *The Three Perils of Woman* (1823): see (S/SC, 2002 rev. paperback), Antony Hasler and Douglas S. Mack, eds., pp. 403–04.

58, l. 29 I sought them last night with the haunch of the deer the reference to the young girl taking food to Foyers is based on tradition. Neil Fraser-Tytler notes, 'the Laird of Foyers, looking out from his cave, saw a soldier following secretly a girl bringing up his food': see 'Tales of Old Days on the Aldourie Estate', *Transactions of the Gaelic Society of Inverness*, vol. 32 (1924–25), 144–157 (155).

58, l. 31 the brown heather-cock the red grouse; a medium-sized game bird of reddish-brown colour found on uplands and heather moors.

Ye Breezes that Spring (p. 59)

Creative Context:
'Ye Breezes that Spring' is one of only two songs (also 'Ohon-A-Righ!' on pp. 124–25) within *Songs* 1831, which comes from Hogg's short political drama of 1822 titled *The Royal Jubilee. A Scottish Mask* (Edinburgh: William Blackwood). This drama included eight songs and this one appeared as 'Song II' where, untitled, it is presented simply as 'By the Sea-Nymphs' to the air 'Birks of Invermay'. More information on the drama can be found in *James Hogg: The Bush Aboon Traquhair and the Royal Jubliee* (S/SC, 2008). In short the play was written for George IV's famous visit to Scotland in August 1822, the first undertaken by a British monarch for over a century. King George travelled to Edinburgh from London by sea and within the context of the play, the 'sea-nymphs' fly out to meet the Royal Ship, while singing this song.

Taking its title from the first line, the song then appeared as 'Ye Breezes that Spring' 'with a 'melody by the Ettrick Shepherd', within *Select & Rare Scotish Melodies*; a collection of thirteen of Hogg's songs published by the London publishers, Goulding & D'Almaine in [1828]. For further information on the collection, Hogg's involvement with it and the song itself: *Contributions to Musical Collections and Miscellaneous Songs*. The first fourteen lines follow the text of 'Song II', with one minor change in l.4 to 'Arabia's spicy gale'. The 'free man's boast from the forest and hall' becomes 'the cottager's boast over lordlings and hall' (l. 13) and the song, understandably removes its specific reference to the King at the end amending the final two lines to: 'Bring these thou breeze of the Forest abroad,/ And welcome be thou to this lowly abode'.

It is not clear if Hogg uses this [1828] text or the original from *The Royal Jubliee* as his copy text for *Songs* 1831. He sticks with the amended 'Arabia's spicy gale!' from *Select & Rare*, but he makes considerable changes to the final six lines. The 'poor man' is still mentioned but 'The good man's pray'r' becomes 'The shepherd's proud boast' in *Songs* 1831. And Hogg changes the final two lines once again from a more general all-embracing welcome to something more romantic and bardic: 'Come laden with these, thou breeze of the hill!/And the lay of the Minstrel shall hail thee still'. His headnote for 1831 makes no mention of the song's previous incarnations.

No manuscript for the song has yet been found. This is one of the songs missing from the fair-copy manuscript for *Songs* 1831 (NLS MS 4805, ff. 26–102 (Blackwood Papers)) see: 'The Genesis of the Text', pp. xli–xlviii.

Publication History:
1822 – as 'Song II' in *The Royal Jubliee: a Scottish Mask*, pp. 13–14 – see *The Bush Aboon Traquhair and The Royal Jubliee* (S/SC, 2008) pp. 125–26 (Text and musical notation) and pp. 185–56 (notes)

[1828] – in *Select & Rare Scotish Melodies*, pp. 19–22 – see *Contributions to Musical Collections and Miscellaneous Songs* (S/SC, 2014)

1831 – in *Songs by the Ettrick Shepherd*, pp. 129–30 – see p. 59 in the present edition

Musical Context:
The song's appearance in *The Royal Jubilee* is with the tune 'The Birks of Invermay' and melodic notation is printed above the words of the first verse (on p. 13). The tune was one of the most popular of the eighteenth century and appeared in many of the major collections including *Orpheus Caledonius* (1725). See Glen, p. 80 for

further details. Hogg's song 'I Lookit East, I Lookit West' (*Songs* 1831, pp. 18–20) was also sung to this tune. Hogg's 1831 headnote states that the setting by Henry Bishop is of 'an original air' but the melody he sets is not 'The Birks of Invermay' and may be Bishop's own composition. For a copy of the setting see: *Contributions to Musical Collections and Miscellaneous Songs*.

Explanatory Notes:
59, l. 4 More sweet than Arabia's spicy gale Scotland had close links with the lucrative spice trade routes of Arabia and India through the British East India Company.
59, l. 16 the lay of the Minstrel echoes the title of Scott's long narrative poem, *The Lay of the Last Minstrel* (1805).

Come Rowe the Boat (pp. 59–60)

Creative Context:
Hogg's headnote to the song suggests that it was written much earlier in his career, and it may possibly connect to his earlier Highland journeys. There are accounts of a number of boat trips in Hogg's *Highland Journey*, but to date no clear evidence has been found for the creation of this song. The song first appeared as one of the thirteen Hogg songs published by the London music publisher Goulding & D'Almaine in *Select & Rare Scotish Melodies* in [1828] with musical settings by Sir Henry Bishop, and Hogg promotes this collection clearly in his headnote. The song may have been one of 'eight more songs for your correspondents' which Hogg sent to Goulding & D'Almaine's agent Robert Purdie on 18 January 1828: see *Letters*, II, 284. For further information about this collection, Hogg's involvement with it and to see the song itself see: *Contributions to Musical Collections and Miscellaneous Songs*.

Unsurprisingly, it is the text from *Select & Rare Scotish Melodies* which Hogg uses as copy text for the song which appears in *Songs* 1831. There is slight textual modification of the spelling in two places: in the title, where 'Row' changes to 'Rowe', and also in the spelling of 'Ben Airtly' (l. 17), which is changed to 'Ben-Aitley'. The usual changes to punctuation and orthography, which come with the change of printer, are present, such as changing capitals to lower case and removing exclamation marks.

As with 'Ye Breezes that Spring' which comes immediately before it in *Songs* 1831, there is no extant manuscript for this song in the fair-copy manuscript of the volume which is at NLS MS 4805, ff. 26–102 (Blackwood Papers).

Publication History:
[1828] – in *Select & Rare Scotish Melodies*, pp. 33–6 – see *Contributions to Musical Collections and Miscellaneous Songs* (S/SC, 2014)
1831 – in *Songs by the Ettrick Shepherd*, pp. 131–2 – see pp. 59–60 in the present edition

Musical Context:
Aside from the fact that Hogg mentions the song being 'a short cross measure' he provides no information about the melody for this song, but states in his headnote that 'it is set in a modern style by Bishop'. It is most likely that Bishop has created his own melody as a nod to the pibroch or *piobaireachd* (Gaelic) which is the music

of the *pib mhor* (Gaelic) or Highland pipe, mentioned by Hogg in the text. The dotted rhythms and the wide leaps in the melody are tokenistic, however, for Bishop's melody is gentle and smooth and does not create that sense of wildness often associated with pibroch. For a copy of the setting see: *Contributions to Musical Collections and Miscellaneous Songs*. The tune does have resonances to 'Fear a' bhata' ('The Boatman') which appeared in Simon Fraser's *Airs and Melodies peculiar to the Highlands of Scotland* of 1816.

Explanatory Notes:
60, l. 17 deer of Ben-Aitley not located. In the *Select & Rare Scotish Melodies* version of the song it is spelt 'Ben Airtly'. Both are possibly a miss-spelling of 'Airtney' or Artney. Glen Artney is a large glen in the Loch Earn area and it is in this region that 'Kilmeny' of *The Queen's Wake* (1813) is set. In the report of the 'Parish of Comrie' it is recorded that there are 'between 200 and 300 deer in the forest of Glen Airtney' (*Statistical Account of Scotland*, vol. 11, 178–188 (p. 182)).

The Highlander's Farewell (pp. 60–61)

Creative Context:
There is no information about the creation of this song, but, like most of the Jacobite songs included in *Songs* 1831, it was first published in *Jacobite Relics* II in 1821 with 'From the Gaelic' beside the title. Hogg's note in the *Relics* states that someone translated the song for him, but that he cannot remember who it was, nor where 'I pickt up the air' and he notes that it feels as though he has 'never seen either of them before'. This places heavy emphasis on the traditional root for the song. Pittock notes that it is most unlikely that the text is from the Gaelic but there is evidence that the tune has Gaelic roots. He also notes that this song is the reverse of the gallant 'Highland Laddie' genre for here 'a defeated, emasculated warrior laments the irretrievable loss of the domestic space which stands for Scotland' (p. 521). This element is much highlighted by Hogg in the headnote for 1831 which includes the terms 'desperate Jacobite effusions' and 'the beastly cruelty of their victors'.

Before choosing to include it in *Songs* 1831 Hogg gave it, along with several other songs, to Robert Archibald Smith and it appears under the shorter title 'The Highlander's Farewell' in the the the fifth volume of *The Scotish Minstrel*, edited by Smith and published by Robert Purdie of Edinburgh in [1823]. For further information about this collection, Hogg's involvement in it and a copy of the song see: *Contributions to Musical Collections and Miscellaneous Songs*.

Hogg most probably used the *Relics* text as copy text for *The Scotish Minstrel*, as there are no changes between the two. In the second and third editions of *The Scotish Minstrel* the song moves to the sixth volume within the collection (p. 97). One slight change occurs on l. 9 in the second edition, where 'might' becomes 'night. This is most likely the result of a printing error, revealing that this is a new plate. The error is carried forward into the third edition where the title is altered to 'The Hielander's Farewell' but otherwise the song is textually unaltered from the *Jacobite Relics* version.

The copy text for *Songs* 1831 is also *Jacobite Relics* though there are now several variants. For example, 'My native land' is changed to 'But Scotland' (l. 7). Other changes tone down the Jacobite sentiment: for example, the 'mean deceiver' of

l. 14 is here the 'ruthless reaver', and the 'helpless rover' of l. 22 becomes the 'hapless rover'. A further, more significant textual alteration occurs at l. 27, where Hogg redrafts the original Jacobite claim, 'A stranger fill thy ancient throne' to the more opaque, 'Strangers have trod thy glory on'. Hogg uses his headnote here to suggest his personal frustration over the failed Jacobite cause, while nodding his head to contemporary monarchy. But he notably uses this opportunity to promote himself as the key composer of national songs and the most prolific of 'all the Bards of Britain put together'.

As with the preceding two songs in *Songs* 1831 there is no extant manuscript of this song in the fair-copy manuscript for the volume at NLS MS 4805, ff. 26–102 (Blackwood Papers).

Publication History:
1821 – in *Jacobite Relics*, II, 185–86 and 369 – see also (S/SC, 2003), p. 521
[1823] – in the *The Scotish Minstrel*, V, 88 – see *Contributions to Musical Collections and Miscellaneous Songs* (S/SC, 2014)
1831 – in *Songs by the Ettrick Shepherd*, pp. 131–32 – see pp. 60–61 in this edition
Unauthorised versions:
1829 – 'The Highlander's Farewell' was published in *The Jacobite Minstrelsy, with Notes* (Glasgow: R. Griffin, 1829), pp. 277–78. The copy text is *Jacobite Relics*. See *Letters*, II, 341 and 343.

Musical Context:
Hogg makes no comment about the melody or the musical setting. Pittock notes that there is good evidence to suggest that the melody which appears beside the song in *Jacobite Relics* is of Gaelic origin. This is not the same melody used by Smith for *The Scotish Minstrel*. The tune presented by Smith is also noted to be a 'Gaelic air' but he gives no title.

Explanatory Notes:
60–61 [headnote] the genuine heir of the Stuarts fills their throne reflects an ideological shift that gradually took place in Scottish society and culture over the decades since 1746. Murray Pittock explains that by the 1822 visit to Edinburgh by George IV, the term 'Jacobite' had made a 'semantic and symbolic shift' and that it now 'simultaneously sealed its old meaning in obsolescence by covering it in the glamour of sentiment while celebrating a rebirth of Jacobite spirit in the unity and pluck of British imperial success and loyalty to the crown in the face of Jacobinism and Bonapartism' (*The Myth of Jacobite Clans* (Edinburgh: Edinburgh University Press, 1995), p. 113). In Summer 1803, while making one of his journeys through the Highlands Hogg had noted: 'I could not help being a bit of a Jacobite in my heart, and blessing myself that in those days I did not exist, or I had certainly been hanged': see *Highland Journeys*, ed. by Hans de Groot (S/SC, forthcoming), p. 81.
61, l. 14 Stole by a ruthless reaver a reference to the actions of the Duke of Cumberland after Culloden: see Explanatory Notes to 'Farewell to Glen-Shalloch", pp. 12–13.
61, ll. 18–19 Thy people have disown'd thee – | Have hunted and have driven thee hence after defeat at Culloden, and with a reward of £30,000 offered for his capture, the Prince sheltered in the Western Highlands and Islands for five months before escaping to France, where he remained until his death in 1788.

61, l. 20 ruined Chiefs a further reference to the devastating consequences of the battle of Culloden in 1746 (see notes to 'Farewell to Glen-Shalloch' and 'Callum-a-Glen' and 'The Three Men of Moriston' pp. 12, and 22–23) and the commercial management of Highland estates that eventually led to the Clearances.

61, l. 25 Caledon a poetic allusion to Scotland, see note to 'Caledonia' (p. 13).

A Witch's Chant (pp. 62–63)

Creative Context:

This song was created for inclusion in *All-Hallow-Eve*, a five-act play in Hogg's two-volume *Dramatic Tales* published in May 1817. It appeared in Volume 1. This song is performed in the third Act during one of the most dramatic scenes of the play set in the Witch's Cot (scene ii) on All Hallow's Eve, or Hallowe'en. The first four lines of the song presented here are sung or chanted in the play and the remaining lines are spoken by the two witches named Nora and Grimald as they summon the spirit of 'Gil-Moules', or the Devil, to reveal the future.

In his headnote for *Songs* 1831 Hogg states that he wrote the song for 'an unearthly tragedy' in 1817, but that in the intervening years he has all but forgotten it. He explains that he rediscovered it in November 1830 with some modest delight: 'the poetry of the play has astounded me'. Not surprisingly after such a lapse of time Hogg redrafts the song for inclusion in 1831. Firstly, he omits both the stage directions and characters' names and also omits nine lines of dialogue. He changes the layout of the main body of the text to quatrains rhyming aabb – with the opening refrain differing (aaba). A substantial part of the original wording is retained. Alterations include, changing 'little star' to 'witching star' (l. 8) and adjusting the wording of l. 20 from 'With aerial blood by angels shed' to 'With blood by guilty angels shed'.

Hogg's 1831 headnote also draws attention to his literary connection with Henry Mackenzie (1745–1831), author and essayist, whose favourable critical appraisal in *The Lounger* referred to Robert Burns as 'the heaven-taught ploughman'. Horst Drescher's edition of *The Literary Correspondence and Notebooks of Henry Mackenzie*. 2 vols (Frankfurt am Main: Peter Lang, 1999) accounts for Mackenzie's influence and interest in theatrical performance and his correspondence to William Blackwood makes several comments about Hogg and his work (Vol. I., 273–74 and 323–24 respectively). Gillian Hughes includes an undated letter from Hogg in which he refers with great delight to Mackenzie's interest in his work and in which he states that he has asked Mackenzie's advice over an unnamed 'pastoral drama'. Hughes dates the letter to the period November 1814 to May 1815 (see *Letters*, I, 225–26).

No early manuscript version of 'The Witches Chant' has been located. This is one of a group of songs missing from the fair-copy manuscript for *Songs* 1831 at NLS MS 4805, ff. 26–102 (Blackwood Papers).

Publication History:

1817 – in *Dramatic Tales* (Edinburgh: John Ballantyne and London: Longman, Hurst, Rees, Orme, and Brown), I, pp. 1–154

1831 – in *Songs by the Ettrick Shepherd*, pp. 136–8 – see pp. 62–63 in the present edition

Musical Context:
There is no music nominated in the original version and Hogg gives no musical information in his headnote for *Songs* 1831. Research to date has not found a copy of the song with musical notation.

Explanatory Notes:
62, l. 8 the witching star is red as blood perhaps the red star Betelguese. It forms the right shoulder of the constellation *Orion* (see below) and is easily spotted with the naked eye in the winter sky of the northern hemisphere.

62, ll. 10–12 The giant form of a naked man, | [...] , | And he holds a sword in his right hand possibly the constellation *Orion* (the hunter) which is prominent in the night sky of the northern hemisphere in the winter months. Orion is usually described as holding a club in his right hand and a sword at his side. In *All-Hallow-Eve* Hindlee, a young Laird in love with Gelon, interrupts the scene in the Witch's Cot as Gelon watches Nora and Grimald perform a ritual to discover her future husband. Hindlee enters half-naked, wielding a sword in his right hand, and proceeds to attack or stab a wax image of Gelon, forecasting the dramatic conclusion of the play.

63, l. 28 Great Gil-Moules a name for the Devil. Hogg frequently uses this denomination in his 'unearthly' fiction. For example, in 'Jocke Taittis Expeditioune till Hell' he is 'Gil-Moullis, the 'shepherdis deille' (l. 77), and in 'Superstition and Grace', 'Gil-moules frae hind the hallan may flee' (l. 193). Both these poems were later published in *A Queer Book* (1832): see the S/SC edition ed. by P. D. Garside (1995), pp. 136–43 (p. 138) and pp. 189–92 (p. 191) respectively.

63, ll. 31–32 long-tailed fiery dragon outfly, | The rocket of heaven, the bomb of the sky possibly *Draco*, the Dragon, a large constellation that winds around *Ursa Minor*.

63, l. 33 the dog-star, [...] the wain the dog star is *Sirius*, *Orion's* main dog. It is the brightest star in the night sky and part of the constellation named *Canis Major*, found just below *Orion*. It is particularly easy to spot during the winter months in the northern hemisphere. 'King Charles' Wain' or the Plough is the constellation *Ursa Major*, a formation of seven main stars.

How Dear to me the Hour (p. 63)

Creative Context:
This is another of the eight Irish songs Hogg choses to include in *Songs* 1831 all of which had been created for inclusion in the first edition of Robert Archibald Smith's *The Irish Minstrel* in [1825]. For further information on this set of songs, Hogg's involvement in Smith's collection and their wrangle with Thomas Moore's publishers, the Power brothers, alluded to in Hogg's headnote by the comment 'This is likewise on the proscription list' see: *Contributions to Musical Collections and Miscellaneous Songs*.

As with the other songs in this group, Hogg's song shares a great deal of similarity with a partner song by Thomas Moore: in this case Moore's 'How Dear to me the Hour' to the tune 'The Twisting of the Rope', which first appeared in in the second number of *Irish Melodies* in 1808 (ii). In common with other of his Irish songs, this Hogg song echoes Moore's original lyric notably in the first line, where Moore's evening setting – 'How dear to me the hour when day-light dies' is replaced by Hogg's daytime setting – 'How dear to me the hour when day-light springs' (l. 1). Even although this is the main reflection of Moore, this song was not retained by Smith for his 'Second Edition' of *The Irish Minstrel* in *c.*1828.

The *Songs* 1831 version of the song is radically different from the version in *The Irish Minstrel*. The wording of the first four lines is retained, but ll. 5 and 6 are completely new. The opening line of the second verse is retained from *The Irish Minstrel*, but ll. 8–9 contains fresh wording, while ll. 10 and 11 are also new. The concluding line is a mixture of new wording 'And in life's cheerless gloaming' and text derived from *The Irish Minstrel* version 'yearn and die'.

This song is included in Hogg's fair-copy manuscript for *Songs* 1831 at NLS MS 4805, f. 57v. While the body of the text is transferred cleanly to the printed page the headnote is altered significantly. Hogg gives only three lines in the manuscript:

> Another of the same like Mr Johnstone's psalm. It was set to the air "Twisting of the Rope" but shared the fate of its companions. It was no great matter' (NLS MS 4805, f. 57v).

But in print it appears as given on p. 63 with more specific reference to the situation with Moore's publishers, the Power brothers. Hogg's change of wording allows him to link it directly to the other Irish songs in *Songs* 1831 which are referred to in similar terms, and he is also able to snipe directly at Moore as 'Mr Little the Great', even though he balances this by admitting that if he has caused offense it was 'through no ill intention'. This song appears on the verso manuscript page of 'The Minstrel Boy' (p. 11), another of Hogg's banned Irish Songs. As the note to 'The Minstrel Boy' states, this song appeared twice in the fair-copy manuscript with entirely different headnotes. It may be that Hogg also prepared a different version of 'How Dear to me the Hour' when preparing the text for the printer, but only one version on f. 57v has been located.

Publication History:
[1825] – in *The Irish Minstrel* p. 73 – see *Contributions to Musical Collections and Miscellaneous Songs* (S/SC, 2014)
1831 – in *Songs by the Ettrick Shepherd*, p. 139 – see p. 63 in the present edition

Musical Context:
As with the other songs in *The Irish Minstrel* Smith appears to have used Moore's *Irish Melodies* as his musical source. 'The Twisting of the Rope' is the tune he uses for Hogg's song and it is in the same key as the tune in Moore's collection. The rhythm of the ending of the song is slightly different and Moore's setting accommodates a number of semiquaver rests (for the singer to breathe) which Smith omits. Moore's semiquaver upbeat is also turned into a quaver by Smith. Otherwise the two are very similar. Moore clearly used Edward Bunting's collection as the source for his melody: namely, Edward Bunting, *A General Collection of the Ancient Irish Music* (London: Preston and son, 1796). Bunting obtained the air from Rose Mooney, the only woman harper to attend the Belfast Harp Festival in 1792. Donal O'Sullivan maintains that the folk tale for the twisting of the rope was prevalent in Connaught and Munster. One night, a poet gains access to a house and makes advances to a young girl but her mother decides to get rid of him by asking him to make a hay-rope with her. While she twists the rope and the distance grows between them, he eventually finds himself back outside the house when she slams the door in his face. The story is retold by W.B. Yeats in *The Secret Rose*, and Douglas Hyde also wrote a play on the subject: see D. J. O'Sullivan, ed.,

The Bunting Collection of Irish Folk Music and Song, I, 67 (NLI catalogue no. Ir 7844 I 3).

Explanatory Notes:
63 [headnote] Mr Little the Great one of Thomas Moore's earliest books was published pseudonymously as *The Poetical Works of the Late Thomas Little, esq.* (London: J. and T. Carpenter, 1801).

The Hill of Lochiel (pp. 64–65)

Creative Context:
There is no information about the creation of this particular song, but, like most of the Jacobite songs included in *Songs* 1831, it was first published in *Jacobite Relics* II in 1821 as Song CIX. In the *Relics* Hogg notes that the song is 'From the Gaelic', translated by 'Captain John Steuart', but Pittock categorises the song as being one of Hogg's own or created during the period. Hogg draws special attention to the air 'under the same title' in Simon Fraser's influential *Airs and Melodies Peculiar to the Highlands of Scotland and the Isles* of 1816 of which Hogg thinks so highly (see 'Musical Context' below).

Before choosing to include the song in *Songs* 1831 Hogg sent it to Robert Archibald Smith for inclusion in *The Scotish Minstrel*. It appeared in the first edition of the fifth volume in [1823] and textually the song is the same as that in the *Relics*, which must have been the copy text. For more information on this collection, Hogg's involvement with it and to see a copy of the song itself see: *Contributions to Musical Collections and Miscellaneous Songs*. Notably it is the song's appearance in *The Scotish Minstrel* which Hogg cites in his 1831 headnote, and not its original appearance in *Relics* thus acting as a promotional tool for Smith's collection.

Hogg also used the *Jacobite Relics* as copy text for the song in *Songs* 1831. However verses three and six are omitted. The third verse in the *Relics* version makes specific reference to Cameron of Lochiel's bravery and heroism and may have been removed to place more emphasis on the Jacobites generally. It is not so clear why verse six has been removed for it shares its general sentiment of loss with the other verses Hogg chose to retain.

This song is included in Hogg's fair-copy manuscript for *Songs* 1831 at NLS MS 4805, ff. 57v–58v. Hogg's unpunctuated text is transferred cleanly to the printed volume.

Publication History:
1821 – in *Jacobite Relics*, II, 209–11 and 377–78 – see also (S/SC, 2003), p. 524
[1823] – in the *The Scotish Minstrel*, V, 12 – see *Contributions to Musical Collections and Miscellaneous Songs* (S/SC, 2014)
1831 – in *Songs by the Ettrick Shepherd*, pp. 140–42 – see pp. 64–65 in the present edition

Musical Context:
In his notes to the song both for *Relics* and *Songs* 1831 Hogg makes a great deal about the air or melody, being the tune with the title 'Bràighe Loch Iall' Iall' ['The Braes of Lochiel'], which is no. 44 in Simon Fraser's collection. But in his 'errata' for *Jacobite Relics* (p. 480) he states that the tune in the *Relics* is in fact a very different tune known as 'The Banks of Devon' ('Bhannerach dhon na chri')

which Glen notes is a Highland melody not found in print before its appearance in *SMM* with Burns's words (see Glen p. 112). Fraser's notes to the melody in his collection refer closely to the events Hogg describes in his song (see Fraser, p. 108). The tune that appears with the song in R.A.Smith's *The Scotish Minstrel*, is, however, the same as the tune in *Relics* – namely 'The Banks of Devon' – and in the same key. So it would appear that Hogg's song never appears in print with his first choice of tune.

A version of 'Bràighe Loch Iall', with musical notation, together with a parallel English translation, is printed in *Songs of Gaelic Scotland*, by Anne Lorne Gillies (Edinburgh: Birlinn, 2005), pp. 257–59. The title and tune are the same, which Gillies translates as 'The Braes of Lochiel' (p. 257). She notes that it is 'a beautiful song of parting' and that is has 'long been a favourite among Gaelic singers and instrumentalists alike' (p. 259).

Explanatory Notes:

64 [Title] the chief of the Clan Cameron was known as 'Lochiel'. In this version of the song, Hogg focuses on the part played by Donald, 'the Gentle or Young Lochiel' (*c*.1700–1748). Details of the Clan Cameron estate at Achnacarry are given in the notes to 'Cameron's Welcome Hame' (pp. 55–56) which concerns the same subject. John Grieve's song 'Culloden, or Lochiel's Farewell', which he contributed to *The Forest Minstrel* in 1810, also covers the same subject matter: see *The Forest Minstrel* (S/SC, 2006), pp. 181–83 and notes on pp. 355–57.

64, l. 18 Young Charlie Stuart Prince Charles Edward Stuart (1720–1788).

64, l. 19 Cameron, that loyal name reflecting the historical royalism of the clan. See Notes for 'Cameron's Welcome Hame', pp. 55–56.

64, l. 31 Fell hall and hamlet low a further reference within *Songs* 1831 to the devastating consequences of the battle of Culloden in 1746. Cumberland's forces destroyed Achnacarry Castle and the Cameron estate was seized by the government.

65, l. 33 Far in a hostile land Lochiel was injured during the battle of Culloden and went into hiding in the hills around Achnacarry, where he sheltered with other Jacobite rebels, including the prince. He fled to France where he died in exile in 1748.

65, l. 39 Now I'm return'd to thee the forfeited Cameron estates were restored to Donald Cameron (1769–1832), the grandson of 'the brave Lochiel' under the General Amnesty of 1784. By 1819, when Southey toured Scotland, he was an absentee landlord, living ' "miserably in London upon 600£, kept needy by his debauched course of life, and eking out this pittance by cutting down his woods!" (*Journal of a Tour in Scotland*, pp. 208–09)', reprinted in *Highland Journeys*, ed. by Hans de Groot (S/SC, forthcoming), n. to 80 (c), p. 52.

The Flowers of Scotland (pp. 65–66)

Creative Context:

Hogg's headnote suggests that this is an older song, but no earlier version has been found, and short of Hogg's explanation given in his 1831 headnote, there is no other information about its creation. Interestingly here Hogg gives the impression that it is a nonsense song, but he also uses the headnote to show his ability and willingness to write songs by request. Several versions of songs written to match the popular tune 'The Blue Bells of Scotland' were in circulation at this time (see 'Musical Context' below), mostly with Scoto-British lyrics and Hogg's lyric about the national flower of Scotland is thus pointedly nationalistic.

As no earlier copy has been found it is impossible to tell which text he used for *Songs* 1831. The song is included in Hogg's fair-copy manuscript for *Songs* 1831 at NLS MS 4805, ff. 58v–59r. Hogg's unpunctuated text is transferred cleanly to the printed volume.

Publication History:
1831 – in *Songs by the Ettrick Shepherd*, pp. 143–44 – see pp. 65–66 in the present edition

Musical Context:
Hogg clearly gives the title of the melody for this song as 'The Blue Bells of Scotland'. No musical copy has been found with Hogg's text, but the tune was very popular at this time. It was thought to have been in circulation from the latter part of the eighteenth century or slightly earlier. But there is some controversy over whether it was composed or merely popularised on the stage by the actress known as 'Mrs Jordan' (namely Dora Jordan nèe Bland) – see Glen, p. 227. Mrs Grant of Laggan's lyric beginning 'O where, tell me where, is your Highland laddie gone?', which was written '"on the Marquis of Huntly's departure for Holland with the British forces under the command of the gallant Sir Ralph Abercrombie, in 1799" ', appeared in her *Poems* of 1803. It was set at the same time by Joseph Haydn and published by George Thomson in his *Select Collection of Original Scottish Airs*, Vol. 2 in 1803.

A different melody with the same name also appeared in 1803 in the *SMM* with accompanying, anonymous lyrics including references to 'George our king' (No. 548, 566–67). In 1823, Robert Archibald Smith included 'The Blue Bells of Scotland' by Mrs Grant of Laggan in *The Scotish Minstrel* where it was accompanied by his arrangement of the *SMM* air (v, 58–59). For further information about the history of the song, see Graham, II, 107. There is no evidence that Hogg did not intend this SMM melody to be used for his song. While different to the Dora Jordan popular tune, it is a bright and upbeat tune which also fits well with Hogg's text.

Explanatory Notes:
65 [headnote] **"is ane shame till heir."** a common Scots phrase that translates as, 'shameful to hear'.
65, ll. 5–6 **The thistle's purple bonnet** the Scottish thistle (*Onopordon Acanthium*), a wild-growing, prickly plant that produces purple or lavender-coloured flowers in the second year of growth. It is a national emblem of Scotland.
65, l. 6 **bonny heather bell** heather (*Erica tetralix*) grows across the moor and heath-lands of Scotland, although Hogg is more likely referring to the blue bell (*Campanula rotundifolia*), another heath flower that has strong associations with the Scottish landscape.
65, l. 9 **England eyes her roses** the rose is a national emblem of England.
65, ll. 13–14 **But the thistle in her bonnet blue, | Still nods outow'r the fell** a reference to the common misconception that Scotland has never been conquered. See also note 133, l. 27.
65, l. 17 **the wee bit leaf o' Ireland** the shamrock, a three-leaved plant of the genus *Trifolium*. It is a national emblem of Ireland.
65, l. 22 **Still bobs aboon them a'** the thistle can reach up to six feet in height.
66, l. 30 **reeky cell** Hell.

The Bonny Lass of Deloraine (pp. 66–67)

Creative Context:
A full account of the textual and publishing history of 'The Bonny Lass of Deloraine' is given in *The Forest Minstrel* (S/SC, 2006). And further information about the song can be sourced in Richard D. Jackson's article '*The Pirate* and the Bonny Lass of Deloraine' in the *Scott Newsletter* (No. 40 (Summer 2002), 9–21). Jackson notes that the 'Elizabeth' or 'Mrs W.B. Shaw' to whom Hogg refers is Eliza Scott (b. 1786), who lived in Wester Deloraine in the Ettrick district from the 1780s and who married the Rev. William Berry Shaw of Langholm in 1813. It would seem then that Hogg composed the song before he left Ettrick in 1804, which also approximately matches the information in his headnote that the song was written 'nearly thirty years ago'.

In summary, as Garside and Jackson note, the earliest known publication of the song is much longer version comprising six verses which first appeared in *The Scots Magazine* in August 1807 immediately below 'Verses on the Earl of Dalkieth's Birthday', 'by the Ettrick Shepherd'. A shortened version of the song, which omits references to 'Scott of Deloraine' and a fifth verse 'in which Hogg by implication proposes himself as a potential suitor' was next published in *The Forest Minstrel* in 1810. The song then appeared once more in the fourth volume of Hogg's 1822 *Poetical Works* of 1822 before Hogg chose to include it in *Songs* 1831. Both of these later versions are based on the song which appears in *The Forest Minstrel* with some changes.

The text in *Songs* 1831 may have been that from *Poetical Works*, although Hogg omits the penultimate or fourth verse beginning 'If Heaven shall keep her aye as good'.

The song is extant within the fair-copy manuscript for *Songs* 1831 at NLS MS 4805, ff. 59v–60r. The manuscript is page-numbered '118' and '119' and it sits within the longest sequential pagination in this manuscript. It is notable that this part of the manuscript includes the majority of the songs Hogg lifts from *The Forest Minstrel*. Hogg's unpunctuated text is transferred reasonably cleanly to the printed page with few non-substantive alterations. For example, 'lye' and 'bye' of l.1 are changed to the less archaic 'lie' and 'by'.

Publication History:
1807 – in *The Scots Magazine*, 69 (August, 1807), 607–08
1810 – in *The Forest Minstrel* pp. 62–64 – see (S/SC, 2006), pp. 67–69 and 264–66
1822 – in *Poetical Works*, IV, 357–59
1831 – in *Songs by the Ettrick Shepherd*, pp. 145–47 – see pp. 66–67 in the present edition
[1834] – in *Original Scottish Melodies* pp. 1–3 – see *Contributions to Musical Collections and Miscellaneous Songs* (S/SC, 2014)

Musical Context:
As Jackson and Garside state in *The Forest Minstrel*, Hogg's 1831 headnote refers to the song having 'never been set to music'. But when it appears in *The Forest Minstrel* it does so with the tune title 'The Maid of Isla'. More information about this tune is given in *The Forest Minstrel*, and the editors choose to present a variant of the tune from Gow's *Fourth Collection of Strathspey Reels* with Hogg's text (p. 266). But after the song's appearance in *Songs* 1831 it was taken up for inclusion

in Peter McLeod's *Original Scottish Melodies* of [1834]. The song was also included in McLeod's revised and extended *Original National Melodies of Scotland* in [1838] but was a reprint from the [1834] musical plates. McLeod, however, does not use the tune 'The Maid of Isla' and gives no title for the tune which is presented in his collection. The text which appears with music in McLeod's collection is clearly derived from *Songs* 1831, though McLeod only sets the first three verses. For further information on McLeod's collection, and a copy of the song itself see: *Contributions to Musical Collections and Miscellaneous Songs.*

Explanatory Notes:
66 [headnote] when both of them have children Jackson notes that Eliza Scott 'had four sons and four daughters' (2002, p. 21).
66, l. 17 Let Athole boast her birchen bowers 'Athole Forest is a part of the district preserved for deer and other game; comprises upwards of 100,000 acres; is famed above every other forest for its hunting attractions and its magnificent scenery' (Groome). Hogg's poem of 1816, *Mador of the Moor*, is set in the Athol district.
66, l. 18 Windermere her woodlands green an alteration in *Songs* 1831 that highlights the soft wooded landscape surrounding the Lake. The previous image of 'Windermere her woodland shores' may have been altered to reflect nineteenth-century development of the shoreline of Windermere following the 'discovery' of the Lake District in the latter part of the eighteenth century and the subsequent need to accommodate the rising numbers of tourists and artists who flocked to the area.
66, l. 19 And Lomond of her lofty shores an alteration in *Songs* 1831. Previously, the image had been of 'Lomond and her isles so green', reflecting the numerous islands on the loch. Hogg now imagines looking outward from the loch and upward to the hills and mountains which surround the loch as it 'lies completely imbedded among different ranges of hills' (Groome), many of them extending from the water's edge, such as Conic Hill (1175 feet), Beinn Bhreae (1922) and Ben Lomond (3192).

The Two Men of Colston: or: The True English Character (pp. 67–71)

Creative Context:
As Hogg's 1831 headnote clearly states this is another of his 'old friends the Jacobites' and it thus sits amongst a large group of Jacobite songs in *Songs* 1831. This song, with 'Red Clan-Ranald's Men' and 'Up an' Rin' Awa', Geordie' provide a short sequence of three Jacobite songs from Cumberland in *Songs* 1831. All three are connected with work Hogg produced following the completion of the of his *Jacobite Relics of Scotland* project in 1821. In June of that year Hogg had received further Jacobite material, some of which was from 'Mr. H. B. Marshall' of Chelsea. This had been passed via the London publisher Cadell to Blackwood who forwarded it on to Hogg on 21 June (see *Letters*, I, p. 98n.). Hogg informs William Blackwood (on 3 July 1821) that 'The Jacobite relics are doubtless very curious but they are totally English. They appear to me to be all the work of one man and I think them Tom D,Urfys I know they are; and I think that perhaps they are in his hand writing'. He asks that Blackwood send Marshall 'a subscription copy of the Wake', presumably as a thank you, as the manuscripts were sent gratis for Hogg's work on Jacobite song: see *Letters*, II, 97–98 (p. 98) and notes.

Hogg subsequently used material from Marshall's collection within several articles published in the *Edinburgh Magazine* under the general title, 'Jacobite Relics, Not Published in Mr Hogg's Collection' in November 1821 and again in January and April 1822. Murray Pittock writes that these songs are 'partly authentic [...], it is the Border derived material which is more doubtful' (p. xxiii). 'The Two Men of Colston, or, the True English Character', was printed in the January number in 1822, with no indication that the song was Hogg's own composition. Indeed, a note below the song states it is 'From Mr Bulmer's collection' and directs the reader to 'our November Number, p. 441'. In this number, along with genuine correspondence from 'Mr. H. B. Marshall' is correspondence from 'Ed. Bulmer' of 'Adderston-House' dated '3 Sept. 1821'. Hogg's original narrative of 'Twommy's beuk', from which this song and the next two in *Songs* 1831 are apparently taken, is found within Bulmer's correspondence here. It is introduced as 'circumstantial and fanciful, but, in all probability not the less true'; a statement that seems designed to create uncertainty about its authenticity (439). Hogg further notes that, in comparison with Marshall's songs that 'relate mostly to the English court' Bulmer's songs are 'all border songs' (441).

The story of 'Twommy's beuk' in its notably thick Cumberland dialect is recounted within Bulmer's correspondence, a section of which is lifted and included by Hogg in his 1831 headnote (from 'Jacobite Relics, Not Published in Mr Hogg's Collection', 9 (November 1821), 440–41). The few verbal variants do not significantly alter the narrative of 'Twommy's beuk', which is used to introduce three Jacobite songs giving the English dimension of the '45 rebellion.

Hogg then uses the text from the *Edinburgh Magazine* January number as copy text for the song in *Songs* 1831, with some variants. For example, 'vile' becomes 'dwom'd' [i.e., 'damned'] (l. 51) while 'dwom'd stupid hussey' of l.93 is changed to 'fusionless hussey'. Overall, though, the *Songs* 1831 version of 'The Two Men of Colston, or, the True English Character' is essentially unchanged from the earlier magazine version.

The song appears in Hogg's fair-copy manuscript for *Songs* 1831 at NLS MS 4805, ff. 60r–63v. Evidence of Hogg's clear involvement in the preparation of the manuscript for Blackwood is found in the changes to the headnote here. Hogg originally writes 'two pretended Cumberland ones', meaning songs, but scores out 'two' and writes 'three' instead, after deciding to add a further song from 'Twommy's beuk'. Hogg's unpunctuated text is transferred relatively cleanly to the printed page. However, Hogg's original wording at l.16 is changed from 'burnd' of the holograph manuscript to 'bworn'.

Publication History:
1821 – in *The Edinburgh Magazine and Literary Miscellany*, 10 (January 1822), 51–52
1831 – in *Songs by the Ettrick Shepherd*, pp. 148–55 – see pp. 67–71 in the present edition

Musical Context:
Hogg makes no mention of the Musical Context for the song in his 1831 headnote. But when the text appears in the *Edinburgh Magazine* in November 1821 it gives the information: 'To a celebrated Scotch air called "Go to the kye wi' me"'. This is similar to the title of Hogg's love song which was set, in *Blackwood's Magazine* in 1823, to the fiddle tune 'The Blathrie o't' and also appeared in *Songs* 1831 (pp. 25–27). However, no musical notation is given in the *Edinburgh Magazine* and singing the printed verses to the tune 'The Blathrie o't' presents some difficulties

with scansion of the lyric. Another traditional tune is found in several eighteenth-century music collections, such as Daniel Dow's *Collection of Ancient Scots Music* (1775), p. 42 [as 'G,iomain na ngauna' or 'Gae to the kye wi' me Johnnie']. Glen notes that this is regarded as a 'very old song' and that it is most likely to be 'A Border tune' and he quotes from Stenhouse's notes, but gives no additional information about the melody itself (Glen, p. 105).

Explanatory Notes:
67 **[Title]** 'Colston' is perhaps another form of Coniston, a community scattered around the northern end of Coniston Water in the Lake District in Cumberland.

67 **[headnote] Cumberland** Hogg's only recorded visit through Cumberland to the Lake District took place after September 1814, although it is likely that he travelled through the area on more than this occasion.

67 **[headnote] old Magazine** referring to the *Edinburgh Magazine* 10 (January 1822), 49–52 (51–52) where this and the next two songs were first printed.

67 **[headnote] the sel o' him** literally, 'to himself'.

67 **[headnote] Caril** 'Carlisle', which is the word used in the original *Edinburgh Magazine* version. Carlisle is a city in the county of Cumberland some thirteen miles from the Scottish border. The Jacobites laid siege to the Castle in November 1745 and held it for three weeks.

68 **[headnote] Mr Palsy [...] Teuk off peur Twommy leyke the shot of a gun** it would seem that 'Twommy' died from a sudden and severe case of 'palsy' or paralysis.

68, l. 11 **haudding and gyetting** property, worldly goods and wealth.

68, l, 17 **meale weyming** 'men women', presumably the kilt-wearing Highlander is meant. John Leonard Roberts notes of the Jacobite army, 'it was not exclusively composed of Highland clansmen, although the men did wear Highland dress [...]'. See *The Jacobite Wars: Scotland and the Military Campaigns of 1715 and 1745* (Edinburgh: Edinburgh University Press, 2002), p. 104.

68, ll. 21–22 **they eat Chreastians lyke robbits, | And bworn all the chworches for fwon** Roberts (see note to l. 17) goes on to note how the 'idea' of the savage Highlander was 'vigorously prompted by contemporary Whig propaganda' (p. 104).

68, l. 25 **a greyt general** George Wade (1673–1748), 'army officer and road builder'. In 1745 he 'headed the military committee responsible for deciding the government's response to the crisis', although his strategic mistakes in the winter of 1745 led to Cumberland taking over from him (*ODNB*).

69, l. 35 **Bwarton's weyld shieling** the inn at the village of Burton was a major staging post on the route through Westmorland, although its records only date from the 1750s. The Jacobite army passed through Burton in 1745.

69, ll. 49–50 **"His feythers have held this ould keyngdom | For a meatter of ten thowsand years** is something of an exaggeration. The line of Royal Stuarts is through Robert II (1316–1390), grandson of Robert the Bruce.

69, ll. 51–52 **a bit dwom'd scrwogy bwody, | A theyvish ould rascal, I hears** a satirical reference to King George II (1683–1760).

69, l. 55 **rewin'd us all with taxations** as with all wars, local taxation was increased to pay for the soaring National Debt.

Red Clan-Ranald's Men (pp. 71–72)

Creative Context:
The context for the creation of this song is given directly above in the note to 'The Two Men of Colston'. In summary, these two songs, and 'Up an' Rin Awa', Geordie', which comes next in *Songs* 1831, were all apparently included in some manuscript materials sent to Hogg after completing work on the *The Jacobite Relics of Scotland* project in 1821. They were subsequently published in the *Edinburgh Magazine* and this particular song appeared in the first number of 'Jacobite Relics, Not Published in Mr Hogg's Collection' in the *Edinburgh Magazine* for November 1821, so it was likely included within Hogg's letter to Cadell of August/September 1821. In this case, then, the song immediately follows the correspondence from 'Ed. Bulmer' discussed above which thus questions its authenticity, and very much suggests that it is by Hogg. Its inclusion in *Songs* 1831 would provide further evidence of Hogg's authorship.

Hogg uses the version of the song in the *Edinburgh Magazine* as copy text for *Songs* 1831. However, the original verse format of quatrains is changed to octets, three of the verses (vs 4, 5, and 6) are arranged in a different order than in the original and verse 7 is omitted entirely from *Songs* 1831. The refrain, 'There's news–news–gallant news' is repeated after each verse in the original, but is here only printed once at the beginning of the song in 1831. The text of the song remains relatively stable with very few verbal variants. One of these is, however, significant. Hogg changes 'carle' to 'Caril' (l. 2 and l. 8). And he includes, beside the song in the *Edinburgh Magazine*, a note in which he states that 'it relates to some particular event, although the precise meaning is inexplicable. Had the term Carle been written *Carlisle*, or even *Caril*, as it is uniformly pronounced in Cumberland, I would have concluded that the song related to the battle of Clifton' ((November 1821), 439–43, p. 442). Hogg is explicit that the *Songs* 1831 version 'relates to a skirmish on Clifton Moor' (headnote, p. 71), so that the change serves to reinforce the song's historical context. The other significant verbal alteration occurs at line 33 where the reference to 'Atholl's bonny lord' becomes a reference to 'Athole's gallant band'.

The song appears in Hogg's fair-copy manuscript for *Songs* 1831 at NLS MS 4805, ff. 63v–64r, where it comes immediately after 'The Two Men of Colston, or, the True English Character'. The song is sequentially paginated '126' and '127' and follows the order of both manuscript and printed versions. A printer's mark '8/161' written at the side of the fourth verse (f. 64r) almost corresponds with the position of the page within the printed volume, at p. 158. Hogg's unpunctuated text is transferred reasonably cleanly to the printed volume. However, a misreading of Hogg's hand results in the word 'slashing' at l. 6 replacing 'flashing', which is also Hogg's original word in the *Edinburgh Magazine* version.

Publication History:
1821 – in *The Edinburgh Magazine and Literary Miscellany* 9, (November 1821), 441–42
1831 – in *Songs by the Ettrick Shepherd*, pp. 156–58 – see pp. 71–72 in the present edition

Musical Context:
Hogg's note with the song in the *Edinburgh Magazine* states that this is 'A Jacobite Song, to the tune of "Paddy of Molla's Hymn".' He further notes: 'I have heard

this fine air. It has manifest resemblance to a Scots tune called 'Honest Duncan' which seems to be taken from it; the two second parts being nearly the same'. No tunes by these titles have been sourced.

Explanatory Notes:

71 [Title] Ranald Macdonald (the younger) of Clan Ranald (*d.* 1766). He was one of the first welcome the Prince to Scotland in 1745: see also notes to 'The Gathering of the Clans' in the present volume.

71 [headnote] the skirmish on Clifton Moor, on the 18th of December, 1745, where a party of M'Donalds, left to guard the baggage, so gallantly repulsed [...]the Highlanders lost only twenty four in all the information from Hogg's headnote is a summary of the original editorial note to the song in the *Edinburgh Magazine* (November 1821), 442.

71, l. 2 Caril Carlisle (see 'Creative Context' above)

71, l. 3 tartan trews for a well-informed discussion of 'tartan's symbolic link with (militant) Jacobitism in the first half of the eighteenth century', see, Murray G. H. Pittock, *The Myth of the Jacobite Clans* (Edinburgh: Edinburgh University Press, 1995), pp. 112–14 (p. 113).

71, l. 5 blinking on the bent turning aside, or flinching on the moorland (*DSL*).

71, l. 7 red-coats the Hanoverian forces.

71, l. 9 by 'zoons a profane euphemism of 'God'. It apparently originated in the 1600s with the phrase 'God's wounds', a reference to the Crucifixion: see *A History of English Words*, by Geoffrey Hughes (Oxford: Blackwell Publishing, 1999), p. 47, p. 186 and also p. 226.

71, l. 13 frumpy froward Duke Prince William Augustus, duke of Cumberland (1721–1765), army officer and the 'second surviving son of George, prince of Wales, the future George II, and his wife, Caroline' (Speck, *ODNB*).

71, l. 15 our Charlie Prince Charles Edward Stuart (1720–1788), see note 3, l. 13

71, ll. 15 hand to hand Cumberland's forces used cannon and artillery against the Highlanders' broadswords: see John Home's *The History of the Rebellion in the Year 1745* (1802), pp. 230–39.

71, l. 16 In a' his Highland gear, joe according to Robin Nicholson, Charles Edward Stuart wore Highland dress, or parts of it, such as a tartan plaid or waistcoat, during the '45 campaign: see *Bonnie Prince Charlie and the Making of a Myth: A Study in Portraiture, 1720–1892* (Lewisburg: Bucknell University Press; London: Associated Presses, 2002), pp. 62–80.

72, l. 33 Athole's gallant band the 'Atholmen' mustered under the command of Lord George Murray (*c.*1700–1760) of Blair Atholl: see also notes to 95, l. 32.

72, l. 34 To Cluny of the Glen, joe Ewan Macpherson of Cluny (1706–1764), Jacobite officer and clan Chieftain [from 1746] (see *ODNB* entry by Davie Horsburgh). See also notes to 95, l. 33.

72, l. 35 To Donald Blue, and Appin true Donald Blue as a Jacobite figure is not recognised, although there is a traditional Scottish tune of that title. The Appin Stuarts were prominent during the Jacobite campaign, which Hogg records more fully in his song 'The Stuarts of Appin', pp. 28–30 and notes.

Up an' Rin Awa', Geordie (pp. 72–74)

Creative Context:

The context for the creation of this song is given above in the note to 'The Two

Men of Colston' and 'Red Clan-Ranald's Men'. In summary, these three songs, which are placed next to each other in *Songs* 1831, were all apparently included in some manuscript materials sent to Hogg after completing work on *The Jacobite Relics of Scotland* project in 1821. They were subsequently published in the *Edinburgh Magazine* and this particular song appeared in the final number of 'Jacobite Relics, Not Published in Mr Hogg's Collection' in the *Edinburgh Magazine*, in April 1822. Here the song is printed as though it was derived from 'Mr Bulmer's Collection', giving a strong indication that it is by Hogg himself (see notes for the above two songs). The article, within which the songs sits in the magazine, also gives notices from 'the journals of the day' which he states are 'by means of explanation' to the reader. The article then includes several stories of the Jacobite march south from Edinburgh into Cumberland and Westmoreland and into Carlisle.

In his 1831 headnote Hogg states that the song is 'an answer to a Whig song of 1746, beginning, "Up an' rin awa', Charlie'. He includes two verses and a refrain of this song in his 'Fragments' at the end of 'Appendix. Part II: Whig Songs' in *Jacobite Relics* II: see (S/SC, 2003), p. 478. Pittock compares it to the Jacobite song 'Up an' waur them a', Willie' which appears on p. 471 and notes that there are multiple Whig variants of this song. Both Jacobite and Whig texts are set to the same tune, known by the Jacobite title 'Up an' waur them a', Willie' (see 'Musical Context' below).

As with the preceding two songs here, Hogg uses the version in the *Edinburgh Magazine* as copy text for *Songs* 1831, with few variants. For example, at l. 78 the original wording 'motley mumps' (referring to the toothless veteran soldiers) is changed to 'motley group', while in the following line 'mony ane may rue the day' is changed to the more definitive statement, 'mony a ane may rue the day'.

The song appears in Hogg's fair-copy manuscript for *Songs* 1831 at NLS MS 4805, ff. 64v–66r, where it follows immediately after 'Red Clan-Ranald's Men'. The song is sequentially paginated from 129' to '131' and follows the order of both manuscript and printed versions. While the *Edinburgh Magazine* prints 'Bran new wig' in l. 52, Hogg notes this word as 'braw' in his manuscript and 'braw' is printed in 1831. In l. 65 the *Magazine* prints 'It fits you to a flaw'. Hogg writes 'It suits you to a flaw'in his manuscript, but in 1831 the text is printed 'It suits you to a straw'.

Publication History:
1822 – in *The Edinburgh Magazine and Literary Miscellany*, 10 (April 1822), 460–61
1831 – in *Songs by the Ettrick Shepherd*, pp. 159–63 – see pp. 72–74 in the present edition

Musical Context:
As with the 1831 headnotes to the preceding two songs, Hogg makes no comment about the song's Musical Context here. But he states, where the song appears in the *Edinburgh Magazine* that this lyric is to the 'Tune– "Up an' war them a', Willie"'. Hogg was evidently familiar with this Jacobite tune, nominating it as the suitable accompaniment to his song 'I'm a' gane wrang, Jamie', in the *Forest Minstrel* in 1810: see (S/SC, 2006), pp. 79–80 and pp. 273–75. This was a popular and well known tune during Hogg's lifetime: Burns had based his song 'When we gaed to the braes o' Mar' to the tune (*SMM* II (1788), no. 181, 195–96) while a version of this Jacobite tune is also found in Oswald's *Caledonian Pocket Companion* (III, 1) and in Joseph Ritson 's influential *Scotish Songs* (1794) (II, 73–74).

Explanatory Notes:

72 [Title] Geordie King George II (1683–1760).

72, l. 6 ague fits a fit of shivering.

72, ll. 7–8 auntie Wade, wi' pick an' spade, | Is delving through the snaw George Wade (1673–1748), 'army officer and road builder'. See also note 68, l. 25.

73, ll. 12 took the spavie in their houghs were afflicted with some form of rheumatic disorder in their joints. 'The spavin' is a disease affecting horses, so that the use here is clearly derogatory.

73, l. 21 like Kendal bend a type of fishing hook: 'the hook we prefer is the Kendal circular bend. It is of a much lighter make than the Limerick, and its shape in the smaller sizes more suitable for hooking trout. [...]' – see: Thomas Tod Stoddart, *The Art of Angling: As Practised in Scotland* (1838), p. 17.

73, ll. 25–26 auld Carlisle, baith tower an' pile, | Has got a waesome fa' The Jacobite siege of Carlisle began on 9 November and lasted for around five days. See *Edinburgh Magazine* 10 (April 1822), 460–63 (461).

73, l. 28 Brave Sir John Pennington is fled eldest son of Sir Joseph Pennington, second baronet. He 'defended Carlisle against the Jacobites in 1745': see *ODNB*, Roland Thorne's entry for 'John Pennington, first Baron Muncaster (*bap.* 1741, *d.* 1813)'.

73, l. 29 An' Doctor Waugh an' a' John Waugh (*bap.* 1701, *d.* 1765), dean of Worcester. 'In 1727 he was appointed by his father [Bishop Waugh] to the posts of vicar of Stanwix, rector of Caldbeck, prebendary of Carlisle Cathedral, and chancellor of the diocese of Carlisle. [...] Waugh established his political reputation by the work he undertook for the government during the Jacobite rising of 1745: see the *ODNB* entry for his father, John Waugh (1661–1734), by David W. V. Weston.

73, l. 30 And Humphrey Stenhouse he is lost not identified.

73, l. 31 And Aeron-bank's but raw Acron bank (from the Saxon for oak) is near to Temple Sowerby at the foot of the Pennines in Westmoreland.

73, l. 32 And Andrew Pattison's laid bye | The prince of provosts a' in his notes to the song in the *Edinburgh Magazine* version, Hogg writes of 'Mr Pattison, the redoubted Mayor of Carlisle', and he reprints part of 'the excuses sent by the Mayor' for surrendering to the Jacobite army (461).

73, l. 40 banish foreign law propagandists for both the Whigs and the Jacobites each portrayed the other as 'foreign': 'the Stuart cause was foreign because Catholic, their Jacobite counterparts had no hesitation in proclaiming the alien nature of the Hanoverians': see *The Hanoverians: The History of a Dynasty*, by Jeremy Black (London: Continuum, 2006), p. 60.

73, l. 41 o'er the Mersey the River Mersey: 'On 1 December, the bulk of the Prince's army marched out of Manchester, crossing the River Mersey at Stockport on the road to Macclesfield', John Leonard Roberts, *The Jacobite Wars: Scotland and the Military Campaigns of 1715 and 1745* (Edinburgh: Edinburgh University Press, 2002), p. 115.

73, ll. 42–43 An' braid claymores an' a', Geordie; | An' awsome forks, an' Highland durks Highland weaponry designed for hand-to-hand combat: see John Home's *The History of the Rebellion in the Year 1745* (1802), pp. 230–39.

74, ll. 50–51 ye maun tak your foreign bike, | Your Turks, an' queans, an' a' Jeremy Black discusses contemporary satirical accounts of significant people within the Royal household of George I that Hogg probably refers to: ' aside from rumours concerning George's relations with women, there were also unfounded suggestions that his relationship with Mustapha and Mehemet, the two Turkish grooms of the chamber, the latter of whom was in charge of George's private accounts, was improper' (*The Hanoverians: The History of a Dynasty* (London: Continuum, 2006), p. 77).

74, l. 64 Hanover's a dainty place Hanover, capital city of the Lower Saxony region of Germany. Following the death of his father in 1727, George Augustus of the House of Hanover, acceded the thrones of England, Scotland and Ireland, reigning as George II. Raised in Hanover, he returned frequently during his reign, 'taking extended summer vacations in his homeland on a dozen different occasions': see Linda Colley, *Britons. Forging the Nation 1707–1837* (1992; London: Pimlico, new ed. 2003) p. 201. He was visiting Hanover when the Prince landed in Scotland.

74, l. 73 the land o' cakes an' weir 'land o' cakes' is a common literary euphemism for Scotland. See Robert Fergusson's 'The King's Birthday in Edinburgh' (1772), and Burns 's 'On the Late Captain Grose's Peregrinations Thro' Scotland' (1789) and also in the closing verse of his 'Election Ballad: At the close of the contest for representing the Dumfries Burghs' (1790). [Brewer's] *Dictionary of Phrase and Fable* (1898) suggest the definition comes from the preponderance of oatmeal cakes in the Scottish diet.

74, l. 74 Auld Caledonia 'Roman name for part of what is now Scotland; literary name for Scotland' (*DSL*). See also 'Caledonia', pp. 13–14 and notes.

74, l. 77 tak leg-bail 'leg-bail' is a portion of land measured as part of one horse's leg, 'the idea being that the possessor of this amount of land contributed one horse's leg i.e. a sixteenth part of the price of the four-horse team to work the plough gate' (*DSL*).

My Love's Bonny (p. 75)

Creative Context:
As is the case with the song 'O, Weel Befa' the Maiden Gay' (pp. 53–15), this song appears to have been created for Hogg's drama *The Haunted Glen*, published as part of Hogg's two volume collection of *Dramatic Tales* in 1817. The song is performed by the character of Lu, a Spirit. Further information on *The Haunted Glen* is provided in the notes to 'O, Weel Befa' the Maiden Gay' (see above), the only other song derived from the play in *Songs* 1831. In the drama it appears under the title 'Song' and, like 'O weel befa' the Maiden Gay', it was also included in Hogg's drama as it appears in the second volume of *Poetical Works* of 1822. Aside from the normal orthographic changes and differences in punctuation, there is only one variant between these (where 'flue' ('the soft down from feathers', *OED*) in l. 14 becomes 'fleece').

Hogg redrafted his song for *Songs* 1831. His headnote suggests that he is remembering the text rather than using *Dramatic Tales* or his *Poetical Works* as his copy text and the changes to the song would support this. The form is changed from four quatrains to two octets and the first two lines are transposed. Indeed the 1831 text is quite different from the original version. There is fresh wording at ll. 3–4, new wording in l. 5, in l. 11 'roseate' becomes 'vernal' and in l. 14 the 'flue of the raven's wing' is changed to 'the blackbird's bonny wing'. Finally 'dear side' on l. 15 is changed to 'bonny breast'.

The song, as it appears in 1831, is in the fair-copy manuscript for *Songs* 1831 at NLS MS 4805, f. 66, where it follows immediately after 'Up an' rin' Awa', Geordie'.

The song is sequentially paginated '131' and '132' and follows the order of both manuscript and printed versions. Hogg's unpunctuated text is transferred cleanly to the printed volume.

It forms the first of a set of three love songs at this point in *Songs* 1831, followed by 'The Gloamin'' and 'Liddel Bower'.

Publication History:

1817 – in *Dramatic Tales* (London: Longman, Hurst, Rees, Orme, and Brown; Edinburgh: John Ballantyne), II, 53–54

1822 – in *Poetical Works*, II, 179–228 (220–21)

1831 – in *Songs by the Ettrick Shepherd* , pp. 164–65 – see p.75 in the present edition

Musical Context:

In his head not Hogg refers to a 'fine ballad air' being used for this song, but gives no title. He also notes that it has 'never been set to music'. No musical copy has yet been found and we have not been able to identify the 'ballad air'.

The Gloamin' (pp. 75–76)

Creative Context:

In his headnote for 1831 Hogg states that this is 'one of my earliest songs'. While this is true, the version printed in *Songs* 1831 is substantially reworked. The song first appeared with the title 'Love Abused' in the *Scots Magazine* in April 1805 where it is end-signed 'Ettrick. A Shepherd'. This suggests that the song may have been written before the summer of 1804 while Hogg was still living in Ettrick. It was subsequently included in all Hogg's major collections (excluding the 1821 edition of *The Mountain Bard*). An account of the publication history of the song and its various textual changes is given in *The Forest Minstrel* (S/SC, 2006).

In summary, after appearing in the *Scots Magazine*, the song was then included in Hogg's *The Mountain Bard* of 1807 (under the title 'Love Abused'). It then appeared in *The Forest Minstrel* of 1810 (under the heading 'The Gloamin'' frae the welkin high') and in his *Poetical Works* of 1822 and Hogg made relatively few changes between these versions. However when he came to include it in *Songs* 1831 he made significant changes. This may have been a result (as with 'My Love's Bonny' above) of Hogg remembering the song rather than using an existing copy as his copy text.

The editorial notes to the song in *The Forest Minstrel* (S/SC, 2006) discuss the interesting way in which Hogg introduces the song in 1831 – by emphasising his literary immaturity at the time of its creation – and Garside and Jackson suggest that some of the major changes to the song as it appears in 1831 are because of the new 'evangelical and moralistic atmosphere' of the 1820s. Substantive changes include the alteration of the name of the female protagonist from 'Betty' to 'Ellen', the inclusion of a new third verse, a change in perspective from internal monologue to third person narrator and a focus, as Garside and Jackson note, 'on Ellen's and her parent's grief and the irreparable nature of their ruin'. Suzanne Gilbert's note to the song in *The Mountain Bard* also provides discussion of the realities of such 'abuses' of love in Hogg's early years as noted by Douglas Mack. And she also states that Hogg's embarrassment about his early writings may have been due to 'decades of painful experience of having his writings ridiculed' (see S/SC (2007), p. 448).

This song sits in the middle of a group of three love songs in *Songs* 1831 which show Hogg's skills at writing love songs of all types: from the light celebration of 'My Love's Bonny', through the personal devastation of 'The Gloamin' to the murderous tragedy of the border ballad 'Liddel Bower'.

The song appears in Hogg's fair-copy manuscript for *Songs* 1831 at NLS, MS 4805, f. 67 (and verso). It is paginated '133' and '134' and is within the longest consecutively paginated portion of the manuscript which runs without a break from '114' to '168'. On l.33 Hogg scores out 'dye' and replaces it with 'die', which appears in the printed text. Hogg's unpunctuated text is transferred reasonably cleanly to the printed page. However, one significant alteration occurs within the title and first line: Hogg writes 'Gloaming' in his manuscript but this is changed to 'Gloamin' in the printed text.

Publication History:

1805 – in the *Scots Magazine*, 76 (April 1805), 295

1807 – in *The Mountain Bard,* pp. 70–71– see (S/SC, 2007), pp. 103–04 and 447–48

1810 – in *The Forest Minstrel,* pp. 25–26 – see (S/SC, 2006), pp. 31–32 and 236–37

1822 – in *Poetical Works,* IV, 351–52

1831 – in *Songs by the Ettrick Shepherd* , pp. 166–68 – see pp. 75–76 in the present
   edition

Musical Context:

Although Hogg writes in his headnote that the song 'has never been set to music' he previously indicated that two different traditional Scottish tunes would provide a suitable accompaniment. 'Ettrick Banks' is written below the title of the first version of the song in the *Scots Magazine* of 1805. However, in the three subsequent versions of the song the tune 'Mary Weep Nae Mair for Me' (more commonly known as 'Mary's Dream') is given. It is likely that Hogg knew the latter tune in association with Alexander Lowe's verses as they appear in the *SMM*, I, (1787), no. 37. This is the tune used in *The Forest Minstrel* (S/SC, 2006), where the two tunes are discussed in detail (pp. 237–39).

Liddel Bower, A Ballad (pp. 77–78)

Creative Context:

Hogg's headnote states that this song was composed for inclusion in Alexander Campbell's musical collection *Albyn's Anthology* where it first appeared in the first volume in 1816. Evidence that this was one of Hogg's first contributions to Campbell's collection is found in the 'Prospectus for Albyn's Anthology', which was written by Walter Scott and circulated in March 1816 (Todd and Bowden, 92A, p. 300). Five of Scott's songs as well as Hogg's 'The Liddel Bower' and 'A Year Owre Young' are advertised as 'written expressly for this Work, as making part of the present Volume': see NLS MS 677, ff. 139–40. For further information about Hogg's involvement in Campbell's collection and to see a copy of the song see *Contributions to Musical Collections and Miscellaneous Songs.*

Hogg' s 'Liddel Bower' simulates a traditional border ballad much like those he was involved in providing for Scott's *Minstrelsy of the Scottish Border* in the early 1800s and relating closely to his own ballads for *The Mountain Bard* of 1807. This ballad relates the circumstances leading to the death or disappearance of 'the heiress of the lands of Nith' through her relationship with an unidentified ancestor of the powerful Douglas family and their meeting 'at Liddel bower' or by Liddel

Water in Liddesdale in the Scottish Borders. His title, setting and references to the key Border families of Douglas, Jardine, Johnstone and Maxwell, give this ballad a very firm place in Border balladry. These four families were all regarded as Border 'Clans': see Appendix XII: Border Clans' in *The Border Antiquities of England and Scotland*, by Walter Scott (Edinburgh: Constable and Co.; London: Longman, Hurst, Rees, Orme, and Brown, 1814) vol. 2.

The background to 'Liddel Bower' also relates closely to Hogg's work searching for extant oral or printed sources surrounding the assassination of William Douglas, Lord of Liddesdale by his kinsman William, Earl of Douglas in Ettrick Forest in 1353, over a jealousy involving 'his lady'. Walter Scott had mentioned this event in his introduction to the *Minstrelsy of the Scottish Border* and it may be this to which Hogg is referring in his 1831 headnote when he states that the ballad is apparently 'founded on some published legend, but where it is to be found I have quite forgot'. Suzanne Gilbert's note on Hogg's ballad 'The Death of Douglas, Lord of Liddisdale' (which had first appeared in the *Scots Magazine* in 1804 and was then included in *The Mountain Bard* in 1807) gives a detailed account of how Hogg pulled together a variety of sources for use in this and later ballads and songs referring to this event (see *The Mountain Bard*, S/SC 2007, pp. 435–36). Other Hogg songs using the Liddesdale connection include: 'Lock the Door, Lariston' (pp. 89–90 of the present volume), 'The Death of Douglas, Lord of Liddisdale' and 'The Laird of Lairistan, or, The Three Champions of Liddisdale', both appearing in *The Mountain Bard* (1807) – pp. 96–102, pp. 137–50 (see S/SC (2007), pp. 67–70 and pp. 86–92. As Suzanne Gilbert's notes to 'The Death of Douglas' state, Liddel Water 'joins the river Esk shortly before the Esk flows into the Solway Firth' and for a short time this water 'marks the border between Scotland and England' (*The Mountain Bard*, S/SC, (2007), p. 437). This is the setting for Hogg's 'Liddel Bower', and explains Hogg's references to the Nith and to Caerlaverock in his ballad.

After appearing in Campbell's work, Hogg included 'Liddel Bower' in the third volume of his *Poetical Works* of 1822, where clearly the copy text was *Albyn's Anthology*: there are no substantive variants. Parts of the song were then redrafted for *Songs* 1831. Although the narrative of the ballad remains the same, the layout changes from typical ballad quatrains to octets. Some are simple revisions: e.g. 'My flocks lie in the Border dales' becomes 'My flocks spread o'er the Border dales' (l. 11), and 'O gae with me to Liddel Bower' becomes 'With Douglas at the Liddel bower' (l. 15). Other variants are more significant. For example, the last four lines of verse five and the first four lines of verse eight are newly created for *Songs* 1831. Originally, the lines in what is now verse five which suggested Douglas's discomfort become notably more threatening. From:

> Red grew the Douglas' dusky cheek,
>   He turned his eye away;
> The gowden hilt fell to his hand;
>   "What can the wee bird say?" (verse 10, ll. 37–40)

To:

> "Lady, beware! Some words there are
>   That secrets may betray
> No utterance gives them to the air
>   What dares your wee bird say?" (verse 5, ll. 37–40)

The four new lines at the beginning of verse eight introduce another Border family – the 'Johnstones' – into the ballad who join the search for the young lady (ll. 57–60).

The only extant holograph version of 'Liddel Bower' known to survive is found in the fair-copy manuscript for *Songs* 1831, at NLS MS 4805, ff. 67v–69r, immediately below 'The Gloaming'. The pages are numbered '134', '135', '137' (mispaged), and '137'. Hogg's unpunctuated text is transferred cleanly to the printed volume without alteration.

Publication History:

1816 – in *Albyn's Anthology*, I, 38–9 – see *Contributions to Musical Collections and Miscellaneous Songs* (S/SC, 2014)

1822 – in *Poetical Works*, III, 361–67

1831 – in *Songs by the Ettrick Shepherd*, pp. 169–73 – see pp. 77–8 in the present edition.

Musical Context:

Hogg's headnote refers his reader to Campbell's choice of 'an old Border air' which Cambpell had 'picked up' to include in his song collection, *Albyn's Anthology*. But the only information given in the collection is 'A Border Melody'. The title of the air has not yet been identified. Walter Scott's introductory letter to Robert Shortreed, Sheriff Substitute of Roxburghshire, written on Campbell's behalf, and dated 18 October 1816, reveals at least one occasion when Campbell could have 'picked up' the air. Scott writes:

> Mr Alexander Campbell a man of great musical talent and an excellent singer is going forward into Liddesdale to try if he can find any original melodies and I will be much obliged to you to give him a recommendation or two to help him on his journey. If a good Scots song can pay for hospitality he is well qualified to give it. I think he may possibly pick up something in our dales though they have been well harried. (*The Letters of Sir Walter Scott*, 10 vols (London: Constable & Co., 1932–36), IV, 104.

Explanatory Notes:

78, l. 62 Tarras linn Tarras Water, a stream in Eskdale, E Dumfriesshire.

Auld Ettrick John (pp. 79–81)

Creative Context:

A full textual and Publication History of the song is provided in *The Forest Minstrel* (S/SC, 2006), where the song is described as 'one of the most frequently printed of Hogg's songs'. In summary, one of Hogg's earliest songs, it was first published as 'Auld Ettrick John. A Scottish Ballad' in the *Scots Magazine* in March 1804 and thereafter was included in all Hogg's main song collections as 'Auld Ettrick John', namely in *The Mountain Bard* (1807) – though not in its 1821 edition – and in *The Forest Minstrel* (1810), and *Poetical Works* (1822). Hogg then picked it up as the first in a set of five songs which he presents in *Songs* 1831 as 'all compositions of my early youth, made for the sphere around the cottage hearth and the farmer's kitchen-ingle, without the most distant prospect of any higher distinction'. This comment is noteworthy. Hogg is clearly declaring the importance of his position as a member of an active oral tradition and celebrating this. His headnote also comments on the fact that this little group of songs needed to be included, even if they were poetically 'below par' because they have been 'such general favourites among the class for which they were framed, for the last thirty years'. But all five songs in his 'quintet' here in 1831, had already appeared in *The Forest Minstrel*, and elsewhere, often in publications, which as Peter Garside and Richard Jackson have stated, were clearly designed within a 'new genteel and musically diverse context' (p. xxv).

The editorial notes in *The Forest Minstrel* account for any earlier textual variants. The version in *Songs* 1831 relates most closely to that in *Poetical Works* of 1822, which had omitted the seventh stanza as found in earlier versions. But Hogg makes other substantial changes for 1831. There are a number of verbal changes; and Hogg adds two new verses (four and seven) and gives four new lines to complete verse 8. Garside and Jackson suggest that some of these changes result in removing 'some of the more 'physical' ingredients in the original wording' (p. 304). But this would rather contradict Hogg's suggestion, in his headnote, that these songs were to represent his earliest songs sung in an earthier setting than the middle-class drawing room. While some of the more physical descriptions are indeed excluded Hogg does not replace the earthy use of Scots here.

The only extant holograph version of this early song known to survive is found in Hogg's fair-copy manuscript for *Songs* 1831 at NLS MS 4805, ff. 69v–71v. The song is paginated from '138' to '142' and is within the longest consecutively paginated portion of the manuscript. There are both substantive and non-substantive alterations to the text. Within the headnote the word 'next' originally preceded 'four songs' in the opening line, but was omitted from the printed version. A further non-substantive change occurs in l. 57 of the song when 'sickan': 'such, of a kind' (*DSL*) is printed as 'sicklike': 'suchlike' (*DSL*). Two substantive alterations occur through misreading: in Hogg's poetic shortened form of 'early' [as in 'late and ear"] is printed as 'air' (l. 61), rendering the phrase meaningless, while the Scots word 'lythe': 'gentle, genial, kindly' (*DSL*) becomes 'blithe': 'joyous, cheerful, happy' in the final stanza of the printed version (l. 81).

Publication History:
1805 – in the *Scots Magazine*, 66 (March, 1804), 217
1807 – in *The Mountain Bard*, pp. 192–96 – see (S/SC, 2007), pp. 114–16 and 457–58
1810 – in *The Forest Minstrel*, pp. 119–23 – see (S/SC, 2006), pp. 120–23 and 303–06
1822 – in *Poetical Works*, III, 375–79
1831 – in *Songs by the Ettrick Shepherd*, pp. 174–79 – see pp. 79–81 in the present edition

Musical Context:
Hogg makes no mention of a melody or a musical setting in 1831, but from its appearance elsewhere from 1810 the song is associated with the popular tune 'Rothiemurchus' Rant' to which Burns had also written two songs: 'Lassie wi' the lintwhite locks' and 'Full-well thou know'st I love thee dear' with the chorus 'Fairest maid on Devon banks'. Hogg's song appears with this melody in *The Forest Minstrel* and there is a detailed note on the history of the melody (S/SC, 2006, pp. 304–06).

Explanatory Notes:
See *The Mountain Bard* (S/SC (2007), pp. 457–58.

Doctor Munroe (pp. 81–82)

Creative Context:
Though there is no headnote to this song it belongs to the quintet of 'compositions from my early youth' referred to in the headnote to the previous song 'Auld Ettrick John' (pp. 79–81). Though apparently one of his earliest, it appears for the first time in print in *The Forest Minstrel* in 1810 as the first song in the 'Humorous' class – though notably with the spelling 'Munro'.

A full textual and Publication History of the song is provided in *The Forest Minstrel* (S/SC, 2006) where Garside and Jackson note that much of the song was revised (as is the case with 'The Gloamin' and 'Auld Ettrick John') for its appearance in 1831. Only ll. 1–12 and 39–40 approximate the wording of the 1810 version. 'Christy', the female protagonist in the 1810 version becomes three different named women – Bell, Sue and Christy – in 1831. And the 1810 consultation between Dr Monro and his patient between ll. 17–32 in the 1810 version is completely rewritten in 1831. Garside and Jackson record, indeed, that Hogg arguably removes elements of the song 'which could have been more vulnerable to accusations of 'indelicacy' in the later 1820s'. They also note that it is the 1831 text which is then used for later publications of the song in Thomas Thomson's edition of Hogg's *Works* and other later nineteenth century editions.

The only extant holograph version of this early song known to survive is found in Hogg's fair-copy manuscript for *Songs* 1831 located at NLS MS 4805, ff. 71v–72r where it begins below 'Auld Ettrick John' (see above). Hogg's unpunctuated text is transferred relatively cleanly to the printed page although several verbal and non-verbal alterations have crept into the printed text. For example, contracted words such as 'an'' are written in full and words changed from lower to upper case. One non-substantive alteration deserving attention occurs in the phrase 'heels-o'er-head' (l. 4), where Hogg's holograph (uncharacteristically) has dashes between the words. These are not transferred to the printed version. However, as these dashes are also found in *The Forest Minstrel* version it would appear to be Hogg's usual practice.

Publication History:
1810 – in *The Forest Minstrel*, pp. 111–13 – see (S/SC, 2006), pp. 113–14 and 297–99
1831 – in *Songs by the Ettrick Shepherd*, pp. 180–82 – see pp. 81–82 in the present edition

Musical Context:
It is strange that Hogg gives no Musical Context for the song in 1831, for the popular tune 'The Humours o'Glen' is given as the tune title alongside the text in 1810. For a full history of the tune see *The Forest Minstrel* (S/SC, 2006), pp. 298–99. Garside and Jackson also refer to the work of Elaine Petrie (*Altrive Chapbooks* no. 3 (September 1986; pp. 106–10) and David Groves (*James Hogg Selected Poems and Songs*, 1986 p. 4) on this particular song and its air. No musical settings of Hogg's song to this air have been located.

Explanatory Notes:
As Garside and Jackson note, the name Doctor Munro(e) refers to 'three father-son generations of Alexander Munro who served as Professors of Anatomy at Edinburgh from the early 1720s into the 19th century' (p. 297).

Sing On, Sing On, my Bonny Bird (pp. 82–83)

Creative Context:
Though there is no headnote in 1831 this song belongs to the quintet of 'compositions from my early youth' referred to in the headnote to 'Auld Ettrick John' (pp. 79–81), which all sit together at this point in *Songs* 1831. A full textual and Publication History of the song, also known as 'Bonny Jean', is provided in *The Forest Minstrel* (S/SC, 2006).

In summary, the song is clearly one of Hogg's earliest, first found in the *Scots Magazine* for May 1803 as having been written 'by a Scots Shepherd' (it had also been referred to back in the issue of March 1803: p. 146). Garside and Jackson note Hogg's debt to Allan Ramsay's 'Bonny Jean' ('Love's goddess in a myrtle grove') from the *Tea-Table Miscellany* (Edinburgh, 1724, pp. 83–4) and also to the popularity of Scottish songs with this title. It is notable that Burns also has a 'Bonny Jean' which Hogg undoubtedly knew (see Kinsley 414). Aside from a notable change in the version which appears in *The Mountain Bard* in 1807 (the second octet of the *Scots Magazine* version is omitted here), all other versions after 1807 are very close, with just a handful of verbal variants.

Unlike several of Hogg's earliest songs, which he substantially rewrites for 1831, this one stays true to its earlier incarnations. In this final version the title alters from 'Bonny Jean' (the title in all previous versions) to the first line of the song 'Sing on, Sing on, My Bonny Bird'. A comprehensive account of all verbal and non-verbal variants in all four versions of the song is found in *The Forest Minstrel* (S/SC, 2006).

Hogg's fair-copy holograph for the version found in *Songs* 1831 is in NLS MS 4805, ff. 72v–73r where it follows immediately after 'Doctor Monroe' (see above). Hogg's unpunctuated text is transferred cleanly to the printed page. Notably, in 1831, Hogg remembered Jean's hair as being 'auburn' in his fair-copy manuscript, but it changes to 'yellow' (l. 31) in *Songs* 1831 to match all previous versions. It is interesting to note Hogg's unusual insistence on grammatical correctness with the insertion in the manuscript (and retained in the printed text) of an apostrophe in the repeated word-phrase 'O weel's me' (ll. 9–11) which does not occur in any previous version of the song. A typed copy of the song is also extant at NLS MS 3581, f. 87. The provenance is not known, although the NLS catalogue entry notes that it is 'taken from a manuscript in Hogg's hand'. Set in quatrains instead of octets and omitting the original second verse, it closely follows all other versions.

Publication History:
1803 – in *Scots Magazine*, 65 (May, 1803), 339 – see also *The Mountain Bard* (S/SC, 2007), pp. 188–89
1807 – in *The Mountain Bard*, pp. 200–02 – see (S/SC, 2007), pp. 118–19, 458, and 469
1810 – in *The Forest Minstrel*, pp. 89–91 – see (S/SC, 2006), pp. 92–93 and 283–85
1831 – in *Songs by the Ettrick Shepherd*, pp. 183–85 – see pp. 82–83 in the present edition

Musical Context:
As with 'Dr Munroe' above, it seems very strange that Hogg should omit to give
the title of the tune which has been associated with his lyrics in earlier publications.
Both *The Forest Minstrel* and *The Mountain Bard* note that the tune 'Prince William
Henry's Delight' is the air associated with Hogg's song. Garside and Jackson note
that 'no tune with precisely this name has been found'. But they give an account
of similarly titled songs which may have provided a suitable accompaniment to
the song: see *The Forest Minstrel* (S/SC, 2006), pp. 285–86.

Jock an' his Mother (pp. 84–85)

Creative Context:
Again though there is no headnote in 1831 this is clearly the fourth of Hogg's
quintet of 'compositions from my early youth' referred to in the headnote to
'Auld Ettrick John' (pp. 79–81), which all sit together in *Songs* 1831. Like the three
immediately preceding it a full textual and Publication History of the song is
provided in *The Forest Minstrel* (S/SC, 2006). In summary, the song first appeared
in 1810 in *The Forest Minstrel* with the title 'Jack and his Mother' (emended to
'Jock' in the S/SC edition). Garside and Jackson note that there is an earlier
version in a manuscript booklet with five songs Hogg had apparently sent to the
Edinburgh Magazine in 1802. They give details of the manuscript now at Boston
Public Library (MS Ch.H.13.1), noting that 'the song comprised six eight-line
stanzas, one more than the *Forest Minstrel* version, which effectively fails to take up
four lines each from the original second and third stanzas.' The language of the
original version is less polished or refined and there are more Scots words than
appears in the *Forest Minstrel* version.

Garside and Jackson suggest that the 1831 version was redrafted from memory.
But Hogg's autograph manuscript that he used in preparation for *Songs* 1831
(NLS MS 4805, ff. 73v–74r), provides two clear pieces of evidence that he copied
the song directly from *The Forest Minstrel* text. The first is found at l.16, the final
line of the second verse, where Hogg originally writes the text exactly as it appears
in *The Forest Minstrel*: 'Dear Jocky be wise an tak warning'. He then scores out these
words, including the 'y' of 'Jocky', and rewrites the text above as 'Dear Jock tak
a thought an some warning', which is printed in *Songs* 1831. Further evidence is
found at l. 25 where Hogg originally writes 'young', as it is in *The Forest Minstrel*
version, but scores this word out and writes 'dear' immediately beside it, as it then
appears in *Songs* 1831.

As well as providing evidence of direct copying, such evidence also helps to
date when Hogg was working on this part of his collection. On 20 October 1830,
within a long letter to William Blackwood, Hogg tells him, 'You must by all
means endeavour to get me a copy of "The Forest Minstrel" published long ago
by Constable I cannot go on without that although out of the whole vol I do not
think I could take above half a dozen' (*Letters* II, 404–406 (405)).

As noted above there are two manuscripts related to this song, the first in
Boston Public Library (MS Ch.H.13.1) which comprises a four-page booklet
dating from 1801–1802. Of the five songs included, apparently intended for the
Edinburgh Magazine, only one song, 'By a Bush' was published there, in January
1803 (see *The Forest Minstrel* (2006), pp. xvii–xviii). The second manuscript is
Hogg's fair-copy manuscript for Songs 1831 at NLS MS 4805, 73v–74r. Here it
follows immediately after 'Sing on, Sing on, My Bonny Bird' as it does in *Songs*
1831. Hogg's unpunctuated text is transferred cleanly to the printed page.

Publication History:
1810 – in *The Forest Minstrel*, pp. 144–6 – see (S/SC, 2006), pp. 138–39 and 321–22
1831 – in *Songs by the Ettrick Shepherd,* pp. 186–88 – see pp. 84–85 in the present
   edition

Musical Context:
Unlike the two songs immediately preceding this one in *Songs* 1831 Hogg does
give a tune title in this case. The song always appears in print alongside the tune
or air entitled 'Jackson's Cog i' the Morning', a tune with Irish origins. Full details
of the Musical Context can be found in *The Forest Minstrel* (2006), pp. 322–23.

Explanatory Notes:
84, l. 15 Send ye to sea (literal) be confused, unable to decide on a course of
   action.
84, l. 19 Perjury black as a crow a black lie. 'From the mid 16th century, rook
   also denoted a cheat or swindler' (*Oxford Dictionary of Phrase and Fable*).

On Ettrick Clear (pp. 85–86)

Creative Context:
This song, like the three before it, has no headnote in 1831 but is intended as the
fifth and final song in the quintet of 'compositions from my early youth', which all
sit together in *Songs* 1831 and are referred to in the headnote to 'Auld Ettrick John'
(pp. 79–81). A full textual and Publication History of the song is provided in *The
Forest Minstrel* (S/SC, 2006), where Garside and Jackson also emphasise the links
with Burns's 'Blythe, blithe and merry was she' (Kinsley, 179).
   In summary, the song, like 'Auld Ettrick John' and 'Sing on, Sing on, my Bonny
Bird' first appeared in the *Scots Magazine*, in this case in July 1803, under the title
'Blythe and Cheary, A Scots Sang'. With the revised title 'Blythe an' Cheery' the
song was next included in *The Forest Minstrel* in 1810. In this and in all subsequent
versions printed in Hogg's lifetime the second verse is omitted and the wording
and line ordering is close to that in *Songs* 1831. Garside and Jackson note that the
changes in 1810 suggest a 'more gentrified and less 'communal'' feeling to the
lyric. The song was subsequently included in the fourth volume of Hogg's *Poetical
Works* of 1822 with some slight alterations (e.g.'lose baith my een' becomes 'tine
baith my een' (l.26)) and the usual orthographic changes (e.g. 'Peggie' for 'Peggy').
   As in 'Sing on, Sing on, My Bonny Bird', the version included in *Songs* 1831
alters the title to a repetition of the first line, 'On Ettrick Clear'. Overall, though,
the text is very close to that of *Poetical Works*, with some verbal differences which
Garside and Jackson suggest are 'indicative of a fresh redrafting from memory'.
The most obvious change occurs at line 20, where Hogg rewrote the original
line of 'An' in my arms at e'ening lie' of all previous versions to the possibly less
offensive, 'An' meet me on the brae at e'en.'
   The only extant holograph version of this early song known to survive is found
in Hogg's fair-copy manuscript for *Songs* 1831 located at NLS MS 4805, f. 74. The
manuscript is page-numbered '147' and '148' and follows immediately below 'Jock
an' his Mother' on f. 74v within the longest consecutively paginated portion of
the manuscript which runs without a break from '114' to '168' ending abruptly at
the headnote to 'I'll No' Wake Wi' Annie' (f. 83v). Hogg's unpunctuated text is
transferred cleanly to the printed page.

Publication History:

1803 – in *Scots Magazine*, 65 (May, 1803), 479–80
1810 – in *The Forest Minstrel*, pp. 55–56 – see (S/SC, 2006), pp. 59–60 and 258–60
1822 – in *Poetical Works*, IV, 355–56
1831 – in *Songs by the Ettrick Shepherd*, pp. 189–90 – see pp. 85–86 in the present
    edition

Musical Context:

Of the quintet of songs only 'Jock and his mother' has a tune title printed alongside
it in *Songs* 1831. Although Hogg fails to include a tune title for 'On Ettrick Clear'
earlier printings do give an air or tune title: 'Cutty Gun' is given alongside the
song in the *Scots Magazine* in 1803 and 'Blythe, blithe, an' merry was she' is given
in *The Forest Minstrel* in 1810. As noted by Garside and Jackson, the change title
most probably nods to Burns (his song first appeared with music in the *SMM* (II,
1788, no. 180). The tune Burns used was 'Andro and his cutty gun' (Kinsley 179),
and was known initially with bawdy verses. A full account of the tune is given in
The Forest Minstrel (S/SC, 2006), pp. 259–60). This tune was also used by Hogg's
friend Thomas Mouncey Cunningham for his humorous love lyric beginning
'Ayont the Mow among the Hay' also printed in *The Forest Minstrel* in 1810 (see
S/SC, 2006, pp. 126–27).

Athol Cummers (p. 86)

Creative Context:

Though not one of the 'quintet' of 'compositions from my early youth', which
immediately precedes it in *Songs* 1831, this song is included as an extra youthful
song and Hogg's headnote dates its creation to 1800 at the request of his mother
Margaret Laidlaw (1730–1813). There is no reason to doubt the Creative Context
he relates in 1831. A full textual and Publication History is included in *The Forest
Minstrel* (S/SC, 2006).

In summary, the song first appeared in *The Forest Minstrel* in 1810 in the class
of 'Humorous Songs' beside 'Jack [Jock] and his Mother' which Hogg had also
chosen to insert at this point in *Songs* 1831. Garside and Jackson note that Hogg's
lyric skilfully captures the rhythm of the strathspey to which it is set along with
the droning sound of the bagpipe mentioned in the first line notably with Hogg's
creation of the word 'bummers'.

The version of 'Athol Cummers' included in *Songs* 1831 shows clear signs
of rewriting on Hogg's part. The first line is different, with 'Duncan, lad, blaw
the bummers' changed to 'Duncan, lad, blaw the cummers', even though Hogg
has written 'bummers' in the manuscript (NLS MS 4805 f.75). The song is now
in octets and the chorus is dropped. Indeed, in the printed copy there is no
indication that the first four lines might be used as a chorus. As well as some
verbal alterations, such as changing 'cry' to the more poetic 'lilt' (l. 12), the
concluding four lines of *The Forest Minstrel* version are rewritten and four new
lines added. Now Hogg compares the 'cummers' of his own district with those
of Athol (mountainous area north of Perthshire), Lomond and Breadalbane (a
district of North West Perthshire), and finds them wanting. Hogg also adds a
clarifying footnote to explain that 'cummers' are 'Maidens'.

Hogg's 1831 headnote highlights the success of the song in performance, with
its references both to Hogg first learning the fiddle tune at home and then with its
reference to Hogg's new song having been sung often by his friend Robert Pearse

Gillies (1788–1858), writer and German scholar (see also 'The Noctes Sang' pp. 14–15). This anecdote emphasises the importance of Hogg's songs as part of enjoyable socialising with family and friends.

The only extant holograph version of this early song known to survive is found in Hogg's fair-copy manuscript for *Songs* 1831 located at NLS MS 4805, f. 75. The manuscript is page-numbered '149' and '150' and follows immediately after 'On Ettrick Clear'. A few substantive alterations and omissions have crept into the printed text. In the headnote, Hogg writes that it was 'In the winter of 1800' but 'One evening' is added to the printed version. Further down the headnote, Hogg adds 'uniformly' next to the word 'then'. But 'then' is subsequently removed before the printing. And at the end of the first octet he then gives 'Duncan lad &c.', clearly suggesting the need for a chorus, but he then scores this through. No chorus appears in the printed version. One alteration is clearly a misreading of Hogg's hand. At the end of the first line the word 'bummers' to denote the droning noise of the bagpipes is printed as 'cummers', which is completely meaningless within the context of the line and the verse.

Publication History:
1810 – in *The Forest Minstrel*, pp. 147–48 – (S/SC, 2006), pp. 140–41 and 323–24
1831 – in *Songs by the Ettrick Shepherd* , pp. 191–92 – see p. 86 in the present edition

Musical Context:
The Forest Minstrel (S/SC, 2006) gives a detailed account of the complexities of finding the tune which Hogg clearly references in his headnote in 1831. Garside and Jackson do note the popularity of the strathspey 'Athole Cummers', citing its inclusion in several published collections and also referencing Elaine Petrie's work on this tune and Hogg's use of it (*Altrive Chapbooks*, No. 2 (September, 1985), pp. 55–57). This indicates the difficulty of recreating exact variants of popular tunes which were often so numerous. Clearly Hogg was creating a lyric to match his own variant of the strathspey as he had learned it and as he performed it on his fiddle.

Love Letter (pp. 87–88)

Creative Context:
This song and 'Mischievous Woman', which follows it in *Songs* 1831, are companion pieces written in the early 1810s (Hogg states 1811) for Hogg's wife-to-be Margaret Philips (1789–1871). Both songs (see p. 88) were first published in Hogg's magazine *The Spy*: 'Mischievous Woman' in December 1810 and 'Love Letter' in May 1811. In his headnote Hogg claims that they were sent as part of 'humorous letters' to Margaret, but these private letters have not been located. Gillian Hughes notes that Hogg was first introduced to Margaret at the home of his friend James Gray in Edinburgh in 1810 and she states that while Margaret's early letters to Hogg are not extant, his to her are 'admiring and playful, affectionate and teasing rather than passionate' (*A Life*, pp. 93–94). Hogg includes words derived from both these songs within an early letter to Margaret Phillips of 27 July 1811, where he states,' "and I would watch thy witching smile and glossy een sae dark and wiley" '. The words are set within quotation marks, which seems to indicate that Hogg is quoting from the printed versions in *The Spy* rather than private communications: see *Letters*, I, 112–113. Another untitled song, beginning 'The bittern's quavering trump on high', that was published the week

before 'Scottish Song', in *The Spy* on 4 May 1811 (No. 36), also uses the phrase 'thy witching smile' and the love interest is also named 'Peggy', so that it was also probably addressed to Margaret Phillips (see below).

'Love Letter' first appeared in a longer version of six verses under the general title 'Scotch Song' in *The Spy* in May 1811. It was then included, with music, as one of Hogg's thirteen songs in Alexander Campbell's *Albyn's Anthology or A Select Collection of the Melodies and Vocal Poetry Peculiar to Scotland the Isles*. 'My Peggy, Thou Art Gane Away' was presented by Campbell in 1818 as 'Written for this Work' and indeed was a new version of 'Scotch Song' from *The Spy*. There are only three verses, and of these the first and third verses are completely new, so that only verse two from the original version remains, albeit with slightly re-arranged wording in l. 13. For further information on Hogg's involvement in Alexander Campbell's project see *Contributions to Musical Collections and Miscellaneous Songs*.

A further version of the song was subsequently included in the fourth volume of Hogg's *Poetical Works* of 1822 under the title, 'Ah, Peggie, since thou'rt gane away'. The copy text, with slight non-verbal variants in spelling and punctuation, is the version in *The Spy* of 1811, with the fourth verse omitted entirely.

Under the new title, 'Love Letter', it was then included in *Songs* 1831. The copy text is the version found in *The Spy* with the fourth verse (not included in the *Poetical Works* version) reinstated and the name Peggy changed to Maggy. However, verse three is omitted. As is the case with several of his early songs at this point in *Songs* 1831, fresh drafting throughout the song shows Hogg reengaging with his earlier material, making a further version of this very personal song – which may explain the removal of verse 3 with its reference to 'ae kiss o' thy cherry mou''.

Hogg's fair-copy holograph version of the text found in *Songs* 1831 is missing from the bulk of the main surviving manuscript portion at NLS MS 4805, ff. 26–102 (Blackwood Papers) and has not been located elsewhere. For more information see 'The Genesis of the Text' in the present volume, pp. xli–xlviii.

Publication History:
1811 – in *The Spy*, No. 37 (11 May 1811), pp. 295–96 – see (S/SC, 2000), pp. 376–77
1818 – in *Albyn's Anthology*, ii, 24–25 – see *Contributions to Musical Collections and Miscellaneous Songs* (S/SC, 2014)
1822 – in *Poetical Works*, iv, 331–33
1831 – in *Songs by the Ettrick Shepherd*, pp. 193–95 – see pp. 87–88 in the present edition

Musical Context:
Hogg gives no tune title for this song, and notably he does not refer the reader to Campbell's *Albyn's Anthology*. This may be because the text underlaid to Campbell's musical setting is not the same as that published in 1831. No musical version of this specific text has been located. The tune to which 'My Peggy, Thou Art Gane Away' is set in Campbell's collection is the 'Royal Highlander's March', an unusually regimental tune for a love song.

Mischievous Woman (p. 88)

Creative Context:
This song shares its Creative Context with 'Love Letter', the preceding song with which it is paired in *Songs* 1831 (see above). Both were written for Hogg's

wife-to-be, Margaret Philips, and 'Mischievous Woman' was first published in Hogg's magazine *The Spy* under the title 'Scotch Song' on 8 December 1810.

It next appears with music in George Thomson's *Select Collection of Original Scottish Airs* in 1818. Hogg's involvement with Thomson and his collection is further discussed in *Contributions to Musical Collections and Miscellaneous Songs*. Hogg sent his revised version of 'Scotch Song' to Thomson in a letter of 18 October 1815. Thomson specifically asked Hogg about his 'beautiful song of Meg, which you sung the last time I had the pleasure of seeing you at the Exchange': see *Letters*, I, 253–54 and notes on p. 255. Hogg redrafts much of the original song, deleting ll. 5–8 and moving the first four lines of verse two into the first verse to make a new opening verse. He adds fresh material at ll. 5–8 as a new opening for the second verse but retains ll. 9–12 (originally ll. 13–16) to complete verse two. The final verse is relatively stable, although 'cheerin' notes' becomes 'wild witch notes' (l. 22).

Thomson's published version of the song remains close to Hogg's fair-copy holograph manuscript (reprinted in *Letters*, I, 254) and he publishes it in his *Select Collection of Original Scottish Airs* in 1818 (Vol. 5) with a musical arrangement by Ludwig van Beethoven with the first line of the song as its title: 'Could this ill warld have been contrived'. The most significant alteration to the version in Thomson's collection occurs in the second line with the contraction of the word 'mischievous' into 'mischief', doubtless because it fits better with Thomson's melody. The song (in German translation beginning 'Wenn doch die arge böse Welt') was then included in Beethoven's *Schottische Lieder* published by Anton Schlesinger in Vienna in 1822, though apparently without Hogg's knowledge. Thomson reprinted the song in 1841 in his sixth and final folio volume now entitled *Melodies of Scotland*. The setting is identical, though with new musical plates. The song is now entitled 'Mischievous Woman' and not 'Could this ill warld have been contriv'd'. The text is stable with only minor variants, notably 'bonnie' at the end of the first verse is now 'bonny'.

A completely revised version of the song was published in the Christmas literary annual *Friendship's Offering for 1830*, with the title, 'A Scots Luve Sang'. Currie and Hughes note: 'There are no indications in Hogg's surviving correspondence of when he sent 'A Scots Luve Sang to London for *Friendship's Offering*', although it was clearly one of several contributions that were handled by Thomas Pringle after his initial approach to Hogg in May 1828' (*Contributions to Annuals and Gift Books* (S/SC, 2006), p. 314). The first verse and the opening four lines of verse two are freshly drafted and clearly aiming at the London literary marketplace with the new setting of 'dale and wood' (l. 9) in this further version of the song, although the wording of verse three remains stable.

The copy text for the song's appearance in *Songs* 1831 is from the version Hogg contributed to Thomson within his letter of 25 October 1818, with the original wording, 'mischievous woman', reinstated at l. 2 and further reinforced with the revised title. Thomson reprinted the song in his 1841 sixth folio volume of *Melodies of Scotland* and there he changed the title to 'Mischievous Woman', although he did not alter the text of the song: see Notes on Musical Collections, p. ??.

A presentation holograph version of the song survives at the Pierpont Morgan Library, New York (MA 2406 R–V Autogr. Misc. Eng), which 'consists of only the first and third stanzas of the poem, signed by Hogg at the end, and was probably produced as an autograph' (*Contributions to Annuals and Gift Books*, p. 314).

Only part of the song appears in Hogg's fair-copy manuscript for *Songs* 1831 at NLS MS 4805, ff. 26–102 (Blackwood Papers). The manuscript breaks off at page number '150' at the end of 'Athol Cummers' (f. 75v) and begins again on page number '153' comprising the last two verses of 'Mischievous Woman' and the title and headnote of 'Lock the Door, Lariston' (f. 76r). The title and first verse of 'Mischievous Woman' are missing and have not been located elsewhere. Of the extant verses, Hogg's unpunctuated text is transferred cleanly to the printed version.

Publication History:
1810 – in *The Spy*, No. 15 (8 December 1810), p. 120 – see (S/SC, 2000), p. 163
1818 – in George Thomson, *A Select Collection of Original Scottish Airs*, v, 204, with a setting by Ludwig van Beethoven – see *Contributions to Musical Collections and Miscellaneous Songs* (S/SC, 2014). The song also appeared with a German translation in Beethoven's *Schottische Lieder mit englischem und deutschem Texte...* (Vienna: Anton Schlesinger, 1822), pp. 18–19 – see Gooch and Thatcher (8768) and *Contributions to Musical Collections and Miscellaneous Songs* (S/SC, 2014)
1830 – in *Friendship's Offering for 1830*, (London: Smith Elder & Co), pp. 185–86 – see *Contributions to Annuals and Gift Books* (S/SC, 2006), pp. 131–32
1831 – in *Songs by the Ettrick Shepherd*, pp. 196–97 – see p. 88 in the present edition
1841 – in George Thomson, *The Melodies of Scotland*, vi (1841), 272 – see *Contributions to Musical Collections and Miscellaneous Songs* (S/SC, 2014)

Musical Context:
The tune title 'Delvin-side' is given alongside the text for this song in *The Spy* and this is also the tune Hogg suggests to Thomson in October 1818 (*Letters*, i, 254). In Thomson's *Select Collection of Original Scottish Airs* and *Melodies of Scotland* the air is named 'Mischievous Woman' and Thomson indicates 'the air composed for the words by a friend of the editor'.

Lock the Door, Lariston (pp. 89–90)

Creative Context:
Hogg's 1831 headnote boldly reclaims the authorship of this song (as his inclusion of songs from *Noctes* also does in *Songs* 1831): 'Mine only, mine solely and mine for ever'. He notes that it is a 'Border Song' which was first published in his magazine *The Spy* in March 1811. But he also notes his chagrin at the general understanding that the song was written by his friend James Gray. Gillian Hughes notes that 'Border Song' was published in the *Dumfries and Galloway Courier* of 3 September 1811 where it was attributed to James Gray (1770–1830), Hogg's early literary mentor: see *Letters*, i, 281n. Gray went to India in 1826 'as chaplain in the East India Company's service. In India he was selected as tutor to the young ruler of Bhuj in Cutch. He died in India on 25 September 1830': see 'Notes on Contributors' in *The Spy* (S/SC, 2000), pp. 562–63. This explains Hogg's reference to the song's wide circulation. The mention of Walter Scott in the headnote here is also notable, for this song features many Border places and names which would be known through the ballads included in Scott's *Minstrelsy of the Scottish Border* (see Explanatory Notes below).

After initially appearing in *The Spy* in 1811, Hogg's rousing 'Border Song' was then revised for inclusion in the fourth volume of his *Poetical Works* in 1822 with its new specific title 'Lock the door, Lariston'. The copy text is the version in *The Spy* with no textual alteration, although the usual changes to orthography and punctuation (such as adding or removing exclamation marks) are consistent with the rest of the *Poetical Works* volumes.

When Hogg chooses to include it in *Songs* 1831 he makes some changes. The addition of new lines created at ll. 21–25 has the effect of foregrounding the gallantry of 'Jock Elliot' (l. 25). One further substantive alteration to the text is at l. 31 where Hogg changes the name 'Ogilvie', found in all earlier versions of the song, to 'Gornberry'. Slighter alterations smooth the antique language, such as at ll. 26–27 where 'know'st thou' becomes 'know you', and also at l. 42 where he replaces the 'Helmit' (or 'Helmet' in 1822) of the earlier two versions of the song with 'Halberd'.

Hogg's authorship is apparently accepted after 1831. Groome's *Ordnance gazetteer of Scotland* (1882–1885) quotes the existence of Hogg's song in his entry for 'Lariston' noting that Lariston Castle 'was once the stronghold of a chief of Elliots, that 'Lion of Liddisdale' whom Hogg has commemorated in his stirring ballad'. In fact, the 'Elliot' of Hogg's ballad is not based on any particular historical figure.

The only extant holograph version known to survive is found in Hogg's fair-copy manuscript for *Songs* 1831 at NLS MS 4805, ff. 26–102 (Blackwood Papers), on ff. 76r–77v. 'Lock the Door, Lariston' is written immediately below the final two verses of 'Mischievous Woman' on page '153', beginning a new sequence of pagination that runs continuously until page number '168' comprising the last eight lines of 'Highland Tay' and the title and headnote to 'I'll No Wake Wi' Annie' (f. 83v). Hogg's unpunctuated text is transferred cleanly to the printed volume with the exception of the word 'deeds' on line 47 which becomes 'hopes' in the published volume.

Publication History:

1811 – in *The Spy*, No. 31 (30 March 1810), 247–48 – see (S/SC, 2000), pp. 318–19 and 608

1822 – in *Poetical Works*, IV, 305–07

1831 – in *Songs by the Ettrick Shepherd*, pp. 198–201– see pp. 89–90 in the present edition

Musical Context:

No music is nominated to accompany any version of the song, although Hogg presumably did have a tune in mind when he composed it. It was one of four songs he offered to John Clarke-Whitfeld on 11 November 1816: see *Letters*, I, 280–81. However, Whitfeld does not appear to have arranged it. For further information on Hogg and Clarke-Whitfeld. See *Contributions to Musical Collections and Miscellaneous Songs*. Gooch and Thatcher list two further musical iterations vof the song: 8617–8618, but neither in Hogg's lifetime.

Explanatory Notes:

89, l. 5 The Castletown's burning, and Oliver's gone the germ of the song is found in an account of Cromwell's destruction of the Border town in 'the sessions records' of Castletown parish church, dated '17th January 1649' and reprinted in the 1790s in the *Statistical Account of Scotland*: ('Parish of Castletown' (vol 16), 68)

89, l. 2 Lowther Hogg follows the normal Scots practice of naming the person after the property or residence, although the particular residence and person of Lowther have not been identified.

89, l. 3 The Armstrongs in his introductory note to the traditional ballad of 'Johnny Armstrang' Scott writes, 'the Armstrongs appear to have been, at an early period, in possession of great part of Liddesdale, and of the Debateable Land. Their immediate neighbourhood to England, rendered them the most lawless of the Border depredators', *Minstrelsy of the Scottish Border*, 3 vols (3ʳᵈ ed., 1806, I, 104).

89, l. 11 Bewcastle a hamlet in Cumberland on the English side of the Anglo/Scottish border.

89, l. 12 Ridley Scott writes that '*Sim of the Cat-hill*' (an Armstrong) was killed by one of the Ridleys of Haltwhistle: see *Minstrelsy of the Scottish Border*, 3 vols (3ʳᵈ ed., 1806, I, 105).

89, ll. 13–14 Hedley and Howard [...] | Wandale and Windermere people and place names in Cumbria, on the English side of the Anglo/Scottish border. Lord William Howard of Naworth Castle, near Brampton, in Cumberland, is a central figure of Scott's *The Lay of the Last Minstrel* (1805).

89, l. 16 Elliot of Lariston in Hogg's earlier tradition-inspired ballad, 'The Laird of Lairiston; or, The Three Champions of Liddisdale', the protagonist is 'the chief warrior of Liddisdale, Elliot Laird of Lairistan' (*The Mountain Bard* (1807)). Suzanne Gilbert discusses how in the original version the chief was named 'Jardine' and the ballad hero was named 'Jock Elliot' but that after corresponding with Scott Hogg changed the name of the protagonist to 'Elliot' and that of the hero to 'Jock Armstrong of Milburn': see *The Mountain Bard* (S/SC, 2007), p. 443.

90, ll. 28–29 Lindhope and Sorby true, | Sundhope and Milburn place-names in Liddesdale.

90, l. 31 Margerton, Gornberry, Raeburn, and Netherby further place-names and people of Liddesdale and Cumberland. The chief of the Armstrongs (according to Scott's version in *Minstrelsy of the Scottish Border*, 3 vols (3ʳᵈ ed., 1806), I, 104) was Armstrong of Mangerton; 'Willie o' Gorrinberry' is mentioned in the ballad of 'Jamie Telfer of the fair Dodhead' in *Minstrelsy of the Scottish Border*, 3 vols (3ʳᵈ ed., 1806), I, 137 (l.108), in the original version of 'Lock the Door, Lariston' the name was Ogilvie; Lessuden House, near the village of St. Boswells was the home of the Scotts of Raeburn; Netherby Hall, seat of the Graham family is on the Cumberland side of the River Esk.

90, l. 32 Old Sim of Whitram Scott mentions 'Sim of Whitram' in his introductory note to 'Johnny Armstrang': (*Minstrelsy of the Scottish Border*, 3 vols (3ʳᵈ ed., 1806), I, 111). In a footnote, Scott explains that 'Whitram is a place in Liddesdale' (p. 111).

90, ll. 33–34 Come all Northumberland, | Teesdale and Cumberland regions on the English side of the Anglo/Scottish border.

90, l. 35 the Breaken Tower 'Martin Elliot of the Preakin Tower was chief of the Liddesdale Elliots': Scott's introductory note to 'Jamie Telfer of the fair Dodhead' (*Minstrelsy of the Scottish Border*, 3 vols (3ʳᵈ ed., 1806), I, 137).

Fair was thy Blossom (pp. 90–91)

Creative Context:

Like the group of early songs which precede it in *Songs* 1831 the first appearance of this song, with the title 'Elegy', is in Hogg's magazine *The Spy* in May 1811. There is little information about the circumstances surrounding its creation, short of the details Hogg gives about the death of a child in his 1831 headnote. Thomas

Richardson notes that Hogg sent his 'Elegy' along with his 'Extempore Song' to William Blackwood in September 1817 for inclusion in *Blackwood's Edinburgh Magazine*. Full textual and publication histories for both songs as they appear in *Blackwood's* are found in *Contributions to Blackwood's Edinburgh Magazine* I (S/SC, 2008).

Richardson notes that the manuscript of Hogg's two songs sent to Blackwood (NLS MS 4805, fols. 99–100) also included Robert Southey's poem 'To Mary'. Gillian Hughes suggests that Hogg was most probably just packaging together some 'little poetical pieces' and 'verses by a respected friend' for the magazine (*Letters*, I, 300–01, 301). But all three poems focus on loss and have a certain mystery about them. Southey's poem had originally appeared in *The Morning Post* of 20 October 1803 under the title 'Stanzas written After a Long Absence', and Linda Pratt has noted recently that the identity of Mary is still a mystery (*Poetical Works 1793–1810*, 5 vols, General Editor, Lynda Pratt (London: Pickering and Chatto, 2004), Vol. 5, 508). Hogg had also published Southey's poem in *The Spy*, No. 21 (19 January 1811). 'Extempore Song' only appears in *Blackwood's* and not elsewhere in Hogg's lifetime. But Richardson notes that images and phrases from this song were resued in later songs by Hogg, notably 'In Memory of Mr Robert Anderson'; a song composed around 1823, which details Hogg's response to the death of his friend's son. See also 'I downa laugh, I downa sing' in *Select & Rare Scotish Melodies*, Hogg's London-based song-collection of 1828 (pp. 15–18) – in *Contributions to Musical Collections and Miscellaneous Songs*. And see also 'A Father's Lament' in *Songs* 1831 (pp. 37–38).

'Elegy', however, was included in several other places. Firstly it appeared, with the same title and using the recent *Blackwood's* text, in the fourth volume of Hogg's *Poetical Works* of 1822. Hogg then decided to include it in *Songs* 1831. He returned to the earliest version in *The Spy*, but, as he states in his headnote for 1831 he has removed 'some of the original stranzas' because the information was 'too particular'. For 1831 Hogg altered the structure of the song from quatrains to octets. The omitted verses do provide additional information about the mother, including, for example, 'How oft thy mother heav'd the sigh | O'er wreaths of honour early shorn' (ll. 5–6); 'Her wrong'd but gentle bosom' (l. 13), and 'faded dreams of past delight' (l. 19), descriptions which, cumulatively, builds a devastating picture of early nineteenth-century Scottish morality. But they certainly do not identify the woman in question. Tellingly, in all versions, Hogg concludes his song by overturning the image of the illegitimate 'child of love, of shame, and woe' to one of, 'the emblem true | Of beauty, innocence, and truth' (ll. 21–22).

NLS, MS 4805, ff. 99–100 is the earliest extant manuscript version of the song as sent to Blackwood in 1817 (see above). The only other extant manuscript is that found in the fair-copy manuscript for *Songs* 1831 at NLS, MS 4805, ff. 77v–78r. The text has been cleanly transmitted to the printed version with no change, aside from the usual insertion of punctuation.

Publication History:

1811 – in *The Spy*, No. 39 (25 May 1811), pp. 311–12 – see also (S/SC, 2000), pp. 395–96

1817 – in *Blackwood's Edinburgh Magazine*, 2 (October 1817), 47 – see also (S/SC, 2008), pp. 25–26 and 407–09

1822 – in *Poetical Works*, IV, 246–48

1831 – in *Songs by the Ettrick Shepherd*, pp. 202–03 – see pp. 90–91 in the present edition

Musical Context:
Hogg gives no tune title here or elsewhere for this song, nor has any musical setting of the lyric been located.

Explantory notes:
91, l.31 And long the daisy, emblem meet Richardson notes that the daisy is the traditional symbol of childhood innocence. The daisy or 'day's eye' opens its white petals in the morning exposing a golden centre and closes them over again at each sunset. The emblematic daisy as grave-flower became a stock image of later nineteenth-century literature.

Courting Song (pp. 91–92)

Creative Context:
Continuing with his grouping of 'early' songs at this point in *Songs* 1831, Hogg's headnote claims that 'Courting Song' dates from 1810 and indeed the first recorded printing entitled 'Scotch Song' is found in Hogg's magazine *The Spy* on 1 December 1810 alongside another of his songs, 'The Dawn of July 1810'. It then appears several times before Hogg decides to include it in *Songs* 1831.

A version of 'Scotch Song' from *The Spy* is found in the literary miscellany *The Nithsdale Minstrel: being, Original Poetry, chiefly by The Bards of Nithsdale* (Dumfries: Preacher and Dunbar) in 1815. It was edited and compiled by the Rev. William Dunbar of Applegirth (1779?–1861) and most of the items in it were unattributed. There is evidence that Dunbar appropriated at least one song, namely Hogg's friend Thomas Mounsey Cunningham's 'The Hill o' Gallowa' ' (pp. 301–02), which sparked a satirical poem by Cunningham and Dunbar's unapologetic response in 'Defence of *The Nithsdale Minstrel*' in the *Scots Magazine* (vol. 78, 1816), 89–91. At least some of Hogg's contributions were authorised and these included: 'Hymn to the Evening Star', pp. 26–28 (see also *Songs* 1831, p. 123); 'The Admonition', pp. 94–97; and 'Scotch Song', pp. 296–98. All three of these pieces had appeared in *The Spy* (see S/SC (2000), pp. 493–94, pp. 443–45, and pp. 151–52). 'Verses Written on hearing of the Death of the Duchess of Buccleuch and Queensberry' (pp. 59–61) which had appeared in the *Edinburgh Evening Courant* of 3 September 1814 was also included: see Gillian Hughes, 'Hogg's Poetic Response to the Unexpected Death of his Patron' in *Studies in Hogg and his World*, 12 (2001), 80–89.

The copy text of 'Scotch Song' in *The Nithsdale Minstrel* is the version in *The Spy*, although it comprises only four verses and some lines are rearranged, so that, for example, ll. 13–16 were originally placed at ll. 17–20, while ll. 17–20 were originally ll. 25–28 of *The Spy* version. Moreover, some 16 lines of text comprising, ll. 13–16 and ll. 29–32 as well as the whole of verse five are omitted. The orthography and punctuation are revised in line with the style of *The Nithsdale Minstrel*, so that some words ending in 'g' are constricted. There is one substantive textual alteration with the removal of the name 'Jeanie' (l. 17 of *The Spy*) which is replaced by the more general 'lassie' (l. 13). Overall, 'Scotch Song' is a new version created especially for *The Nithsdale Minstrel*.

Douglas Mack has noted that it is likely that Hogg began work on his drama

The Bush Aboon Traquair in the early 1810s (S/SC, 2008, p. xv). 'Song III' in the play is a version of 'Courting Song'. There are three different versions of the play extant. However, only one of these was ever published. Comparison with the text as it appears in the first published version of the play in Blackie's *Tales and Sketches* of 1836–37 shows that Hogg clearly uses 'Scotch Song' from *The Spy* as copy text : verses one, two, three, four and six are retained from the original version, although the whole of verse four is omitted. There are several substantive alterations too. The lassie now becomes Mary, to fit the play's protagonist. ll. 1–4 of verse one are redrafted and single words and phrases changed. The opening line now becomes 'The day-beam's unco laith to gang', taking it relatively close to the version in *Songs* 1831. Other changes retain the original sentient. For example, 'This primrose bank shall be our bed' of 'Scotch Song' (l. 41) becomes 'This flowery heath shall be our bed' in 'Song III' (l. 33).

The song next appeared, under the title of its first line 'What gars the parting day-beam blush' as its title, in the fourth volume of Hogg's *Poetical Works* in 1822. Here again the copy text is clearly that from *The Spy* – all six verses are included in 1822 along with the nominated tune 'Gae fetch to me a pint of wine' and excepting the usual orthographic changes there are no substantive variants (see below).

The version Hogg includes in 1831 is substantially revised and combines elements of both 'Scotch Song' from *The Spy* and 'Song III' from *The Bush Aboon Traquair*. Verses one to four are derived from 'Scotch Song'. The sixth verse is removed (as it was in *The Bush Aboon Traquair*) and the final fifth verse in 1831 is new. In all versions, the text of verse two remains the most stable. However, the word 'dew' which completes l.9 in all versions is missing from *Songs* 1831. The word does not appear either in the printed text or Hogg's fair-copy holograph. The opening line of 'Scotch song' in *The Spy* is 'What gars the parting day-beam blush?' which becomes 'The daybeam's unco laith to gang' in *The Bush Aboon Traquair* and is changed to 'The day-beam's unco laith to part' in *Songs* 1831 (l. 1). Other notable variants include l. 2 where 'An' linger o'er yon summit lourin'' becomes 'It lingers o'er yon summit low'ring'. And l.18 which in earlier versions reads 'My flower sae lovely an' sae loving'!' is transformed in *Songs* 1831 to 'The jewel of all my earthly treasure'. The final four lines of verse four and the first four lines of verse five are radically different from the later version. 'Jeany' of the earlier versions and 'Mary' of *The Bush Aboon Traquair* is replaced by the unnamed 'lassie' for 1831.

There are a number of different manuscript sources for this song. Douglas S. Mack notes that *The Bush Aboon Traquair or The Natural Philosophers A Pastoral Drama With Songs by the Ettrick Shepherd*, dated *c*.1820, survives at MS Papers 42, folder 6 (Alexander Turnbull Library, New Zealand), and *The Bush Aboon Traquair or The Rural Philosophers A Pastoral Drama With Songs by the Ettrick Shepherd*, a later version dating from the 1830s, survives at NLS, MS 1869, ff. 1–52. A radically re-written version of the play retitled 'Pastoral Love Scenes or Dramas of Simple Life No II', dated around 1826, is located at MS Papers 42, folder 6 (Alexander Turnbull Library, New Zealand). Further information on the textual variants between Hogg's holograph versions of the play are detailed in Douglas S. Mack's S/SC edition of *The Bush Aboon Traquair*.

The manuscript of 'Courting Song' used by Hogg for its 1831 appearance is found in Hogg's fair-copy manuscript for *Songs* 1831 at NLS MS 4805, ff. 78v–79r. Unusually within MS 4805, ff. 26–102, the song is written horizontally across the page in two equal columns. The folios are page-numbered sequentially '158' and '159'. 'There's Nae Laddie Coming' (the song next in the printed collection), begins immediately below the last line, with the songs separated by a single pen stroke (f. 79r). Hogg's unpunctuated text has been cleanly transferred to the printed version.

Publication History:

1810 – in *The Spy*, No. 14 (1 December 1810), 112 – see also (S/SC, 2000), pp. 151–52

1815 – in *The Nithsdale Minstrel: being, Original Poetry, chiefly by The Bards of Nithsdale* (Dumfries: Preacher and Dunbar), pp. 296–98

1822 – in *Poetical Works*, IV, 325–27

1831 – in *Songs by the Ettrick Shepherd*, pp. 204–05 – see (S/SC, 2014), pp. 91–92.

[1836–37] – in *Tales and Sketches*, published posthumously in 1836 (Glasgow), 6 vols, II, 289–90 – see also S/SC, 2008, pp. 70–71.]

Musical Context:

Hogg's comment in his 1831 headnote that the song has 'since been set to music' is unhelpful, for three different melodies or airs are associated with the variants of his lyrics for this song.

The traditional tune which Burns uses for 'My Bonny Mary' – namely 'Gae fetch to me a pint o' wine' (*SMM*, III, no. 231, p. 240) is given alongside the song in *The Spy* in 1810 and with 'What gars the parting day-beam blush' in *Poetical Works* of 1822. Further information on the history of this tune can be found in *The Forest Minstrel* (S/SC, 2006, pp. 254–56).

The tune 'The Maid that tends the Goats' is given alongside 'Song III' in the Wellington Manuscript for *The Bush Aboon Traquair,* but Hogg has scored this through and replaces it, for the published Blackie version of the play, with the tune entitled 'Tushilaw's Lines'. Douglas Mack suggests that Hogg changed the nominated tune because he had already used 'The Maid that tends the Goats' for the play's first song, 'By a Bush' (see S/SC, 2008, note to 15 (b)). Hogg had already published this song and tune combination in *The Forest Minstrel* in 1810 see (S/SC, 2006, pp. 354–55) . But he had also used the tune 'Tushilaw' in *The Forest Minstrel* (1810) for a song by James Gray titled 'Strathfillan'. Here Hogg noted that the tune 'is an old Border air, never set' (2006), p. 94. In his headnote to the song 'Row On, Row On' in *Songs* 1831 Hogg repeats this by noting that the song 'was written to an old Border air, ycleped "Tushilaw's Lines," which has never been published. The words were meant to suit the plaintive notes of the tune' (see p. 15 of the present volume). Full details of this traditional tune are given in the 'Music Note' to 'Strathfillan' in the recent S/SC edition of *The Forest Minstrel* (2006), p. 287. In summary, the tune was in fact published in Hogg's lifetime, in Hamilton's *Caledonian Museum*, II (*c*.1810), 47. Hogg had earlier named the tune along with 'Song I' of his early collection, *Scottish Pastorals* (1801), p. 33. In an exchange of letters between Hogg, William Laidlaw and Scott in 1803, discussion centred on locating the words of the traditional ballad of the same name and Hogg eventually contributed 'a text for "Tushilaw's Lines"' for inclusion in the third volume of *The Minstrelsy of the Scottish Border*. However, they were never published: information from *The Forest Minstrel* (S/SC, 2006), p. 287; see also *Letters*, I, 33–36.

Hogg's failure to give a tune title in *Songs* 1831 means that we do not know which tune he preferred for this song. No settings of his 1831 text have been located.

Explanatory Notes:
91, l. 5 gloamin' stern 'the planet Venus, the evening star' (Douglas Mack's note in *The Bush Aboon Traquair and The Royal Jubilee* (S/SC, 2008), p. 14 (d)).

There's nae laddie coming (p. 93)

Creative Context:
This song most probably dates to the period 1827–1828 and was one of thirteen songs in *Songs* 1831 which was published in the London musical collection *Select & Rare Scotish Melodies* published by Goulding & D'Almaine with musical settings by Sir Henry Bishop. For further information about Hogg's involvement with this collection and to see copies of all thirteen songs see: *Contributions to Musical Collections and Miscellaneous Songs*. In summary, it is possible that this song was one of those sent to Robert Purdie with Hogg's letter of 18 January 1828 when he informs Purdie that he 'encloses eight more songs for your correspondents': see *Letters*, II, 284. Further details about its creation are not given.

The song only appeared in *Select & Rare Scottish Melodies* and in *Songs* 1831 in Hogg's lifetime and yet he did some redrafting for *Songs*. This involved fine tuning some lines: changing 'wooers' to 'lovers' (l. 5), 'billy' to 'wee brother' (l. 14) and 'young' to 'kind' (l. 17). The wording is also fresh in ll. 15–16: 'I fand your cauld hand often laid on my brow' becomes 'I felt the cool hand, and the kindly embrace' (l. 15). And in ll. 19–20 'It was then that I mark'd a' thy kindness for me, | O what do I owe my dear Sister to thee!' becomes 'And I'll never forget till the day that I dee, | The gratitude due, my dear Jeanie, to thee!'. These are strange emendations, making Hogg's *Songs* 1831 version more angliscised than that published for the London musical market.

The only extant manuscript of the song is found in Hogg's fair-copy manuscript for *Songs* 1831 at NLS MS 4805, ff. 26–102 (Blackwood Papers), on f. 79r immediately below the last line of 'Courting Song'. The folios are page-numbered sequentially '159' and '160' and Hogg's unpunctuated text has been cleanly transferred to the printed volume.

Publication History:
[1828] – in *Select & Rare Scotish Melodies*, pp. 10–14 – see also *Contributions to Musical Collections and Miscellaneous Songs* (S/SC, 2014)
1831 – in *Songs by the Ettrick Shepherd*, pp. 207–08 – see p. 93 in the present edition
Unauthorised versions:
1835 – The song's continuing popularity is revealed in an unauthorised American version of 'There's Nae Laddie Coming, by the Ettrick Shepherd' published in the *Southern Literary Messenger* (Richmond), I, no. 5 (January 1835), 200. The song is introduced by a paragraph explaining the source and reason for publishing Hogg's song:

> At the suggestion of a friend, whose fine taste selected the following effusion of the celebrated "Ettrick Shepherd", from some of the periodicals of the day, we gladly insert it into our columns. It is a most touching tribute of a fraternal affection to an elder sister, from one of the most distinguished bards of modern times. (200)

The copy text is undoubtedly the version in *Songs* 1831 as there are no textual variants, but the 'periodicals of the day' have not been identified. The song may have been taken directly from the American reprinting of *Songs* 1831 that was published in New York in 1832. Further details of the American publication of Hogg's songs can be found in the *Listing of Hogg Items in the American Periodical Press*, by Janette Currie, at the online *James Hogg Research* website hosted by the Division of Literature and Languages, School of Arts and Humanities, Stirling University, http://www.jameshogg.stir.ac.uk.

Musical Context:
In his letter to Purdie of 18 January 1828 Hogg also includes 'such airs as I knew they could not command in London' (*Letters*, II, 284), but the names of these tunes are not stated. In his 1831 headnote Hogg writes that Bishop set the song to 'a sweet original air'. The name of the air has not been identified, but the indication to the performers is that it should be 'very slow with considerable feeling and expression' (p. 10).

Appie M'Gie (pp. 93–94)

Creative Context:
As with 'There's nae laddie coming' directly before it and 'The Gathering of the Clans' immediately following it in *Songs* 1831, this is another of the thirteen Hogg songs included by Goulding & D'Almaine in its collection *Select & Rare Scotish Melodies* with musical settings by Sir Henry Bishop in [1828]. For further information about Hogg's involvement with this collection and to see copies of all thirteen songs see: *Contributions to Musical Collections and Miscellaneous Songs*. It may have been one of the 'eight more songs for your correspondents' that Hogg sent with his letter to Robert Purdie of 18 January 1828: see *Letters*, II, 284. While there is no information about its creation, it was completed by 27 February 1828, when Hogg sent a slightly different version of the song to an unidentified person named 'William': see *Letters*, II, 289 and also the note to 'Manuscript Versions' below.

The version in *Songs* 1831 is the same as that in *Select & Rare Scotish Melodies* with only some verbal emendations, including: 'fell i' the gloaming' to 'fell through the gloaming' (l. 6), 'a tint of the mellow soft-breathings' to 'even a shade of the tincture' (l. 20).

Hogg's 1827 manuscript of the song, sent to the unidentified 'William' noted above, is held by the Scottish Border Archive and Local History Centre in Selkirk (SC/S/10/2/1). The wording is slightly different from the earliest known published version in *Select & Rare Scotish Melodies*. For example, l. 7 begins 'He has pierced the fair bosom' which becomes 'He has woundit the bosom' in later versions. Two phrases in verse three 'The flowers of Glen-Ara' (l. 17) and 'Has some of the sweetness and tincture' (l. 20) are also only found in this version of the song. The full text of Hogg's fair-copy holograph manuscript is reprinted in *Letters*, II, 289.

The manuscript of the song found in *Songs* 1831 is found in Hogg's fair-copy manuscript for *Songs* 1831 at NLS MS 4805, ff. 79v–80r immediately below the last line of 'There's Nae Laddie Coming'. Numbered '161' and '162' the song follows the sequential page-numbering from the previous song and Hogg's unpunctuated text has been cleanly transferred to the printed volume.

Publication History:
[1828] – in *Select & Rare Scotish Melodies*, pp. 37–40 – see also *Contributions to Musical Collections and Miscellaneous Songs* (S/SC, 2014)

1831 – in *Songs by the Ettrick Shepherd*, pp. 209–10 – see pp. 93–94 in the present edition

Unauthorised versions:

1831 – 'Appie M'Gie. By James Hogg, the Ettrick Shepherd', an unauthorised version of the song derived from *Songs* 1831 was published in the Philadelphia *Lady's Book* in May 1831 (p. 253). Further details of the American publication of Hogg's songs can be found in the *Listing of Hogg Items in the American Periodical Press*, by Janette Currie, at the online *James Hogg Research* website hosted by the Division of Literature and Languages, School of Arts and Humanities, Stirling University, http://www.jameshogg.stir.ac.uk.

Musical Context:

Hogg's 1831 headnote suggests that this song is already known by a tune or air in Scotland which is taken from 'Captain Fraser's Collection', namely Simon Fraser's *Airs and Melodies Peculiar to the Highlands and Islands* (1816), which Hogg often uses or cites as a source for tunes. But no tune title is given and no match has been located in Fraser's collection. Bishop's setting for *Select & Rare Scotish Melodies*, gives no title for the melody and is most probably a new tune created by Bishop for the collection.

The Gathering of the Clans (pp. 94–95)

Creative Context:

As with the two songs immediately preceding it in *Songs* 1831 this is one of the thirteen songs in this collection to have also appeared in Goulding & D'Almaine's *Select & Rare Scotish Melodies* with musical settings by Sir Henry Bishop in [1828]. For futher information about Hogg's involvement with this collection for copies of all songs see *Contributions to Musical Collections and Miscellaneous Songs* (S/SC, 2014). As such it may have been one of the 'eight more songs for your correspondents' that Hogg sent with his letter to Robert Purdie of 18 January 1828: see *Letters*, II, 284.

In his headnote, Hogg writes that the song was 'originally composed to the popular Irish air, "St Patrick's Day in the Morning"' (p. 94), indicating that there is perhaps an earlier version, but this has not been located nor has more information about the creation of the song.

Unlike the contemporaneous *The Border Garland* of (*c.*1829) which included a number of Hogg's popular Jacobite songs, *Select & Rare Scotish Melodies* included mostly pastorale love songs, so 'The Gathering of the Clans' seems a strange choice for inclusion. Hogg's song is not included earlier in *The Jacobite Relics of Scotland*, but it does notably share the same title and theme as ' "Song VI": "The Gathering of the Clans" ', written 'by the author of Waverley', and published in the 'Appendix' to *Jacobite Relics*, II, 404–06, 433, and notes on 525. Here, as the Explanatory Notes below illustrate, Hogg's depiction of the mustering of the clans in 1745 under the Stewart standard is highly imaginative and humorous (the 'M'Dumpies and M'Lumpies' are pure invention for literary effect).

Hogg uses the first publication of the song in *Select & Rare Scotish Melodies* as copy text for the version he includes in 1831. A few verbal variants as well as a revised layout show Hogg reengaging with the song, or perhaps writing from memory. For example, ''array | Is in Moidart Bay' replaces 'is landed in Moidart Bay' (l. 10) and 'Are all in array | And hasting away' replaces 'Are all in the field and know not to yield', ll. 24–25. A further alteration in the later version is the omission of line 35 which is not included in the *Songs* 1831 version: 'McLean and McGregor are rising with vigour'.

The only extant manuscript of 'The Gathering of the Clans' is found within Hogg's fair-copy manuscript for *Songs* 1831 at NLS MS 4805, ff. 80r–81r. The manuscript is page-numbered '160', 161' and '162' and follows the sequential order from the previous song. Hogg's unpunctuated text is transferred cleanly to the printed volume without alteration.

Publication History:
[1828] – in *Select & Rare Scotish Melodies*, pp. 51–57– see also *Contributions to Musical Collections and Miscellaneous Songs* (S/SC, 2014)
1831 – in *Songs by the Ettrick Shepherd*, pp. 211–14 – see pp. 94–95 in the present edition

Musical Context:
The popular Irish air, "St Patrick's Day in the Morning" which Hogg refers to in his 1831 headnote is a military tune for bagpipes, dating from at least 1745 when the Irish Brigade pipers played it during the battle of Fontenoy. By the nineteenth century it was also a popular dance tune. For example, a version is found Gow's *Complete Repository of Original Scottish Slow Strathspeys and Dances* (Edinburgh: Gow and Shepherd), 4 parts, (3, no. 18). Hogg's marriage of this tune with his Highland 'gathering' song is entirely appropriate, as the '45 campaign was 'buoyed by the Irish brigade's victory at Fontenoy on 11 May [1745] which meant more British troops would be needed to maintain the war in Flanders': see *ODNB* entry for 'Charles Edward [styled Charles III [...] (1720–1788)', by Murray G. H. Pittock. Notably the Bishop setting has the performance indication that the song is 'With martial spirit and in moderate time'.

Explanatory Notes:
94, **ll. 10–11 Our Prince's array Is in Moidart bay** after first setting down at Eriskay on 23 July 1745, Charles headed for the west coast of Scotland and landed at 'Lochnanuagh, between Moidart and Arisaig' on the mainland on 25 July: see John Home, *The History of the Rebellion in the Year 1745* (1802), p. 39.
94, **ll. 12–13 Come, raise the clamour Of bagpipes' yamour** possibly refers to events of 19 August where the pipes were heard behind the hills round Loch Shiel, 'and nearly 1000 of Lochiel's men came down to the standard with 300 Keppoch MacDonalds'. (*ODNB* entry for 'Charles Edward [styled Charles III [...] (1720–1788)', by Murray G. H. Pittock)
95, **l. 15 brave Lochiel** 'the Gentle or Young Lochiel', Donald, chief of the Clan Cameron (*c.*1700 1748). See above and notes to 8, l. 14, 55(c)–56, ll. 43–44, and 64 (a) 65, l. 39.
95, **l. 17 bold Clan-Ranald** Ranald Macdonald (the younger) of Clan Ranald (*d.* 1766). He was one of the first to board Charles' ship in Moidart bay. See also notes to 22, l. 7.
95, **l. 19 Glengarry** the Macdonnells of Glengarry, a branch of the MacDonald Clan. John MacDonell of Glengarry (*d.* 1754) was their chieftain in 1745.
95, **l. 20 Keppoch** see ll. 12–13 above. Keppoch died heroically at Culloden. See also notes to 22, l. 7, 29, l. 44 and 122, ll. 45–46.
95, **l. 21 Whiggers o' Sky** Sir Alexander Macdonald of Sleat and Macleod of Macleod of Sky refused to support the Jacobite rebellion 'unless he (Charles)

brought over with him a body of regular troops': *The History of the Rebellion in the Year 1745* (1802), p. 38.

95, l. 22 Connal and Donald names to signify general Highlander support for the rebellion.

95, l. 27 Appin the Appin Stuarts were prominent during the Jacobite campaign, which Hogg records more fully in his song 'The Stuarts of Appin', pp. 28–30 and notes.

95, l. 28 stern M'Intosh Aeneas Mackintosh, Chieftain of the Mackintosh clan remained a loyalist during the Jacobite campaign. See also note 8, l. 16 and 29, ll. 41–42.

95, l. 28 M'Kenzie and Fraser possibly George Mackenzie, 'styled third earl of Cromarty (*c.* 1703–1766), Jacobite army officer'. See also 'The Frazer's in the Correi', pp. 58–59 and notes and 'Bauldy Frazer', pp. 121–22 and notes.

95, l. 31 Whiggers of Sutherland Lord Milton explained that the 'Whig Clans' as he saw them included the 'Campbells, Grants, Munros, M'Kays, Sutherlands' see John Home, *The History of the Rebellion in the Year 1745* (1802), 'Appendix No. 19: Letter – Lord Milton to the Marquis of Tweedale, 16 September 1745 (p. 302).

95, l. 32 Atholmen mustered under the command of Lord George Murray (*c.*1700–1760), of Blair Atholl.

95, l. 33 M'Pherson Ewan Macpherson of Cluny (1706–1764), Jacobite officer and clan Chieftain [from 1746] (see *ODNB* entry by Davie Horsburgh). See note 122, ll. 33–36.

95, ll. 34–35 hardy Clan-Donnoch Is up in the Rannoch the estate of Clan Donnachie is at Dun Alister in Loch Rannoch.

95, l. 36 haughty Argyle describes the Duke of Argyll and Greenwich (1680–1743), 'renowned for valour, and of great experience in arms', who commanded the king's troops in suppressing the Jacobite army at the Battle of Sherrifmuir in 1715 (John Home (1802), p. 17).

95, l. 37 lordly Drummond the Drummonds played a crucial part in the Jacobite campaign of 1745. Lord James Drummond, sixth earl of Perth and Jacobite third Duke of Perth (1713–1746) 'was appointed lieutenant-general of the Highland army'. He 'offered in early 1745 to mortgage his estates for £10,000 to aid the Jacobite interest' (*ODNB* entry by John Sibbald Gibson).

95, l. 40 steel to the bane a familiar expression of Hogg's. For example, see 'Donald Macdonald', where the phrase describes the hardiness of Clan Campbell (p. 5, l. 50).

95, l. 42 hae breeks and all that hae nane possibly looking forward to the outlawing of the wearing of traditional Highland dress, including the philabegs, kilt and tartan plaid, one of the severest reprisals imposed by the Hanoverian government following the collapse of the Jacobite campaign in 1746.

95, ll. 44–47 Moidart and Moy, M'Gun and M'Craw, [...] M'Leods an' M'Lumpies these lines are similar to Hogg's earlier listing of real and imaginary Highland clans and mixing loyalist with royalist clans in the closing lines of 'Donald Macdonald', where Hogg mingles real and fictional clan names to express and exaggerate the extent of Highland support for the rebellion.

I Hae Naebody Now (pp. 96–97)

Creative Context:

Hogg states clearly in his 1831 headnote that this song was 'published lately in Fraser's Magazine'. This is one of two songs in *Songs* 1831 also printed in *Fraser's Magazine for Town and Country*, a London-based magazine edited by James Fraser (*d.* 1841): see also 'The Lass o' Carlisle' on p. 101. Hogg's involvement with the magazine began in 1830 through his acquaintance with the writer John Galt (1779–1839) who, Gillian Hughes notes, had written to Hogg on 6 February 1830 soliciting articles for *Fraser's Magazine for Town and Country* on the editor's and publisher's behalf: see *Letters*, II, 387n. Hogg contributed several items to the first number of February 1830. He established a close working relationship with James Fraser that lasted until Hogg's death. 'I hae naebody now' appeared in the magazine in May 1830. Hogg's headnote refers to it having received 'higher encomiums than it deserved'. This is supported by in his letter to James Fraser of 2 June 1830 enclosing 'three more articles for the Town and country Magazine'. Here Hogg explains that he is sending further contributions 'as I percieve [*sic*] from the papers that some of my little pieces have appeared in it with approval': *Letters*, II, 386–87.

The copy text of the version in *Songs* 1831 is that of *Fraser's Magazine* with a few verbal variants. For example, at l. 5 'soft sweet' becomes 'raptured' while l. 23 has some redrafting, from 'softly aneath in the arms of death' to 'calmly aneath the hand o' death'.

The only extant manuscript is that found in Hogg's fair-copy manuscript for *Songs* 1831 at NLS MS 4805, f. 81. The manuscript is page-numbered '162' and '163'and follows the sequential order from the previous song. The final four lines of the headnote do not appear within the manuscript and must have been added, either by Hogg or someone else prior to printing. A further difference between the manuscript and the printed volume occurs on l.23. Hogg writes 'grasp o' death' although this is printed as 'hand o' death'. It is not clear whether these changes are authorial.

Publication history:

1830 – in *Fraser's Magazine for Town and Country* fourth number for May 1830 (p. 398)

1831 – in *Songs by the Ettrick Shepherd*, pp. 215–17 – see pp. 96–97 in the present edition

Unauthorised versions:

The *Fraser's Magazine* version of 'I hae naebody now' was reprinted in several American literary magazines during the 1830s. For example, under the title 'A Father's Lament' it appeared in the New York *Atlas, or Literary, Historical, and Commercial Reporter* of 26 June 1830 (521). Hogg's 1831 headnote, indeed, refers to the fate of a 'disconsolate parent' and the 'desolate condition' of their having lost a child. As such it bears some resemblance to Hogg's other song with the title 'A Father's Lament' also included in *Songs* 1831 (pp. 37–38). Full details of the American printing can be found in the *Listing of Hogg Items in the American Periodical Press*, by Janette Currie, at the online *James Hogg Research* website hosted by the Division of Literature and Languages, School of Arts and Humanities, Stirling University, http://www.jameshogg.stir.ac.uk.

Musical Context:
Hogg gives no tune title for this song in 1831, but he does refer to a contemporary setting by one 'Mr Ebsworth' in Edinburgh. Joseph Ebsworth (1788–1868) was a London-born 'printer, publisher, bookseller and teacher of music'who was based in Edinburgh from 1826 where he was 'for a time an actor and prompter at the Theatre Royal, a post that he relinquished on becoming leader of the choir at St Stephen's (episcopal) Church. [... Ebsworth] gave concerts of both choral and instrumental music at the Hopetoun Rooms in Queen Street from 1830 till his death.' His premises in Edinburgh were at 22 and 23 Elm Road, moving to 46 London Road in 1831 (*Scottish Book Trade Index*). But his setting of 'I hae naebody now' has not been located.

The English composer Edward J. Nielson set the text as it appeared in *Fraser's*. His musical setting, as its ornate coverpage explains, was performed at the 'Nobilities and other Concerts' in London by one 'Miss Bruce'. This song sheet was published in London by W. H. Aldridge of 264 Regent Street between *c.*1833 and 1840. Hogg discusses a newspaper report of a performance of 'I hae naebody now' on the London stage in his letter of 3 August 1833 to 'N. Lamont' (NLS MS 10279, f. 73). So his 1831 headnote that the song had been set to music in both England and Scotland is correct – indeed this letter may refer to an early performance of Nielson's setting as the dates would match the possible publication date. Again, his headnote reveals Hogg's knowledge of the musical popularity of some of his best songs. For more information and to see a copy of the song sheet see: *Contributions to Musical Collections and Miscellaneous Songs*. There is a reproduction of this song sheet also on the *James Hogg Research* website at: http://www.jameshogg.stir.ac.uk.

Nielson set two further Hogg songs: 'Maggy o' Buccleuch' and 'The Woman Fo'k' (see *Contributions to Musical Collections and Miscellaneous Songs*).

American versions of the songs were also produced. 'I hae naebody now, a Scotch Ballad. By the Ettrick Shepherd' comprises a five-page music score produced in 1841 and sold for 50 cents by the New York music publishing firm of C. T. Geslain, 72 Lispernard Street, Nr. Broadway. The title page records it was 'sung by Mrs Hardwick at Public and Private Concerts' and though it gives no composer's name, it is the Nielson setting replicated with only very slight amendments. The music score is reproduced on the *Music for the Nation: American Sheet Music* website at the Library of Congress located at http://memory.lc.gov.

Explanatory Notes:
96, l. 5 **lightsome fay** there are echoes here and also later in the song of 'A Bard's Address to his Youngest Daughter', Hogg's celebratory verses on his daughter, Harriet (*b.* 1827). See *Contributions to Annuals and Gift Books* (S/SC, 2006), pp. 138–39 and notes on pp. 315–16.

96, l. 12 **An' pray for a blessing from heaven** echoed in the concluding lines of 'A Bard's Address to his Youngest Daughter' (ll. 66–69).

96, l. 13 **gleesome face** see also 'My gleesome, gentle Harriet' (l. 2) in 'A Bard's Address to his Youngest Daughter'.

96, ll. 21–22 **To see a flower in its vernal hour | By slow degrees decay** Hogg echoes this same sentiment within his headnote to 'A Father's Lament', a song originally composed shortly after the death of Robert Anderson on 20 November 1823 – (see *Songs* 1831 (S/SC, 2014), pp. 37–38 and notes).

The Forty-Second's Welcome to Scotland (pp. 97–98)

Creative Context:
This is one of the songs Hogg creates for George Thomson's collections of national airs in the 1810s, though Hogg's reference to it appearing in 'Mr Thomson's first volume, small edition' is incorrect. Instead it appeared several times across Thomson's publications both folio and octavo. For further information about Hogg's involvement with Thomson's collections and to see copies of the musical settings see *Contributions to Musical Collections and Miscellaneous Songs.*

The subject matter for this song was initially suggested to Hogg in Thomson's letter of 9 November 1815. Hogg had sent him 'Mischievous Woman' (see *Songs* 1831, p. 88) which greatly pleased Thomson and he had sent Hogg several tunes for further songs. Amongst these was one entitled 'The Highland watch', which Thomson describes as, 'an air well worthy of the Poet's favour, not only from its own intrinsic beauty, but from a consideration of the noble and daring deeds of that corps (the 42nd) in all parts of the globe' (BL. MS Add. 35, 267, ff. 162–163). Hogg's response is not extant but he probably contributed a song to Thomson at the end of 1815 which is now lost.

On 29 November 1817 Thomson wrote again to Hogg repeating his request for lyrics for the tune 'The Highland watch' which Beethoven had set for him. This illustrates clearly Thomson's editorial policy which involved commissioning composers to 'set' or 'arrange' melodies (without texts) while, at the same time, approaching a writer to collect, amend or create new text for the same tune. Thomson makes no mention of an earlier text by Hogg, nor that he had already requested lyrics for the same air. Moreover, Thomson is very specific about the kind of lyrics he now requires and gives Hogg very clear instructions:

> It requires 8 lines of verse and 4 of Chorus, of the measure of the lines written under the notes. The Chorus should not be a repetition of the verse lines, as in the inclosed, but ought to be written in the plural number or expressed in such a way as to suit several voices singing together. I have exemplified the Chorus by a repetition of words because I had no other, and to shew you that the measure of the Chorus verse must be the very same with what precedes it.

Thomson then goes on to outline some ideas for the subject-matter of Hogg's lyrics:

> You of course know The Highland watch, the origin of the 42nd regiment was at first composed of the sons of gentlemen. As the characteristic bravery of the Corps has ever placed it in the hottest part of the field, and left many a baby fatherless & many a *sweet maid* mourning, it will be easy for the Poet to imagine a Subject of the touching kind, a farewell, or an invocation for the safe return of her hero, – such as you may deem appropriate to the music. (BL, MS Add. 35, 268, ff. 13–14)

Hogg responded within the week, sending three verses and a complaint that he had earlier sent Thomson' a song for that tune nearly two years ago [...] and I think it was a very good song too' (see Hogg's letter to Thomson, 29 November 1817 in *Letters*, I, 309–30). By December, Thomson had returned the proofs of the lyrics to Hogg who made few alterations (such as changing 'to echoes wild and weirly' to 'In all its wildest splendors' (l. 2)), which were all accepted by Thomson. The song was published along with three other Hogg contributions in the fifth volume of *A Select Collection of Original Scottish Airs* in 1818 (folio edition) with its musical setting by Beethoven. As Gillian Hughes has noted, the song appears to have been first published by Thomson, but it is clearly connected to the intense celebrations which took place in Edinburgh immediately following the battle of Waterloo in 1814. Between Thomson's first letter to Hogg and his follow up request in 1817 the regiment returned to Edinburgh to overcrowded streets and many dinners and assemblies to mark their victorious role in the battle. Thomson was clearly well aware of their contemporary popularity and so the song was timely (see Gillian Hughes, 'James Hogg and Edinburgh's Triumph over Napoleon' in *Scottish Studies Review* (4:1 (Spring 2003), 98–111).

Thomson subsequently published the song in further editions of his collections (in both octavo and folio formats) issued between 1818 and 1831 (see Publication History below). In all cases the text remains the same and the musical arrangement is by Beethoven.

As it remains stable in Thomson's publications, it is presumably the earliest published version in *A Select Collection of Original Scottish Airs* in 1818 which Hogg uses as copy text for *Songs* 1831. The title becomes 'The Forty-Second's Welcome to Scotland' and in several places the wording is altered. For example, the word 'Then' is deleted from the beginning of the chorus of verses one and two so that the word 'high' is also removed, presumably to keep the scansion regular. There is further fine-tuning in the second verse: 'can carry' becomes 'can sound them' (l. 14) and 'glory kindles' becomes 'glory blazes' (l. 16).

The earliest manuscript version of the song is found in Hogg's letter to George Thomson of 29 November 1817. It is reprinted in *Letters*, I, 309–10. Hogg's corrected copy of 22 December 1817 showing all his alterations and corrections is also reprinted in *Letters*, I, 317–18. In summary, in the revised version, Hogg provides fresh wording at ll. 2, 4, 10–12, 13, 22 and the final chorus on ll. 33–36. This correspondence clearly illustrates how Thomson liked to work with his writers.

The song also appears in Hogg's fair-copy manuscript for *Songs* 1831 at NLS MS 4805 f. 81. It is page numbered '165' and '166' and follows the sequential numbering from the previous song. In the title Hogg does not write out the number 'forty-two' although this is what appears in the printed volume. Aside from this small alteration, Hogg's unpunctuated text is transferred cleanly to the printed volume.

Publication History:
1818 – in George Thomson, *A Select Collection of Original Scottish Airs*, V, 205 – see
    Contributions to Musical Collections and Miscellaneous Songs (S/SC, 2014)
1822–23 – in George Thomson, *The Melodies of Scotland* , V, 15 (octavo collection)
    – see *Contributions to Musical Collections and Miscellaneous Songs* (S/SC, 2014)
1826 – in George Thomson, *A Select Collection of Original Scottish Airs*, II, 205
1831/8 – in George Thomson, *The Melodies of Scotland*, V, 205
1831 – in *Songs by the Ettrick Shepherd*, pp. 218–20 – see (S/SC, 2014), pp. 97–98

Musical Context:
As noted above the known musical setting for this Hogg song is that by Beethoven as found in Thomson's collections. Thomson made mention of the tune 'The Highland Watch' in his letter to Hogg of 23 November 1817 where he noted that

the tune was often played by fiddler Niel Gow, and stated:

> it has never been vocalized, but with verses on any touching or striking
> soldierly theme, it will make one of our most admired national songs. I
> have sung the Music with my daughters at the piano forte, times without
> number, and always with fresh pleasure: one half of which at least is due to
> Beethoven, who has harmonized it with the utmost felicity, and given it a
> chorus. (BL, MS Add. 35, 268, ff. 13–14).

Hogg's song with its Beethoven setting can be found in *Contributions to Musical
Collections and Miscellaneous Songs*. It was also to be published by Beethoven's
Viennese publisher Anton Schlesinger in 1822 in Beethoven's *Schotticshe Lieder* –
see *Contributions to Musical Collections and Miscellaneous Songs*. This is cited by Gooch
and Thatcher, 8652.

A performance of the song by the well known contemporary singer 'Mr
Broadhurst' is advertised in *The Times* of Tuesday,18 September 1821:

> THEATRE-ROYAL, ENGLISH OPERA-HOUSE, STRAND – Mr Broadhurst has the
> honour to inform his friends and the public in general, that his annual
> benefit will take place on Wednesday, September 26, when will be presented
> the melo-drama called "The Blind Boy". In the course of the evening, Mr
> Broadhurst will, for that night only, sing the highly favourite Scotch Songs
> of "My ain kind dearie O" [...] "The Highland Watch, written on the
> return of the 42nd Regiment from Waterloo by the Ettrick Shepherd [...],
> with a variety of other ENTERTAINMENTS, particulars of which will be duly
> announced. (p. 2)

Explanatory Notes:
97 [Title] the 42nd Highland Regiment was initially one of six independent
companies raised in 1729 by the Hanoverian government to keep the peace in
the Highlands. Also referred to as the Black Watch.
97 [headnote] the return of that gallant regiment from Waterloo the 42nd
Highland Regiment were mentioned in despatches for their bravery during
the Waterloo campaign. The regiment returned to England in December 1815
and slowly worked their way northwards on what became a victory tour. Their
entry to Edinburgh brought the city to a standstill and was a great cause for
celebration. See Gillian Hughes, 'James Hogg, and Edinburgh's Triumph over
Napoleon' in *Studies in Scottish Review*, 4:1 (Spring 2003), 98–111 (107–08). In
his letter to Thomson of 29 November 1817 Hogg claims he composed a song
to the air 'nearly two years ago', or around the time the regiment returned to
Britain: see *Letters*, I, 309–10.
97, l. 9 the pibroch the *piobaireachd* (Gaelic) is the music of the *pib mhor* (Gaelic) or
Highland pipe. See note to 60, l. 2.
97, ll. 17–18 Small is the remnant you will see, | Lamented be the others Mary
Cosh writes that during the Waterloo campaign the 42nd Highland Regiment
'lost two flank companies cut to pieces at Quatre Bras, and the rest having
suffered heavily. It was a remnant that had returned to the main battlefield
and rallied for victory' (*Edinburgh, The Golden Age* (Edinburgh: John Donald,
2003), p. 548).
97, l. 23 the chanter yell, and the drone-notes swell A 'chanter' is 'that part of a
bagpipe, resembling an oboe, on which the melody is played' (*DSL*). Frances
Collinson mentions George Buchanan's observation of 'the bagpipe as the

military instrument among the Gaelic-speaking people of Scotland' and points out that 'the two-drone bagpipe was for long the standard instrument of the Highlands' (*The Traditional and National Music of Scotland* (London: Routledge and Kegan Paul, 1966), p. 162).

98, ll. 31–32 the bonnet blue | Behind the nodding feather Hogg cleverly unites the traditional Highland 'blue bonnet' (see note to 3, l. 5) with the uniform of the [British] 42nd Highland Regiment: plumes of 'red-and-white' according to James Nasmyth (see Cosh above) or, more usually, of black ostrich feathers.

Highland Tay (pp. 98–99)

Creative Context:
This song originates from the early 1820s and Hogg's 1831 headnote suggests that it may well be connected with the Izett family, whose summer residence was at Kinnaird House in Athol from 1805 until 1810 when it became their permanent residence: see Janette Currie's essay, 'James Hogg's Literary Friendships with John Grieve and Eliza Izett' in *Mador of the Moor* ed. by James E. Barcus (S/SC, 2005), xliii–lvii. The 'sweetest maiden' is most probably Eliza Izett (1774–1842). Hogg had already written of his feelings about her during the Spring of 1810 in his song titled 'The Bogles', published in *The Forest Minstrel* in 1810. In the song she is described as 'bonny Eliza', 'the flower of our isle' and, more pertinently, 'sweet' (l.1, l. 6 and l. 23): see *The Forest Minstrel* (S/SC, 2006), pp. 90–91 and notes on pp. 282–83.

As an untitled 'Song' this lyric first appeared in the London daily evening newspaper *The Star* of 27 April 1821. *The Star* was printed and edited (after 1789) by John Mayne (1759–1830), 'a Dumfriesshire printer and minor poet', who was assisted occasionally by two other Scotsmen, Andrew Macdonald and Alexander Tilloch. The newspaper 'avoided strong expressions of political sentiment and maintained a steady level of circulation', and was largely confined to London: see *British Fiction, 1800–1829: A Database of Production and Reception, Phase II: Advertisements for Novels in The Star, 1815–1824*, by Jacqueline Belanger, Peter Garside, Anthony Mandal, Sharon Ragaz: http://www.romtext.cf.ac.uk/reports/starlist.html – accessed August 2013. No other earlier version of the song has been found and there is no further information to date about Hogg's involvement with this newspaper.

Hogg's song next appeared, with the title 'The Bower of Tay' in the fourth volume of his *Poetical Works* of 1822 where the copy text is clearly that in *The Star* with only one minor alteration: l. 11 'the restless stream was ey'd' becomes 'the restless stream we eyed'.

When Hogg decided to include it in *Songs* 1831 he retitled it 'Highland Tay', and appears to have returned to the earlier version of the song. Single verbal variants include changing 'blooms' to 'dyes' (l. 2) and 'greenwood' to 'birken' (l. 8). Longer phrase changes occur on l. 24 where 'played within' becomes 'trembled'. Fresh wording occurs over ll. 29–32 giving a new ending to the literary song. For example, the descriptive 'Ettrick's fairy banks are green' become 'On Ettrick's fairy banks at eve', while further local and personal references are removed altogether: 'And Yarrow braes are mooned with grey' becomes 'Though music melts the breeze away' (l. 30) and 'Like I viewed in Bower of Tay' becomes 'A glow like that by Highland Tay' (l. 32).

Only one extant manuscript has been located, and that is the version in Hogg's fair-copy manuscript for *Songs* 1831 at NLS MS 4805, ff. 82v–83r. The pages are numbered '167' and '168' and follow the sequential order from the previous song. Hogg's unpunctuated text is transmitted cleanly to the printed volume.

Publication History:
1821 – in *The Star*, 27 April
1822 – in *Poetical Works*, IV, 310–12
1831 – in *Songs by the Ettrick Shepherd*, pp. 221–23 – see pp. 98–99 in the present edition

Musical Context:
Hogg nominates the tune or air 'The Maid of Isla' for this lyric in all three published versions of it, but no printed musical setting has been located. 'The Maid of Isla' is also nominated as the tune to accompany 'The Bonny Lass of Deloraine' (for further information see *Songs* 1831 pp. 66–67 and notes above). The air or tune was thought to have been 'brought over [from the island of Isla] by Lady Charlotte Campbell'. It is found in several eighteenth-century music collections, such as Gow's collections of *Strathspey Reels* (*c*.1800 and *c*.1810): see *The Forest Minstrel* (S/SC, 2006), p. 266.

Explanatory Notes:
98 [Title] The River Tay, a major river of the Athol valley in Perthshire. The River Tay runs through the Izett's Kinnaird Estate (see below).
98 [headnote] It was never published, that I remember David Radcliffe recently located the earliest known version of the song as an untitled contribution to the *Star* newspaper of 27 April 1821 (information forwarded by email from Gillian Hughes on 24/02/2007).
98, l. 13 Glen-Lyon 'a long narrow glen and a *quoad sacra* parish in Breadlalbane district, Perthshire' (Groome). The hamlet of Dowally, Eliza Izett's birth-place, is in Glen Lyon.
99, l. 29 On Ettrick's fairy banks at eve Hogg writes that his maternal grandfather, Will o' Phaup, or 'Phawhope at the head of the Ettrick valley', 'was the last man of this wild region, who heard, saw, and conversed with the fairies' (*The Shepherd's Calendar*, ed. by Douglas S. Mack (S/SC, 1995; rev. paperback 2002), p. 103 and note on p. 267; p. 107).

I'll no wake wi' Annie (pp. 99–101)

Creative Context:
The exact date of this song's creation is not known, though Hogg's 1831 headnote, referring to Lord Napier would suggest that it dates after 1816. William John Napier (1786–1834) was a major landowner and powerful figure in Selkirkshire descended from the Scotts of Thirlestane. After his marriage in 1816 he settled in the Ettrick district. Hogg was on friendly terms with this 'improving' landlord and assisted in the publication of his book titled *A Treatise on Practical Store-Farming as Applicable to the Mountainous Region of Ettrick Forest* (1822).

The only specific reference to the song is found in Hogg's letter of 1 April 1818 to the musician William Heather (*b*. 1784), concerning the plans for publishing 'seven or eight songs' by Hogg with musical arrangements by Heather. The two had been collaborating on Charles Christmas's publication of *German Hebrew Melodies* which had appeared in [1817]. For further information on this collection and Hogg's involvement in it and with William Heather see: *Contributions to*

Musical Collections and Miscellaneous Songs. But in this letter Hogg was clearly referring to a second collection, this time of Scots songs. 'I'll no wake wi' Annie' appeared as the first of nine songs in *A Border Garland* of [1819] published in Edinburgh by Hogg's musician friend Nathaniel Gow. For further information on this collection and a copy of the song see: *Contributions to Musical Collections and Miscellaneous Songs.*

The song next appears as part of the *Noctes Ambrosianae* (No XXXV (113–114) in *Blackwood's Edinburgh Magazine* in January 1828. The 'Shepherd' sings the (untitled) song to himself while waiting in the 'South East Drawing Room' of Ambrose's Hotel in 'Picardy Place'. He plays a fiddle with 'ae string wantin' and something or ither wrang wi' twa three o' the pegs' (p. 113). The song is presented here with musical notation and is exactly the same tune as had appeared in *A Border Garland* (and in the same key) which reinforces the performative nature of the song. There is no evidence that Hogg sent the song directly to Blackwood for inclusion. Nor does he mention its appearance there in his 1831 headnote. Notably the *Blackwood's* version closely follows the text of *A Border Garland* and it might be that it was simply copied from the earlier song collection. There is apparently no surviving correspondence about the song later than 1818.

Before picking it up for *Songs* 1831 the song appears again in the later collection *The Border Garland* published by Robert Purdie in Edinburgh in *c.*1829 with settings by Edinburgh musician James Dewar. For further information on this collection and a copy of the song see: *Contributions to Musical Collections and Miscellaneous Songs.* The inclusion of the song in *Blackwood's* is exactly contemporary with preparation for this musical collection, but Hogg appears to have made some changes. The text in *The Border Garland* included emendations: 'the glen was lanely' (verse 5, l. 2) becomes 'the glen was lovely', and 'Up in yon glen'(verse 6, l. 6) becomes 'Upon yon glen'. These changes suggest that Hogg wrote the text out afresh. For example, the chorus of the second verse is changed from 'Ill no wake, &c.' to 'He'll no wake, &c.'; a change that follows the *Blackwood's* version rather than the earlier *Border Garland.*

Hogg seems to have undergone a similar process for 1831. There are several spelling alterations which change Scots words to English: e.g. 'skeel' becomes 'skill' (v. 3. l. 7), 'moor' becomes 'muir' (v. 3, l. 8 and v. 5, l. 6). And Hogg creates a new ending: 'I'll ne'er again keep wake wi' ane' is changed to 'An' sit my lane ilk night wi' ane'; suggesting that the shepherd will contine his relationship with Annie, against the parental advice given earlier in the poem.

Aside from the text of the song with Hogg's letter of 1 April 1818, the manuscript used for the song in *Songs* 1831 is that found in Hogg's fair-copy manuscript at NLS, MS 4805, f. 83v. However this manuscript contains only the title and headnote of the song as it appears in *Songs* 1831. In all, some nineteen songs including 'I'll No Wake Wi' Annie' are missing from this section of NLS, MS 4805 and have not apparently survived. For further information see Janette Currie's essay 'The Genesis of the Text', pp. xli–xlviii. The text of Hogg's headnote for the song is reprinted reasonably accurately. However, some harsh words have been softened in the printed text. In his statement about Lord Napier that occurs after details about how he had interdicted Hogg from sailing on St. Mary's Loch Hogg originally wrote 'But he'll be ____ for it that's ay some comfort'. This is softened in the printed version to 'But the credit will be his own, – that is some comfort'; this may be one of the changes directed by Hogg's nephew Robert.

Publication History:

[1819] – in *A Border Garland*, pp. 2–3 – see *Contributions to Musical Collections and Miscellaneous Songs* (S/SC, 2014)

1828 – in *Blackwood's Edinburgh Magazine*, 23 (January 1828) – see (S/SC, 2008), pp. 312–13, 375, and 544

*c.*1829 – in *The Border Garland* , pp. 25–27 – see *Contributions to Musical Collections and Miscellaneous Songs* (S/SC, 2014)

1831 – in *Songs by the Ettrick Shepherd*, pp. 224–27 – see pp. 99–101 in the present edition

Musical Context:

The song's first musical appearance in *A Border Garland* of [1819] notes that the 'Air' is by James Hogg and when the song appears in *The Border Garland* in c.1829 Hogg is also attributed as the creator of the 'melody' as well as the words. In his letter of 1 April 1818 Hogg reminds Heather of a song 'on two flats consisting of three parts, two and a chorus' and includes the first verse and chorus of 'I'll No Wake Wi' Annie', indicating he has sent an earlier version of the song which has not apparently survived (*Letters*, I, 343–45 (p. 344)). Heather does not produce all the musical settings for the nine songs in *A Border Garland* but the correspondence would suggest that the musical setting of this song is by him. The tune in *Blackwood's* is identical to that in the first musical collection. This is a tune which is typical of Hogg's style and it clearly resembles a fiddle tune, with its octave leap (often coinciding with 'O') which is not easy for many to sing. Hogg does refer to both Heather's and Dewar's settings in his 1831 headnote, but directs the reader to the readily available *The Border Garland* which had appeared only two years before *Songs* 1831.

Explanatory Notes:

99 [Title] 'wake' is here derived from the phrase 'Wauking o' the Fauld': the act of watching the sheep-fold, about the end of summer, when the lambs were weaned, and the ewes milked (*DSL*).

99 [headnote] high seas Mack notes that Napier 'served as a Captain in the Royal Navy during the Napoleonic Wars', *The Queen's Wake* (2004, p. 453); see also 'Notes on Correspondents: William John Napier', in *Letters*, II, 509–10.

99 [headnote] interdicting me from sailing in a letter dated 8 March 1818 Hogg sent Napier a preview of some lines from the ballad 'Mary Scott' showing where he had replaced lines referring to Napier's father with one where the revised depiction of 'Red Will of Thirlestane' contains an allusion to an ongoing boat dispute:

> Wildly he looked from side to side
>   No skiff was nigh the chief to save
> "O for a friendly barge" he cried
>   "How I would maul them from the wave!"

> But neither net nor boat nor barge
>   Nor minstrel's skiff was there that day
> For why the knight had given charge
>   In wrath to drive them all away

Hogg advised, 'now lest the bard's song written in fun should have the smallest chance of ever proving prophetic I am sure you will not hinder me to put a half dozen new boats with as m[?] nets and cannons on the loch this year' (*Letters*, I, 334–335, p. 335). Napier obviously took no notice of Hogg's friendly warning. Mack notes that Napier demolished a 'boat and boat house [...] which was ever free to Hogg and his friends' (*The Queen's Wake* (S/SC, 2004), pp. 453–54). A full account of the boat dispute is on pp. 453–54.

99 [headnote] rendered classical Scott provided a vivid description of St. Mary's Loch in the second Canto of *Marmion* (1808) and Wordsworth, too, provided what might be termed 'classical' descriptions of the loch in both 'Yarrow' poems printed before 1831 in 'Yarrow Unvisited' (1803) and 'Yarrow Visited' (1814). Hogg's headnote correctly focuses on a major difference between his descriptive writing of the loch and that produced by his peers. Hogg's descriptions focus on how the landscape reflects the history of particular, sometimes named, people, rather than the vague connections to 'classical' figures, such as the 'swain' or 'Minstrel' of Scott and Wordsworth. For example, in his poem of 1828 titled 'Saint Mary of the Lows', which appeared in the London-based Christmas annual, the *Forget Me Not for 1829* (pp. 25–29), see *Contributions to Annuals and Gift Books* (S/SC, 2006), pp. 44–47, pp. 298–99 and notes on p. 372.

The Lass o' Carlisle (p. 101)

Creative Context:
This is the second of only two songs in *Songs* 1831 which Hogg created for *Fraser's Magazine for Town and Country*, a London-based magazine edited by William Fraser (the other song is 'I hae naebody now' on pp. 96–97). It appears that Hogg had no specific person or situation in mind. He notes that he just quickly created a 'daftlike song' for the specific purpose of sending something to this magazine. It appeared with the title 'The Lass o' Carlisle. An Excellent New Song', in *Fraser's* in July 1830, not long before Hogg was preparing his *Songs* volume, which clearly explains his decision to include it in *Songs* and the reference he makes in his 1831 headnote. Hogg continued to contribute high quality articles of prose and poetry to *Fraser's*.

This song may have been included in Hogg's letter to James Fraser of 2 June 1830 where he sends 'three more articles for the Town and country Magazine' (*Letters*, II, 386–87). And Hogg clearly uses the *Fraser's Magazine* version for 1831 with with only one slight textual alteration within the wording of l. 17 where 'bairns galore' is altered to 'plenty o' weans'.

There is no extant manuscript of the song. It is one of the group of songs missing from the fair-copy manuscript for *Songs* 1831 at NLS MS 4805, ff. 26–102 (Blackwood Papers). See note to 'I'll No Wake Wi' Annie' above.

Publication History:
1830 – in *Fraser's Magazine for Town and Country* (July, 1830), p. 654
1831 – in *Songs by the Ettrick Shepherd*, pp. 228–29 – see p. 101 in the present edition

Musical Context:
There is no melody given for this song and no musical setting has been found.

Explanatory Notes:
101 [headnote] Carlisle is a city in the county of Cumberland some thirteen miles from the Scottish border.

101 [headnote] being averse to his paying for any blank paper prior to the introduction of the 'Uniform Penny Post' in 1840 postal charges were paid for by the addressee. Several different factors affected postal costs, such as the distance travelled and whether any toll roads were used, the weight of the letter, whether it was written on a single or double sheet and whether there were any enclosures.

My love she's but a lassie yet (p. 102)

Creative Context:

Hogg's headnote in *Songs* 1831 states clearly that this was one of the songs created for George Thomson (1757–1851) and his *Select Collection of Original Scottish Airs*. For further information on Thomson, his collections and Hogg's involvement with them see *Contributions to Musical Collections and Miscellaneous Songs*. Hogg's reference to Thomson's criticism of his version of the song is characteristic of Thomson's editorial interventions. Thomson's request for a set of lyrics to match the already well-established tune known as 'My Love she's but a lassie yet' dates back to Hogg's letter of 15 August 1829 (*Letters*, II, 350–51), in which Hogg was responding to Thomson's request to publish his 'Bonny Prince Charlie' (beginning 'Cam ye by Athole', pp. 8–9). Hogg explains that he had given the copyright of this song to Mr Purdie, who had published it as a song sheet and also in *A Border Garland* [1819]. But Hogg promises to write a new set of lyrics for Thomson. He then appears to have forgotton this promise, and when Thomson contacts him again (in an undated letter) he gives instead the tune for 'My love she's but a lassie yet' and asks Hogg to compose new lyrics for it. The song was already known with a set of lyrics by Robert Burns published in the *SMM* in 1790 (see 'Musical Context' below). Thomson enclosed a copy of Joseph Haydn's new arrangement of the traditional tune 'My Love She's but a Lassie Yet' requesting that Hogg 'retain the first line [...] as being identified with the air' and compose new words according to his specific requirement:

> The more light and playful your song is the more appropriate will it be to the music. And I should wish it of that delicate and graceful character which should be acceptable to female hearers and singers. (Thomson's undated letter to Hogg is at BL Add. MS 35, 269, f. 2)

Hogg produced his lyric but, as he states in his headnote, Thomson was not satisfied with Hogg's lyrical playfulness. In a letter of 29 October 1829 Hogg informs Thomson: 'You have fairly puzzled me. For the truth is that I find to make a graceful song to a triple rhythm is impracticable' (see *Letters*, II, 358). Sadly Thomson did not publish Hogg's contribution in any of his song collections though it makes a fine match to Haydn's witty arrangement in performance.

As Hogg indicates in his headnote he recycled the song as a contribution to the *Edinburgh Literary Journal* where it was published in the number for 6 March 1830. It appears that Hogg's holograph manuscript version for Thomson has not survived and so it is not known whether he revised the song prior to its publication in the magazine. Hogg's holograph manuscript of the *Edinburgh Literary Journal* version, however, has several substantive alterations, which may relate to the earlier iteration of the song. Although textually different from any published version it would appear that MS Papers 42, no. 67, (iii), an undated version of the song located among the Hogg papers in the Alexander Turnbull

Library, New Zealand, represents a draft of the version published in the *Edinburgh Literary Journal*. The concluding lines of 'The Flower of Annisley' are written side-ways on the same folio and, as this latter poem was published in *Fraser's Magazine* for April 1830 (308–09), it probably helps to date Hogg's draft of 'My Love She's but a Lassie Yet'. In the draft version, line two refers to a 'blithesome bonny lassie' and not the 'lightsome lovely lassie' of the published version. The opening five lines of the third verse are also radically different from later published versions:

> When I think on what's like to be
> My very heart's in ecstaty
> An frae my een
> The tear drap sheen
> Is rowing down a freak to see

Hogg's holograph manuscript version of 'My Love she's but a Lassie yet' that he prepared for *Songs* 1831 is not part of the substantial portion of the manuscript within NLS MS 4805, ff. 26–102 (Blackwood Papers): see note to 'I'll No Wake Wi' Annie' above.

'My Love She's but a Lassie Yet' appears near the end of *Songs* 1831 where it opens a sequence of five songs out of the ten derived from the *Edinburgh Literary Journal* included within the whole collection. The copy text is the *Edinburgh Literary Journal* version without any major alterations to the text, although there is a slight adjustment of the orthography of 'hinney' which becomes 'hinny', and 'marmelite' which changes to 'marmalete' (l. 17).

Publication History:
1830 – in the *Edinburgh Literary Journal*, 6 March 1830 (No. 69, 147–48)
1831 – in *Songs by the Ettrick Shepherd*, pp. 230–32 – see p. 102 in the present edition
Unauthorised versions:
Gooch and Thatcher list ten unauthorised and later song sheets: 8744–8752 but none in Hogg's lifetime.

Musical Context:
Hogg writes in his headnote that the song 'was written [...] to the old air bearing the same name', although it would appear that he originally composed his version of this popular song to an arrangement of the tune by Joseph Haydn. Thomson informs Hogg that Haydn's arrangement is 'simple, graceful and highly beautiful' (BL Add. MS 35, 269, f. 2). Donald Low's note to the air in *The Songs of Robert Burns* states that: 'The air had been printed in *Bremner's Reels* (1757) as *Miss Farquharson's Reel* and as *My love she's but a lassie yet* in *Airds Airs* (1782)' (London: Routledge, 1993), p. 379. Burns's version of 'My love she's but a lassie yet' was published in *SMM*, III (1790), No. 225 (234).

The Moon (p. 103)

Creative Context:
This song was inspired by John Wilson's proposed article for Blackwood's *Noctes Ambrosianae* about a ride in a hot-air balloon. The idea is mentioned in Hogg's letter to William Blackwood of 11 August 1827 (*Letters*, II, 276) where he states enthusiastically: 'I approve highly of the Baloon [sic] Noctes' and that 'Such songs

are indeed well adapted for my stile'. But he also regrets that he is so busy at this time in the year (with the shooting season) that it will be difficult for him to produce the songs quickly. A year later, in his letter of 8 October 1828 to Blackwood, Hogg requests the return of several items which Blackwood has not published, including his 'Balloon [*sic*] songs' (see *Letters*, II, 308–09). Two years later when Wilson had still not produced his piece Hogg went ahead and wrote his own tale incorporating his 'Balloon songs'. But Blackwood would not publish it, still believing that he would receive Wilson's essay. Hogg's anger over this rejection is clear in his letter to Blackwood of 4 January 1830 (*Letters*, II, 368). In his chagrin Hogg thus sent his essay and its songs on to Henry Glassford Bell for publication in the *Edinburgh Literary Journal* where it appeared soon after as 'Dr David Dale's Account of a Grand Aerial Voyage. By the Ettrick Shepherd' on 23 January 1830.

'The Moon' appears as 'Song Second' within the 'grand aerial voyage' of Dr. David Dale who is accompanied on his experimental tour by the Ettrick Shepherd. The balloon holds 'a keg of at least six gallons' of Glenlivet whisky which caused the poet, as Hogg writes, 'such a spring for joy on his wicker-seat, that he made the balloon bob, and put her so much off her balance, that she kept a rocking motion for an hour afterwards' (p. 51). Influenced by their load, they approach 'a grand sunshine hill' that they initially believe is 'Ben Nevis', the highest mountain in Scotland, but they find that it is actually the moon. The 'Ettrick Shepherd' offers his lyrical description of the scene. Hogg's first letter to Blackwood in August 1827 gives an idea of a balloon voyage over the highlands and Hogg was clearly thinking about this when he wrote the song.

There is no extant manuscript for the song as it appears in *Songs* 1831: it is not part of the substantial portion of the manuscript found in NLS MS 4805, ff. 26–102: see note to 'I'll No Wake Wi' Annie' above. But there are two extant manuscripts of the song. The first is found at NLS MS 4805, ff. 101–02 and is evidently Hogg's manuscript used in the preparation of the earliest version of his 'Baloon Songs' composed between 11 August 1827 and 8 October 1828 referred to above. Under the heading 'Songs for the Baloon' it comprises four untitled songs ranging from 'Song First' to 'Song Fourth' written consecutively over two folios measuring 21 cm x 18 cm. Hogg's unpunctuated text is written neatly although there is evidence of scoring out in several places so that it perhaps represents a draft copy of the songs he originally submitted to William Blackwood. 'The Moon' in this version is untitled and headed 'Song Second' set out in two numbered octets immediately below 'Song First' also known as 'The Witch of Fife' which immediately follows it in *Songs* 1831 (see notes below).

The second extant manuscript is an undated version of Hogg's 'Baloon songs' found at MS Papers 42, Item 41 located among the Hogg papers in the Alexander Turnbull Library, New Zealand (ATL). Here it is alongside other material consisting of draft copies of items Hogg went on to contribute to the *Edinburgh Literary Journal*. Peter Garside gives a detailed account of this manuscript in 'An Annotated Checklist of Hogg's literary manuscripts in the Alexander Turnbull library, Wellington, New Zealand' in *The Bibliotheck*, 5–23 (p. 5). Unlike the earlier manuscript version (above), the AT version has no overall title and the four songs are also untitled. The songs are written in a different order and there are no verse numbers to separate different verses or indeed songs giving rise to the initial impression that the manuscript, as Garside suggests, is for one song. Hogg's untitled draft version of 'The Moon' is written immediately below his draft version of 'The Witch of Fife' and he uses every available space on the paper so that the final four lines are written sideways on the same sheet.

Collation between both surviving manuscript versions of 'The Moon' shows substantial revision. For example, the AT manuscript has an extra line added after l. 10. Lines 15 and 17 in the AT MS are freshly drafted in MS 4805, f. 101. Collation of the final published version of the song reveals further redrafting prior to publication. For example, the original wording of l. 13 in MS 4805 f. 101 reads, 'Thou pale viceregent of the Sun', but this is replaced by 'Fare-ye-weel, bonny Lady Moon' in *Songs* 1831.

The copy text for *Songs* 1831 is that of the *Edinburgh Literary Journal*, with slight textual adjustment. For example, the opening of ll. 5–7 has 'Thy' instead of 'You' and there are two substantive variants so that 'dark' becomes 'still' (l. 2) and 'mortal' becomes 'joyful' (l. 15). In *Songs* 1831 Hogg adds a title, 'The Moon', for the first time and introduces the song with a section of dialogue to provide context. But without a headnote and only giving the words for a character named 'SHEPHERD' the 1831 reader might understandably think this song comes directly from *Noctes* and not from another source.

Publication History:
1830 – with 'Dr David Dale's Account of a Grand Aerial Voyage. By the Ettrick Shepherd' in *the Edinburgh Literary Journal*, 23 January 1830 (50–53 (p. 52))
1831 – in *Songs by the Ettrick Shepherd*, pp. 233–34 – see p. 103 in the present edition

Musical Context:
Hogg gives no air or Musical Context for the song, and no copy with music has yet been located.

Explanatory Notes:
103 [**headnote**] **the prospeck** 'a spy-glass, field glass or telescope' (*DSL*).
103, l. 1 **Lady Moon** in Greek mythology, for example, the moon is associated with feminine qualities.
103, l. 5 **Your lip is like Ben-Lomond's base** 'a mountain in Buchanan parish, Stirlingshire, extending along the E side of the upper part of Loch Lomond' (Groome).
103, l. 7 **the Grampian range** 'the broad fringe of mountains that extends along the eastern side of the Highlands of Scotland'(Groome).
103, l. 9 **still thou bear'st a human face** the 'man in the moon', a mythical person thought to inhabit the moon from the 'imagined semblance of a person or a human face in the disc of the (full) moon' (Brewer's *Dictionary of Phrase and Fable*).

The Witch of Fife (pp. 103–04)

Creative Context:
The history of 'The Witch of Fife' parallels exactly that of the preceding song in *Songs* 1831. Like 'The Moon' it originates in the year 1827 as a planned contribution to *Blackwood's Edinburgh Magazine*, although it was never published there: see the Introduction to 'The Moon' for full details. Like 'The Moon', 'The Witch of Fife' was first published as an untitled 'Song First' in 'Dr David Dale's Account of a Grand Aerial Voyage. By the Ettrick Shepherd' in the *Edinburgh Literary Journal* of 23 January 1830. And like 'The Moon', the 'Ettrick Shepherd'

sings the 'song'. 'Dr Dale' 'lets forth a supply of gas' causing the hot air balloon to rise. 'The Shepherd', 'delirious with joy [...] clapped his hands, waved his bonnet, took a quelch of whisky' [just saved from being thrown overboard] and proceeds to sing 'The Witch of Fife'.

As is also the case with 'the Moon' there is no extant manuscript of 'The Witch of Fife' within the bulk of Hogg's fair-copy manuscript for *Songs* 1831 at NLS MS 4805, ff. 26–102: see note to 'I'll No Wake Wi' Annie' above. But there are two other extant manuscripts. The first is NLS MS 4805, ff. 101–02 and more information is given above in the notes to 'The Moon'. Here 'The Witch of Fife' appears as 'Song First' and is set out in two numbered octets as the lead item in the manuscript. The second extant manuscript is found in MS Papers 42, Item 41 located among the Hogg papers in the Alexander Turnbull Library, New Zealand (ATL). More information on this manuscript of Hogg's 'Baloon Songs' is given above in the notes to 'The Moon'. Suffice it to say that 'The Witch of Fife' is untitled and appears as the first item on the sheet. Hogg's otherwise clean text has a scoring out at line four when 'And' is changed to 'But'.

Collation between both surviving manuscript versions of 'The Witch of Fife' reveals alteration to the layout: in the AT MS it appears as a sixteen-line song rather than two octets which are given in MS 4805, f. 101. Textually there is only one alteration, which is the change from the word 'steed' to 'yaud' (l. 6), its Scots equivalent in the AT version. This emendation does not appear in the printed version, however, as the whole line is completely redrafted. The wording of line nine is found only in the AT version, while ll. 10–12 occurs in both the original and the AT version but is not transferred to the published version, for these lines are replaced by entirely new wording.

In *Songs* 1831 Hogg adds the title 'The Witch of Fife' for the first time and provides a cryptic introductory headnote explaining that this is 'another balloon song', which is the only clue as to its origins in the *Edinburgh Literary Journal*. Indeed, the copy text is the *Edinburgh Literary Journal* version with several textual alterations. For example, 'spirit's' of the opening line in all previous versions refer to the 'Witch of Fife' and this now becomes 'jade', the Scots word for 'a worn-out or worthless horse; a nag' (*DSL*). The tense also changes, from plural to singular, so that 'we're', which had related to 'Dr Dale' and the 'Ettrick Shepherd' in the original story, is rendered as 'I'm (ll. 3 and 5). Hogg adds a little further confusion for readers of *Songs* 1831 who would know his earlier works, beacuse 'The Witch of Fife' is also the title of the song performed by the 'Eighth Bard' during 'Night the First' in *The Queen's Wake* (1813), one of Hogg's most popular works with his contemporary readership: (S/SC 2004), pp. 40–48 and also Mack's important discussion of this song on pp. xliii–xlviii of the introductory essay.

Publication History:
1830 – with 'Dr David Dale's Account of a Grand Aerial Voyage. By the Ettrick Shepherd' in *the Edinburgh Literary Journal* (23 January 1830), 50–53 (p. 53))
1831 – in *Songs by the Ettrick Shepherd* , pp. 235–36 – see pp. 103–04 in the present edition

Musical Context:
Hogg gives no air or Musical Context for the song, and no copy with music has yet been located.

Explanatory Notes:

103, l. 1 the jade's away a Scots word for 'a worn-out or worthless horse; a nag' (*DSL*). Earlier versions of the song at this point had 'Spirit' so that the change more firmly relates the song to that other 'Witch of Fife' in *The Queen's Wake* whose 'stout stallion' 'is made of ane humlocke schaw' (ll. 647–48): see (S/SC, 2004), p. 41.

103, l. 5 ring the skirts o' the gowden wain 'King Charles' Wain' or the Plough is the constellation *Ursa Major*, a formation of seven main stars.

103, l. 7 catch the Bear by the frozen mane the constellation *Ursa Major*.

Row On, Row On (pp. 104–05)

Creative Context:

Like the three songs which precede it in *Songs* 1831, 'Row on, Row on' first appeared in the *Edinburgh Literary Journal*, in this case with the title 'A Song. By the Ettrick Shepherd' on 14 November 1829. But unlike the preceding two songs, written initially with *Blackwood's Edinburgh Magazine* in mind, there appears to be little information about the Creative Context for this song. Indeed Hogg's headnote in 1831 refers only to its Musical Context, and this may well be the only reason for his having created his lyric.

Like the preceding group of songs in *Songs* 1831, 'Row on, Row on' is not part of Hogg's fair-copy manuscript for *Songs* found at NLS MS 4805, ff. 26–102 (Blackwood Papers): see note to 'I'll No Wake Wi' Annie' above. But an extant manuscript which includes an undated and untitled version of the song has been located at MS Papers 42, no.42 in the Alexander Turnbull Library, New Zealand (AT). Further information about this manuscript is given in the notes for 'The Moon' and 'The Witch of Fife' above. Hogg's draft of 'Row on, Row on' is written within the same four-page booklet containing his 'Balloon Songs' and this AT version of the song shows Hogg's revisions and cancellations prior to publication of the song in the *Edinburgh Literary Journal*.

Hogg uses the *Journal* printing as his copy text for *Songs* 1831 where he gives the song the title of its first line. He also redrafts l.16 changing 'That there is nought for me but mourning' in the *Edinburgh Literary Journal* to 'That nought remains for me but mourning'. It seems likely that Hogg simply copied the song from this recent publication.

Publication History:

1829 – in *Edinburgh Literary Journal*, No. 53 (14 November 1829), 346

1831 – in *Songs by the Ettrick Shepherd*, pp. 237–38 – see pp. 104–05 in the present edition

Musical Context:

Hogg's headnote suggests that he was inspired to write this song principally due to a local plaintive border melody entitled 'Tushilaw's Lines'. But although he notes that it has 'never been published' the tune had already appeared in the second volume of John Hamilton's *The Caledonian Museum Containing a favourite collection of Ancient and Modern Scots Tunes, adapted to the German flute or Violin*, 3 vols (Edinburgh, *c*.1810), 47. Full details of the tune can be found in *The Forest Minstrel* (S/SC, 2006, p. 287). This is probably the same air as that named 'Tushilaw' which had been matched to the song 'Strathfillan' written by Hogg's good friend

James Gray and which Hogg had already published in *The Forest Minstrel* in 1810 (p. 92). As Garside and Jackson note, Hogg also nominates 'Tushilaw's Lines' to accompany 'Song I' in his *Scottish Pastorals* of 1801 (p. 33) and it would seem that the song was current within the Borders. See also the notes to 'Courting Song' (pp. 91–92). Garside and Jackson also note that Hogg and William Laidlaw corresponded with Scott about the tune in the early 1800s. Laidlaw referred to the tune as 'plaintively sweet' in his letter to Hogg of 3 January 1803. Writing to Scott on 7 January 1803 with a version of the lyrics, Hogg writes, 'it hath been a popular song in Ettrick forest since the memory of the oldest person living [...] there': see *Letters*, I, 33–37 (p. 36).

Marion Graham (pp. 105–06)

Creative Context:
There is little information about the creation of this song, short of Hogg's headnote in *Songs* 1831 which states that it was written specially for the first number of the *Edinburgh Literary Journal*. As such it follows on nicely to the preceding four songs which also all appeared in the magazine (and there are others in *Songs* 1831 including 'Black Mary', p. 51). This song first appeared in the *Journal* for 15 November 1828 with the heading 'A Pastoral Sang. By the Ettrick Shepherd'. Hogg appears to make no textual changes to the song (though he changes the spelling of the Christian name 'Marrion' to 'Marion') when he decides to include it in *Songs* 1831. Marion Graham appears to be a fictional name.

As with the preceding group of songs 'Marion Graham' is not part of Hogg's fair-copy manuscript for *Songs* found at NLS MS 4805, ff. 26–102 (Blackwood Papers): see note to 'I'll No Wake Wi' Annie' above. No other extant manuscript has been located.

Publication History:
1829 – in *Edinburgh Literary Journal*, No. 53 (15 November 1828), 12
1831 – in *Songs by the Ettrick Shepherd*, pp. 237–38 – see pp. 105–06 in the present edition

Musical Context:
Hogg gives no air title and no musical setting of the song has yet been located.

Explanatory Notes:
106, l. 33 morning's gem– the star of love the planet Venus, visible at dawn and at dusk and therefore popularly known as both 'the morning star' and the 'evening star'.

The Flower (pp. 106–07)

Creative Context:
A full account of the textual and publishing history of 'The Flower' is given in *The Forest Minstrel* (S/SC, 2006). In summary, the song, as Hogg states clearly in his headnote for *Songs* 1831, first appeared in *The Forest Minstrel* in 1810 and its creation dates from the period 1808–1811, when Hogg's social circle widened to include the Izetts and their niece, Chalmers Forest, and James Gray and Margaret Phillips, whom Hogg later married in 1820. Garside and Jackson note that this

song is a fine example of Hogg creating songs for amateur performance amongst a polite circle of friends.

The song appears twice more in Hogg's lifetime, in the fourth volume of his 1822 *Poetical Works* and in *Songs* 1831. Details of textual variants are noted in *The Forest Minstrel*. Although the song is set out in quatrains in *Poetical Works* and there is a reordering of ll. 21–24, the text is essentially that of *The Forest Minstrel*.

The version printed in *Songs* 1831 is altered quite substantially from both previous printings and shows clear signs of Hogg re-engaging with his earlier material. He returns to the octet arrangement and reinstates ll. 21–24. While the content and tone remains constant, Hogg also changes single words, such as 'partial' for 'transient' (l. 7) and whole lines, e.g. 'One sweetly scented summer eve' replaces 'One evening, when the sun was low'.

As with the group of songs immediately preceding it this is one of the songs missing from Hogg's fair-copy manuscript for *Songs* 1831 found at NLS MS 4805, ff. 26–102 (Blackwood Papers): see note for 'I'll No' Wake Wi' Annie' above. No other extant manuscript has been found.

Publication History:
1810 – in *The Forest Minstrel*, pp. 7–8 – see (S/SC, 2006), pp. 14 and 215–16
1822 – in *Poetical Works*, IV, 334–36
1831 – in *Songs by the Ettrick Shepherd*, pp. 242–43 – see pp. 106–07 in the present edition

Musical Context:
Hogg's headnote suggests that there is a Gaelic air for the song and that a songsheet of it, arranged by 'Miss C Forest', is also extant. Chalmers Forest (*b.* 3 March 1790) was the niece of Chalmers Izet and his wife, Eliza. No copy of this song sheet has been found nor has the title of the 'Gaelic air' to which Hogg refers been identified. Garside and Jackson suggest that it may be one and the same tune as Hogg refers to in his letter of 11 December 1808, sent from the farm of Locherben in Dumfriesshire to Eliza Izett: 'My kindest respects to Mr. Izet and the amiable Miss Forest; the next time I come to Edin I will bring verses with me to the tunes of Lord Eglintons auld man and the other gaelic air' (*Letters*, I, 98). Garside and Jackson's note for the song suggests that there may be a link with the tune for Hogg's song 'The Moon was A-Waning' which sits beside it in *The Forest Minstrel*.

Birniebouzle (pp. 107–09)

Creative Context:
A full account of the textual and publishing history of 'Birniebouzle' is given in *The Forest Minstrel* (S/SC, 2006).This headnote for 1831 gives another example of Hogg's modesty topos: he is including the song only because of its clear popularity, not because he thinks of it as one of his best. It is also another example of Hogg clearly illustrating his role within popular song culture, when he states in his that this has been a 'popular street song for nearly thirty years'. Certainly a number of popular chapbook and broadside versions of the song have been identified. Garside and Jackson note that there are no earlier printings of Hogg's song before its inclusion in *The Forest Minstrel* in 1810. They also note that the title possibly derives from the word 'birnie' ('land covered with birns, i.e. scorched stems of heather') and 'bouzy' ('covered with bushes'). They comment on the existence

of a house in West Aberdeenshire called 'Burnieboozle', though no evidence has been found for a link with Hogg.

Between the song's appearance in 1810 and Hogg's inclusion of it in *Songs* 1831, there are a number of other popular printings. The chapbook versions consulted at the National Library of Scotland (RB.m.168 (70) and L.C. 2873 (31)) are probably derived from *The Forest Minstrel* version. These are largely unpunctuated, with several errors ('brook' instead of 'brock', l. 5) and missing letters (such as 'we' for 'wed', l. 28). They remain close to the 'spirit' of Hogg's original, although as is usual for chapbook publication, no author is given. These changes may suggest that the song has been noted from oral performance rather than from the printed text in *The Forest Minstrel*. Hogg's knowledge of the song's popularity is further evidenced by a reference to the song in the long poem 'Eppie and Tam the Piper. A Tale', by William Jamie (1849). In a house on 'Lutherside' in Aberdeenshire the company dance as Tam plays "Birniebouzle" on his bagpipes (*Stray Effusions, or Gleanings of Nature* (Montrose, 1849), pp. 91–120, p. 110).

As Garside and Jackson note, the changes between the texts in *The Forest Minstrel* and *Songs* 1831 include a number of verbal variants suggesting that Hogg is freshly drafting earlier material at this later point in his career. They note a 'radical difference' in the fifth stanza where Hogg has his male narrator continue rather than have the 'lassie' herself to speak. At times, the changes in this new version add an antique gloss to the song, such as 'yird' which replaces 'earth' (l. 3), but on other occasions the changes amount to anglicisation, e.g., 'Ye sall aye hae plenty' to 'Want shall ne'er come near ye' (l. 12).

As with the group of songs immediately preceding it there is no extant holograph of this song in the fair-copy manuscript for *Songs* 1831 at NLS MS 4805, ff. 26–102 (Blackwood Papers): See note to 'I'll No' Wake Wi' Annie'. There is, however, an autograph version of the song under the slightly revised title of 'Birnieboezle' which was published, posthumously, in 1836 in the *Southern Weekly Journal and Magazine of the Arts* (Charleston, South Carolina, vol. 2, no. 4 ((June 1836), 258). It was noted as being the production of 'James Hogg, the Ettrick Shepherd' and, wrongly, that it 'was never before published'. Further details can be found in the note to the song in *The Forest Minstrel* (S/SC, 2006). Garside and Jackson note that this version is very close to the text in *The Forest Minstrel*.

Publication History:
1810 – in *The Forest Minstrel*, pp. 139–41 – see (S/SC, 2006), pp. 134–35 and 317–18
1831 – in *Songs by the Ettrick Shepherd*, pp. 244–46 – see pp. 107–09 in the present edition
Unauthorised versions:
c.1810–1830 – 'The Braes of Birniebouzle' (c.1810–1830), a broadside ballad printed in London by J. Pitts, Printer and Toymaker, Gt. St. Andrews Street, 7 Dials. The text largely follows that of *The Forest Minstrel* of 1810, although several spelling mistakes, such as 'tank the puppy of the seal' instead of 'fank the porpy and the seal' (l. 23) belie its London printing. The broadside is printed with a woodcut of a well-dressed man, probably representing the male protagonist who turns out to be wealthy at the end of the song: See NLS RB.m.168 (070) – also at http://www.nls.uk/broadsides. Another chapbook copy, also at NLS, is bound within L.C. 2873 (31).

Musical Context:
In both of the authorised printed versions Hogg pairs the song with the traditional

Scottish tune, 'The Braes of Tullimet/Tullymet'. As Garside and Jackson note, 'Tulliemet is a hamlet in Strathtay, Perth and Kinross, lying a mile to the east of Ballinluig on the lower slopes of Creagan Ruathair': *The Forest Minstrel* (S/SC, 2006). *The Forest Minstrel* also provides a full history of the tune, which is found in several of the major eighteenth-century musical collections, including McGlashen and Gow.

Explanatory Notes:

107 [headnote] "the multitude are never wrong" Hogg is quoting from Dryden's commentary on critics in *Of Dramatic Poesy. An Essay* (1668). It is an expression Hogg uses frequently in his writing. For example, in 'Charlie Dinmont', *The Border Chronicler*, a short story he contributed to the *Literary Souvenir* in 1825 and also in his comments on the critical failure of *Queen Hynde* in his 'Memoir of the Author's Life' (1832): see *Contributions to Annuals and Gift Books* (S/SC, 2006), p. 10, p. 287 and note on p. 365.

108, l. 27 littit brogues this phrase is glossed in the *Southern Literary Journal* version of 1836 as 'Colored shoes', which accords with *DSL* denotation of 'littit' as 'dyed'.

108, l. 39 drag the larry at my tail a 'larry' is 'a long flat wagon without sides running on four low wheels' (*OED*), presumably in the context of the song it is used to carry the gathered mussels.

I Hae Lost My Love (p. 109)

Creative Context:

Like several of the songs immediately preceding it in *Songs* 1831 this song first appears in the the *Edinburgh Literary Journal*. It is found on 17 January 1829, in its 'Original Poetry' section, under the title 'A Scots Sang. By the Ettrick Shepherd'. Most of Hogg's songs about women present them in a positive light. The same year he published an essay titled 'A Letter about Men and Women' in *Blackwood's Edinburgh Magazine* (vol. 26, 245–50), in which he stated that: 'There is no doubt that the proper study of mankind is WOMAN; and Mr. Pope was wrong; for the endless variety of character among the sex is of itself a mine, endless and inexhaustible; but to study them in their domestic capacity, is the sweetest of all' (246). So this song, with its ironic subtitle 'A BITTER song against the women', is rather uncharacteristic for Hogg. There is little additional information about its creation, or to whom the song refers.

Hogg appears to have lifted the text from the *Journal* for inclusion in *Songs* 1831 and there are only the usual orthographic changes but no substantive variants. Like the songs preceding it in *Songs* 1831 there is no extant holograph for 'I hae lost my love' in the fair-copy manuscript for *Songs* 1831 at at NLS MS 4805, ff. 26–102 (Blackwood Papers): See note to 'I'll No' Wake Wi' Annie'. However, like 'The Moon', 'The Witch of Fife' and 'Row on, Row on' above it, Hogg's fair-copy holograph manuscript of the version he prepared for the *Edinburgh Literary Journal* is extant among the James Hogg papers at the Alexander Turnbull Library, New Zealand, MS Papers 42, no. 62 (i). See Peter Garside, 'An Annotated Checklist of Hogg's literary manuscripts in the Alexander Turnbull library, Wellington, New Zealand' in *The Bibliotheck*, 5–23 (p. 5).

Publication History:

1829 – in *Edinburgh Literary Journal*, No. 10 (17 January 1829), 140

1831 – in *Songs by the Ettrick Shepherd*, pp. 247–48 – see p. 109 in the present edition

Musical Context:
Hogg gives no tune or air title nor any reference to a musical setting of this song. However it does appear with music in *The Cream of Scottish Song* (n.d.) with the heading 'Written by the Ettrick Shepherd for the Edinburgh Literary Journal. Music composed by a Gentleman of Glasgow. Sung by Mr Mackay': see NLS L.C. 2852. D (18).

Explanatory Notes:
109, l. 23 this ill warld wording derived from his early song of the same title composed for Margaret Phillips (later his wife) in the 1810s. As 'Mischievous Woman' it was included in *Songs* 1831: see p. 88 (l. 1) and was one of Hogg's songs to appear with music by Beethoven in George Thomson's collections: see *Contributions to Musical Collections and Miscellaneous Songs*.

Allan Dhu (p. 110)

Creative Context:
Again like several of the songs immediately preceding it in *Songs* 1831 this song originates as a contribution to the *Edinburgh Literary Journal*. It was first published in its 'Original Poetry' section under the slightly longer title 'Allan Dhu–A Love Song. By the Ettrick Shepherd' in October 1830. Allan Dhu appears to be a fictional character and there is little additional information about the song's creation.

Aside from the reduction in the title to 'Allan Dhu', Hogg makes no textual alterations to the song for its appearance in *Songs* 1831.

Like the songs preceding it in *Songs* 1831 there is no extant holograph for 'Allan Dhu' in the fair-copy manuscript for *Songs* 1831 at at NLS MS 4805, ff. 26–102 (Blackwood Papers): See note to 'I'll No' Wake Wi' Annie'. No other manuscript sources have been located.

Publication History:
1830 – in *Edinburgh Literary Journal*, No. 100 (30 October 1830), 232
1831 – in *Songs by the Ettrick Shepherd*, pp. 249–50 – see p. 110 in the present edition

Musical Context:
There is no melody given for this song and no musical setting has been found.

Explanatory Notes:
110, l. 16 Breadalbin's land a 'district of NW Perthshire' (Groome).
110, l. 32 An' greet, an' greet my fill a phrase common in traditional balladry. See, for example, 'The Beggar Laddie' (Child 280). Burns used the phrase in his song 'My Harry was a Gallant Lad', published to the tune 'Highlander's Lament' in *SMM*, III (1790), No. 208 (p. 218).

Love's Visit (p. 111)

Creative Context:
Again like several of the songs immediately preceding it in *Songs* 1831 this song originates as a contribution to the *Edinburgh Literary Journal*. Hogg was a frequent

contributor to this literary rival to *Blackwood's*, beginning with a song in the very first number of 15 November 1828 (see 'Marion Graham' above). Hoping to elicit further contributions from Hogg in the Spring of 1829, the Editor wrote in the section 'To Our Correspondents' in the number for Saturday 19 April 1829:

> The Ettrick Shepherd requests us to mention on what subject we should like his next communication to be. All we can say is, that with the genius he brings to bear upon every subject, we do not think he can go wrong. Let it be grave or gay–verse of prose–just as the mood is on him. The great rule we should like him to attend to is, that the *sooner* he favours us the better. (No. 23, p. 324)

It would appear that Hogg replied immediately as a note 'To our Readers' in the following number advises 'Want of room obliges us to delay till next week [...] "A Real Love Song" by the Ettrick Shepherd' (No. 24 (25 April 1829), p. 338). Under this title, Hogg's song was duly published in the next number of the *Edinburgh Literary Journal* of 2 May 1829. There is no further information about the song's Creative Context not did it appear elsewhere before Hogg picked it up for inclusion in *Songs* 1831.

Aside from the change in title to 'Love's Visit', Hogg makes no textual alterations to this literary song for its appearance in *Songs* 1831. And like the songs preceding it there is no extant holograph for 'Love's Visit' in the fair-copy manuscript for *Songs* 1831 at at NLS MS 4805, ff. 26–102 (Blackwood Papers): see note to 'I'll No' Wake Wi' Annie'. No other manuscript sources have been located.

Publication History:
1829 – in *Edinburgh Literary Journal*, No. 25 (2 May 1829), 352
1831 – in *Songs by the Ettrick Shepherd*, pp. 251–52 – see p. 111 in the present edition
[1834] – in *Original Scottish Melodies*, pp. 63–66 – see *Contributions to Musical Collections and Miscellaneous Songs* (S/SC, 2014)

Musical Context:
Hogg gives no information about a choice of tune or air or any musical settings. But Peter McLeod published an arrangement of the song in his *Original Scottish Melodies* [1834] under the title 'Love Came to the Door O' My Heart. Written by the Ettrick Shepherd', pp. 63–66. It was subsequently reprinted under this title in McLeod's *Original National Melodies of Scotland* [1838], pp. 63–66. For further details about Hogg's involvement with Peter McLeod's collections and a copy of the song see: *Contributions to Musical Collections and Miscellaneous Songs*.

The Moon Was A-Waning (pp. 112–13)

Creative Context:
A full account of the textual and publishing history of 'The Moon was a-waning' is given in *The Forest Minstrel* (S/SC, 2006). This song sits next to Hogg's 'The Flower' in *The Forest Minstrel* and it comes just a few songs after it in *Songs* 1831.

In summary, the first appearance of the song is in *The Forest Minstrel* in 1810 and, as Garside and Jackson note, both songs are potentially suited to an unnamed 'gaelic air' which Hogg mentions in a letter of 11 December 1808 (see note for 'The Flower' above). Hogg's 1831 headnote, however, gives additional information about the song's Creative Context being much earlier in Hogg's career. His reference to it being 'one of the songs of my youth, written long ere I threw aside the shepherd's plaid, and took farewell of my trusty colley, for the bard's perilous and thankless occupation' would suggest the composition date is prior to February 1810, when Hogg claims 'in utter desperation, I took my plaid about my shoulders and marched away to Edinburgh, determined, since no better could be, to push my fortune as a literary man': see James Hogg. *The Mountain Bard* (S/SC, 2007), p. 206. Moreover Hogg's 1831 headnote makes much of its musical and performance context – 'this was the first song of mine I ever heard sung at the piano' – showing, as Garside and Jackson state so forcibly in their new edition of *The Forest Minstrel*, that Hogg was aware of the potential of his songs for wider dissemination and performance. Again Hogg names Chalmers Forest here as the first to set the song to music and to have 'lifted' Hogg's songs away from the 'ewe-bught and milking green' to the drawing room.

The notes to the song in *The Forest Minstrel* (S/SC, 2006) give a clear account of the textual differences between the three publications of the song, noting that there are only 'minimal changes in spelling and punctuation'. Aside from a slight revision of the title to 'The Moon was A-Waning', the text included in the fourth volume of Hogg's *Poetical Works* of 1822 is essentially that of *The Forest Minstrel* with one slight revision to the word 'corpse' to the more poetic 'corse' on the final line. The version included in *Songs* 1831 is closest to the text of *Poetical Works*, although, as Hogg's holograph is not extant, it is unclear which version he used as the copy text. The final version of the song removes the only Scotticism, 'muirland' (l. 8) which becomes 'moorland' but without Hogg's holograph it is not clear whether this is an authorial revision or the work of the printer.

Acting as an advertisement for the newly published *Songs by the Ettrick Shepherd* the song also appears in the February 1831 issue of *Blackwood's Edinburgh Magazine* where it is preceded by a general discussion of Scottish song. 'Christopher North' remarks, 'In their mournfulness are they not almost like the wail of some bird distracted on the bush from which its nest has been harried, and then suddenly flying away for ever into the woods?' He then introduces Hogg's 'snaw-sang' and notes that it is from 'the collection of Songs–published this very day'. Commenting on Hogg's 'delightfully characteristic notes', he writes, 'The poet knows not the magic of his own strains, till he hears their inspiration in the breath of youth and innocence'.

Like the songs preceding it there is no extant holograph for 'The Moon is a-waning' in the fair-copy manuscript for *Songs* 1831 at at NLS MS 4805, ff. 26–102 (Blackwood Papers): see note to 'I'll No' Wake Wi' Annie'. But, as Garside and Jackson note, there is an autograph version of the song amongst George Thomson's papers in the British Library (Add MS 35265, ff. 338–39). In summary, the autograph includes two songs on a four-page booklet with an 1810 watermark and also includes 'What ails my heart what ails my head' to the air, 'Widow are ye wakin'. But Hogg and Thomson did not begin their correspondence until 1815 and so it is more likely that the song was 'remembered' and written down by Hogg for him at a later date. In any case Thomson did not choose to publish this particular song. For further information about Hogg's involvement with Thomson's song collections and for copies of Hogg's songs which appeared therein see: *Contributions to Musical Collections and Miscellaneous Songs*.

Publication History:
1810 – in *The Forest Minstrel*, pp. 9–10 – see (S/SC, 2006), pp. 15–17 and 216–19
1822 – in *Poetical Works*, IV, 337–38

1831 – in *Songs by the Ettrick*, pp. 253–55 – see pp. 112–13 in the present edition
1831 – in *Blackwood's Edinburgh Magazine*, 29 (February 1831), 288–89
Unauthorised versions:
1831 – 'The Moon was a-Waning. From the Songs of James Hogg', in *The Lady's Book* (Philadelphia), vol. 3 (September 1831), 181
1835 – in *The Zodiac, A Monthly Periodical devoted to Science, Literature and the Arts* 2 vols (Albany, New York: E. Perry), I, No. 4 (October 1835), 59. This version of the song has a substantive alteration at l. 4, where the 'fond lover' of all previous versions is here a 'proud lover'. The American edition of *Songs, by the Ettrick Shepherd*, published by William Stodart in New York in 1832 is a reprinting of the first British edition, so that the change in this version may be down to an error by the printer of *The Zodiac*. Although Hogg contributed material for *The Zodiac* in 1834, this item is headed by the note 'Selected for the Zodiac' indicating that it is derived from a printed source. Further details about Hogg and *The Zodiac* can be found in 'From Altrive to Albany: James Hogg's Transatlantic Publication', by Janette Currie, *James Hogg Research* website at http://www.jameshogg.stir.ac.uk.

Musical Context:
As his headnote for 1831 suggests, this song was apparently 'first set to music and sung by Miss C. Forest' and 'has long been a favourite'. But strangely no extant copy of the song setting has been located as a single song sheet nor in any contemporary song collections with, or without music, and it is not listed by Gooch and Thatcher. In the preface to *The Forest Minstrel*, as Garside and Jackson state, Hogg makes mention that the song was written for an unnamed 'sweet and mournful Gaelic air' but he has forgotton what it is called. He also suggests his song will 'sing well' to the popular tune 'I'll Never Leave Thee' full details of which can be found in *The Forest Minstrel*: see pp. 217–19.

Explanatory Notes:
112 **[headnote] I was a poor shepherd half a century ago, and I have never got farther to this day** refers to the 1830s being a fraught time financially for Hogg. He repeats this exact phrase within a letter of 1833 to a Major Robert H. Rose of Silver Lake, Susquehanna, which was published, posthumously, on 16 February 1836, in Adam Waldie's *Journal of Belles Lettres*, a two-page supplement to the *Select Circulating Library* (Philadelphia), unpaginated. The letter is reprinted in full in the *Listing of Hogg Items in the American Periodical Press*, by Janette Currie, at the online *James Hogg Research* website hosted by the Division of Literature and Languages, School of Arts and Humanities, Stirling University, http://www.jameshogg.stir.ac.uk.
113, l. 30 **Where the dead-tapers hover** Garside and Jackson compare this with Hogg's later mention of 'the phosphorescent lights coming from a decaying corpse' in the short story of 'Rob Dodds', published first in *Blackwood's Edinburgh Magazine* (March 1823) and more recently revised in *The Shepherd's Calendar* of 1829: *The Forest Minstrel* (S/SC, 2006), p. 216.

O, What Gart Me Greet (pp. 113–14)

Creative Context:
This song makes a good partner to the preceding 'The Moon Was A-Waning' in content. It is one of the group of eleven Hogg songs which first appeared in *The*

Spy, the weekly newspaper Hogg edited in 1810–11. It first appeared there in the issue for 17 November 1810 with the title 'Poor Little Jessy A Scottish Song, by John Millar'. The figure of John Millar is first introduced in this issue of the newspaper. The editor explains to the readership that Millar came to Edinburgh expressly to 'be introduced to the world in my paper' and that the Editor had agreed to include his work, which features 'a great number of anecdotes illustrative of country manners in general, delineations of many singular characters in Nithsdale and Galloway, old legends, and stories of ghosts and bogles' (p. 122). The issue then includes Miller's 'Description of a Peasant's Funeral' followed by 'Poor Little Jessy' and another melancholic poetic fragment.

Hogg included the song later in 1822 in his *Poetical Works* though there are few changes from the text as it appears in *The Spy*.

For *Songs* 1831 Hogg revised the title so that it now repeats the first line of the song, and amended the format from quatrains to octets. The copy text for the *Songs* 1831 version is that of the original in *The Spy*, although there are several substantive alterations and also fresh drafting. For example, l.3, originally in Scots ('The neibours upbraidit, and said it was sillie') is now in English. Line 20 has some fresh drafting, while the final four lines are newly created for the *Songs* 1831 version. Originally, the song had concluded with the fate of 'Willie' confirmed: 'he's lyin' cauld i' the clay' which is changed to 'I'll lang for the day that shall meet us again' (l. 32).

None of Hogg's holograph manuscript versions of the song have been located. Like the songs preceding it there is no extant holograph of this song in the fair-copy manuscript for *Songs* 1831 at at NLS MS 4805, ff. 26–102 (Blackwood Papers): see note to 'I'll No' Wake Wi' Annie'.

Publication History:
1810 – in *The Spy*, No. 12 (17 November 1810), 95 – see S/SC, 2000), pp. 126–27
1822 – in *Poetical Works*, IV, 328–30
1831 – in *Songs by the Ettrick Shepherd*, pp. 256–57 – see pp. 113–14 in the present edition

Musical Context:
Hogg's headnote for the song in 1831 gives no chosen melody or air for the lyric and makes no mention of a song setting. No musical settings have been located. However, Hogg notes that he has heard the song 'chanted to the tune "Bonny Dundee"'. Hogg's own song with the title 'Bonny Dundee' (beginning 'O will you gang down to the bush i' the meadow') was first published in the *Scots Magazine* for July 1804 (66, p. 534) and was later included in *The Forest Minstrel* (S/SC, 2006) though he does not include it in *Songs* 1831. A full history of this popular contemporary tune is given in *The Forest Minstrel*. In summary, it dates back at least as far as the seventeeth century and has sets of lyrics by both Burns and Walter Scott. With significant variants it is found in several of the key eighteenth century music collections including Oswald's *Caledonian Pocket Companion*, III (*c*.1795) 4, and McGibbon's *Second Collection of Scots Tunes* (1746), p. 36.

A National Song of Triumph (pp. 114–15)

Creative Context:
As Hogg's headnote for the song in *Songs* 1831 states, this song appeared in 1814 'to celebrate the entry of the Allies into Paris'. Gillian Hughes has located the earliest

printing of the song as that in the *Edinburgh Evening Courant* in April that year: for more details see 'James Hogg, and Edinburgh's Triumph Over Napoleon', *Scottish Studies Review*, 4:1 (Spring 2003), 98–111. Hughes suggests that Hogg may have created the song earlier than this when news of Napoleon's defeat reached Edinburgh on 8 April 1811.

It appeared in the *Edinburgh Evening Courant* in 1814 beside a report that 'the dethroning of BONAPARTE was celebrated this morning by the firing of the Castle guns, and the ringing of bells'. The introductory paragraph records the circumstances of the first performance of the song: 'A party of social friends having met on Friday evening last, in honour of the glorious news which arrived that day of the taking of Paris. MR HOGG (the Ettrick shepherd) was called on for a song, when he recited the following verses'.

A revised version of the song next appeared in the first issue of *Blackwood's Edinburgh Magazine* in April 1817 in the section of 'Original Poetry' alongside an unsigned early contribution by John Wilson titled 'The Desolate Village: A Reverie' (p. 72). It was introduced by the phrase: 'Recited by the Author, in a Party of his Countrymen, on the Day that the News arrived of our final victory over the French'. 'Where now the coofs' (l. 13) became the more violent 'Gae hang the coofs' and this version included a new additional verse:

Come, jaw your glasses to the brim!
  Far in the air your bonnets flee!
"Our gude auld king!" I'll drink to him,
  As lang as I hae drink to pree. (ll. 25–28)

Hogg included the song in the fourth volume of his *Poetical Works* of 1822 with another, different title: 'Stanzas Recited in a party of Social Friends, met in honour of the entry into Paris by the Allies – 1814'. In this version, Hogg returns to the text published in the *Edinburgh Evening Courant*, although he omits the eight lines from the middle of the song (ll. 17–24 of *Songs* 1831).

In *Songs* 1831 it appeared with yet another different title: 'A National Song of Triumph'. But Hogg appears to go back to its earliest iteration, in the *Edinburgh Evening Courant*, for this version, amending its form from quatrianes to octets and changing only one or two words: 'Oft; (l. 9) becomes 'Lang'.

None of Hogg's holograph manuscript versions of the song have been located. Like the songs preceding it there is no extant holograph of this song in the fair-copy manuscript for *Songs* 1831 at at NLS MS 4805, ff. 26–102 (Blackwood Papers): see note to 'I'll No' Wake Wi' Annie'.

Publication History:
1814 – in *Edinburgh Evening Courant* (11 April 1814)
1817 – in *Blackwood's Edinburgh Magazine*, 1 (April 1817), 4 – see (S/SC, 2008), pp. 5–6 and 393–95
1822 – in *Poetical Works*, IV, 276–77
1831 – in *Songs by the Ettrick Shepherd*, pp. 258–59 – see pp. 114–15 in the present edition

Musical Context:
Although, as noted above, there is an account of Hogg reciting the song, no information about a musical performance and no musical settings have been located. Hogg does not give a melody or air for the song.

Explanatory Notes:
Full Explanatory Notes appear in Thomas Richardson's note for this song in
Blackwood's Edinburgh Magazine, (S/SC, 2008), I, 394–95.

The Fall of the Leaf (p. 115)

Creative Context:
Like 'O, What Gart Me Greet?', situated only two songs before it in *Songs* 1831,
this is another of the group of eleven songs in this collection which Hogg first
published in his newspaper *The Spy*. This one first appeared on 13 October 1810
and Hogg later claimed it as his own song when he published it almost unchanged
in the fourth volume of his 1822 *Poetical Works*.

In 1831 Hogg changed the format of the song from quatrains to octets. Although
the version in *The Spy* is his copy text, he altered l. 12 from 'It often leaves sorrows
behind' changing to 'That lead to the sorrows behind' and he omitted 28 lines of
text (ll. 17–20, ll. 25–28 and ll. 33–52).

None of Hogg's holograph manuscript versions of the song have been located.
Like the songs preceding it there is no extant holograph of this song in the
fair-copy manuscript for *Songs* 1831 at at NLS MS 4805, ff. 26–102 (Blackwood
Papers): see note to 'I'll No' Wake Wi' Annie'.

Publication History:
1810 – in *The Spy*, No. 12 (13 October 1810), 56 – see (S/SC, 2000), pp. 73–74
1822 – in *Poetical Works*, IV, 263–66
1831 – in *Songs by the Ettrick Shepherd*, pp. 260–61 – see p. 115 in the present edition
Unauthorised versions:
1835 – in *The Zodiac, A Monthly Periodical devoted to Science, Literature and the Arts*
(Albany) of October 1835, p. 49. *The Zodiac* published new writing by Hogg
created specifically for the American market. However, collation reveals the
American version of 'The Fall of the Leaf' is from *Songs* 1831. Further details
of the American publication of Hogg's writing in America, as well as a compete
Listing of Hogg Items in the American Periodical Press is included on the *James Hogg
Research* website hosted by the Division of Literature and Languages, School of
Arts and Humanities, Stirling University, http://www.jameshogg.stir.ac.uk.

Musical Context:
Hogg makes no mention of a melody or air for the song in 1831 and no musical
settings of this song have been located.

The Ancient Banner (pp. 116–17)

Creative Context:
This is one of Hogg's Ettrick songs and as he notes in 1831 it was composed for
an important football match organised by the Duke of Buccleuch and Walter
Scott which took part on 4 December 1815; not the 5 December as Hogg states
in his 1831 headnote. Hogg was involved in the organisation of the event about
which he was most enthusiastic, writing to Scott on 16 November:

> the great match at Ball is finally settled to take place on Carterhaugh on
> *Monday the fourth of Dec.* I never was so much delighted with the prospect
> of any thing I wish no lives may be lost. The two parishes of Yarrow

and Selkirk are to be matched against each other and Lord Hume as I understand to head the Yarrow shepherds against you and the *other* Souters of Selkirk. (*Letters*, I, 256)

On 11 November Scott had already asked Lady Compton to compose music for a song he had been asked to write and he requested that she find or create a 'good rattling tune with a strain of wild character in it which may suit the gathering of our Dalesmen': *The Letters of Sir Walter Scott*, ed. by H. J. C. Grierson, 12 vols (London: Constable and Co., 1932–37), IV, 125–27. But in his letter of 19 November, Scott wrote to the Duke that he wished 'Hogg to give me a little of his best assistance to celebrate the Lifting of the Banner' (see *The Letters of Sir Walter Scott*, IV, 127–28). Scott's letter has not survived but Hogg's response along with the original version of 'The Ancient Banner' is extant at NLS MS 3886, ff. 241–42. The letter accompanying the song suggests that Hogg wrote the song quickly on 24 November after only receiving Scott's letter of invitation the night before. He continues: 'I wrote the following verses this morning judging that there was no time to lose and you know I cannot endure to be behind in a *ploy*'. He notably asks directly for Scott's assistance: 'I beseech you to take them through hand and lop and add what you will. I am not the same person I was this way' (*Letters*, I, 258–59). While Hogg previously protested against Scott's literary advice, writing in his *Memoir*, it was 'with the utmost difficulty that I can be brought to alter one line', he appears to have mellowed. Here he seems to have accepted Scott's suggested alterations, as the published version of the song is radically different from Hogg's original of 24 November.

The textual changes between this early version and that published just three weeks later in an eight-page pamphlet by James Ballantyne are discussed in detail in Douglas S. Mack's article '"The Ettricke Garland" by Scott and Hogg: a Note': see *The Bibliotheck*, 7 no 4 (1975), 105–11. In summary, the song was revised by enlarging the title (from 'To the Ancient Banner of Buccleuch' to 'To the Ancient Banner of the House of Buccleuch'), adding a further verse (now verse three), by creating new wording for ll. 5–8, l. 9, l. 28, ll. 30–31 and l. 34, and by moving ll. 21–24 to ll. 33–36 and ll. 25–28 to 29–32. Mack suggests that 'it seems probable that this re-writing was the work of Scott [...]. It therefore seems reasonable to conclude that the version of 'The ancient banner' published in *The Ettricke Garland* can best be described as a joint work by Hogg and Scott, rather than the work of Hogg alone' (*The Bibliotheck*, p. 109). Mack notes that Hogg's initial attempt is 'itself a poem of some merit' and Hogg's 1831 headnote captures his pride in writing a song to celebrate such an ancient, if tattered, banner. Hogg appears to have been happy with the revised version for he retained the text of the new version for two later publciations.

The song appeared again in the fourth volume of his *Poetical Works* in 1822, now retitled 'On the Lifting of the Banner of Buccleuch' and sub-titled 'at the great football match on Carterhaugh, Dec. 4, 1815'. The copy text is *The Ettricke Garland* with no textual alterations.

Finally he chose to include it in *Songs* 1831 and here he also uses *The Ettricke Garland* as copy text with the title revised once more to 'The Ancient Banner'.

As noted above Hogg's fair-copy holograph manuscript of the original song composed on 24 November 1815 is extant at NLS MS 38886, ff. 241–42. This manuscript is discussed in detail in Douglas Mack's article and Hughes reprints the original version in *Letters*, I, 258–59.

As with the songs immediately preceding it in *Songs* 1831 this is one of the songs missing from the fair-copy manuscript for *Songs* 1831 at at NLS MS 4805, ff. 26–102 (Blackwood Papers): see note to 'I'll No' Wake Wi' Annie'.

Publication History:
1815 – *The Ettricke Garland; being Two Excellent New Songs on The Lifting of the Banner of the House of Buccleuch, at the great football match on Carterhaugh,* Dec. 4, 1815 'To the Ancient Banner of the House of Buccleuch' (Edinburgh: James Ballantyne & Co., 1815): see *The Bibliotheck,* 7 no 4 (1975), 105–11; see also *Contributions to Musical Collections and Miscellaneous Songs* (S/SC, 2014)
1822 – in *Poetical Works,* IV, 287–89
1831 – in *Songs by the Ettrick Shepherd,* pp. 262–63 – see pp. 116–17 in the present edition
Unauthorised versions:
The event was reported in several newspapers in London and Edinburgh and most included the text of the songs reprinted from *The Ettricke Garland*: see, for example, the *Scots Magazine,* 77 (December 1815), 935–36.

Musical Context:
Hogg makes no mention of a melody or air for this song in 1831 or elsewhere and no musical settings of it have been located. While the original intention was to have a performance of both songs at the football match on 4 December 1815, there is no record of this having taken place. Writing after the match, Walter Scott informs Mrs Clephane (Lady Compton), that 'The music was much admired by all who had an opportunity of hearing it but I had no time to train a ballad singer or two to sing our joint minstrelsy upon the field' (*The Letters of Sir Walter Scott,* ed. by H. J. C. Grierson, 12 vols (London: Constable and Co., 1932–37), IV, 141 [misdated 1 Dec].

Explanatory Notes:
116 [headnote] Carterhaugh Carterhaugh is a large level field at the junction of the Yarrow and Ettrick Rivers. According to Scott, 'many came twenty miles and bivouacked in the heather all night', and after the match Carterhaugh 'looked almost like the field of Waterloo from the mode in which it was trampled and torn up': see Scott's letter to Lady Compton (IV, 141–42). A very full account of the match from a contemporary newspaper is reprinted in Lockhart's *Life of Sir Walter Scott,* 7 vols (Edinburgh and London, 1837–38), III, 395–97. It reports, for example, 'Mr James Hogg acted as aide-de-camp to the Earl of Home in the command of the Yarrow men, and Mr Robert Henderson of Selkirk to Mr Clarkson, both of whom contributed not a little to the good order of the day' (III, 396).
116, l. 4 Thou emblem of the days of old! in his letter to Mrs Clephane of 12 November, describing the forthcoming football match, Scott informs her that the pennon 'has not so far as we know been out since the battle of Dryfe-Sands near Lochmaben where Lord Maxwell was slain', which dates the banner to the late 1600s (*The Letters of Sir Walter Scott,* IV, 122–24 (p. 123)).
116, l. 7 the bloodless toil Hogg had earlier expressed a 'wish no lives may be lost' (see his letter to Scott of 16 November 1815 in *Letters* I, 256). In 'A Journey Through the Highlands of Scotland, in the Months of July and August 1802, in a Series of Letters to S– W–', published in the *Scots Magazine* during 1802–1803 Hogg describes 'playing at the ball' as 'the most furious contest of all'; *Highland*

Journeys, ed. by Hans de Groot (S/SC, 2010), p. 8.

116, l. 18 Twas thine thy gleaming moon and star several crescent moons and stars adorn the Buccleuch banner.

117, l. 33 even the days ourselves have known a reference to the Battle of Waterloo of 18 June 1815 when Wellington's victory over Napoleon brought an end to decades of fighting with France.

A Widow's Wail (pp. 117–8)

Creative Context:

Hogg suggests in his headnote that this is one of his early songs, but he also comments that his memory is unreliable as to its creation and indeed there is no evidence of its composition before it first appears in *The Forest Minstrel* in 1810. An account of the textual and publishing history of the song and the popular melody 'Gilderoy', which Hogg names as the air to which it is sung, can be found in *The Forest Minstrel* (S/SC, 2006).

In summary, Garside and Jackson suggest that Hogg's memory of an earlier existence of the song may well refer to an earlier oral provenance and the tune 'Gilderoy' is indeed a popular tune with many variant lyrics so this is entirely possible. They also note similarities between Hogg's song and earlier lyric for this melody by Thomas Campbell in 1799. Hogg's song appears in *The Forest Minstrel* with the title 'The Soldier's Widow' and, as Garside and Jackson persuasively suggest, the reference to 'gallant Moore in Spain' – Scottish general Sir John Moore who had died defending the evacuation at Corunna – clearly places this version of the song around 1810.

The next printing of the song is found in Hogg's 1822 *Poetical Works* with a change in title to 'The Widow's Lament'. Garside and Jackson account for a number of changes to the text in 1822 most of which are kept for the 1831 version. They refer to a possible confusion with another entirely different song entitled 'The Solider's Widow' which also appears in the fourth volume of Hogg's *Poetical Works* (IV, 316–18) but which is, in fact, an earlier version of 'I Lookit East, I Lookit West' which Hogg also includes (in a later version) in Songs 1831 (see pp. 18–20).

Hogg used the text of the version in *Poetical Works* as his copy text for the text in *Songs* 1831. Once more retitled, here to 'A Widow's Wail', most of the changes to the text in 1822 are retained, though ll. 18–20 change from: 'Thy breast is cauld as clay: | An' a' my hope, an a' my joy, | Wi' thee are reft away' to: 'Thy kind wee heart is still, | An' thy dear spirit far away | Beyond the reach of ill'.

There are no extant manuscripts for this song. As with those immediately preceding it in *Songs* 1831 this song is missing from the fair-copy manuscript for *Songs* 1831 at at NLS MS 4805, ff. 26–102 (Blackwood Papers): see note to 'I'll No' Wake Wi' Annie'.

Publication History:

1810 – in *The Forest Minstrel*, pp. 3–4 – see (S/SC, 2006), pp. 11–12 and 209–14

1822 – in *Poetical Works*, IV, 349–50

1831 – in *Songs by the Ettrick Shepherd*, pp. 265–67 – see pp. 117–18 in the present edition

Musical Context:

Hogg nominates the traditional Scottish tune 'Gilderoy' as the melody for his song on all three occasions. The historical context of the tune, which dates back to the seventeenth century, is comprehensively discussed by Garside and Jackson in *The Forest Minstrel* pp. 211–14. They suggest that 'the sorrow expressed by Gilderoy's female companion within the ballads named after him is what led Hogg to associate this tune with his verses'. Hogg also notes that the song 'never was set to music' and indeed no musical settings have been located.

Auld Joe Nicholson's Nanny (pp. 118–9)

Creative Context:
As Hogg states clearly in his headnote, this song, with the slightly different title of 'Auld Joe Nicholson's Bonny Nannie. A Scotch Sang', appeared in the annual *Friendships's Offering* in 1829. Another two of the songs he includes in *Songs* 1831 were also published in the annual: 'The Broken Heart', which is partnered with 'Auld Joe Nicholson's Nanny' in *Songs* 1831, appeared with the title 'Ballad' (pp. 415–16) also in 1829, and 'Mischievous Woman' was included (with the title 'A Scots Love Sang') in the annual for 1830 (pp. 185–86).

Friendship's Offering, the popular London literary annual enjoyed a lengthy run of twenty years between 1824 and 1844. Between 1828 and his death in 1834 it was edited by Hogg's friend, the writer Thomas Pringle (1789–1834). Pringle was keen to enlist the support of Scottish acquaintances, and contributions from Allan Cunningham, D. M. Moir, R. P. Gillies and William Motherwell appeared alongside contributions from John Clare, Amelia Opie, Mary Howitt, Felicia Hemans and James Montgomery, amongst others. Seven of Hogg's contributions were published between 1828 and 1831. Further information on Hogg's long-standing relationship with Pringle can be found in Gillian Hughes's 'Notes on Correspondents' in *Letters*, I, 466–68 and Hogg's contributions are all available in *Contributions to Annuals and Gift Books* (S/SC, 2006), pp. 123–43.

Literary annuals were usually published around October–November of the year prior to their stated date, so that *Friendship's Offering* for 1829 was actually published in time for Christmas in 1828. This would then account for the almost simultaneous printing of Hogg's song within the *Noctes Ambrosianae* section (No. XL) of *Blackwood's Edinburgh Magazine* for December 1828. It fitted neatly into the *Noctean* discussions about literary annuals, and also promoted Hogg's contributions to them. In this issue 'North' asks James, 'Do, my dear James, give us "John Nicholson's Daughter" ', which, after a long digression he does. 'North' remarks, 'Bravo! You have sent that song to our friend Pringle's Friendship's Offering – haven't you, James?' And the 'Shepherd' replies, 'I hae – and anither as gude, or better – .'

Aside from usual orthographic changes 'bonny Nannie' becomes 'bonny Nanny', Hogg's 1831 version is almost identical to the earlier versions. There are only two notable changes between the text as it appears in *Blackwood's* and that in 1831: 'Her looks so gay o'er nature away' (l. 16), is replaced by 'Her looks that stray'd o'er nature away' (l. 16). And in l. 29 'dearest Nanny' becomes 'bonny Nanny' (l. 29).

No manuscript version of Hogg's song has been located. As with those immediately preceding it in *Songs* 1831 this song is missing from the fair-copy manuscript for *Songs* 1831 at at NLS MS 4805, ff. 26–102 (Blackwood Papers): see note to 'I'll No' Wake Wi' Annie'.

Publication History:
1828 – in *Blackwood's Edinburgh Magazine*, 24 (December 1828), 688 – see (S/SC, 2008), pp. 350–51 and 561

1829 – in *Friendship's Offering* (1829), pp. 263–64 – see *Contributions to Annuals and Gift Books*, (S/SC, 2006), pp. 123–24, 311 and 388

1831 – in *Songs by the Ettrick Shepherd*, pp. 268–70 – see pp. 118–19 in the present edition

Musical Context:
Hogg boldly states in his headnote for 1831 that he has 'composed an air for it myself' and, moreover, that he is sure he will always prefer his own tune to any other. He also states that he has 'refused all applications to have it set to music'. He does not name his tune, nor has it been located. But a later, most probably unauthorised, musical setting by John Blewitt has been found: 'Niddity, Noddity, Nannie. A Ballad in the Scottish Style, music by J. Blewit, 'Sung by Mr Wilson with Great Applause at the Theatre Royal, Covent Garden (London: Mori & Lavenu, 28 New Bond Street, *c.*1828–1839) Price 2s.' For a copy of this song and more information see – *Contributions to Musical Collections and Miscellaneous Songs*. Later versions of the song are found with an arrangement by John Fulcher in *The Casquet of Lyric Gems* (Glasgow: Bell and Bain, n.d.), pp. 234–35; and in *The Lyric Gems of Scotland* (Glasgow: David Jack, 1856), p. 129 (with unnamed melody only). Gooch and Thatcher list a further three versions of the song: 8659–8662.

The Broken Heart (pp. 119–20)

Creative Context:
As with the song immediately preceding it in *Songs* 1831 ('Auld Joe Nicholson's Nanny'), this song also first appeared in the annual *Friendship's Offering* in 1829. Further information about this literary annual and Hogg's involvement with it is given in the note above.

'The Broken Heart' appears to have been written specifically for *Friendship's Offering* and was one of four of Hogg's poems published in the annual that year. The editor Thomas Pringle was fastidious; keen to keep a strict moral tone and 'admit not a single expression' into the annual, 'which would call up a blush in the cheek of the most delicate female if reading aloud to a mixt company' (quoted in *Contributions to Annuals and Gift Books*, (S/SC, 2006, p. 310). As a result Hogg's contributions for him were mostly biographical and family-oriented. Under the title, 'Ballad. By the Ettrick Shepherd', this lyric focusses on a doomed romantic love-affair, exactly the kind of subject matter suited to this and other contemporary annuals.

When Hogg chose to include it in *Songs* 1831 he makes much of this personal connection by stating in his headnote that it involves 'a dearly-beloved young relative of my own'. His literary friend James Gray moved to India in 1826, and two of his daughters, Mary and Janet, stayed behind and lived for a time at Mount Benger with the Hoggs. Both were engaged to be married, although both engagements were subsequently broken off. The song was composed for Mary Gray, who was reportedly 'broken-hearted at being jilted' (*Contributions to Annuals and Gift Books*, pp. 311–12). Hogg's comment that it 'turned out a lucky disappointment' refers to her subsequent marriage to a Mr Robert Money, who, as Hogg described in his letter to Allan Cunningham of 18 October 1829, was 'a young English gentleman in the Company's civil service' whose 'character and prospects rank very high': see *Letters*, II, 355–56 (p. 355).

Hogg chose to retitle the song 'The Broken Heart' in *Songs* 1831 and he amended ll. 5–6 replacing 'No earthly sleep' with 'A slumber deep' (l. 5) and 'partially' with 'even a while'. In ll. 25–26 he emphasises the personal and local connections with the song by moving the setting to 'Yarrow' (l. 25) and changing 'primrose' to 'broom' (l. 26). Hogg chose to include a verse of another poem, 'Verses to a Beloved Young Friend', which had also appeared in *Friendship's Offering for 1829*, and which he notes in 1831 was 'written at the same time'. Currie and Hughes note that this poem was also written for Mary Gray on her 'departure from Mount Benger' in 1828 (p. 312).

The substantial portion of manuscript prepared for *Songs* 1831, located at NLS MS 4805, ff. 26–102 (Blackwood Papers), has a long gap beginning at the headnote to the incomplete song 'I'll No' Wake Wi' Annie', paginated '168' (f. 83v). The manuscript continues again at page '193', which is the beginning of the second verse (l. 9) of 'The Broken Heart' (f. 84r), so that the title, headnote and first verse of 'The Broken Heart' are not extant. Evidence that this portion of NLS MS 4805 was used in the final stages of printing is found in the printer's mark '273/S' at the right-hand side of the song which identifies the location of this page within the printed volume of *Songs* 1831, on page number 273 at gathering 'S'. Along with the usual addition of punctuation, the song appears to have been transmitted cleanly to the printed version.

Publication history:
1829 – in *Friendship's Offering* (1829), pp. 415–16 – see *Contributions to Annuals and Gift Books*, (S/SC, 2006), pp. 124–25, 311–12 and 388
1831 – in *Songs by the Ettrick Shepherd*, pp. 271–73 – see pp. 119–20 in the present edition
Unauthorised versions:
1831 – in *The Lady's Book* of Philadelphia: vol. 2 (June 1831), 330
1831 – in *The Lady's Book* of Philadelphia: vol. 3 (July 1831), 41
The copy text of both versions is *Songs* 1831. Further information on the reprinting of Hogg's work in American periodicals is found in Janette Currie's *Listing of Hogg Items in American Periodicals* on the *James Hogg Research* website, hosted by the Division of Literature & Languages, School of Arts & Humanities, at Stirling University: http://www.jameshogg.stir.ac.uk.

Musical Context:
Hogg gives no melody title and no musical setting has been located.

Explanatory Notes:
See *Contributions to Annuals and Gift Books* (S/SC, 2006), p. 388.

John o'Brackadale (pp. 120–21)

Creative Context:
This is one of the six songs in *Songs* 1831 to have originally appeared in Alexander Campbell's musical collection *Albyn's Anthology,* published in Edinburgh by Oliver & Boyd in two volumes in 1816 and 1818. For further information on this collection, Hogg's involvement with it and copies of the songs see: *Contributions to Musical Collections and Miscellaneous Songs.*

There is no evidence of an exact date of composition, but it would appear that Hogg created the song for Campbell's collection and so it must have been written sometime between February 1816 and February 1818. The song first appeared in the second volume in 1818.

The subject was clearly inspired by Hogg's Highland tour in summer 1803 when he visted Skye and the area around Bracadale. He wrote of his first sight of the the area from on board 'the sloop Grace of Greenock': 'about sunset we passed the three astonishing basaltic pillars called McLeods Maidens & shortly after opened Loch-Bracadale'. Hogg was impressed with both the island and its people and formed the opinion, 'there is so much kindness & unanimity amongst them, that I could not help pronouncing the people happy in my own mind And viewing Sky as a little Paradise': see *Highland Journeys*, ed. by Hans de Groot (S/SC, 2010), pp. 136–37.

The song next appeared in 1822 in Hogg's *Poetical Works*, where the copy text is the *Albyn's Anthology* version, without change. The 'air' nominated below the title is 'Nuair a thig an Samhra' (see below).

For its inclusion in *Songs* 1831 Hogg significantly altered the wording from the original. In the refrain he removes the line 'Wae's me gin you should fail' found in the previous two versions. And he completely revises the text of the second verse. The original version comically recounts how the people of 'Portree' and 'myself' will lament the death of John of Brackadale, even although 'the weary usquebae | Will grow cheaper by a third' (ll. 15–21). In the revised version, the song laments John's passing, 'just when the glorious usquebae | Is growing cheaper by a third' (ll. 14–17).

The only extant manuscript of the song is found in the fair-copy manuscript for *Songs* 1831 at NLS MS 4805, ff. 26–102 (Blackwood Papers), f. 84v. The single folio is page-numbered '194' and follows immediately after 'The Broken Heart', a sequence followed in the printed volume. A significant difference in the wording between Hogg's fair-copy holograph and the printed volume occurs at ll. 4 and 25. Hogg clearly writes the word 'drunken' to describe John of Brackadale. However, in the published version of the song the word is changed to 'brave'. The remainder of Hogg's unpunctuated text is transferred cleanly to the printed volume.

Publication History:

1818 – in *Albyn's Anthology*, ii, 78 – see *Contributions to Musical Collections and Miscellaneous Songs* (S/SC, 2014)

1822 – in *Poetical Works*, iv, 319–20

1831 – in *Songs by the Ettrick Shepherd*, pp. 274–75 – see pp. 120–21 in the present edition

Musical Context:

Hogg's version of 'John of Bracadale' in *Albyn's Anthology* was one of three songs Campbell gave for the air 'Nuair a thig an samhra', (on p. 78) which appears to be the opening phrase of the first song titled 'Oran Sugradh'. Campbell explains in his collection that he took down the air whie he was in Skye 'in anno 1815, from the singing of Donald Nicolson, Esq. of Scorbreck' and that the key set of lyrics were by 'his late friend, the Rev. Hugh Macdonald of Portree'.

Explanatory Notes:

120 [Title] **Bracadale** is 'a hamlet and a parish in the W of Skye, Inverness-shire. The hamlet lies at the head of Loch Bracadale, about ½ mile E of Struan hamlet' (Groome).

120, l. 5 **by Moravich** a hamlet some 16 miles east of the Kyle of Lochalsh on the west coast of Scotland. In Hogg's day the main route to Skye passed through Morvich.

120, ll. 7–8 At his nose a siller queich | At his knee a water-pail? a 'quaich' is a two-handled drinking cup, in this case, made from silver. Previous versions of the song the used the word 'copper' here, which more explicitly refers to the traditional method of distilling whisky in copper stills. Water is one of the main ingredients of whisky.

121, ll. 16–17 Just when the glorious usquebae | Is growing cheaper by a third meaning not clear. Taxation on whisky increased during the eighteenth century.

Bauldy Frazer (pp. 121–22)

Creative Context:
This is one of Hogg's early songs (there are clear links to his 'first' song 'Donald MacDonald', pp. 3–5) and he first mentions it in a letter to Walter Scott of 22 February 1805. Here Hogg discusses his plans to publish a collection of 'Ballads in imitation of the Ancients' (ultimately, *The Mountain Bard*) along with some letters of his Highland journeys. Hogg writes: 'In my last I have written some songs. One *Bauldy Frazers description of the battle of Cullodden*' [*sic*] I intend sending to the magazine' (*Letters*, I, 48–49 (p. 48)). 'In my last' might refer to several letters giving biographical information about 'the Ettrick Shepherd', which were written by 'A Constant Reader' and 'Z' and published in the January, March, July and November numbers of the *Scots Magazine* during 1805. The letter of March 1805 reports that '*Two very ingenious pieces will appear in our next*', which refers both to this song and to 'Love Abused', both included in the April issue. The letters to the *Scots Magazine* are published in James Hogg, *The Mountain Bard* (S/SC, 2007), pp. 125–36. Hogg includes both songs in *Songs* 1831 though 'Love Abused' is titled 'The Gloamin' (see pp. 75–76).

In their note to the song in *The Forest Minstrel* (S/SC, 2006) Garside and Jackson suggest that Hogg drew on oral sources from battle-veterans he met during his journeys into the Highlands in the early 1800s and that he may have conflated different elements of the stories he heard. As the 'Explanatory notes' here suggest Hogg may also have drawn extensively from John Home's *The History of the Rebellion in the Year 1745* (London: T. Cadell and W. Davies, 1802) for historical information. In early versions of the song Hogg blames 'Charlie an' the brave Lochyell (l. 17) for choosing Drummossie moor as the theatre of war, which Garside and Jackson note 'is more akin to folk knowledge than historical record' (p. 330). Home records (on pp. 220–25) that, after 'Locheil' joins the rebel army at Culloden-wood 'in the evening of the 14th' of April, Charles 'proposed to march with all his forces' that evening and cross the River Nairn at 'Kilraick, or Kilravock' to Nairn where the Duke's army had set up camp. Locheil opposes this plan and proposes 'that the army would be stronger the next day' (pp. 219–20). The night march went ahead but took longer than planned and around 2 o'clock in the morning, with Nairn some three miles still in the distance, Locheil and others stopped the march and provoked a row over whether to turn back or press ahead and attack in daylight. While Lord George Murray and others argued for abandoning the attack, 'John Hay' (also mentioned by Hogg as taking an active part in the plans), advised Charles 'that unless he came to the front, and ordered Lord George Murray to go on, nothing would be done.' Charles rode out but met the Highland army marching back towards Culloden and did not manage to turn them back. Verse three refers to this altercation and to the battle plans and repeats the opinion, suggested by Home, that the Jacobites would have defeated the King's forces 'had we met wi' Cumberland, | By Athol braes or yonder strand' (ll. 21–22) or, more specifically in later versions, to 'ford of Spey or Prae-Calrook' or Kilvarock. Hogg includes 'Cluny of Macpherson' along with 'Hay' in early versions of the song (ll. 33–34) even although Home provides evidence that Cluny missed the actual battle. While this may, as Garside and Jackson suggest, indicate that Hogg's information is 'anecdotal' (p. 329) it may also indicate careful dafting of the historical information to create an 'authentic' oral account of the battle.

A full account of the textual and publishing history the song is given in *The Forest Minstrel* (S/SC, 2006). Garside and Jackson note the specific changes to the text between its first printing in *The Scots Magazine* in 1805 and subsequent appearance in *The Forest Minstrel* in 1810 where the final stanza is notably omitted. They note the conversion of 'he' to 'she' in l. 38 of the text and explain this by noting that 'the use of the feminine third-person pronoun' is a 'substitiute for 'he' or 'I' in Highland speech in English. There is substantial alteration of the wording when the song appears next in 1821 as 'Song XIV'in the Appendix to the *Jacobite Relics* II. Here the 'broken Highland dialect', as Hogg calls it in his 1831 headnote, is intensified. Hogg's highland dialect is achieved by combining a number of literary and linguistic effects, such as swapping the values of letters or missing out letters: so that 'p' stands for 'b' such as 'pe' or 'be', 't' replaces 'd' such as 'Cullotin' or 'Culloden', 'f' replaces 'v' as in 'nefer' or 'never', 's' replaces 'z' as in 'plase' or blaze, 'c' and 'k' replaces 'g' as in 'cot' or 'got' and 'ket' or 'get', and so on. Words where it is thought Hogg's usage may cause confusion are included in the Glossary. In 1821 Hogg also adds a new stanza entirely beginning 'Macpherson and Macgregor poth'. The version of the song in his 1822 *Poetical Works* sticks closely to that in *Jacobite Relics*.

In *Songs* 1831 Hogg makes some notable changes to his text. While there are clear connections to the 1821/22 appearances of the song, the 1831 text contains several new passages and there is clear evidence, from the fair-copy manuscript, that Hogg has redrafted the text. Notably ll. 5–8 are new and the sixth verse is now omitted, but there is redrafting of specific words in almost every other verse. The Highland dialect is even more overt in 1831 and there are orthographic changes, so that 'Drumboy/Dumbroy' becomes 'Dunvey' (l. 32).

The only extant holograph version of this early song known to survive is found in the fair-copy manuscript for *Songs* 1831 at NLS MS 4805, ff. 26–102 (Blackwood Papers) at f. 85. The song follows immediately after 'John of Brackadale' (f. 84) which is page-numbered '194', following the consequential page ordering of '195' and '196'. The song begins 'My name is' but the 'My' and 'is' are scored out and 'Her' and 'pe' inserted above.

Publication History:

1805 – in *The Scots Magazine,* 67 (April), 295

1810 – in *The Forest Minstrel,* pp. 166–69 – see (S/SC, 2006), pp. 155–57 and 329–32

1821 – in *Jacobite Relics,* II, 415–17 – and (S/SC, 2003), 415–17 and 527

1822 – in *Poetical Works,* IV, 345–48

1831 – *Songs by the Ettrick Shepherd,* pp. 276–79 – see pp. 121–22 in the present edition

Unauthorised versions:

1818 – in *The Harp of Caledonia* (3 vols.) (Glasgow: Khull, Blackie &Co.; Edinburgh:

A. Fullarton, n.d. [*c.*1818]), II, 239–41

1829 – in *The Scottish Songs*, ed. Robert Chambers, (Edinburgh: Ballantyne & Co.)
I, 267–68.

These are both derived from the version printed in *The Forest Minstrel* in 1810.

Musical Context:

The traditional Scottish tune 'Whigs of Fife' is nominated for every version of
the song. Below the version in *Jacobite Relics*, Hogg notes 'For the Air, see Song
XVII', which in the main body of the volume is 'The Whigs of Fife' (pp. 41–42).
Hogg clearly drew on the traditional Jacobite song, which he argues is 'coeval'
with the air, when composing his own Jacobite song. Written against the 'whigs
of fife' who, like Cumberland in later versions of Hogg's song, 'came frae hell', it
describes, as Hogg also does, how 'Thae hunds hae huntit owre the plain' (l. 14).
Full details of the historical and Musical Context are provided in *The Forest
Minstrel* (S/SC, 2006), pp. 332. In summary, the tune is found in most of the major
eighteenth-century music collections, including Bremner's *Collection of Scots Reels or
Country Dances* (1769), p. 98.

Explanatory Notes:

121, l. 1 bauldy 'bauld' is 'brave' in Scots; also the derivative of the name
   Archibald. Sir Simon Fraser, Lord Lovat, sent Clan Fraser under the
   command of his eldest son to reinforce the Jacobite forces. However,
   during the time of the actual battle, the younger Lovat was on his way to
   Inverness to collect reinforcements, so that the song is not based on the
   real Lords Lovat but an imaginary Jacobite rebel, one of the foot-soldiers
   named 'Archibald Fraser'. Lord Lovat (the elder) was executed in England
   in 1747, holding the distinction of being the last nobleman executed for his
   part in the uprising.

121, l. 4 Cullotin the battle at Culloden was fought on Drummossie Moor on 16
   April 1746.

121, l. 12 Heelant mans to flee Fraser [Lord Lovat], 'having gone to his father's
   country, which is near Inverness, to bring up the men wanted to compleat his
   regiment (to which a second battalion had been added), he was coming with
   300 men; and when halfway between Inverness and Culloden, he met the
   Highlanders flying from the field': John Home, *The History of the Rebellion in the
   Year 1745* (1802), p. 239.

121, l. 13 cannon and te pluff dragoon Cumberland's army 'chiefly consisted' of
   'cannon and cavalry': *The History of the Rebellion in the Year 1745* (1802), p. 220.

122, l. 19 To plant tem on te open fell in earlier versions of the song Hogg
   blames 'Charlie and' the brave Lochyell (l. 17) for choosing Drummossie
   moor as the theatre of war. In an 'Appendix' to *The History of the Rebellion in
   the Year 1745* Home published an account by Lord George Murray in which
   he claims to have proposed 'to retire to the other side of the river Nairn, and
   occupy a piece of ground which he said was a much more proper field of battle
   for Highlanders than the plain muir where the army was drawn up' (1802),
   footnote, p. 219 and 'Appendix No. 42'.

122, l. 21 gruesome Tuke Prince William Augustus, Duke of Cumberland
   (1721–1765), army officer and the 'second surviving son of George, prince of
   Wales, the future George II, and his wife, Caroline' (W. A. Speck, *ODNB*). See
   Explanatory Notes for 'Farewell to Glen-Shalloch' (p. 12).

122, l. 22 Spey or Prae-Calrook after leaving their base at Cullen with further reinforcements on 12 April, Cumberland's forces crossed the River Spey 'without opposition, though it was generally expected that the passage of the river would be disputed'. Although 'a considerable part of the rebel army, under the Duke of Perth, lay on the north-west side of the river Spey', they were outnumbered by the King's forces and therefore under 'orders to retreat without coming to an action' (*The History of the Rebellion in the Year 1745* (1802), p. 216).

122, ll. 27–28 **mony a bonny Heelant lad | Lay pleeding on te prae, man** it is estimated that around 3600 Jacobites were killed at Culloden (see W. A. Speck, entry for 'Prince William Augustus' in *ODNB*). See also the Explanatory Notes for 'Farewell to Glen-Shalloch', (p. 12).

122, ll. 29–32 **Fat could she too, fat could she say? | Te crand M'Tonald was away | And her nown chief tat luckless tay | Po far peyond Dunvey** Hogg echoes Home's discussion of the crisis caused by Lovat's failure to raise substantial forces of men in time to reach Culloden prior to the commencement of the battle (*The History of the Rebellion in the Year 1745* (1802), p. 135).

122, ll. 33–36 **M'Pherson and M'Gregor poth, | Te men of Moidart and Glen-quoich, | And cood M'Kenzies of te Doich, | All absent from te field** John Home (1802) records that around '3000' men belonging to the rebel army were absent from the battle (*The History of the Rebellion in the Year 1745*, p. 218)

122, l. 41 **Sharles** Prince Charles Edward Stuart (1720–1788): see the Explanatory Notes for 'Donald MacDonald', (p. 3).

122, ll. 43–44 **"Turn, turn," he cryít, "and face tem yet, | We'll conquer, or we'll tee, man!"** the germ of Hogg's imaginary account of the event is found in Home: 'When Charles saw the Highlanders repulsed and flying, which he had never seen before, he advanced, it is said, to go down and rally them. But the earnest entreaties of his tutor, Sir Thomas Sheridan, and others, who assured him that it was impossible, prevailed upon him to leave the field' (*The History of the Rebellion in the Year 1745* (1802), pp. 239–40).

122, l. 48 **hanging on te tree** the penalty for treason was death by 'hanging, drawing and quartering'. An Act of Attainder passed in June 1746 meant that 'the rights of trial were dispensed with' and rebels could be summarily executed without trial' (Frank McLynn, *Crime and Punishment in Eighteenth-Century England* (Abingdon: Routledge, 1989), pp. 156–59).

122, ll. 49–50 **ploody Tuke, fat ail't her ten, | To rafage every Heelant glen?** For details of 'butcher Cumberland' and the post-Culloden ravaging of the Highland clans, see the Explanatory Notes for 'Farewell to Glen-Shalloch', (p. 12).

Hymn to the Evening Star (p. 123)

Creative Context:
This song is another of Hogg's 1831 songs which was initially written for and included in his weekly magazine, *The Spy*. Hogg states in his 1831 headnote that this song was created in 1811. A longer version comprising some forty lines in quatrains appeared in the magazine in August that year. It then appeared in several different publications across the next two decades.

Around 1815 it was revised for William Dunbar's *The Nithsdale Minstrel*. Nothing is known about Hogg's involvement with this collection, though another three of his songs appeared there, including 'Courting Song' which is also in *Songs* 1831 (pp. 91–92). The copy text for 'Hymn to the Evening Star' is clearly that found in *The Spy* with some variations: for example, 'east' becomes 'west' (l. 7), 'silken' becomes 'purple' (l. 22) and 'radiant' becomes 'orient' (l. 35). The final verse is freshly drafted, so that 'Rapt in devotion's wildest dream' is changed to 'And pay the vows I made to thee' (l. 38). Furthermore, the song concludes with the words 'western sea' replacing 'morning beam' (l. 40).

The song then appeared in 1818 in the second volume of Alexander Campbell's musical collection *Albyn's Anthology*. For further information about Hogg's involvement with this collection and for a copy of the song see *Contributions to Musical Collections and Miscellaneous Songs*. Campbell claims that the song was 'never before published'. This is partly true as Hogg clearly revises his 1815 text substantially for Campbell. Verse seven is omitted and there is fresh wording scattered throughout the song: for example, 'canopy of blue' replaces 'throne so bright and blue' (l. 4) and at l. 21 'O let thy spirit seek the glade' replaces 'Say wilt thou hover o'er my head'. The closing lines receive further revision, with 'modest light' (l. 35) replacing 'silver light' (l. 39) while the final line is again revised with 'Is cradled on the heaving sea' (l. 36) replacing 'Evanish of the western sea' (l. 40). In 1822 Hogg included the song in the fourth volume of his *Poetical Works*. The copy text is the version in *Albyn's Anthology* with one slight variant over ll. 23–24, where the possessive 'my cheek' and 'my careless arm' changes to third person, 'thy cheek' and 'thy careless arm'.

Hogg retains the version in *Albyn's Anthology* as his copy text for the version included in *Songs* 1831 and makes only one significant change: ll. 21–24 are removed and the text is arranged in four octets.

There are two extant manuscripts for 'Hymn to the Evening Star'. Hogg's holograph manuscript prepared around 1815 for *The Nithsdale Minstrel* is extant at the Mitchell Library, Special Collections, Cowie Collection, MS 283 c. The manuscript is watermarked 'Fellows 1812'. Unusually, the text is fully punctuated so that version probably represents Hogg's final fair copy.

Hogg's fair-copy holograph manuscript of the version of the song he prepared for *Songs* 1831 is found among fair-copy manuscript at NLS MS 4805, ff. 26–102 (Blackwood Papers) at f. 86. The song is paginated '197' and '198' and follows immediately after 'Bauldy Frazer' in the same sequential order of the printed volume. Hogg's text is transferred cleanly to the printed volume.

Publication history:
1811– in *The Spy*, No. 49 (3 August 1811), 342 [mispaged] – see (S/SC, 2000), pp. 73–74
1815 – in *The Nithsdale Minstrel: Being Original Poetry Chiefly by the Bards of Nithsdale*, (Dumfries: C. Munro & Co. for Preacher and Dunbar), pp. 26–28
1818 – in *Albyn's Anthology*, II, 39 – see *Contributions to Musical Collections and Miscellaneous Songs* (S/SC, 2014)
1822 – in *Poetical Works*, IV, 240–42
1831 – in *Songs by the Ettrick Shepherd*, pp. 280–82 – see p. 123 in the present edition

Musical Context:
Hogg names no melody or air for 'Hymn to the Evening Star'. In *Albyn's Anthology* the song is placed as second lyric after one beginning 'Young Maidens I to You Consign', 'Written by a lady – both songs are intended to be sung to the arrangement given on the opposite page. In an editorial footnote Campbell

writes, 'This fine Melody is one of the many that have lain long dormant; it was communicated to the Editor by the Hon. Mrs Baron Norton. The words were written by an intimate and lamented friend of hers, a Lady of great worth and elegant acquirements, many years since dead' (II, 39). The melody is unnamed.

Explanatory Notes:
123 [Title] the evening star is the planet Venus the first star to appear in the night sky.

Ohon-A-Righ! (pp. 124–25)

Creative Context:
Like 'Ye Breezes that Spring', also included in *Songs* 1831 (p.59), this song first appeared in Hogg's drama *The Royal Jubilee. A Scottish Mask* (Edinburgh: William Blackwood) in 1822. It is there sung to the traditional tune 'Killiecrankie' and appears as 'Song V' performed by the 'Scottish Fairies' to the 'Genius of the Gael' who, as Douglas Mack notes, is a 'figure representative of the culture of Highland Scotland, and clearly modelled on Ossian, the blind third-century warrior-bard of Gaelic tradition' (S/SC, 2008, p. 187, note 132–33). At this point in the drama, the Fairy Queen (who represents 'the old world' of 'pre-Reformation and pre-Enlightenment Scotland': note to p. 126) discusses how the Highlanders have altered their military position. Whereas they once fought for the Jacobites, they are now fighting on behalf of the Hanoverian King George. But Hogg retains a Jacobite element with the refrain 'Ohon a'righ!' which translates 'Alas for the King'. This refrain is also used in 'The Stuarts of Appin' (see pp. 28–30) and in 'Oh-hon, Oh Righ!' (p. 57). Hogg glosses the Gaelic phrase 'Oh-hon an Rei' in a presentation holograph manuscript of 'The Appin Coronach' (NLS, Acc. 10001). It is the song in *The Royal Jubilee* which Hogg then uses as copy text for *Songs* 1831 and notably he changes the title to 'Ohon-a-Righ!' in this later version. Hogg gives no idea of the original dramatic context, but his 1831 headnote does clearly note that he wanted the song to be 'a humble petition' to King George IV to 'restore the titles of the last remnants of the brave defenders'. Hogg refers here to the estates of Jacobite-supporting Clan chiefs, whose clan-lands were forfeited following Jacobite uprisings in 1680, 1716 and 1745. These estates were managed for the Crown by a committee of Edinburgh lawyers acting as the Forfeited Estates Commission. In 1784, Parliament enacted a bill, proposed by Dundas and seconded by Pitt, 'for the Restoration of the Estates Forfeited in the Rebellion of 1745'. Subsequently, the majority of forfeited estates were restored to 'the heirs of the former proprietors, upon certain terms and conditions', including a fine: see *The Speeches of the Honourable Charles James Fox, in the House of Commons*, 6 vols (London, 1815), III, 14–15. Murray Pittock writes how the occasion of the King's visit to Scotland in 1822 'gave rise to a Memorial requesting the restoration of attainted peerages. In 1824, Parliament duly restored the peerage to Mar, Kenmure, Perth, Strathallan and Nairne': see *Poetry and Jacobite Politics in Eighteenth-Century Britain and Ireland* (Cambridge: Cambridge University Press, 1994), p. 236.

There are few variants between the 1822 and 1831 versions of the song: 'Sovereign' is no longer capitalised in 1831 and in l.42 the Highland 'pe' is anglicised to 'be'.

A manuscript for the 1822 first printing of *The Royal Jubliee* has not been located. Hogg's fair-copy holograph of 'Ohon-a-Righ!' survives the fair-copy manuscript for *Songs* 1831 at NLS MS 4805, ff. 26–102 (Blackwood Papers) at f. 87. Aside from the usual addition of punctuation, the song has been transmitted cleanly to the printed version.

Publication History:

1822 – in *The Royal Jubilee. A Scottish Mask* (Edinburgh: William Blackwood), pp. 24–26 – see *The Bush Aboon Traquair and The Royal Jubilee* (S/SC, 2008), pp. 136–38 and 189–90

1831 – in *Songs by the Ettrick Shepherd*, pp. 283–85 – see pp. 124–25 in the present edition

Musical Context:

Hogg gives no melody or air title in *Songs* 1831, but the song is clearly set for the traditional Scottish melody 'Killiecrankie' when it appears in *The Royal Jubilee* in1822 with musical notation. It was common practice for pamphlets and magazines to include musical notation for melodies only (the same is true for several of Hogg's songs in *Blackwood's Edinburgh Magazine*: see 'When the kye comes hame' pp. 25–27). Hogg knew the melody and had already used it several times. It is the melody named for 'The Auld Highlandman' in *The Forest Minstrel* (1810), pp. 177–80; and Hogg prints it twice in *Jacobite Relics* I: 'Song XVII', 'The Braes of Killiecrankie' (pp. 28–30) and 'Song XIX', 'Killiecrankie' (pp. 189–200). Full details about the history of the melody can be found in the recent S/SC edition of *The Forest Minstrel* (2006), pp. 337–40. In summary, it is one of the most popular Scottish tunes of the period.

Explanatory Notes:

124, l. 36 As Donald does for Geordie 'Donald' signifies all Scotsman. Hogg's eponymous patriotic Highlandman 'Donald Macdonald' had shown how Scots could unite under the British flag in the early 1800s. See *Songs* 1831, pp. 3–5.

125, l. 37 Beannaich-an-righ! 'this Gaelic phrase means "Blessings on the King!"': see *The Royal Jubilee*, ed. by Douglas S. Mack (S/SC, 2008), note to p. 137.

125, l. 45 braolich another Gaelic word, meaning 'make a loud noise' (*The Royal Jubilee* (S/SC, 2008), note to p. 138.

The Laddie That I Ken O' (p. 125)

Creative Context:

This is a late song and is the last of ten songs in *Songs* 1831, which Hogg had already contributed to the *Edinburgh Literary Journal*. Untitled, this song first appeared there in March 1829 as the final song in 'Noctes Bengeriane' No. II By the Ettrick Shepherd'. For further information about 'Noctes Bengeriane' see the note to 'Black Mary' (p.51). The song is part of a brief dramatic scene featuring five characters who converse with one another about love and songs, and Jean completes the scene with this song. The sketch also includes 'O saw ye this sweet bonny lassie o' mine', 'Auld John Nichol' and an Irish love song called 'Denis Delaney'.

Hogg uses this *Edinburgh Literary Journal* appearance as copy text for the song he includes in 1831 and there are one or two changes: l.6 'waled' becomes 'woo'd' in 1831; l.11 'cunning' becomes 'demure'; l.12 Burn's' becomes 'Burns''.

Hogg makes clear reference in the song to his ancestor in Scottish song, Robert Burns, and he chooses to include the names of several of the key women in

Burns's life: Annie, probably refers to to Ann (or [Helen] Anna) Park (*b.* 1770) who bore Burns's daughter, Elizabeth, born on 31 March 1791; Nancy is most probably Mrs Agnes McLehose (1758–1841), the 'Clarinda' with whom Burns corresponded; Mary is most probably a reference to Mary Campbell (1763–1786), known more familiarly as 'Highland Mary'; and Jean is Burns's wife Jean Armour (1765–1834).

There are two manuscript versions of the song. The first is at MS Papers 42, Item No. 60 (Alexander Turnbull Library [ATL], New Zealand) and is an untitled draft of the *Edinburgh Literary Journal* version of the song. Peter Garside records that the song is written on 'a single leaf, 23 x19cm. WM: horn device visible': see 'An Annotated Checklist of Hogg's literary manuscripts in the Alexander Turnbull library, Wellington, New Zealand' in *The Bibliotheck*, 5–23 (p. 19).

The 1831 song is part of the fair-copy manuscript for *Songs* 1831 at NLS MS 4805, ff. 26–102 (Blackwood Papers), f. 88r. The text covers a single folio page-numbered '206' and follows immediately after 'Ohon-a-righ'. Hogg's unpunctuated text is transferred cleanly to the printed version.

Publication History:
1829 – in *Edinburgh Literary Journal*, No. 19 (21 March), 260, as the final song in 'Noctes Bengeriane' No. II By the Ettrick Shepherd' which appears on pp. 257–260
1831 – in *Songs by the Ettrick Shepherd*, pp. 286–87– see p. 125 in the present edition

Musical Context:
Hogg does not give a melody or air for this song. No musical setting been located.

Explanatory Notes:
125, l. 18 An' he'll tirl at the pin rattle or tap at the door latch to draw the attention of the lover within. This phrase also appears in the original text of the Jacobite song 'Charlie is my Darling', which Hogg includes in *Jacobite Relics,* II, ('Song L', pp. 93–94) alongside a modern version of the text. Hogg includes the modern version earlier in *Songs* 1831 (pp. 45–46), but notably it is the original text which has connections with Burns (see *Jacobite Relics,* II, (S/SC, 2003), p. 506).

O Lady Dear (p. 126)

Creative Context:
Hogg's 1831 headnote states that this short lyric was initially included in his long narrative poem *The Queen's Wake: A Legendary Poem* published in Edinburgh in 1813, where it simply appeared as part of the introduction as 'The Song'. In his notes to the recent S/SC edition of the poem Douglas Mack writes of the significance of the song to the poem as a whole: 'the Queen's heart, "to nature true" (l. 197), responds warmly to the "simple native melody" (l. 204) of the "Caledonian lyre" (l. 207). The poem features a singing contest which ranges across three nights and includes a wide range of songs and ballads from all over Scotland, performed by a number of different bards, minstrels and singers. They perform for Mary, who has just arrived from France as Queen of Scots. At the end of the final evening she selects the winning Bard, Gardyn, the Ossianic harper from the North West. But the 'Bard of Ettrick' makes a case for himself, and, in conclusion the Queen

awards him the new 'Caledonian Harp'. 'The Song' in the Introduction is clearly in anticipation of this (p. 405n).

Between 1813 and 1819, as noted by Mack, six editions of *The Queen's Wake* appeared which included four different authorial versions. Collation of 'The Song' in each of these four editions reveals that the text remains stable.

The Queen's Wake is so important to Hogg's output that it assumes the first of the four volumes of Hogg's 1822 *Poetical Works*. As Mack has noted, the sixth edition of 1819 is the text which becomes the standard version and it is the text used for 1822. There are no substantive variants: the variant spelling of the word 'flowret' at l. 8, which becomes 'floweret', is most likely the work of the printer.

Hogg's decision to include the song in *Songs* 1831 may have to do with the song's musical popularity (see 'Musical Context'). At the time of proposing his *Songs by the Ettrick Shepherd* to William Blackwood, Hogg did suggest that he also publish 'a handsome 12mo edition of The Queen's Wake': [letter of 30 September 1830], *Letters*, II, 400–01 (401). While this did not happen it should be little surprise that Hogg would therefore wish to use *Songs* 1831 as a promotional tool for the songs from the poem. Immediately following 'O Lady Dear' he includes 'The Spectre's Cradle-Song' and 'Hymn to the God of the Sea', with the note that these are 'pieces that might be successfully set to music'. Retitled, 'O, Lady dear' from the first line of the song, the layout in *Songs* 1831 is altered from the original two quatrain format to an octet. One substantive alteration occurs at l.7, where 'maiden' of all previous versions becomes 'virgin'.

The only extant holograph version known to survive is found in the fair-copy manuscript for *Songs* 1831 at NLS MS 4805, ff. 26–102 (Blackwood Papers), f 88v. The single folio is page-numbered '202'. Hogg's holograph has evidence of Hogg rethinking his original plan as he put his collection together. Below the text of the song Hogg adds a footnote of further information beginning with the words 'I also composed an air for it', and indicates with an arrow that the additional information should be incorporated in the main headnote. The text is transferred cleanly to the printed volume and Hogg's wishes are carried out with all the information incorporated into the headnote.

Publication History:
1813 – in *The Queen's Wake: A Legendary Poem*, p. 12 – see (S/SC, 2005), p. 12
1822 – in *Poetical Works*, I, 14
1831 – in *Songs by the Ettrick Shepherd*, p. 288 – see p. 126 in the present edition

Musical Context:
The popularity of *The Queen's Wake* may be the reason for the subsequent musical interest in this short lyric. Both Gillian Hughes and Douglas Mack refer to the setting Hogg mentions: 'An advertisement under the 'New Music' section of the *Edinburgh Evening Courant* for 1 July 1813 notes that ' "O Lady Dear" (described as "A Song from *The Queen's Wake*") is this day published" by Penson, Robertson of Edinburgh, as "the first of a series from that work" ', (*The Queen's Wake* (S/SC, 2004), p. 405). However, to date no scholar has been able to locate a copy of Monzanni's song sheet. Monzanni has also not been identified, though there is a popular composer named Joseph Mazzinghi (1765–1844) who had found inspiration in Walter Scott for some of his compositions.

Hogg's note also mentions his composing an air or melody for the song known by the title 'The Cameronian's Midnight Hymn', which he notes is also in his novel *The Brownie of Bodsbeck*. A song titled 'A Cameronian's Midnight Hymn' is printed with musical notation in the first volume of *The Brownie of Bodsbeck*, 2 vols (Edinburgh: William Blackwood; London: Cadell), I, 291. Interestingly, Ian Duncan discusses Hogg's plans in April 1813 for a two-volume edition of *Scottish Rural Tales*, which probably included *The Brownie of Bodsbeck*: see the 'Introduction' to *Winter Evening Tales* (S/SC, revised paperback, 2004), pp. xiv–xvii. 'A Cameronian's Midnight Hymn' might therefore have been composed in the same year that the first version of 'O Lady Dear' was published in *The Queen's Wake*. Hogg's 'O Lady Dear' does indeed match his melody for 'A Cameronian's Midnight Hymn' and the solemnity of the hymn suits the tenor of the lyric well. However, 'O Lady Dear' is two lines too long to fit the printed tune snugly, and it would require a repetition of the final phrase to fit the text properly. No copy of the song with this melody has been located.

Hogg's wish that further songs from the poem be set to music is notable in his inclusion of the three songs in 1831. But his correspondence to George Thomson back in 1815 did raise the issue of their suitability for singing. In his letter to Hogg of 18 October 1815 in which he discusses contributions to his Scottish collection (see 'Mischievous Woman' above), Thomson states: 'The Bard's songs in the Queen's Wake are immortal, but from their length are for reading, not for singing' (BL Add Mss 35,267, ff. 160–61).

Jon Finson records a version of 'The Song', retitled 'The Minstrel's Song', published in 1818 by Thomas Van Dyke Wiesenthal (1790–1831). As Finson comments: 'American-born' Wiesenthal, 'a naval surgeon by profession, set at least one poem from *Rokeby* in 1818, "Oh! Lady Twine no Wreath for Me! ("The Cypress Wreath"), and in the same series he included 'The Minstrel's Song' (Philadelphia: Bacon & Co., 1818) with lyrics from James Hogg's poem, *The Queen's Wake*'. Finson reproduces this in *The Voices that are Gone: Themes in Nineteenth-century American Popular Music* (Oxford: Oxford University Press, 1994), pp. 16–17. For a copy of the song see *Contributions to Musical Collections and Miscellaneous Songs*.

Robert Archibald Smith includes a variant of Hogg's melody 'A Cameronian Midnight Hymn' with the unattributed lyric beginning 'Thy father, my bairnie, will ne'er come hame' in *The Scotish Minstrel*, [1824], VI, 89.

The Spectre's Cradle Song (pp. 126–27)

Creative Context:
As with the song which immediately precedes it in *Songs* 1831, 'The Spectre's Cradle Song' first appears in *The Queen's Wake* in 1813. It is performed by an unidentified Highland minstrel ('Warrior he was in battle maimed' (l. 722)), during 'Night the Second' of the bardic competition at the Palace of Holyrood in Edinburgh in front of Mary, Queen of Scots.

In his notes to the 1813 edition of *The Queen's Wake* Hogg explains that the song 'is founded on a popular Highland tradition' he heard while 'travelling up Glen-Dochart, attended by Donald Fisher, a shepherd of that country'. Fisher pointed out 'some curious green dens' whose name 'in the Gaelic language, signifies, *the abode of the fairies*.' Hogg then goes on to recount how 'a native of that country, who is still living' had stayed overnight at the place:

About midnight he was awaked by the most enchanting music; and on listening, he heard it to be the voice of a woman singing to her child. She sung the verses twice over, so that next morning he had several of them by heart. Fisher had heard them often recited in Gaelic, and he said they were wild beyond human conception. He remembered only a few lines, which were to the same purport as the Spirit's song here inserted, namely, that she (the singer) had brought her babe from the regions below to be cooled by the breeze of the world, and that they would soon be obliged to part, for the child was going to heaven, and she was to remain for a season in purgatory. I had not before heard any thing so truly romantic. (Note, XI, *The Queen's Wake* (S/SC, 2004), pp. 184–85 (p. 185))

As with 'O Lady Dear', the text appeared in the subsequent editions of *The Queen's Wake* throughout the 1810s. Collation between the 'four distinct authorial versions' of 'The Spectre's Cradle Song' reveals some minor fine-tuning in the 1819 sixth edition, which became the standard version. A new line is created: 'O weep not thou for thy mother's ill' appears for the first time (l. 27), and the final line changes from a repetition of the final line of the first verse (l. 14), 'Smile now, my bonny babe! Smile on me!' to a repetition of the first line, 'Hush, my bonny babe! hush and be still!' (l. 28).

The version of the song which appears in the first volume of Hogg's 1822 *Poetical Works* uses the 1819 version as copy text. In l.9 'travail'd' is changed to 'travelled', which is possibly the result of a printer's error and not an authorial change.

In 1831 Hogg appears to use the 1819 text also as copy text. This is suggested by his reverting to 'Smile now, my bonny babe! Smile on me!' at l. 14. But Hogg makes some other significant changes for 1831. He amends the layout, making it appear more like a song rather than a poetic text; changing two 14-line stanzas and presenting four octaves instead. He also creates five new lines, which are added to the concluding two lines of verses two and three, one of which repeats the last line of the first verse as a refrain. A further line is added to the final verse, 'And all yon stars of the milky way' (l. 27). The word 'travail'd' is here reinstated (l. 9) and in l. 11 'soft' becomes 'kind' and 'it' becomes 'I'.

The only extant holograph version known to survive is found in Hogg's fair-copy manuscript for *Songs* 1831 at NLS MS 4805, ff. 26–102 (Blackwood Papers), f. 89. As noted in Janette Currie's essay on 'The Genesis of the Text' (pp. xli–xlviii) the fair-copy manuscript is missing page numbers for 'The Spectre's Cradle Song','Hymn to the God of the Sea' and 'Angel's Morning Song to the Shepherd', all three of which sit together in *Songs* 1831 between 'O Lady Dear' and 'Mary Gray'. It would seem that this group of three songs were added quite late in the preparation of the volume. They sit immediately after 'O Lady Dear', most likely to draw attention to *The Queen's Wake* and to help Hogg persuade Blackwood to produce a new edition to sit alongside *Songs by the Ettrick Shepherd* and *A Queer Book*. Notably three variants from the manuscript have crept into the printed volume. The first alteration occurs on l.7, where the word 'bow' is printed as 'how'. The word 'bow' occurs in all previous versions of the song, which seems to indicate that this version is a misreading of Hogg's handwriting, though it is possible that Hogg simply chose to correct an earlier misreading here. The wording of l.15 changes from 'And weep not so for thy mother's ill' to 'And weep thou not for thy mother's ill'. At l.25 'shall' in the manuscript becomes 'will' in the printed volume. Hogg had an opportunity to oversee the final stages of printing the volume so that these changes may be authorial. The remainder of Hogg's unpunctuated text is transferred cleanly to the printed volume.

Publication History:

1813 – in *The Queen's Wake: A Legendary Poem*, pp. 136–37 – see (S/SC, 2005), pp. 76–77

1822 – in *Poetical Works*, I, 145–46

1831 – in *Songs by the Ettrick Shepherd*, pp. 289–90 – see pp. 126–27 in the present edition

Musical Context:

In the headnote to the next song in *Songs* 1831, namely 'Hymn to the God of the Sea', Hogg notes that 'This and the foregoing songs are copied, with a slight variation, from the Queen's Wake, as pieces that might be successfully set to music'. To date no musical setting of the song has been located.

Explanatory Notes:

126, l. 2 Thy mother's arms a description of the 'Spectre' introduces the song in *The Queen's Wake* ('Night the Second', ll. 801–09) as 'a slender female form/Pale as the moon in Winter storm'.

126, ll. 5–6 The dew shall moisten thy brow so meek, | And the breeze of midnight fan thy cheek in his Editorial notes in *The Queen's Wake* Hogg explains that 'the "Spirit" [...] had brought her babe from the regions below to be cooled by the breeze of the world': (S/SC, 2004), p. 185.

126, ll 11–14 My heart was kind, and I fell in the snare, | Thy father was cruel, but thou wert fair [...] Then O, my bonny babe, smile on me! There are elements here commonly found in popular ballads and songs such as 'Lady Anne Bothwell's Lament' (*SMM*, II, No. 130 (135–36)) and 'The Cruel Mother' (Child 20A). See: Suzanne Gilbert's essay 'The Popular Context' in *Mador of the Moor*, ed. by James E. Barcus (S/SC, 2005), 'Appendix II', pp. 96–103.

127, l. 26 The trees of the forest be weeded away echoes of the familiar refrain from the traditional Scottish song 'The Flowers of the Forest': 'The flowers of the forest are a' wede [withered] away', lamenting the slaughter of the men of Ettrick Forest at the Battle of Flodden in 1513.

127, l. 28 thou shalt bloom for ever and aye Hogg explains, 'the child was going to heaven': see *The Queen's Wake* (S/SC, 2004), p. 185.

127, ll. 29–30 The time will come I shall follow thee, | But long, long hence that time shall be Hogg explains that, although the child was bound for heaven, 'she was to remain for a season in purgatory': see *The Queen's Wake* (S/SC, 2004), p. 185.

Hymn to the God of the Sea (pp. 127–28)

Creative Context:

As with the two songs immediately preceding it in *Songs* 1831, this song originally appeared in *The Queen's Wake* in 1813. Originally titled 'The Monks' Hymn' the song forms part of 'The Abbot M'Kinnon', which is sung by the 'Seventeenth Bard' on 'Night the Third' at the end of the bardic contest. As Douglas S. Mack notes in his recent S/SC edition of *The Queen's Wake*,

> 'the Abbot M'Kinnon' is 'a narrative, set on the holy island of Iona, about the collapse of the old medieval Scottish Catholic church. [...] In Hogg's poem, the Abbot M'Kinnon is a deeply corrupt man who, in his "visioned sleep", is called to account by the spirit of Saint Columba, "the saint of

the isle"('Night the Third' *1813*, ll. 1747, 1727). The Abbot duly gets his comeuppance, through supernatural agency, on the nearby small island of Staffa. ((S/SC, 2004), pp. xlvi– xlvii)

'The Monks' Hymn' is sung soon after they land on Staffa, as they look on the rock formations of Fingal's Cave which, 'dimly seen like the forms of men, | Like giant monks in ages agone, | Whom the God of the ocean had seared to stone' ('Night the Third' *1813*, ll. 1811–13).

As with 'The Spectre's Cradle Song' immediately before it in *Songs* 1831, collation shows that there are two variants occurring in the 1819 sixth edition of the poem, which became the standard version. In l.8 'gatherest' becomes 'bring'st' while in l.10 'bosom'd sail' becomes 'bellied' sail'.

In 1822 in the first volume of his *Poetical Works*, as above, Hogg uses the 1819 version as copy text for 'The Monks' Hymn' and thus retains these changes. But he does, as with 'The Spectre's Cradle Song', revise both the layout and the wording of the *Songs* 1831 version. He gives it a new title: 'Hymn to the God of the Sea', which he takes directly from the line preceding the song in *The Queen's Wake*. There are some small changes: for example, 'gleam' becomes 'lamp' (l. 14) and 'silver' is changed to 'mellow' (l. 27). But Hogg also creates new lines (l. 5, ll. 17–18, ll. 33–34) and the layout is regularised so that there are now five octets comprising six lines and a concluding refrain for each verse: 'To thee! –to thee!– we sing to thee, God of the western wind! God of the Sea!.

The only extant holograph version known to survive is found in the fair-copy manuscript for *Songs* 1831 at NLS MS 4805, ff. 26–102 (Blackwood Papers), ff. 89v–90r, immediately below 'The Spectre's Cradle Song' (see above). Line four of Hogg's holograph manuscript is revised. He originally writes, 'Great Spirit that moves on the face of the deep', which was the wording of the fifth line in all previous versions of the song. However, in the manuscript for *Songs* 1831 he scores through these words thus removing this line. He creates a new fifth line: 'Journeying with everlasting motion' which then rhymes neatly with 'ocean' at the end of l.6. A misreading of Hogg's hand occurs at l. 17, where the word 'b[not clear but not what's printed] is printed as 'leadest'. The remainder of Hogg's unpunctuated text is transferred cleanly to the printed volume.

Publication History:
1813 – in *The Queen's Wake: A Legendary Poem* , pp. 294–95– see (S/SC, 2005), pp. 155–56
1822 – in *Poetical Works*, I, 308–09
1831 – in *Songs by the Ettrick Shepherd*, pp. 291–93 – see pp. 127–28 in the present edition

Musical Context:
See note to the song above: 'The Spectre's Cradle Song'. No musical setting of 'Hymn to the God of the Sea' has been located.

Angel's Morning Song to the Shepherd (p. 128)

Creative Context:
As with the three songs immediately preceding it in *Songs* 1831, Hogg most probably added this one at the final stages of preparing his volume for print. This is one of the songs Hogg created initially for his magazine *The Spy* and it first

appeared there in the issue for 18 May 1811. With the title 'Morning', the version in *The Spy* is significantly longer than that included in *Songs* 1831, comprising 49 lines, and the text makes no mention of an angel or of a shepherd.

Hogg then included the text in the fourth volume of his 1822 *Poetical Works* where it appeared also with the title 'Morning'. The copy text is clearly the poem from *The Spy* but with some alterations in both layout and wording. The format changes from a single longish poem to four unequally-sized verses. Aside from normal changes resulting from the new printer, there are one or two variants. In l. 21 'the' becomes 'their' while at l. 37 'point' becomes 'paint', both of which could be the result of printing errors rather than changes that were authorised by Hogg.

For its appearance in *Songs* 1831 Hogg makes significant changes to the text. Firstly he gives it a new title: 'Angel's Morning Song to the Shepherd'. He also shortens the original: the new text is just sixteen lines formed into two octets. Hogg's copy text appears to be the text from *The Spy* with 'the' reinstated at l. 15. But the removal of the sections of the text which refer to life and death and the human soul, turn the poem into a celebration of the dawning of a new day and the inclusion of 'Shepherd' in the title makes a notable connection with Hogg, the Ettrick Shepherd.

Hogg keeps the first eight lines from the original version, omits ll. 9–14, creates a second verse from ll. 15–22, and omits the rest of the song. In l.11 he changes 'quail' to 'rail'. The word 'rail' often denotes the landrail or corncrake, which, like the quail makes its nest on the ground. According to *DSL* 'rail' is the Scots word for 'game bird'. Corncrakes are related to moorhens and other game birds, so Hogg's change of wording here does not significantly alter the meaning.

The only extant holograph version known to survive is in the fair-copy manuscript for *Songs* 1831 at NLS MS 4805, ff. 26–102 (Blackwood Papers), f. 90v. As with the previous two songs, the single folio is unpaginated, suggesting that it may have been added in December 1830 when Hogg was in Edinburgh overseeing the final stages of the volume in preparation for publication. The only variant here is that mentioned above in l. 11 when Hogg scores out the word 'quail' and writes the word 'rail' alongside it. Otherwise Hogg's unpunctuated text is transferred cleanly to the printed volume.

Publication History:
1811– in *The Spy* No. 38 (18 May 1811), 303–04 – see (S/SC, 2000), pp. 386–07
1822 – in *Poetical Works*, IV, 257–59
1831 – in *Songs by the Ettrick Shepherd*, pp. 294–95 – see (S/SC, 2014), p. 128

Musical Context:
Hogg gives no melody or air for this song and no musical copy has been located.

Explanatory Notes:
128, l. 12 moon-fern the 'moon-wort' (*Botrychium lunaria*). It was thought to possess magical powers (*OED*).

Mary Gray (p. 129)

Creative Context:
As noted in *Contributions to Annuals and Gift Books* (S/SC, 2006, pp. 322–23), this was one of four items Hogg sent to Samuel Carter Hall on 17 April 1829 for potential inclusion in *The Amulet*, a literary annual with a religious theme: See

Hogg's letter to Hall in *Letters*, II, 339–40. However Hall chose not to include this particular piece, and preferred one of Hogg's 'Covenanting Ballads' instead. The song formed part of Hogg's longer poem 'Elen of Reigh' which Hogg then included in *A Queer Book* published by Blackwood in 1832. Peter Garside notes that Hall wrote to Hogg on 25 June 1829 saying: 'the poem Ellen Reigh is also I think most splendid & powerful | but I preferred the "tale of the Martyrs" as embodying a more distinct story' (See *A Queer Book* , (S/SC, 1995), p. 233).

Hogg regarded 'Elen of Reigh' as one of his finest works. Garside notes that he rewrote the piece for inclusion in *Blackwood's Edinburgh Magazine* during July 1829, referring to a letter from Blackwood to Hogg of 8 August in which Blackwood highly commends the poem. It appeared in *Blackwood's* in September that year with the song 'Maria Gray' within it.

The subject of the song has two contexts for Hogg. Firstly, Mary Gray was one of the heroines in the traditional ballad 'Bessie Bell and Mary Gray' (Child, 201). The story was well known. Hogg's friend John Leyden wrote a version, removing the setting from Lednock to Yarrow, and a version of the ballad appeared in Charles Kirkpatrick Sharpe's *A Ballad Book* (1825). John Wilson used the story as the genesis for his poem titled 'The Desolate Village', first printed in the first issue of *Blackwood's Edinburgh Magazine* (1817), and later reprinted in his *Poetical Works* (1825). Interestingly, Wilson's poem included the inset song titled 'Mary Gray's Song', which also adds a Yarrow locality. The background to the ballad had been referred to by Thomas Pennant in his *Tour in Scotland* (1776) and was then included in fuller detail in *Transactions of the Society of the Antiquaries of Scotland*, 1822 (II, 108). In the original story both girls were staying with one another when in 1666 the plague broke out. In order to avoid the illness they built a bower outside the town of Lednock (whence Mary Gray's father lived), but they nevertheless died of the plague, having caught it from 'a young gentleman who was in love with them both' and who had brought them food (Child, IV, 745–46).

As Garside notes in *A Queer Book*, Mary Gray was also the name of one of Hogg's nieces by marriage and both Mary and Janet Gray had lived for a time with Hogg and his family in 1828 while their parents were in India. She was the subject of the song 'The Broken Heart' (pp. 119–20) which Hogg also included in *Songs* 1831. 'Mary Gray' is also the title of a pastoral poem written by Hogg around 1831, when his youngest daughter Mary Gray Hogg was born. A holograph version of 'Mary Gray A Ballad By the Ettrick Shepherd'is located at NLS, Acc 8432. A further version of this same poem is located at the University of Stirling Library, Special Collections, MS 25 box 1 (1). It was published as an Occasional Publication (No. 2) by the University of Stirling Bibliographical Society in 1981.

The connections with the original ballad of 'Bessie Bell and Mary Gray' are notable within the song's appearance in 'Elen of Reigh'. 'Maria Gray. A Song' acts as a bridge from the happy opening section about a loving friendship between two girls, Maria Gray and Elen of Reigh, to the hopelessness of loss following Maria Gray's early death in adolescence. The song is a mournful elegy of loss, sung by Elen of Reigh before her own mysterious death that night. In the poem 'Maria Gray. A Song' is followed by 'Hymn Over A Dying Virgin'.

In transmitting the text to *Songs* 1831, 'Maria' becomes 'Mary', and the text is subtly altered. For example, in the opening words of the first verse, the choric ''Who says' becomes the more general 'Some say' (l. 1 and l. 3), and the specific description of 'virgin', which is unclear without the surrounding poem, substitutes 'human' (l. 12). The song appeared once more after *Songs* 1831 in *A Queer Book* the following year. Garside's notes to the song (S/SC, 1995) give a detailed account of its textual history and of its various manuscript appearances (pp. 234–35). As mentioned above this song should not be confused with Hogg's 'Mary Gray A Ballad By the Ettrick Shepherd' also created around 1831.

Hogg's fair-copy manuscript of the version of 'Mary Gray' of *Songs* 1831 is found at NLS, MS 3112, f. 281, where, as Garside notes, 'the pagination by Hogg (203–04) indicates that it originally belonged to a sequence of autograph materials prepared for *Songs*, a large section of which survives in NLS, MS 4805' (p. 235). Hogg's pagination of 'Mary Gray' follows immediately after the song 'O Lady Dear' which is number '202' in the top left-hand corner of the manuscript, while the songs following after 'O Lady Dear' in MS, 4805, from ff. 89–93, either have no page numbers or are numbered out of sequence. This would seem to suggest that, initially, 'Mary Gray' was to follow 'O Lady Dear' within the collection but that at some point prior to printing, Hogg added further songs from *The Queen's Wake*.

Publication History:
1829 – in *Blackwood's Edinburgh Magazine*, 26 (September 1829), 271–77
1831 – in *Songs by the Ettrick Shepherd*, pp. 296–97 – see p. 129 in the present edition
1832 – in *A Queer Book* (William Blackwood: Edinburgh; T. Cadell: London), pp. 76–93, with 'Maria Gray. A Song' on pp. 89–90: see (S/SC, 1995), pp. 233–35

Musical Context:
Hogg makes no mention of an air or melody for the song and no musical copy has been located.

Explanatory Notes:
129, l. 3 cold death-bed according to tradition, Bessie Bell and Mary Gray were not permitted a Church burial and their bodies lay in the open for some time. Their bones were subsequently interred (Child, IV, 76).
129, l. 8 morning bower Barry writes that the girls built their bower 'in a very retired and romantic place called Burn-braes, on the side of Brauchie-burn': Child, iv, 76.
129, l. 21 She has kiss'd my cheek, she has kaim'd my hair Hogg quotes here from l. 14 of 'The Dowie Howms o' Yarrow', a traditional ballad he contributed to Scott for the *Minstrelsy of the Scottish Border*. The manuscript is located within a batch of 'Scotch Ballad Materials' at the National Library of Scotland, MS 877, f. 250. Scott subsequently printed the ballad with interpolations and revisions in the third volume (1803) under the revised title 'The Dowie Dens of Yarrow'. See Valentina Bold, 'Nouther right spelled nor right setten down': Scott, Child and the Hogg Family Ballads', in *The Ballad in Scottish History* (East Linton: Tuckwell Press, 2000), pp. 116–41.

Ode on Hearing of the Death of Mr Pitt (pp. 130–31)

Creative Context:
This song had only appeared once prior to *Songs* 1831, namely in the fourth volume of Hogg's *Poetical Works* in 1822 where it had the shorter title 'On the Death of Mr Pitt'. However, in *The Forest Minstrel* in 1810 Hogg had included 'Song for the Anniversary of Mr Pitt's Birth' (beginning 'O Willy was a wanton wag'), a song performed by John Ballantyne at a meeting of the Edinburgh Pitt

Club in May 1810. It was attributed by Hogg to 'D', or John Ballantyne, although Garside and Jackson note that 'it is not unlikely that Hogg himself had at least a hand in the 1810 song': see *The Forest Minstrel* (S/SC, 2006).

The song refers to the death of William Pitt, the Younger (1759–1806), politician and able debater in the House of Commons. He held senior positions both in government and in opposition. King George III twice called him to the office of Prime Minister during a political career that spanned from the 1780s until his death.

Hogg had involvement with the Edinburgh Pitt Club from the 1810s. The Pitt Club of Scotland had an exclusive membership of 'gentlemen and noblemen' Tories. As well as an annual dinner held 'either upon the anniversary of the birthday of Mr Pitt, or upon some other day appointed by the Committee of Management', the Club held a 'triennial public dinner' to commemorate Pitt's birthday: see 'The Pitt Clubs of Great Britain' in *The New Monthly Magazine* (vol. V), No. 29 (June 1816), 430–39 and the inset article 'Pitt Club of Scotland' on 433–34.

'On the Death of Mr Pitt' may relate to the annual dinner for 1821 advertised in the *Caledonian Mercury* of 30 December 1820. In a letter of 3 January, Scott invited Hogg to attend this dinner and also to compose a song, noting:

> I have a ticket for your acceptance, and a commission from the committee of management to request that the author of "Donald M'Donald" will favour us with his company. Do come if possible, and tune your pipes to a clever stave for the occasion. (Stirling University Library, MS 25, Box 2/1)

The *Caledonian Mercury* of 13 January 1821 subsequently reported that some 500 people attended the dinner, with Scott presiding over '200' in an ante room while 'the 7th fusileers entertained the company [...] with some excellent pieces of music'. All songs and toasts are mentioned, such as that of 'Mr P. Hill' who 'sang a parody on "A man's a man for a' that"'. Late in the evening, once Scott and his group had rejoined the main party, 'the company were entertained with some volunteered songs [...] and Gow and his band enlivened the remaining part of the night with their performances'. Hogg's name does not appear anywhere in the report so that it seems unlikely he was present. Nonetheless, it is quite possible that he composed 'On the Death of Mr Pitt' for this occasion and, although it was not performed, he included it shortly after in his *Poetical Works*.

This 1822 version of the text appears to be copy text for the song in *Songs* 1831, though the title is expanded. Variants include rewording of l.6 so that 'Of a splendour steadfastly shone' becomes 'Of the splendour that over it shone', and 'motion' is replaced with 'measure' (l. 22). The majority of the changes are confined to the orthography and punctuation. For example, the heavy use of exclamation marks within the 1822 version is toned down while the overuse of capitalisation in the concluding two lines is removed.

The only extant manuscript version known to survive is that in Hogg's fair-copy manuscript for *Songs* 1831 at NLS MS 4805, ff. 26–102 (Blackwood Papers), f. 91. However, 'Ode on hearing of the death of Mr Pitt' is the first of three songs (see also 'Busaco' and 'Ode to the Genius of Shakespeare' following) that are numbered differently from the rest of the holograph manuscript. There are no page numbers, instead, each song is numbered '1' to '3' written in the top right-hand corner. It is probable that they were included within the collection at a relatively late stage of the preparation, possibly during the end of December 1830 when Hogg was in Edinburgh to oversee the final stages of printing the volume. Whatever the case, these three songs also follow the order within the printed collection.

There are three unauthorised changes to Hogg's holograph manuscript version of 'Ode on hearing of the death of Mr Pitt' that probably occurred during transmission to the printed text. The first is the deletion of the word 'pieces' after 'the two following' in the headnote. As the word is repeated later in the same sentence it seems a sensible omission for the sake of clarity. The following two changes to Hogg's holograph manuscript are more problematic. In l.20 the word 'rest' occurs in both the *Poetical Works* version and in Hogg's manuscript. However, the printed version has 'nest' at this point. Further, in l.28 the word 'fumes' occurs in both the *Poetical Works* version and in Hogg's manuscript. However, in the printed version of the song it is rendered 'foams'. Both changes are possibly a result of the printer misreading Hogg's handwriting.

Publication History:
1822 – in *Poetical Works*, IV, 237–39
1831 – in *Songs by the Ettrick Shepherd*, pp. 298–300 — see pp. 130–31 in the present edition

Musical Context:
Hogg states in his headnote that this 'and the two following are inserted as pieces that might be set to music, though as yet they never have been, and probably never will be'. No musical settings have been located.

Explanatory Notes:
130, l. 13–14 **'Twas in the lone wild I first heard of thy name, | With Nature alone for my guide** Pitt first came to public political prominence in 1782 with his appointment to the post of Chancellor of the Exchequer. At this time, Hogg would have been around 11 years old.

130, ll. 7–8 **The darkness is shed, and the storm is gone forth, | Our sun and our moon have both dropp'd to the earth** Hogg echoes words reputedly spoken by Charles Fox (1749–1806) after hearing of Pitt's death when 'he was heard to mutter that there seemed to be "something missing in the world –a chasm or blank that cannot be supplied" ' (quoted in *ODNB* entry on 'William Pitt, the Younger').

130, l. 27 **That minds there are framed like the turbulent ocean, [...] There dash its rude billows for ever** Hogg is employing imagery of Pitt as 'the pilot who weathered the storm' from a song first performed during a public birthday dinner which Canning had arranged for Pitt at Merchant Taylor's Hall on 20 May 1802 (*ODNB* entry on 'William Pitt, the Younger'). The lines were frequently reprinted in newspapers and journals so that by the 1820s the image was familiarly associated with Pitt.

130, l. 31 and 131, l. 135 **They said thou wert proud [...]They call'd thee ambitious** Pitt had a 'declared ambition for power' (ODNB entry on 'William Pitt, the Younger').

130, l. 132 **tried thee by plummet and line** literally, an implement for measuring the depth of the sea or perpendicularity of a wall.

Busaco (pp. 131–32)

Creative Context:

This is another of Hogg's relatively early songs, first appearing in his magazine *The Spy* for 9 February 1811 with the title 'The Battle of Busaco'. The song was created to celebrate Wellington's victory over Napoleon's forces under the command of Marshal André Masséna (1758–1817), Prince of Essling and Duke of Rivoli, at Busaco in Portugal on 27 September 1810. Gillian Hughes notes that Hogg may have been responding to Walter Scott's letter in *The Spy* (No. 9, 27 October 1810) which accompanied the printing of John Leyden's 'The Battle of Assaye', another contemporary battle in the Peninsular Campaign.

With the same title, the song next appeared in the fourth volume of Hogg's 1822 *Poetical Works*. The copy text is clearly the version from *The Spy* and there are no major textual alterations, only normal changes in orthography and punctuation.

Hogg appears to use this text also for the version which appears in *Songs* 1831. He alters the format from quatrains to octets and retains almost all of the original version. In l.6 'cold turf' becomes 'green turf' and the two concluding lines are redrafted: 'Thy sons, O wretched Portugal | Rous'd their feats of chivalry' is replaced with 'For even the slumbering Portugal | Arouses at their chivalry!'.

The only extant holograph version known to survive is found in the fair-copy manuscript for *Songs* 1831 at NLS MS 4805, ff. 26–102 (Blackwood Papers), f. 92. 'Busaco' is the second of three songs that are numbered differently from the rest of the holograph manuscript at this point, suggesting that Hogg probably added them at the final stage of preparation for printing the volume (see note to the previous song 'Ode on hearing of the death of Mr Pitt' and 'Ode to the Genius of Shakespeare' following).

Publication History:

1811– in *The Spy*, No. 24 (9 February 1811), 155–56 – see (S/SC, 2000), pp. 254–56 and 603

1822 – in *Poetical Works*, IV, 243–45

1831 – in *Songs by the Ettrick Shepherd*, pp. 301–03 – see pp. 131–32 in the present edition

Unauthorised versions:

1819 – as 'Song No. VIII' in *The Harp of Renfrewshire: A Collection of Songs and other Poetical Pieces* (Paisley: J. Lawrence,), pp. 11–13. The copy text is the version in *The Spy*. It is published anonymously, but within an extended footnote the Editor 'conjecture[s]' that it is by 'Mr Hogg [...] both from the internal evidence which the piece itself exhibits, and by its appearance first of all in the Spy' (p. 11). The footnote also states: 'The Battle of Busaco is a song of considerable merit, and undoubtedly the production of a master in poetry', and goes on to compare it to Thomas Campbell's 'Hohenlinden' (p. 12).

1839 – in *The New York Literary Gazette* of Saturday 16 March 1839 (p. 56). The copy text is most probably the *Poetical Works* version (above) with some variants: 'sight' for 'scene' (l. 15), and 'feats' for 'deeds' on the final line (l. 40). See *Listing of Hogg Items in the American Periodical* Press, by Janette Currie at the online *James Hogg Research* website hosted by the Division of Literature and Languages, School of Arts and Humanities, Stirling University, http://www.jameshogg.stir.ac.uk.

Musical Context:
See note above for 'Ode on Hearing of the Death of Mr Pitt'. No musical setting has been located. In the unauthorised printing of the song in *The Harp of Renfrewshire* in 1819 the melody title given to match the text is 'Scots wha hae wi' Wallace Bled'. This refers to the Burns song with this title which was set to the stirringly militaristic tune 'Hey tutti taiti'. The melody appears with the lyric beginning 'Landlady count the lawin' in *SMM* (1788), No. 170 (p. 178). The melody with Burns's text first appears in George Thomson's *A Select Collection of Original Scottish Airs*, Vol. 3 (1802) as no. 133 with a musical setting by Joseph Haydn.

Explanatory Notes:
132, ll. 33–5 The thistle waved her bonnet blue [...] Hogg refers here to the national emblems of Scotland (the thistle), Ireland (the harp) and England (the rose), thus emphasising the composition of the British military strength during the Napoleonic wars. See also 'The Flowers of Scotland' (pp. 65–66).

Ode to the Genius of Shakespeare (pp. 132–33)

Creative Context:
Hogg appears to have created this song for a meeting of the Shakespeare Club of Alloa, where he recited it in his capacity as honorary member and Poet Laureate of the Club at the meeting held on Tuesday 23 April 1816 – see also 'The Mermaid's Song' (pp. 40–41). The Club met annually on or around the anniversary of Shakespeare's birthday where the 'memory of Shakespeare' was toasted and an 'Ode to the Genius of Shakespeare' (composed for the occasion) was recited. Although it would appear from his letter to Alexander Bald dated 23 April 1815 that Hogg was invited to the dinner that month, there is no evidence that he attended (*Letters* I, 248). But he did attend the meeting the following year where he recited his 'Ode', evidenced by a report of the proceedings in the *Caledonian Mercury* of 4 May 1816:

'ANNIVERSARY OF SHAKESPEARE'
In no part of his native country could the anniversary of this great man have been celebrated with higher devotion and enthusiasm, than at Alloa, in Clackmannanshire. A Shakespeare Club has for many years existed in that place, the Members of which have always held a literary festival on the day that gave birth to the greatest poet the world ever beheld. Tuesday last, 23rd of April, being the second centenary from the day of his decease, (for he died on the same day and month, and year, in which he was born), a number of their literary friends and acquaintances were invited to join in the social pleasures of the evening. When dinner was over, and a few general toasts were given, the President rose, and after an appropriate eulogy, concluding with a quotation from one of the poet's best plays, gave 'The Memory of Shakespeare", which was drunk standing, and in deep silence. Mr James Hogg, the Ettrick Shepherd, who is now an honorary member, and Poet Laureate of the Club, then produced, and read an ode "To the Genius of Shakespeare"; upon which the President, after a short address most flattering to the bard, and well calculated to encourage him in his poetical career, presented him in the name of the Society, with a handsome silver cup, having the Shakespeare arms beautifully engraved on one side, and the following inscription on the other, "Presented to Mr James Hogg, by his

brethren of the Shakespeare Club of Alloa, in testimony of their esteem of him as a man, and their admiration of him as a poet." A number of songs, and poetical effusions written for the occasion were sung and recited, and the healths of our distinguished living bards were individually given, as well as the memories of departed sons of genius, who have so proudly elevated the intellectual character of their country.

The song was first published in the fourth volume of Hogg's 1822 *Poetical Works* with the shorter title 'To the Genius of Shakespeare' and Hogg then substantially redrafted the song for *Songs* 1831. He omits verses 3 and 7. He rearranges the order of several of the verses: verse 4 is now verse 3, verse 5 is verse 2 and verse 6 is now verse 5. The first and last verses remain as they were in 1822. He amends l.12 from 'thy carols unearthly and boon' to 'thy carols all lightsome and boon' and in l.21, the topical reference to Alloa in the original version with mention of 'the windings of the Forth' becomes a vague reference to the 'vales of the north'. Finally in l.31 the 'Forest and green wood' becomes the 'Torrent and green-wood'.

No earlier manuscript version of the song is extant. Hogg's fair-copy manuscript of the *Songs* 1831 version survives at NLS MS 4805, f. 93. The manuscript is page-numbered '3' and '4' and, as discussed in the notes for the songs immediately preceding it, this seems to be a section of manuscript prepared quite late in the production of the volume. Hogg's unpunctuated text is transmitted relatively cleanly to the printed volume. At l. 6 Hogg originally writes the singular, 'votary', which is printed as the plural, 'votaries' in the volume. As the plural form of the word is more in keeping within the context of the song's original composition for the Shakespeare Club of Alloa dinner, the change is probably authorial. Further, a printing error has crept into the title with the bard's name wrongly printed as 'Shakspeare', although it is correctly spelt in Hogg's holograph manuscript: it is emended to its proper spelling in this new edition.

Publication History:
1822 – in *Poetical Works*, IV, 252–54
1831 – in *Songs by the Ettrick Shepherd*, pp. 304–06 – see pp. 132–33 in the present edition

Musical Context:
The *Caledonian Mercury* (cited above) reports that Hogg 'read' the 'ode' to the Club. No tune is nominated to any published version and no musical setting has been located.

Explanatory Notes:
132, [Title] Hogg writes within a long tradition of celebratory poems, essays, songs, and music composed to honour Shakespeare's literary 'genius': see *The Genius of Shakespeare* (Oxford: Oxford University Press, 1998), especially, pp. 157–87 (p. 184).
132, ll. 9–11 Dream'st in the shadowy brows of the moon; | Or linger'st in fairyland | Mid lovely elves to stand echoes of *A Mid-summer Night's Dream*. Around 1814, Hogg planned *Midsummer Night Dreams,* 'a volume of romantic poems' on dreams and 'other wild and visionary subjects': see Hogg's 'Memoir', pp. 35–36.
133, l. 14 Green grave of Elsinore Ophelia's grave, probably both the 'glassy stream' (4.vii, l.168) where she drowned and her grave in the final Act of

Hamlet, Prince of Denmark. During Hogg's Highland Journey in July and August of 1802 (published in the *Scots Magazine* of February 1803) he included an extensive review of a performance of *Hamlet* that he attended in Edinburgh at the beginning of his journey (*Highland Journeys*, ed. by Hans de Groot (S/SC, forthcoming), pp. 22–24).

133, l. 15 Stay'st o'er the hill of Dunsinnan to hover 'high Dunsinane Hill', (*Macbeth*, IV.i., l. 93), is the location of Macbeth's castle.

133, l. 16 Bosworth or Shrewsbury the Battle of Bosworth (1485) provides the dramatic conclusion to *King Richard III*, while the Battle of Shrewsbury (1401) provides the climax to *Henry IV, Pt I*.

133, l. 17 Egypt or Philippi Mark Antony defeats Caesar's assassins at the Battle of Philippi in the final Act of *Julius Caesar* and is captivated by Cleopatra, Queen of Egypt in *Antony and Cleopatra*.

133, l. 20 thy hallow'd shrine! during the annual Shakespeare Club festivities, 'the beautiful bust of the poet, which is placed in the hall, was crowned with laurel, and adorned with wreaths of flowers. His picture was also hung with garlands': from a report of the proceedings in the *Edinburgh Evening Courant* of 4 May 1815 (quoted in *Letters* I, 248n).

133, l. 26 Caledon a poetic allusion to Scotland, see note to 'Caledonia' (p. 13).

133, l. 27 land of the ardent and free a reference 'to the traditional boast that Scotland was never conquered, in spite of the efforts of (for example) the Roman empire and the Vikings'. Hogg returns to this theme in the opening sequence of his epic poem *Queen Hynde* (1824).'

133, l. 30 wild meteor a further allusion to the self-taught tradition. Hogg used the phrase self-referentially on several subsequent occasions: 'Say, can the meteor of the wild, | Nature's unstaid erratic child' is repeated in, for example, *Queen Hynde* (1824), 'Book First', ll. 1088–89 and also within 'To Miss. MA.C–e', a poem Hogg contribution to the *Amulet*, although not published there: see *Contributions to Annuals and Gift Books* (S/SC, 2006), pp. 203–05 and notes on pp. 335–36.

133, ll. 31–32 by the sounding sea, | Torrent and green-wood tree Hogg's description is of Alloa: a river-port and parish; [..] chief town of Clackmannanshire. Groome notes: 'The situation of Alloa is a pleasant one— in front of the Lime-tree Walk (planted 1714), leading up from the harbour; eastward, close by, the old grey tower and modern mansion of the Earls of Mar and Kellie; westward the bonnie Links of the Forth, with Stirling Castle beyond; and for a background the Ochil Hills'.

The Wee Housie (pp. 133–34)

Creative Context:
This is the final of the eleven songs Hogg includes in *Songs* 1831 which originally appeared in his magazine, *The Spy*. Under the longer title of 'The Auld Man's Farewell to his Little House. By John Miller', a longer version of the song (some 42 lines) appeared there on 16 March 1811. Several songs within *The Spy* are attributed to 'John Miller', a shepherd-figure from Nithsdale who is first introduced in *The Spy* of 17 November 1810 where his song 'Poor Little Jessy' is published: see 'O What Gart me Greet' on pp. 113–14.

The song next appeared in the fourth volume of Hogg's 1822 *Poetical Works* using *The Spy* as its copy text. It has the slightly amended title of 'The Auld Man's Farewell to his Wee House', and verse 7 is omitted. Aside from changes to orthography and punctuation, the text is basically the same.

For *Songs* 1831 Hogg amalgamates the two previous versions of the song and gives the song the shorter title of 'The Wee Housie'. He changes the form from quatrianes to octets and he now omits verse 3. Some of the new orthographic changes made in 1822 are changed back to their original: for example 'cozy' in l.4 becomes 'cozie' in 1822, but reverts to its original in 1831.

A microfilm copy of a fragment of Hogg's fair-copy holograph manuscript of 'The Auld Man's Farewell to his little House' for *The Spy* is extant at NLS MF. MS. 414. It is end-signed in Hogg's hand-writing, 'Written in March 1811 by James Hogg', and comprises the final 18 lines of the song (ll. 31–48). In this earliest version the text is slightly different from the printed version in *The Spy* in two places. On l. 42 'should close' is printed 'had clos'd' in *The Spy*, while the final two lines have been altered more radically prior to publication: 'I'll never find while lingering here, | A hame I like sae weel as thee' (ll. 41–41) becomes 'The wee while I maun sojourn here, | I'll ne'er find a hame like thee'.

The manuscript for the *Songs* 1831 version is extant as part of the fair-copy manuscript for the volume at NLS MS 4805, ff. 26–102 (Blackwood Papers), on f. 94. There are no page-numbers on the manuscript. Instead, it is numbered '2' in the top right-hand corner of the first page and seems to belong to a section of manuscript prepared quite late in the preparation stages as Hogg adjusted the order within the collection. Hogg's unpunctuated text is transmitted cleanly to the printed volume.

Publication History:

1811– in *The Spy*, No. 29 (16 March 1811), 231–32 – see (S/SC, 2000), pp. 299–300 and p. 606

1822 – in *Poetical Works*, IV, 231–34

1831 – in *Songs by the Ettrick Shepherd*, pp. 307–09 – see pp. 133–34 in the present edition

Musical Context:

Hogg gives no tune title for the song and no musical copy has been located.

Explanatory Notes:

134, l. 38 bourtree bush 'This shrub was supposed to possess great virtue in warding off the force of charms and witchcraft. Hence it was customary to plant it round country-houses and barnyards' (*DSL*).

Good Night, and Joy (p. 135)

Creative Context:

As noted by Hogg in his 1831 headnote, this song was created as the final song for Robert Archibald Smith's sixth volume of his musical collection *The Scotish Minstrel* which appeared in [1824]. For more information about Hogg's involvement with this collection and for a copy of the song see: *Contributions to Musical Collections and Miscellaneous Songs*.

Smith must have invited Hogg to produce lyrics for the song sometime in 1823. His letter to Hogg is not extant, but there as a letter from Smith to William Motherwell, dated 14 November 1823, in which Smith refers to Hogg's text. He explains to Motherwell that he is about to complete his collection and commissions Motherwell to supply him with poetry for the last song 'Good night and joy be wi' ye a", asking that the song not be more than three stanzas long and continuing:

> The Ettrick Shepherd is in Edinburgh at present and has been trying his hand, but I do not like the verses he has produced They are extremely coarse, with the exception of one stanza they are far below mediocrity – I am positive if you will sit down for one evening you will produce something infinitely superior – I will give you his first verse as a guide for the measure (GUL MS Robertson, ff. 26–27)

In his response of 18 November, Motherwell sent copies of both his and William Chalmers's attempts, 'for the purpose of being carefully corked up in a bottle of spirits to be kept as a curiosity along with other monstrosities of a similar kind.' Motherwell informed Smith, 'unless you have been more successful in other quarters you will be under the necessity of adopting the Ettrick Shepherds (*sic*) verse which from the specimen sent promises but little' (GUL MS Robertson, ff. 28–29). On the 21 November, Smith replied 'To tell the truth I do not think very highly of the verses sent for "Gude Night" I am to shew them however to the Ladies this morning' (GUL MS Robertson, f. 30). The opinion of 'the Ladies' was clearly persuasive, as it was Hogg's song which Smith published to close his collection.

The song next appeared in *Blackwood's Edinburgh Magazine* in May 1828, sung by the 'Shepherd' in *Noctes Ambrosianae* No. XXXVI, at the conclusion of a Noctean revel, so that the 'night' rather than 'year' is 'wearing to the wane'. In this version the Scots orthography, for example, within the new lines inserted at ll. 2–4 of the first verse, are clearly designed to suit Hogg's 'Noctean' persona:

> And daylight glimmering east awa';'
> The little sternies dance amain,
> And the moon bobs aboon the shaw.

The Shepherd's introduction to the song is that it's 'a bit bonny sang o' my ain – No sae merry, but yet no melancholy' (802).

Although Hogg assigned the publisher Robert Purdie the 'sole Copy-right of my songs contained in the Scottish Minstrel and Irish Minstrel' (see Hogg to Purdie, 17 November 1828 in *Letters*, II, 315–16) he included the proviso of 'reserving to myself the right of publishing any one or all of these songs in any literary work or new edition of the Jacobite Relics'. It was thus understandable that Hogg would wish to use this song as the conlusion to *Songs* 1831. Purdie published two further editions of Hogg's song in the *Scotish Minstrel* during Hogg's lifetime (between 1829–1834). Both versions appear to reuse the original plate and all versions occupy the same important position in the final sixth volume (p. 104).

The version of the text for *Songs* 1831 appears to rely more on the Smith text than on *Blackwood's* as copy text. The first and second verses more closely follow the *Scotish Minstrel* version. And l. 11 also retains the words from the *Scotish Minstrel* rather than from *Blackwood's* ('And mony a bonny flower we've pu'd"). The first three lines of the final verse were newly composed for 1831.

No manuscripts of the Smith or *Blackwood's* versions of the song have been located. NLS MS 3112, f. 280, appears to be Hogg's fair-copy version of the song which he composed as 'an appropriate conclusion' to *Songs* 1831. There is no page number on this leaf, but in style and layout it clearly belongs with NLS MS 4805, ff. 26–102, the longest but incomplete section of Hogg's fair-copy manuscript of *Songs* 1831. Hogg's direction at the head that 'this to be on the last leaf of the vol' indicates that it may have been composed late in the process of compiling the collection, perhaps while Hogg was in Edinburgh during the latter stages of printing and thus separate from the other songs sent from Altrive to Edinburgh from 20 October until around 9 December 1830. The song has been transmitted cleanly to the printed text, aside from the normal alterations, such as insertion of punctuation, shortening and lengthening of conjunctions, and also by placing the footnote as the headnote to the song.

Publication History:
[1824] – in *The Scottish Minstrel*, VI, 104 – see *Contributions to Musical Collections and Miscellaneous Songs* (S/SC, 2014)
1828 – in *Blackwood's Edinburgh Magazine*, 23 (May 1828), 80 – see also S/SC, 2008), pp. 315 and 548
1831 – in *Songs by the Ettrick Shepherd*, pp. 310–11 – see p. 135 in the present edition

Musical Context:
Clearly stated in the headnote for 1831, the musical setting to which Hogg refers is that published in Smith's *The Scotish Minstrel*. However, the tune to which Hogg sets his lyric is much older than this. In a letter dated 'Aug. or Sept. 1795', Burns instructs James Johnson: '"Gude night & Joy be wi' you a'" — let this be your last song of all in the Collection; & set it to the old words; & after them, insert my "Gude night & joy be wi' you a'" which you will find in my Poems' (Letter 684, in *The Letters of Robert Burns*, second edition, edited by G. Ross Roy, 2 vols (Oxford: Clarendon Press), II, 299–371). Burns also used this melody for his song 'The Farewell. To the Brethren of St. James' Lodge, Tarbolton' (Kinsley, 115) which first appeared in his 'Kilmarnock Edition' in 1786. The old words to which Burns refers were traditionally sung at parting during this period. Johnson took his advice and included the song as the final piece in the sixth volume of the *SMM* in 1803 (No. 600, p. 370), but with Burns's text rather than the old song. Glen comments further that a variant of the same tune was found in the Skene Manuscript (*c*.1620) with the title "Good Night, and God be with you". He also notes its Scottish roots as it appeared under the same title in Henry Playford's "Original Scotch Tunes (Full of the Highland Humours) for the Violin; Being the first of this kind yet printed, etc" in 1700. This work was published in London by the son of John Playford. (Glen, p. 241).

The traditional words given by Burns later appeared in *Minstrelsy of the Scottish Border* (1802/03) as a fragment of two verses titled 'Armstrong's Goodnight' where, although he did not mention his source, Scott's note acknowledged that 'the tune is popular in Scotland, but whether these are the original words will admit of some doubt'.

Explanatory Notes:
135 **[Title]** in footnote to 'Good Night, and Joy', which is the last tune in Niel Gow's *Complete Repository of Original Scots Slow Strathspeys and Dances* (second edition, 1800), Gow explains: 'this tune is played at the conclusion of every convivial Dancing meeting throughout Scotland.' Scott cleverly uses the title of the tune in *Waverley* (1814) when the band strikes up the tune to signal the end of the Ball at Holyrood (Oxford: Oxford University Press, World's Classics, 1986), edited by Claire Lamont, p. 210.

135, l. 4 shaw in the second, revised edition of *The Queen's Wake*, Hogg 'replaced the last four Notes of the first edition', which then appeared in subsequent editions. The replacement Notes provided a glossary of selected Scots words, including 'shaw': a Lowland term, whichdenotes the snout, or brow of a hill; but the part so denominated is always understood to be of a particular form, broad at the base, and contracted to a point above' (S/SC, 2004), p. 456 and p. 389.

135, ll. 9–10 O, we hae wander'd far and wide | O'er Scotia's hills, o'er firth an' fell Hogg's early life prior to success with *The Queen's Wake* in 1813 included an unsettled time of shepherding in Nithsdale and frequent journeys into the Highlands and Islands in search of a suitable farm: see 'Memoir', pp. 11–52, and also *Highland Journeys*, ed. by Hans de Groot (S/SC, 2010).

135, ll. 19–20 my strains were often wild | As winds upon a winter day *The Queen's Wake* (1813) concludes with the following lines on Hogg's 'wayward' muse, the demotic harp of Ettrick: 'oft thy erring numbers born | Have taught the wandering winds to sing' (ll. 392–94).

135, l. 21 Minstrel again in *The Queen's Wake* Mack discusses Hogg's self-designated role as the 'Bard of Ettrick', a Minstrel poet figure who 're-tunes the Caledonian harp, the harp of the people […] who gives voice to the experiences and insights of the non-elite people of Scotland' (S/SC, 2004), p. lix.

Index of First Lines and Melody Titles

First Lines

Titles of Melodies / Airs / Tunes

Note: Hogg does not give information about melodies/airs/tunes for all of the songs in *Songs by the Ettrick Shepherd*, nor does he always give the title of a melody, even if he has one in mind. Sometimes a melody title is exactly the same as the general title for the song (see 'Contents' list). The following list thus comprises the titles of melodies/airs/tunes where Hogg has given them in his headnotes, or where they have been identified by other means.

Bibliography

This bibliography includes materials referenced in the preparation of the new S/SC editions of both *Songs by the Ettrick Shepherd* 1831 and *Contributions to Musical Collections and Miscellaneous Songs*. Manuscript sources referred to as part of the preparation of these editions are listed clearly where applicable in editorial notes. Specific articles about Hogg's life and work relating to individual songs are also referenced in full in editorial notes for the songs in question. This bibliography does not include the titles of the musical collections and individual song sheets which are available in full in *Contributions to Musical Collections and Miscellaneous Songs*.

A. General Bibliographical Sources

Bushell, G. H., *Scottish Engravers: a Biographical Dictionary of Scottish Engravers and of Engravers who worked in Scotland, to the beginning of the nineteenth century* (Oxford: Oxford University Press, 1949).

Dichter, Harry, and Elliot Shapiro, *Handbook of Early American Sheet Music, 1768–1889* (New York: Dover Publications, 1941, reprint 1977).

Glen, John, *Early Scottish Melodies* (Edinburgh: R. & J. Glen, 1900).

Gooch, Bryan N. S. and David S. Thatcher, *Musical Settings of British Romantic Literature*, 2 vols (New York & London: Garland, 1982).

Gore, Charles, ed., *The Scottish Fiddle Music Index: The 18ᵗʰ & 19ᵗʰ Century Printed Collections* (Musselburgh: Amaising, 1994).

Hughes, Gillian, ed., *Hogg's Verse and Drama: A Chronological Listing* (Stirling: James Hogg Society, 1990).

Humphries, Charles and William C. Smith, *Music Publishing in the British Isles from the Beginning until the middle of the nineteenth century* (Oxford: Blackwell, 1970).

Kassler, Michael, *Music Entries at Stationers' Hall 1710–1818* (Kent: Ashgate, 2004).

Kidson, Frank, *British Music Publishers, Printers and Engravers* (London: W.E. Hill & Sons, 1900).

Wolfe, Richard J., *Secular Music in America, 1801–1825, A Bibliography* (New York: New York Public Library; Astor, Lenox and Tilden Foundations, 1964).

B. Primary Printed Sources (Music, Song Collections and Song sheets)

Aiken, John, *Essays on Song-Writing: With a Collection of English Songs as are most Eminent for Poetical Merit* (London: Printed for J. Johnson, 1772).

Ballads & Songs. Scotish (Ludlow: George Nicholson, 1799).

The Banquet of Euphrosyne: A selection of the most esteemed songs, Scottish and English (Hawick: R. Armstrong, 1816).

Beauties of the Scottish Poets, or The Harp of Renfrewshire: A Collection of Songs and other Poetical Pieces, Many of which are original, Accompanied with Notes Explanatory, Critical and Biographical and a Short Essay on the Poets of Renfrewshire (Glasgow: William Turnbull, 1821).

Bishop, Henry R., *The Gathering of the Clans. Scotia's Welcome to Queen Victoria. National Song, the Symphonies and Accompaniments composed by Sir Henry R. Bishop. Mus. Bac. Oxon. Conductor of her Majesty's concerts of Ancient Music and The Professor of Music in the University of Edinburgh* (London: Goulding & D'Almaine, 1831).

_____, *Melodies of Various Nations with Symphonies and Accompaniments by Henry R. Bishop. The words by Thomas Bayly Esq.* (London, Dublin : Goulding, D'Almaine, Potter & Co, [1822]).

_____, *A Selection of Popular National airs with Symphonies and Accompaniments by Henry R. Bishop. The words by Thomas Moore, Esqr.* (London: J. Power, 1822).

_____, *Songs of the Old Chateau. The Poetry by Thomas Haynes Bayly. Esq., The Symphonies and Accompaniments composed by Henry R. Bishop* (London: Goulding and D'Almaine, 1831).

'Blue Bonnets over the border' Sung with the most characteristic applause by Mr Braham. At the Theatre Royal, Liverpool, Edinburgh & Dublin Arranged by J. C. Clifton (London: H. Faulkner, 3 Old Bond Street, [n.d.]).

The British Minstrel, A Collection of all the Ancient and Modern Songs, Which possess any Claim to poetical Excellence good Sentiment, or Humour; Consisting of nearly 500 English, Irish and Scotch songs by the best authors, third edition (London: Vernor & Hood, [1820]).

Bunting, E., *A General Collection of the Ancient Irish Music* (London: Preston and son, 1796).

Burns, Robert, *The Letters of Robert Burns* (2nd edn), ed. G. Ross Roy, 2 vols, (Oxford: Clarendon Press, 1985).

_____, *The Merry Muses*, ed. Valentina Bold (Edinburgh: Birlinn, 2009).

_____, *The Merry Muses of Caledonia. With a Prefatory Note and some authentic Burns Texts contributed by J. DeLancey Ferguson*, eds. James Barke and Sydney Goodsir Smith (London: W. H. Allen, 1965).

_____, *Notes on Scottish Song By Robert Burns Written in an Interleaved Copy of The Scots Musical Museum with Additions by Robert Riddell and Others*, ed. James C. Dick (London: Henry Frowde, 1908).

_____, *The Poems and Songs of Robert Burns*, ed. James Kinsley, 3 vols (Oxford: Clarendon, 1968).

_____, *Robert Burns's Commonplace Book 1783–1785*, ed. D. Daiches (Fontwell: Centaur Press, 1965).

_____, *Robert Burns's Tour The Borders 5 May–1 June 1787*, ed. Raymond Lamont Brown (Ipswich: Boydell Press, 1972).

_____, *Robert Burns's Tour of the Highlands and Stirlingshire 1787*, ed. Raymond Lamont Brown (Ipswich: Boydell Press, 1973).

_____, *The Scots Musical Museum 1787–1803*, ed. James Johnson, Introduction by Donald A. Low (Aldershot: Scolar Press, 1991).

_____, *The Songs of Robert Burns*, ed. Donald A. Low (London: Routledge, 1993).

_____, *The Works of Robert Burns. Edited by the Ettrick Shepherd, and William Motherwell*, 5 vols (Glasgow: Archibald Fullarton, 1840).

_____, *The Songs of Robert Burns now first printed with the melodies for which they were Written. A Study in Tone-Poetry with Bibliography, Historical Notes, and Glossary*, ed. James C. Dick (London: Henry Frowde, 1903).

_____, *The Songs of Robert Burns and Notes on Scottish Songs by Robert Burns*, Together with *Annotation of Scottish Songs by Burns*, ed. James C. Dick (Hatboro, Pennsylvania: Folklore Associates, 1962).

Burns, Walter, *Caledonia, A National Scottish Song. Sung by Augustus Braham Esq. the Poetry by The Ettrick Shepherd. To the Music Composed and Dedicated by Permission to the Society for the Vindication of Scottish Rights By Walter Burns Arranged with Symphonies and Accompaniment for the pianoforte by Edward Salter* (Edinburgh, [1855]).

Byron, George Gordon, *A Selection of Hebrew Melodies, Ancient and Modern by Isaac Nathan and Lord Byron*, ed. with introduction and notes by Frederick Burwick and Paul Douglass (Tuscaloosa and London: University of Alabama Press, 1988).

_____, *Fugitive Pieces and Reminiscences of Lord Byron: containing an entire new edition of The Hebrew Melodies, with the addition of Several Never Before Published[...]Also some Original Poetry, Letters and Recollections of Lady Caroline Lamb[...]*, (London: Whittaker, Treacher, and Co., 1829).

Kinloch, George R., *Caledonia Adieu! The melody composed by Geo. Kinloch Esqre of Kinloch. Written and Arranged with symphonies & Accompaniment for the Piano Forte by Charles J. Finlayson* (Edinburgh: Alexander Robertson, 1822).

Calliope or English Harmony, A Collection of the celebrated English and Scots Songs, Neatly Engrav'd and Embellished with Designs, adapted to the Subject of each Song taken from the Compositions of the Best Masters in the most Correct Manner with the thorough Bass and Transpositions for the Flute proper for all the Teachers Scholars and Lovers of Musick, Printed on a fine Paper on each side of which renders theUndertaking more compleat than any thing of the kind ever published (London: Printed for ... J. Simpson, [1746]).

Campbell, Alexander, *Twelve Songs set to Music by Alexander Campbell Organist Edinburgh* (London: Longman & Broderick, 1785).

Chambers, Robert, *The Scottish Songs; Collected and Illustrated by Robert Chambers Author of 'Traditions of Edinburgh', 'The Picture of Scotland &c.',* 2 vols (Edinburgh: Ballantyne & Co for William Tait, 78 Princes Street, 1829).

Chappell, William, *Popular Music of the Olden Time*, 16 vols (London: Cramer, Beale, & Chappell [1855–1859]).

Clio and Euterpe or British Harmony. A collection of Celebrated Songs and Cantatas by the most approv'd Masters Curiously Engrav'd. With the Thorough Bass for the Harpsicord and Transposition for the German Flute. Embelish'd with Designs adapted to each Song. In two Volumes, etc. (London: Henry Roberts, [1762]).

Cromek, R. H., *Remains of Nithsdale and Galloway Song with Historical and Traditional Notices Relative to the Manners and Customs of the Peasantry* (London: T. Cadell and W. Davis, 1810).

Cunningham, Allan, *The Songs of Scotland, Ancient and Modern: With an Introduction and Notes, Historical and Critical, and Characters of the Living Poets*, 4 vols (London: John Taylor, 1825).

Dale's Collection of Sixty Favourite Scotch Songs, Adapted for the Voice & Piano Forte or Harpsichord. With a Thorough Bass Carefully revised. Taken from the Original Manuscripts Of the most Celebrated Scotch Authors & Composers Entered at Stationer's Hall (London: J. Dale, (c.1790)).

Dibdin, Charles, *The Sea Songs of Charles Dibdin: With a Memoir of his Life and Writings by William Kitchiner, M.D.* [...] (London: G. and W. B. Whittaker; Clementi and Co, 1823).

The Edinburgh Musical Miscellany: A Collection of the Most Approved Scotch, English, and Irish Songs, Set to Music, second edition (Edinburgh: Mundell and Son, 1804).

The Ettrick Shepherd Memorial Volume Being the Speeches delivered on the occasion of the Unveiling of the Memorial, erected to commemorate the Birthplace of JAMES HOGG, The Ettrick Shepherd, at Ettrickhall, on 28th June 1898. With an Introductory Sketch by R. Borland, F.S.A. (Scot) Author of "Yarrow: Its Poets and Poetry," "Border Raids and Reivers," &c. (Selkirk: James Lewis, [1898]).

Fraser, Simon, ed., *The Airs and Melodies Peculiar to the Highlands of Scotland and the Isles* (Edinburgh: The Editor, [1816]).

Freiligrath, Ferdinand, *F. F.'s. The Rose, Thistle, and Shamrock, Rose, Distel und Kleeblatt. Eine Sammlung von Blühten britischer Lyrik verpflanzt auf deutsches Gebiet von H. I. D. A. Seeliger. Germ.* (Stuttgart, 1853).

A Garland of New Songs containing the Drunken Cobler, or the Prating Magpye, the complying Shepherdess; What can the matter be, Dicky Gossip (Newcastle: M. Angus and Son, [n.d.]).

Gerhard, Wilhelm, *Minstrelklänge aus Schottland* (Leipzig: Verlag von Otto Wigand, 1853).

Glass, Willison, *Scenes of Gloamin': Original Scottish Songs by Willison Glass, A son of Auld Reekie* (Stirling: M. Randall, 1814).

_____, *Songs of Edina; An Original Scottish Poesy,* second edition (Edinburgh: Wm Blair, 1816).

Graham, George Farqhuar, *The Songs of Scotland Adapted to their Appropriate Melodies, arranged with Pianoforte Accompaniments by G. F. Graham, T. M. Mudie, J. T. Surenne, H. R. Dibdin, Finlay Dun, &c.: Illustrated with Historical, Biographical, and Critical Notices by George Farquhar Graham,* 3 vols in 1 (Edinburgh: Wood and Co, 1848–49).

Graham, John, *The Flowers of Melody: A Select Collection of Scottish, English, Irish and American Songs; Selected and arranged by John Graham,* 2 vols (New York: Clayton & van Norden, 1833).

Grant of Elgin, Donald, *Collection of Strathspeys, Reels, Jigs &c. for the piano forte, violin &violoncello* (Edinburgh: Printed for the author, [1790]).

Goldie, John, *Spirit of British Song with Biographical and Ilustrative Notes, by John Goldie,* 2 vols (Glasgow: W. R. M'Phun; London: Knight and Lacey; Edinburgh: John Sutherlands; Dublin: W. Curry, Jun & Co., 1825).

Gow, Neil, *The Lass o' Gowrie. A popular Scottish Ballad Sung with distinguished applause by Mr Melrose & Mr Thorne. The Melody by Niel Gow Arranged with Symphonies &Accompaniment for the Piano Forte by Alexr. Robertson* (Edinburgh: Alexander Robertson, [1825]).

Hecht, Hans, ed. *Songs from David Herd's Manuscripts* (Edinburgh: William J. Hay, 1973).

The Harp of Caledonia, 2 vols (Glasgow: Khull, Blackie & Co.; Edinburgh: A. Fullarton, [1818]).

Herd, David, *Ancient and Modern Scottish Songs*, 2 vols (Edinburgh: J. Wotherspoon, 1776).

Herder, Johann Gottfried, *Selected Early Works 1764–1767: Addresses, Essays, and Drafts; Fragments on Recent German Literature*, eds. Ernest A. Menze and Karl Menges (transl. Ernest A. Menze with Michael Palma), (Pennsylvania: Pennsylvania State University Press, 1991).

Hodgson's Little Warbler: Select Scotch Songs (London: Orlando Hodgson, [n.d.]).

Hogg, James, *Songs and Ballads by the Ettrick Shepherd.With an Autobiography and Reminiscences of his Cotemporaries [sic]* (Glasgow, Edinburgh and London: Blackie and Son, 1852).

_____, *Songs by the Ettrick Shepherd. Now First Collected. First American Edition* (New York: William Stodart, 1832).

_____, *Songs by the Ettrick Shepherd, 1831*, ed. Jonathan Wordsworth (Oxford: Woodstock, 1989).

The Illustrated Book of Scottish Songs, from the Sixteenth to the Nineteenth Century (London: Illustrated London Library, [n.d.]).

Jacobite Minstrelsy; with Notes Illustrative of the Text, and Containing Historical Details in Relation to the House of Stuart, from 1640–1784 (Glasgow: Richard Griffin and Co., 1829).

Kay, John, *A Series of Original Portraits and Caricature Etchings, by the late John Kay, Miniature Painter, Edinburgh: With Biographical Sketches and Illustrative Anecdotes*, 2 vols (Edinburgh: Hugh Paton, Carver and Gilder, 1838) now (Edinburgh: Birlinn, 2007).

King's Scotch Song Book, Containing a Choice Collection of Comic, Sentimental, and Humourous Scotch Songs, Selected from the Works of Burns, and Other Celebrated Authors (New York: S. King, 1822).

Land, Edward, *Reminiscences of the Jacobite Airs, sung by Mr. Wilson in his ... Scottish Entertainment entitled "The Adventures of Prince Charles". Arranged as a Fantasia for the Piano Forte ... by Edward Land* (London: Duff & Hodgson, [1847]).

The London Melodist: or, Songster's Companion; A Selection of Popular English, Irish, and Scottish Songs, by Celebrated Authors (London: Deprose and Co, [n.d.]).

The London Minstrel: A collection of Approved Songs, Duets, &c. &c. set To Music, Adapted to the voice, violin, flute &c. to which is prefixed an Introduction to Singing, By a Professional Gentleman(London: Printed for Dean and Munday, Threadneedle Street, [n.d.]).

Lockhart, John Gibson, *Memoirs of The life of Walter Scott Bart.*, 7 vols (Edinburgh: Robert Cadell; London: John Murray and Whittaker, 1837).

Lockhart, John Gibson, *Peter's Letters to his Kinsfolk* (Edinburgh: Blackwoood, 1819).

My love's in Germany, A Favourite Jacobite Ballad As Sung with the most distinguished applause at the Concerts and the Theatre Royal Edinburgh, by Miss Noel, the symphonies & accompaniments Composer by Alexr. Robertson (Edinburgh: Alexander Robertson, [n.d.]).

The Lyre: A Collection of the Most Approved Scottish, English and Irish Songs Ancient and Modern (Edinburgh: W. Rollo, 1824).

The Miniature Museum of Scotch Songs and Music. Written by Ramsay, Crawford, Blacklock, Burns, Macniel, Tannahill, Glass, Hogg, &c. With & Without Symphonies. The Whole Arranged for the Voice and Piano Forte by the Most Eminent Composers (Edinburgh: Printed by Walker & Anderson, [1818]).

Mitchison, William, ed., *Hand-book of the Songs of Scotland with Illustrations, Descriptive and Historical Notes, edited by William Mitchison, to which is added, a Biographical Sketch of the Life of the late John Wilson, Esquire, the Celebrated Scottish Vocalist* (London: John J. Griffin & Company; Glasgow: Richard Griffin & Co., 1851).

Music for Allan Ramsay's Collection of Seventy-One Scots Songs in the Tea-Table Miscellany. The Six Parts Complete...Set by Alexr. Stuart, and Engraved by Richard Cooper (Edinburgh: Allan Ramsay, 1726).

The National Melodies of Scotland; united to the Songs of Robert Burns, Allan Ramsay, and other Eminent Lyric Poets; with Symphonies and Accompaniments for the Piano Forte, by Haydn, Pleyel, Kozeluch, and other celebrated composers. A separate arrangement for the flute or violin is given of such airs as require it (London: Jones & Company, 1834).

National Songs of Scotland (London: Printed for Steuart and Panton, 1823).

The New-England Songster; A choice collection of Popular Song, New and Old. Claremont ([1846]).

The New Skylark: being an Entire new Choice Collection Of the most-admired Songs sung at the Theatres, Astley's, the Circus, Vauxhall, and by Mr Dibden (West Smithfield: J. Davenport, [n.d.]).

Oliphant, Carolina, *The Songs of Lady Nairne* (London; Edinburgh: T. N. Foulis, 1911).

O the Voice of Woman's Love Ballad the Poetry by the Northamptonshire Peasant John Clare. The Music by Edwin J Nielson (London: Joseph Alfred Novello, (c. 1829–1834)).

Parry, John, *The Beauties of Caledonia, being a Selection of the Most Popular Scottish Songs, Arranged with new Symphonies and Accompaniments. Also several of them Harmonized for Three Voices* (London: D'Almaine & Co, [1845]).

Phillips, William Lovell, *'Bonnie Prince Charlie', Song* (London: Goulding & D'Almaine for the Author [1830]).

Prelleur, Peter, *An Introduction to Singing after so easy a Method, that Persons of the meanest Capacities may (in a short time) learn to sing (in Tune) any Song that is set to Musick. by Mr PETER PRELLEUR Organist of Christ Church Spittal Fields; To which is added a choice Collection of Songs for one and two Voices, by the most Eminent Masters of the Age* (London: J. Simpson, [n.d.]).

Robertson, Alexander, *Will ye Gang to the Highlands wi' me Leezie Lindsay. An Admired Old Highland Song. Arranged with Symphonies & Accompaniments for the Piano Forte by Alexr. Robertson* (Edinburgh: Alexander Robertson, [1825]).

Rogers, Charles, *Ettrick Forest, The Ettrick Shepherd and his Monument. A Guide to the Romantic Scenery at St Mary's Loch, Ettrick and Yarrow, Illustrated with Original Engravings* (Edinburgh: John Menzies, 1860).

_____, *The modern Scottish minstrel; or, The songs of Scotland of the past half century: with memoirs of the poets, and sketches and specimens in English verse of the most celebrated modern Gaelic bards* (Edinburgh: A. & C. Black, 1855–1857).

The Royal Highlander's Quadrille for the Piano forte Viz. Lady Hopetown, Marchioness of Huntley, Countess of Roseberry, Lady Glenorchy, and the Duchess of Hamilton with new Figures as Danced at the Nobility's Assembles by Charles T. Sykes (London: Goulding D'Almaine, Potter & Co. [n.d.]).

Sangs of the Lowlands of Scotland, Carefully Compared with the Original Editions, and

Embellished with Characteristic Designs Composed and Engraved by the Late David Allan (Edinburgh: Printed and Sold by Andrew Foulis, 1798).

Scott, Sir Walter, *The Letters of Sir Walter Scott*, ed. H. J. C. Grierson (London: Constable & Co., 1932).

_____, *Minstrelsy of the Scottish Border*. 3 vols (Kelso: James Ballantyne, for T. Cadell Jun. and W. Davies, Strand, London; Edinburgh: A. Constable, 1802–1803).

Shuldham-Shaw, Patrick, Emily B. Lyle, et al., eds., *The Greig-Duncan Folk Song Collection*, vols 1–8 (Edinburgh: The Mercat Press for the University of Aberdeen in association with the School of Scottish Studies, University of Edinburgh, 1981–2002).

The Skylark: A Collection of the Best Songs, Ancient and Modern (Lincoln's Inn Fields; London: Wilson & Co., Oriental Press, 1803).

The Sky Lark: Being an Elegant Collection of the Best and Newest Songs in the English Language (London: J. Walker: Longman, Hurst, Rees, Orme and Brown etc., 1813).

The Skylark; Being an Entire new and Choice Collection of the Most Admired songs sung this Season at Vauxhall, Sadler's Wells, and by Mr Dibden (London: J. Evans and Co., [n.d.]).

The Songster's Repository Being a Choice selection of the most esteemed Songs Many of which have not heretofore been published (New York: Nathl. Dearborn, 171 Willm. Street, 1811).

Stenhouse, William, *Illustrations of the Lyric Poetry and Music of Scotland* (Edinburgh: William Blackwood, 1853).

Struthers, John, *The Harp of Caledonia: A Collection of Songs, Ancient and Modern, (chiefly Scottish), with an Essay on Scottish Song Writers*, 2 vols (Glasgow: Edward Khull, 1819).

Dewar, James, *There grows a bonnie Brier Bush. [Song] As sung ... by Miss Stephens, and Miss Noel, arranged with symphonies & accompaniment by J. Dewar* (Edinburgh: Alexr Robertson, [1825]).

The Thistle, or Caledonian Songster; Comprising a Select Collection of Modern Scotch Songs, Including the Most Admired Ballads of Burns, Allan Ramsay, and other Celebrated Scottish Bards (London: H. Gray, 1833).

Thomson, William, *Orpheus Caledonius* (London,: Engrav'd and printed for the author at his house in Leicester Fields [1725/1733]).

Topliff, Robert, *Original Sabbath Melodies. The words selected from the Holy Scriptures* (London: T. E. Purday, [c. 1855]).

Tytler, William, 'Dissertation on the Scottish Music', in *Transactions of the Society of Antiquaries of Scotland* (Edinburgh & London, 1792), pp. 495–96.

The Universal Songster or Museum of Mirth: forming the most Complete, Extensive, and Valuable Collection of Ancient and Modern Songs in the English Language with a Copious and Classified Index…[lists classes of songs] Embellished with humourous characteristic Frontispiece, and Twenty-nine woodcuts designed by George and Robert Cruikshank and engraved by J.R. Marshall, 3 vols (London, 1828–1829).

MacDonald, of Dundee, *The Vain Pursuit by Dr Blacklock. Tune, the Maids of Arochar by Mr McDonald of Dundee* (Edinburgh: Stewart & Co, [1790]).

The Vocal Library, Being The Largest Collection of English, Scottish and Irish Songs, Ever printed in a single volume. Selected from the best Authors, Between the age of Shakespeare, Jonson and Cowley and that of Dibdin, Wolcot and Moore (London: G. B. Whittaker, Ave-Maria Lane, 1824).

The Vocal Melodies of Scotland, Dedicated to his Grace the Duke of Buccleuch & Queensberry. Arranged for the Piano Forte or Harp Violin & Violoncello By Nathaniel Gow (Edinburgh: N. Gow and Son, [1818]).

The Vocal Miscellany of Great Britain and Ireland; or, Union Song Book; Comprising Two Hundred and Sixty-Four of the most approved Scots, Irish, and English Songs; with a Variety of Airs, Catches, and Glees, &c. &c. &c. (Berwick: Printed for W. Phorson, 1797).

Vocal Miscellany by Thomas Moore Esqre. The Music Composed and Selected By Henry R Bishop and Mr Moore. Number 1 (London: J Power, [n.d.]).

When the stars are in the Sky, ballad sung by Mr Wilson, at the Theatre Royal English Opera House, Written by J. W. Davidson, Composed and Dedicated to James King Esq. by G. Alexander McFarren (London: Printed by Coventry and Hollier, 71 Dean Street, Soho [n.d.]).

Wilson, James, *The Musical Cyclopedia: A Collection of English, Scottish, and Irish Songs, with Appropriate Music, Adapted to the Voice, Piano Forte, &c. by James Wilson, Esq. to which is prefixed an Essay on the First Principles of Music, by William Grier* (London: Allan Bell & Co., 1834).

Wilson, John, *Wilson's edition of the songs of Scotland, as sung by him in his entertainments on Scottish music and song* (London: Printed for Mr. Wilson, [1842]).

C. Secondary Material

Ashton, Thomas L., *Byron's Hebrew Melodies* (London: Routledge & Kegan Paul, 1972).

Baptie, David, *Musical Scotland Past and Present Being a Dictionary of Scottish Musicians From About 1400 Till the Present Time to which is added a Bibliography of Musical Publications Connected with Scotland from 1611, compiled and edited by David Baptie* (Paisley: J. and R. Parlane; Edinburgh and Glasgow: John Menzies and Co.; London: Houlston and Sons, 1894).

_____, *A handbook of musical biography, compiled and edited by David Baptie* (London: W. Morley, [1883]).

Bashford, Christina, and Leanne Langley, *Music and British Culture 1785–1914: Essays in Honour of Cyril Ehrlich* (Oxford; New York: Oxford University Press, 2000).

Batho, Edith C., *The Ettrick Shepherd* (Cambridge: Cambridge University Press, 1927).

_____, 'Notes on the Bibliography of James Hogg', *The Library*, 2nd series, 16 (1936), 309–26.

Baxter, Sonia Tingali, 'Italian Music and Musicians in Edinburgh *c.*1720–1800: an historical and critical study', (unpublished Doctoral thesis, University of Glasgow, 1999).

Bayard, Samuel P., 'A Miscellany of Tune Notes', in *Studies in Folklore: In Honor of Distinguished Service Professor Stith Thompson*, ed. W. Edson Richmond (Bloomington: Indiana University Press, 1957), pp. 151–76.

Bold, Valentina, 'The Mountain Bard: James Hogg and Macpherson's Ossian', *Studies in Hogg and his World,* 9 (1998), 32–44.

Brown, Mary Ellen, *Burns and Tradition* (London: Macmillan, 1984).

Burchell, Jenny, *Polite and Commerical Concerts: concert management and orchestral repertoire in Edinburgh, Bath, Oxford, Manchester, and Newcastle, 1730–1799* (London; New York: Garland Pub., 1996).

Campbell, Katherine, 'Scots Song Collectors', in John Beech, et al., eds., *Scottish Life and Society: Oral Literature and Performance Culture* (*A Compendium of Scottish Ethnology,* vol. 10), (Edinburgh: John Donald in association with the European Ethnological Research Centre, 2007), pp. 427–439.

Campbell, Katherine & Emily Lyle, "The Perfect Fusion of Words and Music: The Achievement of Robert Burns", in *Musica Scotica 800 Years of Scottish Music: Proceedings from the 2005 and 2006 Conferences*, eds. Kenneth Elliott , et al. (Glasgow: Musica Scotica Trust, 2008), pp. 19–28.

Carew, Derek, 'The Consumption of Music', in *Cambridge History of Nineteenth century Music*, ed. Jim Samson (Cambridge: Cambridge University Press, 2002), pp. 237–258.

Chambers, Robert, ed., *A Biographical Dictionary of Eminent Scotsmen* (Edinburgh: Blackie, 1847).

Child, Francis James, ed., *The English and Scottish Popular Ballads*, 5 vols (New York: The Folklore Press, 1957).

St Clair, William, *The Reading Nation in the Romantic Period* (Cambridge: Cambridge University Press, 2004).

Collinson, Francis, *The Traditional and National Music of Scotland* (London: Routledge and Kegan Paul, 1966).

Cook, Davidson, 'Annotations of Scottish Songs by Burns: An Essential Supplement to Cromek and Dick', in *The Burns Chronicle and Club Directory*, 31 (1922), 1–21.

Cooper, Barry, *Beethoven's Folksong Settings* (Oxford: Clarendon Press, 1994).

Corder, F., 'The Works of Sir Henry Bishop', *Musical Quarterly*, 4 (1918), 78–97.

Cowan, E. J and M. Paterson, *Folk in Print: Scotland's Chapbook Heritage, 1750–1850* (Edinburgh: John Donald, 2007).

Crawford, Thomas, *Society and the Lyric: A Study of the Song Culture of Eighteenth-Century Scotland* (Edinburgh: Scottish Academic Press, 1976).

Crawford, Thomas, ed., *Love, Labour and Liberty: The Eighteenth-Century Scottish Lyric* (Cheadle: Carcanet Press, 1976).

Currie, Janette & Kirsteen McCue, 'Editing the text and music of *Songs by the Ettrick Shepherd* (1831), in *Scottish Studies Review*, 8.2 (November 2007), 54–68.

Dauney, James C., ed., *Ancient Scottish Melodies from a Manuscript of the Reign of King James VI. With an Introduction Enquiry Illustrative of the History of the Music in Scotland* (Edinburgh: The Edinburgh Printing and Publishing Company; Smith, Elder, & Co., Cornhill, London, 1838).

Davis, Leith, *Music, Postcolonialism and Gender: The Construction of Irish National Identity 1724–1874* (Indiana: University of Notre Dame Press, 2006).

Dayell, John Graham, *Musical Memoirs of Scotland, with Historical Annotations and Numerous Illustrative Plates* (Edinburgh: Thomas G. Stevenson; London: William Pickering, 1849).

Dick, James C., 'The Interleaved Scots Musical Museum Transcript: A New Light on Cromek', in *The Burns Chronicle and Club Directory*, 14 (1905), 66–72.

Donaldson, William, *The Jacobite Song: Political Myth and National Identity* (Aberdeen: Aberdeen University Press, 1988).

Douglas, Sir George, *James Hogg* (Edinburgh & London: Oliphant Anderson and Ferrier, 1899).

Ericson-Roos, Catarina, 'The Songs of Robert Burns: A Study of the Unity of Poetry and Music' (Doctoral Thesis, University of Uppsala, 1977).

Farmer, Henry George, *A History of Music in Scotland* (New York: Da Capo Press, 1970).

Fielding, Penny, *Writing and Orality: Nationality, Culture, and Ninteenth Century Scottish Fiction* (Oxford: Clarendon Press, 1996).

Fiske, Roger, *Scotland in Music: A European Enthusiasm* (Cambridge: Cambridge University Press, 1983).

Fleischmann, Aloys ed., *Sources of Irish Traditional Music c1600–1855*, 2 vols (New York and London: Garland, 1998).

Gaier, Ulrich, ed., *Johann Gottfried Herder Volkslieder Übergragungen Dichtungen*, (Frankfurt: Deutscher Klassiker Verlag, 1990).

Garden, M.G., *Memorials of James Hogg, the Ettrick Shepherd* (Paisley and London: Alexander Gardner, 1881/1887).

Gaskill, Howard, ed., *The Reception of Ossian in Europe* (London/New York: Continuum, 2004/2008).

Gaskill, Howard, ed., *Ossian Revisited* (Edinburgh: Edinburgh University Press, 1991).

Gelbart, Matthew, *The Invention of "Folk Music" and "Art Music"* (Cambridge; New York: Cambridge University Press, 2007).

Giddings, Robert, 'Scott and Opera' in *Sir Walter Scott: The Long Forgotten Melody*, ed. Alan Bold, (London: Barnes & Noble, 1983), pp. 194–218.

Gifford, Douglas, *James Hogg* (Edinburgh: The Ramsay Head Press, 1976).

Groome, Francis H., ed., *Ordnance gazetteer of Scotland: a survey of Scottish topography, statistical, biographical, and historical*, 6 vols (Edinburgh: Thomas C. Jack, 1882–1885).

Groves, David, 'James Hogg on Robert Burns', *The Burns Chronicle and Club Directory*, 100 (1991), 51–59.

_____, *James Hogg: The Growth of a Writer* (Edinburgh: Scottish Academic Press, 1988).

HaCohen, Ruth, 'Between Noise and Harmony: The Oratorical Moment in the Musical Entanglements of Jews and Christians', *Critical Inquiry*, 32 (Winter 2006), 250–77.

Hopkinson, Cecil and Oldham, C. D., *Haydn's settings of Scottish songs in the Collections of Napier and Whyte* (Edinburgh, 1954). [20 copies printed from Edinburgh Bibliographical Society Transactions, vol. III, part 2.]

_____, 'Thomson's Collections of National Song', Transactions of the Edinburgh Bibliographical Society, Vol.II (1940), Part 1, 3–64. Amendments were published in the same journal, Vol.III, Part 2 (1954), 123–4.

Hughes, Gillian, 'Hogg and the *Monthly Musical and Literary Magazine*', *Studies in Hogg and his World*, 15 (2004), 120–25.

_____, 'Hogg's Personal Library', *Studies in Hogg and his World*, 19 (2008), 32–65.

_____, 'Irish Melodies and a Scottish Minstrel', *Studies in Hogg and his World* 13 (2002), 36–45.

_____, *James Hogg: A Life* (Edinburgh: Edinburgh University Press, 2007).

_____, 'James Hogg and the Theatre', *Studies in Hogg and his World*, 15 (2004), 53–66.

_____, '"Native Energy": Byron and Hogg as Scottish Poets'. *The Byron Journal*, 34:2 (2006), 133–42.

Johnson, David, *Music and Society in Lowland Scotland in the Eighteenth Century*, (Oxford: Oxford University Press, 1972), now (Edinburgh: Birlinn, 2003).

_____, *Scottish Fiddle Music in the Eighteenth Century*, second edition (Edinburgh: Mercat Press, 1997).

Langan, Celeste, 'Scotch Drink & Irish Harps: Mediations of the National Air', in *The Figure of Music in Nineteenth Century British Poetry*, ed. Phyllis Weliver (Hampshire: Ashgate, 2005), pp. 25–49.

Langley, Leanne, 'The English Musical Journal in the Early Nineteenth Century' (unpublished PhD dissertation, The University of North Carolina, Chapel Hill, 1983).

Langley, Leanne, 'The Life and Death of "The Harmonicon": An Analysis', *Royal Musical Association Research Chronicle*, 22 (1989), 137–63.

Leask, Nigel, '"A degrading species of alchemy": Ballad Poetics, Oral Tradition, and the Meaning of Popular Culture', in *Romanticism and Popular Culture in Britain and Ireland*, eds. Phillip Connel and Nigel Leask (Cambridge: Cambridge University Press, 2009), pp. 51–71.

Low, Donald A., ed., *Critical Essays on Robert Burns* (London and Boston: Routledge & Kegan Paul, 1975).

McAulay, Karen, *Our ancient national airs: Scottish song collecting from the Enlightenment to the Romantic era* (Farnham, Surrey: Ashgate, 2013).

McCue, Kirsteen, '"An Individual Flowering on a Common Stem": Melody, Performance, and National Song', in Philip Connell and Nigel Leask, eds., *Romanticism and Popular Culture in Britain and Ireland* (Cambridge: Cambridge University Press, 2009), pp. 88–106.

_____, 'Burns's Songs and Poetic Craft', in Gerard Carruthers, ed., *The Edinburgh Companion to Robert Burns* (Edinburgh: Edinburgh University Press, 2009), pp. 74–85.

_____, 'From the Songs of Albyn to German Hebrew Melodies: The Musical Adventures of James Hogg', *Studies in Hogg and his World* 20 (2009), 67–83.

_____, 'George Thomson (1757–1851): his collections of National Airs in their Scottish Cultural Context' (unpublished D.Phil thesis, Oxford, 1993).

_____, '"Magnetic Attraction": The Transatlantic Songs of Robert Burns and Serge Hovey', in *Robert Burns and Transatlantic Culture*, eds. Sharon Alker, Holly Faith Nelson and Leith Davis (Surrey: Ashgate, 2012), pp. 233–246.

_____, '"The most intricate bibliographical enigma": Understanding George Thomson (1757–1851) and his collections of national airs', in *Music Librarianship in the United Kingdom*, ed. Richard Turbet (Aldershot: Ashgate, 2003).

_____, '"O My Luve's like a Red, Red rose": Does Burns's Melody Really Matter?', in *Robert Burns and Friends* (Columbia: University of South Carolina Libraries, 2012), pp. 68–82.

_____, 'Scottish Song, Lyric Poetry and the Romantic Composer' in *The Edinburgh Companion to Scottish Romanticism*, ed. Murray Pittock (Edinburgh: Edinburgh University Press, 2011), pp. 39–48.

_____, '"Schottische Lieder ohne Worte?": what happened to the words for the Scots song arrangements by Beethoven and Weber?', in *Scotland in Europe*, eds. R. D. S. Jack and Tom Hubbard (Amsterdam/New York: Rodopi, 2006), pp. 119–36.

_____, 'Singing "more old songs than ever ploughman could": The Songs of James Hogg and Robert Burns in the Musical Marketplace', in *James Hogg and the Literary Marketplace* (Farnham: Ashgate, 2009), pp. 123–138.

_____, '"The Skylark": the popularity of Hogg's "Bird of the Wilderness"' (2009), on the *James Hogg Research* website, http://www.jameshogg.stir.ac.uk.

McCulloch, Margery Palmer, 'German Responses to Robert Burns', *Studies in Scottish Literature,* 33 (2004), 30–41.

McGuinness, David, 'Tune Accompaniments in Eighteenth-Century Scottish Music Publications', in *Notismusycall: Essays on Music and Scottish Culture inHonour of Kenneth Elliott*, ed. Gordon Munro et al., (Glasgow: Musica Scotica Trust, 2005), pp. 221–229.

Mack, Douglas S., 'Hogg as Poet: Successor to Burns?', in *Love and Liberty: Robert Burns, A Bicentenary Celebration*, ed. Kenneth Simpson (East Linton: Tuckwell Press, 1997), pp. 119–127.

Matheson, William, 'Some Early Collectors of Gaelic Folk-song', *The Proceedings of the Scottish Anthropological and Folklore Society*, 5.2 (1955), 67–82.

Mathison, Hamish, 'Robert Burns and National Song', in David Duff and Catherine Jones, eds., *Scotland, Ireland and the Romantic Aesthetic*, (Lewisburg: Bucknell University Press, 2007), pp. 77–92.

Mergenthal, Silvia, *James Hogg: Selbstbild und Bild* (Frankfurt am Main; Bern; New York; Paris: Peter Lang, 1990).

Miller, Karl, *Electric Shepherd: A Likeness of James Hogg* (London, Faber, 2003).

Millgate, Jane, 'Unclaimed Territory: The Ballad of 'Auld Robin Gray' and the Assertion of Authorial Ownership' in *The Library*, 8:4 (December 2007), 423–441.

Mitchell, Jerome, *The Walter Scott Operas* (Alabama: University of Alabama Press, 1977).

Mole, Tom, 'The Handling of Hebrew Melodies', *Romanticism* 8:1 (2002), 18–33.

Nelson, Clare, 'Tea-table Miscellanies: Song culture in late eighteenth-century Scotland' in *Early Music*, 28:4 (2000), 596–618.

Newman, Steve, 'The Scots Songs of Allan Ramsay: "Lyrick" Transformation, Popular Culture and the Boundaries of the Scottish Enlightenment', *Modern Language Quarterly*, 63:3 (2002), 277–314.

_____, *Ballad collection, lyric, and the canon: the call of the popular from the Restoration to the New Criticism* (Philadelphia: University of Pennsylvania Press, 2007).

Ní Chinnéide, Veronica, 'The Sources of Moore's Irish Melodies', *Journal of the Royal Society of Antiquaries of Ireland* (1959), 109–34.

Northcott, Richard, *The Life of Sir Henry R. Bishop* (London: Press Printers, 1920).

Ogilvie, D. Wilson, 'James Hogg – the Two Monuments', *Burns Chronicle*, 97 (1988), 28–32.

O'Sullivan, D. J., ed., 'The Bunting Collection of Irish Folk Music and Song, edited from the Original Manuscripts'; *Journal of the Irish Folk Song Society*, part 1–VI (1927–1939).

Parr, Nora, *James Hogg at Home* (Dollar: Douglas S. Mack, 1980).

Pelkey, Stanley C., 'Music, Memory, and the People in Selected British Periodicals of the Late Eighteenth and Early Nineteenth Centuries', in *Music and History: Bridging the Disciplines*, eds. Jeffrey H. Jackson and Stanley C. Pelkey (Jackson, Miss.: University Press of Mississippi, 2005), pp. 61–83.

Petrie, Elaine, 'Hogg as Songwriter', *Studies in Hogg and his World*, 1 (1990), 19–29.

_____, 'Lyric Progressions: Ballad to Art Song', *Studies in Hogg and his World*, 2 (1991), 81–90.

Pittock, Murray G. H., 'James Hogg: Scottish Romanticism, Song and the Public Sphere', in *James Hogg and the Literary Marketplace: Scottish Romanticism and the Working-Class Author*, eds. Sharon Alker and Holly Faith Nelson (Farnham/Burlington: Ashgate, 2009), pp. 111–122.

_____, 'James Hogg and the Jacobite Song of Scotland', *Studies in Hogg and his World*, 14 (2003), 73–87.

_____, 'The Making of the Jacobite Relics', *Studies in Hogg and his World*, 3 (1992), 10–17.

_____, ed., *The Reception of Walter Scott in Europe* (London/New York: Continuum, 2006).

Poole, H. Edmund, 'A Day at the Music Publishers: A Description of the Establishment of D'Almaine & Co', *Journal of the Printing Historical Society*, 14 (1979/80), 59–81.

Poole, H., 'Masonic Song and Verse of the Eighteenth Century', in *Ars Quatuor Coronatorum*, XL (1928), 7–29.

Porter, James, 'The Traditional Ballad: Requickened Text or Performative Genre?', *Scottish Studies Review*, 4.1 (Spring 2003), 24–40.

Purser, John, *Scotland's Music: A History of the Traditional and Classical Music of Scotland from the Earliest Times to the Present Day* (Edinburgh: Mainstream Publishing, 2007).

_____, '"The Wee Apollo": Burns and Oswald' in *Love & Liberty: Robert Burns: A Bicentenary Celebration*, ed. Kenneth Simpson (East Linton: Tuckwell Press, 1997), pp. 326–333.

Purser, John and Nick Parkes, eds., *The Caledonian Pocket Companion by James Oswald*, vol. 1 (books 1–6), vol. 2 (books 7–12), available on two CD ROMs (self-published; 2006–2007).

Rechter, David, 'Western and Central European Jewry in the Modern Period: 1750–1933', in *The Oxford Handbook of Jewish Studies*, eds. Martin Goodman, et al. (New York: Oxford University Press, 2002), pp. 378–79.

Ringer, Alexander, ed., *The Early Romantic Era: Between Revolutions: 1789–1848* (London: MacMillan, 1990).

Samson, Jim, 'Nations and Nationalism', in *Cambridge History of Nineteenth century Music*, ed. Jim Samson (Cambridge: Cambridge University Press, 2002), pp. 568–600.

Sands, Mollie, *The Eighteenth-Century Pleasure Gardens of Marylebone* (London: The Society for Theatre Research, 1987).

Scott, Derek, 'Music and Social Class', in *Cambridge History of Nineteenth century Music*, ed. Jim Samson (Cambridge: Cambridge University Press, 2002), pp. 544–567.

Richard B. Sher, *The Enlightenment & the Book: Scottish Authors & Their Publishers in Eighteenth Century Britain, Ireland & America* (Chicago & London: University of Chicago Press, 2006).

Simpson, C. M., *The British Broadside Ballad and its Music* (New Brunswick, N.J.: Rutgers University Press, 1966).

Simpson, Louis, *James Hogg: A Critical Study* (Edinburgh and London: Oliver & Boyd, 1962).

Small, Christopher, 'Ossian in Music', in *The Reception of Ossian in Europe*, ed. Howard Gaskill (London & New York: Continuum, 2004), pp. 375–392.

Kirby-Smith, H.T., *The Celestial Twins: Poetry and Music Through the Ages* (Amherst: University of Massachusetts Press, 1999).

Spink, Gerald W., 'Walter Scott's Musical Acquaintances', *Music and Letters*, 51:1 (January 1970), 61–65.

Steinberg, Michael, 'Mendelssohn's Music and German-Jewish Culture: An Intervention', *The Musical Quarterly*, 83.1 (Spring 1999), 31–44.

Smith, Nelson C., *James Hogg* (Boston: Twayne Publishers, 1980).

Temperley, Nicholas, ed., *The Romantic Age 1800–1914*, Vol 5 of *The Athlone History of music in Britain* (London: The Athlone Press, 1981).

Tomalin, Claire, *Mrs Jordan's Profession: The Story of a Great Actress and a Future King* (London: Penguin, 1994).

Weber, William, 'The Contemporaneity of Eighteenth-century musical taste' *The Musical Quarterly*, 70:1 (winter, 1984), 175–194.

_____, 'The Eighteenth-century Origins of the Musical Canon', *Journal of the Royal Musical Association*, 114:1 (1989), pp. 6–17.

Wroth, Warwick, *The London Pleasure Gardens of the Eighteenth Century* (London: MacMillan, 1896).

D. Digital Sources

American Periodical Series Online (Proquest)
http://www.proquest.co.uk/en-UK/catalogs/databases/detail/aps.shtml

The Bodleian Library Broadside Ballads
http://www.bodley.ox.ac.uk/ballads/ballads

BOSLIT – accessed through the website for the National Library of Scotland
http://www.nls.uk/catalogues/resources/boslit/

British Periodicals Collection (Proquest) 19th Century British Library
http://www.proquest.co.uk/en-UK/catalogs/databases/detail/c19.shtml

Glasgow Broadside Ballads – The Murray Collection
http://www.gla.ac.uk/t4/~dumfries/files/layer2/glasgow_broadside_ballads/

'James Hogg Research' website
http://www.jameshogg.stir.ac.uk/

Musick for Allan Ramsay's Collection of 71 Scots Songs
http://library.sc.edu/digital/collections/ramsaysg.html

National Library of Scotland, Music Collections
http://www.nls.uk/collections/music

The Oxford Dictionary of National Biography online
http://www.oxforddnb.com/

Oxford Music online
http://www.oxfordmusiconline.com/subscriber/

Vauxhall Gardens 1661–1859
http://www.vauxhallgardens.com/

Glossary

Janette Currie

This Glossary provides a guide to Hogg's Scots and English words in *Songs* 1831 that readers may find unfamiliar. In preparing the Glossary the online *Dictionary of the Scottish Language* (DSL) – located at http://www.dsl.ac.uk – has been particularly useful [accessed September 2005–June 2008]. This online resource incorporates both the 12 vol. *Dictionary of the Older Tongue*, ed. by William Craigie, et. al. (Oxford: Oxford University Press, 1931–2002) and the 10 vol. *Scottish National Dictionary*, ed. by William Grant and David Murison (Edinburgh: Scottish National Dictionary Association, 1931–1976). The *Scots Dialect Dictionary*, compiled by Alexander Warrack (New Lanark: Waverley Books, 2000) was also useful. The *Oxford English Dictionary* (OED) was helpful for locating those words that have now fallen out of common usage. Likewise *The Concise Scots Dictionary,* ed. by Mairi Robinson (Aberdeen: Aberdeen University Press, 1985) was used in preparation of the Glossary.

Often a Scots spelling of a word is formed by changing the English 'ed' to 'it' (as in *wantit* for wanted) and 'qu' to 'wh' (as in *quat f*or what). Moreover, often words ending in 'y', are amended by adding 'e' – e.g., *loyaltye* and *courtesye*. These words are not glossed. In several songs Hogg uses a synthetic literary Highland dialect which is achieved by swapping the values of letters, so that 'p' stands for 'b' such as 'pe' or 'be', 't' replaces 'd' such as 'Cullotin' or 'Culloden', 'f' replaces 'v' as in 'nefer' or 'never', 's' replaces 'z' as in 'plase' or blaze, 'c' and 'k' replaces 'g' as in 'cot' or 'got' and 'ket' or 'get', and so on. Only those synthetic words where Hogg's usage might be confusing are glossed. Words requiring longer explanations are given in the Explanatory Notes section at the end of the Editorial Notes to individual songs.

a': all; everyone

abigh: aside, away, apart (from company)

aboon: above, in the heavens

ae: one [numerical]; a

aff: off

affrontit: affronted

afore: before

aft/aftener: often

ain: own (belonging to)

aince: once

air: early

alane: to be alone; lonely

alloy: to mix with something of inferior quality

altar-cloth: linen cloth used at the celebration of Communion or Mass

amang/'mang: among

ane: a person, some one; one [numerical]

aneath: beneath, below, under

anes: once

arles: payments or wages for services

array: to draw up in battle lines

atween: between

auld/aulden/auldest: old; aged; oldest

auld: (of people) advanced in years; aged

ava: at all

awa': away

aweel: used as 'well', such as expressing an agreement, or introducing a statement

ay/aye: always, ever, continually

ayont: on the further side of

bairnly: childlike

bairns/bairnies: children, offspring of any age

baith: both

balloch: a narrow mountain pass

ban: prohibit, interdict; to curse (a person or thing)

bandalet: a small band or streak

banes: bones; the human skeleton

bannets: bonnets

barley bree: a Scots phrase meaning 'malt liquor, whisky'

batten: to grow fat, to thrive (*OED*)

baukit: to avoid, shirk

bauld/bauldy: (of persons) brave

bear: barley

beaver: a hat made of beaver's fur

beetle-bee: a humming beetle

befa': to befall; to happen

begoud: to begin to do something

bein: to be water-tight

bell: the cry of a deer

ben: in, or towards the back or inner parts of a house or dwelling

bent: a strong, coarse, or wiry variety of grass

betide: to happen

beuk: a book

bide: to stay, remain

big/biggin': to build; a building

bike: an insect nest, i.e. ants or bees; a swarm

billman: soldier carrying a weapon, usually a broadsword

birk: the birch tree

bit: a small piece or portion

bladds: a lump or portion (of something)

blasted: blighted

blathrie: trumpery, foolishness, ostentation, harm

blaw: to blow

bleeze: to blaze

blewart: the harebell

blin': to be blind

blithe: joyous, cheerful, happy

blithesome: cheery

blude: blood

bogle: a ghost

bonnet: a cloth cap, often with a peak at the front

booby: a dunce

boordly: stalwart, well built, powerful

bore: to pierce through

bothy: a primitive dwelling house, often the place used by shepherds during the summer months

boud: (verb) had to

bowzy: covered with bushes; bushy

bracken/braken: fern

brae: a hill or hillside, a sloping bank

braid: broad (as in length)

brairding: the first shoots of grain, turnips, etc.; sprouting

brake: breach

braken: fern

brand: a sword

braw: fine, splendid; elegant

bree: the eyebrow, or, broth or juice

breeks: breeches

breery: the rose briar; a prickly shrub

breviary: a book containing the 'Divine Orders' for each day recited by those in holy orders (in Roman Catholicism)

brier: a prickly shrub (often the wild rose)

brochin: a plaid (of tartan)

brock: a badger

brogs/brogues: roughly made shoes worn by Highlanders

broom, bushes

brose: oatmeal

brow: the brow of a hill; or, to face or confront

brownie: a supernatural being in human form (often harmless)

bruiks: bears or endures

buckler: a small round shield

bught: a sheepfold, sheep-pen

bulk: the bosom

bung: part of an item of clothing

burd: a bird

burn/burnie: a brook or a stream; a river

but: also

byre: a building for keeping cattle

ca': to call

cairny: small pile of stones, a marker for the dead, or a boundary mark

callan/callant: a young boy; in older men, a term of endearment or familiarity

cam: to come; came

canna: cannot

cannie/canny: skilfull; careful; shrewd; knowing, wise

canopy: a tent or pavilion

canty: lively, cheerful; contented

caper'd: danced or leapt in frolicsome manner, skipped merrily

carbineer: soldier who carries a fire-arm, a sort of musket

carena: uncaring; careless

carle: a man, fellow (sometimes derogatory term)

carle: man or fellow, old man

cauld/cauldness/cauldest: cold/coldness/coldest

cauld: to be cold

cauldrife: chilly

caup: cup

cauve: a calf

chaperoon: a hooded cloak, formerly worn by nobility

Cherman: German

clay: [literary] the ground

claymore: a two-edged broadsword

cleuch/cleugh: ravine or gorge

cludd: a cloud

coble: a small, flat-bottomed rowing boat

coffer: strong box or chest for storing valuables

cog: wooden vessel, made of hooped staves

coof: a fool, simpleton, dull-witted fellow

coronach: a lament for the dead, a dirge, either sung or played on the bagpipes

coronal: a garland; a circlet of gold worn on the head

corrie/correi: a hollow in a hillside or between hills

cot: a small house or cottage, used poetically to denote size or humbleness

couldnae, could not

counterfeit: not genuine, malformed

courser: a large, powerful horse; a racing horse

couthy: agreeable, sociable, friendly, sympathetic

cove: a cave; a recess

crabbit: in bad humour, cross

crack/ crackit: to boast; to chat; boasted, bragged

craigy: rocky, craggy

craws: crows; to crow

creat: great

cumber: trouble, distress or hardship; a state of difficulty or anxiety

cummer: a female intimate, a gossip; a form of designation

curd: curdled milk

curlew: a bird of the *Nemenius* family, known as a whaup in Scotland

daddin': to plod, to trudge

daft: stupid; foolish

dang: to strike, to knock

darena: dare not (to)

daunder: to stroll, saunter; walk uncertainly

declivity: downward slope or incline.

dee/dee'd: to die/died

deevil/deil: Satan, the Devil

deil: behaving in such a way to indicate a familiar or humorous personification of the spirit of mischief

denty: [colloquial] dainty

deray: a disturbance

dewlaps: the loose skin under the throat of dogs, etc.

dight: to adorn

dike: a low wall or fence of turf or stone serving as a division or enclosure *dilde/dilder:* a frightened state

din: a loud noise

dingle: a deep dell or hollow; 'now usually applied (after Milton) to one that is closely wooded or shaded with trees' (*OED*)

dink: fastidious, prim

dinna: do not; did not

dirk/durk: a Highland dagger

disna: does not

ditty/ditties: a short simple song; often used of the songs of birds, or applied depreciatively; stories or tales

doddit: hornless

doited: (of persons) not of sound mind; impaired intellect

dool: stupid, or stupidity

dort: ill-humoured

dorty: peevish, sulky

dought: strength, ability

doughtna: was not able to, i.e., did not have the strength to perform an act

doup: the buttocks

dover'd: stunned

dowiei/dowye: to be sad, melancholy; [colloquial] stupid

downa: unfit or unable to perform an action; cannot

dowy: dull and lonely, or melancholy

dracht: (Hogg's own spelling) a draught

drappin: dropping

dree: to endure, to bear

drifty: used to denote fallen snow, driven by the wind

drill: a small furrow made in the soil, in which seed is sown; a ridge having such a furrow on its top; also, the row of plants then sown

drouth: thirst

drysome: cold, unemotional

dulefu': sorrowful; distressing

dun: a dull or dingy brown colour

duntin': stamped heavily

dwomony: (dominie) a student at university, one with learning

e'en: evening, dusk

e'er: ever

ee/een/ eebree: the eyes; the eyebrows

ee: in view, within sight

eerie/eery: affected by fear or dread, especially by a fear of the supernatural which gives rise to uneasiness or loneliness; gloomy, dismal, melancholy

ell: a unit of linear measurement equal to around 38 inches of cloth

elwand: a measuring wand

enow: enough

erst: formerly

ether: an adder or poisonous snake or serpent

fa': to fall (down)

fain: gladly; lovingly

faem: foam

fand: put to the test

fank: to catch in a noose, to snare

fat: what

fauldit: folded

fause: false

fay: unearthly; possessing fairylike or supernatural qualities; a fairy

feath: faith (shortened form of 'in good faith')

feint: weak, feeble

fell: [figurative] to cast down, defeat, ruin, humiliate; (of persons) fierce, cruel, severe; a hill or mountain

fend: to defend from want, to provide sustenance

ferly/ferlies: to marvel or wonder; marvellous things

firth: a wood

flang: flung

flaughten: a flake

fleech'd: to coax, wheedle, flatter; to beseech, entreat

fley'd: to be frightened, scared

flichterin': fluttering (as a bird)

flittin': moving house

flosh/flush: a piece of boggy ground especially with water on the surface; a large shallow puddle

flowy: adj. spongy, or boggy

flyting: the act of quarrelling, scolding, or employing abusive language

foggies: a veteran; an army pensioner

forby: besides, in addition to, as well as

forgie: to forgive

forspent: exhausted

forworn: forewarned

foster: nourish; encourage, indulge

foughten: fought

frae: from (indicating departure)

froward: perverse

fu': fully; with force; to be drunk

funk: a strong, unpleasant smell

funkit: to flinch or shrink through fear

fusionless: (of people) fainthearted; spiritless

gadman: a blacksmith

gae/gane/gang/gaed/gaun: to go (on foot); the act of walking or going; went

gaishen: a thin, emaciated person, a skeleton

gaits: goats

gar/gars/gart/: to cause (something) to be done

garret: a turret, or watch-tower

gat: to get

gate: a way or road

gaucy: (of people) plump; cheery

gaw: to irritate, annoy

gear/gier: possessions

gecks: mocks

geen: given

gie: to give

gin: of time: by, before, when, etc.; if

girt/gird: encircle

glen: a valley between hills or mountains

gloamin': evening twilight, dusk

goadman: the man or boy who accompanied the ploughman to direct and incite the team of oxen or horses with his gaud (bar or stick)

gorse: common prickly shrub

goud/gowden : gold (money); golden (colour)

gouk/gowk: the cuckoo

gowl: to howl; to yell

grane: to groan; to suffer

greet/grat: to weep; wept

grews: greyhounds

grist: corn to be ground

Gude: God

gude: good

gudebrither: a brother-in-law

ha': a farm-house, the main dwelling of a farm, less commonly with Eng. sense of a manor-house

hae: to have; possess

haffets/haffits: temples; namely the region on each side of the head in front of the ear and above the cheek bone

haill: whole

halberd: a military weapon, around five feet long comprising a battle-axe and spear head

halberdier: soldier who carries a halberd

hale: sound in body

hallan: an internal wall that prevents wind penetration; a dwelling or house

hame: a dwelling house; a habitation

han': a hand

hapless: unsuccessful

happing: (of tears), to trickle down rapidly

happit: covered; wrapped up

harp: to sing

hart: a stag; a male deer (especially of the red species)

hauberk: a piece of defensive clothing, such as chain mail

haud/hauds: to hold; holds

haw: the hawthorn tree

heath-cock: (*Tetrao tetrix*) the male of the black grouse

herd: a herdsman, denotes a shepherd in Scotland

herry/herried: to harry; harried, robbed; ravaged

hie: hasten

hill cheek: hill side

hind: a female deer; a person; a married farm-worker; a peasant

hing: to look glum or doleful

hinney/hinny: honey

hirple: lameness; walk unevenly

hirst: a threshold

hives: see mussell hives

ho: singular form of hose, such as stockings or socks

holm: a small grassy island

hoody craw: the hooded crow (*Corvidae*) a close relation of the carrion crow

hough: the joint between the knee and fetlock, often an animal, sometimes on a person

hough'd: cut the hamstrings (of a horse or other animal)

hunder: [numerical] a hundred

hurkle: crouch down; to yield

hussey: shortened form of 'housewife'

i': in

ilka/ilk ane: each; every one; all

ill: badly, unsatisfactory; trouble; ill-luck; to take offence; be displeased at

indite: to write; to compose

ingle: the fire on a household hearth

ingle-cheek: the fire-side of a household hearth

ither: other (as person)

jaunt: a trip or journey (usually for pleasure)

jinking/jinks: move around quickly; elusive

kaime/ kem'd: to comb; combed

kebbit: a 'keb-ewe' has lost its lamb

kebbuck: a cabbage

kebbuck: a home-made cheese; a lump of cheese

keekit/keek'd: peeped, glanced at inquisitively

ken/kens/kend: to perceive, recognise or know; knew

kendnae: did not know not to

keust: to cast aside; throw off

kie/kye: cows, cattle

kipple: a rafter

kirk: a church building; parochial church

kirk-stile: a stile, or gate-way for foot-passengers, giving entrance to a church-yard

kirtle: a woman's gown or skirt

knowe: a small rounded hillock or a mound

kyle: a sound or strait; a ninepin or skittle

laith/laigh: averse, reluctant, unwilling, loth

lammie: the lamb (term of endearment)

lance: a lancet, a two-edged surgical instrument with a point like a lance, used for bleeding etc.

lane/lanely/ lanesome: lone, solitary; lonely, lonesome

lang: long (as in measurement); long (with reference to duration of time)

lang: to long for; to hope

langkail: a type of cabbage

langsome: lengthy; tedious

larry: see Explanatory note for 108, l. 39

laverock: the skylark; 'the common lark of Europe, *Alauda arvensis*, so called from its habit of soaring towards the sky while singing' (*OED*)

lea, ground left untilled, fallow

leal/leal-hearted: loyal, faithful

leears/leeing: liars; lying

lee-lang: live-long

leeve: to live
leg-bail: to run away
leifu': solitary, desolate, eerie
leman: lover (often unlawful)
liegeman: a vassal (owing allegiance)
lift: the sky, firmament, upper regions
liltit: sung in a low, clear voice; singing sweetly
lily: the common daffodil
limmers: rascals; mischievous rogues
ling: the fish
lingel: waxed thread (in shoemaking)
links: gorse or grass-land found along the coast
linn: a waterfall, a cataract
list: to hear, listen to
littit: dyed (coloured)
lo'e/loe/loed: to love; loved
lone/loan: to drive cattle to pasture along a loaning
loon: derogatory term, a worthless person
lowe: a flame; to blaze
lucken gowan: the globe-flower
lum: a chimney

mailing: the action of letting or taking for rent
main: a stretch of open or deep water
mair: more; further
maist: most
mak: to make, devise
marmalete: [colloquial] marmalade
marrow: companion
matin: the morning (chorus) or combined song of birds
maun: must
mavis: the starling (*Sturnus*)
meal-pock: a beggar's bag used for holding oatmeal
meed: to reward; a deserved accolade or titled (*OED*)
meetness: to be fit, or qualified for a purpose
mend: to put on weight, to fatten
menzie: a crowd, multitude

micht: might, or strength
mind: give heed to; remember
minister: a Parish clergyman of the Church of Scotland
mirds: obsequiousness
mirk: dark, murky (weather)
mony: many (in number)
mou': the mouth
moudie: the mole
muckle: much, a great amount
mump: to nibble (denotes a toothless person)
mumpit: be deceived
mussel hives: breeding place for mussels

na/nae: no, not, none, not one
naebody: no one
naething: not anything, nothing
nain sell: the self, literary expression pertaining to 'her/his own self'
nane: no one
ne'er: never
neb: the nose; the tip or point; a protuberance
needfu': needful
needna: need not
neist: next
no: not
nor: than
norlan': belonging to the north
nout: collective term for cattle, oxen, etc.
nouther/ nowther: neither
nown: own (as belonging to)
nowther: neither
nummers: numbers

o'er: over
ony: any
oult: old
out-ower: (of motion) outwards and over, over the top of, over to the other side of, across, etc.
ower/owre: over (as in jumped over)

pall: a cloth spread over a coffin or tomb
panniels: possibly dialect for panniers

pavilion: a temporary dwelling ornate or ornamental in style

pawkie/pawky: wily, sly, cunning, crafty

pech: to puff or pant, to gasp

pen: an enclosure (for livestock)

pether: to run hurriedly

philabeg: short kilt, introduced in the eighteenth century

pickle: an indefinite amount of a substance

pingle: contention, open disagreement

plack: [literary] Scottish coinage made of copper out of circulation by the 18c

plaid: a regular piece of woollen cloth, used as an outer garment

pliskie: an awkward or distressing situation; a predicament

ploot: plunging or submerging

plough: to make furrows in and turn up (the earth, land) with a plough, esp. as a preparation for sowing or planting

plover: a short-billed bird of the *Charadriidae* family. Usually found near the shore-line, it is also common to grass-land and mountain regions

plover: the lapwing

pluff: a mild explosion; can be applied to anything that disintegrates easily into dust; also a term for the instrument used to apply hair-powder

pock: type of small bag or pouch; a small sack

popplin: bubbling (as boiling water)

porpy: porpoise

pouches: pockets (in a garment)

pouk or bouk: a body, either of a living or a dead person

pow: head

preen: [figurative] a pin, symbol of something of little or low value

prig: to resist, stand against

prigging: pleading or talking

persuasively; haggling

prinkling: a prickling or tingling sensation

pruved: verified, confirmed; attempted

pu': to pull

pund: a form of Scottish currency ; a measurement of weight

quaich/queich: a drinking vessel

quean: a young, unmarried woman

rant: a tirade

rase: race (as in fight or battle)

reave/reaved: rob (to steal from); to be deprived (of)

reaver: robber or plunderer; a marauder, raider

reck: to reckon

redding: the action of clearing out

reek: smoke, vapour

reft/reif: take by force, such as robbery, etc.

reid: red (colour)

riggin': a roof, the ridge of a roof

rime: a hoar-frost

rin: to run

roopit: a hoarse sound

rouse: to stir up, provoke.

routh: plenty, an abundance

row'd: rolled

ruffed: applauded by making a noise with the feet (*OED*)

sae: so

saftly: softly

sair/ sairer/ sairly: causing mental distress or grief; sore; more painful or distressing; sorely

sall: shall

sang: a song

sauf: save

sauls: souls

saut: salt

sax-an-thretty: thirty-six

saxpence: a sixpence (coinage)

scadd: to scald; to mark or blemish

scimitar: a sword with a curved blade

sclate: a thin piece of slate used as a writing utensil

scour: to search (over a wide area)

screw'd: tightened

serried: (of files or ranks of men) pressed close together; shoulder to shoulder

sey: a trying out, a test, a putting to the proof

seybos: a cut of beef, hollow or rounded in shape

shaw: a small wood (especially one of natural growth), a thicket, etc.

shieling: a rough hut built near to pasture, often used by shepherds; a habitation

shoon: shoes or other articles of footwear

shumpit: jumped

sic/ sicklike: such; similar, of the same kind

siller: silver (colour); coinage

simmer: summer

sin/sinsyne: since; since then

skaith: to damage; to hurt or inflict injury

skeel: skill

skelp: to strike (a blow)

skeugh: to take shelter from (rain, etc.)

skull: a close-fitting hat or cap

slee: sly

slummers: a period of sleep

sma': small

snaw: snow

snool'd: crawled meekly or humbly

sock: a ploughshare

solan: (*Sulidae*) the gannet

sonsy: (of women) comely, attractive, good-looking; buxom, plump

sorde: sword

sorning: living at the expense of others

sough/soughs: (of the wind), a whistling or rushing sound

sourock: sorrel

spavie: a enlargement of the hock, causing lameness in cattle and horses

sparks: a man, fellow (derogatory term)

speer: to ask, enquire

squib: a firework

stamocks: stomachs

stane: a stone

stang'd: stung

starn/sternies: a star; the stars

stoon: stone

stound: to affect with a pang or throb; to cause pain

stown: vernacular form of stolen

strang: strong, solidly constructed

sward: the surface of the ground; dense covering of grass or turf

sweart: swore

sweer: lazy, lacking effort

sweets: pleasant fragrance

tae: the toe; toes

tak: to take

tangleness: involved (a person) in a state of affairs

tauld: to relate (information) (to a person); to let (a person) know (something)

te/ten: the/then

tem/ter/tee: them/their/thee

tent: give heed to

tether: a rope for used to restrain animals (livestock, etc.)

thae: those

theek: to roof (a building) with material , including straw (as in thatch)

thegither: together

thimble: possibly 'thrimble', to jostle, or use roughly; to press or squeeze

thole: to suffer or undergo

thrapple: the throat

thraw: distort by twisting and turning; become crooked

thraward: to be perverse, refractory, contrary

thrawn: difficult or perverse; or mechanical contrivances, etc., which refuse to function properly *thrush:* probably the musical species, the song thrush (*Turdus musicus*)

tirl: to turn or twirl

tine/tines: to lose, suffer loss; decline; wanes, fades

tint: lost

toom: (of a person) thin, lean, lank

tout: to sound a horn

tow: rope

trakoon: dragoon

trapan/trepan/trepann'd: a trick, a trap; beguiled

tree: three

trews: close-fitting trousers worn by Highlanders, usually of a tartan pattern and extended to cover the feet

trifles: a lying story, a fable, a fiction; a jest or joke

trig: neat, in good shape

trow/troth: in truth; to believe or trust (a person)

twa/twain: two (as in number)

unbritherly: unbrotherly

uncanny: incautious

unco: strange, unfamiliar; unusual; very

usquebae: whisky

vaunty: proud, boastful

wa/wa's: a wall, walls

wad, would

wad: to pledge a wager

wadna: would not

wae/waeful/waesome, grieved, wretched, sorrowful; woeful

waik: weak

wain: the Plough or Great Bear constellation

wan: pale or sickly in appearance

wan: won

wantit: lacked the presence of a person

war: were

wardly: wordly

warie: to be aware, be conscious of

wark: to work

warld: world

warst: worst

wasna: was not

wasters: squander; spoiler

wat: to know

waughtin': drinking in large quantities or draughts

wean: a child

weary fa': an expression of exasperation damn! the devil take (*DSL*).

wee: a small quantity or size (measurement)

weel: to be well; wellness

ween/weened: to think; surmise; thought

weigh-bauk: the beam of a pair of scales; scales

weir: war, war-mongering

weird/weirdly: fate; destiny; supernatural, other-wordly

welkin: [poetic] the sky

wert: were

westlin: the western side

wha/wha's/ whase: (pronoun) who; who is; whose

wheedle: to persuade (a person) into a way of thinking or course of action

whigging: urging forward; playing the part of a Whig

whilly-whawp: Scots name for the curlew (*Numenius arquata*)

whisht: hush, be quiet

wi': with (as together)

wicker-work: a hut or dwelling made of wickerwork, most likely of the willow tree

widdy: a wooden pole (derogatory term)

winding-sheet: special clothes used for burial; a shroud

winna: will not

wold: open countryside; the earth

wons: dwells

woo: wool

wrang: a wrong-doing against the moral law

wud: mad, demented, insane
wudna: would not

yarely: quickly, promptly
yaud: old mare
ycleped: called, named
ye: (pronoun) you (singular); you
    (plural)
yepic: epic
yerk: draw together (as in
    shoemaking); to beat, thump

or strike severely
yestreen: yesterday evening; last night
yett: a gate (of a field, or enclosure)
yird: the ground, the earth
yon: that, those, yonder
yout: to howl, roar; to bellow
yowes: ewes

'zoons: abbreviation of the oath, 'by
    God's wounds'

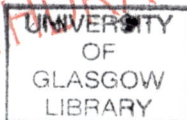